Dialogues
of
Modern Philosophy

ALLYN and BACON, Inc.
BOSTON LONDON SYDNEY TORONTO

PHILIP E. DAVIS

San José State University

DIALOGUES

OF

MODERN

PHILOSOPHY

Library of Congress Cataloging in Publication Data
Main entry under title:

Dialogues of modern philosophy.

    Includes bibliographies and index.
    1. Philosophy, Modern—Collected works.   2. Dia-
logues.   I. Davis, Philip E.
B790.D5   190   76-13560
ISBN 0-205-05511-7

ACKNOWLEDGMENTS

I am grateful to the following publishers and copyright holders for their courtesy in allowing the reproduction of short excerpts from the following published works:

The Idea of History by R. G. Collingwood, copyright 1946, published by Oxford University Press.

Human Knowledge: Its Scope and Limits by Bertrand Russell, copyright 1948 by Bertrand Russell, published by Simon & Schuster Inc., and George Allen & Unwin, Ltd.

Philosophical Investigations by Ludwig Wittgenstein, copyright 1958, published by Basil Blackwell & Mott, Ltd.

Mind and the World Order by Clarence Irving Lewis, copyright 1929 by Clarence Irving Lewis, published by Dover Publications, Inc., 1956.

Process and Reality by Alfred North Whitehead (copyright 1929 by Macmillan Publishing Co., Inc., renewed 1957 by Evelyn Whitehead); published by The Macmillan Publishing Co., Inc., and Cambridge University Press.

Problems of Philosophy by Bertrand Russell, copyright 1912, published by Oxford University Press.

Dilemmas by Gilbert Ryle, copyright 1954, published by Cambridge University Press.

Gottfried Wilhelm Leibniz: Philosophical Papers and Letters, translated and edited by Leroy E. Loemker, 2nd revised edition, published by D. Reidel Publishing Company, 1969.

Acknowledgments to other publishers and copyright holders who have kindly given their permission to reprint longer selections or paraphrases of materials under their control will be found on the bottom of the first page on which the selection or paraphrase begins.

I am also grateful to Professor Leroy E. Loemker for information supplied and advice given; and to my colleagues at San Jose State University, especially Professors Joseph Waterhouse and Calvin Stewart, for many useful discussions on topics related to this book. I am most grateful for the criticism and suggestions provided by Dr. Edwin M. Curley of The Australian National University, Canberra.

PORTRAITS

FRANCIS BACON, a painting by J. Vanderbank. Photographic reproduction by permission of the National Portrait Gallery, London, pg. 9.

THOMAS HOBBES, a painting by J. M. Wright, dated 1679–80, apparently begun shortly before Hobbes' death on Dec. 4, 1679. Photographic reproduction by permission of the National Portrait Gallery, London, pp. 9, 57, 117.

RENÉ DESCARTES, a painting by Frans Hals. The Louvre. Photographic reproduction by permission of Archives Photographiques, Paris, pg. 57.

JOHN LOCKE, a painting by Hermann Verelst, signed and dated 1689, when Locke was about 57 years of age. Photographic reproduction by permission of the National Portrait Gallery, London, pp. 117, 189.

BARUCH SPINOZA. Photographic reproduction by permission of Culver Pictures, Inc., New York, pg. 141.

GOTTFRIED WILHELM LEIBNIZ. Photographic reproduction by permission of Culver Pictures, Inc., New York, pp. 141, 189.

GEORGE BERKELEY, a painting by John Smibert, 1728, the same year that he and Berkeley, along with others, sailed for America to establish a college in the Bermuda Islands. Smibert was to be the college's first Professor of the Arts. Photographic reproduction by permission of the National Portrait Gallery, London, pg. 215.

DAVID HUME, a painting by Allan Ramsay, 1766, when Hume was approximately 55 years old and recently returned from France. Photographic reproduction by permission of the Scottish National Portrait Gallery, Edinburgh, pg. 279.

JAMES BOSWELL, a painting by George Willison. Photographic reproduction by permission of the Scottish National Portrait Gallery, Edinburgh, pg. 281.

JAMES BEATTIE, a painting by Sir Joshua Reynolds known as "The Triumph of Truth," 1773–74. Truth is depicted as an angel pressing her hand against the head of a figure meant to represent Voltaire. One of the other two shadowy figures is alleged to be David Hume. In a letter to Beattie, Reynolds responded: "There is only a figure covering his face with his hands, which they may call 'Hume,' or any body else; it is true it has a tolerable broad back." See James Northcote, *The Life of Sir Joshua Reynolds* (London, 1819), Vol. 1, pg. 321. The painting hangs in Marischal College, University of Aberdeen. Photographic reproduction by permission of the University Court of the University of Aberdeen, pg. 345.

IMMANUEL KANT, an engraving by J. L. Raab from the portrait by Döbler. Photographic reproduction by permission of Historical Pictures Service, Chicago, pp. 321, 381.

To PLATO
who set
the precedent

CONTENTS

5

THE LIMITS OF HUMAN UNDERSTANDING: *Monsieur Gottfried Wilhelm Leibniz and Mr. John Locke*

6

THE PERCEPTION OF REALITY: *Bishop George Berkeley*

7

THE GROUNDS FOR SCEPTICISM: *Mr. David Hume*

8

A DEFENSE OF SCIENCE: *A Critic of Hume's Philosophy and Herr Professor Immanuel Kant*

9

A
Comparative
Biographical
Chronology

FRANCIS BACON	THOMAS HOBBES	RENÉ DESCARTES	JOHN LOCKE	BARUCH de SPINOZA
1561 Born Jan. 22,* York House, London, son of Sir Nicholas Bacon, Lord Keeper of the Seal.				
1573 Enters Trinity College, Cambridge, at age 12.				
1576 Accompanies Queen Elizabeth's ambassador, Sir Amias Paulet, to Paris, at age 15.				
1579 Returns to England; father dies leaving him ill provided; reads law at Gray's Inn.				
1582 Admitted as Utter Barrister of Gray's Inn.				
1584 Member of Parliament for the first time, at age 23.				
1594 First appearance as a pleader in court; awarded M.A. degree by Cambridge University.	*1588* Born prematurely (due to his mother's fright over the approaching Spanish Armada) on April 5, in Westport, an adjunct of Malmesbury; second son of Thomas Hobbes, a poor and ignorant country vicar, who later deserted his family.	*1596* Born March 31, at La Haye, in Touraine, son of a councillor of the *Parlement* of Brittany.		
1597 *Essays* published, first edition.				

*1650 of the civil or fiscal calendar. Listed sometimes as 1560-1. See next footnote relating to Hume and historic calendar changes.

1603 Knighted by James I.	1602 Sent by wealthy uncle to Magdalen Hall, Oxford, at age 14.	1604 Enrolls in the Royal Jesuit College of La Flèche, at age 8.
1605 *The Advancement of Learning* published.		
1606 Marries Alice Barnham.		
1607 Appointed Solicitor General.	1608 Becomes tutor and companion of the son of William Cavendish, Earl of Devonshire.	
	1610 Tours Continent with his pupil.	
1612 *Essays*, second edition.		1612 Leaves La Flèche; proceeds to the University of Poitiers.
1613 Appointed Attorney General.		
1616 Appointed a Privy Councillor; *Proposition to His Majesty Touching the Compiling and Amendment of the Laws of England.*		1616 Receives Bachelor's degree in law, but never enters practice; joins as an unpaid volunteer in the army of Prince Maurice of Nassau.
1617 Appointed Lord Keeper.		
1618 Appointed Lord Chancellor; created Baron Verulam.		

FRANCIS BACON	THOMAS HOBBES	RENÉ DESCARTES	JOHN LOCKE	BARUCH de SPINOZA
1620 *Novum Organum.*		*1619* On the night of Nov. 10, in the German town of Neuberg, has a three-part dream regarding the interconnectedness of all science.		
1621 Created Viscount St. Albans; impeached; sentenced by the House of Lords, May 3, to pay £40,000, imprisoned in the Tower of London during the King's pleasure (4 days), debarred from holding public office, and forbidden to come within the verge of the court (12 miles from London); retires to Gorhambury, June 23. On Oct. 17, receives limited pardon from king.	*1621-26* Period during which he walks and talks with Bacon and serves as his amanuensis at Gorhambury House.			
1622 *History of Henry VII* published end of March.		1622 Returns to France, sells his estate, resumes his travels through Switzerland and Italy.		
1623 *De Augmentis Scientiarum* (Latin version of *The Advancement of Learning*).				
1625 *Essays,* third edition.		*1625-29* In Paris; associates with scientific friends and school-fellow Father Marin Mersenne.		

				1632 Born Nov. 24, at Amsterdam, of Jewish Portuguese parents, refugees from persecution by the Spanish Inquisition.
			1632 Born Aug. 29, at Wrington in Somerset, near Bristol, son of an attorney.	
		1629 *Regulae ad Directionem Ingenii* (Rules for the Direction of the Mind) written (but published posthumously in 1701); leaves Paris to go to Holland where he lives more or less continuously for 20 years, venturing back to Paris for only 3 short visits. 1633 Finishes *Le Monde* (The World), but upon learning from Mersenne of Galileo's condemnation by the Inquisition withholds publication because it reaffirms Copernicus' hypothesis that the earth moves about the sun.		
1626 Dies, April 9, at Highgate, of a chill received after having stuffed a chicken with snow as an experiment in food preservation, at age 65. 1627 *New Atlantis* published.	1628 Publishes translation of Thucydides' *Peloponnesian War*. 1629 Accompanies the son of Sir Gervase Clinton on a journey to the Continent; discovers Euclid and the wonders of geometry. 1630 Returns to the service of the Cavendish family. 1634-36 Third trip to Continent; becomes acquainted with Father Mersenne and his intellectual circle.			

THOMAS HOBBES	RENÉ DESCARTES	JOHN LOCKE	BARUCH de SPINOZA	GOTTFRIED WILHELM LEIBNIZ
1636 Visits Galileo in Florence. 1637 Returns to England. 1640 *Humane Nature, or The Fundamental Elements of Policie*; and *De Corpore Politico, or The Elements of Law* (widely circulated in manuscript form, but published together in 1650); flees England to Paris when Long Parliament takes over; exiled 1640–51. 1641 *Objectiones in Cartesii de Prima Philosophia* (Objections to Descartes' Meditations on First Philosophy) written in response to a request by Mersenne. 1642 *De Cive* (later published and circulated more widely in 1647): English	1637 *Discours de la Method* (Discourse on Method); *La Dioptrique, Les Meteores, et la Geometrie* (Dioptric, Meteors, and Geometry: Essays in this Method). 1641 *Meditationes de Prima Philosophia in qua Dei Existentia et Animae Immortalitas Demonstratur* (Meditations on First Philosophy in which the Existence of God and the Immortality of the Soul Are Demonstrated) first edition published in Paris. 1642 Second edition of the *Meditations* published in Amsterdam with		1638 Mother dies; presumably attends a Jewish school in Amsterdam founded about this time.	

Hobbes	Descartes	Locke	Leibniz
			1646 Born July 1, at Leipzig, son of a professor of moral philosophy.
		1647 Enrolls in Westminster School.	
translation: *Rudiments Concerning Government and Society*, published 1651.	changed title: *Meditationes de Prima Philosophia in quibus Dei Existentia et Animae Humanae a Corpore Distinctio Demonstrantur* (Meditations on First Philosophy in Which the Existence of God and the Distinction between the Mind and the Body Are Demonstrated); dictates his *Principia Philosophia* (Principles of Philosophy) to Princess Elizabeth of Palatinate (published 1644).		
1648 Meets Descartes face-to-face in Paris.	*1648* Tête-à-tête with Hobbes in Paris.		
	1649 *Traité des Passions de L'Âme* (Passions of the Soul); Queen Christina invites him to come to Sweden to instruct her; leaves Amsterdam Sept. 1 and arrives in Stockholm one month later.		
	1650 Dies, Feb. 11, in Stockholm, of a chill brought on by the severe weather and by the Queen's insistence upon having her lessons at 5 o'clock each morning, at age 54.		
1651 *Leviathan*; returns to England.			

THOMAS HOBBES	JOHN LOCKE	BARUCH de SPINOZA	GOTTFRIED WILHELM LEIBNIZ	GEORGE BERKELEY
	1652 Enters Christ Church, Oxford.	1652 Helps with the teaching of school children sometime between 1652 and 1656 at a school opened by Francis van den Enden in 1652; receives help himself with Latin and Greek; becomes acquainted with the philosophy of René Descartes.	1652 Father dies; apparently undertakes own education at age 6.	
1654 Of Liberty and Necessity.		1654 Father dies; litigation with sister over estate; wins case but renounces share except for one bed.	1654 By age 8 has taught himself Latin (by age 12 has begun Greek).	
1655 Elementa Philosophiae Prima de Corpore (Elements of First Philosophy Concerning Body) published in England in 1656.	1656 Graduates from Oxford with B.A. degree.	1656 Excommunicated by the Jewish Community of Amsterdam for "heresies and other enormities," July 27, at age 23; thereafter known as Benedictus; attempt made on his life by unknown enemy.		
1657 De Homine, sive Elementorum Philosophiae Sectio Secunda (Concerning Man, or Elements of Philosophy Second Section).	1658 Awarded M.A. and elected Senior Student (i.e., Fellow) of Christ Church, Oxford. For next few years serves as tutor, studies under Sir Robert Boyle, and begins the study of			

medicine. About this time also becomes acquainted with the philosophy of René Descartes.	1660 Moves to Rijnsburg near Leyden; writes *Korte Verhandeling van God, de Mensch und deszelbs Welstand* (Short Treatise on God, Man and his Wellbeing) and *De Intellectus Emendatione* (On the Improvement of the Understanding); most of his *Renati Des Cartes Principiorum Philosophae* (Principles of Descartes' Philosophy) together with an appendix *Cogitata Metaphysica* (Metaphysical Thoughts) and the first book of his *Ethica* (Ethics).	1661 Enters University of Leipzig at age 15.
	1663 *Renati Des Cartes Principiorum Philosophiae* and *Cogitata Metaphysica* published in Amsterdam by friends; moves to Voorburg near The Hague.	1663 Awarded bachelor's degree; dissertation entitled *De Principio Individui* (Concerning the Principle of Individuation); 1663–66 studies law.
1665–66 Spends time in Germany at Cleves as secretary to a diplomat.		
1666 Gives medical treatment to Lord Ashley, Chancellor of the Exchequer (created Earl of Shaftesbury in 1672) while the		1666 Applies for degree of doctor of law, but is refused because of his youth (20 yrs.); leaves native city; goes to Altdorf
1666 (circa) *A Dialogue Between a Philosopher and a Student of the Common Laws of England* (written but left unfinished; pub-		

THOMAS HOBBES	JOHN LOCKE	BARUCH de SPINOZA	GOTTFRIED WILHELM LEIBNIZ	GEORGE BERKELEY
lished posthumously in 1681).	latter is visiting Oxford, and becomes lifelong friend; by royal mandate allowed to retain Studentship without further qualification. *1667* Joins Lord Ashley's household in London as family physician (operates on Ashley in 1668 and attends birth of third Earl of Shaftesbury in 1671) and as confidential adviser and secretary. Helps draft a constitution for the colony of Carolina in the new world. *1668* Elected Fellow of the Royal Society, sponsored by Sir Paul Neile.		and in Nov. the University of Altdorf accepts his dissertation, *De Casibus Perplexis in Iure* (Concerning Perplexing Cases in Law), grants the doctorate, and offers him a professorship which he declines; *Dissertatio de Arte Combinatoria* (Dissertation on the Art of Combinations) published as well as various legal essays; becomes a member of the Society of Rosicrucians out of curiosity. *1667* Enters service of the elector of Mainz as an assistant in the revision of the statute books and as a political spokesman; concocts a plan for France to conquer Egypt.	

			1670 Writes to Hobbes; receives no reply.
			1671 *Hypothesis Physica Nova* (A New Physical Hypothesis) which maintains that corporeal phenomena should be explained in terms of motion; dedicates first part of essay to the Royal Society of London and the second part to the Paris Academy.
			1672 To Paris at the request of the French Secretary of State.
			1673 In January goes to London, becomes acquainted with Heinrich Oldenburg, secretary of the Royal Society, Robert Boyle, and John Pell, the mathematician; in March returns to Paris and studies advanced geometry under Huygens; in April elected a Fellow of the Royal Society (where earlier he had exhibited a calculating machine which he invented which could add, subtract, divide, and extract square roots).
		1670 *Tractatus Theologico-Politicus* published anonymously; moves to The Hague; begins a Hebrew grammar (left unfinished at his death).	
		1673 Invited to join the faculty of Heidelberg University but declines in order to preserve his intellectual freedom, and because he feels that he would have to "give up philosophical research if I am to find time for teaching a class."	
		1675 Completes *Ethics* but withholds publication; circulates manuscript copies to friends.	
	1675 Awarded B.M. (Bachelor of Medicine) degree; never obtains doctor's degree; goes to France for health reasons (asthma); travels and works on his *Essay Con-*		
1670 Ignores Leibniz's correspondence.			
1672 Writes autobiography in Latin verse at age 84.			
1673 *The Travels of Ulysses*, a rhymed partial translation of the *Odyssey*.			
1675 Publishes a translation of the entire *Odyssey*.			

THOMAS HOBBES	JOHN LOCKE	BARUCH de SPINOZA	GOTTFRIED WILHELM LEIBNIZ	GEORGE BERKELEY
1676 Verse translation of the *Iliad*.	cerning *Human Understanding* begun around 1670-71, developed and reworked for the next 18-19 years.	1676 Visited by Leibniz at The Hague. 1677 Dies Feb. 20, at The Hague, of a pulmonary disease caused by the inhalation of glass dust from the lenses he ground, at age 44. 1677 (near end of year) In accordance with his instructions, previously unpublished manuscripts secretly prepared for press by his friends are published as *B.d.S. Opera Posthuma;* also published in Dutch edition.	1676 Accepts employment as librarian to the Duke of Brunswick-Lüneburg; moves from Paris to Hanover by way of London and Holland; visits Spinoza, reads the manuscript of his *Ethics,* and is allowed to copy parts of it.	
1679 Dies Dec. 4 at Hardwick Hall in Derbyshire, at age 91.	1679 Returns to England; finds Shaftesbury leading opposition against Charles II; undertakes to refute Royalists. 1683 Seeks refuge in Holland to avoid political persecution for his views. 1684 Charles II orders that he be deprived of his Studentship at Christ Church.		1684 Publishes his account of the Infinitesimal Calculus in the *Acta Eruditorum,* Leipzig. 1686 Writes *Systema Theologicum,* an attempt to find a common ground be-	1685 Born March 12, in Kilcrene, near Thomastown, County Kilkenny, Ireland, of English ancestry.

tween Catholic and Protestant Churches.

1686-90 Correspondence with Antoine Arnauld in which he formulates the central doctrines of his own philosophical system. (published as a whole in 1846).

1689 Visits Rome; offered Vatican librarianship on condition that he convert; declines offer.

1687 Settles in Rotterdam with an English Quaker, Benjamin Furly; contributes an abridgement of his *Essay Concerning Human Understanding* to a French periodical, *Bibliothèque Universelle et Historique,* and sends copies to friends for their criticism.

1689 Returns to England following the Revolution of 1688-89 during which James II is deposed and William III subsequently installed as King of England; William III offers him post of Ambassador to Brandenburg, but offer declined; appointed a commissioner of appeals in excise cases; on Aug. 23, 1689, *Two Treatises of Government* licensed for printing, on sale in Nov., dated 1690, and published anonymously. *Epistola de Tolerantia* published anonymously and later in the same year translated and published as *A Letter Concerning Toleration.* In

JOHN LOCKE	GOTTFRIED WILHELM LEIBNIZ	GEORGE BERKELEY	DAVID HUME	IMMANUEL KANT
December, *An Essay Concerning Human Understanding* finally published; dated 1690; and bearing Locke's name.				
1693 *Some Thoughts Concerning Education.*				
1695 *The Reasonableness of Christianity.*				
1696 Appointed member of the Council of Trade and Plantations (resigns 1700).		1696 Enters Kilkenny College, a boarding school.		
1697 Ignores Leibniz's criticisms of his *Essay.*	1697 Sends criticisms of Locke's *Essay* to him; receives no reply.			
	1700 Made a foreign member of the *Académie des Sciences* in Paris; encouraged by Sophia Charlotte, electress of Brandenburg, in his plans for an academy at Berlin; *Akademie der Wissenschaften* founded July 11, with Leibniz elected its first president for life.	1700 Enters Trinity College, Dublin, at age 15.		
1704 Dies at Oates, Oct. 28, at age 72.	1704 *Nouveaux Essais sur l'Entendement Humain* (New Essays on the Human Understanding)	1704 Receives bachelor's degree.		

completed but publication withheld because of Locke's death. (First published in 1765.) *1710 Essais de Théodicée sur la Bonté de Dieu, la Liberté de l'Homme, et l'Origine du Mal* (Essays of Theodicy on the Goodness of God, the Liberty of Man, and the Origin of Evil), the only major work published during his lifetime. *1712-14* In Vienna as Imperial Privy Councillor, with title of *Freiherr* (Baron).	*1707* Awarded M.A. degree; elected Fellow of Trinity College (retains fellowship until 1724); takes Holy Orders and lives in residence as a tutor until 1712. *1709 An Essay Toward a New Theory of Vision* published at age 24; ordained Deacon. *1710 Treatise Concerning the Principles of Human Knowledge* (at age 25); ordained Priest. *1713* Sojourn in London; meets Addison, Steele, Swift, Pope, Samuel Clarke; *Three Dialogues Between Hylas and Philonous* (at age 28).	*1711* Born April 26 (old style; May 7, new style*) in Edinburgh, son of a Scottish laird of modest income.

*Hume's autobiography calls attention to the fact that the "new style" or Gregorian calendar was adopted in Great Britain only during his lifetime in 1751, even though it had been promulgated by Pope Gregory in 1582, and adopted in that year by the principal member states of the Holy Roman Empire. In 1751 and by the same act of Parliament, the beginning of the year in England was changed from March 25 (by the Julian or "old style" calendar) to January 1. Scotland, Hume's homeland, had already carried out this change in the year 1600. The complications for historical calculation are evident, and are perhaps the reason why so many historians of modern philosophy avoid giving exact dates of births and deaths. For further information about this fascinating subject, consult the excellent articles on the calendar in the *Encyclopaedia Britannica*, 1965 edition, Vol. 4, especially pp. 615-19.

GOTTFRIED WILHELM LEIBNIZ	GEORGE BERKELEY	DAVID HUME	IMMANUEL KANT
	1713-14 Tours Continent as secretary and chaplain to the Earl of Peterborough, newly appointed ambassador to the King of Sicily.		
1715-16 Correspondence with Samuel Clarke, acting as Sir Isaac Newton's spokesman.	*1715-16* In London.		
1716 Dies Nov. 14, at Hanover, at age 70, with his secretary Eckhart as his only mourner. Neither the Royal Society nor the Berlin Academy takes notice of his death.	*1716-20* Tours Continent as companion of the son of Bishop Ashe; spends most of time in Italy; loses materials for natural history of Sicily and the incomplete manuscript of Part II of his *Principles* (never rewritten).		
1717 Bernard Fontenelle, secretary of the *Académie des Sciences*, commemorates Leibniz's death with an eloquent address in Paris.	*1721* Takes both B.D. and D.D. degrees at Trinity College, Dublin.		
	1723 Finds himself heir to half the estate of Esther Van Homrigh (Swift's Vanessa) whom he met only once at a dinner party.	*1723* Enters Edinburgh University at age 12; leaves without graduating at age 14 or 15.	
	1724 Appointed Dean of Derry; begins planning and promotion of his project to establish a college in the Bermudas.	*1725/6-29* Studies law.	*1724* Born April 22, at Königsberg, East Prussia, the son of a saddler; grandfather an emigrant from Scotland.

1728 Marries Anne Forster; sails for Rhode Island after obtaining approval for his colonial project from the House of Commons and a promise from the Prime Minister, Sir Robert Walpole, of a grant of £20,000.	*1729* Gives up law at age 18; decides to become a "scholar and philosopher"; has nervous breakdown.	
1729-31 Resides in Newport, R.I., awaiting receipt of the endowment of the proposed College of St. Paul.		*1732-40* Attends Collegium Fridericianum.
1731 In the fall, sails back to England after learning that the money for the college has been diverted to other purposes.		
1731-33 Resides in London.		
1732 *Alciphron, or the Minute Philosopher* (composed in Rhode Island).		
1733 *The Theory of Vision, or Visual Language Vindicated and Explained*; donates books to the libraries of Yale and Harvard.		

GOTTFRIED WILHELM LEIBNIZ	GEORGE BERKELEY	DAVID HUME	IMMANUEL KANT
	1734 *The Analyst*; made Bishop of Cloyne; returns to live in Ireland for 18 years.	1734 Leaves for France; begins writing *A Treatise of Human Nature*.	
	1735 *A Defense of Free Thinking in Mathematics*.	1737 Returns to England.	
	1735-37 *The Querist* (in three parts).	1739 *A Treatise of Human Nature* (Books I & II) falls "dead-born from the press." Book III published in 1740.	1740 Matriculates at the University of Königsberg, at age 16.
		1741-42 *Essays, Moral and Political*.	
		1744 Becomes candidate for the Chair of Moral Philosophy at Edinburgh; fails to obtain it.	
	1744 *Siris* (promotes tar water as a general medicine).	1745-46 Tutor to the mad Marquis of Annandale.	1746-55 Private tutor.
		1746 Secretary to General Sinclair on expedition to Brittany (later secretary to Sinclair on diplomatic missions to the courts of Vienna and Turin, 1748-49).	
	1748 Makes second gift of books to Harvard.	1748 *Three Essays Moral and Political; Philosophical Essays Concerning Human*	

Understanding (a rewriting of Book I of the *Treatise,* better known as *An Enquiry Concerning Human Understanding,* the title he gave it in his revision of 1758).

1751 *Enquiry Concerning the Principles of Morals* (a rewriting of Book III of the *Treatise*); attempts to become Adam Smith's successor in the Chair of Logic at Glasgow University, but unsuccessful because of his reputation for atheism.

1752 Appointed keeper of the Advocates' Library at Edinburgh; begins his *History of England* (published in six volumes between 1754-62); publishes *Political Discourses.*

1754-56 First German translation of Hume's *Essays,* including his *Enquiry Concerning Human Understanding.*

1752 Moves to Oxford to oversee the college education of one of his sons; attempts to resign as bishop since he disapproves of nonresident prelates, but King George II refuses, declaring that he might live where he pleases, but "he should die a bishop in spite of himself."

1753 Dies, Jan. 14, at Oxford, at age 67.

1755 Earns degree of Doctor of Philosophy; appointed Privat-docent (a licensed but unsalaried lecturer) at Königsberg University; publishes *Allgemeine Naturgeschichte und Theorie des*

GOTTFRIED WILHELM LEIBNIZ		DAVID HUME	IMMANUEL KANT	
			Himmels (General Natural History and Theory of the Heavens).	
		1761 All writings placed on the *Index* in Rome.	*1762* Reads Rousseau's *Émile* and is so entranced that for once he neglects his usual afternoon walk.	
		1763 Secretary to the British Ambassador in Paris, well received by French intellectual circles, and given a reception at court.	*1762-64* Johann Gottfried von Herder attends Kant's lectures.	
		1765 Acting Chargé d'Affaires at Paris Embassy.	*1764* Turns down opportunity to become Professor of Poetry.	
1765 *Nouveaux Essais* published for the first time.		*1766* Returns to London with Jean Jacques Rousseau, a refugee from persecution at the time, who suspects Hume's motives, secretly returns to France, and spreads vicious reports about Hume; Hume counters by publishing his correspondence with Rousseau together with an account of their relationship in *A Concise and Genuine Account of the Dispute between Mr. Hume and M. Rousseau.*	*1766* In February appointed sub-librarian in the Schloss (Palace) Library.	

	1770 Obtains full Professorship in Logic and Metaphysics, at Königsberg; inaugural dissertation: *Disputatio de Mundi Sensibilis atque intelligibilis Forma et Principiis* (On the Forms and Principles of the Sensible and Intelligible Worlds).
1769 Reestablishes residence in Edinburgh; issues five editions of his *History* between 1762 and 1773.	
1776 Dies, August 25, at his Edinburgh home, at age 65.	
1777 *The Life of David Hume Written by Himself* (dated April 18, 1776) published posthumously by his friend and literary executor, Adam Smith.	
1779 *Dialogues Concerning Natural Religion* published; faithfully edited by Hume's nephew, David.	1781 *Kritik der reinen Vernunft* (Critique of Pure Reason). 1783 *Prolegomena zu einer jeden künftigen Metaphysik* (Prolegomena to any Future Metaphysics). 1784 *Idee zu einer allgemeinen Geschichte in weltbürgerlicher Absicht* (Idea for a Universal History with a Cosmopolitan Intent).

DAVID HUME	IMMANUEL KANT
	1785 Grundlegung zur Metaphysik der Sitten (Fundamental Principles of the Metaphysics of Morals).
	1786 Metaphysische Anfangsgründe der Naturwissenshaften (Metaphysical Foundations of Natural Science).
	1787 Kritik der reinen Vernunft (Second edition).
	1788 Kritik der praktischen Vernunft (Critique of Practical Reason).
	1790 Kritik der Urteilskraft (Critique of Judgment).
1790-91 First German translation of Hume's *Treatise.*	*1793 Religion innerhalb der Grenzen der blossen Vernunft* (Religion Within the Bounds of Reason Alone).
	1795 Zum ewigen Frieden (Perpetual Peace).
	1797 Metaphysik der Sitten: I. *Metaphysische Anfangsgründe der Rechtslehre;* II. *Metaphysische Anfangsgründe der Tugendlehre* (The Metaphysics of Morals: I. The Metaphysical Principles of Right; II. The Metaphysical Principles of Virtue).

Retires from lecturing because of old age (73 years).

1798 Anthropologie in pragmatischer Hinsicht (Anthropology from a Pragmatic Point of View).

1803 Ueber Pädagogik (On Pedagogy).

1804 Dies, Feb. 12, in Königsberg, at age 79.

INTRODUCTION

THE CONVERSATIONAL CHARACTER
OF PHILOSOPHY

If a person really wants to find out **how** philosophers think, as well as **what** they think, he would do well to imagine them in conversation with each other. Everyone, of course, enjoys talking with other persons who have similar interests and problems, but several factors tend to differentiate the conversations of philosophers from those of non-philosophers. In the first place, philosophical conversations regularly take the form of arguments, that is, the giving of reasons for or against some view or opinion. Light banter, a few jokes, even a little gossip may enter into such a conversation, but the **expected** form of the conversation is argumentative.

This is not generally so, I believe, with other professional groups. Some are content with descriptive discourse. It is often enough merely to report the event or describe the phenomenon. Others, more committed to the idea of supporting their beliefs with evidence, find that they are sometimes **unable** to do so in a conversational context. A scientist's evidence, for instance, may be wholly experimental or observational in character, requiring that it be **seen**, rather than **listened** to; or it may be expressible only in mathematical or statistical terms, requiring that it be **read**.

A lawyer in conversation with another lawyer might indeed discuss a legal decision by examining the reasoning of the judge, or rehearse a brief of his own by providing the reasons in support of his case. Unlike other types of conversation in which the evidence for one's statements is neither expected nor offered, the lawyer's talk may take an argumentative form, and in that respect is very much like philosophical conversation—with one important difference, however. At some point in the legal argument there is bound to be an ultimate appeal to **authority** and to **settled** law. Philosophical arguments, by contrast, are not so restrained. Nothing is finally settled in philosophy in the same way that a law of a particular jurisdiction is settled, and no one in philosophy is an unchallengeable authority.

Philosophers, furthermore, tend to take a much more democratic attitude toward their discussions than do many other professional groups. An example may suffice. A recent Nobel prize winner for physics was asked by the press to explain his theory in words that the average (intelligent) layman could understand. He

1

refused, on the ground that the theory was far too technical for most persons to grasp. Had a comparable request been made of a philosopher, he would have tried, in most instances, to explain his theory. Take the case of Immanuel Kant. His **Critique of Pure Reason** is equally as technical, though perhaps not always as precise, as the theory of any scientist. His is one of the world's most difficult books to read and understand. And yet, after receiving just those complaints, Kant made every effort to be understood, at least by "men of insight, impartiality, and true popularity."[1]

The philosopher John Locke once wrote the following:

> My appearing . . . in print being on purpose to be as useful as I may, I think it necessary to make what I have to say as easy and intelligible to all sorts of readers as I can. And I had much rather the speculative and quick-sighted should complain of my being in some parts tedious, than that any one not accustomed to abstract speculations, or prepossessed with different notions, should mistake or not comprehend my meaning.[2]

The philosopher René Descartes took a similarly egalitarian attitude toward philosophy and even supplied a rationale for it. Good sense, he said, is equally distributed among men, and consequently the chief cause of diverse opinions, misunderstanding, and error is not that some persons are endowed with a larger share of reason than others, but rather that "we conduct our thoughts along different ways, and do not fix our attention on the same objects."[3]

In much the same spirit, G. W. Leibniz aimed at the development of a universal calculus in terms of which every human problem could be expressed, so that whenever a controversy of any sort arose, all that would be necessary to clarify and resolve it would be for the participants to sit down like two accountants, take pens in hand, and say to one another, "Calculemus."[4]

Besides the modern philosopher's generally more egalitarian attitude toward human intelligence, it also happens that the topics that interest him are, generally speaking, those which all persons delight in thinking and talking about (matters of life and death, good and evil, truth and falsity, knowledge and opinion, God and the world, freedom, authority, morality, and the like). These are not esoteric topics, but ones in which laymen can easily become interested.

---

1. *Critique of Pure Reason*, Preface to the Second Edition, F. Max Muller translation (New York: The Macmillan Co., 1949), p. 708; Norman Kemp Smith translation (London: Macmillan & Co. Ltd., 1963), p. 37. Kant's views on his obligation to be intelligible, and his attempts in this direction, are clearly spelled out in the prefaces to the first and second editions of his *Critique*.
2. *An Essay Concerning Human Understanding*, A. S. Pringle-Pattison edition (Oxford: Clarendon Press, 1924), Epistle to the Reader, p. 6.
3. *A Discourse on Method*, Everyman's Library edition (New York: E. P. Dutton, 1951), p. 1.
4. "Let us calculate." Entire passage can be found in *Leibniz: The Monadology and Other Philosophical Writings*, translated by Robert Latta (London: Oxford University Press, 1898), Introduction, pp. 85–86.

One final clue to the nature of philosophical thought: Since philosophers like to argue about matters of common (and uncommon) interest, it often happens that in the absence of a proper antagonist or fellow conversationalist, they invent one. Sometimes this need directly affects the style in which they record their views, and so they write in dialogue form. But it may influence only the order and organization of what they say. For example, if you take a sample of a philosopher's writing and ask yourself what question (or questioner) he is addressing in the first paragraph or section, and then ask yourself what question he is undertaking to answer in the succeeding sections, it will often become apparent that the philosopher, though he has not made it explicit, has been carrying on a conversation with an imaginary or unseen critic. My point, or thesis, if you will, is that, by its very nature, philosophical thought and writing are molded by conversation, whether actual or imaginary.

AN ENLARGED CONCEPT OF CONVERSATION

An attempt has been made in this book to present the problems of modern philosophy through the conversations of the classic modern philosophers. The so-called "modern period" of philosophy, by the way, runs in terms of time—from approximately the beginning of the seventeenth century through the first part of the nineteenth. In terms of active influence, it runs from the seventeenth century up to and including the present century. To indicate this continued influence, and to dispel perhaps the reader's astonishment that a philosopher living in the 1600s is "modern," each introduction to each set of philosophical conversations is preceded by a quotation from a twentieth-century philosopher. These quotations are intended not only to epitomize the problems under discussion but also to indicate that they are still very much with us.

Unfortunately, only a few of the classic philosophers of this period met face-to-face, and so conversations of the ordinary sort between them are practically nonexistent. Even those contemporaries who did meet, such as Bacon and Hobbes, Hobbes and Descartes, and Leibniz and Spinoza, left behind little or no record of what they actually said to each other. Nevertheless, there is plenty of evidence, both of a direct and testimonial sort (e.g., their correspondence, their critiques of each other's views, etc.) and of an indirect and circumstantial sort (e.g., the reports of third parties, the implications of their own views, etc.), to indicate that these philosophers were well aware of their contemporaries and predecessors, and that they often wrote with them consciously in mind.

What we need to do, therefore, if we are to appreciate the full extent of the conversational character of their philosophies, is to enlarge our ordinary conception of conversation. The usual notion is that of an oral interchange of views, a dialogue between two or more persons conducted in each other's physical presence. But obviously there is no need for conversations to be always **face-to-face**, or even that they be **spoken** exchanges. Correspondence as well as written critiques (or lists of objections) and responses are also kinds of conversations. At least I see no good reason why they cannot be so considered. There is even some question whether an actual response is required. A preface to the reader of a book; a prayer to God; a meditation by oneself and directed to oneself ("soliloquies" as well as "colloquies")—may not these forms of communication also be regarded as kinds of conversation?

Of course, we do not want to stretch the notion of a conversation completely out of recognizable shape, or include in it every type of human communication. At a minimum I suppose that a conversation should include some kind of verbalization, whether spoken or written. Also, I suppose that there should be at least some identifiable "parties" to the conversation. We want to be able to distinguish a conversation from a mere chronicle or record addressed to everyone, and thus to no one in particular. Although a verbal response of some kind may not actually be a requirement of "conversation," a verbal response is normally expected. In other words, we should be able to distinguish the kind of "talk" which goes on in a conversation from the kind that is used to express commands, entreaties, requests, and the like. The latter, though directed at determinate persons, is aimed at provoking nonverbal responses.

There is some question, that is, some leeway for argument, whether a lecture, or a straightforward didactic presentation, is conversation. Perhaps it is not what we normally or even occasionally mean by conversation. It seems too one-sided, and the expectation of a verbal response is usually absent. Of course, it is conceivable that, under some special circumstances, a lecture, dictation, narration, or even someone's reading aloud to another, might be construed (without too much damage to the meaning of the term) as a conversation.

THE HISTORICAL IMAGINATION

In making the selections of materials which compose this volume, and organizing them, I have occasionally and inevitably resorted to what R. G. Collingwood calls the "a priori" or "constructive" historical imagination, which he characterizes as follows:

> ... In addition to selecting from among his authorities' statements those which he regards as important, the historian must in two ways go beyond what his authorities tell him. One is the critical way.... The other is the constructive way.... I described constructive history as interpolating between the statements borrowed from our authorities, other statements implied by them. Thus our authorities tell us that on one day Caesar was in Rome and on a later day in Gaul; they tell us nothing about his journey from one place to the other, but we interpolate this with a perfectly good conscience.

This act of interpolation has two significant characteristics. First, it is in no way arbitrary or merely fanciful: it is necessary or, in Kantian language, *a priori*. If we filled up the narrative of Caesar's doings with fanciful details such as the names of the persons he met on the way, and what he said to them, the construction would be arbitrary: it would be in fact the kind of construction which is done by an historical novelist. But if our construction involves nothing that is not necessitated by the evidence, it is a legitimate historical construction of a kind without which there can be no history at all.

Secondly, what is in this way inferred is essentially something imagined. If we look out over the sea and perceive a ship, and five minutes later look again and perceive it in a different place, we find ourselves obliged to imagine it as having occupied intermediate positions when we were not looking. That is already an example of historical thinking; and it is not otherwise that we find ourselves obliged to imagine Caesar as having travelled from Rome to Gaul when we are told that he was in these different places at these successive times.

This activity, with this double character, I shall call *a priori* imagination. . . .[5]

In addition to making selections which I regard as particularly important in the history of modern philosophy from the writings of nine major philosophers, I have attempted to organize them in such a way as to bring out the essentially conversational character of the philosophers' thought. In most cases this was easy and involved no departure from the authors' own written statements. Included in Chapter 1 is a dialogue by Hobbes. The dialogues, correspondence, criticisms, responses, and meditations of other philosophers have similarly been used. Sometimes, however, a difficulty is encountered. For example, suppose we want to bring out the connection between Hobbes' thought about logic and scientific method with that of Bacon. A mere juxtaposition of their writings on the subject provides neither critical analysis nor historical explanation, both of which **can** be supplied through a conversation exchange. We know, as a matter of historical fact, that Bacon and Hobbes walked and talked together at Bacon's country home at Gorhambury. We know the years during which these conversations took place. We know that during these years Bacon was actively concerned with scientific projects. Unfortunately, we do not know exactly what they said. Various bits of circumstantial and implicative evidence (which is subsequently noted) nonetheless justify the assumption that matters of philosophical importance were discussed, and that Hobbes was influenced in his thinking by at least some of Bacon's views. It seems reasonable, then, to weave their otherwise expressed opinions regarding logic and scientific method into what I have called an "exchange of views."

5. R. G. Collingwood, *The Idea of History* (London: Oxford University Press, 1946), pp. 240–241.

Collingwood was quite correct when he insisted that the employment of the historical imagination be neither arbitrary nor merely fanciful. A distinction between history and fiction must be maintained. This means that evidence for one's suppositions must be sought, and negative evidence never ignored. In this respect historians are unlike writers of fiction who sometimes permit to happen what we know actually did not. It also means that the evidence must support "necessary" interpolations. Although conclusive evidence is always lacking in history, we have to be able to say that the event (or conversation) not only could have occurred in just this way, but that we are confident that it did.

There is one possible misunderstanding which Collingwood says "needs only to be mentioned in order to be dispelled." Its mention, however, also helps to explain and to some extent legitimize the use of the historical imagination. The misunderstanding is simply the prejudice that we can imagine only what is fictitious or unreal. If this were so, then of course no employment of the historical imagination would provide us with the truth. Collingwood's illustration is a sufficient refutation: "If I imagine the friend who lately left my house now entering his own, the fact that I imagine this event gives me no reason to believe it unreal. The imaginary, simply as such, is neither unreal nor real."[6]

RULES FOR THE DIRECTION
OF THE HISTORICAL IMAGINATION

In order to ensure that the employment of the historical imagination results in a historical account of the philosophical conversations involved, and not a purely fictional account, I have abided by several self-imposed rules. The first is to use obviously conversational materials insofar as possible, e.g., dialogues, correspondence, etc., and to keep "constructed" conversations to a minimum.

The second is to use the actual words of the authors to the extent possible even in the constructed or invented dialogues. If the words are borrowed from another context (e.g., a letter to someone else) this is carefully footnoted. The justification for taking such a liberty, aside from the fact that it is the author's own language, lies in the reasoning that what we say to one person we often repeat to others, particularly if the views expressed represent fairly settled opinions.

The third is to differentiate, by using different typefaces, the historically imagined parts of the conversations, clearly demarcating what the authors are **known** to have said from what it may be historically **supposed** that they said.

The fourth rule is not to make statements in such invented dialogues about the authors' lives or times which cannot otherwise be substantiated, e.g., the fact that Hobbes was once Bacon's secretary is established in Aubrey's biography.

The fifth rule is to employ, insofar as I know how, the style of speaking, as well as the personal titles and forms of address which were commonly used by

---

6. *Ibid.*, p. 241.

persons in their lifetimes, in order to emphasize the personal and conversational character of the interchanges.

The sixth, final, and perhaps most restrictive rule is to construct philosophical conversations or exchanges only between classic philosophers and other **historically imaginable** conversationalists. That is to say, I do not undertake to imagine a conversation between Kant and Bacon, who died nearly a century before Kant was born. Such an imagined discussion would no doubt be interesting to read, but entirely fanciful, more like a historical novel than a philosophical history. But in saying that the conversationalists must be historically imaginable, I have in mind not merely that the encounter must at least have been **possible** (requiring minimally that their life-spans overlapped), but also that there is some factual basis for supposing that they did in fact converse, in some manner, with one another. We have this kind of basis to substantiate conversations between Bacon and Hobbes, Hobbes and Descartes, and Leibniz and Spinoza, for example, but not between Hobbes and Locke or between Kant and Hume. Although the lives of these last pairs overlapped, there is no good evidence that they ever met or communicated with one another.

It is clearly and historically the case, however, that Hobbes exerted a considerable influence on Locke, as did Hume on Kant. Instead of inventing a conversation between such authors themselves, therefore, I have substituted as parties to the conversations imaginary (but highly probable) characters who, in some cases, share the views of the principal philosophers or, in other cases, hold opposing views. For example, in Chapter 3, the parties to the conversation are a "Hobbesian royalist" named Malmesbury, and a "Lockeian constitutionalist" dubbed Wrington. In Chapter 8, one of the parties is a "Critic of Hume's Philosophy," who, as it turns out, is fairly easy to identify historically with one Professor James Beattie. In Chapter 9, the other conversationalist is a "Student of Ethics," a character invented by Kant himself, just as in Chapter 1 a "Student of the Common Laws of England" was similarly invented by Hobbes.

THE COMPARATIVE STUDY
OF PHILOSOPHICAL PROBLEMS

Most problems that philosophers deal with come in clusters, not singly nor even in pairs. Thus the "problem of error" is difficult, if not impossible, to distinguish from the "problem of method," the "problem of knowledge" (which is itself a cluster of problems), and the "problem of the role of reason" in ethics and other practical disciplines such as law and religion.

Similarly, problems relating to human existence, the nature of thought, the mind-body relation, man's place in the world and his relation to God, all more or less hang together. The problem of evil, problems regarding God's nature and existence, free will, and universal determinism tend to cluster together, as do problems of inductive inference, causation, and scientific knowledge.

It is perhaps no mere coincidence that these different clusters of logically interrelated problems have been the topics of discussion by many pairs and groups of classic modern philosophers. Given any two philosophers with an interest in one or another of these problems, it stands to reason that they are going to end up discussing all the other relevant issues, even if they start from quite different suppositions or even from different problems in the set. Of course not all of the philosophers are interested in the same cluster of problems. Descartes, for example, has very little to say regarding problems of moral conduct; the same for Bacon. Berkeley and Leibniz hardly concern themselves with the problem of inductive inference.[7] None of this is particularly surprising. What is surprising, however, is that these different clusters of problems are discussed in historical sequence. It is at least conceivable that all of these philosophical problems might have been in the air at the same time, perceived by one or another of the philosophers of each generation, and discussed more or less simultaneously. This does not seem to have happened. Although an overlap occurs with respect to some of the discussions, we find that they took place in a definite historical (and more or less logical) order. For example, we find that discussions of inductive inference follow more general metaphysical discussions of the extent of human understanding, and these follow discussions of the need for scientific method. Similarly, discussions of natural religion follow earlier discussions of the problem of evil.

There are lessons to be learned, I think, from the fact that these clusters of philosophical problems have been the preoccupations of specific pairs or groups of philosophers, and from the fact that these discussions have occurred in a roughly logical order which is also a historical order. The first is that, if one wants to know what the problems are, he should carefully compare what each of the interested parties to the conversations has to say about them. If he wants to know where these problems and inquiries lead, he should compare what some of the earlier philosophers have said about the problems with later discussions of the same and related problems. The historical study of philosophical problems is in this double sense comparative.

Because of these considerations, a deliberate attempt has been made in this book to combine a problematic approach to modern philosophy with a historical approach. The conversational format permits both a critical and a historical interconnection between the selections which a mere juxtaposition of materials simply cannot provide. It also gives the reader the opportunity to consider not just one philosopher at a time, but two or more, simultaneously, with respect to the same set of problems. A comparative study of their views is thereby facilitated and encouraged.

---

7. These claims may provoke controversy. It should, therefore, be admitted that Descartes did provide the rudiments of an ethics resembling Stoicism, and that Bacon wrote his *Essays*. Berkeley's views have been used to formulate philosophies of science, and Leibniz was interested in the theory of probability. When all this has been said, however, it remains true that the *primary* interests and contributions of these philosophers lay elsewhere.

Sir Francis Bacon
(1561 – 1626)

Thomas Hobbes
(1588 – 1679)

THE USES OF REASON

Sir Francis Bacon and Mr. Thomas Hobbes

> There is error when a bird flies against a pane of glass which it does not see. We all, like the bird, entertain rash beliefs which may, if erroneous, lead to painful shocks. Scientific method, I suggest, consists mainly in eliminating those beliefs which there is positive reason to think a source of shocks, while retaining those against which no definite argument can be brought.
>
> Bertrand Russell, *Human Knowledge: Its Scope and Limits* (1948)

When Thomas Hobbes was about seventy-six years old, his close friend and biographer, John Aubrey, tried to encourage him to make a study of the law. He even sent him a copy of Bacon's **Elements of the Common Laws of England** in order to pique his interest in the project. Hobbes protested that he did not have enough life left to undertake such a long and difficult task, and Aubrey reports, "I desponded . . . that he should make any **tentamen** [effort] toward this designe."[1] Aubrey's scheme apparently worked, however. Hobbes made such a study and, sometime between 1664 and 1675 (probably in 1666), he wrote his unfinished **Dialogue Between a Philosopher and a Student of the Common Laws of England.**

Many years before, Hobbes had been Bacon's amanuensis, or private secretary, and had no doubt talked to Bacon about matters of law. In any case, Hobbes could not have been unaware of the legal battles between Bacon and his adversary in Parliament, Sir Edward Coke (1552–1634). Coke is frequently referred to in the dialogue as the chief advocate of the autonomy of Parliament and the common-law courts insofar as appeals to the King's representative, the Lord Chancellor, and the courts of equity (Chancery) were concerned. Bacon had argued against Coke that aggrieved parties might appeal decisions of the common-law courts directly to the King through Chancery, and had upheld the position that the King had certain absolute prerogatives. Hobbes generally agreed with Bacon's position.

The "Philosopher" in the dialogue, therefore, represents both Hobbes and Bacon, or perhaps more accurately, Hobbes as influenced by Bacon. The other

---

1. John Aubrey, *Brief Lives,* edited by Anthony Powell (London: The Cresset Press, 1949), p. 247.

participant in the conversation, the "Lawyer," or "Student of the Common Laws," is more difficult to identify: He expresses some of Hobbes' own views, particularly those regarding the origin of civil society, while espousing others that are characteristic of Coke. Yet, since his views are the ones which the Philosopher is most concerned to challenge, perhaps the Lawyer is more accurately looked upon, not so much as Coke himself, as simply an idealized representative of the legal profession.

The chief problems under discussion in the dialogue concern the place of reason in matters of law. For example, may a person justifiably disobey a law if he finds that it is "against reason"? If it is "not wisdom but authority that makes a law," then what role, if any, does reason have in either the formulation or the enforcement of a law? Is it a dictate of reason for people to submit to a sovereign who continually "crosses their wishes"? Is it reasonable, on the other hand, to give the sovereign the authority to make laws without the power to execute them? If all courts ought to judge according to the "law of reason," is it not unnecessary and burdensome to have a separate court of equity?

Throughout his life, Bacon tried to put the chaotic mass of English law into some kind of sensible order. As early as 1616 and again in 1622 he offered to undertake the supervision of the monumental task of compiling and digesting the laws of England. The last offer was made soon after his impeachment as Lord Chancellor by the House of Lords for accepting a bribe. But apparently King James I was not about to offend Parliament by granting Bacon too many favors. Bacon had confessed to the charge, but pleaded that he had only done what was customary and that in no case had his judgment been unduly influenced.

Not being allowed to undertake a reorganization of the English legal system, Bacon turned to another long-standing project, the development and application of a new "organon," or scientific method. On this project he had already done some work. Just prior to his retirement in 1621, he had published his **Novum Organum** (which also included his **Great Instauration**). It was admittedly a kind of patchwork of odds and ends of writing he had done on the subject over the years when he was not otherwise occupied with affairs of state. He feared that he might not live to finish it properly, but nonetheless wanted to leave some record of his discoveries and reflections for posterity. Characteristically, he dedicated this ill-composed volume to King James I and sent him a copy. James, a scholar of sorts himself, expressed his gratitude to Bacon in a letter. Privately to others, however, he is reported to have said that Bacon's book "was like the peace of God. It passeth all understanding."[2]

There is a tremendous novelty and profundity in Bacon's thought, however, which less-probing minds in his own time failed to grasp. Even today his views are usually associated with an exclusively inductive approach to scientific problems. Bacon does emphasize the inductive approach, but he also advocates a dual or compromise approach—a union of reason and experience. Our model in matters of scientific investigation, he says, ought not to be either the ant (who merely collects) nor the spider (who merely spins from its own substance), but rather the bee (who

2. See *Calendar of State Papers, Domestic Series,* CXIX, 64. Cited in A. Wigfall Green, *Sir Francis Bacon* (New York: Twayne Publishers, Inc., 1966), p. 130.

gathers but who also transforms and digests by a power of its own). It was just such a thought as this which the German philosopher, Immanuel Kant, was later to use as the basis of his synthesis of the empirical and rationalistic philosophical traditions.

Hobbes agreed far less with Bacon's views on scientific method than with his views on society and law. But Hobbes is not quite the extreme deductionist he has sometimes been thought to be. The influence of Bacon, even in this department of his thought, was quite substantial. For example, Hobbes agreed with Bacon's conception of the practical end of all knowledge and with Bacon's notion that "knowledge is power." He agreed that all knowledge is derived from the "phantasms" of sense experience and with Bacon's critique of meaningless Aristotelian concepts. Above all, Hobbes agreed with Bacon's concern for the avoidance of verbal fallacies of the kind which Bacon calls "idols of the market-place."

The points of difference between Hobbes and Bacon regarding the scientific uses of reason concern primarily their conceptions of the ultimate causes of human error; their evaluations of the importance of sense experience, experimentation, and natural histories in scientific methodology; and their opinions regarding the value of using mathematics in the investigations of nature. Over and beyond these differences, Hobbes was far more interested than Bacon ever was in developing a total world view.

BACON AND JAMES I

Correspondence

Epistle Dedicatory*

To Our Most Gracious and Mighty Prince and Lord
JAMES
By the Grace of God
Of Great Britain, France, and Ireland King,
Defender of the Faith, Etc.

Most Gracious and Mighty King,

Your Majesty may perhaps accuse me of larceny, having stolen from your affairs so much time as was required for this work. I know not what to say for myself. For of time there can be no restitution unless it be that what has been abstracted from

---

* From *The Great Instauration* in *The Works of Francis Bacon*, edited by James Spedding, Robert L. Ellis, and Douglas D. Heath (London: Longman and Co., 1857–1874), Vol. IV,

your business may perhaps go to the memory of your name and the honour of your age; if these things are indeed worth anything. Certainly they are quite new, totally new in their very kind; and yet they are copied from a very ancient model, even the world itself and the nature of things and of the mind. And to say truth, I am wont for my own part to regard this work as a child of time rather than of wit, the only wonder being that the first notion of the thing, and such great suspicions concerning matters long established, should have come into any man's mind. All the rest follows readily enough. And no doubt there is something of accident (as we call it) and luck as well in what men think as in what they do or say. But for this accident which I speak of, I wish that if there be any good in what I have to offer, it may be ascribed to the infinite mercy and goodness of God, and to the felicity of your Majesty's times; to which as I have been an honest and affectionate servant in my life, so after my death I may yet perhaps, through the kindling of this new light in the darkness of philosophy, be the means of making this age famous to posterity; and surely to the times of the wisest and most learned of kings belongs of right the regeneration and restoration of the sciences. Lastly, I have a request to make—a request no way unworthy of your Majesty, and which especially concerns the work in hand, namely, that you who resemble Solomon in so many things—in the gravity of your judgments, in the peacefulness of your reign, in the largeness of your heart, in the noble variety of the books which you have composed—would further follow his example in taking order for the collecting and perfecting of a natural and experimental history, true and severe (unincumbered with literature and book-learning), such as philosophy may be built upon—such, in fact, as I shall in its proper place describe: that so at length, after the lapse of so many ages, philosophy and the sciences may no longer float in air, but rest on the solid foundation of experience of every kind, and the same well examined and weighed. I have provided the machine, but the stuff must be gathered from the facts of nature. May God Almighty long preserve your Majesty!

Your Majesty's
Most bounden and devoted Servant,
FRANCIS VERULAM
Chancellor

Correspondence

*Regarding Bacon's New Method**

To the King's Most Excellent Majesty

It may please your most excellent Majesty,
It being one thing to speak or write, specially to a King, in public, another in private, although I have dedicated a work, or rather a portion of a work, which at

---

pp. 11–12. Some changes have been made in punctuation.

* From *The Works of Francis Bacon*, Vol. XIV, pp. 119–120, 122.

last I have overcome, to your Majesty by a public epistle, where I speak to you in the hearing of others; yet I thought fit also humbly to seek access for the same, not so much to your person as to your judgment, by these private lines.

The work, in what colours soever it may be set forth, is no more but a new logic, teaching to invent and judge by induction, (as finding syllogism incompetent for sciences of nature) and thereby to make philosophy and sciences both more true and more active.

This, tending to enlarge the bounds of Reason and to endow man's estate with new value, was no improper oblation to your Majesty, who, of men, is the greatest master of reason, and author of beneficence.

There be two of your council, and one other bishop of this land, that know I have been about some such work near thirty years; so as I made no haste. And the reason why I have published it now, specially being unperfect, is, to speak plainly, because I number my days, and would have it saved. There is another reason of my so doing, which is to try whether I can get help in one intended part of this work, namely the compiling of a natural and experimental history, which must be the main foundation of a true and active philosophy.

This work is but a new body of clay, whereinto your Majesty by your countenance and protection, may breathe life. And, to tell your Majesty truly what I think, I account your favour may be to this work as much as an hundred years' time: for I am persuaded the work will gain upon men's minds in ages, but your gracing it may make it take hold more swiftly; which I would be glad of, it being a work meant not for praise or glory, but for practice, and the good of men. One thing, I confess, I am ambitious of, with hope, which is, that after these beginnings, and the wheel once set on going, men shall suck more truth out of Christian pens, than hitherto they have done out of heathen. I say with hope; because I hear my former book of the Advancement of Learning is well tasted in the universities here, and the English colleges abroad: and this is the same argument sunk deeper.

And so I ever humbly rest in prayers, and all other duties,

Your Majesty's most bounden
and devoted servant,
FR. VERULAM, Canc.

York-house, this 12th
of October, 1620.

From the King

My Lord,

I have received your letter and your book, than the which you could not have sent a more acceptable present unto me. How thankful I am for it cannot better be expressed by me, than a firm resolution I have taken; first, to read it thorough with care and attention, though I should steal some hours from my sleep: having otherwise as little spare time to read it as you had to write it. And then to use the liberty of a true friend, in not sparing to ask you the question in any point whereof I shall stand in doubt: (*nam ejus est explicare, cujus est condere*)[3] as, on the other part, I will willingly give a due commendation to such places as in my opinion shall deserve it. In the meantime, I can with comfort assure you, that you could not have made choice of a subject more befitting your place, and your universal and methodick knowledge; and in the general, I have already observed, that you jump with me, in keeping the mid way between the two extremes; as also in some particulars I have found that you agree fully with my opinion. And so praying God to give your work as good success as your heart can wish and your labours deserve, I bid you heartily farewell.

JAMES R.

Octob. 16, 1620.

Correspondence

Regarding Bacon's Retirement and Renewed Offer of a Digest of the Laws of England*

To the King's Most Excellent Majesty

May it please your Majesty,

I acknowledge myself in all humbleness infinitely bounden to your Majesty's grace and goodness, for that at the intercession of my noble and constant friend my Lord Marquis [of Buckingham], your Majesty hath been pleased to grant me that which the civilians say is *Res Inaestimabilis*, my liberty [to come within the verge of the Court]; so that now, whenever God calleth me, I shall not die a prisoner. Nay further, your Majesty hath vouchsafed to cast a second and iterate aspect of your eye of compassion upon me in referring the consideration of my broken estate to my good Lord the Lord Treasurer; which as it is a singular bounty in your Majesty, so I have yet so much left of a late commissioner of your treasure, as I would be sorry to sue for any thing that [might] seem immodest.

These your Majesty's great benefits in casting your bread upon the waters (as the Scriptures saith) because my thanks cannot any ways be sufficient to attain, I have raised your progenitor of famous memory (and now I hope of more famous memory than before) King Henry the 7th, to give your Majesty thanks for me; which work, most humbly kissing your Majesty's hands, I do present. And because in the beginning of my trouble, when in the midst of the tempest I had a kenning of

---

3. "For he must explain who is the author."

* From *The Works of Francis Bacon*, XIV, pp. 357–358.

the harbour which I hope now by your Majesty's favour I am entering into, I made a tender to your Majesty of two works, *An history of England* and *A digest of your laws*; as I have (by a figure of *pars pro toto*) performed the one, so I have herewith sent your Majesty, by way of an epistle, a new offer of the other. But my desire is further, if it stand with your Majesty's good pleasure, since now my study is my exchange and my pen my factor for the use of my talent, that your Majesty (who is a great master in these things) would be pleased to appoint me some task to write, and that I shall take for an oracle.

And because my *Instauration* (which I esteem my great work, and do still go on with in silence) was dedicated to your Majesty; and this History of King Henry the 7th to your lively and excellent image the Prince; if now your Majesty will be pleased to give me a theme to dedicate to my Lord of Buckingham, whom I have so much reason to honour, I should with more alacrity embrace your Majesty's direction than mine own choice. Your Majesty will pardon me for troubling you thus long. God evermore preserve and prosper you.

Your Majesty's poor beadsman most devoted,
FR. ST. ALBAN.

Gorham[bury], 20 Mar., 162[2.]

BACON AND HOBBES

An Exchange of Views Regarding Logic and Scientific Method[4]

Gorhambury House, circa Fall, 1622

Sir Francis.   You come well recommended to me, sir. My good Lord Cavendish has informed me of your scholarship. Are you sure you desire the position as my amanuensis? Because of my recently enforced retirement, I can pay you but little for your services.

---

4. What follows is a speculative reconstruction of the kind of discussions Bacon and Hobbes may have had at Bacon's residence, Gorhambury House, during the period of Bacon's retirement, from 1621 until his death in 1626. It is known that Hobbes served as Bacon's

Mr. Hobbes.   Your lordship does me a great honor even to offer the position. I do hope to "advance my own learning"—if I may borrow upon your most excellent book's title—by my association with you, and that, my lord, is compensation quite adequate.

Sir Francis.   Well, then, if you do not object to being secretary to a former Lord Chancellor, let us begin the work. I find in books that it is accounted a great bliss for a man to have Leisure with Honour. That was never my fortune; nor is. For time was, I had Honour without Leisure; and now I have Leisure without Honour. But my desire is now to have Leisure without Loitering, and not to become an abbey-lubber, as the old proverb was, but to yield some fruit of my private life.[5] You are no doubt aware that my *History of the Reign of Henry VII* came out earlier this year. It was a project I had postponed many years, and yet after I had started, I managed to complete it in only four month's time. I next offered to oversee the recompilement and digest of the laws of England, but his Majesty, the King, has deigned neither to approve the project nor provide me with the necessary helps. So I am inclined, and quite naturally too, to return to my *Instauratio*, my first love and greatest work. There are many natural histories to be investigated and written up regarding the winds, density and rarity, heaviness and lightness, the sympathy and antipathy of things, sulphur, mercury, salt, life and death, and the like. Then too I should like to have my *Advancement of Learning*, my *Henry VII*, and my *Essays* well translated into Latin by the help of some good pens which forsake me not. For these modern languages will at one time or other play the [bankrupts] with books; and since I have lost much time with this age, I would be glad, as God shall give me leave, to recover it with posterity.[6] I have an idea also for a philosophical romance to be called *The New Atlantis* and another for a book of jests or *Apophthegms*. If God wills and time permits I would also indulge my favorite pastime and recreation to add a few more pieces to my *Essays*, with a view to the publication of yet a third edition thereof.[7] With respect to all these matters and projects, Mr. Hobbes, you can be a most welcome assistant.

Mr. Hobbes.   I shall do my best, my lord, and am ready with pen and ink to take down your thoughts, if that be your pleasure at this time.

---

secretary sometime during this period, and that John Aubrey, the biographer, obtained his account of Bacon's death from Hobbes himself. Very few direct references to Bacon are found in Hobbes' writings and apparently none at all in Bacon's regarding Hobbes, so the actual content of their conversations must of necessity be speculative. It appears reasonable, however, to assume that matters of considerable philosophical significance were discussed, given the philosophical and scientific temperaments of both, plus Bacon's acknowledgement (according to Aubrey's account) "that he better liked Mr. Hobbes' taking his thoughts than any of the others, because he understood what he wrote." The statements in the "quotation typeface" are taken from each philosopher's actual writings, as indicated by the footnote citations.

5. Letter to the Queen of Bohemia, sister of Prince Charles, later Charles I of England, April 20, 1622. *The Works of Francis Bacon*, XIV, pp. 364–365.

6. Letter to Mr. Tobie Matthew, replying to his of June 26, 1623. *The Works of Francis Bacon*, XIV, pp. 428–429.

7. All of these projects, and more, Bacon commenced and, for the most part, completed in the five years before his death.

Sir Francis. I think I should like today to reconsider what I previously wrote concerning my "new organon," and perhaps go on from there to augment that very unperfect and incomplete second division of my grand design for a total reconstruction of the sciences. Let me find the book and read you a few selections. I shall want to hear your opinions before I proceed further with the subject.

Mr. Hobbes. I should be delighted to give you the fruit of some of my own thinking on these same matters and to tell you wherein we agree and wherein, per chance, we disagree.

Sir Francis. Ah, here's the passage.[8] It goes as follows:

Now my method, though hard to practice, is easy to explain; and it is this. I propose to establish progressive stages of certainty. The evidence of the sense, helped and guarded by a certain process of correction, I retain. But the mental operation which follows the act of sense I for the most part reject; and instead of it, I open and lay out a new and certain path for the mind to proceed in, starting directly from the simple sensuous perception. The necessity of this was felt no doubt by those who attributed so much importance to logic; showing thereby that they were in search of helps for the understanding, and had no confidence in the native and spontaneous process of the mind. But this remedy comes too late to do any good, when the mind is already, through the daily intercourse and conversation of life, occupied with unsound doctrines and beset on all sides by vain imaginations. And therefore that art of logic, coming (as I said) too late to the rescue, and no way able to set matters right again, has had the effect of fixing errors rather than disclosing truth. There remains but one course for the recovery of a sound and healthy condition,—namely, that the entire work of the understanding be commenced afresh, and the mind itself be from the very outset not left to take its own course, but guided at every step; and the business be done as if by machinery. Certainly if in things mechanical men had set to work with their naked hands, without help or force of instruments, just as in things intellectual they have set to work with little else then the naked forces of the understanding, very small would the matters have been which, even with their best efforts applied in conjunction, they could have attempted or accomplished. Now (to pause awhile upon this example and look in it as in a glass) let us suppose that some vast obelisk were (for the decoration of a triumph or some such magnificence) to be removed from its place, and that men should set to work upon it with their naked hands; would not any sober spectator think them mad? And if they should then send for more people, thinking that in that way they might manage it, would he not think them all the madder? And if they then proceeded to make a selection, putting away the weaker hands, and using only the strong and vigorous, would he not think them madder than ever? And if lastly, not content with this, they resolved to call in aid the art of athletics, and required all their men to come with hands, arms,

---

8. From the Preface, *The New Organon,* in *The Works of Francis Bacon,* Vol. IV, pp. 40–42.

and sinews well anointed and medicated according to the rules of art, would he not cry out that they were only taking pains to show a kind of method and discretion in their madness? Yet just so it is that men proceed in matters intellectual,—with just the same kind of mad effort and useless combination of forces,—when they hope great things either from the number and co-operation or from the excellency and acuteness of individual wits; yea, and when they endeavor by logic (which may be considered as a kind of athletic art) to strengthen the sinews of the understanding: and yet with all this study and endeavor it is apparent to any true judgment that they are but applying the naked intellect all the time; whereas in every great work to be done by the hand of man it is manifestly impossible, without instruments and machinery, either for the strength of each to be exerted or the strength of all to be united.

Upon these premises two things occur to me of which, that they may not be overlooked, I would have men reminded. First it falls out fortunately as I think for the allaying of contradictions and heart-burnings, that the honor and reverence due to the ancients remains untouched and undiminished; while I may carry out my designs and at the same time reap the fruit of my modesty. For if I should profess that I, going the same road as the ancients, have something better to produce, there must needs have been some comparison or rivalry between us (not to be avoided by any art of words) in respect of excellency or ability of wit; and though in this there would be nothing unlawful or new (for if there be anything misapprehended by them, or falsely laid down, why may not I, using a liberty common to all, take exception to it?), yet the contest, however just and allowable, would have been an unequal one perhaps, in respect of the measure of my own powers. As it is, however,—my object being to open a new way for the understanding, a way by them untried and unknown,—the case is altered; party zeal and emulation are at an end; and I appear merely as a guide to point out the road; an office of small authority, and depending more upon a kind of luck than upon any ability or excellency. And thus much relates to the persons only. The other point of which I would have men reminded relates to the matter itself.

Be it remembered then that I am far from wishing to interfere with the philosophy which now flourishes, or with any other philosophy more correct and complete than this which has been or may hereafter be propounded. For I do not object to the use of this received philosophy, or others like it, for supplying matter for disputations or ornaments for discourse,—for the professor's lecture and for the business of life. Nay more, I declare openly that for these uses the philosophy which I bring forward will not be much available. It does not lie in the way. It cannot be caught up in passage. It does not flatter the understanding by conformity with preconceived notions. Nor will it come down to the apprehension of the vulgar except by its utility and effects.

Let there be therefore (and may it be for the benefit of both) two streams and two dispensations of knowledge; and in like manner two tribes or kindreds of students in philosophy—tribes not hostile or alien to each other, but bound together by mutual services;—let there in short be one method for the cultivation, another for the invention, of knowledge.

And for those who prefer the former, either from hurry or from considerations of business or for want of mental power to take in and embrace the other (which must needs to be most men's case), I wish that they may succeed to their desire in what they are about, and obtain what they are pursuing. But if any man there be who, not content to rest in and use the knowledge which has already been discovered, aspires to penetrate further; to overcome, not an adversary in argument, but nature in action; to seek, not pretty and probable conjectures, but certain and demonstrable knowledge;—I invite all such to join themselves, as true sons of knowledge, with me, that passing by the outer courts of nature, which numbers have trodden, we may find a way at length into her inner chambers. And to make my meaning clearer and to familiarize the thing by giving it a name, I have chosen to call one of these methods or ways *Anticipation of the Mind,* the other *Interpretation of Nature.* . . .

Sir Francis. And elsewhere[9] I add the following by way of further explanation:

. . . The art which I introduce with this view (which I call *Interpretation of Nature*) is a kind of logic; though the difference between it and the ordinary logic is great, indeed immense. For the ordinary logic professes to contrive and prepare helps and guards for the understanding, as mine does; and in this one point they agree. But mine differs from it in three points especially: viz., in the end aimed at, in the order of demonstration, and in the starting point of the inquiry.

For the end which this science of mine proposes is the invention not of arguments but of arts; not of things in accordance with principles, but of principles themselves; not of probable reasons, but of designations and directions for works. And as the intention is different, so accordingly is the effect: the effect of the one being to overcome an opponent in argument, of the other to command nature in action.

In accordance with this end is also the nature and order of the demonstrations. For in the ordinary logic almost all the work is spent about the syllogism. Of induction the logicians seem hardly to have taken any serious thought, but they pass it by with a slight notice, and hasten on to the formulae of disputation. I on the contrary, reject demonstration by syllogism, as acting too confusedly, and letting nature slip out of its hands. For although no one can doubt that things which agree in a middle term agree with one another (which is a proposition of mathematical certainty), yet it leaves an opening for deception; which is this. The syllogism consists of propositions; propositions of words; and words are the tokens and signs of notions. Now if the very notions of the mind (which are as the soul of words and the basis of the whole structure) be improperly and overhastily abstracted from facts, vague, not sufficiently definite, faulty in short in many ways, the whole edifice tumbles. I therefore reject the syllogism; and that not only as regards principles (for to principles the logicians themselves do not apply it) but also as regards middle propositions;

---

9. From The Plan of *The Great Instauration,* in *The Works of Francis Bacon,* Vol. IV, pp. 23–33.

which, though obtainable no doubt by the syllogism, are, when so obtained, barren of works, remote from practice, and altogether unavailable for the active department of the sciences. Although therefore I leave to the syllogism and these famous and boasted modes of demonstration their jurisdiction over popular arts and such as are matter of opinion (in which department I leave all as it is), yet in dealing with the nature of things I use induction throughout, and that in the minor propositions as well as the major. For I consider induction to be that form of demonstration which upholds the sense, and closes with nature, and comes to the very brink of operation, if it does not actually deal with it.

Hence it follows that the order of demonstration is likewise inverted. For hitherto the proceeding has been to fly at once from the sense and particulars, up to the most general propositions, as certain fixed poles for the argument to turn upon, and from these to derive the rest by middle terms: a short way, no doubt, but precipitate; and one which will never lead to nature, though it offers an easy and ready way to disputation. Now my plan is to proceed regularly and gradually from one axiom to another, so that the most general are not reached till the last; but then when you do come to them you find them to be not empty notions, but well defined, and such as nature would really recognize as her first principles, and such as lie at the heart and marrow of things.

But the greatest change I introduce is in the form itself of induction and the judgment made thereby. For the induction of which the logicians speak, which proceeds by simple enumeration, is a puerile thing; concludes at hazard; is always liable to be upset by contradictory instance; takes into account only what is known and ordinary; and leads to no result.

Now what the sciences stand in need of is a form of induction which shall analyze experience and take it to pieces, and by a due process of exclusion and rejection lead to an inevitable conclusion. And if that ordinary mode of judgment practiced by the logicians was so laborious, and found exercise for such great wits, how much more labor must we be prepared to bestow upon this other, which is extracted not merely out of the depths of the mind, but out of the very bowels of nature.

Nor is this all. For I also sink the foundations of the sciences deeper and firmer; and I begin the inquiry nearer the source than men have done heretofore; submitting to examination those things which the common logic takes on trust. For first, the logicians borrow the principles of each science from the science itself; secondly, they hold in reverence the first notions of the mind; and lastly, they receive as conclusive the immediate informations of the sense, when well disposed. Now upon the first point, I hold that true logic ought to enter the several provinces of science armed with a higher authority than belongs to the principles of those sciences themselves, and ought to call those putative principles to account until they are fully established. Then with regard to the first notions of the intellect: there is not one of the impressions taken by the intellect when left to go its own way, but I hold it for suspected, and no way established, until it has submitted to a new trial and a fresh judgment has been thereupon pronounced. And lastly, the information of the sense itself I sift and examine in many ways. For certain it is that the senses deceive; but then at the same time they supply the means of discovering their own errors; only the errors are here, the means of discovery are to seek.

The sense fails in two ways. Sometimes it gives no information, sometimes it gives false information. For first, there are very many things which escape the sense, even when best disposed and no way obstructed; by reason either of the subtlety of the whole body, or the minuteness of the parts, or distance of place, or slowness or else swiftness of motion, or familiarity of the object, or other causes. And again when the sense does apprehend a thing its apprehension is not much to be relied upon. For the testimony and information of the sense has reference always to man, not to the universe; and it is a great error to assert that the sense is the measure of things.

To meet these difficulties, I have sought on all sides diligently and faithfully to provide helps for the sense-substitutes to supply its failures, rectifications to correct its errors; and this I endeavor to accomplish not so much by instruments as by experiments. For the subtlety of experiments is far greater than that of the sense itself, even when assisted by exquisite instruments; such experiments, I mean, as are skillfully and artificially devised for the express purpose of determining the point in question. To the immediate and proper perception of the sense therefore I do not give much weight; but I contrive that the office of the sense shall be only to judge of the experiment, and that the experiment itself shall judge of the thing. And thus I conceive that I perform the office of a true priest of the sense (from which all knowledge in nature must be sought, unless men mean to go mad) and a not unskillful interpreter of its oracles; and that while others only profess to uphold and cultivate the sense, I do so in fact. Such then are the provisions I make for finding the genuine light of nature and kindling and bringing it to bear. . . .

But I design not only to indicate and mark out the ways, but also to enter them. And therefore the third part of the work[10] embraces the Phenomena of the Universe; that is to say, experience of every kind, and such a natural history as may serve for a foundation to build philosophy upon. For a good method of demonstrating or form of interpreting nature may keep the mind from going astray or stumbling, but it is not any excellence of method that can supply it with the material of knowledge. Those however who aspire not to guess and divine, but to discover and know; who propose not to devise mimic and fabulous worlds of their own, but to examine and dissect the nature of this very world itself; must go to facts themselves for everything. Nor can the place of this labor and search and world-wide perambulation be supplied by any genius or meditation or argumentation; no, not if all men's wits could meet in one. This therefore we must have, or the business must be forever abandoned. But up to this day such has been the condition of men in this matter, that it is no wonder if nature will not give herself into their hands.

---

10. *The Great Instauration* has six parts named as follows: I. The Divisions of the Sciences; II. The New Organon; or, Directions Concerning the Interpretation of Nature; III. The Phenomena of the Universe; or, a Natural and Experimental History for the Foundation of Philosophy; IV. The Ladder of the Intellect; V. The Forerunners; or, Anticipations of the New Philosophy; VI. The New Philosophy; or, Active Science.

For first, the information of the sense itself, sometimes failing, sometimes false; observation, careless, irregular, and led by chance; tradition, vain and fed on rumor; practice, slavishly bent upon its work; experiment, blind, stupid, vague, and prematurely broken off; lastly, natural history trivial and poor:—all these have contributed to supply the understanding with very bad materials for philosophy and the sciences.

Then an attempt is made to mend the matter by a preposterous subtlety and winnowing of argument. But this comes too late, the case being already past remedy; and is far from setting the business right or sifting away the errors. The only hope therefore of any greater increase or progress lies in a reconstruction of the sciences.

Of this reconstruction the foundation must be laid in natural history, and that of a new kind and gathered on a new principle. For it is in vain that you polish the mirror if there are no images to be reflected; and it is as necessary that the intellect should be supplied with fit matter to work upon, as with safeguards to guide its working. But my history differs from that in use (as my logic does) in many things,—in end and office, in mass and composition, in subtlety, in selection also and setting forth, with a view to the operations which are to follow.

For first, the object of the natural history which I propose is not so much to delight with variety of matter, or to help with present use of experiments, as to give light to the discovery of causes and supply a suckling philosophy with its first food. For though it be true that I am principally in pursuit of works and the active department of the sciences, yet I wait for harvest-time, and do not attempt to mow the moss or to reap the green corn. For I well know that axioms once rightly discovered will carry whole troops of works along with them; and produce them, not here and there one, but in clusters. And that unseasonable and puerile hurry to snatch by way of earnest at the first works which come within reach, I utterly condemn and reject, as an Atalanta's apple that hinders the race. Such then is the office of this natural history of mine.

Next, with regard to the mass and composition of it: I mean it to be a history not only of nature free and at large (when she is left to her own course and does her work her own way),—such as that of the heavenly bodies, meteors, earth and sea, minerals, plants, animals,—but much more of nature under constraint and vexed; that is to say, when by art and the hand of man she is forced out of her natural state, and squeezed and molded. Therefore I set down at length all experiments of the mechanical arts, of the operative part of the liberal arts, of the many crafts which have not yet grown into arts properly so called, so far as I have been able to examine them and as they conduce to the end in view. Nay (to say the plain truth) I do in fact (low and vulgar as men may think it) count more upon this part both for helps and safeguards than upon the other; seeing that the nature of things betrays itself more readily under the vexations of art than in its natural freedom. . . .

Further, in the selection of the relations and experiments I conceive I have been a more cautious purveyor than those who have hitherto dealt with natural history. For I admit nothing but on the faith of eyes, or at least of

23

careful and severe examination; so that nothing is exaggerated for wonder's sake, but what I state is sound and without mixture of fables or vanity. All received or current falsehoods also (which by strange negligence have been allowed for many ages to prevail and become established) I proscribe and brand by name; that the sciences may be no more troubled with them. For it has been well observed that the fables and superstitions and follies which nurses instill into children do serious injury to their minds; and the same consideration makes me anxious, having the management of the childhood as it were of philosophy in its course of natural history, not to let it accustom itself in the beginning to any vanity. Moreover, whenever I come to a new experiment of any subtlety (though it be in my own opinion certain and approved), I nevertheless subjoin a clear account of the manner in which I made it; that men knowing exactly how each point was made out, may see whether there be any error connected with it, and may arouse themselves to devise proofs more trustworthy and exquisite, if such can be found; and finally, I interpose everywhere admonitions and scruples and cautions, with a religious care to eject, repress, and as it were exorcise every kind of phantasm.

Lastly, knowing how much the sight of man's mind is distracted by experience and history, and how hard it is at the first (especially for minds either tender or preoccupied) to become familiar with nature, I not unfrequently subjoin observations of my own, being as the first offers, inclinations, and as it were glances of history towards philosophy; both by way of an assurance to men that they will not be kept for ever tossing on the waves of experience, and also that when the time comes for the intellect to begin its work, it may find everything the more ready. By such a natural history then as I have described, I conceive that a safe and convenient approach may be made to nature, and matter supplied of good quality and well prepared for the understanding to work upon. . . .

The sixth part of my work (to which the rest is subservient and ministrant) discloses and sets forth that philosophy which by the legitimate, chaste, and severe course of inquiry which I have explained and provided is at length developed and established. The completion however of this last part is a thing both above my strength and beyond my hopes. I have made a beginning of the work—a beginning, as I hope, not unimportant:—the fortune of the human race will give the issue;—such an issue, it may be, as in the present condition of things and men's minds cannot easily be conceived or imagined. For the matter in hand is no mere felicity of speculation, but the real business and fortunes of the human race, and all power of operation. For man is but the servant and interpreter of nature: what he does and what he knows is only what he has observed of nature's order in fact or in thought; beyond this he knows nothing and can do nothing. For the chain of causes cannot by any force be loosed or broken, nor can nature be commanded except by being obeyed. And so those twin objects, *human knowledge* and *human power,* do really meet in one; and it is from ignorance of causes that operation fails.

And all depends on keeping the eye steadily fixed upon the facts of nature and so receiving their images simply as they are. For God forbid that we should give out a dream of our own imagination for a pattern of the world; rather may He graciously grant to us to write an apocalypse or true vision of the footsteps of the Creator imprinted on his creatures. . . .

There. I think that is enough of a review of my method. Allow me to benefit from your opinions, Mr. Hobbes.

Mr. Hobbes. I am much impressed, my lord, by what you have just read to me. Perhaps I can best convey my own reflections on these and similar matters by first presenting some of my ideas about the nature of Philosophy generally, and then some of my more specific views about scientific method.

Sir Francis. Please proceed.

Mr. Hobbes. 1. Philosophy[11] seems to me to be amongst men now, in the same manner as corn and wine are said to have been in the world in ancient time.[12] For from the beginning there were vines and ears of corn growing here and there in the fields; but no care was taken for the planting and sowing of them. Men lived therefore upon acorns; or if any were so bold as to venture upon the eating of those unknown and doubtful fruits, they did it with danger of their health. In like manner, every man brought Philosophy, that is, Natural Reason, into the world with him; for all men can reason to some degree, and concerning some things: but most men wander out of the way, and fall into error for want of method, as it were for want of sowing and planting, that is of improving their reason. And from hence it comes to pass, that they who content themselves with daily experience, which may be likened to feeding upon acorns, and either reject, or not much regard philosophy, are commonly esteemed, and are, indeed, men of sounder judgment than those who, from opinions, though not vulgar, yet full of uncertainty, and carelessly received, do nothing but dispute and wrangle, like men that are not well in their wits. I confess, indeed, that that part of philosophy by which magnitudes and figures are computed, is highly improved. But because I have not observed the like advancement in the other parts of it, my purpose is, as far forth as I am able, to lay open the few and first Elements of Philosophy in general, as so many seeds from which pure and true Philosophy may hereafter spring up by little and little. . . .

2. *Philosophy is such knowledge of effects or appearances, as we acquire*

---

11. From *De Corpore,* edited by Sir William Molesworth (1839), Vol. I of *The English Works of Thomas Hobbes,* Ch. 1. It should be realized that for Hobbes, as well as Bacon, "philosophy" and "science" are more or less synonymous terms.

12. Cf. Plato's picture of members of primitive society, their production of "corn and wine" and eating of acorns, in *The Republic,* II, 372. As a classical scholar it may be assumed that Hobbes was aware of this and other works of Plato long before he undertook the explicit formulation of his own ideas. Taken together with the fact that he was trained in Aristotelian logic at Oxford and considered himself good at it, there is ample reason to doubt the frequent suggestion that Hobbes' philosophical inspiration dates from his discovery of geometry in 1629, and that his preference for a deductive method was acquired only years after his meetings with Bacon. For an expression of this latter view, however, see Richard Peters' excellent book, *Hobbes* (Penguin, 1956) pp. 48, 18, but see also pp. 14 and 19 for evidence to the contrary.— P.E.D.

by true ratiocination from the knowledge we have first of their causes or generation: And again, of such causes or generations as may be from knowing first their effects.

For the better understanding of which definition, we must consider, first, that although Sense and Memory of things, which are common to man and all living creatures, be knowledge, yet because they are given us immediately by nature, and not gotten by ratiocination, they are not philosophy.

Secondly, seeing Experience is nothing but memory; and Prudence, or prospect into the future time, nothing but expectation of such things as we have already had experience of, Prudence also is not to be esteemed philosophy.

By *ratiocination,* I mean *computation.* Now to compute, is either to collect the sum of many things that are added together, or to know what remains when one thing is taken out of another. *Ratiocination,* therefore, is the same with *addition* and *substraction;* and if any man add *multiplication* and *division,* I will not be against it, seeing multiplication is nothing but addition of equals one to another, and division is nothing but a substraction of equals one from another, as often as is possible. So that all ratiocination is comprehended in these two operations of the mind, addition and substraction.

3. But how by the *ratiocination* of our mind, we add and subtract in our silent thoughts, without the use of words, it will be necessary for me to make intelligible by an example. . . . If therefore a man see something afar off and obscurely, although no appellation had yet been given to anything, he will, notwithstanding, have the same idea of that thing for which now, by imposing a name on it, we call it *body.* Again, when, by coming nearer, he sees the same thing thus and thus, now in one place and now in another, he will have a new idea thereof, namely, that for which we now call such a thing *animated.* Thirdly, when standing nearer, he perceives the figure, hears the voice, and sees other things which are signs of a rational mind, he has a third idea, though it have yet no appellation, namely, that for which we now call anything *rational.* Lastly, when, by looking fully and distinctly upon it, he conceives all that he has seen as one thing, the idea he has now is compounded of his former ideas, which are put together in the mind in the same order in which these three single names, *body, animated, rational,* are in speech compounded into this one name, *body-animated-rational,* or *man.* . . .

We must not therefore think that computation, that is, ratiocination, has place only in numbers, as if man were distinguished from other living creatures (which is said to have been the opinion of *Pythagoras*) by nothing but the faculty of numbering; for *magnitude, body, motion, time, degrees of quality, action, conception, proportion, speech and names* (in which all the kinds of philosophy consist) are capable of addition and substraction. . . .

4. But *effects* and the *appearances* of things to sense, are faculties or powers of bodies, which make us distinguish them from one another; that is to say, conceive one body to be equal or unequal, like or unlike to another body; as in the example above, when by coming near enough to any body, we perceive the motion and going of the same, we distinguish it thereby from a tree, a column, and other fixed bodies; and so that motion or going is the *property*

thereof, as being proper to living creatures, and a faculty by which they make us distinguish them from other bodies.

5. How the knowledge of any effect may be gotten from the knowledge of the generation thereof, may easily be understood by the example of a circle: for if there be set before us a plain figure, having, as near as may be, the figure of a circle, we cannot possibly perceive by sense whether it be a true circle or no; than which, nevertheless, nothing is more easy to be known to him that knows first the generation of the propounded figure. For let it be known that the figure was made by the circumduction of a body whereof one end remained unmoved, and we may reason thus; a body carried about, retaining always the same length, applies itself first to one *radius,* then to another, to a third, a fourth, and successively to all; and, therefore, the same length, from the same point, toucheth the circumference in every part thereof, which is as much as to say, as all the *radii* are equal. We know, therefore, that from such generation proceeds a figure, from whose one middle point all the extreme points are reached unto by equal *radii.* And in like manner, by knowing first what figure is set before us, we may come by ratiocination to some generation of the same, though perhaps not that by which it was made, yet that by which it might have been made; for he that knows that a circle has the property above declared, will easily know whether a body carried about, as is said, will generate a circle or no.

6. The *end* or *scope* of philosophy is, that we may make use to our benefit of effects formerly seen; or that, by application of bodies to one another, we may produce the like effects of those we conceive in our mind, as far forth as matter, strength, and industry, will permit, for the commodity of human life. For the inward glory and triumph of mind that a man may have for the mastering of some difficult and doubtful matter, or for the discovery of some hidden truth, is not worth so much pains as the study of Philosophy requires; nor need any man care much to teach another what he knows himself, if he think that will be the only benefit of his labour. The end of knowledge is power; and the use of theorems (which, among geometricians, serve for the finding out of properties) is for the construction of problems; and, lastly, the scope of all speculation is the performing of some action, or thing to be done.

7. But what the *utility* of philosophy is, especially of natural philosophy and geometry, will be best understood by reckoning up the chief commodities of which mankind is capable, and by comparing the manner of life of such as enjoy them, with that of others which want the same. Now, the greatest commodities of mankind are the arts; namely, of measuring matter and motion; of moving ponderous bodies; of architecture; of navigation; of making instruments for all uses; of calculating the celestial motions, the aspects of the stars, and the parts of time; of geography, &c. By which sciences, how great benefits men receive is more easily understood than expressed. These benefits are enjoyed by almost all the people of Europe, by most of those of Asia, and by some of Africa: but the Americans, and they that live near the Poles, do totally want them. But why? Have they sharper wits then those? Have not all men one kind of soul, and the same faculties of mind? What, then, makes this difference, except philosophy? Philosophy, therefore, is the cause of all these benefits. But

the utility of moral and civil philosophy is to be estimated, not so much by the commodities we have by knowing these sciences, as by the calamities we receive from not knowing them. Now, all such calamities as may be avoided by human industry, arise from war, but chiefly from civil war; for from this proceed slaughter, solitude, and the want of all things. But the cause of war is not that men are willing to have it; for the will has nothing for object but good, at least that which seemeth good. Nor is it from this, that men know not that the effects of war are evil; for who is there that thinks not poverty and loss of life to be great evils? The cause, therefore, of civil war is, that men know not the causes neither of war nor peace, there being but few in the world that have learned those duties which unite and keep men in peace, that is to say, that have learned the rules of civil life sufficiently. Now, the knowledge of these rules is moral philosophy. But why have they not learned them, unless for this reason, that none hitherto have taught them in a clear and exact method? . . .

8. The *subject* of Philosophy, or the matter it treats of, is every body of which we can conceive any generation, and which we may, by any consideration thereof, compare with other bodies, or which is capable of composition and resolution; that is to say, every body of whose generation or properties we can have any knowledge. And this may be deduced from the definition of philosophy, whose profession it is to search out the properties of bodies from their generation, or their generation from their properties; and, therefore, where there is no generation or property, there is no philosophy. Therefore it excludes *Theology*, I mean the doctrine of God, eternal, ingenerable, incomprehensible, and in whom there is nothing neither to divide nor compound, nor any generation to be conceived.

It excludes the doctrine of *angels,* and all such things as are thought to be neither bodies nor properties of bodies; there being in them no place neither for composition nor division, nor any capacity of more or less, that is to say, no place for ratiocination.

It excludes *history,* as well *natural* as *political,* though most useful (nay necessary) to philosophy; because such knowledge is but experience, or authority, and not ratiocination.

It excludes all such knowledge as is acquired by Divine inspiration, or relevation, as not derived to us by reason, but by Divine grace in an instant, and, as it were, by some sense supernatural.

It excludes not only all doctrines which are false, but such also as are not well-grounded; for whatsoever we know by right ratiocination, can neither be false nor doubtful; and, therefore, *astrology,* as it is now held forth, and all such divinations rather than sciences, are excluded.

Lastly, the doctrine of *God's worship* is excluded from philosophy, as being not to be known by natural reason, but by the authority of the Church; and as being the object of faith, and not of knowledge.

9. The principal parts of philosophy are two. For two chief kinds of bodies, and very different from one another, offer themselves to such as search after their generation and properties; one whereof being the work of nature, is called a *natural body,* the other is called a *commonwealth,* and is made by the

wills and agreement of men. And from these spring the two parts of philosophy, called *natural* and *civil.* But seeing that, for the knowledge of the properties of a commonwealth, it is necessary first to know the dispositions, affections, and manners of men, civil philosophy is again commonly divided into two parts, whereof one, which treats a men's dispositions and manners, is called *ethics;* and the other, which takes cognizance of their civil duties, is called *politics,* or simply *civil philosophy.* . . .

Sir Francis.   I think I comprehend your notion of philosophy. I'm glad we agree that knowledge ends in power, and aims at human welfare. But you seem to me to take at once a narrower and a broader conception of science than I do.

Mr. Hobbes.   How so, my lord?

Sir Francis.   You take a narrower conception in that you tend to exclude from it all sense experience, even experiments and natural histories, whereas I tend to incorporate them as the very foundation of my philosophy.

Mr. Hobbes.   Aye, in a sense, I do, but still I also say, nay, insist, that they are useful and necessary to philosophy, although they are not a part of philosophy in the strict sense, nor of true science.

Sir Francis.   Your view is broader than mine in that you appear to apply your method not only to the interpretation of the Phenomena of Nature (to "natural bodies," I suppose you would prefer to say), but also to such matters as ethics and politics ("civil philosophy," as you call it). Is that not right?

Mr. Hobbes.   Indeed it is.

Sir Francis.   For myself I am quite content to leave to the syllogism jurisdiction over the popular arts, business concerns, and matters of disputation and mere opinion. I don't envisage my inductive method's extending so far. But enough, I'm sure there are other points of agreement and difference between us regarding the nature of science and/or philosophy. What say you more specifically of method itself?

Mr. Hobbes.   . . . Method,[13] . . . in the study of philosophy, *is the shortest way of finding out effects by their known causes, or of causes by their known effects.* But we are then said to know any effect, when we know *that there be causes of the same,* and *in what subject those causes are,* and *in what subject they produce that effect,* and *in what manner they work the same.* And this is the science of causes. . . . All other science . . . is either perception by sense, or the imagination, or memory remaining after such perception.

The first beginnings, therefore, of knowledge, are the phantasms of sense and imagination; and that there be such phantasms we know well enough by nature; but to know why they be, or from what cause they proceed, is the work of ratiocination; which consists . . . in *composition,* and *division* or *resolution.* There is therefore no method, by which we find out the causes of things, but is

---

13.   From Molesworth, *De Corpore,* Ch. 6.

either *compositive* or *resolutive,* or *partly compositive,* and *partly resolutive.*
And the resolutive is commonly called *analytical* method, as the compositive is
called synthetical.

2. It is common to all sorts of method, to proceed from known things to
unknown; and this is manifest from the cited definition of philosophy. But in
knowledge by sense, the whole object is more known, than any part thereof; as
when we see a man, the conception or whole idea of that man is first or more
known, than the particular ideas of his being *figurate, animate,* and *rational;*
that is, we first see the whole man, and take notice of his being, before we
observe in him those other particulars. And therefore in any knowledge . . . that
any thing *is,* the beginning of our search is from the whole idea; and contrarily,
in our knowledge . . . of the causes of any thing, that is, in the sciences, we have
more knowledge of the causes of the parts than of the whole. For the cause of
the whole is compounded of the causes of the parts; but it is necessary that we
know the whole compound. Now, by parts, I do not here mean parts of the
thing itself, but parts of its nature; as, by the parts of man, I do not understand
his head, his shoulders, his arms, &c. but his figure, quantity, motion, sense,
reason, and the like; which accidents being compounded or put together, constitute the whole nature of man, but not the man himself. And this is the meaning
of that common saying, namely, that some things are more known to us, others
more known to nature; for I do not think that they, which so distinguish, mean
that something is known to nature, which is known to no man; and therefore,
by those things, that are more known to us, we are to understand things we
take notice of by our senses, and, by more known to nature, those we acquire
the knowledge of by reason; for in this sense it is, that the *whole,* that is, those
things that have universal names (which, for brevity's sake, I call *universal*) are
more known to us that the *parts,* that is, such things as have names less universal, (which I therefore call *singular*); and the causes of the parts are more known
to nature than the causes of the whole; that is, universals than singulars.

3. In the study of philosophy, men search after science either simply
or indefinitely; that is, to know as much as they can, without propounding to
themselves any limited question; or they enquire into the cause of some determined appearance, or endeavour to find out the certainty of something in
question, as what is the cause of *light,* of *heat,* of *gravity,* of a *figure* propounded, and the like; or in what *subject* any propounded *accident* in inherent;
or what may conduce most to the generation of some propounded *effect* from
many *accidents;* or in what manner particular causes ought to be compounded
for the production of some certain effect. Now, according to this variety of
things in question, sometimes the *analytical method* is to be used, and sometimes the *synthetical.*

4. But to those that search after science indefinitely, which consists in the
knowledge of the causes of all things, as far forth as it may be attained, (and the
causes of singular things are compounded of the causes of universal or simple
things) it is necessary that they know the causes of universal things, or of such
accidents as are common to all bodies, that is, to all matter, before they can
know the causes of singular things, that is, of those accidents by which one

thing is distinguished from another. And, again, they must know what those universal things are, before they can know their causes. Moreover, seeing universal things are contained in the nature of singular things, the knowledge of them is to be acquired by reason, that is, by resolution. For example, if there be propounded a conception or *idea* of some singular thing, as of a *square,* this square is to be resolved into a *plane, terminated with a certain number of equal and straight lines and right angles.* For by this resolution we have these things universal or agreeable to all matter, namely, *line, plane,* (which contains *superficies*) *terminated, angle, straightness, rectitude,* and *equality;* and if we find out the causes of these, we may compound them altogether into the cause of a square. Again, if any man propound to himself the conception of *gold,* he may, by resolving, come to the ideas of *solid, visible, heavy,* (that is, tending to the centre of the earth, or downwards) and many other more universal than gold itself; and these he may resolve again, till he come to such things as are most universal. And in this manner, by resolving continually, we may come to know what those things are, whose causes being first known severally, and afterwards compounded, bring us to the knowledge of singular things. I conclude, therefore, that the method of attaining to the universal knowledge of things, is purely *analytical.*

5. But the causes of universal things (of those, at least, that have any cause) are manifest of themselves, or (as they say commonly) known to nature; so that they need no method at all; for they have all but one universal cause, which is motion. For the variety of all figures arises out of the variety of those motions by which they are made; and motion cannot be understood to have any other cause besides motion; nor has the variety of those things we perceive by sense, as of *colours, sounds, savours, &c.* any other cause than motion. . . .

6. By the knowledge therefore of universals, and of their causes . . . we have in the first place their definitions, (which are nothing but the explication of our simple conceptions). For example, he that has a true conception of *place,* cannot be ignorant of this definition, *place is that space which is possessed or filled adequately by some body;* and so, he that conceives *motion* aright, cannot but know that *motion is the privation of one place, and the acquisition of another.* In the next place, we have their generations or descriptions; as (for example) that *a line is made by the motion of a point, superficies by the motion of a line,* and *one motion by another motion, &c.* It remains, that we enquire what motion begets such and such effects; as, what motion makes a straight line, and what a circular; what motion thrusts, what draws, and by what way; what makes a thing which is seen or heard, to be seen or heard sometimes in one manner, sometimes in another. Now the method of this kind of enquiry, is *compositive.* For first we are to observe what effect a body moved produceth, when we consider nothing in it besides its motion; and we see presently that this makes a line, or length; next, what the motion of a long body produces, which we find to be superficies; and so forwards, till we see what the effects of simple motion are; and then, in like manner, we are to observe what proceeds from the addition, multiplication, substraction, and division, of these motions, and what effects, what figures, and what properties,

they produce; from which kind of contemplation sprung that part of philosophy which is called *geometry.*

From this consideration of what is produced by simple motion, we are to pass to the consideration of what effects one body moved worketh upon another; and because there may be motion in all the several parts of a body, yet so as that the whole body remain still in the same place, we must enquire first, what motion causeth such and such motion in the whole, that is, when one body invades another body which is either at rest or in motion, what way, and with what swiftness, the invaded body shall move; and, again, what motion this second body will generate in a third, and so forwards. From which contemplation shall be drawn that part of philosophy which treats of motion. . . .

After *physics* we must come to *moral philosophy;* in which we are to consider the motions of the mind, namely, *appetite, aversion, love, benevolence, hope, fear, anger, emulation, envy, &c.;* what causes they have, and of what they be causes. And the reason why these are to be considered after *physics* is, that they have their causes in sense and imagination, which are the subject of *physical* contemplation. . . .

7. *Civil* and *moral philosophy* do not so adhere to one another, but that they may be severed. For the causes of the mind are known, not only by ratiocination, but also by the experiences of every man that takes the pains to observe those motions within himself. And, therefore, not only they that have attained the knowledge of the passions and perturbations of the mind, by the *synthetical method,* and from the very first principles of philosophy, may be proceeding in the same way, come to the causes and necessity of constituting commonwealths, and to get the knowledge of what is natural right, and what are civil duties; and, in every kind of government, what are the rights of the commonwealth, and all other knowledge appertaining to civil philosophy; for this reason, that the principles of the politics consist in the knowledge of the motions of the mind, and the knowledge of these motions from the knowledge of sense and imagination; but even they also that have not learned the first part of philosophy, namely, *geometry* and *physics,* may, not withstanding, attain the principles of civil philosophy, by the *analytical method.* For if a question be propounded, as, *whether such an action be just or unjust;* if that *unjust* be resolved into *fact against law,* and that notion *law* into the *command* of him or them that have *coercive power;* and that *power* be derived from the *wills* of men that constitute such power, to the end they may live in peace, they may at last come to this, that the appetites of men and the passions of their minds are such, that, unless they be restrained by some power, they will always be making war upon one another; which may be known to be so by any man's experience, that will but examine his own mind. And, therefore, from hence he may proceed, by compounding, to the determination of the justice or injustice of any propounded action. So that it is manifest, by what has been said, that the method of philosophy, to such as seek science simply, without propounding to themselves the solution of any particular question, is partly analytical, and partly synthetical; namely, that which proceeds from sense to the invention of principles, analytical; and the rest synthetical.

Sir Francis. From what you've said, I see that we concur in the belief that the immediate aim of scientific method is finding out the causes of things.

Mr. Hobbes. And by the shortest way, too.

Sir Francis. Still, I cannot but feel that your dual approach, combining conceptual analysis (your "analytical" method) and deductive inference (your "synthetical" method), fails to meet my objections regarding the deficiencies of the older logic.

Mr. Hobbes. You should bear in mind, my lord, that there are differences between Aristotle's approach and mine. According to my thought, the universal cause of all things is motion, and my entire analytical method is predicated thereon. Furthermore, although I do not hold the syllogism in such disrepute as you do, still I advocate, as pertains to my synthetical method, that all inferences from universal concepts and names be informed by the example of the mathematics, in particular, of geometry.

Sir Francis. And with these emendations and innovations, you expect that your method, unlike Aristotle's, will not let Nature slip out of hand, nor merely fix past errors?

Mr. Hobbes. I do indeed, sir.

Sir Francis. Well, at least we agree that a proper method is absolutely essential, though I doubt that we shall ever agree about its character. Nonetheless, I don't think that either of us should overlook the fact that the human mind is subject to many fallacies, or "idols," as I like to call them.

Mr. Hobbes. I quite agree.

Sir Francis. I am convinced that the provisions and helps I have attempted to supply for the assistance of the mind would be sufficient of themselves to prevent error, if searchers after truth would only make use of them, and if one other thing were so.

Mr. Hobbes. Pray sir, what is that?

Sir Francis. If the human intellect were even, and like a fair sheet of paper with no writing on it. But since the minds of men are strangely possessed and beset, so that there is no true and even surface left to reflect the genuine rays of things, it is necessary to seek a remedy for this also.[14]

Mr. Hobbes. Please tell me more of your theory of the idols of the mind, and your proposals to eradicate them.

Sir Francis. I would be happy to do so.

Now the idols, or phantoms, by which the mind is occupied are either adventitious or innate. The adventitious come into the mind from without;

---

14. This quotation and the next, which is a continuation of it, are from the Plan of *The Great Instauration,* in *The Works of Francis Bacon,* Vol. IV, pp. 26–27.

namely, either from the doctrines and sects of philosophers, or from perverse rules of demonstration. But the innate are inherent in the very nature of the intellect, which is far more prone to error than the sense is. For let men please themselves as they will in admiring and almost adoring the human mind, this is certain: that as an uneven mirror distorts the rays of objects according to its own figure and section, so the mind, when it receives impressions of objects through the sense, cannot be trusted to report them truly, but in forming its notions mixes up its own nature with the nature of things.

And as the first two kinds of idols are hard to eradicate, so idols of this last kind cannot be eradicated at all. All that can be done is to point them out, so that this insidious action of the mind may be marked and reproved (else as fast as old errors are destroyed new ones will spring up out of the ill complexion of the mind itself, and so we shall have but a change of errors, and not a clearance); and to lay it down once for all as a fixed and established maxim, that the intellect is not qualified to judge except by means of induction, and induction in its legitimate form.

Sir Francis. I have developed my views regarding the idols of the mind further in the first part of my Novum Organum. The relevant Aphorisms[15] are as follows:

Aphorisms XXXIX–XLIV: The Four Classes of Idols

There are four classes of idols which beset men's minds. To these for distinction's sake I have assigned names,—calling the first class *Idols of the Tribe;* the second, *Idols of the Cave;* the third, *Idols of the Market-place;* the fourth, *Idols of the Theater.*

The formation of ideas and axioms by true induction is no doubt the proper remedy to be applied for the keeping off and clearing away of idols. To point them out, however, is of great use, for the doctrine of idols is to the interpretation of nature what the doctrine of the refutation of sophisms is to common logic.

The Idols of the Tribe have their foundation in human nature itself, and in the tribe or race of men. For it is a false assertion that the sense of man is the measure of things. On the contrary, all perceptions, as well of the sense as of the mind, are according to the measure of the individual and not according to the measure of the universe. And the human understanding is like a false mirror, which, receiving rays irregularly, distorts and discolors the nature of things by mingling its own nature with it.

The Idols of the Cave are the idols of the individual man. For everyone (besides the errors common to human nature in general) has a cave or den of his

---

15. Bacon lists 130 aphorisms (roughly meaning "theses") in his first book of "aphorisms concerning the interpretation of nature and the kingdom of man." Instead of listing the relevant aphorisms singly as he does, they have been grouped together according to the topic of discussion. From *The New Organon,* in *The Works of Francis Bacon,* Vol. IV, pp. 53–66, 92–93.

own, which refracts and discolors the light of nature; owing either to his own proper and peculiar nature or to his education and conversation with others; or to the reading of books, and the authority of those whom he esteems and admires; or to the differences of impressions, accordingly as they take place in a mind preoccupied and predisposed or in a mind indifferent and settled; or the like. So that the spirit of man (according as it is meted out to different individuals) is in fact a thing variable and full of perturbation, and governed as it were by chance. Whence it was well observed by Heraclitus that men look for sciences in their own lesser worlds, and not in the greater or common world.

There are also idols formed by the intercourse and association of men with each other, which I call Idols of the Market-place, on account of the commerce and consort of men there. For it is by discourse that men associate; and words are imposed according to the apprehension of the vulgar. And therefore the ill and unfit choice of words wonderfully obstructs the understanding. Nor do the definitions or explanations wherewith in some things learned men are wont to guard and defend themselves, by any means set the matter right. But words plainly force and overrule the understanding, and throw all into confusion, and lead men away into numberless empty controversies and idle fancies.

Lastly, there are idols which have immigrated into men's minds from the various dogmas of philosophies, and also from wrong laws of demonstration. These I call Idols of the Theater; because in my judgment all the received systems are but so many stage-plays, representing worlds of their own creation after an unreal and scenic fashion. Nor is it only of the systems now in vogue, or only of the ancient sects and philosophies, that I speak: for many more plays of the same kind may yet be composed and in like artificial manner set forth; seeing that errors the most widely different have nevertheless causes for the most part alike. Neither again do I mean this only of entire systems, but also of many principles and axioms in science, which by tradition, credulity, and negligence have come to be received.

But of these several kinds of idols I must speak more largely and exactly, that the understanding may be duly cautioned.

Aphorisms XLV–LII: The Idols of the Tribe

The human understanding is of its own nature prone to suppose the existence of more order and regularity in the world than it finds. And though there be many things in nature which are singular and unmatched, yet it devises for them parallels and conjugates and relatives which do not exist. Hence the fiction that all celestial bodies move in perfect circles; spirals and dragons being (except in name) utterly rejected. Hence too the element of fire with its orb is brought in, to make up the square with the other three which the sense perceives. Hence also the ratio of density of the so-called elements is arbitrarily fixed at ten to one. And so on of other dreams. And these fancies affect not dogmas only, but simple notions also.

The human understanding when it has once adopted an opinion (either as being the received opinion or as being agreeable to itself) draws all things else to support and agree with it. And though there be a greater number and weight of instances to be found on the other side, yet these it either neglects and despises, or else by some distinction sets aside and rejects; in order that by this great and pernicious predetermination the authority of its former conclusions may remain inviolate. And therefore it was a good answer that was made by one who when they showed him hanging in a temple a picture of those who had paid their vows as having escaped shipwreck, and would have him say whether he did not now acknowledge the power of the gods,—"Aye," asked he again, "but where are they painted that were drowned after their vows?" And such is the way of all superstition, whether in astrology, dreams, omens, divine judgments, or the like; wherein men, having a delight in such vanities, mark the events where they are fulfilled, but where they fail, though this happen much oftener, neglect and pass them by. But with far more subtlety does this mischief insinuate itself into philosophy and the sciences; in which the first conclusion colors and brings into conformity with itself all that come after, though far sounder and better. Besides, independently of that delight and vanity which I have described, it is the peculiar and perpetual error of the human intellect to be more moved and excited by affirmatives than by negatives; whereas it ought properly to hold itself indifferently disposed towards both alike. Indeed in the establishment of any true axiom, the negative instance is the more forcible of the two.

The human understanding is moved by those things most which strike and enter the mind simultaneously and suddenly, and so fill the imagination; and then it feigns and supposes all other things to be somehow, though it cannot see how, similar to those few things by which it is surrounded. But for that going to and fro to remote and heterogeneous instances, by which axioms are tried as in the fire, the intellect is altogether slow and unfit, unless it be forced thereto by severe laws and overruling authority.

The human understanding is unquiet; it cannot stop or rest, and still presses onward, but in vain. Therefore it is that we cannot conceive of any end or limit to the world; but always as of necessity it occurs to us that there is something beyond. Neither again can it be conceived how eternity has flowed down to the present day: for that distinction which is commonly received of infinity in time past and in time to come can by no means hold; for it would thence follow that one infinity is greater than another, and that infinity is wasting away and tending to become finite. The like subtlety arises touching the infinite divisibility of lines, from the same inability of thought to stop. But this inability interferes more mischievously in the discovery of causes: for although the most general principles in nature ought to be held merely positive, as they are discovered, and cannot with truth be referred to a cause; nevertheless the human understanding being unable to rest still seeks something prior in the order of nature. And then it is that in struggling towards that which is further off it falls back upon that which is more nigh at hand,—namely, on final causes; which have relation clearly to the nature of man rather than to the nature of the universe, and from this source have strangely defiled philosophy. But he is no less an unskilled and shallow philosopher who seeks causes of that which is most general, than he who in things subordinate and subaltern omits to do so.

The human understanding is no dry light, but receives an infusion from the will and affections; whence proceed sciences which may be called "sciences as one would." For what a man had rather were true he more readily believes. Therefore he rejects difficult things from impatience of research; sober things, because they narrow hope; the deeper things of nature, from superstition; the light of experience, from arrogance and pride, lest his mind should seem to be occupied with things mean and transitory; things not commonly believed, out of deference to the opinion of the vulgar. Numberless in short are the ways, and sometimes imperceptible, in which the affections color and infect the understanding.

But by far the greatest hindrance and aberration of the human understanding proceeds from the dullness, incompetency, and deceptions of the senses; in that things which strike the sense outweigh things which do not immediately strike it, though they be more important. Hence it is that speculation commonly ceases where sight ceases, insomuch that of things invisible there is little or no observation. Hence all the working of the spirits inclosed in tangible bodies lies hid and unobserved of men. So also all the more subtle changes of form in the parts of coarser substances (which they commonly call alteration, though it is in truth local motion through exceedingly small spaces) is in like manner unobserved. And yet unless these two things just mentioned be searched out and brought to light, nothing great can be achieved in nature, as far as the production of works is concerned. So again the essential nature of our common air, and of all bodies less dense than air (which are very many), is almost unknown. For the sense by itself is a thing infirm and erring; neither can instruments for enlarging or sharpening the senses do much: but all the truer kind of interpretation of nature is effected by instances and experiments fit and apposite; wherein the sense decides touching the experiment only, and the experiment touching the point in nature and the thing itself.

The human understanding is of its own nature prone to abstractions and gives a substance and reality to things which are fleeting. But to resolve nature into abstractions is less to our purpose than to dissect her into parts; as did the school of Democritus, which went further into nature than the rest. Matter rather than forms should be the object of our attention, its configurations and changes of configuration, and simple action, and law of action or motion; for forms are figments of the human mind, unless you will call those laws of action forms.

Such then are the idols which I call *Idols of the Tribe;* and which take their rise either from the homogeneity of the substance of the human spirit, or from its preoccupation, or from its narrowness, or from its restless motion, or from an infusion of the affections, or from the incompetency of the senses, or from the mode of impression.

Aphorisms LIII–LVIII: The Idols of the Cave

The *Idols of the Cave* take their rise in the peculiar constitution, mental or bodily, of each individual; and also in education, habit, and accident. Of this kind there is a great number and variety; but I will instance those the pointing out of which contains the most important caution, and which have most effect in disturbing the clearness of the understanding.

Men become attached to certain particular sciences and speculations, either because they fancy themselves the authors and inventors thereof, or because they have bestowed the greatest pains upon them and become most habituated to them. But men of this kind, if they betake themselves to philosophy and contemplations of a general character, distort and color them in obedience to their former fancies; a thing especially to be noticed in Aristotle, who made his natural philosophy a mere bondservant to his logic, thereby rendering it contentious and well nigh useless. The race of chemists again out of a few experiments of the furnace have built up a fantastic philosophy, framed with reference to a few things; and Gilbert also, after he had employed himself most laboriously in the study and observation of the lodestone, proceeded at once to construct an entire system in accordance with his favorite subject.

There is one principal and as it were radical distinction between different minds, in respect of philosophy and the sciences; which is this: that some minds are stronger and apter to mark the differences of things, others to mark their resemblances. The steady and acute mind can fix its contemplations and dwell and fasten on the subtlest distinctions; the lofty and discursive mind recognizes and puts together the finest and most general resemblances. Both kinds however easily err in excess, by catching the one at gradations the other at shadows.

There are found some minds given to an extreme admiration of antiquity, others to an extreme love and appetite for novelty; but few so duly tempered that they can hold the mean, neither carping at what has been well laid down by the ancients, nor despising what is well introduced by the moderns. This however turns to the great injury of the sciences and philosophy: since these affectations of antiquity and novelty are the humors of partisans rather than judgments; and truth is to be sought for not in the felicity of any age, which is an unstable thing, but in the light of nature and experience, which is eternal. These factions therefore must be abjured, and care must be taken that the intellect be not hurried by them into assent.

Contemplations of nature and of bodies in their simple form break up and distract the understanding, while contemplations of nature and bodies in their composition and configuration overpower and dissolve the understanding: a distinction well seen in the school of Leucippus and Democritus as compared with the other philosophies. For that school is so busied with the particles that it hardly attends to the structure; while the others are so lost in admiration of the structure that they do not penetrate to the simplicity of nature. These kinds of contemplation should therefore be alternated and taken by turns; that so the understanding may be rendered at once penetrating and comprehensive, and the inconveniences above mentioned, with the idols which proceed from them, may be avoided.

Let such then be our provision and contemplative prudence for keeping off and dislodging the Idols of the Cave, which grow for the most part either out of the predominance of a favorite subject, or out of an excessive tendency to compare or to distinguish, or out of partiality for particular ages, or out of the largeness or minuteness of the objects contemplated. And generally let every student of nature take this as a rule,—that whatever his mind seizes and dwells upon with peculiar satisfaction is to be held in suspicion, and that so much the more care is to be taken in dealing with such questions to keep the understanding even and clear.

Aphorisms LIX–LX: The Idols of the Market-place

But the *Idols of the Market-place* are the most troublesome of all: idols which have crept into the understanding through the alliances of words and names. For men believe that their reason governs words; but it is also true that words react on the understanding; and this it is that has rendered philosophy and the sciences sophistical and inactive. Now words, being commonly framed and applied according to the capacity of the vulgar, follow those lines of division which are most obvious to the vulgar understanding. And whenever an understanding of greater acuteness or a more diligent observation would alter those lines to suit the true divisions of nature, words stand in the way and resist the change. Whence it comes to pass that the high and formal discussions of learned men end oftentimes in disputes about words and names; with which (according to the use and wisdom of the mathematicians) it would be more prudent to begin, and so by means of definitions reduce them to order. Yet even definitions cannot cure this evil in dealing with natural and material things; since the definitions themselves consist of words, and those words beget others: so that it is necessary to recur to individual instances, and those in due series and order; as I shall say presently when I come to the method and scheme for the formation of notions and axioms.

The idols imposed by words on the understanding are of two kinds. They are either names of things which do not exist (for as there are things left unnamed through lack of observation, so likewise are there names which result from fantastic suppositions and to which nothing in reality corresponds), or they are names of things which exist, but yet confused and ill-defined, and hastily and irregularly derived from realities. Of the former kind are Fortune, the Prime Mover, Planetary Orbits, Elements of Fire, and like fictions which owe their origin to false and idle theories. And this class of idols is more easily expelled, because to get rid of them it is only necessary that all theories should be steadily rejected and dismissed as obsolete.

But the other class, which springs out of a faulty and unskillful abstraction, is intricate and deeply rooted. Let us take for example such a word as *humid,* and see how far the several things which the word is used to signify agree with each other; and we shall find the word *humid* to be nothing else than a mark loosely and confusedly applied to denote a variety of actions which will not bear to be reduced to any constant meaning. For it both signifies that which easily spreads itself round any other body; and that which in itself is indeterminate and cannot solidize; and that which readily yields in every direction; and that which easily divides and scatters itself; and that which easily unites and collects itself; and that which readily flows and is put in motion; and that which readily clings to another body and wets it; and that which is easily reduced to a liquid, or being solid easily melts. Accordingly when you come to apply the word,—if you take it in one sense, flame is humid; if in another, air is not humid; if in another, fine dust is humid; if in another, glass is humid. So that it is easy to see that the notion is taken by abstraction only from water and common and ordinary liquids, without any due verification.

There are however in words certain degrees of distortion and error. One of the least faulty kinds is that of names of substances, especially of lowest species and well-deduced (for the notion of *chalk* and of *mud* is good, of *earth* bad); a more faulty kind is that of actions, as *to generate, to corrupt, to alter;* the most faulty is of qualities (except such as are the immediate objects of the sense) as *heavy, light, rare, dense,* and the like. Yet in all these cases some notions are of necessity a little better than others, in proportion to the greater variety of subjects that fall within the range of the human sense.

Aphorisms LXI–LXVI: The Idols of the Theater

But the *Idols of the Theater* are not innate, nor do they steal into the understanding secretly, but are plainly impressed and received into the mind from the play-books of philosophical systems and the perverted rules of demonstration. To attempt refutations in this case would be merely inconsistent with what I have already said: for since we agree neither upon principles nor upon demonstrations there is no place for argument. And this is so far well, inasmuch as it leaves the honor of the ancients untouched. For they are no wise disparaged— the question between them and me being only as to the way. For as the saying is, the lame man who keeps the right road outstrips the runner who takes a wrong one. Nay it is obvious that when a man runs the wrong way, the more active and swift he is the further he will go astray.

But the course I propose for the discovery of sciences is such as leaves but little to the acuteness and strength of wits, but places all wits and understandings nearly on a level. For as in the drawing of a straight line or a perfect circle, much depends on the steadiness and practice of the hand, if it be done by aim of hand only, but if with the aid of rule or compass, little or nothing; so is it exactly with my plan. But though particular confutations would be of no avail, yet touching the sects and general divisions of such systems I must say something; something also touching the external signs which show that they are unsound; and finally something touching the causes of such great infelicity and of such lasting and general agreement in error; that so the access to truth may be made less difficult, and the human understanding may the more willingly submit to its purgation and dismiss its idols.

Idols of the Theater, or of Systems, are many, and there can be and perhaps will be yet many more. For were it not that now for many ages men's minds have been busied with religion and theology; and were it not that civil governments, especially monarchies, have been averse to such novelties, even in matters speculative; so that men labor therein to the peril and harming of their fortunes,—not only unrewarded, but exposed also to contempt and envy: doubtless there would have arisen many other philosophical sects like to those which in great variety flourished once among the Greeks. For as on the phenomena of the heavens many hypotheses may be constructed, so likewise (and more also) many various dogmas may be set up and established on the phenomena of philosophy. And in the plays of this philosophical theater you may observe the same thing which is found in the theater of the poets, that stories invented for the stage are more compact and elegant, and more as one would wish them to be, than true stories out of history.

In general however there is taken for the material of philosophy either a great deal out of a few things, or a very little out of many things; so that on both sides philosophy is based on too narrow a foundation of experiment and natural history, and decides on the authority of too few cases. For the rational school of philosophers snatches from experience a variety of common instances, neither duly ascertained nor diligently examined and weighed, and leaves all the rest to meditation and agitation of wit.

There is also another class of philosophers, who having bestowed much diligent and careful labor on a few experiments, have thence made bold to educe and construct systems; wresting all other facts in a strange fashion to conformity therewith.

And there is yet a third class, consisting of those who out of faith and veneration mix their philosophy with theology and traditions; among whom the vanity of some has gone so far aside as to seek the origin of science among spirits and genii. So that this parent stock of errors—this false philosophy—is of three kinds; the *sophistical,* the *empirical,* and the *superstitious.*

The most conspicuous example of the first class was Aristotle, who corrupted natural philosophy by his logic: fashioning the world out of categories; assigning to the human soul, the noblest of substances, a genus from words of the second intention; doing the business of density and rarity (which is to make bodies of greater or less dimensions, that is, occupy greater or less spaces), by the frigid distinction of act and power; asserting that single bodies have each a single and proper motion, and that if they participate in any other, then this results from an external cause; and imposing countless other arbitrary restrictions on the nature of things: being always more solicitous to provide an answer to the question and affirm something positive in words, than about the inner truth of things; a failing best shown when his philosophy is compared with other systems of note among the Greeks. For the *homoeomera* of Anaxagoras; the atoms of Leucippus and Democritus; the Heaven and Earth of Parmenides; the Strife and Friendship of Empedocles; Heraclitus's doctrine how bodies are resolved into the indifferent nature of fire, and remolded into solids; have all of them some taste of the natural philosopher,—some savor of the nature of things, and experience, and bodies; whereas in the physics of Aristotle you hear hardly anything but the words of logic; which in his metaphysics also, under a more imposing name, and more forsooth as a realist than a nominalist, he has handled over again. Nor let any weight be given to the fact that in his books on animals, and his Problems, and other of his treatises, there is frequent dealing with experiments. For he had come to his conclusion before: he did not consult experience, as he should have done, in order to the framing of his decisions and axioms; but having first determined the question according to his will, he then resorts to experience, and bending her into conformity with his placets leads her about like a captive in a procession: so that even on this count he is more guilty than his modern followers, the schoolmen, who have abandoned experience altogether.

But the empirical school of philosophy gives birth to dogmas more deformed and monstrous than the sophistical or rational school. For it has its foundations not in the light of common notions (which, though it be a faint and superficial light, is yet in a manner universal, and has reference to many things) but in the narrowness and darkness of a few experiments. To those therefore who are daily busied with these experiments, and have infected their imagination with them, such a philosophy seems probable and all but certain; to all men else incredible and vain. Of this there is a notable instance in the alchemists and their dogmas; though it is hardly to be found elsewhere in these times, except perhaps in the philosophy of Gilbert. Nevertheless with regard to philosophies of this kind there is one caution not to be omitted; for I foresee that if ever men are roused by my admonitions to betake themselves seriously to experiment and bid farewell to sophistical doctrines, then indeed through the premature hurry of the understanding to leap or fly to universals and principles of things, great danger may be apprehended from philosophies of this kind; against which evil we ought even now to prepare.

But the corruption of philosophy by superstition and an admixture of theology is far more widely spread, and does the greatest harm, whether to entire systems or to their parts. For the human understanding is obnoxious to the influence of the imagination no less than to the influence of common notions. For the contentious and sophistical kind of philosophy ensnares the understanding; but this kind, being fanciful and tumid and half poetical, misleads it more by flattery. For there is in man an ambition of the understanding, no less than of the will, especially in high and lofty spirits.

Of this kind we have among the Greeks a striking example of Pythagoras, though he united with it a coarser and more cumbrous superstition; another in Plato and his school, more dangerous and subtle. It shows itself likewise in parts of other philosophies, in the introduction of abstract forms and final causes and first causes, with the omission in most cases of causes intermediate, and the like. Upon this point the greatest caution should be used. For nothing is so mischievous as the apotheosis of error; and it is a very plague of the understanding for vanity to become the object of veneration. Yet in this vanity some of the moderns have with extreme levity indulged so far as to attempt to found a system of natural philosophy on the first chapters of Genesis, on the book of Job, and other parts of the sacred writings; seeking for the dead among the living: which also makes the inhibition and repression of it the more important, because from this unwholesome mixture of things human and divine there arises not only a fantastic philosophy but also an heretical religion. Very meet it is therefore that we be sober-minded, and give to faith that only which is faith's.

So much then for the mischievous authorities of systems, which are founded either on common notions, or on a few experiments, or on superstition. . . .

Aphorism XCV:
Experiment Versus Dogma: The Middle Course

Those who have handled sciences have been either men of experiment or men of dogmas. The men of experiment are like the ant; they only collect and use: the reasoners resemble spiders, who make cobwebs out of their own substance. But the bee takes a middle course, it gathers its material from the flowers of the garden and of the field, but transforms and digests it by a power of its own. Not unlike this is the true business of philosophy: for it neither relies solely or chiefly on the powers of the mind, nor does it take the matter which it gathers from natural history and mechanical experiments and lay it up in the memory whole, as it finds it; but lays it up in the understanding altered and digested. Therefore from a closer and purer league between these two faculties, the experimental and the rational, (such as has never yet been made) much may be hoped.

Mr. Hobbes. I'm afraid I cannot accept your maxim which you "lay down once for all," namely, that the intellect is not qualified to judge except by means of induction. For my part, human reason is not so "possessed" or "beset" as you have suggested. By nature all men reason alike and if they are attentive and industrious and adopt an orderly method of proceeding to and from the basic elements and principles, they reason well.

Sir Francis. But I thought you agreed with me that there are idols of the mind and errors of procedure which lead men to falsehood and away from truth.

Mr. Hobbes. I do, but I believe that these stem mainly from a want of method and an abuse of speech, rather than from some distortion of the mind itself.

Sir Francis. Then I suppose that you must be taken with what I call "idols of the market-place."

Mr. Hobbes. To be sure I am; I have thought considerably about such errors.

Sir Francis. Please tell me some of your conclusions.

Mr. Hobbes.[16] The general use of speech is to transfer our mental discourse into

16. From *Leviathan*, in *The English Works of Thomas Hobbes*, Part I, Chapters IV and V.

verbal, or the train of our thoughts into a train of words; and that for two commodities, whereof one is the registering of the consequences of our thoughts; which, being apt to slip out of our memory and put us to a new labor, may again be recalled by such words as they were marked by. So that the first use of names is to serve for *marks,* or *notes* of remembrance. Another is, when many use the same words, to signify, by their connection and order, one to another, what they conceive, or think of each matter; and also what they desire, fear, or have any other passion for. And for this use they are called *signs.* Special uses of speech are these: first, to register what by cogitation we find to be the cause of anything, present or past, and what we find things present or past may produce or effect; which, in sum, is acquiring of arts. Secondly, to show to others that knowledge which we have attained; which is, to counsel and teach one another. Thirdly, to make known to others our wills and purposes, that we may have the mutual help of one another. Fourthly, to please and delight ourselves and others, by playing with our words, for pleasure or ornament, innocently.

To these uses, there are also four correspondent abuses. First, when men register their thoughts wrong, by the inconstancy of the signification of their words; by which they register for their conception, that which they never conceived, and so deceive themselves. Secondly, when they use words metaphorically; that is, in other sense than that they are ordained for; and thereby deceive others. Thirdly, by words, when they declare that to be their will which is not. Fourthly, when they use them to grieve one another; for seeing nature hath armed living creatures, some with teeth, some with horns, and some with hands, to grieve an enemy, it is but an abuse of speech, to grieve him with the tongue, unless it be one whom we are obliged to govern; and then it is not to grieve, but to correct and amend. . . .

Seeing then that truth consisteth in the right ordering of names in our affirmations, a man that seeketh precise truth had need to remember what every name he uses stands for, and to place it accordingly, or else he will find himself entangled in words, as a bird in lime twigs, the more he struggles the more belimed. And therefore in geometry, which is the only science that it hath pleased God hitherto to bestow on mankind, men begin at settling the significations of their words; which settling of significations they call *definitions,* and place them in the beginning of their reckoning. By this it appears how necessary it is for any man that aspires to true knowledge, to examine the definitions of former authors; and either to correct them, where they are negligently set down, or to make them himself. For the errors of definitions multiply themselves according as the reckoning proceeds, and lead men into absurdities, which at last they see, but cannot avoid without reckoning anew from the beginning, in which lies the foundation of their errors. From whence it happens that they which trust to books do as they that cast up many little sums into a greater, without considering whether those little sums were rightly cast up or not; and at last finding the error visible, and not mistrusting their first grounds, know not which way to clear themselves, but spend time in fluttering over their books; as birds that entering by the chimney, and finding themselves enclosed in a chamber, flutter at the false light of a glass window, for want of wit to consider which way they came in. So that in the right definition of names lies the first use of speech, which is the acquisition of science; and in wrong, or no definitions, lies the first abuse, from which proceed all false and senseless tenets: which make those men that take their instruction from the authority of books, and not from their own meditation, to be as much below the condition of ignorant men as men endued with true science are above it. For between true science and erroneous doctrines, ignorance is in the middle. Natural sense and imagination are not subject to absurdity. Nature itself cannot err; and as men abound in copiousness of language, so they become more wise, or more mad, than ordinary. Nor is it possible without letters for any man to become either excellently wise, or, unless his memory be hurt by disease or ill constitution of organs, excellently foolish. For words are wise men's counters, they do but reckon by them; but they are the money of fools, that value them by the authority of an Aristotle, a Cicero, or a Thomas, or any other doctor whatsoever, if but a man. . . .

For reason . . . is nothing but *reckoning,* that is adding and subtracting, of the consequences of general names agreed upon for the marking and signifying of our thoughts: I say *marking* them when we reckon by ourselves, and *signifying* when we demonstrate or approve our reckonings to other men. . . .

When a man reckons without the use of words, which may be done in particular things, as when upon the sight of any one thing, we conjecture what was likely to have preceded, or is likely to follow upon it; if that which he thought likely to follow, follows not, or that which he thought likely to have preceded it, hath not preceded it, this is called *error;* to which even the most prudent men are subject. But when we reason in words of general signification, and fall upon a general inference which is false, though it be commonly called error, it is indeed an *absurdity,* or senseless speech. For error is but a deception, in presuming that somewhat is past or to come; of which, though it were not past, or not to come, yet there was no impossibility discoverable. But when we make a general assertion, unless it be a true one, the possibility of it is inconceivable. And words whereby we conceive nothing but the sound, are those we call absurd, insignificant, and nonsense. And therefore if a man should talk to me of a round quadrangle, or, accidents of bread in cheese, of immaterial substances, or of a free subject, a free will, or any *free,* but free from being hindered by opposition; I should not say he were in error, but that his words were without meaning, that is to say, absurd.

I have said before . . . that a man did excel all other animals in this faculty, that when he conceived anything whatsoever, he was apt to inquire the consequences of it, and what effects he could do with it. And now I add this other degree of the same excellence, that he can by words reduce the consequences he finds to general rules, called *theorems,* or *aphorisms;* that is, he can reason, or reckon, not only in number, but in all other things whereof one may be added unto, or subtracted from another.

But this privilege is allayed by another; and that is, by the privilege of absurdity, to which no living creature is subject but man only. And of men, those are of all most subject to it that profess philosophy. For it is most true that Cicero saith of them somewhere, that there can be nothing so absurd but may be found in the books of philosophers. And the reason is manifest. For there is not one of them that begins his ratiocination from the definitions, or explications of the names they are to use; which is a method that hath been used only in geometry, whose conclusions have thereby been made indisputable.

(i) The first cause of absurd conclusions I ascribe to the want of method, in that they begin not their ratiocination from definitions; that is, from settled significations of their words: as if they could cast account without knowing the value of the numeral words, one, two, and three.

And whereas all bodies enter into account upon divers considerations, . . . these considerations being diversely named, divers absurdities proceed from the confusion, and unfit connection of their names into assertions. And therefore:

(ii) The second cause of absurd assertions, I ascribe to the giving of names of *bodies* to *accidents,* or of *accidents* to *bodies;* as they do that say, faith is "infused," or "inspired"; when nothing can be poured, or breathed into anything, but body; and that, extension is body; that phantasms are spirits, etc.

(iii) The third I ascribe to the giving of names of the *accidents of bodies without us,* to the *accidents of our own bodies;* as they do that say the color is in the body, the sound is in the air, etc.

(iv) The fourth, to the giving of the names of *bodies* to *names or speeches;* as they do that say that there be things universal; that a living creature is genus, or a general thing, etc.

(v) The fifth, to the giving of the names of *accidents* to *names and speeches;* as they do that say the nature of a thing is its definition, a man's command is his will, and the like.

(vi) The sixth, to the use of metaphors, tropes, and other rhetorical figures, instead of words proper. For though it be lawful to say, for example, in common speech, "the way goeth, or leadeth hither, or thither"; "the proverb says this or that," whereas ways cannot go, nor proverbs speak; yet in reckoning, and seeking of truth, such speeches are not to be admitted.

(vii) The seventh, to names that signify nothing, but are taken up and learned by rote from the schools, as "hypostatical," "transubstantiate," "consubstantiate," "eternal-now," and the like canting of schoolmen.

To him that can avoid these things it is not easy to fall into any absurdity, unless it be by the length of an account; wherein he may perhaps forget what went before. For all men by nature reason alike, and well, when they have good principles. For who is so stupid, as both to mistake in geometry, and also to persist in it when another detects his error to him?

By this it appears that reason is not, as sense and memory, born with us; nor gotten by experience only, as prudence is: but attained by industry; first in apt imposing of names; and secondly by getting a good and orderly method in proceeding from the elements, which are names, to assertions made by connection of one of them to another; and so to syllogisms, which are the connections of one assertion to another, till we come to a knowledge of all the consequences of names appertaining to the subject in hand; and that is it, men call *science.*

HOBBES

*A Dialogue Between a Philosopher and a Student of the Common Laws of England**

[1. Is the law a rational enterprise?]

Lawyer. What makes you say that the study of the law is less rational than the study of the mathematics?

Philosopher. I say not that, for all study is rational, or nothing worth; but I say that the great masters of the mathematics do not so often err as the great professors of the law.

Lawyer. If you had applied your reason to the law, perhaps you would have been of another mind.

Philosopher. In whatsoever study, I examine whether my inference be rational, and have looked over the titles of the statutes from *Magna Charta* downward to this present time. I left not one unread, which I thought might concern myself, which was enough for me, that meant not to plead for any but myself. But I did not much examine which of them was more or less rational; because I read

---

* From *The English Works of Thomas Hobbes,* edited by Sir William Molesworth (1839), Vol. VI. Hobbes' own subtitles have been omitted and others substituted. The punctuation has been altered slightly.

them not to dispute, but to obey them, and saw in all of them sufficient reason for my obedience, and that the same reason, though the Statutes themselves were changed, remained constant. I have also diligently read over Littleton's book of *Tenures,* with the commentaries thereupon of the renowned lawyer Sir Edward Coke, in which I confess I found great subtlety, not of the law, but of inference from law, and especially from the law of human nature, which is the law of reason; and I confess that it is truth which he says in the epilogue to his book, that by arguments and reason in the law, a man shall sooner come to the certainty and knowledge of the law; and I agree with Sir Edward Coke, who upon that text farther says that reason is the soul of the law; and upon section 138, *nihil quod est contra rationem, est licitum;* that is to say, nothing is law that is against reason; and that reason is the life of the law, nay the common law itself is nothing else but reason; and upon section 21, *aequitas est perfecta quaedam ratio, quae jus scriptum interpretatur et emendat, nulla scriptura comprehensa, sed solum in vera ratione consistens, i.e.,* equity is a certain perfect reason that interpreteth and amendeth the law written, itself being unwritten, and consisting in nothing else but right reason. When I consider this, and find it to be true, and so evident as not to be denied by any man of right sense, I find my own reason at a stand; for it frustrates all the laws in the world. For upon this ground any man, of any law whatsoever, may say it is against reason, and thereupon make a pretense for his disobedience. I pray you clear this passage, that we may proceed.

Lawyer. I clear it thus out of Sir Edward Coke (1 Inst. sect. 138) that this is to be understood of an artificial perfection of reason, gotten by long study, observation, and experience, and not of every man's natural reason; for *nemo nascitur artifex* [no one is born an artificer]. This legal reason is *summa ratio* [highest reason]; and therefore if all the reason that is dispersed into so many several heads were united into one, yet could he not make such a law as the law of England is, because by so many successions of ages it hath been fined and refined by an infinite number of grave and learned men.

Philosopher. This does not clear the place, as being partly obscure, and partly untrue. That the reason which is the life of the law should be not natural, but artificial, I cannot conceive. I understand well enough that the knowledge of the law is gotten by much study, as all other sciences are, which when they are studied and obtained, it is still done by natural, and not by artificial reason. I grant you that the knowledge of the law is an art, but not that any art of one man, or of many, how wise soever they be, or the work of one or more artificers, how perfect soever it be, is law. It is not wisdom, but authority that makes a law. Obscure also are the words *legal reason.* There is no reason in earthly creatures, but human reason. But I suppose that he means that the reason of a judge, or of all the judges together without the King, is that *summa ratio,* and the very law, which I deny, because none can make a law but he that hath the legislative power. That the law hath been fined by grave and learned men, meaning the professors of the law, is manifestly untrue; for all the laws of England have been made by the kings of England, consulting with the nobility and commons in parliament, of which not one of twenty was a learned lawyer.

Lawyer. You speak of the statute law, and I speak of the common law.

Philosopher. I speak generally of law.

Lawyer. Thus far I agree with you, that statute law taken away, there would not be left, either here, or any where, any law at all that would conduce to the peace of a nation; yet equity and reason (laws Divine and eternal, which oblige all men at all times, and in all places) would still remain, but be obeyed by few; and though the breach of them be not punished in this world, yet they will be punished sufficiently in the world to come. Sir Edward Coke, for drawing to the men of his own profession as much authority as lawfully he might, is not to be reprehended; but to the gravity and learning of the judges they ought to have added in the making of laws, the authority of the King, which hath the sovereignty; for of these laws of reason, every subject that is in his wits is bound to take notice at his peril, because reason is part of his nature, which he continually carries about with him, and may read it, if he will.

Philosopher. It is very true; and upon this ground, if I pretend within a month or two to make myself able to perform the office of a judge, you are not to think it arrogance; for you arc to allow to me, as well as to other men, my pretense to reason, which is the common law (remember this, that I may not need again to put you in mind that reason is the common law); and for statute law, seeing it is printed, and that there be indexes to point me to every matter contained in them, I think a man may profit in them very much in two months.

Lawyer. But you will be but an ill pleader.

Philosopher. A pleader commonly thinks he ought to say all he can for the benefit of his client, and therefore has need of a faculty to wrest the sense of words from their truc meaning, the faculty of *rhetoric* to seduce the jury, and sometimes the judge also, and many other arts which I neither have, nor intend to study.

Lawyer. But let the judge, how good soever he thinks his reasoning, take heed that he depart not too much from the letter of the statute; for it is not without danger.

Philosopher. He may without danger recede from the letter, if he do not from the meaning and sense of the law, which may be by a learned man (such as judges commonly are) easily found out by the preamble, the time when it was made, and the incommodities for which it was made. But I pray tell me, to what end were statute laws ordained, seeing the law of reason ought to be applied to every controversy that can arise. . . .

[2. What are the purposes of law?]

Lawyer. I say . . . that the scope of all human law is peace, and justice in every nation amongst themselves, and defense against foreign enemies.

Philosopher. But what is justice?

Lawyer. Justice is giving to every man his own.

Philosopher. The definition is good, and yet it is Aristotle's. What is the definition agreed upon as a principle in the science of the common law?

Lawyer. The same with that of Aristotle.

Philosopher. See, you lawyers, how much you are beholden to the philosopher; and it is but reason; for the more general and noble science and law of all the world is true philosophy, of which the common law of England is a very little part.

Lawyer. It is so, if you mean by philosophy nothing but the study of reason, as I think you do.

Philosopher. When you say that justice gives to every man his own, what mean you by his own? How can that be given me which is my own already? Or, if it be not my own, how can justice make it mine?

Lawyer. Without law, every thing is in such sort every man's, as he may take, possess, and enjoy, without wrong to any man; every thing, lands, beasts, fruits, and even the bodies of other men, if his reason tell him he cannot otherwise live securely. For the dictates of reason are little worth, if they tended not to the preservation and improvement of men's lives. Seeing then without human law all things would be common, and this community a cause of encroachment, envy, slaughter, and continual war of one upon another, the same law of reason dictates to mankind, for their own preservation, a distribution of lands and goods, that each man may know what is proper to him, so as none other might pretend a right thereunto, or disturb him in the use of the same. This distribution is justice, and this properly is the same which we say is one's own; by which you may see the great necessity there was of statute laws for preservation of all mankind. It is also a dictate of the law of reason that statute laws are a necessary means of the safety and well-being of man in the present world, and are to be obeyed by all subjects, as the law of reason ought to be obeyed, both by King and subjects, because it is the law of God.

Philosopher. All this is very rational; but how can any laws secure one man from another when the greatest part of men are so unreasonable, and so partial to themselves as they are, and the laws of themselves are but a dead letter, which of itself is not able to compel a man to do otherwise than himself pleaseth, nor punish or hurt him when he hath done a mischief?

Lawyer. By the laws, I mean laws living and armed. For you must suppose that a nation that is subdued by war to an absolute submission to a conqueror may, by the same arm that compelled it to submission, be compelled to obey his laws. Also, if a nation choose a man, or an assembly of men, to govern them by laws, it must furnish him also with armed men and money, and all things necessary to his office, or else his laws will be of no force, and the nation remains, as before it was, in confusion. It is not therefore the word of the law, but the power of a man that has the strength of a nation, that makes the laws effectual. It was not Solon that made Athenian laws, though he devised them, but the supreme court of the people; nor, the lawyers of Rome that made the imperial law in Justinian's time, but Justinian himself.

Philosopher. We agree then in this, that in England it is the King that makes the laws, whosoever pens them, and in this, that the King cannot make his laws effectual, nor defend his people against their enemies, without a power to levy soldiers, and consequently, that he may lawfully, as oft as he shall really think it necessary to raise an army (which in some occasions be very great) I say, raise it, and money to maintain it. I doubt not but you will allow this to be according to the law, at least of reason.

[3. Is it reasonable to confer absolute power upon a sovereign?]

Lawyer. For my part I allow it. But you have heard how, in and before the late troubles the people were of another mind. Shall the King, said they, take from us what he pleases, upon pretense of a necessity whereof he makes himself the judge? What worse condition can we be in from an ememy? . . .

Philosopher. I know what it is that troubles your conscience in this point. All men are troubled at the crossing of their wishes; but it is our own fault. First, we wish impossibilities; we would have our security against all the world upon right of property, without paying for it; this is impossible. We may as well expect that fish and fowl should boil, roast, and dish themselves, and come to the table, and that grapes should squeeze themselves into our mouths, and have all other the contentments and ease which some pleasant men have related of the land of Cocagne. Secondly, there is no nation in the world where he or they that have the sovereignty, do not take what money they please for the defense of those respective nations, when they think it necessary for their safety. The late Long Parliament denied this; but why? Because there was a design amongst them to depose the King. Thirdly, there is no example of any King of England that I have read of, that ever pretended any such necessity for levying money against his conscience. The greatest sums that ever were levied, comparing the value of money, as it was at that time, with what it is now, were levied by King Edward III and King Henry V, kings in whom we glory now, and think their actions great ornaments to the English history. Lastly, as to the enriching now and then a favourite, it is neither sensible to the kingdom, nor is any treasure thereby conveyed out of the realm, but so spent as it falls down again upon the common people. To think that our condition being human should be subject to no incommodity, were injuriously to quarrel with God Almighty for our own faults.

Lawyer. I know not what to say.

Philosopher. If you allow this that I have said, then say that the people never were, shall be, or ought to be, free from being taxed at the will of one or other;

that if civil war come, they must levy all they have, and that dearly, from the one or from the other, or from both sides. Say that adhering to the King, their victory is an end of their trouble; that adhering to his enemies there is no end; for the war will continue by a perpetual subdivision, and when it ends, they will be in the same estate they were before. That they are often abused by men who to them seem wise, when then their wisdom is nothing else but envy of those that are in grace and in profitable employments; and that those men do but abuse the common people to their own ends, that set up a private man's propriety against the public safety. But say withal, that the King is subject to the laws of God, both written and unwritten, and to no other; and so was William the Conqueror, whose right is all descended to our present King. . . .

[4. How should law be defined?]

Philosopher.   We have hitherto spoken of laws without considering anything of the nature and essence of a law; and now unless we define the word *law,* we can go no farther without ambiguity and fallacy, which will be but loss of time; whereas, on the contrary, the agreement upon our words will enlighten all we have to say hereafter.

Lawyer.   I do not remember the definition of *law* in any statute.

Philosopher.   I think so; for the statutes were made by authority, and not drawn from any other principles than the care of the safety of the people. Statutes are not philosophy, as is the common-law, and other disputable arts, but are commands or prohibitions, which ought to be obeyed, because assented to by submission made to the Conqueror here in England, and to whosoever had the sovereign power in other commonwealths; so that the positive laws of all places are statutes. The definition of law was therefore unnecessary for the makers of statutes, though very necessary to them whose work it is to teach the sense of the law.

Lawyer.   There is an accurate definition of a law in Bracton, cited by Sir Edward Coke: *Lex est sanctio justa, jubens honesta, et prohibens contraria.*

Philosopher.   That is to say, law is a just statute, commanding things which are honest, and forbidding the contrary. From whence it followeth that in all cases it must be the honesty or dishonesty that makes the command a law; whereas you know that but for the law we could not, as saith St. Paul, have known what is sin. Therefore this definition is no ground at all for any farther discourse of law. Besides, you know the rule of honest and dishonest refers to honor, and that it is justice only, and injustice, that the law respecteth. But that which I most except against in this definition is that it supposes that a statute made by the sovereign power of a nation may be unjust. There may indeed in a statute-law, made by men, be found iniquity, but not injustice.

Lawyer.   This is somewhat subtle. I pray deal plainly. What is the difference between injustice and iniquity?

Philosopher. I pray you tell me first, what is the difference between a court of justice and a court of equity?

Lawyer. A court of justice is that which hath cognizance of such causes as are to be ended by the positive laws of the land; and a court of equity is that, to which belong such causes as are to be determined by equity, that is to say, by the law of reason.

Philosopher. You see then that the difference between injustice and iniquity in this; that injustice is the transgression of a statute-law, and iniquity the transgression of the law of reason. But perhaps you mean by common-law, not the law itself, but the manner of proceeding in the law, as to matter of fact, by twelve men, freeholders; though those twelve men are no court of equity, nor of justice, because they determine not what is just or unjust, but only whether it be done or not done; and their judgment is nothing else but a confirmation of that which is properly the judgment of the witnesses. For to speak exactly, there cannot possibly be any judge of fact besides the witnesses.

Lawyer. How would you have a law defined?

Philosopher. Thus: a law is the command of him or them that have the sovereign power, given to those that be his or their subjects, declaring publicly and plainly what every of them may do, and what they must forbear to do.

Lawyer. Seeing all judges in all courts ought to judge according to equity, which is the law of reason, a distinct court of equity seemeth to me to be unnecessary, and but a burthen to the people, since common-law and equity are the same law.

Philosopher. It were so indeed, if judges could not err, but since they may err, and that the King is not bound to any other law but that of equity, it belongs to him alone to give remedy to them that, by the ignorance or corruption of a judge, shall suffer damage. . . . Now define what justice is, and what actions and men are to be called just.

[5. What is the relation of law to justice?]

Lawyer. Justice is the constant will of giving to every man his own, that is to say, of giving to every man that which is his right, in such manner as to exclude the right of all men else to the same thing. A just action is that which is not against the law. A just man is he that hath a constant will to live justly; if you require more, I doubt there will no man living be comprehended within the definition.

Philosopher. Seeing then that a just action, according to your definition, is that which is not against the law, it is manifest that before there was a law, there could be no injustice; and therefore laws are in their nature antecedent to justice and injustice. And you cannot deny but there must be law-makers, before there were any laws, and consequently before there was any justice (I speak of human justice); and that law-makers were before that which you call *own*, or property of goods or lands, distinguished by *meum, tuum, alienum.*

53

Lawyer. That must be granted; for without statute-laws, all men have right to all things; and we have had experience, when our laws were silenced by civil war, there was not a man, that of any goods could say assuredly they were his own.

Philosopher. You see then that no private man can claim a propriety in any lands, or other goods, from any title from any man but the King, or them that have the sovereign power; because it is in virtue of the sovereignty that every man may not enter into and possess what he pleaseth; and consequently to deny the sovereign anything necessary to the sustaining of his sovereign power is to destroy the propriety he pretends to.

COMPARATIVE STUDY QUESTIONS

Review Questions

1. What difficulty does the Philosopher in Hobbes' dialogue find with Sir Edward Coke's dictum, "Nothing that is against reason is law"?
2. Explain what Hobbes (the Philosopher) means by saying, "It is not wisdom but authority that makes a law."
3. Bacon leaves to the syllogism and "ordinary logic" jurisdiction over which departments of human life?
4. In what respects does Bacon's new logic (called "The Interpretation of Nature") differ from the older logic?
5. How does Hobbes define "philosophy"?
6. What does Hobbes mean by a "phantasm"?
7. Explain what Bacon means to describe by each of his four "idols of the mind."
8. Why does Bacon say that the idols of the market-place are the most troublesome of all?
9. What does Hobbes mean by reasoning or "reckoning"?
10. Which would Bacon have scientists emulate: the ant, the spider, or the bee? Why?

Discussion Questions

1. What are the main points of **difference** between the position of the Lawyer or Student of the Common Laws (Coke-Others) and that of the Philosopher (Bacon-Hobbes)? On what points do they agree?
2. Implicit in both Hobbes' dialogue and Bacon's offers to King James I to compile and digest the laws of England is the suggestion that the uncontrolled development and tradition of the common law is chaotic and irrational. Do you see any parallel between this and Bacon's insistence that the senses, unaided by controlled experiments, are liable to error and confusion?
3. Recalling that for both Bacon and Hobbes "philosophy" and "science" are more or less interchangeable terms, compare their conceptions of the subject matter of philosophy.
4. Both Bacon and Hobbes agree that "knowledge is power." Explain what they have in mind.
5. Carefully examine the role that sense experience, including experiments and natural histories, has in the scientific methods of Hobbes and Bacon respectively.
6. What roles do deductive reasoning, the syllogism, and mathematics specifically have in Bacon's **Great Instauration,** his project to reconstruct the sciences, as

compared with Hobbes' grand plan to devise a universal philosophy of matter or body in terms of which literally everything would be understood?

7. List Bacon's criticisms of "demonstration by syllogism" (those advanced in his **Plan of the Great Instauration**). Does Hobbes' analytical-synthetical (resolutive-compositive) method meet any of these objections?

8. According to Bacon, "the intellect is far more prone to error than sense is"; and according to Hobbes, "natural sense and imagination are not subject to absurdity. Nature itself cannot err." Do they agree or disagree regarding human fallibility? What is Hobbes' distinction between absurdity and error? Can all errors and/or absurdities be eradicated, or only with practice avoided, according to these authors?

9. What does Hobbes mean by saying that words are a wise man's "counters," but the "money" of fools? Would Bacon agree?

10. What grounds are there for saying that both Bacon and Hobbes are anti-authoritarian as far as knowledge and scientific procedure are concerned?

René Descartes
(1596 – 1650)

Thomas Hobbes
(1588 – 1679)

MIND, BODY, AND
THE WORLD ORDER

Monsieur René Descartes and Mr. Thomas Hobbes

> But isn't it absurd to say of a *body* that it has pain?—And
> why does one feel an absurdity in that? In what sense is it
> true that my hand does not feel pain, but I in my hand?
>
> Ludwig Wittgenstein, *Philosophical Investi-*
> *gations* (1958)

Although Hobbes and Descartes disagreed with one another on practically everything, they did come to respect each other in later years. According to Hobbes'
biographer, John Aubrey, "Descartes and he were acquainted and mutually respected one another. He would say that had [Descartes] kept himself to Geometry
he had been the best Geometer in the world but that his head did not lye for
Philosophy."[1] Descartes was similarly contemptuous, as were many English mathematicians, of Hobbes' efforts at geometry, but Descartes nonetheless thought him
competent in ethics.

Hobbes and Descartes actually met one another for the first time in Paris in
1648. Prior to that time their communication with each other was entirely written
and in Latin. It all started with an invitation in 1641 from Father Marin Mersenne
(1588–1648), a close friend and former school-fellow of Descartes at La Flèche,
who was now the leader of an intellectual circle in Paris. Mersenne asked Hobbes to
read and comment on a manuscript which he was busy circulating among various
philosophers. It belonged to Descartes and was soon to be published under the title,
Meditations on First Philosophy. Hobbes agreed and submitted anonymously no
less than sixteen objections, which were identified in a later French version as those
"urged by a Celebrated English Philosopher." Descartes dutifully responded to each
of them, barely concealing his irritation with regard to some of them.

The extent of the disagreement between the two philosophers is, from one
perspective, somewhat surprising. Both appreciated geometry and urged the adop-
tion of a generally deductive approach to science. Descartes, of course, is credited
with the invention of analytic geometry. Hobbes was less inventive regarding it, but

---

1. *Aubrey's Brief Lives*, edited by Oliver L. Dick (London: Secker and Warburg, 1950), p.
158.

perhaps more passionately devoted to it. Aubrey tells the following story about Hobbes while he was on one of his trips to the Continent in the year 1629:

> Being in a Gentleman's Library, Euclid's *Elements* lay open, and 'twas the [47th theorem of Book I]. "By G——," sayd he (he would now and then sweare an emphatical Oath by way of emphasis), "this is impossible!" So he reads the Demonstration of it, which referred him back to such a Proposition; which proposition he read. That referred him back to another, which he also read. *Et sic deinceps* [and so on] that at last he was demonstratively convinced of that trueth. This made him in love with Geometry.[2]

Perhaps a retraction is due for saying that Hobbes was not "inventive" with respect to geometry. For later, in 1655, Hobbes published an attempt on his part to square the circle! It was in his book, **De Corpore,** Chapter 20, entitled "Of the Dimensions of a Circle, and the Division of Angles or Arches." Two Oxford professors, John Wallis and Seth Ward, had very little difficulty in establishing the invalidity of Hobbes' proof. Not one to give up a fight however, Hobbes replied to their criticisms in **Six Lessons to the Professors of Mathematics in the University of Oxford.** Wallis responded with his **Due Corrections for Mr. Hobbes on School-discipline for Not Saying His Lessons Right.** Hobbes continued to publish his excursions into mathematics and geometry right up to the ripe age of eighty-six, long after Wallis and the others had ceased their futile attempts to reform him.

But besides the agreement of Hobbes and Descartes regarding the importance of geometry and a deductive method, they were also both concerned to replace the traditional Aristotelian mode of thought with a new philosophy which would be more in keeping with the discoveries and ideas of such men as Copernicus and Galileo. Descartes and Hobbes both wrote works on optics, over which, expectedly, they quarreled. Both claimed originality for their distinction between primary and secondary qualities, i.e., between qualities such as spatial extension in the object and qualities such as color and smell which are attributed to the object but are really in or dependent upon the observer. Galileo, incidentally, had made the distinction long before either of them in his book, **Il Saggiatore,** published in 1623.

Despite this apparent unanimity, or rather, these grounds for unanimity, an enormous chasm existed between Descartes and Hobbes regarding the metaphysical presuppositions and implications of modern science. The cluster of problems that interested them especially, and to which they each gave radically divergent answers, are the following: What is man's place in the (Copernican) world? Is there a God who created it? Is it wholly a deterministic universe governed inexorably by Galileo's and other laws of motion and causation, or is there perhaps an oasis of freedom in man's will? Is everything, including the human mind, explicable in terms of matter in motion, or is there a real distinction between the mind and the body?

Descartes' answer to the first is that man occupies a rather special place in the world. "I am a thing that thinks," he says. "Quite correct," says Hobbes, who then proceeds to claim that that fact in itself does not prove minds, or persons with minds, to be essentially different from any other corporeal "things."

---

2. *Ibid.*, p. 150.

Regarding Descartes' proofs of God's existence, Hobbes complains that they are not conclusive because we have no idea of God. Descartes, he says, should have explained his idea of God better, if indeed he had one at all; furthermore, he should, in that case, have gone on to deduce from it the creation of the world which, he claims, Descartes had not done.

Hobbes' own views regarding God's existence are far from clear. It would seem that if his materialistic conception of the world is correct, there would hardly be a place for God in it, at least as God is ordinarily conceived, though there might be a place if God were conceived as a supreme principle of motion, a world-soul, perhaps, or some such **thing.** Nowhere in his writings does Hobbes deny that there is a God (though he has a lot of critical remarks to make regarding religious belief in general). His restraint so far as pronouncements on God's nature and existence are concerned is perhaps traceable more to political fears than to any lack of metaphysical conviction. After all, for blasphemy or for undermining the state religion, one could get beheaded or sent to the Tower or the Bastille. (At the time Hobbes wrote his objections to Descartes' **Meditations,** he was living in France in voluntary exile at the pleasure of the French king and his chief minister, Cardinal Richelieu.) In general, Hobbes made it a point not to quarrel with royalty.

Regarding the question of determinism, there is really no doubt in the minds of either Descartes or Hobbes that as far as the physical universe is concerned, it is thoroughly deterministic. Descartes insists, however, that man's will is free. Our reason may be limited, but our wills are completely unlimited, according to Descartes. Hobbes, on the other hand, finds the whole notion of a "free will" absurd and meaningless.

The basic opposition between the two philosophers reveals itself best in their views with respect to the nature of the human mind and its relationship to the body. Descartes adopts a dualistic view which asserts that minds exist as well as bodies, are separate kinds of substances, and are more easily known than bodies. Hobbes subscribes to the view that minds are wholly explicable in terms of matter in motion. Mind, he says, is "nothing but the motions in certain parts of an organic body."

DESCARTES

Meditations on the First Philosophy *

In Which
The Existence of God, and the Real Distinction
of Mind and Body, are Demonstrated

Meditation I

Of the Things of Which We May Doubt

Several years have now elapsed since I first became aware that I had accepted, even from my youth, many false opinions for true, and that consequently what I afterwards based on such principles was highly doubtful; and from that time I was convinced of the necessity of undertaking once in my life to rid myself of all the opinions I had adopted, and of commencing anew the work of building from the foundation, if I desired to establish a firm and abiding superstructure in the sciences. But as this enterprise appeared to me to be one of great magnitude, I waited until I had attained an age so mature as to leave me no hope that at any stage of life more advanced I should be better able to execute my design. On this account, I have delayed so long that I should henceforth consider I was going wrong were I still to consume in deliberation any of the time that now remains for action. To-day, then, since I have opportunely freed my mind from all cares [and am happily disturbed by no passions], and since I am in the secure possession of leisure in a peaceable retirement, I will at length apply myself earnestly and freely to the general overthrow of all my former opinions. But, to this end, it will not be necessary for me to show that the whole of these are false—a point, perhaps, which I shall never reach; but as even now my reason convinces me that I ought not the less carefully to withhold belief from what is not entirely certain and indubitable, than from what is manifestly false, it will be sufficient to justify the rejection of the whole if I shall find in each some ground for doubt. Nor for this purpose will it be necessary even to deal with each belief individually, which would be truly an endless labour; but, as the removal from below of the foundation necessarily involves the downfall of the whole edifice, I will at once approach the criticism of the principles on which all my former beliefs rested.

All that I have, up to this moment, accepted as possessed of the highest truth and certainty, I received either from or through the senses. I observed, however, that these sometimes misled us; and it is the part of prudence not to place absolute confidence in that by which we have even once been deceived.

But it may be said, perhaps, that, although the senses occasionally mislead us respecting minute objects, and such as are so far removed from us as to be beyond

---

* From Descartes' *Meditations,* translated by John Veitch, 1853.

the reach of close observation, there are yet many other of their informations (presentations), of the truth of which it is manifestly impossible to doubt; as for example, that I am in this place, seated by the fire, clothed in a winter dressing-gown, that I hold in my hands this piece of paper, with other intimations of the same nature. But how could I deny that I possess these hands and this body, and withal escape being classed with persons in a state of insanity, whose brains are so disordered and clouded by dark bilious vapours as to cause them pertinaciously to assert that they are monarchs when they are in the greatest poverty; or clothed [in gold] and purple when destitute of any covering; or that their head is made of clay, their body of glass, or that they are gourds? I should certainly be not less insane than they, were I to regulate my procedure according to examples so extravagant.

Though this be true, I must nevertheless here consider that I am a man, and that, consequently, I am in the habit of sleeping, and representing to myself in dreams those same things, or even sometimes others less probable, which the insane think are presented to them in their waking moments. How often have I dreamt that I was in these familiar circumstances—that I was dressed, and occupied this place by the fire, when I was lying undressed in bed? At the present moment, however, I certainly look upon this paper with eyes wide awake; the head which I now move is not asleep; I extend this hand consciously and with express purpose, and I perceive it; the occurrences in sleep are not so distinct as all this. But I cannot forget that, at other times, I have been deceived in sleep by similar illusions; and, attentively considering those cases, I perceive so clearly that there exist no certain marks by which the state of waking can ever be distinguished from sleep, that I feel greatly astonished; and in amazement I almost persuade myself that I am now dreaming.

Let us suppose, then, that we are dreaming, and that all these particulars—namely, the opening of the eyes, the motion of the head, the forthputting of the hands—are merely illusions; and even that we really possess neither an entire body nor hands such as we see. Nevertheless, it must be admitted at least that the objects which appear to us in sleep are, as it were, painted representations which could not have been formed unless in the likeness of realities; and, therefore, that those general objects, at all events—namely, eyes, a head, hands, and an entire body—are not simply imaginary, but really existent. For, in truth, painters themselves, even when they study to represent sirens and satyrs by forms the most fantastic and extraordinary, cannot bestow upon them natures absolutely new, but can only make a certain medley of the members of different animals; or if they chance to imagine something so novel that nothing at all similar has ever been seen before, and such as is, therefore, purely fictitious and absolutely false, it is at least certain that the colours of which this is composed are real.

And on the same principle, although these general objects, viz. [a body], eyes, a head, hands, and the like, be imaginary, we are nevertheless absolutely necessitated to admit the reality at least of some other objects still more simple and universal than these, of which, just as of certain real colours, all those images of things, whether true and real, or false and fantastic, that are found in our conscious-ness (*cogitatio*), are formed.

To this class of objects seem to belong corporeal nature in general and its extension; the figure of extended things, their quantity or magnitude, and their number, as also the place in, and the time during, which they exist, and other things of the same sort. We will not, therefore, perhaps reason illegitimately if we conclude from this that physics, astronomy, medicine, and all the other sciences that have for their end the consideration of composite objects, are indeed of a doubtful character; but that arithmetic, geometry, and the other sciences of the same class, which regard merely the simplest and most general objects, and scarcely inquire whether or not these are really existent, contain somewhat that is certain and indubitable: for whether I am awake or dreaming, it remains true that two and three make five, and that a square has but four sides; nor does it seem possible that truths so apparent can ever fall under a suspicion of falsity [or incertitude].

Nevertheless, the belief that there is a God who is all-powerful, and who created me, such as I am, has for a long time, obtained steady possession of my mind. How, then, do I know that he has not arranged that there should be neither earth, nor sky, nor any extended thing, nor figure, nor magnitude, nor place, providing at the same time, however, for [the rise in me of the perceptions of all these objects, and] the persuasion that these do not exist otherwise than as I perceive them? And further, as I sometimes think that others are in error respecting matters of which they believe themselves to possess a perfect knowledge, how do I know that I am not also deceived each time I add together two and three, or number the sides of a square, or form some judgment still more simple, if more simple indeed can be imagined? But perhaps Deity has not been willing that I should be thus deceived, for He is said to be supremely good. If, however, it were repugnant to the goodness of Deity to have created me subject to constant deception, it would seem likewise to be contrary to his goodness to allow me to be occasionally deceived; and yet it is clear that this is permitted. Some, indeed, might perhaps be found who would be disposed rather to deny the existence of a being so powerful than to believe that there is nothing certain. But let us for the present refrain from opposing this opinion, and grant that all which is here said of a Deity is fabulous: nevertheless, in whatever way it be supposed that I reached the state in which I exist, whether by fate, or chance, or by an endless series of antecedents and consequents, or by any other means, it is clear (since to be deceived and to err is a certain defect) that the probability of my being so imperfect as to be the constant victim of deception, will be increased exactly in proportion as the power possessed by the cause, to which they assign my origin, is lessened. To these reasonings I have assuredly nothing to reply, but am constrained at last to avow that there is nothing at all that I formerly believed to be true of which it is impossible to doubt, and that not through thoughtlessness or levity, but from cogent and maturely considered reasons; so that henceforward, if I desire to discover anything certain, I ought not the less carefully to refrain from assenting to those same opinions than to what might be shown to be manifestly false.

But it is not sufficient to have made these observations; care must be taken likewise to keep them in remembrance. For those old and customary opinions perpetually recur—long and familiar usage giving them the right of occupying my mind, even almost against my will, and subduing my belief; nor will I lose the habit of deferring to them and confiding in them so long as I shall consider them to be what in truth they are, viz., opinions to some extent doubtful, as I have already shown, but still highly probable, and such as it is much more reasonable to believe than deny. It is for this reason I am persuaded that I shall not be doing wrong, if, taking an opposite judgment of deliberate design, I become my own deceiver, by supposing, for a time, that all those opinions are entirely false and imaginary, until at length, having thus balanced my old by my new prejudices, my judgment shall no longer be turned aside by perverted usage from the path that may conduct to the perception of truth. For I am assured that, meanwhile, there will arise neither peril nor error from this course, and that I cannot for the present yield too much to distrust, since the end I now seek is not action but knowledge.

I will suppose, then, not that Deity, who is sovereignly good and the fountain of truth, but that some malignant demon, who is at once exceedingly potent and deceitful, has employed all his artifice to deceive me; I will suppose that the sky, the air, the earth, colours, figures, sounds, and all external things, are nothing better than the illusions of dreams, by means of which this being has laid snares for my credulity; I will consider myself as without hands, eyes, flesh, blood, or any of the senses, and as falsely believing that I am possessed of these; I will continue resolutely fixed in this belief, and if indeed by this means it be not in my power to arrive at the knowledge of truth, I shall at least do what is in my power, viz. [suspend my judgment], and guard with settled purpose against giving my assent to what is false, and being imposed upon by this deceiver, whatever be his power and artifice.

But this undertaking is arduous, and a certain indolence insensibly leads me back to my ordinary course of life; and just as the captive, who, perchance, was enjoying in his dreams an imaginary liberty, when he begins to suspect that it is but a vision, dreads awakening, and conspires with the agreeable illusions that the deception may be prolonged; so I, of my own accord, fall back into the train of my former beliefs, and fear to arouse myself from my slumber, lest the time of laborious wakefulness that would succeed this quiet rest, in place of bringing any light of day, should prove inadequate to dispel the darkness that will arise from the difficulties that have now been raised.

Meditation II

*Of the Nature of the Human Mind;
and That It Is More Easily Known
Than the Body*

The Meditation of yesterday has filled my mind with so many doubts, that it is no longer in my power to forget them. Nor do I see, meanwhile, any principle on which they can be resolved; and, just as if I had fallen all of a sudden into very deep water, I am so greatly disconcerted as to be made unable either to plant my feet firmly on the bottom or sustain myself by swimming on the surface. I will, nevertheless, make an effort, and try anew the same path on which I had entered yesterday, that is, proceed by casting aside all that admits of the slightest doubt, not less than if I had discovered it to be absolutely false; and I will continue always in this track until I shall find something that is certain, or at least, if I can do nothing more, until I shall know with certainty that there is nothing certain. Archimedes, that he might transport the entire globe from the place it occupied to another, demanded only a point that was firm and immovable; so also, I shall be entitled to entertain the highest expectations, if I am fortunate enough to discover only one thing that is certain and indubitable.

I suppose, accordingly, that all the things which I see are false (fictitious); I believe that none of those objects which my fallacious memory represents ever existed; I suppose that I possess no senses; I believe that body, figure, extension, motion, and place are merely fictions of my mind. What is there, then, that can be esteemed true? Perhaps this only, that there is absolutely nothing certain.

But how do I know that there is not something different altogether from the objects I have now enumerated, of which it is impossible to entertain the slightest doubt? Is there not a God, or some being, by whatever name I may designate him, who causes these thoughts to arise in my mind? But why suppose such a being, for it may be I myself am capable of producing them? Am I, then, at least not something? But I before denied that I possessed senses or a body; I hesitate, however, for what follows from that? Am I so dependent on the body and the senses that without these I cannot exist? But I had the persuasion that there was absolutely nothing in the world, that there was no sky and no earth, neither minds nor bodies; was I not, therefore, at the same time, persuaded that I did not exist? Far from it; I assuredly existed, since I was persuaded. But there is I know not what being, who is possessed at once of the highest power and the deepest cunning, who is constantly employing all his ingenuity in deceiving me. Doubtless, then, I exist, since I am deceived; and, let him deceive me as he may, he can never bring it about that I am nothing, so long as I shall be conscious that I am something. So that it must, in fine, be maintained, all things being maturely and carefully considered, that this proposition (*pronunciatum*) I am, I exist, is necessarily true each time it is expressed by me, or conceived in my mind.

But I do not yet know with sufficient clearness what I am, though assured that I am; and hence, in the next place, I must take care, lest perchance I inconsiderately substitute some other object in room of what is properly myself, and thus wander from truth, even in that knowledge (cognition) which I hold to be of all others the most certain and evident. For this reason, I will now consider anew what I formerly believed myself to be, before I entered on the present train of thought; and of my previous opinion I will retrench all that can in the least be invalidated by the grounds of doubt I have adduced, in order that there may at length remain nothing but what is certain and indubitable. What then did I formerly think I was? Undoubtedly I judged that I was a man. But what is a man? Shall I say a rational animal? Assuredly not; for it would be necessary forthwith to inquire into what is meant by animal, and what by rational, and thus, from a single question, I should insensibly glide into others, and these more difficult than the first; nor do I now possess enough of leisure to warrant me in wasting my time amid subtleties of this sort. I prefer here to attend to the thoughts that sprung up of themselves in my mind, and were inspired by my own nature alone, when I applied myself to the consideration of what I was. In the first place, then, I thought that I possessed a countenance, hands, arms, and all the fabric of members that appears in a corpse, and which I called by the name of body. It further occurred to me that I was nourished, that I walked, perceived, and thought, and all those actions I referred to the soul; but what the soul itself was I either did not stay to consider, or, if I did, I imagined that it was something extremely rare and subtile, like wind, or flame, or ether, spread through my grosser parts. As regarded the body, I did not even doubt of its nature, but thought I distinctly knew it, and if I had wished to describe it according to the notions I then entertained, I should have explained myself in this manner: By body I understand all that can be terminated by a certain figure; that can be comprised in a certain place, and so fill a certain space as therefrom to exclude every other body; that can be perceived either by touch, sight, hearing, taste, or smell; that can be moved in different ways, not indeed of itself, but by something foreign to it by which it is touched [and from which it receives the impression]; for the power of self-motion, as likewise that of perceiving and thinking, I held as by no means pertaining to the nature of body; on the contrary, I was somewhat astonished to find such faculties existing in some bodies.

But [as to myself, what can I now say that I am], since I suppose there exists an extremely powerful, and, if I may so speak, malignant being, whose whole endeavours are directed towards deceiving me? Can I affirm that I possess any one of all those attributes of which I have lately spoken as belonging to the nature of body? After attentively considering them in my own mind, I find none of them that can properly be said to belong to myself. To recount them were idle and tedious. Let us pass, then, to the attributes of the soul. The first mentioned were the powers of nutrition and walking; but, if it be true that I have no body, it is true likewise that I am capable neither of walking nor of being nourished. Perception is another attribute of the soul; but perception too is impossible without the body: besides, I have frequently, during sleep, believed that I perceived objects which I afterwards observed I did not in reality perceive. Thinking is another attribute of the soul; and here I discover what properly belongs to myself. This alone is inseparable from me. I am—I exist: this is certain; but how often? As often as I think; for perhaps it would even happen, if I should wholly cease to think, that I should at the same time altogether cease to be. I now admit nothing that is not necessarily true: I am therefore, precisely speaking, only a thinking thing, that is, a mind (*mens sive animus*), understanding, or reason,—terms whose signification was before unknown to me. I am, however, a real thing, and really existent; but what thing? The answer was, a thinking thing. The question now arises, am I aught besides? I will stimulate my imagination with a view to discover whether I am not still something more than a thinking being. Now it is plain I am not the assemblage of members called the human body; I am not a thin and penetrating air diffused through all these members, or wind, or flame, or vapour, or breath, or any of all the things I can imagine; for I supposed that all these were not, and, without changing the supposition, I find that I still feel assured of my existence.

But it is true, perhaps, that those very things which I suppose to be nonexistent, because they are unknown to me, are not in truth different from myself whom I know. This is a point I cannot determine, and do not now enter into any dispute regarding it. I can only judge of things that are known to me: I am conscious that I exist, and I who know that I exist inquire into what I am. It is, however, perfectly certain that the knowledge of my existence, thus precisely taken, is not dependent on things, the existence of which is as yet unknown to me: and consequently it is not dependent on any of the things I can feign in imagination. Moreover, the phrase itself, I frame an image (*effingo*), reminds me of my error; for I should in truth frame one if I were to imagine myself to be anything, since to imagine is nothing more than to contemplate the figure or image of a corporeal thing; but I already know that I exist, and that it is possible at the same time that all those images, and in general all that relates to the nature of body, are merely dreams [or chimeras]. From this I discover that it is not more reasonable to say, I will excite my imagination that I may know more distinctly what I am, than to express myself as follows: I am now awake, and perceive something real; but because my perception is not sufficiently clear, I will of express purpose go to sleep that my dreams may represent to me the object of my perception with more truth and clearness. And, therefore, I know that nothing of all that I can embrace in imagination belongs to the knowledge which I have of myself, and that there is need to recall with the utmost care the mind from this mode of thinking, that it may be able to know its own nature with perfect distinctness.

But what, then, am I? A thinking thing, it has been said. But what is a thinking thing? It is a thing that doubts, understands [conceives], affirms, denies, wills, refuses, that imagines also, and perceives. Assuredly it is not little, if all these properties belong to my nature. But why should they not belong to it? Am I not that very being who now doubts of almost everything; who, for all that, understands and conceives certain things, who affirms one alone as true, and denies the others; who desires to know more of them, and does not wish to be deceived; who imagines many things, sometimes even despite his will; and is likewise percipient of many, as if through the medium of the senses. Is there nothing of all this as true as that I am, even although I should be always dreaming, and although he who gave me being employed all his ingenuity to deceive me? Is there also any one of these attributes that can be properly distinguished from my thought, or that can be said to be separate from myself? For it is of itself so evident that it is I who doubt, I who understand, and I who desire, that it is here unnecessary to add anything by way of rendering it more clear. And I am as certainly the same being who imagines; for, although it may be (as I before supposed) that nothing I imagine is true, still the power of imagination does not cease really to exist in me and to form part of my thoughts. In fine, I am the same being who perceives, that is, who apprehends certain objects as by the organs of sense, since, in truth, I see light, hear a noise, and feel heat. But it will be said that these presentations are false, and that I am dreaming. Let it be so. At all events it is certain that I seem to see light, hear a noise, and feel heat; this cannot be false, and this is what in me is properly called perceiving (*sentire*), which is nothing else than thinking. From this I begin to know what I am with somewhat greater clearness and distinctness than heretofore.

But, nevertheless, it still seems to me, and I cannot help believing, that corporeal things, whose images are formed by thought [which fall under the senses], and are examined by the same, are known with much greater distinctness than that

I know not what part of myself which is not imaginable; although, in truth, it may seem strange to say that I know and comprehend with greater distinctness things whose existence appears to me doubtful, that are unknown, and do not belong to me, than others of whose reality I am persuaded, that are known to me, and appertain to my proper nature; in a word, than myself. But I see clearly what is the state of the case. My mind is apt to wander, and will not yet submit to be restrained within the limits of truth. Let us therefore leave the mind to itself once more, and, according to it every kind of liberty [permit it to consider the objects that appear to it from without], in order that, having afterwards withdrawn it from these gently and opportunely [and fixed it on the consideration of its being and the properties it finds in itself], it may then be the more easily controlled.

Let us now accordingly consider the objects that are commonly thought to be [the most easily, and likewise] the most distinctly known, viz., the bodies we touch and see; not, indeed, bodies in general, for these general notions are usually somewhat more confused, but one body in particular. Take, for example, this piece of wax; it is quite fresh, having been but recently taken from the beehive; it has not yet lost the sweetness of the honey it contained; it still retains somewhat of the odour of the flowers from which it was gathered; its colour, figure, size, are apparent (to the sight); it is hard, cold, easily handled; and sounds when struck upon with the finger. In fine, all that contributes to make a body as distinctly known as possible, is found in the one before us. But, while I am speaking, let it be placed near the fire—what remained of the taste exhales, the smell evaporates, the colour changes, its figure is destroyed, its size increases, it becomes liquid, it grows hot, it can hardly be handled, and, although struck upon, it emits no sound. Does the same wax still remain after this change? It must be admitted that it does remain; no one doubts it, or judges otherwise. What, then, was it I knew with so much distinctness in the piece of wax? Assuredly, it could be nothing of all that I observed by means of the senses, since all the things that fell under taste, smell, sight, touch, and hearing are changed, and yet the same wax remains. It was perhaps what I now think, viz., that this wax was neither the sweetness of honey, the pleasant odour of flowers, the whiteness, the figure, nor the sound, but only a body that a little before appeared to me conspicuous under these forms, and which is now perceived under others. But, to speak precisely, what is it that I imagine when I think of it in this way? Let it be attentively considered, and, retrenching all that does not belong to the wax, let us see what remains. There certainly remains nothing, except something extended, flexible, and movable. But what is meant by flexible and movable? Is it not that I imagine that the piece of wax, being round, is capable of becoming square, or of passing from a square into a triangular figure? Assuredly such is not the case, because I conceive that it admits of an infinity of similar changes; and I am, moreover, unable to compass this infinity by imagination, and consequently this conception which I have of the wax is not the product of the faculty of imagination. But what now is this extension? Is it not also unknown? for it becomes greater when the wax is melted, greater when it is boiled, and greater still when the heat increases; and I should not conceive [clearly and] according to truth, the wax as it is, if I did not suppose that the piece we are considering admitted even of a wider variety of extension than I ever imagined. I must, therefore, admit that I cannot even comprehend by imagination what the piece of wax is, and that it is the mind alone (*mens*, Lat.; *entendement*, F.) which perceives it. I speak of one piece in particular; for, as to wax in general, this is still more evident. But what is the piece of wax that can be perceived only by the [understanding of] mind? It is certainly the same which I see, touch, imagine; and, in fine, it is the same which, from the beginning, I believed it to be. But (and this it is of moment to observe) the perception of it is neither an act of sight, of touch, nor of imagination, and never was either of these, though it might formerly seem so, but is simply an intuition (*inspectio*) of the mind, which may be imperfect and confused, as it formerly was, or very clear and distinct, as it is at present, according as the attention is more or less directed to the elements which it contains, and of which it is composed.

But, meanwhile, I feel greatly astonished when I observe [the weakness of my mind, and] its proneness to error. For although, without at all giving expression to what I think, I consider all this in my own mind, words yet occasionally impede my progress, and I am almost led into error by the terms of ordinary language. We say, for example, that we see the same wax when it is before us, and not that we judge it to be the same from its retaining the same colour and figure: whence I should forthwith be disposed to conclude that the wax is known by the act of sight, and not by the intuition of the mind alone, were it not for the analogous instance of human beings passing on in the street below, as observed from a window. In this case I do not fail to say that I see the men themselves, just as I say that I see the wax; and yet what do I see from the window beyond hats and cloaks that might cover artificial machines, whose motions might be determined by springs? But I judge that there are human beings from these appearances, and thus I comprehend, by the faculty of judgment alone which is in the mind, what I believed I saw with my eyes.

The man who makes it his aim to rise to knowledge superior to the common, ought to be ashamed to seek occasions of doubting from the vulgar forms of speech: instead, therefore, of doing this, I shall proceed with the matter in hand, and inquire whether I had a clearer and more perfect perception of the piece of wax when I first saw it, and when I thought I knew it by means of the external sense itself, or, at all events, by the common sense (*sensus communis*), as it is called, that is, by the imaginative faculty; or whether I rather apprehend it more clearly at present, after having examined with greater care, both what it is, and in what way it can be known. It would certainly be ridiculous to entertain any doubt on this point. For what, in that first perception, was there distinct? What did I perceive which any animal might not have perceived? But when I distinguish the wax from its exterior forms, and when, as if I had stripped it of its vestments, I consider it quite naked, it is certain, although some error may still be found in my judgment, that I cannot, nevertheless, thus apprehend it without possessing a human mind.

But, finally, what shall I say of the mind itself, that is, of myself? for as yet I do not admit that I am anything but mind. What, then! I who seem to possess so distinct an apprehension of the piece of wax,—do I not know myself, both with greater truth and certitude, and also much more distinctly and clearly? For if I judge that the wax exists because I see it, it assuredly follows, much more evidently, that I myself am or exist, for the same reason: for it is possible that what I see may not in truth be wax, and that I do not even possess eyes with which to see anything; but it cannot be that when I see, or, which comes to the same thing, when I think I see, I myself who think am nothing. So likewise, if I judge that the wax exists because I touch it, it will still also follow that I am; and if I determine that my imagination, or any other cause, whatever it be, persuades me of the existence of the wax, I will still draw the same conclusion. And what is here remarked of the piece of wax is applicable to all the other things that are external to me. And further, if the [notion or] perception of wax appeared to me more precise and distinct, after that not only sight and touch, but many other causes besides, rendered it manifest to my apprehension, with how much greater distinct- ness must I now know myself, since all the reasons that contribute to the know- ledge of the nature of wax, or of any body whatever, manifest still better the nature of my mind? And there are besides so many other things in the mind itself that contribute to the illustration of its nature, that those dependent on the body, to which I have here referred, scarcely merit to be taken into account.

But, in conclusion, I find I have insensibly reverted to the point I desired; for, since it is now manifest to me that bodies themselves are not properly perceived by the senses nor by the faculty of imagination, but by the intellect alone; and since they are not perceived because they are seen and touched, but only because they are understood [or rightly comprehended by thought], I readily discover that there is nothing more easily or clearly apprehended than my own mind. But because it is difficult to rid one's self so promptly of an opinion to which one has been long accustomed, it will be desirable to tarry for some time at this stage, that, by long continued meditation, I may more deeply impress upon my memory this new knowledge.

Meditation III

Of God: That He Exists

I will now close my eyes, I will stop my ears, I will turn away my senses from their objects, I will even efface from my consciousness all the images of corporeal things; or at least, because this can hardly be accomplished, I will consider them as empty and false; and thus, holding converse only with myself, and closely examining my nature, I will endeavour to obtain by degrees a more intimate and familiar know- ledge of myself. I am a thinking (conscious) thing, that is, a being who doubts, affirms, denies, knows a few objects, and is ignorant of many,—[who loves, hates], wills, refuses,—who imagines likewise, and perceives; for, as I before remarked, although the things which I perceive or imagine are perhaps nothing at all apart from me [and in themselves], I am nevertheless assured that those modes of con- sciousness which I call perceptions and imaginations, in as far only as they are modes of consciousness, exist in me. And in the little I have said I think I have summed up all that I really know, or at least all that up to this time I was aware I knew. Now, as I am endeavouring to extend my knowledge more widely, I will use circumspection, and consider with care whether I can still discover in myself anything further which I have not yet hitherto observed. I am certain that I am a thinking thing; but do I not therefore likewise know what is required to render me certain of a truth? In this first knowledge, doubtless, there is nothing that gives me assurance of its truth except the clear and distinct perception of what I affirm, which would not indeed be sufficient to give me the assurance that what I say is true, if it could ever happen that anything I thus clearly and distinctly perceived should prove false; and accordingly it seems to me that I may now take as a general rule, that all that is very clearly and distinctly apprehended (conceived) is true.

Nevertheless I before received and admitted many things as wholly certain and manifest, which yet I afterwards found to be doubtful. What, then, were those? They were the earth, the sky, the stars, and all the other objects which I was in the habit of perceiving by the senses. But what was it that I clearly [and distinctly] perceived in them? Nothing more than that the ideas and the thoughts of those objects were presented to my mind. And even now I do not deny that these ideas are found in my mind. But there was yet another thing which I affirmed, and which, from having been accustomed to believe it, I thought I clearly perceived, although, in truth, I did not perceive it at all; I mean the existence of objects external to me, from which those ideas proceeded, and to which they had a perfect resemblance; and it was here I was mistaken, or if I judged correctly, this assuredly was not to be traced to any knowledge I possessed (the force of my perception, Lat.).

But when I considered any matter in arithmetic and geometry, that was very simple and easy, as, for example, that two and three added together make five, and things of this sort, did I not view them with at least sufficient clearness to warrant me in affirming their truth? Indeed, if I afterwards judged that we ought to doubt of these things, it was for no other reason than because it occurred to me that a God might perhaps have given me such a nature as that I should be deceived, even respecting the matters that appeared to me the most evidently true. But as often as this preconceived opinion of the sovereign power of a God presents itself to my mind, I am constrained to admit that it is easy for him, if he wishes it, to cause me to err, even in matters where I think I possess the highest evidence; and, on the other hand, as often as I direct my attention to things which I think I apprehend with great clearness I am so persuaded of their truth that I naturally break out into expressions such as these: Deceive me who may, no one will yet ever be able to bring it about that I am not, so long as I shall be conscious that I am, or at any future time cause it to be true that I have never been, it being now true that I am, or make two and three more or less than five, in supposing which, and other like absurdities, I discover a manifest contradiction.

And in truth, as I have no ground for believing that Deity is deceitful, and as, indeed, I have not even considered the reasons by which the existence of a Deity of any kind is established, the ground of doubt that rests only on this supposition is very slight, and, so to speak, metaphysical. But, that I may be able wholly to remove it, I must inquire whether there is a God, as soon as an opportunity of doing so shall present itself; and if I find that there is a God, I must examine likewise whether he can be a deceiver; for, without the knowledge of these two truths, I do not see that I can ever be certain of anything. And that I may be enabled to examine this without interrupting the order of meditation I have proposed to myself [which is, to pass by degrees from the notions that I shall find first in my mind to those I shall afterwards discover in it], it is necessary at this stage to divide all my thoughts into certain classes, and to consider in which of these truth and error are, strictly speaking, to be found.

Of my thoughts some are, as it were, images of things, and to these alone properly belongs the name *idea;* as when I think [represent to my mind] a man, a chimera, the sky, an angel, or God. Others, again, have certain other forms; as when I will, fear, affirm, or deny, I always, indeed, apprehend something as the object of my thought, but I also embrace in thought something more than the representation of the object; and of this class of thoughts some are called volitions or affections, and others judgments.

Now, with respect to ideas, if these are considered only in themselves, and are not referred to any object beyond them, they cannot, properly speaking, be false; for whether I imagine a goat or a chimera, it is not less true that I imagine the one than the other. Nor need we fear that falsity may exist in the will or affections; for, although I may desire objects that are wrong, and even that never existed, it is still true that I desire them. There thus only remain our judgments, in which we must take diligent heed that we be not deceived. But the chief and most ordinary error that arises in them consists in judging that the ideas which are in us are like or conformed to the things that are external to us; for assuredly, if we but considered the ideas themselves as certain modes of our thought (consciousness), without referring them to anything beyond, they would hardly afford any occasion of error.

But, among these ideas, some appear to me to be innate, others adventitious, and others to be made by myself (factitious); for, as I have the power of conceiving what is called a thing, or a truth, or a thought, it seems to me that I hold this power from no other source than my own nature; but if I now hear a noise, if I see the sun, or if I feel heat, I have all along judged that these sensations proceeded from certain objects existing out of myself; and, in fine, it appears to me that sirens, hippogryphs, and the like, are inventions of my own mind. But I may even perhaps come to be of opinion that all my ideas are of the class which I call adventitious, or that they are all innate, or that they are all factitious, for I have not clearly discovered their true origin; and what I have here principally to do is to consider, with reference to those that appear to come from certain objects without me, what grounds there are for thinking them like these objects.

The first of these grounds is that it seems to me I am so taught by nature; and the second that I am conscious that those ideas are not dependent on my will, and therefore not on myself, for they are frequently presented to me against my will,— as at present, whether I will or not, I feel heat; and I am thus persuaded that this sensation or idea (*sensum vel ideam*) of heat is produced in me by something different from myself, viz., by the heat of the fire by which I sit. And it is very reasonable to suppose that this object impresses me with its own likeness rather than any other thing.

But I must consider whether these reasons are sufficiently strong and convincing. When I speak of being taught by nature in this matter, I understand by the word nature only a certain spontaneous impetus that impels me to believe in a resemblance between ideas and their objects, and not a natural light that affords a knowledge of its truth. But these two things are widely different; for what the natural light shows to be true can be in no degree doubtful, as, for example, that I am because I doubt, and other truths of the like kind: inasmuch as I possess no other faculty whereby to distinguish truth from error, which can teach me the falsity of what the natural light declares to be true, and which is equally trust-worthy; but with respect to [seemingly] natural impulses, I have observed, when the question related to the choice of right or wrong in action, that they frequently led me to take the worse part; nor do I see that I have any better ground for following them in what relates to truth and error. Then, with respect to the other reason, which is that because these ideas do not depend on my will, they must arise from objects existing without me, I do not find it more convincing than the former; for, just as those natural impulses, of which I have lately spoken, are found in me, notwithstanding that they are not always in harmony with my will, so likewise it may be that I possess some power not sufficiently known to myself capable of producing ideas without the aid of external objects, and, indeed, it has always hitherto appeared to me that they are formed during sleep, by some power of this nature, without the aid of aught external. And, in fine, although I should grant that they proceeded from those objects, it is not a necessary consequence that they must be like them. On the contrary, I have observed, in a number of instances, that there was a great difference between the object and its idea. Thus, for example, I find in my mind two wholly diverse ideas of the sun; the one, by which it appears to me extremely small, draws its origin from the senses, and should be placed in the class of adventitious ideas; the other, by which it seems to me many times larger than the whole earth, is taken up on astronomical grounds, that is, elicited from certain notions born with me, or is framed by myself in some other manner. These two ideas cannot certainly both resemble the same sun; and reason teaches me that the one which seems to have immediately emanated from it is the most unlike. And these things sufficiently prove that hitherto it has not been from a certain and deliberate judgment, but only from a sort of blind impulse, that I believed in the existence of certain things different from myself, which, by the organs of sense, or by whatever other means it might be, conveyed their ideas or images into my mind [and impressed it with their likenesses].

But there is still another way of inquiring whether, of the objects whose ideas are in my mind, there are any that exist out of me. If ideas are taken in so far only as they are certain modes of consciousness, I do not remark any difference or inequality among them, and all seem, in the same manner, to proceed from myself; but, considering them as images, of which one represents one thing and another a different, it is evident that a great diversity obtains among them. For, without doubt, those that represent substances are something more, and contain in them-selves, so to speak, more objective reality [that is, participate by representation in higher degrees of being or perfection] than those that represent only modes of accidents; and again, the idea by which I conceive a God [sovereign], eternal, infinite [immutable], all-knowing, all-powerful, and the creator of all things that are out of himself,—this, I say, has certainly in it more objective reality than those ideas by which finite substances are represented.

Now, it is manifest by the natural light that there must at least be as much reality in the efficient and total cause as in its effect; for whence can the effect draw its reality if not from its cause? and how could the cause communicate to it this reality unless it possessed it in itself? And hence it follows, not only that what is cannot be produced by what is not, but likewise that the more perfect,—in other words, that which contains in itself more reality,—cannot be the effect of the less perfect: and this is not only evidently true of those effects, whose reality is actual or formal, but likewise of ideas, whose reality is only considered as objective. Thus, for example, the stone that is not yet in existence, not only cannot now commence to be, unless it be produced by that which possesses in itself, formally or eminently, all that enters into its composition [in other words, by that which contains in itself the same properties that are in the stone, or others superior to them] ; and heat can only be produced in a subject that was before devoid of it, by a cause that is of an order [degree or kind] at least as perfect as heat; and so of the others. But further, even the idea of the heat, or of the stone, cannot exist in me unless it be put there by a cause that contains, at least, as much reality as I conceive existent in the heat or in the stone: for, although that cause may not transmit into my idea anything of its actual or formal reality, we ought not on this account to imagine that it is less real; but we ought to consider that [as every idea is a work of the mind], its nature is such as of itself to demand no other formal reality than that which it borrows from our consciousness, of which it is but a mode [that is, a manner or way of thinking]. But in order that an idea may contain this objective reality rather than that, it must doubtless derive it from some cause in which is found at least as much formal reality as the idea contains an objective; for, if we suppose that there is found in an idea anything which was not in its cause, it must of course *derive this from nothing.* But, however imperfect may be the mode of existence by which a thing is objectively [or by representation] in the understanding by its idea, we certainly cannot, for all that, allege that this mode of existence is nothing, nor, consequently, that the idea owes its origin to nothing. Nor must it be imagined that, since the reality which is considered in these ideas is only objective, the same reality need not be formally (actually) in the causes of these ideas, but only objectively; for, just as the mode of existing objectively belongs to ideas by their peculiar nature, so likewise the mode of existing formally appertains to the causes of these ideas (at least to the first and principal), by their peculiar nature. And although an idea may give rise to another idea, this regress cannot, nevertheless, be infinite; we must in the end reach a first idea, the cause of which is, as it were, the archetype in which all the reality [or perfection] that is found objectively [or by representation] in these ideas is contained formally [and in act]. I am thus clearly taught by the natural light that ideas exist in me as pictures or images, which may in truth readily fall short of the perfection of the objects from which they are taken, but can never contain anything greater or more perfect.

And in proportion to the time and care with which I examine all those matters, the conviction of their truth brightens and becomes distinct. But, to sum up, what conclusion shall I draw from it all? It is this;—if the objective reality [or perfection] of any one of my ideas be such as clearly to convince me, that this same reality exists in me neither formally nor eminently, and if, as follows from this, I myself cannot be the cause of it, it is a necessary consequence that I am not alone in the world, but that there is besides myself some other being who exists as the cause of that idea; while, on the contrary, if no such idea be found in my mind, I shall have no sufficient ground of assurance of the existence of any other being besides myself, for, after a most careful search, I have, up to this moment, been unable to discover any other ground.

But, among these my ideas, besides that which represents myself, respecting which there can be here no difficulty, there is one that represents a God; others that represent corporeal and inanimate things; others angels; others animals; and, finally, there are some that represent men like myself. But with respect to the ideas that represent other men, or animals, or angels, I can easily suppose that they were formed by the mingling and composition of the other ideas which I have of myself, of corporeal things, and of God, although there were, apart from myself, neither men, animals, nor angels. And with regard to the ideas of corporeal objects, I never discovered in them anything so great or excellent which I myself did not appear capable of originating; for, by considering these ideas closely and scrutinising them individually, in the same way that I yesterday examined the idea of wax, I find that there is but little in them that is clearly and distinctly perceived. As belonging to the class of things that are clearly apprehended, I recognise the following, viz., magnitude or extension in length, breadth, and depth; figure, which results from the termination of extension; situation, which bodies of diverse figures preserve with reference to each other; and motion or the change of situation; to which may be added substance, duration, and number. But with regard to light, colours, sounds, odours, tastes, heat, cold and the other tactile qualities, they are thought with so much obscurity and confusion, that I cannot determine even whether they are true or false; in other words, whether or not the ideas I have of these qualities are in truth the ideas of real objects. For although I before remarked that it is only in judgments that formal falsity, or falsity properly so called, can be met with, there may nevertheless be found in ideas a certain material falsity, which arises when they represent what is nothing as if it were something. Thus, for example, the ideas I have of cold and heat are so far from being clear and distinct, that I am unable from them to discover whether cold is only the privation of heat, or heat the privation of cold; or whether they are or are not real qualities: and since, ideas being as it were images, there can be none that does not seem to us to represent some object, the idea which represents cold as something real and positive will not improperly be called false, if it be correct to say that cold is nothing but a privation of heat; and so in other cases. To ideas of this kind, indeed, it is not necessary that I should assign any author besides myself: for if they are false, that is, represent objects that are unreal, the natural light teaches me that they proceed from nothing; in other words, that they are in me only because something is wanting to the perfection of my nature; but if these ideas are true, yet because they exhibit to me so little reality that I cannot even distinguish the object represented from non-being, I do not see why I should not be the author of them.

With reference to those ideas of corporeal things that are clear and distinct, there are some which, as appears to me, might have been taken from the idea I have of myself, as those of substance, duration, number, and the like. For when I think that a stone is a substance, or a thing capable of existing of itself, and that I am likewise a substance, although I conceive that I am a thinking and non-extended thing, and that the stone, on the contrary, is extended and unconscious, there being thus the greatest diversity between the two concepts,—yet these two ideas seem to have this in common that they both represent substances. In the same way, when I think of myself as now existing, and recollect besides that I existed some time ago, and when I am conscious of various thoughts whose number I know, I then acquire the ideas of duration and number, which I can afterwards transfer to as many objects as I please. With respect to the other qualities that go to make up the ideas of corporeal objects, viz., extension, figure, situation, and motion, it is true that they are not formally in me, since I am merely a thinking being; but because they are only certain modes of substance, and because I myself am a substance, it seems possible that they may be contained in me eminently.

There only remains, therefore, the idea of God, in which I must consider whether there is anything that cannot be supposed to originate with myself. By the name God, I understand a substance infinite [eternal, immutable], independent, all-knowing, all-powerful, and by which I myself, and every other thing that exists, if any such there be, were created. But these properties are so great and excellent, that the more attentively I consider them the less I feel persuaded that the idea I have of them owes its origin to myself alone. And thus it is absolutely necessary to conclude, from all that I have before said, that God exists: for though the idea of substance be in my mind owing to this, that I myself am a substance, I should not, however, have the idea of an infinite substance, seeing I am a finite being, unless it were given me by some substance in reality infinite.

And I must not imagine that I do not apprehend the infinite by a true idea, but only by the negation of the finite, in the same way that I comprehend repose and darkness by the negation of motion and light: since, on the contrary, I clearly perceive that there is more reality in the infinite substance than in the finite, and therefore that in some way I possess the perception (notion) of the infinite before that of the finite, that is, the perception of God before that of myself, for how could I know that I doubt, desire, or that something is wanting to me, and that I am not wholly perfect, if I possessed no idea of a being more perfect than myself, by comparison of which I knew the deficiencies of my nature?

And it cannot be said that this idea of God is perhaps materially false, and consequently that it may have arisen from nothing [in other words, that it may exist in me from my imperfection], as I before said of the ideas of heat and cold, and the like: for, on the contrary, as this idea is very clear and distinct, and contains in itself more objective reality than any other, there can be no one of itself more true, or less open to the suspicion of falsity.

The idea, I say, of a being supremely perfect, and infinite, is in the highest degree true; for although, perhaps, we may imagine that such a being does not exist, we cannot, nevertheless, suppose that his idea represents nothing real, as I have already said of the idea of cold. It is likewise clear and distinct in the highest degree, since whatever the mind clearly and distinctly conceives as real or true, and as implying any perfection, is contained entire in this idea. And this is true, nevertheless, although I do not comprehend the infinite, and although there may be in

God an infinity of things that I cannot comprehend, nor perhaps even compass by thought in any way; for it is of the nature of the infinite that it should not be comprehended by the finite; and it is enough that I rightly understand this, and judge that all which I clearly perceive, and in which I know there is some perfection, and perhaps also an infinity of properties of which I am ignorant, are formally or eminently in God, in order that the idea I have of him may become the most true, clear, and distinct of all the ideas in my mind.

But perhaps I am something more than I suppose myself to be, and it may be that all those perfections which I attribute to God, in some way exist potentially in me, although they do not yet show themselves, and are not reduced to act. Indeed, I am already conscious that my knowledge is being increased [and perfected] by degrees; and I see nothing to prevent it from thus gradually increasing to infinity, nor any reason why, after such increase and perfection, I should not be able thereby to acquire all the other perfections of the Divine nature; nor, in fine, why the power I possess of acquiring those perfections, if it really now exist in me, should not be sufficient to produce the ideas of them. Yet, on looking more closely into the matter, I discover that this cannot be; for, in the first place, although it were true that my knowledge daily acquired new degrees of perfection, and although there were potentially in my nature much that was not as yet actually in it, still all these excellences make not the slightest approach to the idea I have of the Deity, in whom there is no perfection merely potentially [but all actually] existent; for it is even an unmistakable token of imperfection in my knowledge, that it is augmented by degrees. Further, although my knowledge increase more and more, nevertheless I am not, therefore, induced to think that it will ever be actually infinite, since it can never reach that point beyond which it shall be incapable of further increase. But I conceive God as actually infinite, so that nothing can be added to his perfection. And, in fine, I readily perceive that the objective being of an idea cannot be produced by a being that is merely potentially existent, which, properly speaking, is nothing, but only by a being existing formally or actually.

And, truly, I see nothing in all that I have now said which it is not easy for any one, who shall carefully consider it, to discern by the natural light; but when I allow my attention in some degree to relax, the vision of my mind being obscured, and, as it were, blinded by the images of sensible objects, I do not readily remember the reason why the idea of a being more perfect than myself, must of necessity have proceeded from a being in reality more perfect. On this account I am here desirous to inquire further, whether I, who possess this idea of God, could exist supposing there were no God. And I ask, from whom could I, in that case, derive my existence? Perhaps from myself, or from my parents, or from some other causes less perfect than God; for anything more perfect, or even equal to God, cannot be thought or imagined. But if I [were independent of every other existence, and] were myself the author of my being, I should doubt of nothing, I should desire nothing, and, in fine, no perfection would be awanting to me; for I should have bestowed upon myself every perfection of which I possess the idea, and I should thus be God. And it must not be imagined that what is now wanting to me is perhaps of more difficult acquisition than that of which I am already possessed; for, on the contrary, it is quite manifest that it was a matter of much higher difficulty that I, a thinking being, should arise from nothing, than it would be for me to acquire the knowledge of many things of which I am ignorant, and which are merely the accidents of a thinking substance; and certainly, if I possessed of myself the greater perfection of which I have now spoken [in other words, if I were the author of my own existence] , I would not at least have denied to myself things that may be more easily obtained [as that infinite variety of knowledge of which I am at present destitute] . I could not, indeed, have denied to myself any property which I perceive is contained in the idea of God, because there is none of these that seems to me to be more difficult to make or acquire; and if there were any that should happen to be more difficult to acquire, they would certainly appear so to me (supposing that I myself were the source of the other things I possess), because I should discover in them a limit to my power. And though I were to suppose that I always was as I now am, I should not, on this ground, escape the force of these reasonings, since it would not follow, even on this supposition, that no author of my existence needed to be sought after. For the whole time of my life may be divided into an infinity of parts, each of which is in no way dependent on any other; and, accordingly, because I was in existence a short time ago, it does not follow that I must now exist, unless in this moment some cause create me anew, as it were,—that is, conserve me. In truth, it is perfectly clear and evident to all who will attentively consider the nature of duration that the conservation of a sub-stance, in each moment of its duration, requires the same power and act that would be necessary to create it, supposing it were not yet in existence; so that it is manifestly a dictate of the natural light that conservation and creation differ merely in respect of our mode of thinking [and not in reality] . All that is here required, therefore, is that I interrogate myself to discover whether I possess any power by means of which I can bring it about that I, who now am, shall exist a moment afterwards: for, since I am merely a thinking thing (or since, at least, the precise question, in the meantime, is only of that part of myself), if such a power resided in me, I should without doubt, be conscious of it; but I am conscious of no such power, and thereby I manifestly know that I am dependent upon some being different from myself.

But perhaps the being upon whom I am dependent is not God, and I have been produced either by my parents, or by some causes less perfect than Deity. This cannot be: for, as I before said, it is perfectly evident that there must at least be as much reality in the cause as in its effect; and accordingly, since I am a thinking thing, and possess in myself an idea of God, whatever in the end be the cause of my existence, it must of necessity be admitted that it is likewise a thinking being, and that it possesses in itself the idea and all the perfections I attribute to Deity. Then it may again be inquired whether this cause owes its origin and existence to itself, or to some other cause. For if it be self-existent, it follows, from what I have before laid down, that this cause is God; for, since it possesses the perfection of self-existence, it must likewise, without doubt, have the power of actually possessing every perfection of which it has the idea,—in other words, all the perfections I conceive to belong to God. But if it owe its existence to another cause than itself, we demand again, for a similar reason, whether this second cause exists of itself or through some other, until, from stage to stage, we at length arrive at an ultimate cause, which will be God. And it is quite manifest that in this matter there can be no infinite regress of causes, seeing that the question raised respects not so much the cause which once produced me, as that by which I am at this present moment conserved.

Nor can it be supposed that several causes concerned in my production, and that from one I received the idea of one of the perfections I attribute to Deity, and from another the idea of some other, and thus that all those perfections are indeed found somewhere in the universe, but do not all exist together in a single being who is God; for, on the contrary, the unity, the simplicity or inseparability of all the properties of Deity, is one of the chief perfections I conceive him to possess; and the idea of this unity of all the perfections of Deity could certainly not be put into my mind by any cause from which I did not likewise receive the ideas of all the other perfections; for no power could enable me to embrace them in an inseparable unity, without at the same time giving me the knowledge of what they were [and of their existence in a particular mode].

Finally, with regard to my parents [from whom it appears I sprung], although all that I believed respecting them be true, it does not, nevertheless, follow that I am conserved by them, or even that I was produced by them, in so far as I am a thinking being. All that, at the most, they contributed to my origin was the giving of certain dispositions (modifications) to the matter in which I have hitherto judged that I or my mind, which is what alone I now consider to be myself, is enclosed; and thus there can here be no difficulty with respect to them, and it is absolutely necessary to conclude from this alone that I am, and possess the idea of a being absolutely perfect, that is, of God, that his existence is most clearly demonstrated.

There remains only the inquiry as to the way in which I received this idea from God; for I have not drawn it from the senses, nor is it even presented to me unexpectedly, as is usual with the ideas of sensible objects, when these are presented or appear to be presented to the external organs of the senses; it is not even a pure production or fiction of my mind, for it is not in my power to take from or add to it; and consequently there but remains the alternative that it is innate, in the same way as is the idea of myself. And, in truth, it is not to be wondered at that God, at my creation, implanted this idea in me, that it might serve, as it were, for the mark of the workman impressed on his work; and it is not also necessary that the mark should be something different from the work itself; but considering only that God is my creator, it is highly probable that he in some way fashioned me after his own image and likeness, and that I perceive this likeness, in which is contained the idea of God, by the same faculty by which I apprehend myself,—in other words, when I make myself the object of reflection, I not only find that I am an incomplete [imperfect] and dependent being, and one who unceasingly aspires after something better and greater than he is; but, at the same time, I am assured likewise that he upon whom I am dependent possesses in himself all the goods after which I aspire [and the ideas of which I find in my mind], and that not merely indefinitely and potentially, but infinitely and actually, and that he is thus God. And the whole force of the argument of which I have here availed myself to establish the existence of God, consists in this, that I perceive I could not possibly be of such a nature as I am, and yet have in my mind the idea of a God, if God did not in reality exist,—this same God, I say, whose idea is in my mind—that is, a being who possesses all those lofty perfections, of which the mind may have some slight conception, without, however, being able fully to comprehend them,—and who is wholly superior to all defect [and has nothing that marks imperfection] : whence it is sufficiently manifest that he cannot be a deceiver, since it is a dictate of the natural light that all fraud and deception spring from some defect.

But before I examine this with more attention, and pass on to the consideration of other truths that may be evolved out of it, I think it proper to remain here for some time in the contemplation of God himself—that I may ponder at leisure his marvellous attributes—and behold, admire, and adore the beauty of this light so unspeakably great, as far, at least, as the strength of my mind, which is to some degree dazzled by the sight, will permit. For just as we learn by faith that the supreme felicity of another life consists in the contemplation of the Divine majesty alone, so even now we learn from experience that a like meditation, though incomparably less perfect, is the source of the highest satisfaction of which we are susceptible in this life.

Meditation IV

Of Truth and Error

I have been habituated these bygone days to detach my mind from the senses, and I have accurately observed that there is exceedingly little which is known with certainty respecting corporeal objects,—that we know much more of the human mind, and still more of God himself. I am thus able now without difficulty to abstract my mind from the contemplation of [sensible or] imaginable objects, and apply it to those which, as disengaged from all matter, are purely intelligible. And certainly the idea I have of the human mind in so far as it is a thinking thing, and not extended in length, breadth, and depth, and participating in none of the properties of body, is incomparably more distinct than the idea of any corporeal object; and when I consider that I doubt, in other words, that I am an incomplete and dependent being, the idea of a complete and independent being, that is to say of God, occurs to my mind with so much clearness and distinctness,—and from the fact alone that this idea is found in me, or that I who possess it exist, the conclusions that God exists, and that my own existence, each moment of its continuance, is absolutely dependent upon him, are so manifest,—as to lead me to believe it impossible that the human mind can know anything with more clearness and certitude. And now I seem to discover a path that will conduct us from the contemplation of the true God, in whom are contained all the treasures of science and wisdom, to the knowledge of the other things in the universe.

For, in the first place, I discover that it is impossible for him ever to deceive me, for in all fraud and deceit there is a certain imperfection: and although it may seem that the ability to deceive is a mark of subtlety or power, yet the will testifies without doubt of malice and weakness; and such, accordingly, can be found in God. In the next place, I am conscious that I possess a certain faculty of judging [or discerning truth from error], which I doubtless received from God, along with whatever else is mine; and since it is impossible that he should will to deceive me, it is likewise certain that he has not given me a faculty that will ever lead me into error, provided I use it aright.

And there would remain no doubt on this head, did it not seem to follow from this, that I can never therefore be deceived; for if all I possess be from God, and if he planted in me no faculty that is deceitful, it seems to follow that I can never fall into error. Accordingly, it is true that when I think only of God (when I look upon myself as coming from God, Fr.), and turn wholly to him, I discover [in myself] no cause of error or falsity: but immediately thereafter, recurring to myself, experience assures me that I am nevertheless subject to innumerable errors. When I come to inquire into the cause of these, I observe that there is not only present to my consciousness a real and positive idea of God, or of a being supremely perfect, but also, so to speak, a certain negative idea of nothing,—in other words, of that which is at an infinite distance from every sort of perfection, and that I am, as it were, a mean between God and nothing, or placed in such a way between absolute existence and non-existence, that there is in truth nothing in me to lead me into error, in so far as an absolute being is my creator; but that, on the other hand, as I thus likewise participate in some degree of nothing or of non-being, in other words, as I am not myself the supreme Being, and as I am wanting in many perfections, it is not surprising I should fall into error. And I hence discern that error, as far as error is not something real, which depends for its existence on God, but is simply defect; and therefore that, in order to fall into it, it is not necessary God should have given me a faculty expressly for this end, but that my being deceived arises from the circumstance that the power which God has given me of discerning truth from error is not infinite.

Nevertheless this is not yet quite satisfactory; for error is not a pure negation [in other words, it is not the simple deficiency or want of some knowledge which is not due], but the privation or want of some knowledge which it would seem I ought to possess. But, on considering the nature of God, it seems impossible that he should have planted in his creature any faculty not perfect in its kind, that is, wanting in some perfection due to it: for if it be true, that in proportion to the skill of the maker the perfection of his work is greater, what thing can have been produced by the supreme Creator of the universe that is not absolutely perfect in all its parts? And assuredly there is no doubt that God could have created me such as that I should never be deceived; it is certain, likewise, that he always wills what is best: is it better, then, that I should be capable of being deceived than that I should not?

Considering this more attentively, the first thing that occurs to me is the reflection that I must not be surprised if I am not always capable of comprehending the reasons why God acts as he does; nor must I doubt of his existence because I find, perhaps, that there are several other things, besides the present respecting which I understand neither why nor how they were created by him; for knowing already that my nature is extremely weak and limited, and that the nature of God, on the other hand, is immense, incomprehensible, and infinite, I have no longer any difficulty in discerning that there is an infinity of things in his power whose causes transcend the grasp of my mind: and this consideration alone is sufficient to convince me, that the whole class of final causes is of no avail in physical [or natural] things; for it appears to me that I cannot, without exposing myself to the charge of temerity, seek to discover the [impenetrable] ends of Deity.

It further occurs to me that we must not consider only one creature apart from the others, if we wish to determine the perfection of the works of Deity, but generally all his creatures together; for the same object that might perhaps, with some show of reason, be deemed highly imperfect if it were alone in the world, may for all that be the most perfect possible, considered as forming part of the whole universe: and although, as it was my purpose to doubt of everything, I only as yet know with certainty my own existence and that of God, nevertheless, after having remarked the infinite power of Deity, I cannot deny that he may have produced many other objects, or at least that he is able to produce them, so that I may occupy a place in the relation of a part to the great whole of his creatures.

Whereupon, regarding myself more closely, and considering what my errors are (which alone testify to the existence of imperfection in me), I observe that these depend on the concurrence of two causes, viz., the faculty of cognition which I possess, and that of election or the power of free choices,—in other words, the understanding and the will. For by the understanding alone, I [neither affirm nor deny anything, but] merely apprehend (*percipio*) the ideas regarding which I may form a judgment; nor is any error, properly so called, found in it thus accurately taken. And although there are perhaps innumerable objects in the world of which I have no idea in my understanding, it cannot, on that account, be said that I am deprived of those ideas [as of something that is due to my nature], but simply that I do not possess them, because, in truth, there is no ground to prove that Deity ought to have endowed me with a larger faculty of cognition than he has actually bestowed upon me; and however skillful a workman I suppose him to be, I have no reason, on that account, to think that it was obligatory on him to give to each of his works all the perfections he is able to bestow upon some. Nor, moreover, can I complain that God has not given me freedom of choice, or a will sufficiently ample and perfect, since, in truth, I am conscious of will so ample and extended as to be superior to all limits. And what appears to me here to be highly remarkable is that, of all the other properties I possess, there is none so great and perfect as that I do not clearly discern it could be still greater and more perfect. For, to take an example, if I consider the faculty of understanding which I possess, I find that it is of very small extent, and greatly limited, and at the same time I form the idea of another faculty of the same nature, much more ample and even infinite; and seeing that I can frame the idea of it, I discover, from this circumstance alone, that it pertains to the nature of God. In the same way, if I examine the faculty of memory or imagination, or any other faculty I possess, I find none that is not small and circumscribed, and in God immense [and infinite]. It is the faculty of will only, or freedom of choice, which I experience to be so great that I am unable to conceive the idea of another that shall be more ample and extended; so that it is chiefly my will which leads me to discern that I bear a certain image and similitude of Deity. For although the faculty of will is incomparably greater in God than in myself, as well in respect of the knowledge and power that are conjoined with it, and that render it stronger and more efficacious, as in respect of the object, since in him it extends to a greater number of things, it does not, nevertheless, appear to me greater, considered in itself formally and precisely: for the power of will consists only in this, that we are able to do or not to do the same thing (that is, to affirm or deny, to pursue or shun it), or rather in this alone, that in affirming or denying, pursuing or shunning, what is proposed to us by the understanding, we so act that we are not conscious of being determined to a particular action by any external force. For, to the possession of freedom, it is not necessary that I be alike indifferent towards each of two contraries; but on the contrary, the more I am inclined towards the one, whether because I clearly know that in it there is the reason of truth and goodness, or because God thus internally disposes my thought, the more freely do I choose and embrace it; and assuredly divine grace and natural knowledge, very far from diminishing liberty, rather augment and fortify it. But the indifference of which I am conscious when I am not impelled to one side rather than to another for want of a reason, is the lowest grade of liberty, and manifests defect or negation of knowledge rather than perfection, of will; for if I always clearly knew what was true and good, I should never have any difficulty in determining what judgment I ought to come to, and what choice I ought to make, and I should thus be entirely free without ever being indifferent.

From all this I discover, however, that neither the power of willing, which I have received from God, is of itself the source of my errors, for it is exceedingly ample and perfect in its kind; nor even the power of understanding, for as I conceive no object unless by means of the faculty that God bestowed upon me, all that I conceive is doubtless rightly conceived by me, and it is impossible for me to be deceived in it.

Whence, then, spring my errors? They arise from this cause alone, that I do not restrain the will, which is of much wider range than the understanding, within the same limits, but extend it even to things I do not understand, and as the will is of itself indifferent to such, it readily falls into error and sin by choosing the false in room of the true, and evil instead of good.

For example, when I lately considered whether aught really existed in the world, and found that because I considered this question, it very manifestly followed that I myself existed, I could not but judge that what I so clearly conceived was true, not that I was forced to this judgment by any external cause, but simply because great clearness of the understanding was succeeded by strong inclination in the will; and I believed this the more freely and spontaneously in proportion as I was less indifferent with respect to it. But now I not only know that I exist, in so far as I am thinking being, but there is likewise presented to my mind a certain idea of corporeal nature; hence I am in doubt as to whether the thinking nature which is in me, or rather which I myself am, is different from that corporeal nature, or whether both are merely one and the same thing, and I here suppose that I am as yet ignorant of any reason that would determine me to adopt the one belief in preference to the other: whence it happens that it is a matter of perfect indifference to me which of the two suppositions I affirm or deny, or whether I form any judgment at all in the matter.

This indifference, moreover, extends not only to things of which the understanding has no knowledge at all, but in general also to all those which it does not discover with perfect clearness at the moment the will is deliberating upon them;

for, however probably the conjectures may be that dispose me to form a judgment in a particular matter, the simple knowledge that these are merely conjectures, and not certain and indubitable reasons, is sufficient to lead me to form one that is directly the opposite. Of this I lately had abundant experience, when I laid aside as false all that I had before held for true, on the single ground that I could in some degree doubt of it. But if I abstain from judging of a thing when I do not conceive it with sufficient clearness and distinctness, it is plain that I act rightly, and am not deceived; but if I resolve to deny or affirm, I then do not make a right use of my free will; and if I affirm what is false, it is evident that I am deceived: moreover, even although I judge according to truth, I stumble upon it by chance, and do not therefore escape the imputation of a wrong use of my freedom; for it is a dictate of the natural light, that the knowledge of the understanding ought always to precede the determination of the will.

And it is this wrong use of freedom of the will in which is found the privation that constitutes the form of error. Privation, I say, is found in the act, in so far as it proceeds from myself, but it does not exist in the faculty which I received from God, nor even in the act, in so far as it depends on him; for I have assuredly no reason to complain that God has not given me a greater power of intelligence or more perfect natural light than he has actually bestowed, since it is of the nature of a finite understanding not to comprehend many things, and of the nature of a created understanding to be finite; on the contrary, I have every reason to render thanks to God, who owed me nothing, for having given me all the perfections I possess, and I should be far from thinking that he has unjustly deprived me of, or kept back, the other perfections which he has not bestowed upon me.

I have no reason, moreover, to complain because he has given me a will more ample than my understanding, since, as the will consists only of a single element, and that indivisible, it would appear that this faculty is of such a nature that nothing could be taken from it [without destroying it]; and certainly, the more extensive it is, the more cause I have to thank the goodness of him who bestowed it upon me.

And, finally, I ought not also to complain that God concurs with me in forming the acts of this will, or the judgments in which I am deceived, because those acts are wholly true and good, in so far as they depend on God; and the ability to form them is a higher degree of perfection in my nature than the want of it would be. With regard to privation, in which alone consists the formal reason of error and sin, this does not require the concurrence of Deity, because it is not a thing [or existence], and if it be referred to God as to its cause, it ought not to be called privation, but negation [according to the signification of these words in the schools]. For in truth it is no imperfection in Deity that he has accorded to me the power of giving or withholding my assent from certain things of which he has not put a clear and distinct knowledge in my understanding; but it is doubtless an imperfection in me that I do not use my freedom aright, and readily give my judgment on matters which I only obscurely and confusedly conceive.

I perceive, nevertheless, that it was easy for Deity so to have constituted me as that I should never be deceived, although I still remained free and possessed of a limited knowledge, viz., by implanting in my understanding a clear and distinct knowledge of all the objects respecting which I should ever have to deliberate; or simply by so deeply engraving on my memory the resolution to judge of nothing without previously possessing a clear and distinct conception of it, that I should never forget it. And I easily understand that, in so far as I consider myself as a single whole, without reference to any other being in the universe, I should have been much more perfect that I now am, had Deity created me superior to error; but I cannot therefore deny that it is not somehow a greater perfection in the universe, that certain of its parts are not exempt from defect, as others are, than if they were all perfectly alike.

And I have no right to complain because God, who placed me in the world, was not willing that I should sustain that character which of all others is the chief and most perfect; I have even good reason to remain satisfied on the ground that, if he has not given me the perfection of being superior to error by the first means I have pointed out above, which depends on a clear and evident knowledge of all the matters regarding which I can deliberate, he has at least left in my power the other means, which is, firmly to retain the resolution never to judge where the truth is not clearly known to me: for, although I am conscious of the weakness of not being able to keep my mind continually fixed on the same thought, I can nevertheless, by attentive and oft-repeated meditation, impress it so strongly on my memory that I shall never fail to recollect it as often as I require it, and I can acquire in this way the habitude of not erring; and since it is in being superior to error that the highest and chief perfection of man consists, I deem that I have not gained little by this day's meditation, in having discovered the source of error and falsity.

And certainly this can be no other than what I have now explained: for as often as I so restrain my will within the limits of my knowledge, that it forms no judgment except regarding objects which are clearly and distinctly represented to it by the understanding, I can never be deceived; because every clear and distinct conception is doubtless something, and as such cannot owe its origin to nothing, but must of necessity have God for its author—God, I say, who, as supremely perfect, cannot, without a contradiction, be the cause of any error; and consequently it is necessary to conclude that every such conception [or judgment] is true. Nor have I merely learned to-day what I must avoid to escape error but also what I must do to arrive at the knowledge of truth; for I will assuredly reach truth if I only fix my attention sufficiently on all the things I conceive perfectly, and separate these from others which I conceive more confusedly and obscurely: to which for the future I shall give diligent heed.

Meditation V

Of the Essence of Material Things; and, Again, of God; That He Exists

Several other questions remain for consideration respecting the attributes of God and my own nature or mind. I will, however, on some other occasion perhaps resume the investigation of these. Meanwhile, as I have discovered what must be done, and what avoided to arrive at the knowledge of truth, what I have chiefly to do is to essay to emerge from the state of doubt in which I have for some time been, and to discover whether anything can be known with certainty regarding material objects. But before considering whether such objects as I conceive exist without me, I must examine their ideas in so far as these are to be found in my consciousness, and discover which of them are distinct and which confused.

In the first place, I distinctly imagine that quantity which the philosophers commonly call continuous, or the extension in length, breadth, and depth that is in this quantity, or rather in the object to which it is attributed. Further, I can enumerate in it many diverse parts, and attribute to each of these all sorts of sizes, figures, situations, and local motions; and, in fine, I can assign to each of these motions all degrees of duration. And I not only distinctly know these things when I thus consider them in general; but besides, by a little attention, I discover innumerable particulars respecting figures, numbers, motion, and the like, which are so evidently true, and so accordant with my nature, that when I now discover them I do not so much appear to learn anything new, as to call to remembrance what I before knew, or for the first time to remark what was before in my mind, but to which I had not hitherto directed my attention. And what I here find of most importance is, that I discover in my mind innumerable ideas of certain objects, which cannot be esteemed pure negations, although perhaps they possess no reality beyond my thought, and which are not framed by me though it may be in my power to think, or not to think them, but possess true and immutable natures of their own. As, for example, when I imagine a triangle, although there is not perhaps and never was in any place in the universe apart from my thought one such figure, it remains true nevertheless that this figure possesses a certain determinate nature, form, or essence, which is immutable and eternal, and not framed by me, nor in any degree dependent on my thought; as appears from the circumstance, that diverse properties of the triangle may be demonstrated, viz., that its three angles are equal to two right, that its greatest side is subtended by its greatest angle, and the like, which, whether I will or not, I now clearly discern to belong to it, although before I did not at all think of them, when, for the first time, I imagined a triangle, and which accordingly cannot be said to have been invented by me. Nor is it a valid objection to allege, that perhaps this idea of a triangle came into my mind by the medium of the senses, through my having seen bodies of a triangular figure; for I am able to form in thought an innumerable variety of figures with regard to which it cannot be supposed that they were ever objects of sense, and I can nevertheless demonstrate diverse properties of their nature no less than of the triangle, all of which are assuredly true since I clearly conceive them; and they are therefore something, and not mere negations; for it is highly evident that all that is true is something [truth being identical with existence] ; and I have already fully shown the truth of the principle, that whatever is clearly and distinctly known is true. And although this had not been demonstrated, yet the nature of my mind is such as to compel me to assent to what I clearly conceive while I so conceive it; and I recollect that even when I still strongly adhered to the objects of sense, I reckoned among the number of the most certain truths those I clearly conceived relating to figures, numbers, and other matters and pertain to arithmetic and geometry, and in general to the pure mathematics.

But now if because I can draw from my thought the idea of an object, it follows that all I clearly and distinctly apprehend to pertain to this object, does in truth belong to it, may I not from this derive an argument for the existence of God? It is certain that I no less find the idea of a God in my consciousness, that is, the idea of a being supremely perfect, than that of any figure or number whatever: and I know with not less clearness and distinctness than an [actual and] eternal existence pertains to his nature than that all which is demonstrable of any figure or number really belongs to the nature of that figure or number; and, therefore, although all the conclusions of the preceding Meditations were false, the existence of God would pass with me for a truth at least as certain as I ever judged any truth of mathematics to be, although indeed such a doctrine may at first sight appear to contain more sophistry than truth. For, as I have been accustomed in every other matter to distinguish between existence and essence, I easily believe that the exis- tence can be separated from the essence of God, and that thus God may be conceived as not actually existing. But, nevertheless, when I think of it more atten- tively, it appears that the existence can no more be separated from the essence of God than the idea of a mountain from that of a valley, or the equality of its three angles to two right angles, from the essence of a [rectilineal] triangle; so that it is not less impossible to conceive a God, that is, a being supremely perfect, to whom existence is awanting, or who is devoid of a certain perfection, than to conceive a mountain without a valley.

But though, in truth, I cannot conceive a God unless as existing, any more than I can a mountain without a valley, yet, just as it does not follow that there is any mountain in the world merely because I conceive a mountain with a valley, so likewise, though I conceive God as existing, it does not seem to follow on that account that God exists; for my thought imposes no necessity on things; and as I may imagine a winged horse, though there be none such, so I could perhaps attri- bute existence to God, though no God existed. But the cases are not analogous, and a fallacy lurks under the semblance of this objection: for because I cannot conceive a mountain without a valley, it does not follow that there is any mountain or valley in existence, but simply that the mountain or valley, whether they do or do not exist, are inseparable from each other; whereas, on the other hand, because I cannot conceive God unless as existing, it follows that existence is inseparable from him, and therefore that he really exists: not that this is brought about by my thought, or that it imposes any necessity on things, but, on the contrary, the necessity which lies in the thing itself, that is, the necessity of the existence of God, determines me to think in this way, for it is not in my power to conceive a God without existence, that is a being supremely perfect, and yet devoid of an absolute perfection, as I am free to imagine a horse with or without wings.

Nor must it be alleged here as an objection, that it is in truth necessary to admit that God exists, after having supposed him to possess all perfections, since existence is one of them, but that my original supposition was not necessary; just as it is not necessary to think that all quadrilateral figures can be inscribed in the circle, since, if I supposed this, I should be constrained to admit that the rhombus, being a figure of four sides, can be therein inscribed, which, however, is manifestly false. This objection is, I say, incompetent; for although it may not be necessary

87

that I shall at any time entertain the notion of Deity, yet each time I happen to think of a first and sovereign being, and to draw, so to speak, the idea of him from the store-house of the mind, I am necessitated to attribute to him all kinds of perfections, though I may not then enumerate them all, nor think of each of them in particular. And this necessity is sufficient, as soon as I discover that existence is a perfection, to cause me to infer the existence of this first and sovereign being; just as it is not necessary that I should ever imagine any triangle, but whenever I am desirous of considering a rectilineal figure composed of only three angles, it is absolutely necessary to attribute those properties to it from which it is correctly inferred that its three angles are not greater than two right angles, although perhaps I may not then advert to this relation in particular. But when I consider what figures are capable of being inscribed in the circle, it is by no means necessary to hold that all quadrilateral figures are of this number; on the contrary, I cannot even imagine such to be the case, so long as I shall be unwilling to accept in thought aught that I do not clearly and distinctly conceive: and consequently there is a vast difference between false suppositions, as is the one in question, and the true ideas that were born with me, the first and chief of which is the idea of God. For indeed I discern on many grounds that this idea is not factitious, depending simply on my thought, but that it is the representation of a true and immutable nature: in the first place, because I can conceive no other being, except God, to whose essence existence [necessarily] pertains; in the second, because it is impossible to conceive two or more gods of this kind; and it being supposed that one such God exists, I clearly see that he must have existed from all eternity, and will exist to all eternity; and finally, because I apprehend many other properties in God, none of which I can either diminish or change.

But, indeed, whatever mode of probation I in the end adopt, it always returns to this, that it is only the things I clearly and distinctly conceive which have the power of completely persuading me. And although, of the objects I conceive in this manner, some, indeed, are obvious to every one, while others are only discovered after close and careful investigation; nevertheless, after they are once discovered, the latter are not esteemed less certain than the former. Thus, for example, to take the case of a right-angled triangle, although it is not so manifest at first that the square of the base is equal to the squares of the other two sides, as that the base is opposite to the greatest angle; nevertheless, after it is once apprehended, we are as firmly persuaded of the truth of the former as of the latter. And, with respect to God, if I were not preoccupied by prejudices, and my thoughts beset on all sides by the continual presence of the images of sensible objects, I should know nothing sooner or more easily than the fact of his being. For is there any truth more clear than the existence of a Supreme Being, or of God, seeing it is to his essence alone that [necessary and eternal] existence pertains? And although the right conception of this truth has cost me much close thinking, nevertheless at present I feel not only as assured of it as of what I deem most certain, but I remark further that the certitude of all other truths is so absolutely dependent on it, that without this knowledge it is impossible ever to know anything perfectly.

For although I am of such a nature as to be unable, while I possess a very clear and distinct apprehension of a matter, to resist the conviction of its truth, yet because my constitution is also such as to incapacitate me from keeping my mind continually fixed on the same object, and as I frequently recollect a past judgment without at the same time being able to recall the grounds of it, it may happen meanwhile that other reasons are presented to me which would readily cause me to change my opinion, if I did not know that God existed; and thus I should possess no true and certain knowledge, but merely vague and vacillating opinions. Thus, for example, when I consider the nature of the [rectilineal] triangle, it most clearly appears to me, who have been instructed in the principles of geometry, that its three angles are equal to two right angles, and I find it impossible to believe otherwise, while I apply my mind to the demonstration; but as soon as I cease from attending to the process of proof, although I still remember that I had a clear comprehension of it, yet I may readily come to doubt of the truth demonstrated, if I do not know that there is a God: for I may persuade myself that I have been so constituted by nature as to be sometimes deceived, even in matters which I think I apprehend with the greatest evidence and certitude, especially when I recollect that I frequently considered many things to be true and certain which other reasons afterwards constrained me to reckon as wholly false.

But after I have discovered that God exists, seeing I also at the same time observed that all things depend on him, and that he is no deceiver, and thence inferred that all which I clearly and distinctly perceive is of necessity true: although I no longer attend to the grounds of a judgment, no opposite reason can be alleged sufficient to lead me to doubt of its truth, provided only I remember that I once possessed a clear and distinct comprehension of it. My knowledge of it thus becomes true and certain. And this same knowledge extends likewise to whatever I remember to have formerly demonstrated, as the truths of geometry and the like: for what can be alleged against them to lead me to doubt of them? Will it be that my nature is such that I may be frequently deceived? But I already know that I cannot be deceived in judgments of the grounds of which I possess a clear knowledge. Will it be that I formerly deemed things to be true and certain which I afterwards discovered to be false? But I had no clear and distinct knowledge of any of those things, and, being as yet ignorant of the rule by which I am assured of the truth of a judgment, I was led to give my assent to them on grounds which I afterwards discovered were less strong than at the time I imagined them to be. What further objection, then, is there? Will it be said that perhaps I am dreaming (an objection I lately myself raised), or that all the thoughts of which I am now conscious have no more truth than the reveries of my dreams? But although, in truth, I should be dreaming, the rule still holds that all which is clearly presented to my intellect is indisputably true.

And thus I very clearly see that the certitude and truth of all science depends on the knowledge alone of the true God, insomuch that, before I knew him, I could have no perfect knowledge of any other thing. And now that I know him, I possess the means of acquiring a perfect knowledge respecting innumerable matters, as well relative to God himself and other intellectual objects as to corporeal nature, in so far as it is the object of pure mathematics [which do not consider whether it exists or not].

Meditation VI

Of the Existence of Material Things, and of the Real
Distinction Between the Mind and Body of Man

There now only remains the inquiry as to whether material things exist. With regard to this question, I at least know with certainty that such things may exist, in as far as they constitute the object of the pure mathematics, since, regarding them in this aspect, I can conceive them clearly and distinctly. For there can be no doubt that God possesses the power of producing all the objects I am able distinctly to conceive, and I never considered anything impossible to him, unless when I experienced a contradiction in the attempt to conceive it aright. Further, the faculty of imagination which I possess, and of which I am conscious that I make use when I apply myself to the consideration of material things, is sufficient to persuade me of their existence: for, when I attentively consider what imagination is, I find that is simply a certain application of the cognitive faculty (*facultas cognoscitiva*) to a body which is immediately present to it, and which therefore exists.

And to render this quite clear, I remark, in the first place, the difference that subsists between imagination and pure intellection [or conception]. For example, when I imagine a triangle I not only conceive (*intelligo*) that it is a figure comprehended by three lines, but at the same time also I look upon (*intueor*) these three lines as present by the power and internal application of my mind (*acie mentis*), and this is what I call imagining. But if I desire to think of a chiliogon, I indeed rightly conceive that it is a figure composed of a thousand sides, as easily as I conceive that a triangle is a figure composed of only three sides; but I cannot imagine the thousand sides of a chilogon as I do the three sides of a triangle, nor, so to speak, view them as present [with the eyes of my mind]. And although, in accordance with the habit I have of always imagining something when I think of corporeal things, it may happen that, in conceiving a chiliogon, I confusedly represent some figure to myself, yet it is quite evident that this is not a chiliogon, since it in no wise differs from that which I would represent to myself, if I were to think of a myriogon, or any other figure of many sides; nor would this representation be of any use in discovering and unfolding the properties that constitute the difference between a chiliogon and other polygons. But if the question turns on a pentagon, it is quite true that I can conceive its figure, as well as that of a chiliogon, without the aid of imagination; but I can likewise imagine it by applying the attention of my mind to its five sides, and at the same time to the area which they contain. Thus I observe that a special effort of mind is necessary to the act of imagination, which is not required to conceiving or understanding (*ad intelligendum*); and this special exertion of mind clearly shows the difference between imagination and pure intellection (*imaginatio et intellectio pura*). I remark, besides, that this power of imagination which I possess, in as far as it differs from the power of conceiving, is in no way necessary to my [nature or] essence, that is, to the essence of my mind; for although I did not possess it, I should still remain the same that I now am, from which it seems we may conclude that it depends on something different from the mind. And I easily understand that, if some body exists, with which my mind is so

90

conjoined and united as to be able, as it were, to consider it when it chooses, it may thus imagine corporeal objects; so that this mode of thinking differs from pure intellection only in this respect, that the mind in conceiving turns in some way upon itself, and considers some one of the ideas it possesses within itself; but in imagining it turns towards the body, and contemplates in it some object conformed to the idea which it either of itself conceived or apprehended by sense. I easily understand, I say, that imagination may be thus formed, if it is true that there are bodies; and because I find no other obvious mode of explaining it, I thence, with probability, conjecture that they exist, but only with probability; and although I carefully examine all things, nevertheless I do not find that, from the distinct idea of corporeal nature I have in my imagination, I can necessarily infer the existence of any body.

But I am accustomed to imagine many other objects besides that corporeal nature which is the object of the pure mathematics, as, for example, colours, sounds, tastes, pain, and the like, although with less distinctness; and, inasmuch as I perceive these objects much better by the senses, through the medium of which and of memory, they seem to have reached the imagination, I believe that, in order the more advantageously to examine them, it is proper I should at the same time examine what sense-perception is, and inquire whether from those ideas that are apprehended by this mode of thinking (consciousness), I cannot obtain a certain proof of the existence of corporeal objects.

And, in the first place, I will recall to my mind the things I have hitherto held as true, because perceived by the senses, and the foundations upon which my belief in their truth rested; I will, in the second place, examine the reasons that afterwards constrained me to doubt of them; and, finally, I will consider what of them I ought now to believe.

Firstly, then, I perceived that I had a head, hands, feet, and other members composing that body which I considered as part, or perhaps even as the whole, of myself. I perceived further, that that body was placed among many others, by which it was capable of being affected in diverse ways, both beneficial and hurtful; and what was beneficial I remarked by a certain sensation of pleasure, and what was hurtful by a sensation of pain. And, besides this pleasure and pain, I was likewise conscious of hunger, thirst, and other appetites, as well as certain corporeal inclinations towards joy, sadness, anger, and similar passions. And, out of myself, besides the extension, figure, and motions of bodies, I likewise perceived in them hardness, heat, and the other tactile qualities, and, in addition, light, colours, odours, tastes, and sounds, the variety of which gave me the means of distinguishing the sky, the earth, the sea, and generally all the other bodies, from one another. And certainly, considering the ideas of all these qualities, which were presented to my mind, and which alone I properly and immediately perceived, it was not without reason that I thought I perceived certain objects wholly different from my thought, namely, bodies from which those ideas proceeded; for I was conscious that the ideas were presented to me without my consent being required, so that I could not perceive any object, however desirous I might be, unless it were present to the organ of sense; and it was wholly out of my power not to perceive it when it was thus present. And because the ideas I perceived by the senses were much more lively and clear, and even, in their own way, more distinct than any of those I could of myself frame by meditation, or which I found impressed on my memory, it seemed that they could not have proceeded from myself, and must therefore have been caused in me by some other objects: and as of those objects I had no knowledge beyond what the ideas themselves gave me, nothing was so likely to occur to my mind as the supposition that the objects were similar to the ideas which they caused. And because I recollected also that I had formerly trusted to the senses, rather than to reason, and that the ideas which I myself formed were not so clear as those I perceived by sense, and that they were even for the most part composed of parts of the latter, I was readily persuaded that I had no idea in my intellect which had not formerly passed through the senses. Nor was I altogether wrong in likewise believing that the body which, by a special right, I called my own, pertained to me more properly and strictly than any of the others; for in truth, I could never be separated from it as from other bodies: I felt in it and on account of it all my appetites and affections, and in fine I was affected in its parts by pain and the titillation of pleasure, and not in the parts of the other bodies that were separated from it. But when I inquired into the reason why, from this I know not what sensation of pain, sadness of mind should follow, and why from the sensation of pleasure joy should arise, or why this indescribable twitching of the stomach, which I call hunger, should put me in mind of taking food, and the parchedness of the throat of drink, and so in other cases, I was unable to give any explanation, unless that I was so taught by nature; for there is assuredly no affinity, at least none that I am able to comprehend, between this irritation of the stomach and the desire of food, and more than between the perception of an object that causes pain and the conscious-ness of sadness which springs from the perception. And in the same way it seemed to me that all the other judgments I had formed regarding the objects of sense, were dictates of nature; because I remarked that those judgments were formed in me, before I had leisure to weigh and consider the reasons that might constrain me to form them.

But, afterwards, a wide experience by degrees sapped the faith I had reposed in my senses; for I frequently observed that towers, which at a distance seemed round, appeared square when more closely viewed, and that colossal figures, raised on the summits of these towers, looked like small statues, when viewed from the bottom of them; and, in other instances without number, I also discovered error in judgments founded on the external senses; and not only in those founded on the external, but even in those that rested on the internal senses; for is there aught more internal than pain? and yet I have sometimes been informed by parties whose arm or leg had been amputated, that they still occasionally seemed to feel pain in that part of the body which they had lost,—a circumstance that led me to think that I could not be quite certain even that any one of my members was affected when I felt pain in it. And to these grounds of doubt I shortly afterwards also added two others of very wide generality: the first of them was that I believed I never perceived anything when awake which I could not occasionally think I also perceived when asleep, and as I do not believe that the ideas I seem to perceive in my sleep proceed from objects external to me, I did not any more observe any ground for believing this of such as I seem to perceive when awake; the second was that since I was as yet ignorant of the author of my being, or at least supposed myself to be so, I saw nothing to prevent my having been so constituted by nature as that I should be deceived even in matters that appeared to me to possess the greatest truth. And, with respect to the grounds on which I had before been persuaded of the existence of sensible objects, I had no great difficulty in finding suitable answers to them; for as nature seemed to incline me to many things from which reason made me averse, I thought that I ought not to confide much in its teachings. And although the perceptions of the senses were not dependent on my will, I did not think that I ought on that ground to conclude that they proceeded from things different from myself, since perhaps there might be found in me some faculty, though hitherto unknown to me, which produced them.

But now that I begin to know myself better, and to discover more clearly the author of my being, I do not, indeed, think that I ought rashly to admit all which the senses seem to teach, nor, on the other hand, is it my conviction that I ought to doubt in general of their teachings.

And, firstly, because I know that all which I clearly and distinctly conceive can be produced by God exactly as I conceive it, it is sufficient that I am able clearly and distinctly to conceive one thing apart from another, in order to be certain that the one is different from the other, seeing they may at least be made to exist separately, by the omnipotence of God; and it matters not by what power this separation is made, in order to be compelled to judge them different; and, therefore, merely because I know with certitude that I exist, and because, in the meantime, I do not observe that aught necessarily belongs to my nature or essence beyond my being a thinking thing, I rightly conclude that my essence consists only in my being a thinking thing [or a substance whose whole essence or nature is merely thinking]. And although I may, or rather, as I will shortly say, although I certainly do possess a body with which I am very closely conjoined; nevertheless, because, on the one hand, I have a clear and distinct idea of myself, in as far as I am only a thinking and unextended thing, and as, on the other hand, I possess a distinct idea of body, in as far as it is only an extended and unthinking thing, it is certain that I [that is, my mind, by which I am what I am] is entirely and truly distinct from my body, and may exist without it.

Moreover, I find in myself diverse faculties of thinking that have each their special mode: for example, I find I possess the faculties of imagining and perceiving, without which I can indeed clearly and distinctly conceive myself as entire, but I cannot reciprocally conceive them without conceiving myself, that is to say, without an intelligent substance in which they reside, for [in the notion we have of them, or to use the terms of the schools] in their formal concept, they comprise some sort of intellection; whence I perceive that they are distinct from myself as modes are from things. I remark likewise certain other faculties, as the power of changing place, of assuming diverse figures, and the like, that cannot be conceived and cannot therefore exist, any more than the preceding, apart from a substance in which they inhere. It is very evident, however, that these faculties, if they really exist, must belong to some corporeal or extended substance, since in their clear and distinct concept there is contained some sort of extension, but no intellection at all. Farther, I cannot doubt but that there is in me a certain passive faculty of perception, that is, of receiving and taking knowledge of the ideas of sensible things; but this would be useless to me, if there did not also exist in me, or in some other thing, another active faculty capable of forming and producing those ideas. But this active faculty cannot be in me [in so far as I am but a thinking thing], seeing that it does not presuppose thought, and also that those ideas are frequently produced in my mind without my contributing to it in any way, and even frequently contrary to my will. This faculty must therefore exist in some substance different from me, in which all the objective reality of the ideas that are produced by this faculty is contained formally or eminently, as I before remarked: and this substance is either a body, that is to say, a corporeal nature in which is contained formally [and in effect] all that is objectively [and by representation] in those ideas; or it is God himself, or some other creature, of a rank superior to body, in which the same is contained eminently. But as God is no deceiver, it is manifest that he does not himself and immediately communicate those ideas to me, nor even by the intervention of any creature in which their objective reality is not formally, but only eminently, contained. For as he has given me no faculty whereby I can discover this to be the case, but, on the contrary, a very strong inclination to believe that those ideas arise from corporeal objects, I do not see how he could be vindicated from the charge of deceit, if in truth they proceeded from any other source, or were produced by other causes than corporeal things: and accordingly it must be concluded, that corporeal objects exist. Nevertheless they are not perhaps exactly such as we perceive by the senses, for their comprehension by the senses is, in many instances, very obscure and confused; but it is at least necessary to admit that all which I clearly and distinctly conceive as in them, that is, generally speaking, all that is comprehended in the object of speculative geometry, really exists external to me.

But with respect to other things which are either only particular, as, for example, that the sun is of such a size and figure, etc., or are conceived with less clearness and distinctness, as light, sound, pain, and the like, although they are highly dubious and uncertain, nevertheless on the ground alone that God is no deceiver, and that consequently he has permitted no falsity in my opinions which he has not likewise given me a faculty of correcting, I think I may with safety conclude that I possess in myself the means of arriving at the truth. And, in the first place, it cannot be doubted that in each of the dictates of nature there is some truth: for by nature, considered in general, I now understand nothing more than God himself, or the order and disposition established by God in created things; and by my nature in particular I understand the assemblage of all that God has given me.

But there is nothing which that nature teaches me more expressly [or more sensibly] than that I have a body which is ill affected when I feel pain, and stands in need of food and drink when I experience the sensations of hunger and thirst, etc. And therefore I ought not to doubt but that there is some truth in these informations.

Nature likewise teaches me by these sensations of pain, hunger, thirst, etc., that I am not only lodged in my body as a pilot in a vessel, but that I am besides so intimately conjoined, and as it were intermixed with it, that my mind and body compose a certain unity. For if this were not the case, I should not feel pain when my body is hurt, seeing I am merely a thinking thing, but should perceive the wound by the understanding alone, just as a pilot perceives by sight when any part of his vessel is damaged; and when my body has need of food or drink, I should have a clear knowledge of this, and not be made aware of it by the confused sensations of hunger and thirst: for, in truth, all these sensations of hunger, thirst, pain, etc., are nothing more than certain confused modes of thinking, arising from the union and apparent fusion of mind and body.

Besides this, nature teaches me that my own body is surrounded by many other bodies, some of which I have to seek after, and others to shun. And indeed, as I perceive different sorts of colours, sounds, odours, tastes, heat, hardness, etc., I safely conclude that there are in the bodies from which the diverse perceptions of the senses proceed, certain varieties corresponding to them, although, perhaps, not in reality like them; and since, among these diverse perceptions of the senses, some are agreeable, and others disagreeable, there can be no doubt that my body, or rather my entire self, in as far as I am composed of body and mind, may be variously affected, both beneficially and hurtfully, by surrounding bodies.

But there are many other beliefs which, though seemingly the teaching of nature, are not in reality so, but which obtained a place in my mind through a habit of judging inconsiderately of things. It may thus easily happen that such judgments shall contain error: thus, for example, the opinion I have that all space in which there is nothing to affect [or make an impression on] my senses is void; that in a hot body there is something in every respect similar to the idea of heat in my mind; that in a white or green body there is the same whiteness or greenness which I perceive; that in a bitter or sweet body there is the same taste, and so in other instances; that the stars, towers, and all distant bodies, are of the same size and figure as they appear to our eyes, etc. But that I may avoid everything like indistinctness of conception, I must accurately define what I properly understand by being taught by nature. For nature is here taken in a narrower sense than when it signifies the sum of all the things which God has given me; seeing that in that meaning the notion comprehends much that belongs only to the mind [to which I am not here to be understood as referring when I use the term nature]; as, for example, the notion I have of the truth, that what is done cannot be undone, and all the other truths I discern by the natural light [without the aid of the body]; and seeing that it comprehends likewise much besides that belongs only to body, and is not here any more contained under the name nature, as the quality of heaviness, and the like, of which I do not speak,—the term being reserved exclusively to designate the things which God has given to me as a being composed of mind and body. But nature, taking the term in the sense explained, teaches me to shun what causes in me the sensation of pain, and to pursue what affords me the sensation of pleasure, and other things of this sort; but I do not discover what it teaches me, in addition to this, from these diverse perceptions of the senses, to draw any conclusions respecting external objects without a previous [careful and mature] consideration of them by the mind: for it is, as appears to me, the office of the mind alone, and not of the composite whole of mind and body, to discern the truth in those matters. Thus, although the impression a star makes on my eye is not larger than that from the flame of a candle, I do not, nevertheless, experience any real or positive impulse determining me to believe that the star is not greater than the flame; the true account of the matter being merely that I have so judged from my youth without any ·rational ground. And, though on approaching the fire I feel heat, and even pain on approaching it too closely, I have, however, from this no ground for holding that something resembling the heat I feel is in the fire, any more than that there is something similar to the pain; all that I have ground for believing is, that there is something in it, whatever it may be, which excites in me those sensations of heat or pain. So also, although there are spaces in which I find nothing to excite and affect my senses, I must not therefore conclude that those spaces contain in them no body; for I see that in this, as in many other similar matters, I have been accustomed to pervert the order of nature, because these perceptions of the senses, although given me by nature merely to signify to my mind what things are beneficial and hurtful to the composite whole of which it is a part, and being sufficiently clear and distinct for that purpose, are nevertheless used by me as infallible rules by which to determine immediately the essence of the bodies that exist out of me, of which they can of course afford me only the most obscure and confused knowledge.

But I have already sufficiently considered how it happens that, notwithstanding the supreme goodness of God, there is falsity in my judgments. A difficulty, however, here presents itself, respecting the things which I am taught by nature must be pursued or avoided, and also respecting the internal sensations in which I seem to have occasionally detected error [and thus to be directly deceived by nature]: thus, for example, I may be so deceived by the agreeable taste of some viand with which poison has been mixed, as to be induced to take the poison. In this case, however, nature may be excused, for it simply leads me to desire the viand for its agreeable taste, and not the poison, which is unknown to it; and thus we can infer nothing from this circumstance beyond that our nature is not omniscient; at which there is assuredly no ground for surprise, since, man being of a finite nature, his knowledge must likewise be of limited perfection. But we also not unfrequently err in that to which we are directly impelled by nature, as is the case with invalids who desire drink or food that would be hurtful to them. It will here, perhaps, be alleged that the reason why such persons are deceived is that their nature is corrupted; but this leaves the difficulty untouched, for a sick man is not less really the creature of God than a man who is in full health; and therefore it is as repugnant to the goodness of God that the nature of the former should be deceitful as it is for that of the latter to be so. And, as a clock, composed of wheels and counter-weights, observes not the less accurately all the laws of nature when it is ill made, and points out the hours incorrectly, than when it satisfies the desire of the maker in every respect; so likewise if the body of man be considered as a kind of machine, so made up and composed of bones, nerves, muscles, veins, blood, and skin, that although there were in it no mind, it would still exhibit the same motions which it at present manifests involuntarily, and therefore without the aid of the mind [and simply by the dispositions of its organs], I easily discern that it would also be as natural for such a body, supposing it dropsical, for example, to experience the parchedness of the throat that is usually accompanied in the mind by the sensation of thirst, and to be disposed by this parchedness to move its nerves and its other parts in the way required for drinking, and thus increase its malady and do itself harm, as it is natural for it, when it is not indisposed to be stimulated to drink for its good by a similar cause; and although looking to the use for which a clock was destined by its maker, I may say that it is deflected from its proper nature when it incorrectly indicates the hours, and on the same principle, considering the machine of the human body as having been formed by God for the sake of the motions which it usually manifests, although I may likewise have ground for thinking that it does not follow the order of its nature when the throat is parched and drink does not tend to its preservation, nevertheless I yet plainly discern that this latter acceptation of the term nature is very different from the other; for this is nothing more than a certain denomination, depending entirely on my thought, and hence called extrinsic, by which I compare a sick man and an imperfectly constructed clock with the idea I have of a man in good health and a well-made clock; while by the other acceptation of nature is understood something which is truly found in things, and therefore possessed of some truth.

But certainly, although in respect of a dropsical body, it is only by way of exterior denomination that we say its nature is corrupted, when, without requiring drink, the throat is parched; yet, in respect of the composite whole, that is, of the mind in its union with the body, it is not a pure denomination, but really an error of nature, for it to feel thirst when drink would be hurtful to it: and, accordingly, it still remains to be considered why it is that the goodness of God does not prevent the nature of man thus taken from being fallacious.

To commence this examination accordingly, I here remark, in the first place, that there is a vast difference between mind and body, in respect that body, from its nature, is always divisible, and that mind is entirely indivisible. For in truth, when I consider the mind, that is, when I consider myself in so far only as I am a thinking being, I can distinguish in myself no parts, but I very clearly discern that I am somewhat absolutely one and entire; and although the whole mind seems to be united to the whole body, yet, when a foot, an arm, or any other part is cut off, I am conscious that nothing has been taken from my mind; nor can the faculties of willing, perceiving, conceiving, etc., properly be called its parts, for it is the same mind that is exercised [all entire] in willing, in perceiving, and in conceiving, etc. But quite the opposite holds in corporeal or extended things; for I cannot imagine any one of them [how small soever it may be], which I cannot easily sunder in thought, and which, therefore, I do not know to be divisible. This would be sufficient to teach me that the mind or soul of man is entirely different from the body, if I had not already been apprised of it on other grounds.

I remark, in the next place, that the mind does not immediately receive the impression from all the parts of the body, but only from the brain, or perhaps even from one small part of it, viz., that in which the common sense (*sensus communis*) is said to be, which as often as it is affected in the same way, gives rise to the same perception in the mind, although meanwhile the other parts of the body may be diversely disposed, as is proved by innumerable experiments, which it is unnecessary here to enumerate.

I remark, besides, that the nature of body is such that none of its parts can be moved by another part a little removed from the other, which cannot likewise be moved in the same way by any one of the parts that lie between those two, although the most remote part does not act at all. As, for example, in the cord A, B, C, D, [which is in tension], if its last part D be pulled, the first part A will not be moved in a different way than it would be were one of the intermediate parts B or C to be pulled, and the last part D meanwhile to remain fixed. And in the same way, when I feel pain in the foot, the science of physics teaches me that this sensation is experienced by means of the nerves dispersed over the foot, which, extending like cords from it to the brain, when they are contracted in the foot, contract at the same time the inmost parts of the brain in which they have their origin, and excite in these parts a certain motion appointed by nature to cause in the mind a sensation of pain, as if existing in the foot: but as these nerves must pass through the tibia, the leg, the loins, the back, and neck, in order to reach the brain, it may happen that although their extremities in the foot are not affected, but only certain of their parts that pass through the loins or neck, the same movements, nevertheless, are excited in the brain by this motion as would have been caused there by a hurt received in the foot, and hence the mind will necessarily feel pain in the foot, just as if it had been hurt; and the same is true of all the other perceptions of our senses.

I remark, finally, that as each of the movements that are made in the part of the brain by which the mind is immediately affected, impresses it with but a single sensation, the most likely supposition in the circumstances is, that this movement causes the mind to experience, among all the sensations which it is capable of impressing upon it, that one which is the best fitted, and generally the most useful for the preservation of the human body when it is in full health. But experience shows us that all the perceptions which nature has given us are of such a kind as I have mentioned; and accordingly, there is nothing found in them that does not manifest the power and goodness of God. Thus, for example, when the nerves of the foot are violently or more than usually shaken, the motion passing through the medulla of the spine to the innermost parts of the brain affords a sign to the mind on which it experiences a sensation, viz., of pain, as if it were in the foot, by which the mind is admonished and excited to do its utmost to remove the cause of it as dangerous and hurtful to the foot. It is true that God could have so constituted the nature of man as that the same motion in the brain would have informed the mind of something altogether different: the motion might, for example, have been the occasion on which the mind became conscious of itself, in so far as it is in the brain, or in so far as it is in some place intermediate between the foot and the brain, or, finally, the occasion on which it perceived some other object quite different, whatever that might be; but nothing of all this would have so well contributed to the preservation of the body as that which the mind actually feels. In the same way, when we stand in need of drink, there arises from this want a certain parchedness in the throat that moves its nerves, and by means of them the internal parts of the brain, and this movement affects the mind with the sensation of thirst, because there is nothing on that occasion which is more useful for us than to be made aware that we have need of drink for the preservation of our health; and so in other instances.

Whence it is quite manifest, that notwithstanding the sovereign goodness of God, the nature of man, in so far as it is composed of mind and body, cannot but be sometimes fallacious. For, if there is any cause which excites, not in the foot, but in some one of the parts of the nerves that stretch from the foot to the brain, or even in the brain itself, the same movement that is ordinarily created when the foot is ill affected, pain will be felt, as it were, in the foot, and the sense will thus be naturally deceived; for as the same movement in the brain can but impress the mind with the same sensation, and as this sensation is much more frequently excited by a cause which hurts the foot than by one acting in a different quarter, it is reasonable that it should lead the mind to feel pain in the foot rather than in any other part of the body. And if it sometimes happens that the parchedness of the throat does not arise, as is usual, from drink being necessary for the health of the body, but from quite the opposite cause, as is the case with the dropsical yet it is much better that it should be deceitful in that instance, than if, on the contrary, it were continually fallacious when the body is well-disposed; and the same holds true in other cases.

And certainly this consideration is of great service, not only in enabling me to recognise the errors to which my nature is liable, but likewise in rendering it more easy to avoid or correct them: for, knowing that all my senses more usually indicate to me what is true than what is false, in matters relating to the advantage of the body, and being able almost always to make use of more than a single sense in examining the same object, and besides this, being able to use my memory in connecting present with past knowledge, and my understanding which has already discovered all the causes of my errors, I ought no longer to fear that falsity may be met with in what is daily presented to me by the senses. And I ought to reject all the doubts of those bygone days as hyperbolical and ridiculous, especially the general uncertainty respecting sleep, which I could not distinguish from the waking state: for I now find a very marked difference between the two states, in respect that our memory can never connect our dreams with each other and with the course of life, in the way it is in the habit of doing with events that occur when we are awake. And, in truth, if some one, when I am awake, appeared to me all of a sudden and as suddenly disappeared, as do the images I see in sleep, so that I could not observe either whence he came or whither he went, I should not without reason esteem it either a spectre or phantom formed in my brain, rather than a real man. But when I perceive objects with regard to which I can distinctly determine both the place whence they come, and that in which they are, and the time at which they appear to me, and when, without interruption, I can connect the perception I have of them with the whole of the other parts of my life, I am perfectly sure that what I thus perceive occurs while I am awake and not during sleep. And I ought not in the least degree to doubt of the truth of those presentations, if, after having called together all my senses, my memory, and my understanding for the purpose of examining them, no deliverance is given by any one of these faculties which is repugnant to that of any other: for since God is no deceiver, it necessarily follows that I am not herein deceived. But because the necessities of action frequently oblige us to come to a determination before we have had leisure for so careful an examination, it must be confessed that the life of man is frequently obnoxious to error with respect to individual objects; and we must, in conclusion, acknowledge the weakness of our nature.

HOBBES AND DESCARTES

Objections and Replies*

[Hobbes'] First Objection

(In reference to Meditation I, *Concerning those matters that may be brought within the sphere of the doubtful.*)

It is sufficiently obvious from what is said in this Meditation, that we have no criterion for distinguishing dreaming from waking and from what the senses truly tell us; and that hence the images present to us when we are awake and using our senses are not accidents inhering in external objects, and fail to prove that such external objects do as a fact exist. And therefore, if we follow our senses without using any train of reasoning, we shall be justified in doubting whether or not anything exists. Hence we acknowledge the truth of this Meditation. But, since Plato and other ancient Philosophers have talked about this want of certitude in the matters of sense, and since the difficulty in distinguishing the waking state from dreams is a matter of common observation, I should have been glad if our author, so distinguished in the handling of modern speculations, had refrained from publishing those matters of ancient lore.

[Descartes'] Reply

The reasons for doubt here admitted as true by this Philosopher were propounded by me only as possessing verisimilitude, and my reason for employing them was not that I might retail them as new, but partly that I might prepare my readers' minds for the study of intellectual matters and for distinguishing them from matters corporeal, a purpose for which such arguments seem wholly necessary; in part also because I intended to reply to these very arguments in the subsequent Meditations; and partly in order to show the strength of the truths I afterwards propound, by the fact that such metaphysical doubts cannot shake them. Hence, while I have sought no praise from their rehearsal, I believe that it was impossible for me to omit them, as impossible as it would be for a medical writer to omit the description of a disease when trying to teach the method of curing it.

Objection II

(In opposition to the Second Meditation, *Concerning the nature of the Human Mind.*)

I am a thing that thinks; quite correct. From the fact that I think, or have an image, whether sleeping or waking, it is inferred that I am exercising thought; for *I*

* From *The Philosophical Works of Descartes*, Vol. II, pp. 60–78, translated by Elizabeth S. Haldane and G. R. T. Ross (Cambridge: Cambridge University Press, 1934), by permission of the publisher.

think and *I am exercising thought* mean the same thing. From the fact that I am exercising thought it follows that *I am*, since that which thinks is not nothing. But, where it is added, *this is the mind, the spirit, the understanding, the reason,* a doubt arises. For it does not seem to be good reasoning to say: *I am exercising thought,* hence *I am thought;* or *I am using my intellect,* hence *I am intellect.* For in the same way I might say, *I am walking;* hence *I am the walking.* It is hence an assumption on the part of M. Descartes that that which understands is the same as the exercise of understanding which is an act of that which understands, or, at least, that that which understands is the same as the understanding, which is a power possessed by that which thinks. Yet all Philosophers distinguish a subject from its faculties and activities, i.e. from its properties and essences; for the *entity* itself is one thing, its *essence* another. Hence it is possible for a thing that thinks to be the subject of the mind, reason, or understanding, and hence to be something corporeal; and the opposite of this has been assumed, not proved. Yet this inference is the basis of the conclusion that M. Descartes seems to wish to establish.

In the same place he says, *I know that I exist; the question is, who am I—the being that I know? It is certain that the knowledge of this being thus accurately determined does not depend on those things which I do not yet know to exist.*[3]

It is quite certain that the knowledge of this proposition, *I exist,* depends upon that other one, *I think,* as he has himself correctly shown us. But whence comes our knowledge of this proposition, *I think?* Certainly from that fact alone, that we can conceive no activity whatsoever apart from its subject, e.g. we cannot think of leaping apart from that which leaps, of knowing apart from a knower, or of thinking without a thinker.

And hence it seems to follow that that which thinks is something corporeal; for, as it appears, the subjects of all activities can be conceived only after a corporeal fashion, or as in material guise, as M. Descartes himself afterwards shows, when he illustrates by means of wax, this wax was understood to be always the same thing, i.e. the identical matter underlying the many successive changes, though its colour, consistency, figure and other activities were altered. Moreover it is not by another thought that I infer that I think; for though anyone may think that he has thought (to think so is precisely the same as remembering), yet we cannot think that we are thinking, nor similarly know that we know. For this would entail the repetition of the question an infinite number of times; whence do you know, that you know, that you know, that you know?

Hence, since the knowledge of this proposition, *I exist,* depends upon the knowledge of that other, *I think,* and the knowledge of it upon the fact that we cannot separate thought from a matter that thinks, the proper inference seems to be that that which thinks is material rather than immaterial.

Reply

Where I have said, *this is the mind, the spirit, the intellect, or the reason,* I understood by these names not merely faculties, but rather what is endowed with the

---

3. Cf. Med. II, above, p. 67.

faculty of thinking; and this sense the two former terms commonly, the latter frequently bear. But I used them in this sense so expressly and in so many places that I cannot see what occasion there was for any doubt about their meaning.

Further, there is here no parity between walking and thinking; for walking is usually held to refer only to that action itself, while thinking applies now to the action, now to the faculty of thinking, and again to that in which the faculty exists.

Again I do not assert that that which understands and the activity of understanding are the same thing, nor indeed do I mean that the thing that understands and the understanding are the same, if the term understanding be taken to refer to the faculty of understanding; they are identical only when the understanding means the thing itself that understands. I admit also quite gladly that, in order to designate that thing or substance, which I wished to strip of everything that did not belong to it, I employed the most highly abstract terms I could; just as, on the contrary this Philosopher uses terms that are as concrete as possible, e.g. *subject, matter, body,* to signify that which thinks, fearing to let it be sundered from the body.

But I have no fear of anyone thinking that his method of coupling diverse things together is better adapted to the discovery of the truth than mine, that gives the greatest possible distinctness to every single thing. But, dropping the verbal controversy, let us look to the facts in dispute.

A thing that thinks, he says, *may be something corporeal; and the opposite of this has been assumed; not proved.* But really I did not assume the opposite, neither did I use it as a basis for my argument; I left it wholly undetermined until Meditation VI, in which its proof is given.

Next he quite correctly says, that *we cannot conceive any activity apart from its subject,* e.g. thought apart from that which thinks, since that which thinks is not nothing. But, wholly without any reason, and in opposition to the ordinary use of language and good Logic, he adds, *hence it seems to follow that that which thinks is something corporeal;* for *the subjects of all activities are* indeed *understood as falling within the sphere of substance* (or even, if you care, *as wearing the guise of matter,* viz. metaphysical matter), but not on that account are they to be defined as bodies.

On the other hand both logicians and as a rule all men are wont to say that substances are of two kinds, spiritual and corporeal. And all that I proved, when I took wax as an example, was that its colour, hardness, and figure did not belong to the formal nature of the wax itself [i.e. that we can comprehend everything that exists necessarily in the wax, without thinking of these]. I did not there treat either of the formal nature of the mind, or even of the formal nature of body.

Again it is irrelevant to say, as this Philosopher here does, that one thought cannot be the subject of another thought. Who, except my antagonist himself, ever imagined that it could? But now, for a brief explanation of the matter,—it is certain that no thought can exist apart from a thing that thinks; no activity, no accident can be without a substance in which to exist. Moreover, since we do not apprehend the substance itself immediately through itself, but by means only of the fact that it is the subject of certain activities, it is highly rational, and a requirement forced on us by custom, to give diverse names to those substances that we recognize to be the subjects of clearly diverse activities or accidents, and afterwards to inquire whether those diverse names refer to one and the same or to diverse things. But there are *certain* activities, which we call *corporeal,* e.g. magnitude, figure, motion, and all those that cannot be thought of apart from extension in space; and the substance in which they exist is called *body.* It cannot be pretended that the substance that is the subject of figure is different from that which is the subject of spatial motion, etc., since all these activities agree in presupposing extension. Further, there are other activities, which we call *thinking* activities, e.g. understanding, willing, imagining, feeling, etc., which agree in falling under the description of thought, perception, or consciousness. The substance in which they reside we call a *thinking thing* or *the mind,* or any other name we care, provided only we do not confound it with corporeal substance, since thinking activities have no affinity with corporeal activities, and thought, which is the common nature in which the former agree, is totally different from extension, the common term for describing the latter.

But after we have formed two distinct concepts of those two substances, it is easy, from what has been said in the sixth Meditation, to determine whether they are one and the same or distinct.

Objection III

What then is there distinct from my thought? What can be said to be separate from me myself?[4]

Perchance some one will answer the question thus—I, the very self that thinks, am held to be distinct from my own thought; and, though it is not really separate from me, my thought is held to be diverse from me, just in the way (as has been said before) that leaping is distinguished from the leaper. But if M. Descartes shows that he who understands and the understanding are identical we shall lapse back into the scholastic mode of speaking. The understanding understands, the vision sees, will wills, and by exact analogy, walking, or at least the faculty of walking will walk. Now all this is obscure, incorrect, and quite unworthy of M. Descartes' wonted clearness.

Reply

I do not deny that I, the thinker, am distinct from my own thought, in the way in which a thing is distinct from its mode. But when I ask, *what then is there distinct from my thought,* this is to be taken to refer to the various modes of thought there recounted, not to my substance; and when I add, *what can be said to be separate from me myself,* I mean only that these modes of thinking exist entirely in me. I cannot see on what pretext the imputation here of doubt and obscurity rests.

---

4. Quotation from Med. II, cf. above, p. 67.

Objection IV

Hence it is left for me to concede that I do not even understand by the imagination what this wax is, but conceive it by the mind alone.[5]

There is a great difference between imagining, i.e. having some idea, and conceiving with the mind, i.e. inferring, as the result of a train of reasoning, that something is, or exists. But M. Descartes has not explained to us the sense in which they differ. The ancient peripatetics also have taught clearly enough that substance is not perceived by the senses, but is known as a result of reasoning.

But what shall we now say, if reasoning chance to be nothing more than the uniting and stringing together of names or designations by the word *is?* It will be a consequence of this that reason gives us no conclusion about the nature of things, but only about the terms that designate them, whether, indeed, or not there is a convention (arbitrarily made about their meanings) according to which we join these names together. If this be so, as is possible, reasoning will depend on names, names on the imagination, and imagination, perchance, as I think, on the motion of the corporeal organs. Thus mind will be nothing but the motions in certain parts of an organic body.

Reply

I have here explained the difference between imagination and a pure mental concept, as when in my illustration I enumerated the features in wax that were given by the imagination and those solely due to a conception of the mind. But elsewhere also I have explained how it is that one and the same thing, e.g. a pentagon, is in one way an object of the understanding, in another way of the imagination [for example how in order to imagine a pentagon a particular mental act is required which gives us this figure (i.e. its five sides and the space they enclose) which we dispense with wholly in our conception]. Moreover, in reasoning we unite not names but the things signified by the names; and I marvel that the opposite can occur to anyone. For who doubts whether a Frenchman and a German are able to reason in exactly the same way about the same things, though they yet conceive the words in an entirely diverse way? And has not my opponent condemned himself in talking of conventions arbitrarily made about the meanings of words? For, if he admits that words signify anything, why will he not allow our reasonings to refer to this something that is signified, rather than to the words alone? But, really, it will be as correct to infer that earth is heaven or anything else that is desired, as to conclude that mind is motion [for there are no other two things in the world between which there is not as much agreement as there is between motion and spirit, which are of two entirely different natures].

Objection V

In reference to the third Meditation—concerning God—*some of these* (thoughts of man) *are, so to speak, images of things, and to these alone is the title 'idea' properly*

---

5. Cf. Med. II, pp. 68–69.

applied; examples are my thought of a man, or of a Chimera, of Heavens, of an Angel, or [even] of God.[6]

When I think of a man, I recognize an idea, or image, with figure and colour as its constituents; and concerning this I can raise the question whether or not it is the likeness of a man. So it is also when I think of the heavens. When I think of the chimera, I recognize an idea or image, being able at the same time to doubt whether or not it is the likeness of an animal, which, though it does not exist, may yet exist or has at some other time existed.

But when one thinks of an Angel, what is noticed in the mind is now the image of a flame, now that of a fair winged child, and this, I may be sure, has no likeness to an Angel, and hence is not the idea of an Angel. But believing that created beings exist that are the ministers of God, invisible and immaterial, we give the name of Angel to this object of belief, this supposed being, though the idea used in imagining an Angel is, nevertheless, constructed out of the ideas of visible things.

It is the same way with the most holy name of God; we have no image, no idea corresponding to it. Hence we are forbidden to worship God in the form of an image, lest we should think we could conceive Him who is inconceivable.

Hence it appears that we have no idea of God. But just as one born blind who has frequently been brought close to a fire and has felt himself growing warm, recognizes that there is something which made him warm, and, if he hears it called fire, concludes that fire exists, though he has no acquaintance with its shape or colour, and has no idea of fire nor image that he can discover in his mind; so a man, recognizing that there must be some cause of his images and ideas, and another previous cause of this cause and so on continuously, is finally carried on to a conclusion, or to the supposition of some eternal cause, which, never having begun to be, can have no cause prior to it: and hence he necessarily concludes that something eternal exists. But nevertheless he has no idea that he can assert to be that of this eternal being, and he merely gives a name to the object of his faith or reasoning and calls it God.

Since now it is from this position, viz. that there is an idea of God in our soul, that M. Descartes proceeds to prove the theorem that God (an all-powerful, all-wise Being, the creator of the world) exists, he should have explained this idea of God better, and he should have deduced from it not only God's existence, but also the creation of the world.

Reply

Here the meaning assigned to the term idea is merely that of images depicted in the corporeal imagination; and, that being agreed on, it is easy for my critic to prove that there is no proper idea of Angel or of God. But I have, everywhere, from time to time, and principally in this place, shown that I take the term idea to stand for whatever the mind directly perceives; and so when I will or when I fear, since at the same time I perceive that I will and fear, that very volition and apprehension are

---

6. Cf. Med. III, p. 72.

ranked among my ideas. I employed this term because it was the term currently used by Philosophers for the forms of perception of the Divine mind, though we can discover no imagery in God; besides I had no other more suitable term. But I think I have sufficiently well explained what the idea of God is for those who care to follow my meaning; those who prefer to wrest my words from the sense I give them, I can never satisfy. The objection that here follows, relative to the creation of the world, is plainly irrelevant [for I proved that God exists, before asking whether there is a world created by him, and from the mere fact that God, i.e. a supremely prefect being exists, it follows that if there be a world it must have been created by him].

Objection VI

But other (thoughts) *possess other forms as well. For example, in willing, fearing, affirming, denying, though I always perceive something as the subject of my thought, yet in my thought I embrace something more than the similitude of that thing; and, of the thoughts of this kind, some are called volitions or affections, and others judgments.* [7]

When a man wills or fears, he has indeed an image of the thing he fears or of the action he wills; but no explanation is given of what is further embraced in the thought of him who wills or fears. If indeed fearing be thinking, I fail to see how it can be anything other than the thought of the thing feared. In what respect does the fear produced by the onrush of a lion differ from the idea of the lion as it rushes on us, together with its effect (produced by such an idea in the heart), which impels the fearful man towards that animal motion we call flight? Now this motion of flight is not thought; whence we are left to infer that in fearing there is no thinking save that which consists in the representation of the thing feared. The same account holds true of volition.

Further you do not have affirmation and negation without words and names; consequently brute creatures cannot affirm or deny, not even in thought, and hence are likewise unable to judge. Yet a man and a beast may have similar thoughts. For, when we assert that a man runs, our thought does not differ from that which a dog has when it sees its master running. Hence neither affirmation nor negation add anything to the bare thought, unless that increment be our thinking that the names of which the affirmation consists are the names of the same thing in [the mind of] him who affirms. But this does not mean that anything more is contained in our thought than the representation of the thing, but merely that that representation is there twice over.

Reply

It is self-evident that seeing a lion and fearing it at the same time is different from merely seeing it. So, too, it is one thing to see a man running, another thing to

---

7. Cf. Med. III, p. 72.

affirm to oneself that one sees it, an act that needs no language. I can see nothing here that needs an answer.

Objection VII

It remains for me to examine in what way I have received that idea from God. I have neither derived it from the senses; nor has it ever come to me contrary to my expectation, as the ideas of sensible things are wont to do, when these very things present themselves to the external organs of sense or seem to do so. Neither also has it been constructed as a fictitious idea by me, for I can take nothing from it and am quite unable to add to it. Hence the conclusion is left that it is innate in me, just as the idea of my own self is innate in me. [8]

If there is no idea of God (now it has not been proved that it exists), as seems to be the case, the whole of this argument collapses. Further (if it is my body that is being considered) the idea of my own self proceeds [principally] from sight; but (if it is a question of the soul) there is no idea of the soul. We only infer by means of the reason that there is something internal in the human body, which imparts to it its animal motion, and by means of which it feels and moves; and this, whatever it be, we name the soul, without employing any idea.

Reply

If there is an idea of God (as it is manifest there is), the whole of this objection collapses. When it is said further that we have no idea of the soul but that we arrive at it by an inference of reason, that is the same as saying that there is no image of the soul depicted in the imagination, but that that which I have called its idea does, nevertheless, exist.

Objection VIII

But the other idea of the sun is derived from astronomical reasonings, i.e. is elicited from certain notions that are innate in me. [9]

It seems that at one and the same time the idea of the sun must be single whether it is beheld by the eyes, or is given by our intelligence as many times larger than it appears. For this latter thought is not an idea of the sun, but an inference by argument that the idea of the sun would be many times larger if we viewed the sun from a much nearer distance.

But at different times the ideas of the sun may differ, e.g. when one looks at it with the naked eye and through a telescope. But astronomical reasonings do not increase or decrease the idea of the sun; rather they show that the sensible idea is misleading.

---

8. Cf. Med. III, p. 79.
9. Cf. Med. III, p. 73.

Reply

Here too what is said not to be an idea of the sun, but is, nevertheless, described, is exactly what I call an idea. [But as long as my critic refuses to come to terms with me about the meaning of words, none of his objections can be other than frivolous.]

Objection IX

For without doubt those ideas, which reveal substance to me, are something greater, and, so to speak, contain within them more objective reality than those which represent only modes or accidents. And again, that by means of which I apprehend a supreme God who is eternal, infinite, omniscient, all-powerful, and the creator of all else there is besides, assuredly possesses more objective reality than those ideas that reveal to us finite substances. [10]

I have frequently remarked above that there is no idea either of God or of the soul; I now add that there is no idea of substance. For substance (the substance that is a material, subject to accidents and changes) is perceived and demonstrated by the reason alone, without yet being conceived by us, or furnishing us with any idea. If that is true, how can it be maintained that the ideas which reveal substance to me are anything greater or possess more objective reality than those revealing accidents to us? Further I pray M. Descartes to investigate the meaning of *more reality*. Does reality admit of more and less? Or, if he thinks that one thing can be more a thing than another, let him see how he is to explain it to our intelligence with the clearness called for in demonstration, and such as he himself has at other times employed.

Reply

I have frequently remarked that I give the name idea to that with which reason makes us acquainted just as I also do to anything else that is in any way perceived by us. I have likewise explained how reality admits of more and less: viz. in the way in which substance is greater than mode; and if there be real qualities or incomplete substances, they are things to a greater extent than modes are, but less than complete substances. Finally, if there be an infinite and independent substance, it is more a thing than a substance that is finite and dependent. Now all this is quite self-evident [and so needs no further explanation].

Objection X

Hence there remains alone the idea of God, concerning which we must consider whether it is not something that is capable of proceeding from me myself. By the

---

10. Cf. Med. III, p. 73.

*name God I understand a substance that is infinite [eternal, immutable],
independent, all-knowing, all-powerful, and by which both I myself and everything
else, if anything else does exist, have been created. Now all these characteristics are
such that, the more diligently I attend to them, the less do they appear capable of
proceeding from me alone; hence, from what has been already said, we must
conclude that God necessarily exists.*[11]

When I consider the attributes of God, in order to gather thence the idea of
God, and see whether there is anything contained in it that cannot proceed from
ourselves, I find, unless I am mistaken, that what we assign in thought to the name
of God neither proceeds from ourselves nor needs to come from any other source
than external objects. For by the word God I mean a *substance,* i.e. I understand
that God exists (not by means of an idea but by reasoning). This substance is
infinite (i.e. I can neither conceive nor imagine its boundaries or extreme parts,
without imagining further parts beyond them): whence it follows that corresponding to the term *infinite* there arises an idea not of the Divine infinity, but of
my own bounds or limitations. It is also *independent,* i.e. I have no conception of a
cause from which God originates; whence it is evident that I have no idea corresponding to the term *independent,* save the memory of my own ideas with their
commencement at divers times and their consequent dependence.

Wherefore to say that God is *independent,* is merely to say that God is to be
reckoned among the number of those things, of the origin of which we have no
image. Similarly to say that God is *infinite,* is identical with saying that He is among
those objects of the limits of which we have no conception. Thus any idea of God is
ruled out; for what sort of idea is that which has neither origin nor termination?

Take the term *all-knowing.* Here I ask: what idea does M. Descartes employ in
apprehending the intellectual activity of God?

All-powerful. So too, what is the idea by which we apprehend power, which is
relative to that which lies in the future, i.e. does not exist? I certainly understand
what power is by means of an image, or memory of past events, inferring it in this
wise—Thus did He, hence thus was He able to do; therefore as long as the same
agent exists He will be able to act so again, i.e. He has the power of acting. Now
these are all ideas that can arise from external objects.

Creator of everything that exists. Of creation some image can be constructed
by me out of the objects I behold, e.g. the birth of a human being or its growth
from something small as a point to the size and figure it now possesses. We have no
other idea than this corresponding to the term creator. But in order to prove
creation it is not enough to be able to imagine the creation of the world. Hence
although it had been demonstrated that an *infinite, independent, all-powerful, etc.*
being exists, nevertheless it does not follow that a creator exists. Unless anyone
thinks that it is correct to infer, from the fact that there is a being which we believe
to have created everything, that hence the world was at some time created by him.

Further, when M. Descartes says that the idea of God and that of the soul are
innate in us, I should like to know whether the minds of those who are in a
profound and dreamless sleep yet think. If not, they have at that time no ideas.
Whence no idea is innate, for what is innate is always present.

---

11. Cf. Med. III, p. 76.

Reply

Nothing that we attribute to God can come from external objects as a copy proceeds from its exemplar, because in God there is nothing similar to what is found in external things, i.e. in corporeal objects. But whatever is unlike them in our thought [of God], must come manifestly not from them, but from the cause of that diversity existing in our thought [of God].

Further I ask how my critic derives the intellectual comprehension of God from external things. But I can easily explain the idea which I have of it, by saying that by idea I mean whatever is the form of any perception. For does anyone who understands something not perceive that he does so? and hence does he not possess that form or idea of mental action? It is by extending this indefinitely that we form the idea of the intellectual activity of God; similarly also with God's other attributes.

But, since we have employed the idea of God existing in us for the purpose of proving His existence, and such mighty power is comprised in this idea, that we comprehend that it would be contradictory, if God exists, for anything besides Him to exist, unless it were created by Him; it clearly follows, from the fact that His existence has been demonstrated, that it has been also proved that the whole world, or whatever things other than God exist, have been created by Him.

Finally when I say that an idea is innate in us [or imprinted in our souls by nature], I do not mean that it is always present to us. This would make no idea innate. I mean merely that we possess the faculty of summoning up this idea.

Objection XI

The whole force of the argument lies in this—that I know I could not exist, and possess the nature I have, that nature which puts me in possession of the idea of God, unless God did really exist, the God, I repeat, the idea of whom is found in me.[12]

Since then, it has not been proved that we possess an idea of God, and the Christian religion obliges us to believe that God is inconceivable, which amounts, in my opinion, to saying that we have no idea of Him, it follows that no proof of His existence has been effected, much less of His work of creation.

Reply

When it it said that we cannot conceive God, to conceive means to comprehend adequately. For the rest, I am tired of repeating how it is that we can have an idea of God. There is nothing in these objections that invalidates my demonstrations.

---

12. Cf. Med. III, pp. 79–80.

Objection XII

(Directed against the fourth Meditation, *Concerning the true and the false.*)

And thus I am quite sure that error, in so far as it is error, is nothing real, but merely defect. Hence in order to go astray, it is not necessary for me to have a faculty specially assigned to me by God for this purpose. [13]

It is true that ignorance is merely a defect, and that we stand in need of no special positive faculty in order to be ignorant; but about error the case is not so clear. For it appears that stones and inanimate things are unable to err solely because they have no faculty of reasoning, or imagining. Hence it is a very direct inference that, in order to err, a faculty of reasoning, or at least of imagination is required; now both of these are positive faculties with which all beings that err, and only beings that err, have been endowed.

Further, M. Descartes says—*I perceive that they* (viz. my mistakes) *depend upon the cooperation of two causes, viz. my faculty of cognition, and my faculty of choice, or the freedom of my will.* [14] But this seems to be contradictory to what went before. And we must note here also that the freedom of the will has been assumed without proof, and in opposition to the opinion of the Calvinists.

Reply

Although in order to err the faculty of reasoning (or rather of judging, or affirming and denying) is required, because error is a lack of this power it does not hence follow that this defect is anything real, just as it does not follow that blindness is anything real, although stones are not said to be blind merely because they are incapable of vision. I marvel that in these objections I have as yet found nothing that is properly argued out. Further I made no assumption concerning freedom which is not a matter of universal experience; our natural light makes this most evident and I cannot make out why it is said to be contradictory to previous statements.

But though there are many who, looking to the Divine foreordination, cannot conceive how that is compatible with liberty on our part, nevertheless no one, when he considers himself alone, fails to experience the fact that to will and to be free are the same thing [or rather that there is no difference between what is voluntary and what is free]. But this is no place for examining other people's opinions about this matter.

Objection XIII

For example, whilst I, during these days, sought to discuss whether anything at all existed, and noted that, from the very fact that I raised this question, it was an

---

13. Cf. Med. IV, p. 81.
14. Cf. Med. IV, p. 82.

evident consequence that I myself existed, I could not indeed refrain from judging that what I understood so clearly was true; this was not owing to compulsion by some external force, but because the consequence of the great mental illumination was a strong inclination of the will, and I believed the above truth the more willingly and freely, the less indifferent I was towards it.[15]

This term, *great mental illumination,* is metaphorical, and consequently is not adapted to the purposes of argument. Moreover everyone who is free from doubt claims to possess a similar illumination, and in his will there is the same inclination to believe that of which he does not doubt, as in that of one who truly knows. Hence while this illumination may be the cause that makes a man obstinately defend or hold some opinion, it is not the cause of his knowing it to be true.

Further, not only to know a thing to be true, but also to believe it or give assent to it, have nothing to do with the will. For, what is proved by valid argument or is recounted as credible, is believed by us whether we will or no. It is true that affirming and denying, maintaining or refuting propositions, are acts of will; but it does not follow on that account that internal assent depends upon the will.

Therefore the demonstration of the truth that follows is not adequate—*and it is in this misuse of our free-will, that this privation consists that constitutes the form of error.*[16]

Reply

It does not at all matter whether or not the term *great illumination* is proper to argument, so long as it is serviceable for explanation, as in fact it is. For no one can be unaware that by mental illumination is meant clearness of cognition, which perhaps is not possessed by everyone who thinks he possesses it. But this does not prevent it from being very different from a bigoted opinion, to the formation of which there goes no perceptual evidence.

Moreover when it is here said that when a thing is clearly perceived we give our assent whether we will or no, that is the same as saying that we desire what we clearly know to be good whether willing or unwilling; for the word *unwilling* finds no entrance in such circumstances, implying as it does that we will and do not will the same thing.

Objection XIV

(To the fifth Meditation, *On the essence of material things.*)

As, for example, when I imagine a triangle, though perhaps such a figure does not exist at all outside my thought, or never has existed, it has nevertheless a determinate nature, or essence, or immutable and eternal form, which is not a fiction of my construction, and does not depend on my mind, as is evident from

---

15. Cf. Med. IV, p. 83.
16. Cf. Med. IV, p. 84.

the fact that various properties of that triangle may be demonstrated. [17]

If the triangle exists nowhere at all, I do not understand how it can have any nature; for that which exists nowhere does not exist. Hence it has no existence or nature. The triangle in the mind comes from the triangle we have seen, or from one imaginatively constructed out of triangles we have beheld. Now when we have once called the thing (from which we think that the idea of triangle originates) by the name triangle, although the triangle itself perishes, yet the name remains. In the same way if, in our thought, we have once conceived that the angles of a triangle are together all equal to two right angles, and have given this other name to the triangle—*possessed of three angles equal to two right angles*—although there were no angle at all in existence, yet the name would remain; and the truth of this proposition will be of eternal duration—*a triangle is possessed of three angles equal to two right angles.* But the nature of the triangle will not be of eternal duration, if it should chance that triangle perished.

In like manner the proposition, *man is animal,* will be eternally true, because the names it employs are eternal, but if the human race were to perish there would no longer be a human nature.

Whence it is evident that essence in so far as it is distinguished from existence is nothing else than a union of names by means of the verb *is.* And thus essence without existence is a fiction of our mind. And it appears that as the image of a man in the mind is to the man so is essence to existence; or that the essence of Socrates bears to his existence the relation that this proposition, *Socrates is a man,* to this other, *Socrates is or exists.* Now the proposition, *Socrates is a man,* means, when Socrates does not exist, merely the connection of its terms; and *is,* or *to be,* has underlying it the image of the unity of a thing designated by two names.

Reply

The distinction between essence and existence is known to all; and all that is here said about eternal names in place of concepts or ideas of an eternal truth, has been already satisfactorily refuted.

Objection XV

(Directed against the sixth Meditation, *Concerning the existence of material things.*)

For since God has evidently given me no faculty by which to know this (whether or not our ideas proceed from bodies), but on the contrary has given me a strong propensity towards the belief that they do proceed from corporeal things, I fail to see how it could be made out that He is not a deceiver, if our ideas proceeded from some other source than corporeal things. Consequently corporeal objects must exist. [18]

---

17. Cf. Med. V, p. 86
18. Cf. Med. VI, p. 94.

It is the common belief that no fault is committed by medical men who deceive sick people for their health's sake, nor by parents who mislead their children for their good; and that the evil in deception lies not in the falsity of what is said, but in the bad intent of those who practise it. M. Descartes must therefore look to this proposition, *God can in no case deceive us,* taken universally, and see whether it is true; for if it is not true, thus universally taken, the conclusion, *hence corporeal things exist,* does not follow.

Reply

For the security of my conclusion we do not need to assume that we can never be deceived (for I have gladly admitted that we are often deceived), but that we are not deceived when that error of ours would argue an intention to deceive on the part of God, an intention it is contradictory to impute to Him. Once more this is bad reasoning on my critic's part.

Final Objection

For now I perceive how great the difference is between the two (i.e. between waking and dreaming) from the fact that our dreams are never conjoined by our memory [with each other and] with the whole of the rest of our life's action [as happens with the things which occur in waking moments].[19]

I ask whether it is really the case that one, who dreams he doubts whether he dreams or no, is unable to dream that his dream is connected with the idea of a long series of past events. If he can, those things which to the dreamer appear to be the actions of his past life may be regarded as true just as though he had been awake. Besides, since, as M. Descartes himself asserts, all certitude and truth in knowledge depend alone upon our knowing the true God, either it will be impossible for an Atheist to infer from the memory of his previous life that he wakes, or it will be possible for a man to know that he is awake, apart from knowledge of the true God.

Reply

One who dreams cannot effect a real connection between what he dreams and the ideas of past events, though he can dream that he does connect them. For who denies that in his sleep a man may be deceived? But yet when he has awakened he will easily detect his error.

But an Atheist is able to infer from the memory of his past life that he is awake; still he cannot know that this sign is sufficient to give him the certainty that he is not in error, unless he knows that it has been created by a God who does not deceive.

---

19. Cf. Med. VI, p. 99.

COMPARATIVE STUDY QUESTIONS

Review Questions

1. Mention several things which Descartes finds some grounds to doubt.
2. On the basis of what supposition does Descartes find that he can doubt that $2 + 3 = 5$?
3. Restate the considerations that led Descartes to conclude that because "I think" (**Cogito**), therefore (**ergo**), "I am" (**sum**).
4. What does Descartes mean to illustrate by his example of the piece of wax?
5. Explain the difference between innate, adventitious, and factitious ideas.
6. Restate one of Descartes' causal arguments for the existence of God. Is it convincing?
7. How does Descartes account for human error?
8. What is Descartes' criterion of truth?
9. Restate Descartes' version of the ontological argument.
10. How does Descartes go about reestablishing our commonsense belief in an independently existing physical world?

Discussion Questions

1. In his reply to Hobbes' eleventh objection, Descartes says, with undisguised exasperation, that he is "tired of repeating how it is that we have an idea of God." Why is Hobbes so insistent that we have no such idea? Do Descartes and Hobbes understand the term "idea" differently?
2. According to Hobbes (Obj. II), "It does not seem to be good reasoning to say: I am exercising thought, hence I am thought. . . . For in the same way I might say, I am walking, hence I am the walking." Is this a fair criticism of Descartes?
3. How does Hobbes make use of Descartes' illustration of the piece of wax to support his own materialistic philosophy?
4. Compare Hobbes' conception of reasoning as described in Obj. IV with Descartes' conception. Hobbes derives a theory of mind as "nothing but the motions in certain parts of an organic body." Do any comparable metaphysical consequences follow from Descartes' conception?
5. Hobbes questions whether reality admits of "more or less" (Obj. IX). Descartes also distinguishes between objective and formal reality (Med. III). Do either of these distinctions between the **degrees** and **kinds** of reality make sense?
6. Examine Hobbes' argument at the end of Obj. X. He attempts to prove that no ideas are innate. Does Descartes agree that persons in a profound and dreamless sleep yet think? (Cf. Med. II).

7. Human error, according to Descartes, involves both judgment and volition. Evaluate Hobbes' objection (XII) that Descartes' theory is "contradictory" and assumes without proof the freedom of the will.

8. Descartes' proof of the existence of a material world depends on the proposition that God is not a deceiver. Hobbes (Obj. XV) argues (analogously) that "no fault is committed by medical men who deceive sick people for their health's sake." Is this "bad reasoning," as Descartes says it is?

9. Descartes frequently complains that his critic "refuses to come to terms with me about the meaning of words" (Reply to Obj. VIII) or to accept distinctions which "all men" are wont to make (Replies to Obj. II, XIV). Is Hobbes merely being perverse, or is Descartes perhaps too uncritical in his use of language?

10. Hobbes' final objection, as well as his first, deals with the question of dreaming. He asks whether "one, who dreams he doubts whether he dreams or not, is unable to dream that his dream is connected with the idea of past events." Untangle this thought, and evaluate its significance as a basis of criticism.

Thomas Hobbes
(1588 – 1679)

John Locke
(1632 – 1704)

THE PRESUPPOSITIONS
OF POLITICAL LIFE

Mr. Thomas Hobbes and Mr. John Locke

I admit that the Constitution establishes a representative government, not a pure democracy. It establishes a General Court which is to be the law-making power. But the question is whether it puts a limit upon the power of that body to make laws. In my opinion the Legislature has the whole law-making power except so far as the words of the Constitution expressly or impliedly withhold it. . . .

It has been asked whether the Legislature could pass an act subject to the approval of a single man. I am, not clear that it could not. . . . The contrary view seems to me an echo of Hobbes' theory that the surrender of sovereignty by the people was final. I notice that the case from which most of the reasoning against the power of the Legislature has been taken . . . states that theory in language which almost is borrowed from the *Leviathan*. [*Rice* v. *Foster*, 4 Harringt. (Del.) 479, 488.] Hobbes urged his notion in the interest of the absolute power of King Charles I, and one of the objects of the Constitution of Massachusetts was to deny it.

O. W. Holmes, Jr., *Advisory Opinion*,
160 Mass. 586 (1894)

The age difference between Hobbes and Locke is comparable to that between Plato and Aristotle. Plato was forty-three years old when Aristotle was born; Hobbes was forty-four when Locke arrived. Aristotle entered Plato's Academy when he was seventeen or eighteen; Locke entered Oxford, Hobbes' university, when he was twenty. Hobbes' major work, **Leviathan,** was published in 1651, a year before Locke began his college studies. Plato's **Republic** was completed perhaps even before the founding of the Academy, soon after Plato turned forty.[1] As a consequence, both Aristotle and Locke were able during their most intellectually receptive years to study in detail the chief philosophical works of their famous predecessors.

---

1. See A.E. Taylor, *Plato, The Man and His Work* (London: Methuen, 6th ed. 1949), p. 20.

The extent of Plato's influence on Aristotle is fairly easy to trace. As one might reasonably expect, Aristotle mentions his teacher by name many times, and though he disagrees with him often—feeling obligated to "honor truth" even above friends—his indebtedness to Plato is plainly discoverable. The same statement, unfortunately, cannot be made with respect to the intellectual and literary relationship between Locke and Hobbes. The champion of absolute monarchy whom Locke undertakes to refute in the first of his **Two Treatises of Government** is not Thomas Hobbes, as one might expect, but the philosophical lightweight, Sir Robert Filmer. In the second of the **Two Treatises,** Locke does not even mention Hobbes by name. According to Peter Laslett, "If it were not for the passages in the **Second Treatise** which are Hobbesian in flavour or seem to have been directed particularly at him, we should not know that Locke was concerned in any way with Hobbes as a thinker at that time, for his notes, his diaries, his letters, his book lists and purchases show no sign of such an interest."[2]

Why this apparent disinterest? Why this silence with respect to Hobbes? Perhaps it is not so remarkable. After all, Hobbes was not Locke's tutor, as Plato was Aristotle's; they were not friends, perhaps not even acquaintances; no special bond of loyalty existed between them; why should Locke bother to criticize, or even dissociate himself from, an absolutist who had already been rejected by most of the royalists of the time because of his seemingly heretical views on religion? Filmer, who believed that Adam was the first king and Charles I his rightful heir in England, was by far a more attractive target for Locke's polemical shots.

Plausible as these considerations may appear, students of both Hobbes and Locke are today still divided regarding the motives and purposes of Locke's **Two Treatises of Government.** Several "interpretations" have been advanced. The first, which is also the oldest, is that although Filmer was the nominal object of Locke's criticism, it was Hobbes in fact whom he was attacking. The view assumes that Locke, in the words of Sir Frederick Pollock,[3] "must have seen that . . . Hobbes was the really formidable adversary," and that their views were radically opposed. It alleges that the only reason Locke chose Filmer as a target instead of Hobbes was because Filmer was by far the more fashionable royalist of the time. It is argued that, though differing in important respects, Filmer and Hobbes had many points in common, and so it made sense for Locke to attack Hobbes through this particular intermediary. In partial support of this contention, Filmer is quoted as saying, in the Preface to his **Observations Concerning the Original of Government,** the following:

> With no small content I read Mr. Hobbes's book *De Cive,* and his *Leviathan,* about the rights of sovereignty, which no man, that I know, hath so amply and judiciously handled: I consent with him

---

2. A critical edition of John Locke, *Two Treatises of Government,* edited by Peter Laslett (Cambridge University Press, second ed. 1970), Introduction, p. 71.

3. "Locke's Theory of the State," *Proceedings of the British Academy,* vol. 1, 1904, reprinted in Pollock, *Essays in the Law* (Archon Books, 1969), p. 82. Peter Laslett (*op. cit.,* p. 67n) credits Pollock with having "done the most to establish the view that Locke was really writing against Hobbes."

about the rights of exercising government, but I cannot agree to his means of acquiring it.[4]

A second interpretation—a somewhat modified version of the first—is that whereas Locke was indeed concerned in the **First Treatise** to attack Filmer and his "patriarchalism," Locke's concern in the **Second Treatise** was (tacitly) to attack Hobbes' conception of the state of nature and natural law.[5] Richard H. Cox finds many difficulties with this view, one of which is that it supplies no adequate explanation of Locke's failure to mention Hobbes by name in the whole of the **Second Treatise.** Cox finds it strange that Locke is supposed to be attacking a man in whom, as Locke himself later claimed, he was not "well read." Why, Cox asks, would Locke have gone to enormous pains to study and refute a second-rate political thinker like Filmer, and yet not even bother to read or explicitly refer to the arguments of a great political philosopher like Hobbes?[6]

Others, too, have found it difficult to reconcile these kinds of considerations with either of the first two interpretations. A third interpretation asserts that Locke did not write the **Two Treatises** with Thomas Hobbes either "in hand or in mind."[7] Peter Laslett, who advances this view, admits, however, that Locke rejected Hobbes' absolutism along with Filmer's; that there are phrases and whole arguments in Locke's book which echo the Hobbesian position; and that when Locke wrote **Two Treatises,** "**Leviathan** was an influence, a gravitational constant exercised by a large body though at a great distance."[8] His connection is nonetheless that Locke's work is what it purports to be: a polemic against Filmer and a statement of Locke's own political principles.

A fourth interpretation also adopts the position that Locke was not attacking Hobbes via Filmer as a kind of proxy, for the simple reason that Locke himself was a confirmed "Hobbesian." Richard H. Cox, who advocates this interpretation,[9] states his thesis as follows:

> ... Locke's idea of the original state of nature is, as abundant passages seem to make clear, fundamentally antithetical to that of Hobbes. But it is the main argument of the present study that, contrary to the surface impression which I believe Locke deliberately seeks to convey, his conception of the state of nature— whether with regard to individuals or states—is in fact fundamentally Hobbesian in character. . . .[10]

---

4. *Patriarcha and Other Political Works of Sir Robert Filmer,* edited by Peter Laslett (Oxford: Basil Blackwell, 1949), p. 239. Quoted by Pollock, *op. cit.,* p. 82. The passage down to the word "handled" was even copied down by Locke himself in a notebook he kept. Cf. Peter Laslett's Introduction to his edition of the *Two Treatises* previously cited, p. 46.

5. Cf. the list of proponents of this interpretation given by Richard H. Cox in his *Locke on War and Peace* (Oxford: Clarendon Press, 1960), pp. 2 and 205 (Note A), which includes Sterling P. Lamprecht and T.D. Weldon.

6. Cf. Cox, *op. cit.,* pp. 2–4.

7. Laslett, Introduction, *Two Treatises,* pp. x, 67–78.

8. *Ibid.,* p. 74.

9. See also Leo Strauss, *Natural Right and History* (Chicago: University of Chicago Press, 1953), pp. 202–251.

10. Cox, *op. cit.,* pp. xix–xx.

It is simply not possible in this introduction to present all the evidence which has been mustered in behalf of each of these competitive interpretations. For that the reader will have to consult the authors and writings referred to in the footnotes and the bibliography. A final assessment, however, will of necessity require a careful examination of the texts themselves, Locke's **Second Treatise** and Hobbes' **Leviathan.** Hopefully, the political conversations which are constructed from those texts and included in this section will provide an initial basis for the kind of comparative study required.

But just as these historical and interpretive questions regarding Locke's relationship to Hobbes are still very much alive today, so also are the specifically philosophical issues which the views of Hobbes and Locke have generated. As the excerpt from Justice Oliver Wendell Holmes' advisory opinion suggests, the proper limits of governmental power is as much an issue in our time as it was in theirs. Every constitutional amendment, every impeachment proceeding, every suit against the government itself, raises this question in new and sometimes troubling ways. Are there indeed some things that government, however framed, cannot do? But why, it can be asked, should we recognize any government at all? Why should anyone give up his freedom to do as he pleases, and agree to obey laws which may work against his own wishes? Are the laws of society founded upon another set called "natural laws"? Is there such a thing as a "right of revolution"?

These are but some of the questions about the presuppositions of political life which Hobbes and Locke discuss. We should be reminded, and warned, by the controversies over Locke's relationship to Hobbes that although these philosophers do not always agree, they do not always disagree with respect to the answers they give to these questions. And sometimes, their points of agreement are as interesting and instructive as their differences.

MALMESBURY *v.* WRINGTON

A Political Discussion [11]

After a meeting of the Royal Society at Gresham College in London. Two Fellows are discussing a recent vote.

Malmesbury.   I find it completely absurd for this Society to exclude Mr. Hobbes from membership.

---

11. What follows is a discussion between two wholly imaginary characters, the royalist Malmesbury, who represents the views of Hobbes, and Wrington, the constitutionalist, who

Wrington. Not absurd at all. You yourself heard what Professor Wallis[12] and Mr. Boyle recounted regarding his so-called mathematical discoveries.

Malmesbury. Yes, I know, but shouldn't we be able to overlook such eccentricities in a man whose political writings and contributions to natural philosophy have been so celebrated—at least in years past?

Wrington. Can't say that I agree with them, though I know you find them reasonable.

Malmesbury. Indeed, I still do. Regarding the natural condition of mankind I cannot help but think that Hobbes was absolutely correct when he said that Nature hath made men so equal, in the faculties of the body and mind, as that, though there be found one man sometimes manifestly stronger in body or of quicker mind than another, yet when all is reckoned together, the difference between man and man is not so considerable, as that one man can thereupon claim to himself any benefit to which another may not pretend as well as he. For as to the strength of the body, the weakest has strength enough to kill the strongest, either by secret machination or by confederacy with others that are in the same danger with himself. . . . (xiii)

Wrington. I confess that I am not "well read" in Hobbes.[13] It has been some time since I perused Leviathan.[14] Please continue to refresh my memory of his views.

Malmesbury. Very well. According to Mr. Hobbes: From this equality of ability ariseth equality of hope in the attaining of our ends. And therefore, if any two

---

represents the views of Locke. Except for the introductory and connective dialogue provided by the editor, the statements of Malmesbury are taken from Hobbes' *Leviathan* (Molesworth ed. 1839), and those of Wrington from Locke's Book II of *Two Treatises of Government* (reprinted by A. Millar, 1764). Roman numerals following the Hobbes quotations indicate chapter references; numbers following the Locke quotations indicate section references. There is, as far as I am aware, no evidence that Locke and Hobbes ever engaged in conversation or otherwise communicated. It is historically possible, however, that they could have. In any case, Locke's reputation as a controversialist was well established before he wrote his polemic against Filmer, and he very likely did engage in controversies with royalists of a Hobbesian persuasion. As far as the setting of the discussion is concerned, it is a matter of hard fact that Locke became a fellow of the Royal Society in 1668, and that Hobbes was never elected even though he desired to be. According to John Aubrey, Hobbes "had a high esteeme for the Royall Societie, having sayd that Naturall Philosophy was removed from the Universities to Gresham Colledge, meaning the Royall Societie that meets there; and the Royall Societie (generally) had the like for him: and he would long since have been ascribed a Member there, but for the sake of one or two persons, whom he tooke to be his enemies: viz. Dr. Wallis (surely their Mercuries are in opposition) and Mr. Boyle. I might add Sir Paul Neile, who disobliges everybody." John Aubrey, *Brief Lives,* edited by Oliver Lawson Dick (London: Secker and Warburg, 1950), p. 158.

12. For a further account of the controversy and resultant hostility between Wallis and Hobbes, see p. 59.

13. Cf. Locke's claim to this effect, made in a controversy with the Bishop of Worcester in 1698. *The Works of John Locke* (London: Tegg, 1823), Vol. IV, p. 477. Reprinted by Scientia Verlag Aalen, 1963.

14. According to Locke's journal, he lent his copy of *Leviathan* to his friend, James Tyrrell, in 1674. He seems not to have got it back until 1691. Cf. Peter Laslett, Introduction, *Two Treatises,* p. 71; also pp. 139, 55–58.

men desire the same thing, which nevertheless they cannot both enjoy, they become enemies; and in the way to their end, which is principally their own conservation, and sometimes their delectation only, endeavor to destroy or subdue one another. . . . (xiii)

So that in the first place, [says Mr. Hobbes] , I put for a general inclination of all mankind a perpetual and restless desire of power after power that ceaseth only in death. And the cause of this is not always that a man hopes for a more intensive delight than he has already attained to, or that he cannot be content with a moderate power, but because he cannot assure the power and means to live well, which he hath present, without the acquisition of more. . . . (xi)

It may seem strange to some man that has not well weighed these things that nature should thus dissociate, and render men apt to invade and destroy one another; and he may therefore, not trusting to this inference made from the passions, desire perhaps to have the same confirmed by experience. Let him therefore consider with himself, when taking a journey, he arms himself and seeks to go well accompanied; when going to sleep, he locks his doors; when even in his house he locks his chests; and this when he knows there be laws, and public officers, armed, to revenge all injuries shall be done him; what opinion he has of his fellow-subjects, when he rides armed; of his fellow-citizens, when he locks his doors; and of his children and servants, when he locks his chests. Does he not there as much accuse mankind by his actions, as I do by my words? . . . (xiii)

Hereby it is manifest that during the time men live without a common power to keep them all in awe, they are in that condition which is called war; and such a war as is of every man against every man. For *war* consisteth not in battle only, or the act of fighting, but in a tract of time wherein the will to contend by battle is sufficiently known, and therefore the notion of *time* is to be considered in the nature of war, as it is in the nature of weather. For as the nature of foul weather lieth not in a shower or two of rain, but in an inclination thereto of many days together, so the nature of war consisteth not in actual fighting, but in the known disposition thereto, during all the time there is no assurance to the contrary. All other time is *peace.*

Whatsoever therefore is consequent to a time of war, where every man is enemy to every man; the same is consequent to the time wherein men live without other security than what their own strength and their own invention shall furnish them withal. In such condition there is no place for industry, because the fruit thereof is uncertain; and consequently no culture of the earth; no navigation, nor use of the commodities that may be imported by sea; no commodious building; no instruments of moving and removing such things as require much force; no knowledge of the face of the earth; no account of time; no arts; no letters; no society; and which is worst of all, continual fear, and danger of violent death; and the life of man, solitary, poor, nasty, brutish, and short. . . .

To this war of every man against every man, this also is consequent: *that nothing can be unjust.* The notions of right and wrong, justice and injustice, have there no place. Where there is no common power, there is no law; where no law, no injustice. Force and fraud are in war the two cardinal virtues. Justice and injustice are none of the faculties niether of the body nor mind. If they were, they might be in a man that were alone in the world, as well as his senses and passions. They are qualities that relate to men in society, not in solitude. It is consequent also to the same condition that there be no propriety, no dominion, no *mine* and *thine* distinct; but only that to be every man's that he can get, and for so long as he can keep it. And thus much for the ill condition which man by mere nature is actually placed in. . . . (xiii)

It may peradventure be thought there was never such a time nor condition of war as this; and . . . [Mr. Hobbes himself believes] it was never generally so, over all the world; but there are many places where they live so now. For the savage people in many places of America, except the government of small families, the concord whereof dependeth on natural lust, have no government at all; and live at this day in that brutish manner. . . . Howsoever, it may be perceived what manner of life there would be, where there were no common power to fear, by the manner of life which men that have formerly lived under a peaceful government . . . degenerate into in a civil war. (xiii)

Wrington. I tend to agree with Mr. Hobbes that to understand political power right, and derive it from its original, we must consider what state all men are naturally in, but I fear that my conception of the state of nature is somewhat different from his. I view men as being naturally in a state of perfect freedom to order their actions and dispose of their possessions and persons as they think fit, within the bounds of the law of nature, without asking leave, or depending upon the will of any other man.

A state also of equality, wherein all the power and jurisdiction is reciprocal, no one having more than another; there being nothing more evident than that creatures of the same species and rank, promiscuously born to all the same advantages of nature, and the use of the same faculties, should also be equal one amongst another without subordination or subjection, unless the Lord and Master of them all should by any manifest declaration of His will set one above another, and confer on him by an evident and clear appointment an undoubted right to dominion and sovereignty. (4)

But though this be a state of liberty, yet it is not a state of license; though man in that state have an uncontrollable liberty to dispose of his person or or possessions, yet he has not liberty to destroy himself, or so much as any creature in his possession, but where some nobler use than its bare preservation calls for it. The state of nature has a law of nature to govern it, which obliges everyone; and reason, which is that law, teaches all mankind who will but consult it, that being all equal and independent, no one ought to harm another in his life, health, liberty, or possessions; for men being all the workmanship of one omnipotent and infinitely wise Maker—all the servants of one sovereign Master, sent into the world by His order, and about His business—they are His property, whose workmanship they are, made to last during His, not one another's pleasure; and being furnished with like faculties, sharing all in one community of nature, there cannot be supposed any such subordination among us that may authorize us to destroy one another, as if we were made for one another's uses, as the inferior ranks of creatures are for ours. Everyone, as he is bound to preserve himself, and not to quit his station willfully, so, by the like reason, when his own preservation comes not in competition, ought he, as much as he can, to preserve the rest of mankind, and may not, unless it be to do justice on an offender, take away or impair the life, or what tends to the preservation of the life, the liberty, health, limb, or goods of another. (6)

And that all men may be restrained from invading others' rights, and from doing hurt to one another, and the law of nature observed, which willeth the peace and preservation of all mankind, the execution of the law of nature is, in that state, put into every man's hand, whereby everyone has a right to punish the transgressors of that law to such a degree as may hinder its violation. For the law of nature would, as all other laws that concern men in this world, be in vain if there were nobody that, in the state of nature, had a power to execute that law, and thereby preserve the innocent and restrain offenders. And if anyone in the state of nature may punish another for any evil he has done, everyone may do so. For in that state of perfect equality, where naturally there is no superiority or jurisdiction of one over another, what any may do in prosecution of that law, everyone must needs have a right to do. (7)

And thus, in the state of nature one man comes by a power over another; but yet no absolute or arbitrary power, to use a criminal, when he has got him in his hands, according to the passionate heats or boundless extravagance of his own will; but only to retribute to him, so far as calm reason and conscience dictate, what is proportionate to his transgression, which is so much as may serve for reparation and restraint. For these two are the only reasons why one man may lawfully do harm to another, which is that we call *punishment*. In transgressing the law of nature, the offender declares himself to live by another rule than that of reason and common equity, which is that measure God has set to the actions of men for their mutual security; and so he becomes dangerous to mankind, the tie which is to secure them from injury and violence being slighted and broken by him. Which, being a trespass against the whole species, and the peace and safety of it, provided for by the law of nature, every man upon this score, by the right he hath to preserve mankind in general, may restrain, or, where it is necessary, destroy things noxious to them, and so may bring such evil on anyone who hath transgressed that law, as may make him repent the doing of it, and thereby deter him, and by his example others, from doing the like mischief. And in this case, and upon this ground, *every man hath a right to punish the offender, and be executioner of the law of nature.* (8)

To this strange doctrine—viz., that in the state of nature everyone has the executive power of the law of nature—I doubt not but it will be objected that it is unreasonable for men to be judges in their own cases, that self-love will make men partial to themselves and their friends, and on the other side, that ill-nature, passion, and revenge will carry them too far in punishing others; and hence nothing but confusion and disorder will follow; and that therefore God hath certainly appointed government to restrain the partiality and violence of men. I easily grant that civil government is the proper remedy for the inconveniences of the state of nature, which must certainly be great where men may be judges in their own case, since 'tis easy to be imagined that he who was so unjust as to do his brother an injury will scarce be so just as to condemn himself for it. But I shall desire those who make this objection to remember that absolute monarchs are but men, and if government is to be the remedy of those evils which necessarily follow from men's being judges in their own cases, and the state of nature is therefore not to be endured, I desire to know what kind of government that is, and how much better it is than the state of nature, where one man commanding a multitude has the liberty to be judge in his own case, and may do to all his subjects whatever he pleases, without the least liberty to any one to question or control those who execute his pleasure; and in whatsoever he doth, whether led by reason, mistake, or passion, must be submitted to? Much better it is in the state of nature, wherein men are not bound to submit to the unjust will of another; and if he that judges, judges amiss in his own or any other case, he is answerable for it to the rest of mankind. (13)

'Tis often asked as a mighty objection, "Where are, or ever were there, any men in such a state of nature?" To which it may suffice as an answer at present that, since all princes and rulers of independent governments all through the world are in a state of nature, 'tis plain the world never was, nor ever will be, without numbers of men in that state. . . . (14)

To those that say there were never any men in the state of nature, I will not only oppose the authority of the judicious Hooker (*Eccl. Pol.,* lib. i., sect. 10) . . . but I moreover affirm that all men are naturally in that state, and remain so, till by their own consents they make themselves members of some politic society. . . . (15)

The state of nature and the state of war, which however some men have confounded, are as far distant as a state of peace, good-will, mutual assistance and preservation, and a state of enmity, malice, violence and mutual destruction, are one from another. Men living together according to reason, without a common superior on earth with authority to judge between them, is properly the state of nature. But force, or a declared design of force, upon the person of another, where there is no common superior on earth to appeal to for relief, is the state of war; and 'tis the want of such an appeal gives a man the right of war even against an aggressor, though he be in society and a fellow-subject. Thus a thief, whom I cannot harm but by appeal to the law for having stolen all that I am worth, I may kill when he sets on me to rob me but of my horse or coat; because the law, which was made for my preservation, where it cannot interpose to secure my life from present force, which if lost is capable of no reparation, permits me my own defence, and the right of war, a liberty to kill the aggressor, because the aggressor allows not time to appeal to our common judge, nor the decision of the law, for a remedy in a case where the mischief may be irreparable. Want of a common judge with authority puts all men in a state of nature; force without right upon a man's person makes a state of war both where there is, and is not, a common judge. (19)

Malmesbury. 'Tis plain you view life, liberty, and law in the natural condition (or "state of nature," as you prefer), much differently from the manner in which

Mr. Hobbes perceives them. According to him, the right of nature, which writers commonly call *jus naturale,* is the liberty each man hath to use his own power, as he will himself, for the preservation of his own nature; that is to say, of his own life; and consequently, of doing anything, which in his own judgment and reason, he shall conceive to be the aptest means thereunto.

By *liberty* . . . [Mr. Hobbes understands] the absence of external impediments. . . . A *law of nature, lex naturalis,* is a precept or general rule, found out by reason, by which a man is forbidden to do that which is destructive of his life, or taketh away the means of preserving the same, and to omit that by which he thinketh it may be best preserved. For though they that speak of this subject use to confound *jus* and *lex, right* and *law,* yet they ought to be distinguished, because *right* consisteth in liberty to do or to forbear, whereas *law* determineth and bindeth to one of them; so that law and right differ as much as obligation and liberty, which in one and the same matter are inconsistent.

And because the condition of man, . . . [as Mr. Hobbes sees it] , is a condition of war of everyone against everyone; in which case everyone is governed by his own reason, and there is nothing he can make use of that may not be a help unto him in preserving his life against his enemies; it followeth that in such a condition every man has a right to everything, even to one another's body. And therefore, as long as this natural right of every man to everything endureth, there can be no security to any man, how strong or wise soever he be, of living out the time which nature ordinarily alloweth men to live. And consequently it is a precept, or general rule of reason that *every man ought to endeavor peace, as far as he has hope of obtaining it; and when he cannot obtain it, that he may seek and use all helps and advantages of war.* The first branch of which rule containeth the first and fundamental law of nature, which is, *to seek peace and follow it.* The second, the sum of the right of nature, which is, *by all means we can, to defend ourselves.*

From this fundamental law of nature, by which men are commanded to endeavor peace, is derived this second law: *that a man be willing, when others are so too, as far forth as for peace and defense of himself he shall think it necessary, to lay down this right to all things; and be contented with so much liberty against other men as he would allow other men against himself. . . .*

To lay down a man's right to anything is to divest himself of the liberty of hindering another of the benefit of his own right to the same. . . . Right is laid aside either by simply renouncing it or by transferring it to another. . . . The mutual transferring of right is that which men call *contract.* . . . (xiv)

From that law of nature by which we are obliged to transfer to another such rights as, being retained, hinder the peace of mankind, there followeth a third, which is this: *that men perform their covenants made;* without which, covenants are in vain, and but empty words; and the right of all men to all things remaining, we are still in the condition of war.

And in this law of nature consisteth the fountain and original of justice. For where no covenant hath preceded, there hath no right been transferred, and every man has right to everything; and consequently, no action can be unjust. But when a covenant is made, then to break it is *unjust* and the definition of *injustice* is no other than *the not performance of covenant.* And whatsoever is not unjust, is *just.*

But because covenants of mutual trust, where there is a fear of not performance on either part . . . are invalid; . . . yet injustice actually there can be none, till the cause of such fear be taken away; which while men are in the natural condition of war cannot be done. Therefore before the names of just and unjust can have place, there must be some coercive power to compel men equally to the performance of their covenants, by the terror of some punishment greater than the benefit they expect by the breach of their covenant; and to make good that propriety which by mutual contract men acquire, in recompense of the universal right they abandon; and such power there is none before the erection of a commonwealth. And this is also to be gathered out of the ordinary definition of justice in the Schools; for they say that *justice is the constant will of giving to every man his own.* And therefore where there is no *own,* that is, no propriety, there is no injustice; and where is no coercive power erected, that is, where there is no commonwealth, there is no propriety. . . . (xv)

Wrington. Allow me to postpone for a time my views regarding the way in which mankind passes from the state of nature to a state of political or civil society. I would first like to contrast my views regarding natural liberty, property rights, and the end of law with those you have just expressed. As I see it, the natural liberty of man is to be free from any superior power on earth, and not to be under the will or legislative authority of man, but to have only the law of nature for his rule. The liberty of man in society is to be under no other legislative power but that established by consent in the commonwealth; nor under the dominion of any will or restraint of any law, but what that legislative shall enact according to the trust put in it. Freedom then is not what Sir Robert Filmer tells us . . . "a liberty for everyone to do what he lists, to live as he pleases, and not to be tied by any laws." But freedom of men under government is to have a standing rule to live by, common to everyone of that society, and made by the legislative power erected in it; a liberty to follow my own will in all things where that rule prescribes not; and not to be subject to the inconstant, uncertain, unknown, arbitrary will of another man; as freedom of nature is to be under no other restraint but the law of nature. (22)

This freedom from absolute arbitrary power is so necessary to, and closely joined with a man's preservation that he cannot part with it but by what forfeits his preservation and life together. For a man not having the power of his own life cannot by compact, or his own consent, enslave himself to anyone, nor put himself under the absolute arbitrary power of another to take away his life when he pleases. Nobody can give more power than he has himself; and he that cannot take away his own life cannot give another power over it. . . . (23)

[Regarding the institution of property or "propriety," as you and Mr. Hobbes choose to say, it is my view that] God, who hath given the world to men in common, hath also given them reason to make use of it to the best advantage of life and convenience. The earth and all that is therein is given to men for the support and comfort of their being. And though all the fruits it naturally produces, and beasts it feeds, belong to mankind in common, as they are produced by the spontaneous hand of nature; and nobody has originally a private dominion exclusive of the rest of mankind in any of them as they are thus in their natural state; yet being given for the use of men, there must of necessity be a means to appropriate them some way or other before they can be of any use or at all beneficial to any particular man. . . . (26)

Though the earth and all inferior creatures be common to all men, yet every man has a property in his own person; this nobody has any right to but himself. The labour of his body and the work of his hands, we may say, are properly his. Whatsoever, then, he removes out of the state of nature hath provided and left it in, he hath mixed his labour with, and joined to it something that is his own, and thereby makes it his property. It being by him removed from the common state nature placed it in, it hath by this labour something annexed to it that excludes the common right of other men. . . . (27)

It will perhaps be objected to this that if gathering the acorns or other fruits of the earth, etc., makes a right to them, then anyone may engross as much as he will. To which I answer, Not so. The same law of nature that does by this means give us property does also bound that property too. "God has given us all things richly" (1 Tim. vi. 17), is the voice of reason confirmed by inspiration. But how far has He given it us? To enjoy. As much as anyone can make use of to any advantage of life before it spoils, so much he may by his labour fix a property in; whatever is beyond this is more than his share, and belongs to others. Nothing was made by God for man to spoil or destroy. . . . (31)

But since gold and silver, being little useful to the life of man in proportion to food, raiment, and carriage, has its value only from the consent of men, whereof labour yet makes, in great part, the measure, it is plain that men have agreed to a disproportionate and unequal possession of the earth; they having, by a tacit and voluntary consent, found out a way how a man may fairly possess more land than he himself can use the product of, by receiving in exchange for the overplus, gold and silver, which may be hoarded up without injury to any one; these metals not spoiling or decaying in the hands of the possessor. . . . (50)

[But perhaps enough has been said regarding the natural rights of property. There remains the question whether, as Mr. Hobbes says, the notions of right and law are (like liberty and obligation), in one and the same matter, inconsistent. This does not seem to me to be correct] : For law, in its true notion, is not so much the limitation as the direction of a free and intelligent agent to his proper interest, and prescribes no farther than is for the general good of those under that law. Could they be happier without it, the law, as a useless thing, would of itself vanish; and that ill deserves the name of confinement which hedges us in only from bogs and precipices.[15] So that however it

---

15. Cf. Hobbes' statement in *Leviathan,* Chapter XXX: "For the use of laws, which are but rules authorized, is not to bind the people from all voluntary actions, but to direct and keep them in such a motion as not to hurt themselves by their own impetuous desires, rashness, or indiscretion; as hedges are set, not to stop travellers, but to keep them in the way."

may be mistaken, the end of law is not to abolish or restrain, but to preserve and enlarge freedom. For in all the states of created beings capable of laws, where there is no law there is no freedom. For liberty is to be free from restraint and violence from others; which cannot be where there is no law; but freedom is not, as we are told, "a liberty for every man to do what he lists" (for who could be free, when every other man's humour might domineer over him?), but a liberty to dispose and order as he lists his person, actions, possessions, and his whole property, within the allowance of those laws under which he is, and therein not to be subject to the arbitrary will of another, but freely follow his own. (57)

Malmesbury.   Surely Mr. Hobbes does agree that the true end of law is to direct, not to frustrate, human action; but he nonetheless thinks that the laws of nature,[16] as justice, equity, modesty, mercy, and, in sum, doing to others as we would be done to, of themselves, without the terror of some power to cause them to be observed, are contrary to our natural passions that carry us to partiality, pride, revenge, and the like. And covenants, without the sword, are but words, and of no strength to secure a man at all. . . .

The only way to erect such a common power, as may be able to defend [the people] from the invasion of foreigners and the injuries of one another, and thereby to secure them in such sort as that, by their own industry, and by the fruits of the earth, they may nourish themselves and live contentedly, is to confer all their power and strength upon one man, or upon one assembly of men that may reduce all their wills, by plurality of voices, unto one will; which is as much as to say, to appoint one man, or assembly of men, to bear their person, and everyone to own and acknowledge himself to be author of whatsoever he that so beareth their person shall act or cause to be acted in those things which concern the common peace and safety; and therein to submit their wills, everyone in his will, and their judgments, to his judgments. This is more than consent or concord; it is a real unity of them all, in one and the same person made by covenant of every man with every man, in such manner as if every man should say to every man, "I authorize and give up my right of governing myself to this man, or to this assembly of men, on this condition, that thou give up thy right to him, and authorize all his actions in like manner." This done, the multitude so united in one person is called a *commonwealth*, in Latin *civitas*. This is the generation of that great *Leviathan*, or rather, to speak more reverently, of that *mortal god*, to which we owe under the *immortal God*, our peace and defense. For by this authority, given him by every particular man in the commonwealth, he hath the use of so much power and strength conferred on him that, by terror thereof, he is enabled to perform the wills of them all, to peace at home and mutual aid against their enemies abroad. And in him

---

16. Cf. Hobbes, Chapter XV: "The laws of nature oblige *in foro interno;* that is to say, they bind to a desire they should take place; but *in foro externo,* that is, to the putting them in act, not always. . . . These dictates of reason men used to call by the name of laws, but improperly, for they are but conclusions, or theorems, concerning what conduceth to the conservation and defense of themselves; whereas law, properly, is the word of him that by right hath command over others. . . ."

consisteth the essence of the commonwealth; which, to define it, is "one person, of whose acts a great multitude, by mutual covenants one with another, have made themselves every one the author, to the end he may use the strength and means of them all as he shall think expedient for their peace and common defense." And he that carrieth this person is called *sovereign,* and said to have sovereign power; and everyone besides, his *subject.* . . . (xvii)

The difference of commonwealths consisteth in the difference of the sovereign, or the person representative of all and every one of the multitude. . . . When the representative is one man, then the commonwealth is a monarchy; when an assembly of all that will come together, then it is a democracy, or popular commonwealth; when an assembly of a part only, then it is called an aristocracy. Other kind of commonwealth there can be none, for either one, or more, or all, must have the sovereign power. . . .

The difference between these three kinds of commonwealth consisteth not in the difference of power, but in the difference of convenience or aptitude to produce the peace and security of the people, for which end they were instituted. And to compare monarchy with the other two, we may observe first that . . . where the public and private interest are most closely united, there is the public most advanced. Now in monarchy the private interest is the same with the public. The riches, power, and honor of a monarch arise only from the riches, strength, and reputation of his subjects. For no king can be rich, nor glorious, nor secure, whose subjects are either poor, or contemptible, or too weak[17]. . . . (xix)

A commonwealth is said to be *instituted* when a multitude of men do agree and covenant, everyone with everyone, that . . . [some] man, or assembly of men, shall be given by the major part the right to present the person of them all, that is to say, to be their *representative.* . . . From this institution of a commonwealth are derived all the *rights* and *faculties* of him, or them, on whom sovereign power is conferred by the consent of the people assembled.

First, because they covenant, it is to be understood they are not obliged by former covenant to anything repugnant thereunto; and . . . cannot lawfully make a new covenant amongst themselves to be obedient to any other, in anything whatsoever, without his permission. And therefore, they that are subject to a monarch, cannot without his leave cast off monarchy, and return to the confusion of a disunited multitude, nor transfer their person from him that beareth it, to another man, or other assembly of men; for they are bound every man to every man to own and be reputed author of all that he that already is their sovereign shall do. . . .

Secondly, because the right of being the person of them all is given to him they make sovereign, by covenant only of one to another and not of him to any of them, there can happen no breach of covenant on the part of the sovereign; and consequently none of his subjects, by any pretense of forfeiture, can be freed from his subjection. . . .

---

17. Hobbes advances five additional arguments in favor of monarchy over the other types of government.

Thirdly, because the major part hath by consenting voices declared a sovereign, he that dissented must now consent with the rest; that is, be contented to avow all the actions he shall do, or else justly be destroyed by the rest. For if he voluntarily entered into the congregation of them that were assembled, he sufficiently declared thereby his will, and therefore tacitly covenanted to stand to what the major part should ordain. . . .

Fourthly, because every subject is by this institution author of all the actions and judgments of the sovereign instituted, it follows that whatsoever he doth, it can be no injury to any of his subjects, nor ought he to be by any of them accused of injustice. For he that doth anything by authority from another, doth therein no injury to him by whose authority he acteth; but by this institution of a commonwealth, every particular man is author of all the sovereign doth; and consequently he that complaineth of injury from his sovereign complaineth of that whereof he himself is author; and therefore ought not to accuse any man but himself; no, nor himself of injury, because to do injury to one's self is impossible. It is true that they that have sovereign power may commit iniquity, but not injustice, nor injury, in the proper signification.

Fifthly, and consequently to that which was said last, no man that hath sovereign power can justly be put to death, or otherwise in any manner by his subjects punished. . . .

Sixthly, it is annexed to the sovereignty, to be judge of what opinions and doctrines are averse, and what conducing to peace; and consequently, on what occasions, how far, and what men are to be trusted withal, in speaking to multitudes of people; and who shall examine the doctrines of all books before they be published. . . .

Seventhly, is annexed to the sovereignty, the whole power of prescribing the rules, whereby every man may know what goods he may enjoy, and what actions he may do, without being molested by any of his fellow-subjects. . . .

Eightly, is annexed to the sovereignty, the right of judicature; that is to say, of hearing and deciding all controversies which may arise concerning law, either civil or natural, or concerning fact. . . .

Ninthly, is annexed to the sovereignty, the right of making war and peace with other nations and commonwealths . . . and to levy money upon the subjects, to defray the expenses thereof. . . .

These are the rights which make the essence of sovereignty, and which are the marks whereby a man may discern in what man, or assembly of men, the sovereign power is placed and resideth. . . .

But a man may here object [says Mr. Hobbes in anticipation of the usual criticism of an absolute sovereign] that the condition of subjects is very miserable, as being obnoxious to the lusts, and other irregular passions, of him or them that have so unlimited a power in their hands. And commonly they that live under a monarch think it the fault of monarchy; and they that live under the government of democracy, or other sovereign assembly, attribute all the inconvenience to that form of commonwealth; whereas the power in all forms, if they be perfect enough to protect them, is the same. . . . [The critics fail to consider] that the state of man can never be without some incommodity or other; and that the greatest that in any form of government can possibly happen to the people in general is scarce sensible . . . [in comparison to] the miseries and horrible calamities that accompany a civil war, or that dissolute condition of masterless men without subjection to laws and a coercive power to tie their hands from rapine and revenge. . . . (xviii)

Wrington. You (and Mr. Hobbes) have indeed anticipated a criticism I would make of the notion of absolute or unlimited government, but with your permission I would like to rephrase it in terms of my own way of conceiving the transition from a state of nature to a state of civil society, and then give in more detail my reasons for preferring a limited form of government.

Malmesbury. You have my permission.

Wrington. Well, then, my view is as follows: Wherever . . . any number of men are so united into one society as to quit everyone his executive power of the law of nature, and to resign it to the public, there, and there only is a political or civil society. And this is done wherever any number of men in the state of nature enter into society to make one people, one body politic, under one supreme government, or else when anyone joins himself to, and incorporates with, any government already made. For hereby he authorizes the society, or, which is all one, the legislative thereof, to make laws for him, as the public good of the society shall require, to the execution whereof his own assistance (as to his own decrees) is due. And this puts men out of a state of nature into that of a commonwealth, by setting up a judge on earth with authority to determine all the controversies and redress the injuries that may happen to any member of the commonwealth; which judge is the legislative, or magistrates appointed by it. And wherever there are any number of men, however associated, that have no such decisive power to appeal to, there they are still in the state of nature. (89)

Hence it is evident that absolute monarchy, which by some men is counted the only government in the world, is indeed inconsistent with civil society, and so can be no form of civil government at all. For the end of civil society being to avoid and remedy those inconveniences of the state of nature which necessarily follow from every man's being judge in his own case, by setting up a known authority to which everyone of that society may appeal upon any injury received or controversy that may arise, and which every one of the society ought to obey. Wherever any persons are who have not such an authority to appeal to and decide any difference between them there, those persons are still in the state of nature. And so is every absolute prince, in respect of those who are under his dominion. (90)

In absolute monarchies, indeed, as well as other governments of the world, the subjects have an appeal to the law, and judges to decide any controversies and restrain any violence that may happen betwixt the subjects themselves, one amongst another. This everyone thinks necessary, and believes he deserves to be thought a declared enemy to society and mankind who should go about to take it away. But whether this be from a true love of mankind and society, and such a charity as we owe all one to another, there is reason to doubt. For this is no more than what every man who loves his own power, profit, or greatness may, and naturally must do, keep those animals from hurting or destroying one another who labour and drudge only for his pleasure and advantage; and so are taken care of, not out of any love the master has for them, but love of himself, and the profit they bring him. For if it be asked, what security, what fence is there, in such a state, against the violence and oppression of this absolute rule, the very question can scarce be borne. They are ready to tell you that it deserves death only to ask after safety. Betwixt subject and subject they will grant there must be measures, laws, and judges, for their mutual peace and security; but as for the ruler, he ought to be absolute, and is above all such circumstances; because he has power to do more hurt and wrong, 'tis right when he does it. To ask how you may be guarded from harm or injury on that side where the strongest hand is to do it, is presently the voice of faction and rebellion. As if when men quitting the state of nature entered into society, they agreed that all of them but one should be under the restraint of laws, but that he should still retain all the liberty of the state of nature, increased with power, and made licentious by impunity. This is to think that men are so foolish that they take care to avoid what mischiefs may be done them by polecats or foxes, but are content, nay, think it safety, to be devoured by lions. . . . (93)

Men being, as has been said, by nature all free, equal, and independent, no one can be put out of this estate, and subjected to the political power of another, without his consent. . . . (95) For when any number of men have, by the consent of every individual, made a community, they have thereby made that community one body, with a power to act as one body, which is only by the will and determination of the majority. . . . (96) And thus every man, by consenting with others to make one body politic under one government, puts himself under an obligation to every one of that society to submit to the determination of the majority, and to be concluded by it; or else this original compact, whereby he with others incorporates into one society, would signify nothing, and be no compact, if he be left free and under no other ties than he was in before in the state of nature. . . . (97)

Whosoever, therefore, . . . unite into a community must be understood to give up all the power necessary to the ends for which they unite into society, to the majority of the community, unless they expressly agreed in any number greater than the majority. And this is done by barely agreeing to unite into one political society, which is all the compact that is, or needs be, between the individuals that enter into or make up a commonwealth. And thus that which begins and actually constitutes any political society is nothing but the consent of any number of freemen capable of a majority to unite and incorporate into such a society. And this is that, and that only, which did or could give beginning to any lawful government in the world. (99)

Every man being . . . naturally free, and nothing being able to put him into subjection to any earthly power but only his own consent, it is to be considered what shall be understood to be a sufficient declaration of a man's consent to make him subject to the laws of any government. There is a common distinction of an express and a tacit consent. . . . Nobody doubts but an express consent of any man entering into any society makes him a perfect member of that society. . . . The difficulty is, what ought to be looked upon as a tacit consent, and how far it binds. . . . And to this I say that every man that hath any possessions, or enjoyment of any part of the dominions of any government, doth thereby give his tacit consent, and is as far obliged to obedience to the laws of that government during such enjoyment as anyone under it; whether this his possession be of land to him and his heirs for ever, or a lodging only for a week, or whether it be barely travelling freely on the highway; and in effect it reaches as far as the very being of anyone within the territories of that government. (119)

If man in the state of nature be so free, as has been said; if he be absolute lord of his own person and possessions, equal to the greatest, and subject to nobody, why will he part with his freedom? Why will he give up this empire, and subject himself to the dominion and control of any other power? To which 'tis obvious to answer, that though in the state of nature he hath such a right, yet the enjoyment of it is very uncertain, and constantly exposed to the invasions of others. For all being kings as much as he, every man his equal, and the greater part no strict observers of equity and justice, the enjoyment of the property he has in this state is very unsafe, very unsecure. This makes him willing to quit a condition which, however free, is full of fears and continual dangers; and it is not without reason that he seeks out and is willing to join in society with others who are already united, or have a mind to unite, for the mutual preservation of their lives, liberties, and estates,[18] which I call by the general name, *property*. (123)

The great and chief end, therefore, of men's uniting into commonwealths, and putting themselves under government, is the preservation of their property; to which in the state of nature there are many things wanting:

First, there wants an established, settled, known law, received and allowed by common consent to be the standard of right and wrong, and the common measure to decide all controversies between them. For though the law of nature be plain and intelligible to all rational creatures, yet men, being biased by their interests, as well as ignorant for want of study of it, are not apt to allow of it as a law binding them in the application of it to their particular cases. (124)

Secondly, in the state of nature there wants a known and indifferent judge, with authority to determine all differences according to the established law. For everyone in that state, being both judge and executioner of the law of nature, men being partial to themselves, passion and revenge is very apt to carry them too far and with too much heat in their own cases, as well as negligence and unconcernedness, to make them too remiss in other men's. (125)

Thirdly, in the state of nature there often wants power to back and support the sentence when right, and to give it due execution. They who by any injustice offend will seldom fail, where they are able, by force to make

---

18. Cf. The Declaration of Independence; also, The Constitution of the United States, Amendment XIV.

good their injustice; such resistance many times makes the punishment dangerous, and frequently destructive to those who attempt it. (126)

The great end of men's entering into society being the enjoyment of their
properties in peace and safety, and the great instrument and means of that
being the laws established in that society: the *first and fundamental positive law*
of all commonwealths is the establishing of the legislative power; as the *first and
fundamental natural law,* which is to govern even the legislative itself, is the
preservation of the society, and (as far as will consist with the public good) of
every person in it. This legislative is not only the supreme power of the commonwealth, but sacred and unalterable in the hands where the community have
once placed it; nor can any edict of anyone else, in what form soever conceived,
or by what power soever backed, have the force and obligation of a law, which
has not its sanction from that legislative which the public has chosen and
appointed. For without this the law could not have that which is absolutely
necessary to its being a law, the consent of the society over whom nobody can
have a power to make laws; but by their own consent, and by authority received from them; and therefore all the obedience, which by the most solemn
ties anyone can be obliged to pay, ultimately terminates in this supreme power,
and is directed by those laws which it enacts; nor can any oaths to any foreign
power whatsoever, or any domestic subordinate power, discharge any member
of the society from his obedience to the legislative, acting pursuant to their
trust; nor oblige him to any obedience contrary to the laws so enacted, or
farther than they do allow; it being ridiculous to imagine one can be tied
ultimately to obey any power in the society which is not the supreme. (134)

Though the legislative, whether placed in one or more, . . . be the supreme
power in every commonwealth, yet: . . . (135)

These are the bounds which the trust that is put in them by the society,
and the law of God and nature, have set to the legislative power of every
commonwealth, in all forms of government:

First, they are to govern by promulgated established laws, not to be varied
in particular cases, but to have one rule for rich and poor, for the favourite at court and the countryman at plough.

Secondly, these laws also ought to be designed for no other end ultimately but the good of the people.

Thirdly, they must not raise taxes on the property of the people without
the consent of the people, given by themselves or their deputies. . . .

Fourthly, the legislative neither must nor can transfer the power of
making laws to anybody else, or place it anywhere but where the people
have. (142)

Malmesbury. You speak of the bounds or limits of the supreme governmental
power. The notion strikes me as most peculiar. How can the same thing be both
"supreme" and "limited"? Still, I do recall that Mr. Hobbes, while speaking of
the liberty of subjects, mentioned something akin to this notion. He suggested
two conditions under which men might be free, as he put it, of those "artificial
chains" called civil laws, which are in all other cases fastened at one end to the
lips of the sovereign and at the other end to their own ears. The first exemption

from, or limitation of, the laws he based on the fact that there is no common-wealth in the world wherein there be rules enough set down for the regulating of all the actions and words of men; as being a thing impossible. It followeth necessarily that in all kinds of actions by the laws pretermitted [not prescribed by law], men have the liberty of doing what their own reasons shall suggest. . . . The liberty of a subject lieth therefore only in those things which in regulating their actions, the sovereign hath pretermitted; such as is the liberty to buy and sell, and otherwise contract with one another; to choose their own abode, their own diet, their own trade of life, and institute their children as they themselves think fit; and the like.

Nevertheless [Mr. Hobbes cautions us], we are not to understand that by such liberty the sovereign power of life and death is either abolished or limited. For it has been already shown that nothing the sovereign representative can do to a subject, on what pretense soever, can properly be called injustice or injury. . . .

[The second kind of exemption is based on a consideration of the rights which the subject does and does not give up when he enters a common-wealth. To the question], What are the things which, though commanded by the sovereign, he may nevertheless without injustice refuse to do? Mr. Hobbes answers: It is manifest that every subject has liberty in all those things the right whereof cannot by covenant be transferred. . . . Therefore:

If the sovereign command a man, though justly condemned, to kill, wound, or maim himself; or not to resist those that assault him; or to abstain from the use of food, air, medicine, or any other thing, without which he cannot live; yet hath that man the liberty to disobey.

If a man be interrogated by the sovereign, or his authority, concerning a crime done by himself, he is not bound, without assurance of pardon, to confess it. . . .

A man that is commanded as a soldier to fight against the enemy, though his sovereign have right enough to punish his refusal with death, may nevertheless in many cases refuse without injustice; as when he substituteth a sufficient soldier in his place, for in this case he deserteth not the service of the commonwealth. . . .

If a subject have a controversy with his sovereign, . . . he hath the same liberty to sue for his right as if it were against a subject. . . .

The obligation of subjects to the sovereign is understood to last as long, and no longer, than the power lasteth by which he is able to protect them. . . .

If a subject be taken prisoner in war, or his person or his means of life be within the guards of the enemy, and hath his life and corporal liberty given him on condition to be subject to the victor, he hath liberty to accept the condition. . . .

If a man be held in prison, or bonds, or is not trusted with the liberty of his body, he cannot be understood to be bound by covenant to subjection; and therefore may, if he can, make his escape by any means whatsoever.

If a monarch shall relinquish the sovereignty both for himself and his heirs, his subjects return to the absolute liberty of nature. . . .

If the sovereign banish his subject; during the banishment, he is not subject. . . .

If a monarch subdued by war, render himself subject to the victor, his subjects are delivered from their former obligation, and become obliged to the victor. . . . (xxi)

Wrington. It seems to me that Mr. Hobbes says perhaps too much regarding the usurpation of power and too little regarding the tyranny of power.

Malmesbury. Pray, explain your meaning.

Wrington. Gladly. As usurpation is the exercise of power which another hath a right to, so tyranny is the exercise of power beyond right, which nobody can have a right to. And this is making use of the power anyone has in his hands, not for the good of those who are under it, but for his own private, separate advantage. When the governor, however entitled, makes not the law, but his will, the rule, and his commands and actions are not directed to the preservation of the properties of his people, but the satisfaction of his own ambition, revenge, covetousness, or any other irregular passion. (199)

'Tis a mistake to think this fault is proper only to monarchies; other forms of government are liable to it as well as that. For wherever the power that is put in any hands for the government of the people and the preservation of their properties is applied to other ends, and made use of to impoverish, harass, or subdue them to the arbitrary and irregular commands of those that have it, there it presently becomes tyranny, whether those that thus use it are one or many. . . . (201)

Wherever law ends, tyranny begins, if the law be transgressed to another's harm. And whosoever in authority exceeds the power given him by the law, and makes use of the force he has under his command to compass that upon the subject which the law allows not, ceases in that to be a magistrate; and, acting without authority, may be opposed, as any other man who by force invades the right of another. . . . (202)

May the commands, then, of a prince be opposed? May he be resisted as often as anyone shall find himself aggrieved, and but imagine he has not right done him? This will unhinge and overturn all polities, and instead of government and order, leave nothing but anarchy and confusion. (203)

To this I answer that force is to be opposed to nothing but to unjust and unlawful force. Whoever makes any opposition in any other case draws on himself a just condemnation, both from God and man. . . . (204)

COMPARATIVE STUDY QUESTIONS

Review Questions

1. According to Hobbes, all men are by nature equal. Explain.
2. Although the state of nature is a state of liberty, it is not a state of license, says Locke (Wrington). Explain.
3. What does Hobbes mean by "war"?
4. What is the "executive power of the state of nature," according to Locke?
5. Is there any justice or injustice in the state of nature, according to Hobbes? Locke?
6. What status do the laws of nature have outside civil society, according to Hobbes?
7. With whom is the social contract made, and what are its terms, according to Hobbes? Locke?
8. Explain what Hobbes and Locke (Wrington) mean by "liberty"?
9. Why do men choose to enter a civil society, according to Hobbes? Locke?
10. What are the things which, though commanded by the sovereign, a subject may nevertheless, without injustice, refuse to do, according to Hobbes?

Discussion Questions

1. Locke claims that some persons have confounded the "state of nature" with a "state of war." What is the difference, as he views them? Do you think he has Hobbes in mind?
2. According to Hobbes, in a state of nature there is "no **mine** and **thine**," in other words, no institution of property. Critically compare this view with Locke's.
3. What is the "first and fundamental law of nature," according to Hobbes? Compare it with Locke's (Wrington's) "first and fundamental natural law." Is there any difference? What according to Locke is the "first and fundamental positive law"? Would Hobbes concur?
4. Compare Hobbes' and Locke's views regarding the nature and function of law.
5. It is generally agreed that Locke had a profound influence on the U.S. Constitution and on Thomas Jefferson who wrote the Declaration of Independence. Identify some of these influences. Are there Hobbesian influences as well?
6. Why does Locke (Wrington) argue for limited governmental power? In what sense does Hobbes regard the sovereign as possessing absolute power, and in what sense can it be argued that Hobbes' sovereign is not absolute? Is Hobbes consistent?

7. Is there something inconsistent about the notion of a sovereign's being both "supreme" and "limited"?
8. In arguing for the necessity of a concentration of governmental power, does Hobbes mean to say that the only legitimate form of government is monarchy? In arguing against absolutism, does Locke mean to oppose monarchy?
9. What do Hobbes and Locke each say regarding the distinct possibility that the sovereign, whether individual or assembly, may, if unrestricted, become despotic with respect to the people's wishes and welfare?
10. How do Hobbes and Locke each stand with respect to the question of a "right of revolution"?

Gottfried Wilhelm Leibniz
(1646 – 1716)

Benedictus (Baruch) de Spinoza
(1634 – 1677)

GOD IN AN APPARENTLY EVIL WORLD

Gottfried Wilhelm Leibniz[1]
and Benedictus (Baruch) de Spinoza

> The normal process of life contains moments as bad as any of those which insane melancholy is filled with, moments in which radical evil gets its innings and takes its solid turn. The lunatic's visions of horror are all drawn from the material of daily fact. . . . Here on our very hearths and in our gardens the infernal cat plays with the panting mouse, or holds the hot bird fluttering in her jaws. . . .
>
> William James, *The Varieties of Religious Experience* (1902)

During the years 1672–1676, Leibniz lived in Paris. He was invited there initially to explain to King Louis XIV a scheme of his for the conquest of Egypt. It was a diplomatic venture aimed at redirecting French aggrandizement away from the Christian countries of Europe and toward the Turks of northern Africa. His plan was never formally presented to the King, nor acted upon until a century later, when Napoleon, unaware that a German philosopher had already concocted the scheme, accomplished substantially what Leibniz had had in mind.

Leibniz stayed on in France in order to study mathematics with Christiaan Huygens and to discuss Descartes' philosophy with Nicolas Malebranche and other Cartesians. His study of mathematics at this time eventually led him to the discovery of the differential calculus. His study of Descartes' philosophy, the most influential of the day, led him to have very serious doubts about it.

---

1. The philosophers whose exchanges constitute the fourth set of conversations are named here without the usual prefixed titles. The first named often signed himself simply "Leibniz," or used his initials, "G. W. v. L." Spinoza was even more self-effacing. During his lifetime only one of his books had his name on it, and that was because it was published by friends; his *Tractatus Theologico-Politicus* was published anonymously. Even his posthumous works indicated authorship merely by the initials "B. d. S." which was the way he frequently signed his letters. Leibniz had numerous titles which he could have used, and did whenever he wished to impress someone of reputation. In addition to the title of the post he happened to have at the time, and as a

It was during this sojourn in Paris that Leibniz met a certain Bohemian Count named Ehrenfried Walter von Tschirnhaus who happened to be a friend and correspondent of Spinoza. Tschirnhaus had in his possession some of Spinoza's unpublished manuscripts which he had been told not to release to others without Spinoza's express permission. Leibniz and Tschirnhaus became close friends. Tschirnhaus apparently kept his word about the manuscripts, but he must have said enough to Leibniz to suggest that Spinoza's new system might resolve some of his misgivings about Descartes' philosophy. In any case, Tschirnhaus wrote to Dr. G.H. Schuller, a younger mutual friend, informing him of his acquaintance with Leibniz, and asking him to seek Spinoza's permission to show the manuscripts to Leibniz.

Leibniz was not at this time wholly unacquainted with Spinoza. He had read Spinoza's **Tractatus Theologico-Politicus**, and probably also his earlier book, **The Principles of Descartes' Philosophy.** In October, 1671, he had written to Spinoza about a matter of optics. Spinoza, an expert on the subject, had not only studied optics theoretically, as had Descartes and Hobbes, but was by daily occupation a lens grinder and polisher. According to Schuller, there was also possibly some correspondence between Leibniz and Spinoza regarding the **Tractatus,** but it seems not to have survived.

Spinoza's refusal to allow Leibniz access to the manuscripts must have made him all the more eager to see them. Spinoza wanted to know more about what Leibniz was doing in France, and whether he could be trusted. Leibniz's curiosity remained unsatisfied until about a year later. In October, 1676, he left Paris to assume a position as librarian to the Duke of Brunswick at Hanover, traveling first to London and then to Amsterdam where he stayed with Schuller for about a month. Finally in November, 1676, Leibniz met with Spinoza in The Hague. According to Leibniz's own account, they had many long conversations together. Spinoza allowed him not only to see the **Ethics** manuscript, but also to copy parts of it. The following February (1677) Spinoza died. Toward the end of the same year, in accordance with his instructions, all his manuscripts were published. Schuller, who incidentally was the only person present at Spinoza's death, soon afterwards sent Leibniz a copy of the **Opera Posthuma.**

The detailed marginal notes which Leibniz made in his copy of the **Ethics,** his separate reading notes on Part I, as well as his **Refutation of Spinoza,** which is here reprinted, all indicate that Leibniz gave Spinoza's works a very careful scrutiny. In a letter to Henry Justel, dated February 4/14, 1678, Leibniz made the following comments:

---

recipient of a doctorate (in law), he was entitled to use the degree letters J.U.D. after his name, and I suppose to be called "Herr Doktor." Later in his diplomatic career the title of "Freiherr" (or Baron) was conferred upon him (library card catalogues, I find, make use of this one). And although he once advocated the use of the German language as a vehicle for philosophical conversation, he himself wrote mostly in French. Perhaps because of this, and possibly because both of them at different times were diplomats in Paris, the Scottish philosopher David Hume often refers to him in his writings as "Monsieur Leibniz." For the purpose of the present topic of discussion, however, the first names of both philosophers are all the titles either of them needs: "Gottfried," meaning "Peace of God"; and "Benedictus" or "Baruch," meaning "Blessed."

The posthumous works of the late Mr. Spinoza have at last been published. The most important part is the *Ethics,* composed of five treatises: On God, on mind, on human servitude to affections or on the force of the affections, and on human freedom or the power of the understanding. I have found there a number of excellent thoughts which agree with my own, as some of my friends know who have also learned from Spinoza. But there are also paradoxes which I do not find true or even plausible. As, for example, that there is only one substance, namely, God; that creatures are modes or accidents of God; that our mind perceives nothing further after this life; that God himself does indeed think but neither understands nor wills; that all things happen by a kind of fatal necessity; that God does not act for the sake of ends but only from a certain necessity of nature. This is to retain in word but to deny in fact, providence and immortality.

I consider this book dangerous for those who wish to take the pains to master it. For the rest will not make the effort to understand it.[2]

It is fairly easy to see why Leibniz should have taken such an avid interest in Spinoza's thought. Both men were concerned with the same cluster of philosophical problems. In his letter to Schuller, Tschirnhaus describes Leibniz as "very expert in metaphysical studies about God." Novalis later described Spinoza as a "God-intoxicated man." Neither Spinoza nor Leibniz deny the existence of God; both, in fact, rely on similar kinds of proofs. But they differ radically regarding the nature of God. Spinoza identifies God with Nature, or the Whole of Reality, whereas Leibniz retains, more or less, the traditional theistic conception.

For both, the so-called "problem of evil" is a major difficulty. Neither wishes to deny the existence of disease, natural calamities, human suffering, error, immorality, or sin. Yet, how can such "evils" be compatible with a God conceived **either** as an infinitely perfect Substance, or more traditionally as an all-powerful, all-good Creator? Spinoza makes "good" and "evil" dependent upon a relation to the individual person. We do not desire things because they are good; they are good because we desire them. Similarly, things are evil because we have an aversion to them, and not the other way around. Consequently Spinoza treats Nature itself as value-neutral, i.e., as neither good nor bad. He also denies that God has a will or is in any way purposive. Leibniz rejects these approaches to a solution of the problem, and in fact regards all such doctrines as both paradoxical and "dangerous." Yet, despite their differences, Leibniz and Spinoza share at least one solution of the problem of evil. They both regard the evil of the world as in some sense "necessary." For Spinoza, everything that exists is a part of and is necessarily derived from the nature of God. For Leibniz, evil (which both he and Spinoza conceive of as a "privation" rather than anything positive) is a necessary ingredient even in "the best of all possible worlds."

2. *Gottfried Wilhelm Leibniz: Philosophical Papers and Letters,* translated and edited by Leroy E. Loemker (Dordrecht, Holland: D. Reidel Publishing Co., 2nd revised edition, 1969), note 6, p. 195.

This suggests another problem. Is there no freedom of will? Spinoza denies that there is: We think we are free only because we are ignorant of the causes of our behavior. Leibniz retains the idea of free choice, not only with respect to God's creation and providence, but also with respect to ordinary human wills. Yet, he too talks of "moral necessity," and rejects the notion that a will is free if it chooses evil, or is in any sense better than one which is necessitated by the person's character.

SPINOZA AND G. H. SCHULLER

*Correspondence Regarding Leibniz**

To the Very Eminent and Acute Philosopher
B. d. S.

Most Learned and Excellent Sir,
Most Honoured Patron,

I hope that my last letter, together with the *Process* of an anonymous writer, has been duly delivered to you, and also that you are now very well, even as I am very well. I had, however, received no letter from our friend Tschirnhaus for a space of three months, whence I had made the sad conjecture that his journey from England to France was ill-starred. But now, having received a letter, I am full of joy, and in accordance with his request it is my duty to communicate it to you, Sir, to convey to you his most dutiful greetings, to inform you that he has reached Paris safely, that he has met there Mr. Huygens, as we had advised him to do, and that for the same reason he has in every way adapted himself to his way of thinking so as to be highly esteemed by him. He mentioned that you, Sir, had advised him to associate with him (Huygens), and that you esteem his person very highly. This greatly pleased him, so that he replied that he likewise esteems your person greatly, and that he had lately obtained from you the *Tractatus Theologico-Politicus*. This is esteemed by very many there, and inquiries are eagerly made whether any other words of the same author are published. To this Mr. Tschirnhaus replied that he knew of none save the *Proofs of the First and Second Part of Descartes' Principles.*

---

*From *The Correspondence of Spinoza*, translated and edited by A. Wolf (London: George Allen & Unwin Ltd., 1928), pp. 336–339, 340–342, Letters LXX, LXXII, by permission of the publisher.

Otherwise he related nothing else about you, Sir, than the remarks just reported; hence he hopes that this will not displease you.

Huygens has recently had our Tschirnhaus summoned to him and informed him that Mr. Colbert desired some one to instruct his son in mathematics, and that if a position of this kind pleased him, he would arrange it. To this our friend replied by asking for some delay, and eventually declared that he was ready to accept. Huygens returned with the answer that the proposal pleased Mr. Colbert very much, especially as, owing to his ignorance of French, he will be compelled to speak to his son in Latin.

To the objection made most recently, he replies that the few words which I had written by your instruction, Sir, have revealed to him your meaning more deeply, and that he had already entertained these thoughts (since they chiefly admit of an explanation in these two ways) but that he has been led to follow that which was lately contained in his objection by the two following reasons. The first is that otherwise Propositions V and VII of Book II would seem to be opposed. In the former of these it is stated that the Ideata are the efficient causes of ideas, whereas the contrary seems to be shown by the proof of the latter, on account of the cited Axion, 4, Part I. Maybe (as I rather persuade myself) I do not rightly apply the axiom in accordance with the Author's intention, which I would most willingly learn from him, if his affairs permit. The second cause which hindered me from following the given explanation was that in this way the Attribute Thought is made much more extensive than the other attributes; but since each of the Attributes constitutes the Essence of God, I certainly do not see how the one does not contradict the other. I will only add that if I may judge the minds of others by my own, then Propositions VII and VIII of Book II will be exceedingly difficult to understand, and this for no other reason than that it has pleased the Author (since I have no doubt that they seemed so clear to him) to explain the proofs added to them in such brief and sparing explanations.

He relates, moreover, that he has met in Paris a man called Leibniz, of uncommon learning, well versed in many Sciences, and free from the vulgar prejudices of Theology. He has formed an intimate friendship with him because it happens that like himself he is working at the problem of the continued perfecting of the understanding, than which, indeed, he thinks there is nothing better, and considers nothing more useful. In Morals, he says that he is perfectly disciplined, and speaks from the mere dictates of reason, without any influence of the feelings. In Physics and especially in Metaphysical studies about God and the soul, he continues, he is very expert. Lastly, he concludes that he is most worthy of having communicated to him your writings, Sir, if consent has been first obtained, since he believes that thus great advantage will come to the Author, as he promises to show more fully if it please you, Sir. But if not, then let it cause no uneasiness lest he may not keep them secret conscientiously according to the promise he gave, as he has not made the slightest mention of them. This same Leibniz thinks very highly of the *Tractatus Theologico-Politicus,* on which subject, if you remember, he once wrote a letter to you, Sir.

I would therefore pray you, Sir, unless there is some special reason against it, not to mind giving this permission, in your generous kindliness. If possible, tell me your decision as soon as you can, for as soon as I have received your reply, I shall be able to answer our friend Tschirnhaus, which I am anxious to do on Tuesday evening, unless rather weighty grounds for delay compel you, Sir, to put the matter off.

Mr. Bresser has returned from Cleves, and has sent hither a large quantity of the beer of his country. I advised him to let you, Sir, have half a barrel, which he promised to do with his most friendly greeting.

Lastly, I pray you to forgive the roughness of my style, and the haste of my pen, and to command me to do you some service, so that I may have a real opportunity of proving that I am,

Most distinguished sir,
Your most devoted servant
G. H. SCHULLER.

Amsterdam, 14 November 1675.

To the Very Learned and Expert
Mr. G. H. Schuller

Most Experienced Sir,
Most Honoured Friend,

I was much pleased to understand from your letter received today that you are well, and that our friend Tschirnhaus has happily accomplished his journey to France. In the conversations which he had with Huygens about me he bore himself, in my opinion, very prudently. Moreover, I greatly rejoice that he has found such a fortunate opportunity for the end which he had set himself.

I do not see what he finds in Axiom 4, Part I, to contradict Proposition V, Part II. For in this proposition it is asserted that the essence of every idea has God for its cause in so far as He is considered as a thinking thing; whereas, in that axiom, it is asserted that the knowledge or the idea of the effect depends on the knowledge or the idea of the cause. But to confess the truth, I do not sufficiently follow the meaning of your letter on this point, and I believe that either in your letter, or in the original letter, there is an error due to haste in writing. For you write that it is asserted in Proposition V that the ideata are the efficient causes of ideas, whereas this very thing is expressly denied in this proposition. Hence, I now think, arises the whole confusion, and therefore any endeavour to write more fully on this matter would be vain, and I must therefore wait until you explain to me his meaning more clearly, and I know whether the original letter is sufficiently correct.

I think I know the Leibniz of whom he writes, through his letters, but I do not know why he has gone to France, when he was a Councillor of Frankfort. As far as I could surmise from his letters, he seemed to me a man of liberal mind, and versed in every science. But still I consider it imprudent to entrust my writings to him so soon. I should like to know first what he is doing in France, and to hear the opinion of our friend Tschirnhaus, after he has associated with him longer, and knows his character more intimately. However, greet that friend of ours most dutifully in my name, and if I can be of service to him in anything, let him say what he wants, and he will find me most ready to comply with all his wishes.

I congratulate Mr. Bresser, my most honoured friend, on his arrival or return. For the promised beer I am very grateful, and I will repay in whatever way I may.

Lastly, I have not yet attempted to make trial of the process of your kinsman, nor do I believe that I shall be able to apply my mind to the attempt. For the more I consider the thing itself, the more I am persuaded that you have not made gold, but had not sufficiently separated what was latent in the antimony. But more of this on another occasion; now I am prevented for want of time.

Meanwhile, if I can be of service to you in anything, here I am whom you will always find,

Most distinguished Sir,
Your most friendly and devoted servant,
B. de SPINOZA

The Hague, 18 November 1675
Mr. G. H. Schuller,
Doctor of Medicine
in De Kortsteegh in De Gestofeerde Hoet,
T'Amsterdam

SPINOZA

The Ethics*

Part I. Concerning God

Definitions

I. By that which is *self-caused,* I mean that of which the essence involves existence, or that of which the nature is only conceivable as existent.

II. A thing is called *finite after its kind,* when it can be limited by another thing of the same nature; for instance, a body is called finite because we always

---

*From the translation by R. H. M. Elwes, 1898.

conceive another greater body. So, also, a thought is limited by another thought, but a body is not limited by thought, nor a thought by body.

III. By *substance,* I mean that which is in itself, and is conceived through itself; in other words, that of which a conception can be formed independently of any other conception.

IV. By *attribute,* I mean that which the intellect perceives as constituting the essence of substance.

V. By *mode,* I mean the modifications of substance, or that which exists in, and is conceived through, something other than itself.

VI. By *God,* I mean a being absolutely infinite—that is, a substance consisting in infinite attributes, of which each expresses eternal and infinite essentiality.

Explanation.—I say absolutely infinite, not infinite after its kind: for, a thing infinite only after its kind, infinite attributes may be denied; but that which is absolutely infinite, contains in its essence whatever expresses reality, and involves no negation.

VII. That thing is called *free,* which exists solely by the necessity of its own nature, and of which the action is determined by itself alone. On the other hand, that thing is necessary, or rather constrained, which is determined by something external to itself to a fixed and definite method of existence or action.

VIII. By *eternity,* I mean existence itself, in so far as it is conceived necessarily to follow solely from the definition of that which is eternal.

Explanation.—Existence of this kind is conceived as an eternal truth, like the essence of a thing, and, therefore, cannot be explained by means of continuance or time, though continuance may be conceived without a beginning or end.

Axioms

I. Everything which exists, exists either in itself or in something else.

II. That which cannot be conceived through anything else must be conceived through itself.

III. From a given definite cause an effect necessarily follows; and, on the other hand, if no definite cause be granted, it is impossible that an effect can follow.

IV. The knowledge of an effect depends on and involves the knowledge of a cause.

V. Things which have nothing in common cannot be understood, the one by means of the other; the conception of one does not involve the conception of the other.

VI. A true idea must correspond with its ideate or object.

VII. If a thing can be conceived as non-existing, its essence does not involve existence.

Propositions

Prop. I. Substance is by nature prior to its modifications.
Proof.—This is clear from Def. iii. and v.

Prop. II. Two substances, whose attributes are different, have nothing in common.

Proof.—Also evident from Def. iii. For each must exist in itself, and be conceived through itself; in other words, the conception of one does not imply the conception of the other.

Prop. III. Things which have nothing in common cannot be one the cause of the other.

Proof.—If they have nothing in common, it follows that one cannot be apprehended by means of the other (Ax. v.), and, therefore, one cannot be the cause of the other (Ax. iv.). Q.E.D.

Prop. IV. Two or more distinct things are distinguished one from the other either by the difference of the attributes of the substances, or by the difference of their modifications.

Proof.—Everything which exists, exists either in itself or in something else (Ax. i.),—that is (by Def. iii. and v.), nothing is granted in addition to the understanding, except substance and its modifications. Nothing is, therefore, given besides the understanding, by which several things may be distinguished one from the other, except the substances, or, in other words (see Ax. iv.), their attributes and modifications. Q.E.D.

Prop. V. There cannot exist in the universe two or more substances having the same nature or attribute.

Proof.—If several distinct substances be granted, they must be distinguished one from the other, either by the difference of their attributes, or by the difference of their modifications (Prop. iv.). If only by the difference of their attributes, it will be granted that there cannot be more than one with an identical attribute. If by the difference of their modifications—as substance is naturally prior to its modifications (Prop. i.),—it follows that setting the modifications aside, and considering substance in itself, that is truly (Def. iii. and vi.), there cannot be conceived one substance different from another,—that is (by Prop. iv.), there cannot be granted several substances, but one substance only. Q.E.D.

Prop VI. One substance cannot be produced by another substance.

Proof.—It is impossible that there should be in the universe two substances with an identical attribute, *i.e.,* which have anything in common to them both (Prop. ii.), and, therefore (Prop. iii.), one cannot be the cause of another, neither can one be produced by the other. Q.E.D.

Corollary.—Hence it follows that a substance cannot be produced by anything external to itself. For in the universe nothing is granted, save substances and their modifications (as appears from Ax. i. and Def. iii. and v.). Now (by the last Prop.) substance cannot be produced by another substance, therefore it cannot be produced by anything external to itself. Q.E.D. This is shown still more readily by the absurdity of the contradictory. For, if substance be produced by an external cause, the knowledge of it would depend on the knowledge of its cause (Ax. iv.), and (by Def. iii.) it would itself not be substance.

Prop. VII. Existence belongs to the nature of substance.

Proof.—Substance cannot be produced by anything external (Corollary, Prop. vi.), it must, therefore, be its own cause—that is, its essence necessarily involves existence. . . .

Prop. VIII. Every substance is necessarily infinite. . . .

Note I.—As finite existence involves a partial negation, and infinite existence is the absolute affirmation of the given nature, it follows (solely from Prop. vii.) that every substance is necessarily infinite.

Note II.—. . . And we can hence conclude by another process of reasoning— that there is but one such substance. I think that this may profitably be done at once; and, in order to proceed regularly with the demonstration, we must premise:

1. The true definition of a thing neither involves nor expresses anything beyond the nature of the thing defined. From this it follows that—

2. No definition implies or expresses a certain number of individuals, inasmuch as it expresses nothing beyond the nature of the thing defined. For instance, the definition of a triangle expresses nothing beyond the actual nature of a triangle: it does not imply any fixed number of triangles.

3. There is necessarily for each individual existent thing a cause why it should exist.

4. This cause of existence must either be contained in the nature and definition of the thing defined, or must be postulated apart from such definition.

It therefore follows that, if a given number of individual things exist in nature, there must be some cause for the existence of exactly that number, neither more nor less. For example, if twenty men exist in the universe (for simplicity's sake, I will suppose them existing simultaneously, and to have had no predecessors), and we want to account for the existence of these twenty men, it will not be enough to show the cause of human existence in general; we must also show why there are exactly twenty men, neither more or less: for a cause must be assigned for the existence of each individual. Now this cause cannot be contained in the actual nature of man, for the true definition of man does not involve any consideration of the number twenty. Consequently, the cause for the existence of these twenty men, and, consequently, of each of them, must necessarily be sought externally to each individual. Hence we may lay down the absolute rule, that everything which may consist of several individuals must have an external cause. And, as it has been shown already that existence appertains to the nature of substance, existence must necessarily be included in its definition; and from its definition alone existence must be deducible. But from its definition (as we have shown, Notes ii., iii.), we cannot infer the existence of several substances; therefore it follows that there is only one substance of the same nature. Q.E.D.

Prop. IX. The more reality or being a thing has the greater the number of its attributes (Def. iv.).

Prop. X. Each particular attribute of the one substance must be conceived through itself.

Proof.—An attribute is that which the intellect perceives of substance, as constituting its essence (Def. iv.), and, therefore, must be conceived through itself (Def. iii.). Q.E.D.

Note.—It is thus evident that, though two attributes are, in fact, conceived as distinct—that is, one without the help of the other—yet we cannot, therefore, conclude that they constitute two entities, or two different substances. For it is the nature of substance that each of its attributes is conceived through itself, inasmuch as all the attributes it has have always existed simultaneously in it, and none could be produced by any other; but each expresses the reality or being of substance. It is, then, far from an absurdity to ascribe several attributes to one substance: for nothing in nature is more clear than that each and every entity must be conceived under some attribute, and that its reality or being is in proportion to the number of its attributes expressing necessity or eternity and infinity. Consequently it is abundantly clear, that an absolutely infinite being must necessarily be defined as consisting in infinite attributes each of which expresses a certain eternal and infinite essence.

If any one now ask, by what sign shall he be able to distinguish different substances, let him read the following propositions, which show that there is but one substance in the universe, and that it is absolutely infinite, wherefore such a sign would be sought for in vain.

Prop. XI. God, or substance, consisting of infinite attributes, of which each expresses eternal and infinite essentiality, necessarily exists.

Proof.—If this be denied, conceive, if possible, that God does not exist: then his essence does not involve existence. But this (by Prop. vii.) is absurd. Therefore God necessarily exists.

Another proof.—Of everything whatsoever a cause or reason must be assigned, either for its existence, or for its non-existence— *e.g.,* if a triangle exist, a reason or cause must be granted for its existence; if, on the contrary, it does not exist, a cause must also be granted, which prevents it from existing, or annuls its existence. This reason or cause must either be contained in the nature of the thing in question, or be external to it. For instance, the reason for the non-existence of a square circle is indicated in its nature, namely, because it would involve a contradiction. On the other hand, the existence of substance follows also solely from its nature, inasmuch as its nature involves existence. (See Prop. vii.)

But the reason for the existence of a triangle or a circle does not follow from the nature of those figures, but from the order of universal nature in extension. From the latter it must follow, either that a triangle necessarily exists, or that it is impossible that it should exist. So much is self-evident. It follows therefrom that a thing necessarily exists, if no cause or reason be granted which prevents its existence.

If, then, no cause or reason can be given, which prevents the existence of God, or which destroys his existence, we must certainly conclude that he necessarily does exist. If such a reason or cause should be given, it must either be drawn from the very nature of God, or be external to him—that is, drawn from another substance of another nature. For if it were of the same nature, God, by that very fact, would be admitted to exist. But substance of another nature could have nothing in common with God (by Prop. ii.), and therefore would be unable either to cause or to destroy his existence.

As, then, a reason or cause which would annul the divine existence cannot be drawn from anything external to the divine nature, such cause must, perforce, if God does not exist, be drawn from God's own nature, which would involve a contradiction. To make such an affirmation about a being absolutely infinite and supremely perfect, is absurd; therefore, neither in the nature of God, nor externally to his nature, can a cause or reason be assigned which would annul his existence. Therefore, God necessarily exists. Q.E.D.

Another proof.—The potentiality of non-existence is a negation of power, and contrariwise the potentiality of existence is a power, as is obvious. If, then, that which necessarily exists is nothing but finite beings, such finite beings are more powerful than a being absolutely infinite, which is obviously absurd; therefore, either nothing exists, or else a being absolutely infinite necessarily exists also. Now we exist either in ourselves, or in something else which necessarily exists (see Axiom i. and Prop. vii.). Therefore, a being absolutely infinite—in other words, God (Def. vi.)—necessarily exists. Q.E.D. . . .

Prop. XII. No attribute of substance can be conceived from which it would follow that substance can be divided. . . .

Prop. XIII. Substance absolutely infinite is indivisible. . . .

Prop. XIV. Besides God no substance can be granted or conceived.

Proof.—As God is a being absolutely infinite, of whom no attribute that expresses the essence of substance can be denied (by Def. vi.), and he necessarily exists (by Prop. xi.); if any substance besides God were granted it would have to be explained by some attribute of God, and thus two substances with the same attribute would exist, which (by Prop. v.) is absurd; therefore, besides God no substance can be granted, or consequently, be conceived. Q.E.D. . . .

Prop. XV. Whatsoever is, is in God, and without God nothing can be, or be conceived.

Proof.—Besides God, no substance is granted or can be conceived (by Prop. xiv.), that is (by Def. iii.) nothing which is in itself and is conceived through itself. But modes (by Def. v.) can neither be, nor be conceived without substance; wherefore they can only be in the divine nature, and can only through it be conceived. But substances and modes form the sum total of existence (by Ax. i.), therefore, without God nothing can be, or be conceived. Q.E.D.

Note.—Some assert that God, like a man, consists of body and mind, and is susceptible of passions. How far such persons have strayed from the truth is sufficiently evident from what has been said. But these I pass over. For all who have in anywise reflected on the divine nature deny that God has a body. Of this they find excellent proof in the fact that we understand by body a definite quantity, so long, so broad, so deep, bounded by a certain shape, and it is the height of absurdity to predicate such a thing of God, a being absolutely infinite. But meanwhile by the other reasons with which they try to prove their point, they show that they think corporeal or extended substance wholly apart from the divine nature, and say it was created by God. Wherefrom the divine nature can have been created, they are wholly ignorant; thus they clearly show, that they do not know the meaning of their own words. I myself have proved sufficiently clearly, at any rate in my own judgment (Coroll. Prop. vi., and Note 2, Prop. viii.), that no substance can be produced or created by anything other than itself. Further, I showed (in Prop. xiv.), that besides God no substance can be granted or conceived. Hence we drew the conclusion that extended substance is one of the infinite attributes of God. However, in order to explain more fully, I will refute the arguments of my adversaries, which all start from the following points:—

Extended substance, in so far as it is substance, consists, as they think, in parts, wherefore they deny that it can be infinite, or, consequently, that it can appertain to God. This they illustrate with many examples, of which I will take one or two. If extended substance, they say, is infinite, let it be conceived to be divided into two parts: each part will then be either finite or infinite. If the former, then infinite substance is composed of two finite parts, which is absurd. If the latter, then one infinite will be twice as large as another infinite, which is also absurd.

Further, if an infinite line be measured out in foot lengths, it will consist of an infinite number of such parts; it would equally consist of an infinite number of parts, if each part measured only an inch: therefore, one infinity would be twelve times as great as the other.

Lastly, if from a single point there be conceived to be drawn two diverging lines which at first are at a definite distance apart, but are produced to infinity, it is certain that the distance between the two lines will be continually increased, until at length it changes from definite to indefinable. As these absurdities follow, it is said, from considering quantity as infinite, the conclusion is drawn, that extended substance must necessarily be finite, and, consequently, cannot appertain to the nature of God.

The second argument is also drawn from God's supreme perfection. God, it is said, inasmuch as he is a supremely perfect being, cannot be passive; but extended substance, in so far as it is divisible, is passive. It follows, therefore, that extended substance does not appertain to the essence of God.

Such are the arguments I find on the subject in writers, who by them try to prove that extended substance is unworthy of the divine nature, and cannot possibly appertain thereto. However, I think an attentive reader will see that I have already answered their propositions; for all their arguments are founded on the hypothesis that extended substance is composed of parts, and such a hypothesis I have shown (Prop. xii., and Coroll. Prop. xiii.) to be absurd. Moreover, any one who reflects will see that all these absurdities (if absurdities they be, which I am not now discussing), from which it is sought to extract the conclusion that extended substance is finite, do not at all follow from the notion of an infinite quantity, but merely from the notion that an infinite quantity is measureable, and composed of finite parts; therefore, the only fair conclusion to be drawn is that infinite quantity is not measureable, and cannot be composed of finite parts. This is exactly what we have already proved (in Prop. xii.). Wherefore the weapon which they aimed at us has in reality recoiled upon themselves. If, from this absurdity of theirs, they persist in drawing the conclusion that extended substance must be finite, they will in good sooth be acting like a man who asserts that circles have the properties of squares, and, finding himself thereby landed in absurdities, proceeds to deny that circles have any centre, from which all lines drawn to the circumference are equal. For, taking extended substance, which can only be conceived as infinite, one, and indivisible (Props. viii., v., xii.) they assert, in order to prove that it is finite, that it is composed of finite parts, and that it can be multiplied and divided.

So, also, others, after asserting that a line is composed of points, can produce many arguments to prove that a line cannot be infinitely divided. Assuredly it is not less absurd to assert that extended substance is made up of bodies or parts, then it would be to assert that a solid is made up of surfaces, a surface of lines, and a line of points. This must be admitted by all who know clear reason to be infallible, and most of all by those who deny the possibility of a vacuum. For if extended substance could be so divided that its parts were really separate, why should not one part admit of being destroyed, the others remaining joined together as before? And why should all be so fitted into one another as to leave no vacuum? Surely in the case of things, which are really distinct one from the other, one can exist without the other, and can remain in its original condition. As then, there does not exist a vacuum in nature (of which anon), but all parts are bound to come together to prevent it, it follows from this also that the parts cannot be really distinguished, and that extended substance in so far as it is substance cannot be divided.

If any one asks me the further question, Why are we naturally so prone to divide quantity? I answer, that quantity is conceived by us in two ways; in the abstract and superficially, as we imagine it; or as substance, as we conceive it solely by the intellect. If, then, we regard quantity as it is represented in our imagination, which we often and more easily do, we shall find that it is finite, divisible, and compounded of parts; but if we regard it as it is represented in our intellect, and conceive it as substance, which it is very difficult to do, we shall then, as I have sufficiently proved, find that it is infinite, one, and indivisible. This will be plain enough to all, who make a distinction between the intellect and the imagination, especially if it be remembered, that matter is everywhere the same, that its parts are not distinguishable, except in so far as we conceive matter as diversely modified, whence its parts are distinguished, not really, but modally. For instance, water, in so far as it is water, we conceive to be divided, and its parts to be separated one from the other; but not in so far as it is extended substance; from this point of view it is neither separated nor divisible. Further, water, in so far as it is water, is produced and corrupted; but, in so far as it is substance, it is neither produced nor corrupted.

I think I have now answered the second argument; it is, in fact, founded on the same assumption as the first—namely, that matter, in so far as it is substance, is divisible, and composed of parts. Even if it were so, I do not know why it should be considered unworthy of the divine nature, inasmuch as besides God (by Prop. xiv.) no substance can be granted, wherefrom it could receive its modifications. All things, I repeat, are in God, and all things which come to pass, come to pass solely through the laws of the infinite nature of God, and follow (as I will shortly show) from the necessity of his essence. Wherefore it can in nowise be said, that God is passive in respect to anything other than himself, or that extended substance is unworthy of the Divine nature, even if it be supposed divisible, so long as it is granted to be infinite and eternal. But enough of this for the present.

Prop. XVI. From the necessity of the divine nature must follow an infinite number of things in infinite ways—that is, all things which can fall within the sphere of infinite intellect. . . .

Prop. XVII. God acts solely by the laws of his own nature, and is not constrained by any one. . . .

Corollary II.—It follows: . . . That God is the sole free cause. For God alone exists by the sole necessity of his nature (by Prop. xi. and Prop. xiv., Coroll. i.), and acts by the sole necessity of his nature, wherefore God is (by Def. vii.) the sole free cause. Q.E.D.

Note.—Others think that God is a free cause, because he can, as they think, bring it about, that those things which we have said follow from his nature—that is, which are in his power, should not come to pass, or should not be produced by him. But this is the same as if they said, that God could bring it about, that it should not follow from the nature of a triangle, that its three interior angles should not be equal to two right angles; or that from a given cause no effect should follow, which is absurd.

Moreover, I will show below, without the aid of this proposition, that neither intellect nor will appertain to God's nature. I know that there are many who think that they can show, that supreme intellect and free will do appertain to God's nature; for they say they know of nothing more perfect, which they can attribute to God, than that which is the highest perfection in ourselves. Further, although they conceive God as actually supremely intelligent, they yet do not believe, that he can bring into existence everything which he actually understands, for they think that they would thus destroy God's power. If, they contend, God had created everything which is in his intellect, he would not be able to create anything more, and this, they think, would clash with God's omnipotence; therefore, they prefer to assert that God is indifferent to all things, and that he creates nothing except that which he has decided, by some absolute exercise of will, to create. However, I think I have shown sufficiently clearly (by Prop. xvi.), that from God's supreme power, or infinite nature, an infinite number of things—that is, all things have necessarily flowed forth in an infinite number of ways, or always follow from the same necessity; in the same way as from the nature of a triangle it follows from eternity and for eternity, that its three interior angles are equal to two right angles. Wherefore the omnipotence of God has been displayed from all eternity, and will for all eternity remain in the same state of activity. This manner of treating the question attributes to God an omnipotence, in my opinion, far more perfect. For, otherwise, we are compelled to confess that God understands an infinite number of creatable things, which he will never be able to create, for, if he created all that he understands, he would, according to this showing, exhaust his omnipotence, and render himself imperfect. Wherefore, in order to establish that God is perfect, we should be reduced to establishing at the same time, that he cannot bring to pass everything over which his power extends; this seems to be an hypothesis most absurd, and most repugnant to God's omnipotence.

Further (to say a word here concerning the intellect and the will which we attribute to God), if intellect and will appertain to the eternal essence of God, we must take these words in some significations quite different from those they usually bear. For intellect and will, which should constitute the essence of God, would perforce be as far apart as the poles from the human intellect and will, in fact, would have nothing in common with them but the name; there would be about as much correspondence between the two as there is between the Dog, the heavenly constellation, and a dog, an animal that barks. This I will prove as follows: If intellect belongs to the divine nature, it cannot be in nature, as ours is generally thought to be, posterior to, or simultaneous with the things understood, inasmuch as God is prior to all things by reason of his causality (Prop. xvi. Coroll. i.). On the contrary, the truth and formal essence of things is as it is, because it exists by representation as such in the intellect of God. Wherefore the intellect of God, in so far as it is conceived to constitute God's essence, is, in reality, the cause of things, both of their essence and of their existence. This seems to have been recognized by those who have asserted, that God's intellect, God's will, and God's power, are one and the same. As, therefore, God's intellect is the sole cause of things, namely, both of their essence and existence, it must necessarily differ from them in respect to its essence, and in respect to its existence. For a cause differs from a thing it causes, precisely in the quality which the latter gains from the former.

For example, a man is the cause of another man's existence, but not of his essence (for the latter is an eternal truth), and, therefore, the two men may be entirely similar in essence, but must be different in existence; and hence if the existence of one of them cease, the existence of the other will not necessarily cease also; but if the essence of one could be destroyed, and be made false, the essence of the other would be destroyed also. Wherefore, a thing which is the cause both of the essence and of the existence of a given effect, must differ from such effect both in respect to its essence, and also in respect to its existence. Now the intellect of God is the cause of both the essence and the existence of our intellect; therefore the intellect of God in so far as it is conceived to constitute the divine essence, differs from our intellect both in respect to essence and in respect to existence, nor can it in anywise agree therewith save in name, as we said before. The reasoning would be identical, in the case of the will, as any one can easily see. . . .

Prop. XXI. All things which follow from the absolute nature of any attribute of God must always exist and be infinite, or, in other words, are eternal and infinite through the said attribute. . . .

Prop. XXIV. The essence of things produced by God does not involve existence. . . .

Prop. XXVI. A thing which is conditioned to act in a particular manner, has necessarily been thus conditioned by God; and that which has not been conditioned by God cannot condition itself to act. . . .

Prop. XXVIII. Every individual thing, or everything which is finite and has a conditioned existence, cannot exist or be conditioned to act, unless it be conditioned for existence and action by a cause other than itself, which also is finite, and has a conditioned existence; and likewise this cause cannot in its turn exist, or be conditioned to act, unless it be conditioned for existence and action by another cause, which also is finite, and has a conditioned existence, and so on to infinity.

Proof.—Whatsoever is conditioned to exist and act, has been thus conditioned by God (by Prop. xxvi. and Prop. xxiv., Coroll.)

But that which is finite and has a conditioned existence, cannot be produced by the absolute nature of any attribute of God; for whatsoever follows from the absolute nature of any attribute of God is infinite and eternal (by Prop. xxi). It must, therefore, follow from some attribute of God, in so far as the said attribute is considered as in some way modified; for substance and modes make up the sum total of existence (by Ax. i. and Def. iii., v.), while modes are merely modifications of the attributes of God. But from God, or from any of his attributes, in so far as the latter is modified by a modification infinite and eternal, a conditioned thing cannot follow. Wherefore it must follow from, or be conditioned for, existence and action by God or one of his attributes, in so far as the latter are modified by some modification which is finite and has a conditioned existence. This is our first point. Again, this cause or this modification (for the reason by which we established the first part of this proof) must in its turn be conditioned by another cause, which also is finite, and has a conditioned existence, and again, this last by another (for the same reason); and so on (for the same reason) to infinity. Q.E.D.

Note.—As certain things must be produced immediately by God, namely those things which necessarily follow from his absolute nature, through the means of these primary attributes, which, nevertheless, can neither exist nor be conceived without God, it follows:—1. That God is absolutely the proximate cause of those things immediately produced by him. I say absolutely, not after his kind, as is usually stated. For the effects of God cannot either exist or be conceived without a cause (Prop. xv. and Prop. xxiv., Coroll.). 2. That God cannot properly be styled the remote cause of individual things, except for the sake of distinguishing these from what he immediately produces, or rather from what follows from his absolute nature. For, by a remote cause, we understand a cause which is in no way conjoined to the effect. But all things which are, are in God, and so depend on God, that without him they can neither be nor be conceived.

Prop. XXIX. Nothing in the universe is contingent, but all things are conditioned to exist and operate in a particular manner by the necessity of the divine nature. . . .

Note.—Before going any further, I wish here to explain, what we should understand by nature viewed as active (*natura naturans*), and nature viewed as passive (*natura naturata*). I say to explain, or rather call attention to it, for I think that, from what has been said, it is sufficiently clear, that by nature viewed as active we should understand that which is in itself, and is conceived through itself, or those attributes of substance, which express eternal and infinite essence, in other words (Prop. xiv., Coroll. i., and Prop. xvii., Coroll. ii.) God, in so far as he is considered as a free cause.

By nature viewed as passive I understand all that which follows from the necessity of the nature of God, or of any of the attributes of God, that is, all the modes of the attributes of God, in so far as they are considered as things which are in God, and which without God cannot exist or be conceived. . . .

Prop. XXXII. Will cannot be called a free cause, but only a necessary cause.

Proof.—Will is only a particular mode of thinking, like intellect; therefore (by Prop. xxviii.) no volition can exist, nor be conditioned to act, unless it be conditioned by some cause other than itself, which cause is conditioned by a third cause, and so on to infinity. But if will be supposed infinite, it must also be conditioned to exist and act by God, not by virtue of his being substance absolutely infinite, but by virtue of his possessing an attribute which expresses the infinite and eternal essence of thought (by Prop. xxiii.). Thus, however it be conceived, whether as finite or infinite, it requires a cause by which it should be conditioned to exist and act. Thus (Def. vii.) it cannot be called a free cause, but only a necessary or constrained cause. Q.E.D.

Corollary. I. – Hence it follows, first, that God does not act according to freedom of the will.

Corollary. II. – It follows secondly, that will and intellect stand in the same relation to the nature of God as do motion, and rest, and absolutely all natural phenomena, which must be conditioned by God (Prop. xxix.) to exist and act in a particular manner. For will, like the rest, stands in need of a cause, by which it is conditioned to exist and act in a particular manner. And although, when will or intellect be granted, an infinite number of results may follow, yet God cannot on that account be said to act from freedom of the will, any more than the infinite number of results from motion and rest would justify us in saying that motion and rest act by free will. Wherefore will no more appertains to God than does anything else in nature, but stands in the same relation to him as motion, rest, and the like, which we have shown to follow from the necessity of the divine nature, and to be conditioned by it to exist and act in a particular manner. . . .

Appendix. – In the foregoing I have explained the nature and properties of God. I have shown that he necessarily exists, that he is one: that he is, and acts solely by the necessity of his own nature; that he is the free cause of all things, and how he is so; that all things are in God, and so depend on him, that without him they could neither exist nor be conceived; lastly, that all things are pre-determined by God, not through his free will or absolute fiat, but from the very nature of God or infinite power. I have further, where occasion offered, taken care to remove the prejudices, which might impede the comprehension of my demonstrations. Yet there still remain misconceptions not a few, which might and may prove very grave hindrances to the understanding of the concatenation of things, as I have explained it above. I have therefore thought it worth while to bring these misconceptions before the bar of reason.

All such opinions spring from the notion commonly entertained, that all things in nature act as men themselves act, namely, with an end in view. It is accepted as certain, that God himself directs all things to a definite goal (for it is said that God made all things for man, and man that he might worship him). I will, therefore, consider this opinion, asking first, why it obtains general credence, and why all men are naturally so prone to adopt it? Secondly, I will point out its falsity; and, lastly, I will show how it has given rise to prejudices about good and bad, right and wrong, praise and blame, order and confusion, beauty and ugliness, and the like. However, this is not the place to deduce these misconceptions from the nature of the human mind: it will be sufficient here, if I assume as a starting point, what ought to be universally admitted, namely, that all men are born ignorant of the causes of things, that all have the desire to seek for what is useful to them, and that they are conscious of such desire. Herefrom it follows first, that men think themselves free, inasmuch as they are conscious of their volitions and desires, and never even dream, in their ignorance, of the causes which have disposed them to wish and desire. Secondly, that men do all things for an end, namely, for that which is useful to them, and which they seek. Thus it comes to pass that they only look for a knowledge of the final causes of events, and when these are learned, they are content, as having no cause for further doubt. If they cannot learn such causes from external sources, they are compelled to turn to considering themselves, and reflecting what end would have induced them personally to bring about the given event, and thus they necessarily judge other natures by their own. Further, as they find in themselves and outside themselves many means which assist them not a little in their search for what is useful, for instance, eyes for seeing, teeth for chewing, herbs and animals for yielding food, the sun for giving light, the sea for breeding fish, etc., they come to look on the whole of nature as a means for obtaining such conveniences. Now as they are aware, that they found these conveniences and did not make them they think they have cause for believing, that some other being has made them for their use. As they look upon things as means, they cannot believe them to be self-created; but, judging from the means which they are accustomed to prepare for themselves, they are bound to believe in some ruler or rulers of the universe endowed with human freedom, who have arranged and adapted everything for human use. They are bound to estimate the nature of such rulers (having no information on the subject) in accordance with their own nature, and therefore they assert that the gods ordained everything for the use of man, in order to bind man to themselves and obtain from him the highest honors. Hence also it follows, that everyone thought out for himself, according to his abilities, a different way of worshipping God, so that God might love him more than his fellows, and direct the whole course of nature for the satisfaction of his blind cupidity and insatiable avarice. Thus the prejudice developed into superstition, and took deep root in the human mind; and for this reason everyone strove most zealously to understand and explain the final causes of things; but in their endeavor to show that nature does nothing in vain, *i.e.,* nothing which is useless to man, they only seem to have demonstrated that nature, the gods, and men are all mad together. Consider, I pray you, the result: among the many helps of nature they were bound to find some hindrances, such as storms, earthquakes, diseases, etc.: so they declared that such things happen, because the gods are angry at some wrong done them by men, or at some fault committed in their worship. Experience day by day protested and showed by infinite examples, that good and evil fortunes fall to the lot of pious and impious alike; still they would not abandon their inveterate prejudice, for it was more easy for them to class such contradictions among other unknown things of whose use they were ignorant, and thus to retain their actual and innate condition of ignorance, than to destroy the whole fabric of their reasoning and start afresh. They therefore laid down as an axiom, that God's judgments far transcend human understanding. Such a doctrine might well have sufficed to conceal the truth from the human race for all eternity, if mathematics had not furnished another standard of verity in considering solely the essence and properties of figures without regard to their final causes. There are other reasons (which I need not mention here) besides mathematics, which might have caused men's minds to be directed to these general prejudices, and have led them to the knowledge of the truth.

I have now sufficiently explained my first point. There is no need to show at length, that nature has no particular goal in view, and that final causes are mere human figments. This, I think, is already evident enough, both from the causes and foundations on which I have shown such prejudice to be based, and also from Prop. xvi., and the Corollary of Prop. xxxii., and, in fact, all those propositions in which I have shown, that everything in nature proceeds from a sort of necessity, and with the utmost perfection. However, I will add a few remarks, in order to overthrow this doctrine of a final cause utterly. That which is really a cause it considers as an effect, and *vice versa:* it makes that which is by nature first to be last, and that which is highest and most perfect to be most imperfect. Passing over the questions of cause and priority as self-evident, it is plain from Props. xxi., xxii., xxiii. that that effect, is most perfect which is produced immediately by God; the effect which requires for its production several intermediate causes is, in that respect, more imperfect. But if those things which were made immediately by God were made to enable him to attain his end, then the things which come after, for the sake of which the first were made, are necessarily the most excellent of all.

Further, this doctrine does away with the perfection of God: for, if God acts for an object, he necessarily desires something which he lacks. Certainly, theologians and metaphysicians draw a distinction between the object of want and the object of assimilation; still they confess that God made all things for the sake of himself, not for the sake of creation. They are unable to point to anything prior to creation, except God himself, as an object for which God should act, and are therefore driven to admit (as they clearly must), that God lacked those things for whose attainment he created means, and further that he desired them.

We must not omit to notice that the followers of this doctrine, anxious to display their talent in assigning final causes, have imported a new method of argument in proof of their theory—namely, a reduction, not to the impossible, but to ignorance; thus showing that they have no other method of exhibiting their doctrine. For example, if a stone falls from a roof on to some one's head and kills him, they will demonstrate by their new method, that the stone fell in order to kill the man; for, if it had not by God's will fallen with that object, how could so many circumstances (and there are often many concurrent circumstances) have all happened together by chance? Perhaps you will answer that the event is due to the facts that the wind was blowing, and the man was walking that way. "But why," they will insist, "was the wind blowing, and why was the man at that very time walking that way?" If you again answer, that the wind had then sprung up because the sea had begun to be agitated the day before, the weather being previously calm, and that the man had been invited by a friend, they will again insist: "But why was the sea agitated, and why was the man invited at that time?" So they will pursue their questions from cause to cause, till at last you take refuge in the will of God—in other words, the sanctuary of ignorance. So, again, when they survey the frame of the human body, they are amazed; and being ignorant of the causes of so great a work of art conclude that it has been fashioned, not mechanically, but by divine and supernatural skill, and has been so put together that one part shall not hurt another.

Hence any one who seeks for the true causes of miracles, and strives to understand natural phenomena as an intelligent being, and not to gaze at them like a fool, is set down and denounced as an impious heretic by those, whom the masses adore as the interpreters of nature and the gods. Such persons know that, with the removal of ignorance, the wonder which forms their only available means for proving and preserving their authority would vanish also. But I now quit this subject, and pass on to my third point.

After men persuaded themselves, that everything which is created is created for their sake, they were bound to consider as the chief quality in everything that which is most useful to themselves, and to account those things the best of all which have the most beneficial effect on mankind. Further, they were bound to form abstract notions for the explanation of the nature of things, such as *goodness, badness, order, confusion, warmth, cold, beauty, deformity,* and so on; and from the belief that they are free agents arose the further notions *praise* and *blame, sin* and *merit.*

I will speak of these latter hereafter, when I treat of human nature; the former I will briefly explain here.

Everything which conduces to health and the worship of God they have called *good,* everything which hinders these objects they have styled *bad;* and inasmuch as those who do not understand the nature of things do not verify phenomena in any way, but merely imagine them after a fashion, and mistake their imagination for understanding, such persons firmly believe that there is an *order* in things, being really ignorant both of things and their own nature. When phenomena are of such a kind, that the impression they make on our senses requires little effort of imagination, and can consequently be easily remembered, we say that they are *well-ordered;* if the contrary, that they are *ill-ordered* or *confused.* Further, as things which are easily imagined are more pleasing to us, men prefer order to confusion— as though there were any order in nature, except in relation to our imagination— and say that God has created all things in order; thus, without knowing it, at-tributing imagination to God, unless, indeed, they would have it that God foresaw human imagination, and arranged everything, so that it should be most easily imagined. If this be their theory they would not, perhaps, be daunted by the fact that we find an infinite number of phenomena, far surpassing our imagination, and very many others which confound its weakness. But enough has been said on this subject. The other abstract notions are nothing but modes of imagining, in which the imagination is differently affected, though they are considered by the ignorant as the chief attributes of things, inasmuch as they believe that everything was created for the sake of themselves; and, according as they are affected by it, style it good or bad, healthy or rotten and corrupt. For instance, if the motion [by] which objects . . . [are communicated] to our nerves be conducive to health, the objects causing it are styled *beautiful*; if a contrary motion be excited, they are styled *ugly*.

Things which are perceived through our sense of smell are styled fragrant or fetid; if through our taste, sweet or bitter, full-flavored or insipid, if through our touch, hard or soft, rough or smooth, etc.

Whatsoever affects our ears is said to give rise to noise, sound, or harmony. In this last case, there are men lunatic enough to believe that even God himself takes pleasure in harmony; and philosophers are not lacking who have persuaded themselves, that the motion of the heavenly bodies gives rise to harmony—all of which instances sufficiently show that everyone judges of things according to the state of his brain, or rather mistakes for things the forms of his imagination. We need no longer wonder that there have arisen all the controversies we have witnessed and finally scepticism: for, although human bodies in many respects agree, yet in very many others they differ; so that what seems good to one seems bad to another; what seems well ordered to one seems confused to another; what is pleasing to one displeases another, and so on. I need not further enumerate, because this is not the place to treat the subject at length, and also because the fact is sufficiently well known. It is commonly said: "So many men, so many minds; everyone is wise in his own way; brains differ as completely as palates." All of which proverbs show, that men judge of things according to their mental disposition, and rather imagine than understand: for, if they understood phenomena, they would, as mathematics attest, be convinced, if not attracted, by what I have urged.

We have now perceived, that all the explanations commonly given of nature are mere modes of imagining, and do not indicate the true nature of anything, but only the constitution of the imagination; and, although they have names, as though they were entities, existing externally to the imagination, I call them entities imaginary rather than real; and, therefore, all arguments against us drawn from such abstractions are easily rebutted.

Many argue in this way. If all things follow from a necessity of the absolutely perfect nature of God, why are there so many imperfections in nature? Such, for instance, as things corrupt to the point of putridity, loathsome deformity, confusion, evil, sin, etc. But these reasoners are, as I have said, easily confuted, for the perfection of things is to be reckoned only from their own nature and power; things are not more or less perfect, according as they delight or offend human senses, or according as they are serviceable or repugnant to mankind. To those who ask why God did not so create all men, that they should be governed only by reason, I give no answer but this: because matter was not lacking to him for the creation of every degree of perfection from highest to lowest; or, more strictly, because the laws of his nature are so vast, as to suffice for the production of everything conceivable by an infinite intelligence, as I have shown in Prop. xvi.

Such are the misconceptions I have undertaken to note; if there are any more of the same sort, everyone may easily dissipate them for himself with the aid of a little reflection.

Part IV. Of Human Bondage, or the Strength of the Emotions

Preface

Human infirmity in moderating and checking the emotions I name bondage; for, when a man is a prey to his emotions, he is not his own master, but lies at the mercy of fortune: so much so, that he is often compelled, while seeing that which is better for him, to follow that which is worse. Why this is so, and what is good or evil in the emotions, I propose to show in this part of my treatise. But, before I begin, it would be well to make a few prefatory observations on perfection and imperfection, good and evil.

When a man has purposed to make a given thing, and has brought it to perfection, his work will be pronounced perfect, not only by himself, but by everyone who rightly knows, or thinks that he knows, the intention and aim of its author. For instance, suppose anyone sees a work (which I assume to be not yet completed) and knows that the aim of the author of that work is to build a house, he will call the work imperfect; he will, on the other hand, call it perfect, as soon as he sees that it is carried through to the end, which its author had purposed for it. But if a man sees a work, the like whereof he has never seen before, and if he knows not the intention of the artificer, he plainly cannot know, whether that work be perfect or imperfect. Such seems to be the primary meaning of these terms.

But, after men began to form general ideas, to think out types of houses, buildings, towers, etc., and to prefer certain types to others, it came about, that each man called perfect that which he saw agree with the general idea he had formed of the thing in question, and called imperfect that which he saw agree less with his own preconceived type, even though it had evidently been completed in accordance with the idea of its artificer. This seems to be the only reason for calling natural phenomena, which, indeed, are not made with human hands, perfect or imperfect: for men are wont to form general ideas of things natural, no less than of things artificial, and such ideas they hold as types, believing that Nature (who they think does nothing without an object) has them in view, and has set them as types before herself. Therefore, when they behold something in Nature, which does not wholly conform to the preconceived type which they have formed of the thing in question, they say that Nature has fallen short or has blundered, and has left her work incomplete. Thus we see that men are wont to style natural phenomena perfect or imperfect rather from their own prejudices, than from true knowledge of what they pronounce upon.

Now we showed in the Appendix to Part I., that nature does not work with an end in view. For the eternal and infinite being, which we call God or nature, acts by the same necessity as that whereby it exists. For we have shown that by the same necessity of its nature, whereby it exists, it likewise works (I. xvi.). The reason or cause why God or nature exists, and the reason why he acts, are one and the same. Therefore, as he does not exist for the sake of an end, so neither does he act for the sake of an end; of his existence and of his action there is neither origin nor end. Wherefore, a cause which is called final is nothing else but human desire, in so far as it is considered as the origin or cause of anything. For example, when we say that to be inhabited is the final cause of this or that house, we mean nothing more than that a man, conceiving the convenience of household life, had a desire to build a house. Wherefore, the being inhabited, in so far as it is regarded as a final cause, is nothing else but this particular desire, which is really the efficient cause; it is regarded as the primary cause, because men are generally ignorant of the causes of their desires. They are, as I have often said already, conscious of their own actions and appetites, but ignorant of the causes whereby they are determined to any particular desire. Therefore, the common saying that nature sometimes falls short, or blunders, and produces things which are imperfect, I set down among the glosses treated of in the Appendix to Part I. Perfection and imperfection, then, are in reality merely modes of thinking, or notions which we form from a comparison among one another of individuals of the same species; hence I said above (II. Def. vi.), that by reality and perfection I mean the same thing. For we are wont to refer all the individual things in nature to one genus, which is called the highest genus, namely, to the category of being, whereto absolutely all individuals in nature belong. Thus, in so far as we refer the individuals in nature to this category, and comparing them one with another, find that some possess more of being or reality than others, we, to this extent, say that some are more perfect than others. Again, in so far as we attribute to them anything implying negation—as term, end, infirmity, etc.,—we, to this extent, call them imperfect, because they do not affect our mind so much as the things which we call perfect, not because they have any intrinsic deficiency, or because nature has blundered. For nothing lies within the scope of a thing's nature, save that which follows from the necessity of the nature of its efficient cause, and whatsoever follows from the necessity of the nature of its efficient cause necessarily comes to pass.

As for the terms *good* and *bad,* they indicate no positive quality in things regarded in themselves, but are merely modes of thinking, or notions which we form from the comparison of things one with another. Thus one and the same thing can be at the same time good, bad, and indifferent. For instance, music is good for him that is melancholy, bad for him that mourns; for him that is deaf, it is neither good nor bad.

Nevertheless, though this be so, the terms should still be retained. For, inasmuch as we desire to form an idea of man as a type of human nature which we may hold in view, it will be useful for us to retain the terms in question, in the sense I have indicated.

In what follows, then, I shall mean by "good" that which we certainly know to be a means of approaching more nearly to the type of human nature, which we have set before ourselves; by "bad," that which we certainly know to be a hindrance to us in approaching the said type. Again, we shall say that men are more perfect, or more imperfect, in proportion as they approach more or less nearly to the said type. For it must be specially remarked that, when I say that a man passes from a lesser to a greater perfection, or *vice versa,* I do not mean that he is changed from one essence or reality to another; for instance, a horse would be as completely destroyed by being changed into a man, as by being changed into an insect. What I mean is, that we conceive the thing's power of action, in so far as this is understood by its nature, to be increased or diminished. Lastly, by perfection in general I shall, as I have said, mean reality—in other words, each thing's essence, in so far as it exists, and operates in a particular manner, and without paying any regard to its duration. For no given thing can be said to be more perfect, because it has passed a longer time in existence. The duration of things cannot be determined by their essence, for the essence of things involves no fixed and definite period of existence;

but everything, whether it be more perfect or less perfect, will always be able to persist in existence with the same force wherewith it began to exist; wherefore, in this respect, all things are equal.

Definitions

I. By *good* I mean that which we certainly know to be useful to us.[3]

II. By *evil* I mean that which we certainly know to be a hindrance to us in the attainment of any good. . . .

[The Intellectual Love of God: Related Passages]

Part IV., Prop. XXVIII. The mind's highest good is the knowledge of God, and the mind's highest virtue is to know God.

Proof.—The mind is not capable of understanding anything higher than God, that is (I. Def. vi.), than a Being absolutely infinite, and without which (I. xv.) nothing can either be or be conceived; therefore (IV. xxvi. and xxvii.), the mind's highest utility or (IV. Def. i.) good is the knowledge of God. Again, the mind is active only in so far as it understands, and only to the same extent can it be said absolutely to act virtuously. The mind's absolute virtue is therefore to understand. Now, as we have already shown, the highest that the mind can understand is God; therefore the highest virtue of the mind is to understand or to know God. Q.E.D.

Part V. Prop. XXV. The highest endeavor of the mind, and the highest virtue is to understand things by the third kind of knowledge.[4]

Proof.—The third kind of knowledge proceeds from an adequate idea of certain attributes of God to an adequate knowledge of the essence of things (see its definition II. xl. note ii.); and, in proportion as we understand things more in this way, we better understand God (by the last Prop.); therefore (IV. xxviii.) the highest virtue of the mind, that is (IV. Def. viii.) the power, or nature, or (III. vii.) highest endeavor of the mind, is to understand things by the third kind of knowledge. Q.E.D.

Part V., Prop. XXVII. From this third kind of knowledge arises the highest possible mental acquiescence.

Proof.—The highest virtue of the mind is to know God (IV. xxviii.), or to understand things by the third kind of knowledge (V. xxv.), and this virtue is greater in proportion as the mind knows things more by the said kind of knowledge (V. xxiv.); consequently, he who knows things by this kind of knowledge passes to the summit of human perfection, and is therefore (Def. of the Emotions, ii.) affected by the highest pleasure, such pleasure being accompanied by the idea of

---

3. Cf. the following: ". . . in no case do we strive for, wish for, long for, or desire anything, because we deem it to be good, but on the other hand we deem a thing to be good, because we strive for it, wish for it, long for it, or desire it." Part III, Prop. IX, Note.–P.E.D.

4. The third kind of knowledge is *intuitive knowledge,* as compared with opinion or *imaginative knowledge* (the first kind), and *universal knowledge* or the possession of adequate ideas (the second kind). Cf. Part II., Prop. XL, Note II.–P.E.D.

himself and his own virtue: thus (Def. of the Emotions, xxv.), from this kind of knowledge arises the highest possible acquiescence. Q.E.D.

Part V., Prop. XXXII. Whatsoever we understand by the third kind of knowledge, we take delight in, and our delight is accompanied by the idea of God as cause. . . .

Corollary.—From the third kind of knowledge necessarily arises the intellectual love of God. From this kind of knowledge arises pleasure accompanied by the idea of God as cause, that is (Def. of the Emotions, vi.), the love of God; not in so far as we imagine him as present (V. xxix.), but in so far as we understand him to be eternal; this is what I call the intellectual love of God.

Part V., Prop. XXXVI. The intellectual love of the mind toward God is that very love of God whereby God loves himself, not in so far as he is infinite, but in so far as he can be explained through the essence of the human mind regarded under the form of eternity; in other words, the intellectual love of the mind toward God is part of the infinite love wherewith God loves himself. . . .

Corollary.—Hence it follows that God, in so far as he loves himself, loves man, and consequently, that the love of God toward men, and the intellectual love of the mind toward God are identical.

Note.—From what has been said we clearly understand, wherein our salvation, or blessedness, or freedom, consists: namely, in the constant and eternal love toward God, or in God's love toward men. This love or blessedness is, in the Bible, called Glory, and not undeservedly. For whether this love be referred to God or to the mind, it may rightly be called acquiescence of spirit, which (Def. of the Emotions, xxv. xxx.) is not really distinguished from glory. In so far as it is referred to God, it is (V. xxxv.) pleasure, if we may still use that term, accompanied by the idea of itself, and, in so far as it is referred to the mind, it is the same (V. xxvii.).

Again, since the essence of our mind consists solely in knowledge, whereof the beginning and the foundation is God (I. xv. and II. xlvii. note), it becomes clear to us, in what manner and way our mind, as to its essence and existence, follows from the divine nature and constantly depends on God. I have thought it worth while here to call attention to this, in order to show by this example how the knowledge of particular things, which I have called intuitive or of the third kind (II. xl. note ii.), is potent, and more powerful than the universal knowledge, which I have styled knowledge of the second kind. For, although in Part I. I showed in general terms, that all things (and consequently, also, the human mind) depend as to their essence and existence on God, yet that demonstration, though legitimate and placed beyond the chances of doubt, does not affect our mind so much, as when the same conclusion is derived from the actual essence of some particular thing, which we say depends on God.

Part V., Prop. XLII. Blessedness is not the reward of virtue, but virtue itself; neither do we rejoice therein, because we control our lusts, but contrariwise, because we rejoice therein, we are able to control our lusts. . . .

Note.—I have thus completed all I wished to set forth touching the mind's power over the emotions and the mind's freedom. Whence it appears, how potent is the wise man, and how much he surpasses the ignorant man, who is driven only by his lusts. For the ignorant man is not only distracted in various ways by external causes without ever gaining the true acquiescence of his spirit, but moveover lives, as it were unwitting of himself, and of God, and of things, and as soon as he ceases to suffer, ceases also to be.

Whereas the wise man, in so far as he is regarded as such, is scarcely at all disturbed in spirit, but, being conscious of himself, and of God, and of things, by a certain eternal necessity, never ceases to be, but always possesses true acquiescence of his spirit.

If the way which I have pointed out as leading to this result seems exceedingly hard, it may nevertheless be discovered. Needs must it be hard, since it is so seldom found. How would it be possible, if salvation were ready to our hand, and could without great labour be found, that it should be by almost all men neglected? But all things excellent are as difficult as they are rare.

LEIBNIZ

*Refutation of Spinoza**

The author [Wachter][5] passes on (ch. 4) to Spinoza, whom he compares with the cabalists. Spinoza (Eth., pt. 2, prop. 10, schol.) says: "Every one must admit that nothing is or can be conceived without God. For it is acknowledged by everyone that God is the sole cause of all things, of their essence as well as of their existence; that is, God is the cause of things, not only in respect to their being made (*secundum fieri*), but also in respect to their being (*secundum esse*)." This, from Spinoza, the author [Wachter] appears to approve. And it is true that we must speak of created things only as permitted by the nature of God. But I do not think that Spinoza has succeeded in this. Essences can in a certain way be conceived of without God, but existences involve God. And the very reality of essences by which they exert an influence upon existences is from God. The essences of things are co-eternal with God. And the very essence of God embraces all other essences to such a degree that God cannot be perfectly conceived without them. But existence cannot be conceived of without God, who is the final reason of things.

This axiom, "To the essence of a thing belongs that without which it can

---

*Excerpts are reprinted by permission of Charles Scribner's Sons from *Leibniz Selections*, edited by Philip P. Wiener. Copyright 1951 Charles Scribner's Sons.

5. Johann George Wachter, whose book on "recondite Hebrew philosophy," as Leibniz himself describes it, is here the subject of Leibniz's criticisms.

neither be nor be conceived," is to be applied in necessary things or in species, but not in individual or contingent things. For individuals cannot be distinctly conceived. Hence they have no necessary connection with God, but are produced freely. God has been inclined toward these by a determining reason, but he has not been necessitated. . . .

Spinoza believed that matter, as commonly understood, did not exist. Hence he often warns us that matter is badly defined by Descartes as extension (Ep. 73), and extension is poorly explained as a very low thing which must be divisible in space, "since (de Emend. Intel., p. 385) matter ought to be explained as an attribute expressing an eternal and infinite essence." I reply that extension, or if you prefer, primary matter, is nothing but a certain indefinite repetition of things as far as they are similar to each other or indiscernible. But just as number supposes numbered things, so extension supposes things which are repeated, and which have, in addition to common characteristics, others peculiar to themselves. These accidents, peculiar to each other, render the limits of size and shape, before only possible, actual. Merely passive matter is something very low, that is, wanting in all force, but such a thing consists only in the incomplete or in abstraction.

Spinoza (Eth., pt. 1, prop. 13, corol. and prop. 15, schol.) says: "No substance, not even corporeal substance, is divisible." This statement is not surprising according to his system, since he admits but one substance; but it is equally true in mine, although I admit innumerable substances, for, in my system, all are indivisible or *monads*. . . .

What Spinoza (Eth., pt. 1, prop. 34) says, that "God is, by the same necessity, the cause of himself and the cause of all things," and (Polit. Tract., p. 270, c. 2, no. 2) that "the power of things is the power of God," I do not admit. God exists necessarily, but he produces things freely, and the power of things is produced by God but is different from the divine power, and things themselves operate, although they have received their power to act.

Spinoza (Ep. 21) says: "That everything is in God and moves in God, I assert with Paul and perhaps with all other philosophers, although in a different manner. I would even dare to say that this was the opinion of all the ancient Hebrews, so far as it can be conjectured from certain traditions, although these are in many ways corrupted." I think that everything is in God, not as the part in the whole, nor as an accident in a subject, but as place, yet a place spiritual and enduring and not one measured or divided, is in that which is placed, namely, just as God is immense or everywhere; the world is present to him. And it is thus that all things are in him; for he is where they are and where they are not, and he remains when they pass away and he has already been there when they come into existence.

The author [Wachter] says that it is the concordant opinion of the cabalists that God produced certain things mediately and others immediately. Whence he next speaks of a certain created first principle which God made to proceed immediately from himself, and by the mediation of which all other things have been produced in series and in order, and this they are wont to salute by various names: Adam, Cadmon, Messiah, the Christ, Logos, the word, the first-born, the first man, the celestial man, the guide, the shepherd, the mediator, etc. Elsewhere he gives a reason for this assertion, The fact itself is recognized by Spinoza, so that nothing is wanting except the name. "It follows," he says (Eth., pt. 1, prop. 28, schol.), "in

169

the second place, that God cannot properly be called the remote cause of individual things, except to distinguish these from those which God produces immediately or rather which follow from his absolute nature." Moreover what those things are which are said to follow from the absolute nature of God, he explained (prop. 21) thus: "All things which follow from the absolute nature of any attribute of God must exist always and be infinite or are eternal and infinite through the same attribute."—These propositions of Spinoza, which the author cites, are wholly without foundation. God produces no infinite creature, nor could it be shown or pointed out by any argument in what respect such a creature would differ from God.

The theory of Spinoza, namely, that from each attribute there springs a particular infinite thing, from extension a certain something infinite in extension, from thought a certain infinite understanding, arises from his varied imagination of certain heterogeneous divine attributes, like thought and extension, and perhaps innumerable others. For in reality extension is not an attribute of itself since it is only the repetition of perceptions. An infinitely extended thing is only imaginary: an infinite thinking being is God himself. The things which are necessary and which proceed from the infinite nature of God, are the eternal truths. A particular creature is produced by another, and this again by another. Thus, therefore, by no conception could we reach God even if we should suppose a progress *ad infinitum,* and notwithstanding, the last no less than the one which precedes is dependent upon God. . . .

Spinoza (Eth., pt. 1, prop. 16) says: "From the necessity of the divine nature must follow an infinite number of things in infinite modes, that is to say, all things which can fall under infinite intellect." This is a most false opinion, and this error is the same as that which Descartes insinuated, viz., that matter successively assumes all forms. Spinoza begins where Descartes ended, *in Naturalism.* He is wrong also in saying (Ep. 58) that "the world is the effect of the divine nature," although he almost adds that it was not made by chance. There is a mean between what is necessary and what is fortuitous, namely, what is free. The world is a voluntary effect of God, but on account of inclining or prevailing reasons. And even if the world should be supposed perpetual nevertheless it would not be necessary. God could either not have created it or have created it otherwise, but he was not to do it. Spinoza thinks (Ep. 49) that "God produces the world by that necessity by which he knows himself." But it must be replied that things are possible in many ways, whereas it was altogether impossible that God should not know himself.— Spinoza says (Eth., pt. 1, prop. 17, schol.): "I know that there are many who believe that they can prove that sovereign intelligence and free will belong to the nature of God; for they say they know nothing more perfect to attribute to God than that which is the highest perfection in us. . . . Therefore, they prefer to assert that God is indifferent to all things, and that he creates nothing except what he has decided, by some absolute will, to create. But I think I have shown (prop. 16) sufficiently clearly that all things follow from the sovereign power of God by the same necessity; in the same way as it follows from the nature of a triangle that its three angles are equal to two right angles."—From the first words it is evident that Spinoza does not attribute to God intellect and will. He is right in denying that God is indifferent and that he decrees anything by absolute will: he decrees by a will which is based on reasons. That things proceed from God as the properties of a triangle proceed from its nature is proved by no argument, besides there is no analogy between essences and existing things.

In the scholium of Proposition 17, Spinoza says that "the intellect and the will of God agree with ours only in name, because ours are posterior and God's are prior to things"; but it does not follow from this, that they agree only in name. Elsewhere, nevertheless, he says that "thought is an attribute of God, and that particular modes of thought must be referred to it" (Eth., pt. 2, prop. 1). . . .

Further, Spinoza says (Tract. Polit., c. 2, no. 6), "Men conceive themselves in nature as an empire within an empire (Malcuth in Malcuth, adds the author). For they think that the human mind is not the product of natural causes, but that it is immediately created by God so independent of other things that it has absolute power of determining itself and of using rightly its reason. But experience proves to us over-abundantly that it is no more in our power to have a sound mind than to have a sound body." So Spinoza. In my opinion, each substance is an empire within an empire; but harmonizing exactly with all the rest it receives no influence from any being except it be from God, but, nevertheless, through God, its author, it depends upon all the others. It comes immediately from God and yet it is created in conformity to the other things. For the rest, not all things are equally in our power. For we are inclined more to this or to that. Malcuth, or the realm of God, does not suppress either divine or human liberty, but only the indifference of equilibrium, as they say who think there are no reasons for those actions which they do not understand.

Spinoza thinks that the mind is greatly strengthened if it knows that what happens happens necessarily: but by this compulsion he does not render the heart of the sufferer content nor cause him to feel his malady the less. He is, on the contrary, happy if he understands that good results from evil and that those things which happen are the best for us if we are wise.

From what precedes it is seen that what Spinoza says on the intellectual love of God (Eth., pt. 4, prop. 28) is only trappings for the people, since there is nothing loveable in a God who produces without choice and by necessity, without discrimination of good and evil. The true love of God is founded not in necessity but in goodness. Spinoza (de Emend. Intel., p. 388) says that "there is no science, but that we have only experience of particular things, that is, of things such that their existence has no connection with their essence, and which, consequently, are not eternal truths."—This contradicts what he said elsewhere, viz.: that all things are necessary, that all things proceed necessarily from the divine essence. Likewise he combats (Eth., pt. 2, prop. 10, schol.) those who claim that the nature of God belongs to the essence of created things, and yet he had established before [Eth., pt. 1, prop. 15] that things do not exist and cannot be conceived without God, and that they necessarily arise from him. He maintains (Eth., pt. 1, prop. 21), for this reason, that finite and temporal things cannot be produced immediately by an infinite cause, but that (Prop. 28) they are produced by other causes, individual and finite. But how will they finally then spring from God? For they cannot come from him mediately in this case, since we could never reach in this way things which are not similarly produced by another finite thing. It cannot, therefore, be said that God acts by mediating secondary causes, unless he produces secondary causes. Therefore, it is rather to be said that God produces substances and not their actions, in which he only concurs.

LEIBNIZ

The Theodicy: Abridgement of the Argument Reduced to Syllogistic Form *

Some intelligent persons have desired that this supplement be made [to the Theodicy], and I have the more readily yielded to their wishes as in this way I have an opportunity again to remove certain difficulties and to make some observations which were not sufficiently emphasized in the work itself.

I. *Objection.* Whoever does not choose the best is lacking in power, or in knowledge, or in goodness.

God did not choose the best in creating this world.

Therefore, God has been lacking in power, or in knowledge, or in goodness.

Answer. I deny the minor, that is, the second premise of this syllogism; and our opponent proves it by this

Prosyllogism. Whoever makes things in which there is evil, which could have been made without any evil, or the making of which could have been omitted, does not choose the best.

God has made a world in which there is evil; a world, I say, which could have been made without any evil, or the making of which could have been omitted altogether.

Therefore, God has not chosen the best.

Answer. I grant the minor of this prosyllogism; for it must be confessed that there is evil in this world which God has made, and that it was possible to make a world without evil, or even not to create a world at all, for its creation has de-

*Reprinted by permission of Charles Scribner's Sons from *Leibniz Selections,* edited by Philip P. Wiener. Copyright 1951 Charles Scribner's Sons.

pended on the free will of God; but I deny the major, that is, the first of the two premises of the prosyllogism, and I might content myself with simply demanding its proof; but in order to make the matter clearer, I have wished to justify this denial by showing that the best plan is not always that which seeks to avoid evil, since it may happen that *the evil is accompanied by a greater good.* For example, a general of an army will prefer a great victory with a slight wound to a condition without wound and without victory. We have proved this more fully in the large work by making it clear, by instances taken from mathematics and elsewhere, that an imperfection in the part may be required for a greater perfection in the whole. In this I have followed the opinion of St. Augustine, who has said a hundred times, that God has permitted evil in order to bring about good, that is, a greater good; and that of Thomas Aquinas (in libr. II. sent. Dist. 32, qu. I, art. 1), that the permitting of evil tends to the good of the universe. I have shown that the ancients called Adam's fall *felix culpa,* a happy sin, because it had been retrieved with immense advantage by the incarnation of the Son of God, who has given to the universe something nobler than anything that ever would have been among creatures except for it. For the sake of a clearer understanding, I have added, following many good authors, that it was in accordance with order and the general good that God allowed to certain creatures the opportunity of exercising their liberty, even when he foresaw that they would turn to evil, but which he could so well rectify; because it was not fitting that, in order to hinder sin, God should always act in an extraordinary manner. To overthrow this objection, therefore, it is sufficient to show that a world with evil might be better than a world without evil; but I have gone ever farther, in the work, and have even proved that this universe must be in reality better than every other possible universe.

II. *Objection.* If there is more evil than good in intelligent creatures, then there is more evil than good in the whole work of God.

Now, there is more evil than good in intelligent creatures.

Therefore, there is more evil than good in the whole work of God.

Answer. I deny the major and the minor of this conditional syllogism. As to the major, I do not admit it at all, because this pretended deduction from a part to the whole, from intelligent creatures to all creatures, supposes tacitly and without proof that creatures destitute of reason cannot enter into comparison nor into account with those which possess it. But why may it not be that the surplus of good in the non-intelligent creatures which fill the world, compensates for, and even incomparably surpasses, the surplus of evil in the rational creatures? It is true that the value of the latter is greater; but, in compensation, the others are beyond comparison the more numerous, and it may be that the proportion of number and quantity surpasses that of value and of quality.

As to the minor, that is no more to be admitted; that is, it is not at all to be admitted that there is more evil than good in the intelligent creatures. There is no need even of granting that there is more evil than good in the human race, because it is possible, and in fact very probable, that the glory and the perfection of the blessed are incomparably greater than the misery and the imperfection of the damned, and that here the excellence of the total good in the smaller number exceeds the total evil in the greater number. The blessed approach the Divinity, by means of a Divine Mediator, as near as may suit these creatures, and make such progress in good as is impossible for the damned to make in evil, approach as nearly as they may to the nature of demons. God is infinite, and the devil is limited; the good may and does go to infinity, while evil has its bounds. It is therefore possible, and is credible, that in the comparison of the blessed and the damned, the contrary of that which I have said might happen in the comparison of intelligent and non-intelligent creatures, takes place; namely, it is possible that in the comparison of the happy and the unhappy, the proportion of degree exceeds that of number, and that in the comparison of intelligent and non-intelligent creatures, the proportion of number is greater than that of value. I have the right to suppose that a thing is possible so long as its impossibility is not proved; and indeed that which I have here advanced is more than a supposition.

But in the second place, if I should admit that there is more evil than good in the human race, I have still good grounds for not admitting that there is more evil than good in all intelligent creatures. For there is an inconceivable number of genii, and perhaps of other rational creatures. And an opponent could not prove that in all the City of God, composed as well of genii as of rational animals without number and of an infinity of kinds, evil exceeds good. And although in order to answer an objection, there is no need of proving that a thing is, when its mere possibility suffices; yet, in this work, I have not omitted to show that it is a consequence of the supreme perfection of the Sovereign of the universe, that the kingdom of God is the most perfect of all possible states or governments, and that consequently the little evil there is, is required for the consummation of the immense good which is found there.

III. *Objection.* If it is always impossible not to sin, it is always unjust to punish.

Now, it is always impossible not to sin; or, in other words, every sin is necessary.

Therefore, it is always unjust to punish.

The minor of this is proved thus:

1. *Prosyllogism.* All that is predetermined is necessary.

Every event is predetermined.

Therefore, every event (and consequently sin also) is necessary.

Again this second minor is proved thus:

2. *Prosyllogism.* That which is future, that which is foreseen, that which is involved in the causes, is predetermined.

Every event is such.

Therefore, every event is predetermined.

Answer. I admit in a certain sense the conclusion of the second prosyllogism, which is the minor of the first; but I shall deny the major of the first prosyllogism, namely, that every thing predetermined is necessary; understanding by the *necessity* of sinning, for example, or by the impossibility of not sinning, or of not performing any action, the necessity with which we are here concerned, that is, that which is essential and absolute, and which destroys the morality of an action and the justice of punishments. For if anyone understood another necessity or impossibility, namely, a necessity which should be only moral, or which was only hypothetical (as will be explained shortly); it is clear that I should deny the major of the objection itself. I might content myself with this answer and demand the proof of the proposition denied; but I have again desired to explain my procedure in this work, in order to better elucidate the matter and to throw more light on the whole subject, by explaining the necessity which ought to be rejected and the determination which must take place. That *necessity* which is contrary to morality, and which ought to be rejected, and which would render punishment unjust, is an insurmountable necessity which would make all opposition useless, even if we should wish with all our heart to avoid the necessary action, and should make all possible efforts to that end. Now, it is manifest that this is not applicable to voluntary actions, because we would not perform them if we did not choose to. Also their prevision and predetermination are not absolute, but presuppose the will: if it is certain that we shall perform them, it is not less certain that we shall choose to perform them. These voluntary actions and their consequences will not take place no matter what we do or whether we wish them or not; but, *through* that which we shall do and through that which we shall wish to do, which leads to them. And this is involved in prevision and in predetermination, and even constitutes their ground. And the necessity of such an event is called conditional or hypothetical, or the necessity of consequence, because it supposed the will, and the other *requisites;* whereas the necessity which destroys morality and renders punishment unjust and reward useless, exists in things which will be whatever we may do or whatever we may wish to do, and, in a word, is in that which is essential; and this is what is called an absolute necessity. Thus it is to no purpose, as regards what is absolutely necessary, to make prohibitions or commands, to propose penalties or prizes, to praise or to blame; it will be none the less. On the other hand, in voluntary actions and in that which depends upon them, precepts armed with power to punish and to recompense are very often of use and are included in the order of causes which make an action exist. And it is for this reason that not only cares and labors but also prayers are useful; God having had these prayers in view before he regulated things and having had that consideration for them which was proper. This is why the precept which says *ora et labora* (pray and work), holds altogether good; and not only those who (under the vain pretext of the necessity of events) pretend that the care which business demands may be neglected, but also those who reason against prayer, fall into what the ancients even then called the *lazy sophism.* Thus the predetermination of events by causes is just what contributes to morality instead of destroying it, and causes incline the will, without compelling it. This is why the *determination* in question is not a necessitation—it is certain (to him who knows all) that the effect will follow this inclination; but this effect does not follow by a necessary consequence, that is, one the contrary of which implies contradiction. It is also by an internal inclination such as this that the will is determined, without there being any necessity. Suppose that one had the greatest passion in the world (a great thirst, for example), you will admit to me that the soul can find some reason for resisting it, if it were only that of showing its power. Thus, although one may never be in a perfect indifference of equilibrium and there may be always a preponderance of inclination for the side taken, it, nevertheless, never renders the resolution taken absolutely necessary.

IV. *Objection.* Whoever can prevent the sin of another and does not do so, but rather contributes to it although he is well informed of it, is accessory to it.

God can prevent the sin of intelligent creatures; but he does not do so, and rather contributes to it by his concurrence and by the opportunities which he brings about, although he has a perfect knowledge of it.

Hence, etc.

Answer. I deny the major of this syllogism. For it is possible that one could prevent sin, but ought not, because he could not do it without himself committing a sin, or (when God is in question) without performing an unreasonable action. Examples have been given and the application to God himself has been made. It is possible also that we contribute to evil and that sometimes we even open the road to it, in doing things which we are obliged to do; and, when we do our duty or (in speaking of God) when, after thorough consideration, we do that which reason demands, we are not responsible for the results, even when we foresee them. We do not desire these evils; but we are willing to permit them for the sake of a greater good which we cannot reasonably help preferring to other considerations. And this is a *consequent* will, which results from *antecedent* wills by which we will the good. I know that some persons, in speaking of the antecedent and consequent will of God, have understood by the *antecedent* that which wills that all men should be saved; and by the *consequent,* that which wills, in consequence of persistent sin, that some should be damned. But these are merely illustrations of a more general idea, and it may be said for the same reason that God, by his antecedent will, wills that men should not sin; and by his consequent or final and decreeing will (that which is always followed by its effect), he wills to permit them to sin, this permission being the result of superior reasons. And we have the right to say in general that the antecedent will of God tends to the production of good and the prevention of evil, each taken in itself and as if alone (*particulariter et secundum quid,* Thom. I, qu. 19, art. 6), according to the measure of the degree of each good and of each evil; but that the divine consequent or final or total will tends toward the production of as many goods as may be put together, the combination of which becomes in this way determined, and includes also the permission of some evils and the exclusion of some goods, as the best possible plan for the universe demands. Arminius, in his *Anti-perkinsus,* has very well explained that the will of God may be called consequent, not only in relation to the action of the creature considered beforehand in the divine understanding, but also in relation to other anterior divine acts of will. But this consideration of the passage cited from Thomas Aquinas, and that from Scotus (I. dist. 46, qu. XI), is enough to show that they make this distinction as I have done here. Nevertheless, if anyone objects to this use of terms let him substitute *deliberating* will, in place of antecedent, and *final* or decreeing will, in place of consequent. For I do not wish to dispute over words.

V. *Objection.* Whoever produces all that is real in a thing, is its cause. God produces all that is real in sin.

Hence, God is the cause of sin.

Answer. I might content myself with denying the major or the minor, since the term *real* admits of interpretations which would render these propositions false. But in order to explain more clearly, I will make a distinction. *Real* signifies either that which is positive only, or, it includes also privative beings: in the first case, I deny the major and admit the minor; in the second case, I do the contrary. I might have limited myself to this, but I have chosen to proceed still farther and give the reason for this distinction. I have been very glad therefore to draw attention to the fact that every reality purely positive or absolute is a perfection; and that imperfection comes from limitation, that is, from the privative: for to limit is to refuse progress, or the greatest possible progress. Now God is the cause of all perfections and consequently of all realities considered as purely positive. But limitations or privations result from the original imperfection of creatures, which limits their receptivity. And it is with them as with a loaded vessel, which the river causes to move more or less slowly according to the weight which it carries: thus its speed depends upon the river, but the retardation which limits this speed comes from the load. Thus in the *Theodicy,* we have shown how the creature, in causing sin, is a defective cause; how errors and evil inclinations are born of privation; and how privation is accidentally efficient; and I have justified the opinion of St. Augustine (lib. I. ad Simpl. qu. 2) who explains, for example, how God makes the soul obdurate, not by giving it something evil, but because the effect of his good impression is limited by the soul's resistance and by the circumstances which contribute to this resistance, so that he does not give it all the good which would overcome its evil. *Nec* (inquit) *ab illo erogatur aliquid quo homo fit deterior, sed tantum quo fit melior non erogatur.* But if God had wished to do more, he would have had to make either other natures for creatures or other miracles to change their natures, things which the best plan could not admit. It is as if the current of the river must be more rapid than its fall admitted or that the boats should be loaded more lightly, if it were necessary to make them move more quickly. And the original limitation or imperfection of creatures requires that even the best plan of the universe could not receive more good, and could not be exempt from certain evils, which, however, are to result in a greater good. There are certain disorders in the parts which marvellously enhance the beauty of the whole; just as certain dissonances, when properly used, render harmony more beautiful. But this depends on what has already been said in answer to the first objection.

VI. *Objection.* Whoever punishes those who have done as well as it was in their power to do, is unjust.

God does so.

Hence, etc.

Answer. I deny the minor of this argument. And I believe that God always gives sufficient aid and grace to those who have a good will, that is, to those who do not reject this grace by new sin. Thus I do not admit the damnation of infants who have died without baptism or outside of the church; nor the damnation of adults who have acted according to the light which God has given them. And I believe that if *any one has followed the light which has been given him,* he will undoubtedly receive greater light when he has need of it, as the late M. Hulseman, a profound and celebrated theologian at Leipsig, has somewhere remarked; and if such a man has failed to receive it during his lifetime he will at least receive it when at the point of death.

VII. *Objection.* Whoever gives only to some, and not to all, the means which produces in them effectively a good will and salutary final faith, has not sufficient goodness.

God does this.

Hence, etc.

Answer. I deny the major of this. It is true that God could overcome the greatest resistance of the human heart; and does it, too, sometimes, either by internal grace, or by external circumstances which have a great effect on souls; but he does not always do this. Whence comes this distinction? it may be asked, and why does his goodness seem limited? It is because, as I have already said in answering the first objection, it would not have been in order always to act in an extraordinary manner, and to reverse the connection of things. The reasons of this connection, by means of which one is placed in more favorable circumstances than another, are hidden in the depths of the wisdom of God: they depend upon the universal harmony. The best plan of the universe, which God could not fail to choose, made it so. We judge from the event itself; since God has made it, it was not possible to do better. Far from being true that this conduct is contrary to goodness, it is supreme goodness which led him to it. This objection with its solution might have been drawn from what was said in regard to the first objection; but it seemed useful to touch upon it separately.

VIII. *Objection.* Whoever cannot fail to choose the best, is not free.

God cannot fail to choose the best.

Hence, God is not free.

Answer. I deny the major of this argument; it is rather true liberty, and the most perfect, to be able to use one's free will for the best, and to always exercise this power, without ever being turned aside either by external force or by internal passions, the first of which causes slavery of the body, the second, slavery of the soul. There is nothing less servile, and nothing more in accordance with the highest degree of freedom, than to be always led toward the good, and always by one's own inclination, without any constraint and without any displeasure. And to object therefore that God had need of external things, is only a sophism. He created them freely; but having proposed to himself an end, which is to exercise his goodness, wisdom has determined him to choose the means best fitted to attain this end. To call this a *need,* is to take that term in an unusual sense which frees it from all imperfection, just as when we speak of the wrath of God.

Seneca has somewhere said that God commanded but once but that he obeys always, because he obeys laws which he willed to prescribe to himself: *semel jussit, semper paret.* But he might better have said that God always commands and that he is always obeyed; for in willing, he always follows the inclination of his own nature, and all other things always follow his will. And as this will is always the same, it cannot be said that he obeys only that will which he formerly had. Nevertheless, although his will is always infallible and always tends toward the best, the evil, or the lesser good, which he rejects, does not cease to be possible in itself; otherwise the necessity of the good would be geometrical (so to speak), or metaphysical, and altogether absolute; the contingency of things would be destroyed, and there would be no choice. But this sort of necessity, which does not destroy the possibility of the contrary, has this name only by analogy; it becomes effective, not by the pure essence of things, but by that which is outside of them, above them, namely, by the will of God. This necessity is called moral, because, to the sage, *necessity* and *what ought to be* are equivalent things; and when it always has its effect, as it really has in the perfect sage, that is, in God, it may be said that is is a happy necessity. The nearer creatures approach to it, the nearer they approach to perfect happiness. Also this kind of necessity is not that which we try to avoid and which destroys morality, rewards and praise. For that which it brings, does not happen whatever we may do or will, but because we will it so. And a will to which it is natural to choose well, merits praise so much the more; also it carries its reward with it, which is sovereign happiness. And as this constitution of the divine nature gives entire satisfaction to him who possesses it, it is also the best and the most desirable for the creatures who are all dependent on God. If the will of God did not have for a rule the principle of the best, it would either tend toward evil, which would be the worst; or it would be in some way indifferent to good and to evil, and would be guided by chance: but a will which would allow itself always to act by chance, would not be worth more for the government of the universe than the fortuitous concourse of atoms, without there being any divinity therein. And even if God should abandon himself to chance only in some cases and in a certain way (as he would do, if he did not always work entirely for the best and if he were capable of preferring a lesser work to a greater, that is, an evil to a good, since that which prevents a greater good is an evil), he would be imperfect, as well as the object of his choice; he would not merit entire confidence; he would act without reason in such a case, and the government of the universe would be like certain games, equally divided between reason and chance. All this proves that this objection which is made against the choice of the best, perverts the notions of the free and of the necessary, and represents to us the best even as evil: which is either malicious or ridiculous.

LEIBNIZ

The Principles of Nature and of Grace, Based on Reason *

1. *Substance* is a being capable of action. It is simple or compound. *Simple substance* is that which has no parts. *Compound* substance is the collection of simple substances or *monads. Monas* is a Greek word which signifies unity, or that which is one.

    Compounds, or bodies, are multitudes; and simple substances, lives, souls, spirits are unities. And there must be simple substances everywhere, because without simple substances there would be no compounds; and consequently all nature is full of life.

    2. Monads, having no parts, cannot be formed or decomposed. They cannot begin or end naturally; and consequently last as long as the universe, which will be changed but will not be destroyed. They cannot have shapes; otherwise they would have parts. And consequently a monad, in itself and at a given moment, could not be distinguished from another except by its internal qualities and actions, which can be nothing else than its *perceptions* (that is, representations of the compound, or of what is external, in the simple), and its *appetitions* (that is, its tendencies to pass from one perception to another), which are the principles of change. For the simplicity of substance does not prevent multiplicity of modifications, which must be found together in this same simple substance, and must consist in the variety of relations to things which are external. Just as in a *centre* or point, entirely simple as it is, there is an infinity of angles formed by the lines which meet at the point.

    3. All nature is a *plenum.* There are everywhere simple substances, separated in effect from one another by activities of their own which continually change their relations; and each important simple substance, or monad, which forms the centre of a composite substance (as, for example, of an animal) and the principle of its unity, is surrounded by a *mass* composed of an infinity of other monads, which constitute the body proper of this central monad; and in accordance with the affections of its body the monad represents, as in a *centre,* the things which are outside of itself. And this *body* is *organic,* though it forms a sort of automaton or natural machine, which is a machine not only in its entirety, but also in its smallest perceptible parts. And as, because the world is a *plenum,* everything is connected and each body acts upon every other body, more or less, according to the distance, and by reaction is itself affected thereby, it follows that each monad is a living mirror, or endowed with internal activity, representative according to its point of view of the universe, and as regulated as the universe itself. And the perceptions in the monad spring one from the other, by the laws of desires [*appétits*] or of the *final causes of good and evil,* which consist in observable, regulated or unregulated,

perceptions; just as the changes of bodies and external phenomena spring one from another, by the laws of *efficient causes,* that is, of motions. Thus there is a perfect *harmony* between the perceptions of the monad and the motions of bodies, pre-established at the beginning between the system of efficient causes and that of final causes. And in this consists the accord and physical union of the soul and the body, although neither one can change the laws of the other.

4. Each monad, with a particular body, makes a living substance. Thus there is not only life everywhere, accompanied with members or organs, but there is also an infinity of degrees among monads, some dominating more or less over others. But when the monad has organs so adjusted that by their means prominence and distinctness appear in the impressions which they receive, and consequently in the perceptions which represent these (as, for example, when by means of the shape of the humors of the eyes, the rays of light are concentrated and act with more force), this may lead to *feeling [sentiment]*, that is, to a perception accompanied by *memory,* namely, by a certain reverberation lasting a long time, so as to make itself heard upon occasion. And such a living being is called an *animal,* as its monad is called a soul. And when this soul is elevated to *reason,* it is something more sublime and is reckoned among spirits, as will soon be explained. It is true that animals are sometimes in the condition of simple living beings, and their souls in the condition of simple monads, namely, when their perceptions are not sufficiently distinct to be remembered, as happens in a deep dreamless sleep, or in a swoon. But perceptions, which have become entirely confused must be re-developed in animals, for reasons which I shall shortly (§12) enumerate. Thus it is well to make distinction between the *perception,* which is the inner state of the monad representing external things, and *apperception,* which is *consciousness* or the reflective knowledge of this inner state; the latter not being given to all souls, nor at all times to the same soul. And it is for want of this distinction that the Cartesians have failed, taking no account of the perceptions of which we are not conscious as people take no account of imperceptible bodies. It is this also which made the same Cartesians believe that only spirits are monads, that there is no soul of brutes, and still less other *principles of life.* And as they shocked too much the common opinion of men by refusing feeling to brutes, they have, on the other hand, accommodated themselves too much to the prejudices of the multitude, by confounding a *long swoon,* caused by a great confusion of perceptions, with *death strictly speaking,* where all perception would cease. This has confirmed the ill-founded belief in the destruction of some souls, and the bad opinion of some so-called strong minds, who have contended against the immortality of our soul.

5. There is a connection in the perfections of animals which bears some resemblance to reason; but it is only founded in the memory of *facts* or effects, and not at all in the knowledge of *causes.* Thus a dog shuns the stick with which it has been beaten, because memory represents to it the pain which the stick had caused it. And men, in so far as they are empirics, that is to say, in three-fourths of their actions, act simply as the brutes do. For example, we expect that there will be daylight to-morrow because we have always had the experience; only an astronomer foresees it by reason, and even this prediction will finally fail when the cause of

day, which is not eternal, shall cease. But *true reasoning* depends upon necessary or eternal truths, such as those of logic, of numbers, of geometry, which establish an indubitable connection of ideas and unfailing inferences. The animals in whom these inferences are not noticed, are called *brutes;* but those which know these necessary truths are properly those which are called *rational animals,* and their souls are called *spirits.* These souls are capable of performing acts of reflection, and of considering that which is called the *ego, substance, monad, soul, spirit,* in a word, immaterial things and truths. And it is this which renders us capable of the sciences and of demonstrative knowledge.

6. Modern researches have taught us, and reason approves of it, that living beings whose organs are known to us, that is to say, plants and animals, do not come from putrefaction or from chaos, as the ancients believed, but from *pre-formed* seeds, and consequently by the transformation of pre-existing living beings. There are animalcules in the seeds of larger animals, which by means of conception assume a new dress, which they make their own, and by means of which they can nourish themselves and increase their size, in order to pass to a larger theatre and to accomplish the propagation of the large animal. It is true that the souls of spermatic human animals are not rational, and do not become so until conception destines [*determine*] these animals to human nature. And as in general animals are not born entirely in conception or *generation,* neither do they perish entirely in what we call *death;* for it is reasonable that what does not begin naturally, should not end either in the order of nature. Therefore, quitting their mask or their rags, they merely return to a more minute theatre, where they can, nevertheless, be just as sensitive and just as well ordered as in the larger. And what we have just said of the large animals, takes place also in the generation and death of spermatic animals them-selves, that is to say, they are growths of other smaller spermatic animals, in comparison with which they may pass for large; for everything extends *ad infinitum* in nature. Thus not only souls, but also animals, are ingenerable and imperishable: they are only developed, enveloped, reclothed, unclothed, transformed: souls never quit their entire body and do not pass from one body into another which is entirely new to them. There is therefore no *metempsychosis,* but there is *metamorphosis;* animals change, take and leave only parts: the same thing which happens little by little and by small invisible particles, but continually, in nutrition; and suddenly, visibly, but rarely, in conception or in death, which cause a gain or loss all at one time.

7. Thus far we have spoken as simple *physicists:* now we must advance to *metaphysics,* making use of the *great principle,* little employed in general, which teaches that *nothing happens without a sufficient reason;* that is to say, that nothing happens without its being possible for him who should sufficiently under-stand things, to give a reason sufficient to determine why it is so and not otherwise. This principle laid down, the first question which should rightly be asked, will be, *Why is there something rather than nothing?* For nothing is simpler and easier than something. Further, suppose that things must exist, we must be able to give a reason *why they must exist so* and not otherwise.

8. Now this sufficient reason for the existence of the universe cannot be found *in the series of contingent things,* that is, of bodies and of their representations in souls; for matter being indifferent in itself to motion and to rest, and to this or another motion, we cannot find the reason of motion in it, and still less of a certain motion. And although the present motion which is in matter, comes from the preceding motion, and that from still another preceding, yet in this way we make no progress, go as far as we may; for the same question always remains. Thus it must be that the sufficient reason, which has no need of another reason, be outside this series of contingent things and be found in a substance which is its cause, or which is a necessary being, carrying the reason of its existence within itself; otherwise we should still not have a sufficient reason in which we could rest. And this final reason of things is called *God.*

9. This primitive simple substance must contain in itself eminently the perfections contained in the derivative substances which are its effects; thus it will have perfect power, knowledge and will: that is, it will have supreme omnipotence, omniscience and goodness. And as *justice,* taken very generally, is only goodness conformed to wisdom, there must too be supreme justice in God. The reason which has caused things to exist by him, makes them still dependent upon him in existing and in working: and they continually receive from him that which gives them any perfection; but the imperfection which remains in them, comes from the essential and original limitation of the creature.

10. It follows from the supreme perfection of God, that in creating the universe he has chosen the best possible plan, in which there is the greatest variety together with the greatest order; the best arranged ground, place, time; the most results produced in the most simple ways; the most of power, knowledge, happiness and goodness in the creatures that the universe could permit. For since all the possibles in the understanding of God laid claim to existence in proportion to their perfections, the result of all these claims must be the most perfect actual world that is possible. And without this it would not be possible to give a reason why things have turned out so rather than otherwise.

11. The supreme wisdom of God led him to choose the *laws of motion* best adjusted and most suited to abstract or metaphysical reasons. There is preserved the same quantity of total and absolute force, or of action; the same quantity of respective force or of reaction; lastly the same quantity of directive force. Farther, action is always equal to reaction, and the whole effect is always equivalent to its full cause. And it is not surprising that we could not by the mere consideration of the *efficient causes* or of matter, account for those laws of motion which have been discovered in our time, and a part of which have been discovered by myself. For I have found that it was necessary to have recourse to *final causes,* and that these laws do not depend upon the *principle of necessity,* like logical, arithmetical and geometrical truths, but upon the *principle of fitness,* that is, upon the choice of wisdom. And this is one of the most effective and evident proofs of the existence of God, to those who can examine these matters thoroughly.

12. It follows, farther, from the perfection of the supreme author, that not only is the order of the entire universe the most perfect possible, but also that each living mirror representing the universe in accordance with its point of view, that is to say, that each *monad,* each substantial centre, must have its perceptions and its desires as well regulated as is compatible with all the rest. Whence it follows, still farther, that *souls,* that is, the most dominating monads, or rather, animals themselves, cannot fail to awaken from the state of stupor in which death or some other accident may put them.

13. For all is regulated in things, once for all, with as much order and harmony as is possible, supreme wisdom and goodness not being able to act except with perfect harmony. The present is big with the future, the future might be read in the past, the distant is expressed in the near. One could become acquainted with the beauty of the universe in each soul, if one could unfold all its folds, which only develop perceptibly in time. But as each distinct perception of the soul includes innumerable confused perceptions, which embrace the whole universe, the soul itself knows the things of which it has perception only so far as it has distinct and clear perceptions of them; and it has perfection in proportion to its distinct perfections. Each soul knows the infinite, knows all, but confusedly; as in walking on the seashore and hearing the great noise which it makes, I hear the particular sounds of each wave, of which the total sound is composed, but without distinguishing them. Our confused perceptions are the result of the impressions which the whole universe makes upon us. It is the same with each monad. God alone has a distinct knowledge of all, for he is the source of all. It has been well said that he is as centre everywhere, but his circumference is nowhere, since everything is immediately present to him without any distance from this centre.

14. As regards the rational soul, or *spirit,* there is something in it more than in the monads, or even in simple souls. It is not only a mirror of the universe of creatures, but also an image of the Divinity. The *spirit* has not only a perception of the works of God, but it is even capable of producing something which resembles them, although in miniature. For, to say nothing of the marvels of dreams, in which we invent without trouble (but also involuntarily) things which, when awake, we should have to think a long time in order to hit upon, our soul is architectonic also in its voluntary actions, and, discovering the sciences according to which God has regulated things (*pondere, mensura, numero, etc.*), it imitates, in its department and in its little world, where it is permitted to exercise itself, what God does in the large world.

15. This is why all spirits, whether of men or of genii, entering by virtue of reason and of eternal truths into a sort of society with God, are members of the City of God, that is to say, of the most perfect state, formed and governed by the greatest and best of monarchs; where there is no crime without punishment, no good actions without proportionate recompense; and, finally, as much virtue and happiness as is possible; and this is not by a derangement of nature, as if what God prepares for souls disturbed the laws of bodies, but by the very order of natural

things, in virtue of the harmony pre-established for all time between the *realms of nature and of grace,* between God as Architect and God as Monarch; so that *nature* itself leads to grace, and *grace,* in making use of nature, perfects it.

16. Thus although reason cannot teach us the details, reserved to Revelation, of the great future, we can be assured by this same reason that things are made in a manner surpassing our desires. God also being the most perfect and most happy, and consequently, the most lovable of substances, and *truly pure love* consisting in the state which finds pleasure in the perfections and happiness of the loved object, this love ought to give us the greatest pleasure of which we are capable, when God is its object.

17. And it is easy to love him as we ought, if we know him as I have just described. For although God is not visible to our external senses, he does not cease to be very lovable and to give very great pleasure. We see how much pleasure honors give men, although they do not at all consist in the qualities of the external senses. Martyrs and fanatics (although the emotion of the latter is ill-regulated) show what pleasure of the spirit can accomplish; and, what is more, even sensuous pleasures are really confusedly known intellectual pleasures. Music charms us, although its beauty only consists in the harmonies of numbers and in the reckoning of the beats or vibrations of sounding bodies, which meet at certain intervals, reckonings of which we are not conscious and which the soul nevertheless does make. The pleasures which sight finds in proportions are of the same nature; and those caused by the other senses amount to almost the same thing, although we may not be able to explain it so distinctly.

18. It may even be said that from the present time on, the *love of God* makes us enjoy a foretaste of future felicity. And although it is disinterested, it itself constitutes our greatest good and interest even if we should not seek these therein and should consider only the pleasure which it gives, without regard to the utility it produces; for it gives us perfect confidence in the goodness of our author and master, producing a true tranquillity of mind; not as with the Stoics who force themselves to patience, but by a present contentment, assuring to us also a future happiness. And besides the present pleasure, nothing can be more useful for the future; for the love of God fulfills also our hopes, and leads us in the road of supreme happiness, because by virtue of the perfect order established in the universe, everything is done in the best possible way, as much for the general good as for the greatest individual good of those who are convinced of this and are content with the divine government; this conviction cannot be wanting to those who know how to love the source of all good. It is true that supreme felicity, by whatever *beatific vision* or knowledge of God it be accompanied, can never be full; because, since God is infinite, he cannot be wholly known. Therefore our happiness will never, and ought not, consist in full joy, where there would be nothing farther to desire, rendering our mind stupid; but in a perpetual progress to new pleasures and to new perfections.

COMPARATIVE STUDY QUESTIONS

Review Questions

1. How do Spinoza and Leibniz each define "substance"?
2. How many attributes does God have, according to Spinoza, and how many of them do we know?
3. What is a "monad," according to Leibniz, and how is one distinguished from another?
4. How are monads related to each other if they are without parts, shapes, or "windows"?
5. In Leibniz's theory of monads, how is God to be described?
6. Does Spinoza assert that God has a body? Does he say that God is extended? Is God divisible?
7. Why does Leibniz say that "the best plan is not always that which seeks to avoid evil"?
8. Explain Leibniz's Principle of Sufficient Reason. To what use does he put it?
9. How does Spinoza understand the terms "good" and "bad" (or "evil")?
10. State Leibniz's answer to the objection that God is not free, because God cannot fail to choose the best, and whoever cannot fail to choose the best is not free.

Discussion Questions

1. Compare Spinoza and Leibniz with respect to the indivisibility of substance(s).
2. Examine the similarities between Spinoza's proofs of God's existence (**Ethics,** Pt. I, Props. VII; VIII, Note II; XI) and those of Descartes (**Med.** III & V) and Leibniz (**Principles of Nature and of Grace,** Nos. 7–8).
3. According to Spinoza (Pt. I, Prop. XV), "nothing can be, or be conceived, without God." In his **Refutation,** Leibniz grants that things cannot exist without God, but thinks that "essences can in a certain way be conceived of without God." What metaphysical consequences follow from this difference of opinion?
4. Spinoza claims that "all things are pre-determined by God, not through his free will or absolute fiat, but from the very nature of God or infinite power" (Appendix to Pt. I; also, Prop. XVII, Cor. II, Note). Leibniz disagrees. The world, he says, is a voluntary effect of God. It is not necessary, but contingent. Assess these different points of view.
5. Spinoza objects to thinking of man in Nature as a "kingdom within a kingdom." Leibniz universalizes the notion: Every substance (monad) is an "empire within an empire." How different is his notion from the one Spinoza

objects to? How does his doctrine of pre-established harmony fit into the picture?

6. How does Spinoza answer the question: "If all things follow from a necessity of the absolutely perfect nature of God, why are there so many imperfections in nature?"

7. According to Leibniz, what Spinoza says about the "intellectual love of God" is only "trappings for the people." Is this charge justified, and does it square with his own discussion of the love of God at the end of **The Principles of Nature and of Grace?**

8. Restate the problem of evil as Leibniz understands it, and compare his solution with Spinoza's account.

9. What is the mind's highest good, according to Spinoza? Is God good, according to his view?

10. Both Leibniz and Spinoza subscribe to forms of determinism, and yet both talk about "freedom" and the lack of it (Spinoza's famous phrase is "human bondage"). Is there an inconsistency here? Which set of views makes better sense?

Gottfried Wilhelm Leibniz
(1646 – 1716)

John Locke
(1632 – 1704)

THE LIMITS OF HUMAN UNDERSTANDING

Monsieur Gottfried Wilhelm Leibniz and Mr. John Locke

What we find in the *Nouveaux Essais* is a comparison of the ideas of Locke with those of Leibniz himself, a testing of the former by the latter as a standard. . . . What of Locke? How about him who is the recipient of the criticism?. . . His thought is an inheritance into which every English-speaking person at least is born. Only he who does not think escapes this inheritance. . . . It may be that one who is a lineal descendant of Locke in the spiritual generations of thought would not state a single important truth as Locke stated it. . . . But the fundamental principles of empiricism: its conception of intelligence as an individual possession; its idea of reality as something over against and distinct from mind; its explanation of knowledge as a process of action and reaction between these separate things; its account of our inability to know things as they really are—these principles are congenital with our thinking.

John Dewey, *Leibniz's New Essays: A Critical Exposition* (1888)

It is not uncommon in the history of philosophy for philosophers to begin by addressing one problem and to end by discussing another. This is particularly true in the history of ethics. For example, Plato's dialogue, **Meno,** begins by addressing the question, "Can virtue be taught?" and ends by discussing a problem in geometry.[1] In the preface to his book, **An Analysis of Knowledge and Valuation,** C. I. Lewis admits that:

> The first studies toward this book were addressed to topics in the field of ethics. But . . . it became apparent that the conceptions

---

1. I do not, of course, mean to suggest that a lesson in geometry is all the dialogue is about, but only that the initial question is by-passed, for the time being, in favor of others.

which I wished to develop should not stand by themselves. . . . In particular, they depended on the premise that valuation is a form of empirical knowledge. And the development of that thesis would, in turn, call for much which must be antecedent. In consequence, the studies in ethics were put aside for the time being. . . .[2]

Locke apparently had a somewhat similar experience. Sometime during the winter of 1670–1671, he and five or six of his friends were meeting in his quarters discussing the "principles of morality and revealed religion." Locke reports that they "found themselves quickly at a stand by the difficulties that rose on every side."[3] After they had puzzled a while, without coming any nearer to a resolution of their doubts, it occurred to Locke that "we took a wrong course; and that, before we set ourselves upon enquiries of that nature, it was necessary to examine our own abilities, and see what objects our understandings were or were not fitted to deal with." The eventual outcome—twenty years later—was his book, **An Essay Concerning Human Understanding,** which only very incidentally has to do with matters of morality,[4] but which has much to do with matters of knowledge and reality.

If John Dewey's claim is correct—that Locke's philosophy of experience represents an inheritance into which every English-speaking person who bothers to think is born—then it should not even be necessary to restate it. But for the person who does not regard himself an heir to the English philosophical tradition, or has for some reason neglected to think about these matters, a brief summary should perhaps be given.[5] It is all the more appropriate since the Leibniz dialogue which follows is quite obviously slanted toward his own point of view, which few philosophers today would say is "congenital with our thinking."[6]

According to Locke, the objects which our understandings are most "fitted to deal with" are ideas. In fact, it is this observation which suggests his definition of an idea: "Whatsoever is the object of the understanding when a man thinks" (**Essay,** I, I, 8). He takes it for granted that men have ideas in their minds, such as those expressed by the words, "whiteness, hardness, sweetness, thinking, willing, motion,

---

2. C.I. Lewis, *An Analysis of Knowledge and Valuation* (LaSalle, Ill.: Open Court Publishing Co., 1946), Preface, p. vii.

3. Epistle to the Reader, in *An Essay Concerning Human Understanding*, A.S. Pringle-Pattison edition (Oxford: Clarendon Press, 1924), p. 4.

4. Cf. his brief but suggestive discussion of morality and law in Bk. II, Ch. XXVIII, *Of Other Relations*, sections 4–12.

5. It may be wondered why a summary is given and not excerpts from the *Essay* itself. Partly the reason lies in the manner in which the book was written—"by catches" and "after long intervals of neglect," as Locke says in his "Epistle to the Reader." The result is a tediously repetitive style. Both Leibniz's dialogue and the following summary provide numerous direct quotations from Locke's *Essay*. Still, for those readers for whom nothing but Locke's own presentation will do, the following chunks of the *Essay* are recommended: Bk. I, Chaps. i, ii; Bk. II, Chaps. i–ix, xi–xiii, xxi–xxiii, xxvii–xxviii; Bk. IV, Chaps. i–iv, ix–xii.

6. At least not yet. Novel philosophical ideas have a tendency to infiltrate the common consciousness only after years of criticism and rejection. Many of Leibniz's views have indeed become fashionable, but mainly among logicians.

elephant, and army." His task is to account for their sources and explain their function in knowledge.

The first task leads Locke to attack the notion that we have certain innate ideas and principles in our minds—ideas and principles which we are born with. The entire first book of his **Essay** is concerned with this problem. "If it were true in matter of fact that there were certain truths wherein all mankind agreed, it would not prove them innate, if there can be any other way shown, how men may come to that universal agreement. . ." (I, II, 3). Locke goes on to deny that there is any such universal agreement. Even the principles "What is, is" and "It is impossible for the same thing to be and not be" are not universally assented to, nor even universally known (Section 4). These principles are unknown to children and idiots, and yet if innate they should be known to them as well (Section 5). Some persons think the idea of God is innate, but this view too is mistaken. For there are many who deny that they are even aware of such an idea in themselves (I, IV, 8).

The underlying presupposition of Locke's whole argument against innate ideas is his assumption that "No proposition [or idea] can be said to be in the mind which it never yet knew, which it was never yet conscious of" (I, II, 5). On this basis and the kinds of arguments just suggested, he concludes that there are neither innate ideas nor principles, and that the mind of man is not, as it were, "stamped" with certain characters (I, II, 1), but is instead a "white paper,[7] void of all characters, without any ideas" (II, I, 2). To the question, "Whence has it all the materials of reason and knowledge?" Locke answers, in one word: from **experience.** All our ideas come from either sensation or reflection, i.e., "observation employed either about external objects or about the internal operations of our minds" (II, I, 2–5).

Ideas are either simple or complex. Locke admits that "though the qualities that affect our senses are, in the things themselves, so united and blended that there is no separation, no distance between them; yet it is plain the ideas they produce in the mind enter by the senses simple and unmixed" (II, II, 1). Ideas of whiteness and sweetness are simple; ideas of an elephant or an army are complex. The mind composes complex ideas out of simple ones as a builder does a house out of building blocks.

The "mental state" psychology in which Locke engages may seem to us now as not only crude but extremely dubious. Certainly no psychologist or philosopher today adopts this account of the matter of knowledge. But two observations must be made. In the first place, a person such as Leibniz, with his monadic view of the world, is not about to question this aspect of Locke's epistemology, since he himself is just as committed to the "composition" approach to an understanding of things as Locke was. Secondly, it is an approach that is wholly in accord with

---

7. Locke also likens the mind to an "empty cabinet" (I, II, 15), and a "dark room" or "closet" (II, XI, 17): "I pretend not to teach, but to enquire; and therefore cannot but confess here again that external and internal sensation are the only passages that I can find of knowledge to the understanding. These alone, as far as I can discover, are the windows by which light is let into this *dark room.* For methinks the understanding is not much unlike a closet wholly shut from light, with only some little opening left to let in external visible resemblances or ideas of things without."

Locke's own "historical plain method." Tracing the complex back to its simplest components is but an application of his general idea of following our ideas back to their sources or "originals," as he called them.

The "historical plain method," however, is also intended by Locke to provide "measures of the certainty of our knowledge" (I, I, 2). Locke does not always clearly distinguish this second **epistemological** task of evaluating claims to knowledge from the previous **psychological** task of accounting for the origin and derivation of ideas. Still, he does recognize that knowledge is not just a matter of having ideas. Some men have "false" ideas; others entertain contradictory "persuasions"; some combinations of ideas are perhaps unverifiable, e.g., "We have the idea of matter and thinking, but possibly shall never be able to know whether any mere material being thinks or no" (IV, III, 6). We need a "measure," or standard, for deciding these kinds of questions, and Locke's historical plain method is supposed to supply it.

Locke puts the connection between having ideas and having knowledge fairly succinctly as follows:

> Since the mind, in all its thoughts and reasonings, hath no other immediate object but its own ideas, which it alone does or can contemplate, it is evident that our knowledge is only conversant about them. . . . Knowledge then seems to me to be nothing but the perception of the connexion and agreement, or disagreement and repugnancy, of any of our ideas (IV, I, 1–2).

"White is not black" and "Three angles of a triangle are equal to two right ones" are items of knowledge, the first being the perception of a disagreement between two ideas, and the second a perception of an agreement.

Obviously the ways in which we perceive these agreements and disagreements may vary and so different "degrees" of knowledge are possible. Locke distinguishes **intuitive, demonstrative,** and **sensitive** knowledge. Using the Cartesian criterion of "self-evidence," Locke classes intuitive knowledge as "the clearest and most certain" knowledge that human frailty is capable of. The mind perceives the truth of "white is not black" or "a square is not a circle" as simply and irresistibly as "the eye doth light." Demonstrative knowledge is similarly certain but being a "train" of intuitions, it is not as clear or "easy." Sensitive knowledge is knowledge about the particular existence of finite things. Strictly speaking, it lacks the certitude which Locke reserves for knowledge; perhaps, he says, it should be called faith or opinion; nonetheless, he classes it as a "degree of knowledge."

Contrary to Locke's initial premise, our knowledge of the real world ("real existence") does not involve a relation **between ideas** at all, but rather between an idea and the supposed object or person which is the cause of it. Locke contends that we have an intuitive knowledge of our own existence, a demonstrative knowledge of God's, and a sensitive knowledge of other selves and physical things.

Despite his respect for his good friend, Sir Isaac Newton, and his many accomplishments (cf. **Essay,** Epistle to the Reader; IV, I, 9; IV, VII, 10), Locke doubted that "how far soever human industry may advance useful and experimental philosophy in physical things, **scientifical** [knowledge] will still be out of our reach" (IV, III, 26). Or again:

> This way of getting and improving our knowledge in substances only by experience and history, which is all that the weakness of our faculties . . . can attain to, makes me suspect that natural philosophy is not capable of being made a science. We are able, I imagine, to reach very little general knowledge concerning the species of bodies and their several properties. Experiments and historical observations we may have, from which we may draw advantages of ease and health, and thereby increase our stock of conveniences for this life; but beyond this I fear our talents reach out, nor are our faculties, as I guess, able to advance (IV, XII, 10).

Although these words may sound apologetic and defeatist, they are consistent with Locke's overall attempt to determine the limits of the human understanding. They form a part of his critique, not of Newton's "experimental" conception of science, which he approves, but of the more thoroughly mathematical and deductionist interpretations of Descartes and Leibniz. As a physician himself, with some pretty miraculous operations to his credit[8] and some remarkably advanced notions about the practice of medicine,[9] it is hardly likely that he meant to belittle the empirical approach to scientific matters. Contrast, for example, the above passage with the following from his unfinished essay on **The Art of Medicine:**

> He that in physic shall lay down fundamental maxims, and, from thence drawing consequences and raising disputes, shall reduce it into the regular form of a science, has indeed done something to enlarge the art of talking and perhaps laid a foundation for endless disputes; but, if he hopes to bring men by such a system to the knowledge of the . . . nature, signs, changes, and history of diseases, . . . [he] takes much . . . [the same] course with him that should walk up and down in a thick wood, overgrown with briars and thorns, with a design to take a view and draw a map of the country. These speculative theorems . . . [are of] little advantage . . . , and he that thinks he came to be skilled in diseases by studying the doctrine of the humours . . . may as rationally believe that his cook owes his skill in roasting and boiling to his study of the elements.[10]

Locke clearly intends to oppose the speculative and mathematical to the experimental and "historical." The latter method is the only one mankind is capable of

---

8. Cf. Peter Laslett who quotes a recent medical opinion that Locke's operation on Shaftesbury saved his life and that its success was almost miraculous. *Two Treatises of Government,* edited by Peter Laslett (Cambridge University Press, second ed., 1970), Introduction, p. 26.
9. Cf. Maurice Cranston, *John Locke, A Biography* (London: Longmans, 1957), pp. 113 (consultation); 139 (prevention of miscarriage); 173 (diagnosis).
10. Reprinted in H.R.F. Bourne, *The Life of John Locke* (London edition, 1876), Vol. I, p. 224.

using successfully, but it is sufficient, he thinks, to provide all the knowledge we really need. After all, says Locke,

> Our business here is not to know all things, but those which concern our conduct. If we can find out those measures whereby a rational creature . . . may and ought to govern his opinions, and actions depending thereon, we need not be troubled that some other things escape our knowledge (I, I, 6).

LEIBNIZ

*New Essays on the Human Understanding**

Introduction

Since the *Essay on the Human Understanding,* by a famous Englishman,[11] is one of the finest and most highly esteemed works of our time, I have resolved to make some remarks on it, because, having long meditated on the same subject and on the greater part of the matters therein considered, I thought this would be a good opportunity for publishing something under the title of *New Essays on the Human Understanding,* and for securing a favourable reception for my reflections by putting them in such good company. I further thought that I might profit by someone else's labour, not only to diminish my own (since in fact it is less trouble to follow the thread of a good author than to work at everything afresh), but also to add something to what he has given us, which is always an easier task than making a start; for I think I have removed certain difficulties which he had left entirely on one side. Thus his reputation is of advantage to me; and since I am moreover

---

*From *Philosophical Writings* by Gottfried Wilhelm Leibniz, edited and translated by Mary Morris. Introduction, notes, and revisions copyright © 1973 by J. M. Dent & Sons Ltd. An Everyman's Library Edition. Published in the United States by E. P. Dutton & Co., Inc., and reprinted with their permission.

11. John Locke (1632–1704). When his *Essay* was published in 1690 Leibniz sent him some short papers in criticism. Locke seems to have paid little attention to these. In 1700, Coste's translation of the *Essay* into French was published, and Leibniz set himself to write the *New Essays,* an elaborate work in which he examines and criticizes Locke's doctrines in a running commentary; he delayed publication, however, as a new edition of the French translation of the *Essay* was promised. Then in 1704 Locke died; and the *New Essays* were not published until 1765, nearly fifty years after the death of Leibniz.

inclined to do justice to him, and am very far from wishing to lessen the high opinion commonly entertained of his work, I shall increase his reputation if my approval has any weight. It is true that I am often of another opinion from him, but, far from denying the merit of famous writers, we bear witness to it by showing wherein and wherefore we differ from them, since we deem it necessary to prevent their authority from prevailing against reason in certain important points; besides the fact that, in convincing such excellent men, we make the truth more acceptable, and it is to be supposed that it is chiefly for truth's sake that they are labouring.

In fact, although the author of the *Essay* says a thousand fine things of which I approve, our systems are very different. His bears more relation to Aristotle, mine to Plato; although we both of us depart in many things from the doctrine of these two ancient philosophers. He is more popular, while I am sometimes compelled to be a little more *acroamatic* and abstract, which is not an advantage to me, especially when writing in a living language. But I think that by making two characters speak, of whom one expounds the views derived from our author's *Essay*,[12] while the other gives my observations, I shall show the relation between us in a way that will be more to the reader's taste than dry remarks, the reading of which would have to be constantly interrupted by the necessity of referring to his book in order to understand mine. Nevertheless it will be well sometimes to compare our writings and to judge of his opinions by his own work only, although I have as a rule retained his expressions. It is true that the necessity of having to follow the thread of another person's argument in making my remarks has meant that I have been unable to think of achieving the graces of which the dialogue form is capable: but I hope the matter will make up for this defect in the manner. . . .

Book I. Of Innate Notions

Chapter I

Whether There Are Any Innate Principles in the Human Mind

§21.[13] *Philalethes.*   If the mind assents so promptly to certain truths, may this not come from the consideration of the nature of things, which does not suffer it to think otherwise, rather than because these propositions have been printed naturally in the mind?

---

12. Philalethes gives Locke's views, and Theophilus those of Leibniz. The words of Philalethes are sometimes obviously a translation of Locke's own words, sometimes a paraphrase or summary of a particular passage in Locke, and sometimes a free re-statement of Locke's doctrine. Where his words are obviously meant to be a translation, instead of retranslating them I have printed Locke's own words in italics, as it may be of advantage to the reader to see at a glance what is the original Locke, and what is Leibniz's summary or re-statement. In some places of course it is difficult to tell whether to treat the French as translation or as paraphrase; but as a general rule it is clear enough.

13. The number of the section refers to the section in the corresponding chapter and book of Locke's *Essay;* i.e., in this case to *Essay*, Bk. I, ch. i, §21. It will be seen that Leibniz does not always follow the order of Locke's sections, but sometimes takes the points in an order that suits his own argument. A large part of the present chapter is omitted here.

Theophilus. Both these doctrines are true. The nature of things and the nature of the mind here agree. And since you oppose the consideration of the thing to the apperception of what is printed in the mind, your objection shows, sir, that those whose doctrines you are upholding understand by *innate truths,* only such as would be approved naturally, as if by *instinct,* and without apprehending them except confusedly. There are some of this nature, and I shall have occasion to speak of them. But what is called the *natural light* presupposes a distinct knowledge, and often enough the consideration of the nature of things is nothing else than the knowledge of the nature of our mind and of these innate ideas, for which there is no need to search outside. Thus I call innate those truths which have no need of such consideration for their verification. . . .

§23. *Philalethes.* . . . But what do you say, sir, to this challenge of one of my friends? *I would gladly have any one name,*[14] he says, *that proposition whose terms or ideas were either of them innate.*

Theophilus. I should name the propositions of arithmetic and geometry, which are all of that nature; and as regards necessary truths, it is not possible to find any others.

§25. *Philalethes.* Many people will find that very strange. Can it be said that the most difficult and profoundest sciences are innate?

Theophilus. Actual knowledge of them is not innate, but rather what may be called virtual knowledge; just as the figure traced by the veins of the marble is in the marble, before they are uncovered by the workman.

Philalethes. But is it possible that children, when they receive notions which come to them from outside, and give to them their assent, should still have no knowledge of those which are supposed to be innate and to form part of their mind, on which, it is said, they are *imprinted in indelible characters* to serve as a foundation? *This would be to make nature take pains to no purpose; or at least, to write very ill, since its characters could not be read by those eyes which saw other things very well.*

Theophilus. The apperception of what is in us depends upon the presence of attention and upon order. Now it is not only possible, it is also fitting, that children should pay more attention to the notions of sense, because attention is regulated by need. The event, however, makes it clear in the sequel that nature did not take pains to no purpose in printing in us innate knowledge, since without such knowledge there would be no means of arriving at actual knowledge of necessary truths in the demonstrative sciences, and at the reasons of facts; and so we should have nothing more than the brutes.

§5. *Philalethes.* . . . But you will have rather more difficulty in answering what I am now going to propound to you, namely that if any one particular proposition can be said to be innate, then the same reasoning will enable it to be maintained

14. In the speeches of Philalethes italics indicate Locke's own exact words; in those of Theophilus the italics are Leibniz's.

that all propositions that are reasonable, and that the mind is ever capable of regarding as such, are already imprinted in the soul. . . . Even supposing that there are truths which can be imprinted in the understanding, without the understanding perceiving them, I do not see how *in respect of their original* they can differ from the truths which it is simply capable of knowing.

Theophilus. The mind is not simply capable of knowing them, but also of finding them in itself. If it had only the simple capacity to receive knowledge, or the passive potency necessary for that, as much without determinations as that which the wax has to receive shapes and the *tabula rasa* to receive letters, then it would not be the source of necessary truths, as I have just proved that in fact it is. For it is incontestable that the senses are not sufficient to make us see their necessity, and so the mind has the dispositions (as much active as passive) to draw them itself out of its own depths; though the senses are necessary to give to it the occasion and the attention required for this, and to lead it rather to the one sort than to the other. Thus you see, sir, that these people, clever as they are in other respects, who are of a different opinion, seem not to have reflected sufficiently about the consequences of the difference between truths which are necessary or eternal and truths of experience, as I have already remarked and as our whole dispute makes clear. The original proof of necessary truths comes from the understanding alone, and all other truths come from experiences or from observations of the senses. Our mind is capable of knowing both the one sort and the other, but it is the source of the first; whatever number of particular experiences we may have of a universal truth, we cannot assure ourselves of it for always by induction, without apprehending its necessity by reason.

Philalethes. But is it not true that if these words, *to be in the understanding,* have any positive meaning they mean to be perceived and apprehended by the understanding?

Theophilus. To me they mean something quite different. It is sufficient if that which is in the understanding is capable of being found there, and if the original sources of proofs of the truths which are here in question are simply in the understanding: the senses may suggest, justify, and confirm these truths, but they cannot demonstrate their infallible and perpetual certainty.

§18. *Theophilus.* . . . Thoughts are actions, and apprehensions or truths, in so far as they are in us, even though we are not thinking of them, are habits or dispositions; and we have clear knowledge of things of which we hardly think at all.

Philalethes. It is very difficult to conceive how a truth can be in the mind, if the mind has never thought of that truth.

Theophilus. To say that is like saying that it is difficult to conceive that there are veins in the marble before they are uncovered. It appears, too, that this objection comes very near to a *petitio principii.* All those who allow innate truths, without making them dependent on a Platonic reminiscence, allow some of which the mind has not yet thought. Besides, this reasoning proves too much. If truths are thoughts, it will deprive us, not only of truths of which we have never thought, but also of those of which we have thought but are not actually thinking now. If truths are not thoughts, but habits and aptitudes, natural or acquired, then there is nothing to prevent the existence in us of truths of which we have never thought, no, nor ever shall think.

Book II. Of Ideas

Chapter I

In Which the Author Treats of Ideas
in General, and Examines by the Way
Whether the Soul of Man Thinks Always

§1. *Philalethes.* Having now examined whether ideas are innate, let us consider their nature and their differences. Is it not true that an *idea is the object of thinking?*

Theophilus. I agree, provided that you add that it is an immediate internal object, and that this object is an expression of the nature or of the qualities of things. If an idea were the *form* of thinking, it would come into being and cease with the actual thoughts which correspond to it; but being the *object* of thought, it can exist anterior to and posterior to the thoughts. External sensible objects are only *mediate,* because they cannot act immediately on the soul. God alone is the *immediate external* object. It might be said that the soul itself is its own immediate *internal* object; but it is so only as containing ideas, or that which corresponds to things. For the soul is a little world, in which distinct ideas are a representation of God and confused ideas are a representation of the universe.

§2. *Philalethes.* Our friends, who supposed that at the beginning the soul is a blank tablet, void of all characters and without any ideas, ask themselves how it comes to receive ideas, and by what means it acquires such a vast store. To this they answer in one word: from experience.

Theophilus. This *tabula rasa* of which they talk so much, is nothing in my opinion but a fiction which nature does not admit, and which is founded only in the incomplete notions of the philosophers, like the void, atoms, rest (whether absolute rest or the relative rest of two parts of a whole in relation to one another), or like primary matter conceived as quite formless. Things which are uniform and contain no variety are never anything but abstractions, like time, space, and the other entities of pure mathematics. There is no body whose parts are at rest, and there is no substance which has not something to distinguish it from every other substance. Human souls differ not only from other souls, but also among themselves, although the difference is not of the nature of those which are called specific. And in accordance with the proofs which I think I can supply, every substantial thing, be it soul or body, has its relation to every other substantial thing, which is peculiar to itself; and one must always differ from another by *intrinsic denominations*. It need hardly be said that those who talk so much of this *tabula rasa,* after emptying it of all ideas, could not say what remains, just as the Schoolmen have nothing left for their primary matter. I shall be told, perhaps, that this *tabula rasa* of the philosophers means that the soul has naturally and originally nothing but bare faculties. But faculties without any activity, in a word the pure potencies of the Schools, these too are nothing but fictions, of which nature knows nothing, and which are obtained by making abstractions. For where in the world will you find a faculty which shuts itself up in a mere potency and never exercises any activity? There is always a particular disposition to action, and to one action rather than another. And besides the disposition there is always a tendency to action; indeed there is always an infinite number of them in every subject at any given time; and these tendencies are never without some effect. Experience is necessary, I allow, for the soul to be determined to such and such particular thoughts, and for it to take notice of the ideas which are in us. But by what means can experience and the senses provide ideas? Has the soul windows? Does it resemble a tablet? Is it like wax? It is evident that all those who speak thus of the soul treat it at bottom as corporeal. I shall have brought against me the axiom, accepted among the philosophers, that *there is nothing in the soul save that which comes from the senses.* But we must except the soul itself and its affections. *Nihil est in intellectu, quod non fuerit in sensu;* excipe, *nisi ipse intellectus.*[15] Now the soul contains existence, substance, unity, identity, cause, perception, reasoning, and a quantity of other notions which the senses could not afford. This is in agreement with your friend the author of the *Essay,* who finds the source of a good part of our ideas in the reflection of the mind upon its own nature.

Philalethes. I hope, then, that you will agree with this able author that all our ideas come from sensation or from reflection, that is to say, from the observations we make either of external, sensible objects or of the internal operations of our soul.

Theophilus. To avoid a dispute over which we have delayed too long, I must make it quite clear at the outset, sir, that when you say that ideas come to us from the one or the other of these causes I understand you to speak of the actual perception of them, for I think I have shown that they are in us before they are apperceived in so far as they contain anything distinct.[16]

Chapter IX

Of Perception

§1. *Philalethes.* Let us now turn to the ideas of reflection in detail. *Perception, as it is the first faculty of the mind exercised about our ideas, so it is the first and*

---

15. "There is nothing in the intellect which was not previously in the senses; *provided we make the reservation,* except the intellect itself."

16. In the remainder of this chapter Leibniz discusses Locke's contention that *the mind thinks not always.*

simplest idea we have from reflection. Thinking signifies that sort of operation of the mind about our ideas, wherein the mind is active; where it, with some degree of voluntary attention, considers anything. For in bare naked perception, the mind is, for the most part, only passive; and what it perceives, it cannot avoid perceiving.

Theophilus. We might perhaps add that brutes have perception, and that it is not necessary that they should have thought, that is to say, should have reflection or anything that can be the object of reflection. Moreover, we ourselves have minute *perceptions* which we do not apperceive in our present state. It is true that we could quite well apperceive them or reflect on them, if we were not deterred by their multitude, which distracts our mind, and if they were not effaced or rather obscured by greater ones.

§4. *Philalethes.* I admit that *whilst the mind is intently employed in the contemplation of some objects it takes no notice of impressions of sounding bodies made upon the organ of hearing. A sufficient impulse there may be on the organ; but if not reaching the observation of the mind, there follows no perception.*

Theophilus. I should prefer to distinguish between *perception* and *apperceiving.* The perception of the light or of the colour, for example, which we do apperceive, is composed of a number of minute perceptions, which we do not apperceive; and a noise of which we have perception, but of which we do not take notice, becomes *apperceptible* by a slight addition or increase. For if what precedes made no impression on the soul, neither would this little addition make any, and the whole would make none either. I have already touched on this point in ch. i of this book, §§ 11, 12, and 15.

§8. *Philalethes. We are further to consider concerning perception, that the ideas we receive by sensation are often in grown people altered by the judgment, without our taking notice of it.* The idea imprinted on the mind by a globe of uniform colour is that of *a flat circle variously shadowed and with several degrees of light and brightness coming to our eyes. But we have by use been accustomed to perceive what kind of appearance convex bodies are wont to make in us, what alterations are made in the reflections of light by the difference of the sensible figures of bodies;* and so we put in the place of what appears to us the actual cause of the image, and confuse judgment with vision.

Theophilus. Nothing is more true, and this it is which provides the painter with the means of deceiving us by the artifice of a perspective which we can well understand. When bodies have flat surfaces, we can represent them without making use of shadows, by employing outlines only, and by simply making pictures in the fashion of the Chinese, only more in proportion than theirs. This is the usual way of drawing medals, so that the draughtsman may keep closer to the precise features of the originals. But there is no way by drawing, of exactly distinguishing the inside of a circle from the inside of a spherical surface bounded by that circle, without the assistance of shadows, since the insides have in neither case any distinct points or distinguishing features, although there is all the same a great difference which must be shown. This is why M. Des Argues laid down precepts about the effect of tints and shadows. When a painting deceives us there is a double error in our judgments; for in the first place we substitute the cause for the effect, and think we are seeing immediately that which is the cause of the image, rather like a dog who barks at a mirror. For, strictly speaking, we only see the image, and are affected by nothing but rays of light. And since these rays of light need time (however short), it is possible that the object might have been destroyed during this interval and no longer exist by the time the ray reaches the eye; and what no longer exists cannot be the present object of vision. In the second place we are mistaken in substituting one cause for another, and thinking that what only comes from a flat painting is derived from a body; so that in this case there is in our judgments at the same time both a *metonymy* and a *metaphor;* for the very figures of rhetoric become *sophisms* when they impose upon us. This confusion of the effect with the cause, whether real or alleged, often enters into our judgments in other places as well. It is involved when we feel our bodies, or what touches them, and when we move our arms, by an immediate physical influence, which we think constitutes the communion of the soul and the body; whereas the truth is that we feel and change in this way only what is within us.

§8. *Philalethes.*   I shall here insert a problem which was sent to the illustrious Mr. Locke by that very ingenious and studious promoter of real knowledge, the learned Mr. Molyneux. It was stated very much as follows: *Suppose a man born blind, and now adult, and taught by his touch to distinguish between a cube and a sphere of the same metal, and nighly of the same bigness, so as to tell, when he felt one and the other, which is the cube, which the sphere. Suppose, then, the cube and sphere placed on a table, and the blind man be made to see: quaere, whether by his sight, before he touched them, he could now distinguish and tell which is the globe, which the cube?* I beg you, sir, to tell me your opinion on this matter.

Theophilus.   I should need time to think about this question, which seems to me a remarkable one; but since you urge me to reply on the spot, I venture to say, between ourselves, that I believe that if the blind man knew that the two figures he was looking at were the cube and the globe, he would be able to distinguish them, and say without touching them: This is the globe, this the cube.

Philalethes.   I fear that you must be numbered with the crowd of those who have wrongly answered Mr. Molyneux. For in the letter which contained this question, he stated that he had propounded it to various men of acute mind, apropos of Mr. Locke's *Essay on the Human Understanding,* and had found hardly one who began by giving him what he considered the right answer, although they became convinced of their mistake on hearing his reasons. This acute and judicious author answers: *Not. For, though he* (the blind man) *has obtained the experience of how a globe, how a cube affects his touch, yet he has not obtained the experience, that what affects his touch so or so must affect his sight so or so; or that a protuberant angle in the cube, that pressed his hand unequally, shall appear to his eye as it does in the cube.* The author of the *Essay* declares that he is altogether of the same opinion.

Theophilus. Perhaps Mr. Molyneux and the author of the *Essay* are not as far removed from my opinion as at first appears, and perhaps the reasons for their view, which were apparently contained in the letter of Mr. Molyneux, who had successfully made use of them to convince people of their mistake, were purposely suppressed by Mr. Locke so as further to exercise the minds of his readers. If you will closely consider my answer, you will find that I have included in it a condition which may be taken to be implied in the question, that is, that it is only a question of distinguishing; and that the blind man knows that the two shaped bodies which he has to distinguish are there, and therefore that each of the appearances he sees is either that of the cube or that of the globe. In this case it seems to me certain that the blind man who has just ceased to be blind can distinguish them by the principles of reason, combined with what sensuous knowledge he has previously acquired by touch. I am not speaking of what he perhaps will do actually and on the spot; for he will be dazzled and confused by novelty, as well as little accustomed to drawing conclusions. The foundation of my opinion is, that in the globe there are no points distinguished from the side of the globe itself, all of it being uniform and without angles, whereas in the cube there are eight points distinguished from all the others. If there were not this method of distinguishing figures, a blind man could not learn the rudiments of geometry by means of touch. Yet we see that men born blind are capable of learning geometry, and even have always some rudiments of a natural geometry; moreover geometry is most often learnt simply by sight, without the use of touch, as it could be, and indeed would have to be, learnt in the case of a paralytic or any other person who was more or less incapable of touch. And these two geometries, the geometry of the blind man and that of the paralytic, must meet and agree and even come back to the same ideas, although they have no common images. This shows again how necessary it is to distinguish *images* from *exact ideas,* which consist of definitions. Indeed, it would be most interesting and even instructive thoroughly to examine the ideas of a man born blind, and to hear his descriptions of figures. For he can give such descriptions, and can even understand the doctrine of optics, in so far as it is dependent on ideas that are distinct and mathematical, although he cannot manage to conceive anything which is chiaroscuro, that is to say the image of light and colours. This is why a certain man, born blind, after listening to some lessons on optics, which he seemed to understand pretty well, when asked what he thought about light replied that he imagined it must be something pleasant like sugar. In the same way it would be very important to examine the ideas of a man born deaf and dumb about things without shapes, ideas which we ordinarily describe in words, and which he must acquire in a quite different way, although it may be equivalent to ours, as the writing of the Chinese has the same effect as our alphabet, although it is infinitely different from it, and might seem to have been invented by a deaf man. I have heard, through the courtesy of a great prince, of a man in Paris, born deaf and dumb, whose ears finally came to perform their proper office; this man has now learnt French (for it was from the French Court that he was summoned not long ago) and can tell many curious things about the conceptions he had in his former state, and about the change in his ideas, when his sense of hearing began to function. These people who are born deaf and dumb can go further than we think. There was one at Oldenburg in the time of the last count, who became a good painter, and showed himself very rational in other respects. A very learned man, Breton by nationality, told me that at Blainville, a place ten leagues from Nantes, belonging to the Duke of Rohan, there was about 1690 a poor man living in a hut, near to the castle outside the town, who was born deaf and dumb, and who took letters and other things to the town, finding the houses by means of signs made him by the people who used to employ him. At last the poor man became blind too, and still did not give up performing services, and carrying letters to the town on the strength of what he was told by touch. He had in his hut a plank which went from the door to the place where his feet were, and which made him aware by its movement when any one came in. People are most negligent not to acquire exact knowledge of the ways of thinking of such persons. If he is no longer alive, there is likely to be someone in the vicinity who could still give us some information about him, and make us understand how he was shown the things he was to do. But to return to what the man born blind, who is beginning to see, will think about the globe and the cube, when he sees them without touching them, I answer that he will distinguish them in the way I have said, if someone informs him that one or the other of the appearances or perceptions he has of them belongs to the cube or to the globe; but without this preliminary instruction, I admit that it would not at first occur to him to think that these sorts of paintings which he received of them in the depths of his eyes, and which might arise from a flat painting on the table, represented bodies, until touch had convinced him of it, or until, by dint of reasoning about rays according to the laws of optics, he understood by the lights and the shadows that there was something there which arrested these rays, and that it was this which remained present to his sense of touch. He would arrive at this view finally, when he saw the globe and cube rolling along, and changing shadows and appearances as the result of their motion, or even when, the two bodies remaining at rest, the light which illuminated them changed its place, or his eyes changed their position. For these are more or less our methods of distinguishing at a distance between a picture or a perspective representing a body, and an actual body itself.

§11. *Philalethes.* Let us return to perception in general. *Perception puts the difference between animals and inferior beings.*

Theophilus. I am inclined to think that there is some perception and appetition in plants also, on account of the important analogy which exists between plants and animals; and if there is a vegetable soul, as is the common view, it must have perception. But I none the less attribute to mechanism all that takes place in the bodies of plants and animals, except their original formation. Thus I agree that the motion of the plant which is commonly called sensitive arises from mechanism, and I do not approve of having recourse to the soul for explaining the detail of the phenomena of plants and of animals.

§14. *Philalethes.* It is true that I myself cannot but think that even in such kinds of animals, as oysters and cockles, *there is some small dull perception: for would not quickness of sensation be an inconvenience to an animal that must lie still where chance has once placed it, and there receive the afflux of colder or warmer, clean or foul water, as it happens to come to it?*

Theophilus. Very true; and I hold that nearly as much could be said of plants; but as to man, his perceptions are accompanied by the power of reflection, which passes into action when need arises. But when he is reduced to a state like that of one who is in a lethargy, and is almost without sensation, reflection and apperception cease, and there is no longer any thought of universal truths. Nevertheless, his faculties and dispositions, innate and acquired, and even the impressions he has received in this state of confusion, do not for that reason cease, and are not wiped out, even though they are forgotten; they will even take their turn in contributing one day to some notable result. For nothing in nature is useless; every confusion is bound to be cleared up; the very animals, reduced to a state of stupidity, must one day return to more exalted perceptions; and since simple substances endure for ever, we must not judge of eternity by a few years.

Book IV. Of Knowledge

Chapter II

Of the Degrees of Our Knowledge

§1. *Philalethes.* *Knowledge* is *intuitive* when *the mind perceives the agreement or disagreement of two ideas immediately by themselves, without the intervention of any other.* In this case *the mind is at no pains of proving or examining* the truth. As the eye sees the light, the mind sees that white is not black, that a circle is not a triangle, that three is two and one. *This kind of knowledge is the clearest and most certain that human frailty is capable of;* it acts in a manner that is irresistible, and it leaves no room in the mind for hesitation. It is to know that the idea in the mind is such as it is perceived to be. *He that demands a greater certainty than this, demands he knows not what.*

Theophilus. The *primary* truths which are known by *intuition* are of two kinds, like *derivative* truths. They are either *truths of reason* or *truths of fact.* Truths of reason are necessary, those of fact are contingent. The primary truths of reason are those which I call by the general name of *identical,* because it appears that they do nothing but repeat the same thing, without teaching us anything. They are affirmative or negative. . . .[17]

---

17. Here follows about a page of instances of identical propositions, affirmative and negative, hypothetical, disjunctive, etc.

Someone perhaps, after listening patiently to all that I have just said, will at last lose patience and say that I am amusing myself with frivolous enunciations, and that identical truths serve no purpose whatever. But such a judgment would be due to insufficient reflection on these matters. The consequences of logic, for example, are proved by principles which are identical; and geometry relies upon the principle of contradiction in those demonstrations which reduce *ad impossibile*. I will content myself here with showing the value of identical propositions in the demonstrations of the consequences of reasoning. I say then that the principle of contradiction alone is sufficient to demonstrate the second and third figures of the syllogism from the first. Take an example in the first figure, in *Barbara:*

All *B* is *C*

All *A* is *B*

∴ all *A* is *C.*

Let us suppose that the conclusion is false (or that it is true that some *A* is not *C*), then the one or the other of the premises will be false also. Suppose the second is true: then the first, which asserts that all *B* is *C,* must be false. Then its contrary will be true; that is to say, some *B* is not *C*. And this will be the conclusion of a new argument, drawn from the falsity of the conclusion and the truth of one of the premises of the preceding argument. Here is the new argument:

Some *A* is not *C*

(which is opposite to the previous conclusion, supposed to be false).

All *A* is *B*

(this is the previous premise, supposed to be true).

∴ some *B* is not *C*

(this is the present conclusion, which is true, the opposite of the previous premise, which was false).

This argument is in the mood *Disamis* of the third figure, which is thus demonstrated obviously and at a flash from the mood *Barbara* of the first figure, without involving anything but the principle of contradiction. And I observed in my youth, when I was criticizing these things, that all the moods of the second and third figures can be obtained from the first by this one method, if we suppose that the mood of the first is valid, and consequently that, the conclusion being false and its contrary being taken for true, and one of the premises being taken for true also, it follows that the contrary of the other premise must be true. It is true that in the Schools of logic they prefer to make use of conversions. . . .[18] Since the demonstration of conversions also shows the value of *identical affirmative* propositions, which some take to be utterly frivolous, it is all the more relevant to include it here. I will only mention conversions without contraposition, which are sufficient for my purpose here, and which are either simple or *per accidens*, as they are called. Simple conversions are of two kinds: the universal negative, like *No square is obtuse-angled, therefore no obtuse-angled figure is square;* and the particular affirmative, such as *Some triangles are obtuse-angled, therefore some obtuse-angled figures are triangles.* But conversion *per accidens*, as it is called, concerns the universal affirmative, such as *All squares are rectangles, therefore some rectangles are squares.* By *rectangle* here is always understood a figure whose angles are right angles, and by *square* a regular quadrilateral. We have now to demonstrate these three kinds of conversions, which are:

(1) No A is B, $\therefore$ no B is A.
(2) Some A is B, $\therefore$ some B is A.
(3) All A is B, $\therefore$ some B is A.

Demonstration of the first conversion in *Cesare*, which is of the second figure:

No A is B
All B is B
$\therefore$ no B is A.

Demonstration of the second conversion in *Datisi*, which is of the third figure:

All A is A
Some A is B
$\therefore$ some B is A.

Demonstration of the third conversion in *Darapti*, which is of the third figure:

All A is A
All A is B
$\therefore$ some B is A.

This shows that identical propositions which are most pure and appear to be most useless have considerable value in the abstract and in general. And that should teach us not to despise any truth. As regards the proposition that *three is equal to two and one*, which you adduce, Sir, as an example of intuitive knowledge, my comment is that it is simply the definition of the term *three;* for

18. The validity of conversions themselves, Leibniz says, must be demonstrated from the primary principle, that of contradiction; it is therefore better to demonstrate the second and third figures direct, as above, and not to use conversion.

the simplest definitions of numbers are formed in this manner—*two* is one and one, *three* is two and one, *four* is three and one, and so on. It is true that there is hidden within these definitions an enunciation, which I have already mentioned, namely that these ideas are possible; and that is known in this case *intuitively*, so that we may say that there is intuitive knowledge contained in definitions when their possibility first appears. And in this way all *adequate* definitions contain primary truths of reason, and consequently intuitive knowledge. Finally, we may say in general that all primary truths of reason are immediate with an *immediacy of ideas*.

As regards *primary truths of fact*, these are the immediate internal experiences of an *immediacy of sensation*. It is among these that is included the first truth of the Cartesians or of Saint Augustine: *I think, therefore I am*, that is to say, *I am a thing which thinks*. But it is to be noted that the same is true of primary truths of fact as of identicals, that is to say that they can be either general or particular, and are as clear in the one case as in the other (since it is as clear to say that *A* is *A* as to say that *a thing is what it is*.) For not only is it clear to me immediately that *I think*, but it is just as clear to me that I have *different thoughts*, that now *I think of A* and now *I think of B*, etc. Thus the Cartesian principle is sound, but it is not the only one of its kind. So we see that all *primary truths* of reason or of fact have this in common that they cannot be proved by something more certain.

§2. *Philalethes.* I am very much pleased, sir, that you have developed further my remarks, in which I did no more than touch upon *intuitive* knowledge. Now *demonstrative knowledge* is simply a linking together of intuitive apprehensions in all the connections of the mediate ideas. For often the mind cannot join, compare, or apply its ideas to one another immediately, and so it is obliged to make use of other mediating ideas (one or more, as it happens) in order to discover the agreement or disagreement it is looking for; and this is called *reasoning*. For instance, in demonstrating that the three angles of a triangle are equal to two right angles, it finds out some other angles which it sees to be equal both to the three angles of the triangle and to two right angles. §3. These intervening ideas are called *proofs;* and a quickness of the mind to find them is what is called *sagacity*. §4. Even when these ideas have been found, it is not without pains and attention, nor by a single transient view, that this knowledge can be acquired; there must be *a progression of ideas by steps and degrees*. §5. Before the demonstration there is a doubt. §6. It is less clear than intuitive knowledge; just as a face reflected by several mirrors one to another grows weaker and weaker at each successive reflection, and is not at first sight so knowable, especially to weak eyes. *Thus it is with knowledge made out by a long train of proof*. §7. And though in each step which reason makes in demonstrating there is an intuitive knowledge, or knowledge at sight, yet because in this long succession of proofs the memory does not retain so exactly this chain of ideas, men often embrace falsehoods for demonstrations.

Theophilus. Over and above sagacity, whether natural or acquired by exercise, there is an art of finding mediating ideas (the *medium*); and this art is *Analysis*. Now it is well to consider here that it is sometimes a question of finding out the truth or falsity of a given proposition, that is, simply to answer the question *whether ?*—that is to say, Is it or is it not? At other times it is a matter of answering a question which is much more difficult (*ceteris paribus*); for instance, where it is asked *by what means ?* or *how ?*—and where there is more to be supplied. It is these questions only, which leave part of the proposition blank, which mathematicians call *problems:* for instance when we are asked to find a mirror which collects all the rays of the sun at a point; that is to say we are asked its shape, or how it is made. As for the first kind of questions, where it is simply a matter of true and false, and where there is nothing to supply in the subject or predicate, here there is less *invention;* still there is some, and judgment alone is not sufficient. It is true that a man of judgment, that is to say, one who is capable of attention and restraint, and who has the necessary leisure and patience and is open-minded enough, can understand the most difficult demonstration if it is properly put to him. But the most judicious man in the world will not always be able to find the demonstration without assistance. Thus there is some invention in that too; and in geometry there used to be more in earlier times than there is now. For when the art of Analysis was less cultivated, it required more sagacity to arrive at it. . . . It also happens that induction provides us with some truths about numbers and figures, for which the general reason has not yet been discovered. For we are far from having arrived at the perfection of Analysis in geometry and in numbers. . . .

But it is much more difficult to find out important truths, and even more so to find out means of doing what is wanted, just when it is wanted, than it is to find out the demonstration of what someone else has discovered. Often beautiful truths are arrived at by *Synthesis,* by passing from the simple to the compound; but when it is a matter of finding out exactly the means for doing what is required, Synthesis is ordinarily not sufficient; and often a man might as well try to drink up the sea as to make all the required combinations, even though it is often possible to gain some assistance from the *method of exclusions,* which cuts out a considerable number of useless combinations; and often the nature of the case does not admit of any other method. But there are not always available the means for properly following this method. So it is to Analysis that we must look for a thread in the labyrinth, whenever it is possible; for there are cases where the very nature of the question requires that we should proceed by trial and error throughout, short cuts not always being possible.

§8. *Philalethes.* Now since demonstration always presupposes intuitive knowledge, it is this, I imagine, which gave occasion to the axiom that *all reasoning is from things previously known and previously granted (ex praecognitis et praeconcessis).* But we shall have occasion to speak of the faults of this axiom, when we come to speak of the *maxims* which are mistakenly supposed to be the foundations of our reasonings.

Theophilus. I shall be curious to learn what fault you can find with an axiom which appears so reasonable. If it was necessary to reduce everything to intuitive apprehensions, demonstrations would often be of unbearable prolixity. . . . But there is another hindrance, namely that it is not easy to demonstrate all the axioms, and entirely to reduce demonstrations to intuitive apprehensions. And if attempts had been made to do this, perhaps we should still be without the science of geometry. . . .

§ 14. *Philalethes.* Besides *intuition* and *demonstration,* which are the two degrees of our knowledge, all the rest is *faith or opinion, but not knowledge, at least in all general truths.* There is, however, *another perception of the mind employed about the particular existence of finite beings without us;* and this is called *sensitive knowledge. . . .*

Sensitive knowledge, or the knowledge which establishes the existence of particular beings without us, goes beyond bare probability; but it does not possess all the certainty of the two degrees of knowledge of which we have been speaking. *There can be nothing more certain than that the idea we receive from an external object is in our minds. But whether we can thence certainly infer the existence of anything without us which corresponds to that idea, is that whereof some men think there may be a question made; because men may have such ideas in their minds when no such thing exists, no such object affects their senses. But yet here I think we are provided with an evidence which puts us past doubting.* We are invincibly conscious of a different perception when we look on the sun by day and think on it by night; and the idea which is revived by the aid of memory is very different from the one which actually comes into our minds by our senses. *If any one says a dream may do the same thing, I make him this answer: (1) That it is no great matter whether I remove this scruple or no: where all is but dream, reasoning and arguments are of no use, truth and knowledge nothing. (2) That I believe he will allow a very manifest difference between dreaming of being in the fire and being actually in it.* And if he persists in appearing sceptical, I will tell him that it is enough that we certainly find *that pleasure or pain follows upon the application of certain objects to us, whose existence we perceive, or dream that we perceive, by our senses: this certainty is as great as our happiness or misery; beyond which we have no concernment to know or to be.* So that I think we may reckon *three degrees of knowledge; viz., intuitive, demonstrative, and sensitive.*

Theophilus. I believe you are right, and I even think that to these kinds of *certainty* or *certain knowledge* you might add *knowledge of the probable;* thus there will be two sorts of *knowledge* as there are two sorts of *proofs,* of which the one produces *certainty,* while the other arrives at *probability* only. But let us turn to the quarrel between the Sceptics and the Dogmatists over the existence of things without us. We have already touched upon it, but we must return to it here. I have in the past had much argument about this both personally and by letter with the late M. l'Abbé Foucher, Canon of Dijon, a man both learned and subtle, but somewhat too much engrossed in the Academics, whose sect he would gladly have revived, just as M. Gassendi brought back upon the scene the sect of Epicurus. His criticism of the *Recherche de la Vérité,* and other small treatises which he had printed subsequently, have brought their author some fame. He also published in the *Journal des Savans* some objections to my System of Pre-established Harmony, when I communicated it to the public, after meditating on it for some years; but death prevented him from answering my reply. He always preached that we ought to guard against prejudices and to insist on great exactitude; but not only did he not devote himself to practising what he preached, wherein he was excusable enough, but he also seemed to me not to heed whether others did so, foreseeing no doubt that no one ever would. Now I pointed out to him that the truth of sensible things only consisted in the connection of phenomena, for which there must be a reason, and which is the thing that distinguishes them from dreams; but that the truth of our existence and of the cause of phenomena is of another nature, because it establishes some substances. I urged that the Sceptics spoil what is good in their statements, by carrying them too far, even wishing to extend their doubts to immediate experiences, and even to geometrical truths (which, however, M. Foucher did not do), and to other truths of reason, which he did a little too much. But, to return to you, Sir, you are right in saying that there is a difference ordinarily between sensations and imaginings; but the Sceptics would say that a difference of more and less is not a difference of kind. Besides, though sensations are habitually more vivacious than imaginings, there are none the less cases where imaginative people are as much or perhaps more struck by their imaginings than others are by the truth of things; so that I hold that the true criterion regarding the objects of the senses is the connection between phenomena, that is to say the linking up of what occurs in different places and times, and in the experience of different men, who are themselves very important phenomena to one another in this regard. And the connection of phenomena, which guarantees *truths of fact* with regard to sensible things outside us, is verified by means of *truths of reason;* as appearances in optics have light thrown upon them by geometry. Still it must be admitted that none of this certitude is of the highest order, as you have rightly recognized. For it is not impossible, metaphysically speaking, for there to be a dream which is consecutive and enduring like the life of a man; but it is a thing as contrary to reason as it would be for a book to be composed by chance through the type being jumbled up together anyhow. Besides it is also true, that provided phenomena are linked up, it matters not whether they are called dreams or not, since experience shows that we are not mistaken in the measures we take with phenomena, when they are taken in accordance with the truths of reason.

§15. *Philalethes.* For the rest, *knowledge is not always clear, where the ideas are so. A man that has as clear ideas of the angles of a triangle, and of equality to two right ones, as any mathematician in the world, may yet have but a very obscure perception of their agreement.*

Theophilus. Usually, when ideas are fundamentally understood, their agreements and disagreements appear. Nevertheless, I admit that there are sometimes ideas so compounded that much care is needed to develop what is hidden in them; and considering this, some agreements and disagreements may still remain obscure. As to your example, my comment is that the fact that we have the angles of a triangle in the imagination does not mean that we therefore have clear ideas of them. Imagination is incapable of providing us with an image common to acute-angled and obtuse-angled triangles, and yet the idea of triangle is common to both. Thus this idea does not consist in the images, and it is not as easy as one might think fundamentally to understand the angles of a triangle.

COMPARATIVE STUDY QUESTIONS

Review Questions

1. What is an innate idea, according to Locke (Philalethes)?
2. What does Leibniz (Theophilus) mean by his distinction between "active" and "virtual" knowledge?
3. How does Locke define "idea"?
4. Name several metaphors that Locke uses to describe the nature of the mind.
5. What does Leibniz (Theophilus) mean by saying that "the soul is a little world"?
6. From what source does the mind obtain all the materials of knowledge, according to Locke?
7. What is an "idea of reflection," according to Locke?
8. What does Leibniz mean by "apperception"?
9. What three kinds or "degrees" of knowledge does Locke distinguish?
10. Of what kinds of things do we have sensitive knowledge, according to Locke?

Discussion Questions

1. What is the underlying presupposition of Locke's critique of innate ideas? How does Leibniz challenge this assumption?
2. Compare Locke's "dark closet" conception of the mind with Leibniz's notion of a "windowless monad."
3. On Leibniz's view, are **all** our ideas innate in some sense?
4. Why does Locke (Philalethes) find it strange to regard the propositions of arithmetic and geometry as innate? How does Leibniz account for the ignorance children have of these sciences?
5. Locke accepts the old axiom: "There is nothing in the intellect which was not previously in the senses." Leibniz agrees with one qualification. Assess its significance.
6. What was Mr. Molyneux's problem? Contrast the different answers given by Locke (Philalethes) and Leibniz (Theophilus). Does Locke's answer imply that the objects of sight and touch are ideas which have nothing in common? Does Leibniz think that the two sets of ideas have something in common? If so, what? Would Leibniz have been convinced by an appropriate psychological experiment?
7. Explain Locke's "historical plain method." Contrast it with the **more geo-metrico,** or method of geometry, which Descartes, Spinoza, and Leibniz tended to favor.

8. If knowledge is a perception of the agreement or disagreement of our ideas, and the only **immediate** objects we are acquainted with are ideas, can Locke really claim to know anything else, e.g., external physical objects? How does Leibniz, while agreeing with Locke's basic premise, avoid Locke's epistemological embarrassment?

9. Restate Locke's correspondence or representational theory of knowledge. Does he account satisfactorily for the difference between the world of dreams and the real world?

10. What does Leibniz (Theophilus) mean by saying that "the connection of phenomena, which guarantees **truths of fact** with regard to sensible things outside us, is verified by means of **truths of reason**"? In this context, how does he deal with the dream problem?

George Berkeley
(1685 – 1753)

THE PERCEPTION OF REALITY

Bishop George Berkeley

> Berkeley pointed out that we can never test the validity of
> knowledge by comparing an idea in the mind with an object
> outside the mind. We can only compare ideas among them-
> selves. This is a pertinent consideration about the *criteria* of
> knowledge, whether one agrees with Berkeley's idealism or
> not.
> C. I. Lewis, *Mind and the World Order*
> (1929)

On September 4, 1728, George Berkeley, Dean of Derry, set sail from London for
America. He was forty-three years old, recently married, and inspired with the idea
of founding a college in the Bermuda Islands to educate the sons of English
colonists and "a number of young American savages." He had received a charter
from King George I for St. Paul's College, as it was to be called, and a vote of
approval from the House of Commons for the project. He was also armed with the
promise of a government grant of £20,000, and private subscriptions of about
£3,000. To await the actual receipt of the grant, establish "mainland" connections,
and make other preparations, he chose Newport, Rhode Island, as his immediate
destination, arriving there after a stormy voyage and a brief stopover in Virginia, on
January 23, 1729.

Why had he come? Why had Berkeley left what was described as "the best
deanery in the Kingdom,"[1] a position worth the handsome sum of £1500 a year?
Why had he separated himself from his friends, Jonathan Swift, Richard Steele,
Joseph Addison, and Alexander Pope, and their civilized life in London, for the
wilds of the New World? Why had he abandoned his acquaintances at Court, where
he was always warmly received, and at the Universities of Trinity and Oxford,
where he felt equally at home?

Perhaps part of the answer is given in the following poem which he wrote in
1726 and entitled, "America, or the Muse's Refuge, A Prophecy," published years
later (in 1752) in his **Miscellany** under the title, "Verses on the Prospect of Planting
Arts and Learning in America."

---

1. Cf. Benjamin Rand, *Berkeley's American Sojourn* (Cambridge: Harvard University Press,
1932), p. 10.

The Muse, disgusted at an age and clime
  Barren of every glorious theme
In distant lands now waits a better time,
  Producing subjects worthy fame:

In happy climes, where from the genial sun
  And virgin earth such scenes ensue,
The force of art by nature seems outdone,
  And fancied beauties by the true:

In happy climes the seat of innocence,
  Where nature guides and virtue rules,
Where men shall not impose for truth and sense,
  The pedantry of courts and schools:

There shall be sung another golden age,
  The rise of empire and of arts,
The good and great inspiring epic rage,
  The wisest heads and noblest hearts.

Not such as Europe breeds in her decay;
  Such as she bred when fresh and young,
When heavenly flame did animate her clay,
  By future poets shall be sung.

Westward the course of empire takes its way;
  The four first Acts already past,
A fifth shall close the Drama with the day;
  Time's noblest offspring is the last.[2]

Stanzas one, three, and five express his dissatisfaction with European culture. The first suggests his disgust with the rather unglorious political scandal of his time known as the South Sea Bubble. In reaction to that event Berkeley published in 1721 **An Essay toward Preventing the Ruin of Great Britain.** The third stanza reveals Berkeley's disenchantment with the "pedantry of courts and schools." Although welcomed as an amiable and witty person in both polite and scholarly company, the actual reception of Berkeley's books was cold and uncomplimentary. After the publication of his **Treatise Concerning the Principles of Human Knowledge** in 1710, Sir John Percival wrote to Berkeley that he "did but name the subject matter of your book of **Principles** to some ingenious friends of mine and they immediately treated it with ridicule, at the same time refusing to read it."[3] Berkeley's **Three Dialogues Between Hylas and Philonous,** which is now acknowledged as a literary as well as a philosophical masterpiece, was written specifically to overcome the prejudices against his **Principles,** but apparently it fared no better when it appeared in 1713.

The fifth stanza, although indefinite in its reference, is perhaps somewhat unfair in its accusation. Berkeley knew most of the truly great and learned men of

---

2. *The Works of George Berkeley*, edited by A. C. Fraser (Oxford: Clarendon Press, 1901), Vol. IV, pp. 365–366.
3. Quoted in *The Works of George Berkeley*, Vol. I, p. 352.

his time, either personally or indirectly through their works or close associates. He knew ambassadors and kings, clergymen and politicians, literary people of all sorts, philosophers and scientists. He knew of Newton's physical and mathematical discoveries not only through his writings, but also through many debates which he had had with Newton's spokesman, Dr. Samuel Clarke. But Berkeley also knew that some of these eminent persons, too many to his way of thinking, were atheists and sceptics. Not surprisingly then, the subtitle of his **Three Dialogues** is "In Opposition to Sceptics and Atheists."

His dreams for America envisage, in good Baconian style, another "golden age," a veritable New Atlantis where Truth, Beauty, and Goodness are pursued. His hopes were not fulfilled. Berkeley waited in Rhode Island for nearly three years before the Prime Minister, Sir Robert Walpole, let it be known that the funds for the Bermuda college would not be forthcoming and that Berkeley had better "return home to Europe, and give up his present expectations."[4] Some eight to ten thousand pounds of Berkeley's promised sum were subsequently diverted to the dowry of the Princess Royal, and the rest to a scheme for establishing a colony in Georgia.[5] Berkeley and his family departed from Boston for England on September 21, 1731.

Although disappointing, Berkeley's sojourn in America was not wholly unproductive.[6] During his stay he wrote **Alciphron, or the Minute Philosopher,** seven dialogues patterned after the Platonic model. He also participated in the discussions of the Literary and Philosophical Society of Newport which he may have had a hand in founding in 1730. He conducted an important philosophical correspondence with the Reverend Samuel Johnson of Stratford, Connecticut, also a member of the Society. Through his preaching and other activities he advanced the cause of religious tolerance. People of other faiths attended his sermons and Berkeley himself tried his utmost to cultivate friendlier relations between the Church of England and "dissenters" such as Quakers, Congregationalists, and Baptists. He sought to change the prejudices and policies of his own church against the baptism of black slaves. In fact, he baptized three of his own black servants, which was perhaps only a gesture toward racial justice from today's standpoint, but no doubt a very courageous act in early colonial America.

Even after his project was officially abandoned, Berkeley did what he could to advance learning in America. He donated about one thousand books to Yale which Yale still possesses, and a lesser number to Harvard, all of which unfortunately were destroyed by fire in 1764. He also donated Whitehall, his Newport residence, to Yale. His American friend and disciple, Samuel Johnson, later became the first president of King's College (now Columbia University) and founded it on a model proposed by Berkeley. Other institutions which benefited from the advice or inspiration of Berkeley include the University of Pennsylvania, The Berkeley

---

4. Cf. Rand, *op. cit.,* pp. 39–40; A. A. Luce, *The Life of George Berkeley* (Edinburgh & London: Thomas Nelson & Sons, Ltd., 1949) p. 142.

5. Cf. Rand, *op. cit.,* p. 57; Luce, *op. cit.,* pp. 138–139.

6. The following account of Berkeley's accomplishments and influence is largely indebted to Rand, *op. cit.,* especially pp. 27–30, 67–70.

Divinity School in New Haven, and Trinity College in Hartford, Connecticut. It seems only fitting that the city of Berkeley, California, was named in 1866 by the Trustees of the College of California (later merged with the University of California) in honor of Berkeley's contributions to higher education in America.[7]

Berkeley's conviction, which he expresses in his preface to his **Three Dialogues,** that "the end of speculation [is] practice or the improvement and regulation of our lives and actions" places him squarely in the tradition of pragmatism which extends through Charles S. Peirce to William James, John Dewey, and C. I. Lewis, all of whom were profoundly influenced by Berkeley's views. In contrast to those who, in his words, "perplex the plainest things," Berkeley proposes principles which he thinks will, among other things, destroy atheism and scepticism, retrench science, and reduce men from paradoxes to common sense. It is hardly any wonder that he was so well received in the New World, with its political and religious idealism on the one hand, and its practical common sense on the other.

The central problems around which his thought focuses concern the trustworthiness of the senses as a means of acquiring knowledge, and the supposed distinction between things as they really are and things as they appear to us. To those who doubt that we can immediately perceive things as they really are and suppose that objects nonetheless exist independently of all perception, Berkeley gives the name of "materialist," literally the meaning of the name of "Hylas" of the **Dialogues.** The term is used broadly. It applies to a philosopher like Descartes who believes in the independent existence of things, and also to one like Hobbes who, in addition, believes that all things, including minds, can be wholly explained in terms of matter (i.e., bodies) in motion. Berkeley's own position, that of Philonous, a "lover of mind," is called "immaterialism," or more lately, "idealism." He holds that the senses provide sufficient evidence for knowledge, even knowledge of God's existence and the world at large. In addition to this claim, however, Berkeley makes another, even more far-reaching. He argues that "to be" is "to be perceived," or (in Latin) **esse est percipi.** That is to say, an object's existence is exhausted by the ideas or perceptions we have of it. Totally unperceived things and substances simply do not exist. Finally, Berkeley claims that besides ideas and collections of ideas, the only other ultimate realities are minds.

---

7. See the article on the city of Berkeley, *Encyclopedia Britannica*, 1965 ed., Vol. 3, p. 510.

BERKELEY

Three Dialogues

*Between Hylas and Philonous, in Opposition to Sceptics and Atheists**

The First Dialogue

Philonous. Good morrow, Hylas. I did not expect to find you abroad so early.

Hylas. It is indeed something unusual; but my thoughts were so taken up with a subject I was discoursing of last night that, finding I could not sleep, I resolved to rise and take a turn in the garden.

Philonous. It happened well, to let you see what innocent and agreeable pleasures you lose every morning. Can there be a pleasanter time of the day, or a more delightful season of the year? That purple sky, these wild but sweet notes of birds, the fragrant bloom upon the trees and flowers, the gentle influence of the rising sun, these and a thousand nameless beauties of nature inspire the soul with secret transports; its faculties, too, being at this time fresh and lively, are fit for those meditations which the solitude of a garden and tranquillity of the morning naturally dispose us to. But I am afraid I interrupt your thoughts, for you seemed very intent on something.

Hylas. It is true, I was, and shall be obliged to you if you will permit me to go on in the same vein; not that I would by any means deprive myself of your company, for my thoughts always flow more easily in conversation with a friend than when I am alone; but my request is that you would suffer me to impart my reflexions to you.

Philonous. With all my heart, it is what I should have requested myself if you had not prevented me.

Hylas. I was considering the odd fate of those men who have in all ages, through an affectation of being distinguished from the vulgar, or some unaccountable turn of thought, pretended either to believe nothing at all or to believe the most extravagant things in the world. This, however, might be borne if their paradoxes and scepticism did not draw after them some consequences of general disadvantage to mankind. But the mischief lieth here: that when men of less leisure see them who are supposed to have spent their whole time in the pur-

---

*From Berkeley's *Three Dialogues,* the third and final edition of 1734. The punctuation has been modernized, except for Berkeley's use of italics which has been retained. He consistently uses italics both to place emphasis and to mention or name, and often to do both simultaneously. His capitalization has, for the most part, been retained, as has the old-fashioned spelling, in order to capture some of the flavor of eighteenth-century style.

suits of knowledge professing an entire ignorance of all things, or advancing such notions as are repugnant to plain and commonly received principles, they will be tempted to entertain suspicions concerning the most important truths, which they had hitherto held sacred and unquestionable.

Philonous. I entirely agree with you, as to the ill tendency of the affected doubts of some philosophers, and fantastical conceits of others. I am even so far gone of late in this way of thinking that I have quitted several of the sublime notions I had got in their schools for vulgar opinions. And I give it you on my word, since this revolt from metaphysical notions to the plain dictates of nature and common sense, I find my understanding strangely enlightened, so that I can now easily comprehend a great many things which before were all mystery and riddle.

Hylas. I am glad to find there was nothing in the accounts I heard of you.

Philonous. Pray, what were those?

Hylas. You were represented in last night's conversation as one who maintained the most extravagant opinion that ever entered into the mind of man, to wit, that there is no such thing as *material substance* in the world.

Philonous. That there is no such thing as what *philosophers* call *material substance,* I am seriously persuaded; but if I were made to see anything absurd or sceptical in this, I should then have the same reason to renounce this that I imagine I have now to reject the contrary opinion.

Hylas. What! Can anything be more fantastical, more repugnant to Common Sense, or a more manifest piece of Scepticism than to believe there is no such thing as *matter?*

Philonous. Softly, good Hylas. What if it should prove that you, who hold there is, are, by virtue of that opinion, a greater sceptic and maintain more paradoxes and repugnances to Common Sense than I who believe no such thing?

Hylas. You may as soon persuade me, the part is greater than the whole, as that, in order to avoid absurdity and Scepticism, I should ever be obliged to give up my opinion in this point.

Philonous. Well then, are you content to admit that opinion for true which, upon examination, shall appear most agreeable to Common Sense and remote from Scepticism?

Hylas. With all my heart. Since you are for raising disputes about the plainest things in nature, I am content for once to hear what you have to say.

Philonous. Pray, Hylas, what do you mean by a *sceptic?*

Hylas. I mean what all men mean, one that doubts of everything.

Philonous. He then who entertains no doubt concerning some particular point, with regard to that point cannot be thought a sceptic.

Hylas. I agree with you.

Philonous. Whether doth doubting consist in embracing the affirmative or negative side of a question?

Hylas. In neither; for whoever understands English cannot but know that *doubting* signifies a suspense between both.

Philonous. He then that denieth any point can no more be said to doubt of it than he who affirmeth it with the same degree of assurance.

Hylas. True.

Philonous. And, consequently, for such his denial is no more to be esteemed a sceptic than the other.

Hylas. I acknowledge it.

Philonous. How cometh it to pass then, Hylas, that you pronounce me a *sceptic* because I deny what you affirm, to wit, the existence of Matter? Since, for aught you can tell, I am as peremptory in my denial as you in your affirmation.

Hylas. Hold, Philonous, I have been a little out in my definition; but every false step a man makes in discourse is not to be insisted on. I said indeed that a *sceptic* was one who doubted of everything; but I should have added: or who denieth the reality and truth of things.

Philonous. What things? Do you mean the principles and theorems of sciences? But these you know are universal intellectual notions, and consequently independent of Matter; the denial therefore of this doth not imply the denying them.

Hylas. I grant it. But are there no other things? What think you of distrusting the senses, of denying the real existence of sensible things, or pretending to know nothing of them. Is not this sufficient to denominate a man a *sceptic?*

Philonous. Shall we therefore examine which of us it is that denies the reality of sensible things or professes the greatest ignorance of them, since, if I take you rightly, he is to be esteemed the greatest *sceptic?*

Hylas. That is what I desire.

Philonous. What mean you by Sensible Things?

Hylas. Those things which are perceived by the senses. Can you imagine that I mean anything else?

Philonous. Pardon me, Hylas, if I am desirous clearly to apprehend your notions, since this may much shorten our inquiry. Suffer me then to ask you this further question. Are those things only perceived by the senses which are perceived immediately? Or may those things properly be said to be *sensible* which are perceived mediately, or not without the intervention of others?

Hylas. I do not sufficiently understand you.

Philonous. In reading a book, what I immediately perceive are the letters, but mediately, or by means of these, are suggested to my mind the notions of God, virtue, truth, etc. Now, that the letters are truly sensible things, or perceived by sense, there is no doubt; but I would know whether you take the things suggested by them to be so too.

Hylas. No, certainly; it were absurd to think *God* or *virtue* sensible things, though they may be signified and suggested to the mind by sensible marks with which they have an arbitrary connection.

Philonous. It seems, then, that by *sensible things* you mean those only which can be perceived *immediately* by sense.

Hylas. Right.

Philonous. Doth it not follow from this that, though I see one part of the sky red, and another blue, and that my reason doth thence evidently conclude there must be some cause of that diversity of colours, yet that cause cannot be said to be a sensible thing or perceived by the sense of seeing?

Hylas. It doth.

Philonous. In like manner, though I hear variety of sounds, yet I cannot be said to hear the causes of those sounds.

Hylas. You cannot.

Philonous. And when by my touch I perceive a thing to be hot and heavy, I cannot say, with any truth or propriety, that I feel the cause of its heat or weight.

Hylas. To prevent any more questions of this kind, I tell you once for all that by *sensible things* I mean those only which are perceived by sense, and that in truth the senses perceive nothing which they do not perceive *immediately,* for they make no inferences. The deducing therefore of causes or occasions from effects and appearances, which alone are perceived by sense, entirely relates to reason.

Philonous. This point then is agreed between us—that *sensible things are those only which are immediately perceived by sense.* You will farther inform me whether we immediately perceive by sight anything besides light and colours and figures; or by hearing, anything but sounds; by the palate, anything beside tastes; by the smell, besides odours; or by the touch, more than tangible qualities.

Hylas. We do not.

Philonous. It seems, therefore, that if you take away all sensible qualities, there remains nothing sensible?

Hylas. I grant it.

Philonous. Sensible things therefore are nothing else but so many sensible qualities or combinations of sensible qualities?

Hylas. Nothing else.

Philonous. *Heat* is then a sensible thing?

Hylas. Certainly.

Philonous. Doth the *reality* of sensible things consist in being perceived, or is it something distinct from their being perceived, and that bears no relation to the mind?

Hylas. To *exist* is one thing, and to be *perceived* is another.

Philonous. I speak with regard to sensible things only; and of these I ask, whether by their real existence you mean a subsistence exterior to the mind and distinct from their being perceived?

Hylas. I mean a real absolute being, distinct from and without any relation to their being perceived.

Philonous. Heat therefore, if it be allowed a real being, must exist without the mind?

Hylas. It must.

Philonous. Tell me, Hylas, is this real existence equally compatible to all degrees of heat which we perceive, or is there any reason why we should attribute it to some, and deny it to others? And if there be, pray let me know that reason.

Hylas. Whatever degree of heat we perceive by sense, we may be sure the same exists in the object that occasions it.

Philonous. What! The greatest as well as the least?

Hylas. I tell you, the reason is plainly the same in respect of both. They are both perceived by sense; nay, the greater degree of heat is more sensibly perceived; and consequently, if there is any difference, we are more certain of its real existence than we can be of the reality of a lesser degree.

Philonous. But is not the most vehement and intense degree of heat a very great pain?

Hylas. No one can deny it.

Philonous. And is any unperceiving thing capable of pain or pleasure?

Hylas. No, certainly.

Philonous. Is your material substance a senseless being or a being endowed with sense and perception?

Hylas. It is senseless, without doubt.

Philonous. It cannot, therefore, be the subject of pain?

Hylas. By no means.

Philonous. Nor, consequently, of the greatest heat perceived by sense, since you acknowledge this to be no small pain?

Hylas. I grant it.

Philonous. What shall we say then of your external object: is it a material Substance, or no?

Hylas. It is a material substance with the sensible qualities inhering in it.

Philonous. How then can a great heat exist in it, since you own it cannot in a material substance? I desire you would clear this point.

Hylas. Hold, Philonous, I fear I was out in yielding intense heat to be a pain. It should seem rather that pain is something distinct from heat, and the consequence or effect of it.

Philonous. Upon putting your hand near the fire, do you perceive one simple uniform sensation or two distinct sensations?

Hylas. But one simple sensation.

Philonous. Is not the heat immediately perceived?

Hylas. It is.

Philonous. And the pain?

Hylas. True.

Philonous. Seeing therefore they are both immediately perceived at the same time, and the fire affects you only with one simple or uncompounded idea, it follows that this same simple idea is both the intense heat immediately perceived and the pain; and, consequently, that the intense heat immediately perceived is nothing distinct from a particular sort of pain.

Hylas. It seems so.

Philonous. Again, try in your thoughts, Hylas, if you can conceive a vehement sensation to be without pain or pleasure.

Hylas. I cannot.

Philonous. Or can you frame to yourself an idea of sensible pain or pleasure, in general, abstracted from every particular idea of heat, cold, tastes, smells, etc.?

Hylas. I do not find that I can.

Philonous. Doth it not therefore follow that sensible pain is nothing distinct from those sensations or ideas, in an intense degree?

Hylas. It is undeniable; and, to speak the truth, I begin to suspect a very great heat cannot exist but in a mind perceiving it.

Philonous. What! are you then in that sceptical state of suspense, between affirming and denying?

Hylas. I think I may be positive in the point. A very violent and painful heat cannot exist without the mind.

Philonous. It hath not therefore, according to you, any *real* being?

Hylas. I own it.

Philonous. Is it therefore certain that there is no body in nature really hot?

Hylas. I have not denied there is any real heat in bodies. I only say there is no such thing as an intense real heat.

Philonous. But did you not say before that all degrees of heat were equally real, or, if there was any difference, that the greater were more undoubtedly real than the lesser?

Hylas. True; but it was because I did not then consider the ground there is for distinguishing between them, which I now plainly see. And it is this: because intense heat is nothing else but a particular kind of painful sensation, and pain cannot exist but in a perceiving being, it follows that no intense heat can really exist in an unperceiving corporeal substance. But this is no reason why we should deny heat in an inferior degree to exist in such a substance.

Philonous. But how shall we be able to discern those degrees of heat which exist only in the mind from those which exist without it?

Hylas. That is no difficult matter. You know the least pain cannot exist unperceived; whatever, therefore, degree of heat is a pain exists only in the mind. But as for all other degrees of heat, nothing obliges us to think the same of them.

Philonous. I think you granted before that no unperceiving being was capable of pleasure any more than of pain.

Hylas. I did.

Philonous. And is not warmth, or a more gentle degree of heat than what causes uneasiness, a pleasure?

Hylas. What then?

Philonous. Consequently, it cannot exist without the mind in an unperceiving substance, or body.

Hylas. So it seems.

Philonous. Since, therefore, as well those degrees of heat that are not painful, as those that are, can exist only in a thinking substance, may we not conclude that external bodies are absolutely incapable of any degree of heat whatsoever?

Hylas. On second thoughts, I do not think it is so evident that warmth is a pleasure as that a great degree of heat is a pain.

Philonous. I do not pretend that warmth is as great a pleasure as heat is a pain. But if you grant it to be even a small pleasure, it serves to make good my conclusion.

Hylas. I could rather call it an *indolence.* It seems to be nothing more than a privation of both pain and pleasure. And that such a quality or state as this may agree to an unthinking substance, I hope you will not deny.

Philonous. If you are resolved to maintain that warmth, or a gentle degree of heat, is no pleasure, I know not how to convince you otherwise than by appealing to your own sense. But what think you of cold?

Hylas. The same that I do of heat. An intense degree of cold is a pain; for to feel a very great cold is to perceive a great uneasiness; it cannot therefore exist without the mind; but a lesser degree of cold may, as well as a lesser degree of heat.

Philonous. Those bodies, therefore, upon whose application to our own we perceive a moderate degree of heat must be concluded to have a moderate degree of heat or warmth in them; and those upon whose application we feel a like degree of cold must be thought to have cold in them.

Hylas. They must.

Philonous. Can any doctrine be true that necessarily leads a man into an absurdity?

Hylas. Without doubt it cannot.

Philonous. Is it not an absurdity to think that the same thing should be at the same time cold and warm?

Hylas. It is.

Philonous. Suppose now one of your hands hot, and the other cold, and that they are both at once put into the same vessel of water, in an intermediate state, will not the water seem cold to one hand, and warm to the other?

Hylas. It will.

Philonous. Ought we not therefore, by your principles, to conclude it is really both cold and warm at the same time, that is, according to your own concession, to believe an absurdity?

Hylas. I confess it seems so.

Philonous. Consequently, the principles themselves are false, since you have granted that no true principle leads to an absurdity.

Hylas. But, after all, can anything be more absurd than to say, *there is no heat in the fire?*

Philonous. To make the point still clearer; tell me whether, in two cases exactly alike, we ought not to make the same judgment?

Hylas. We ought.

Philonous. When a pin pricks your finger, does it not rend and divide the fibres of your flesh?

Hylas. It doth.

Philonous. And when a coal burns your finger, does it any more?

Hylas. It doth not.

Philonous. Since, therefore, you neither judge the sensation itself occasioned by the pin, nor anything like it to be in the pin, you should not, conformably to what you have now granted, judge the sensation occasioned by the fire, or anything like it, to be in the fire.

Hylas. Well, since it must be so, I am content to yield this point, and acknowledge that heat and cold are only sensations existing in our minds. But there still remain qualities enough to secure the reality of external things.

Philonous. But what will you say, Hylas, if it shall appear that the case is the same with regard to all other sensible qualities, and that they can no more be supposed to exist without the mind than heat and cold?

Hylas. Then, indeed, you will have done something to the purpose; but that is what I despair of seeing proved.

Philonous. Let us examine them in order. What think you of tastes—do they exist without the mind, or no?

Hylas. Can any man in his senses doubt whether sugar is sweet, or wormwood bitter?

Philonous. Inform me, Hylas. Is a sweet taste a particular kind of pleasure or pleasant sensation, or is it not?

Hylas. It is.

Philonous. And is not bitterness some kind of uneasiness or pain?

Hylas. I grant it.

Philonous. If, therefore, sugar and wormwood are unthinking corporeal substances existing without the mind, how can sweetness and bitterness, that is, pleasure and pain, agree to them?

Hylas. Hold, Philonous. I now see what it was deluded me all this time. You asked whether heat and cold, sweetness and bitterness, were not particular sorts of pleasure and pain; to which I answered simply that they were. Whereas I should have thus distinguished: those qualities as perceived by us are pleasures or pains, but not as existing in the external objects. We must not therefore conclude absolutely that there is no heat in the fire or sweetness in the sugar, but only that heat or sweetness, as perceived by us, are not in the fire or sugar. What say you to this?

Philonous. I say it is nothing to the purpose. Our discourse proceeded altogether concerning sensible things, which you defined to be *the things we immediately perceive by our senses.* Whatever other qualities, therefore, you speak of, as distinct from these, I know nothing of them, neither do they at all belong to the point in dispute. You may, indeed, pretend to have discovered certain qualities which you do not perceive, and assert those insensible qualities exist in fire and sugar. But what use can be made of this to your present purpose, I am at a loss to conceive. Tell me then once more, do you acknowledge that heat and cold, sweetness and bitterness (meaning those qualities which are perceived by the senses), do not exist without the mind?

Hylas. I see it is to no purpose to hold out, so I give up the cause as to those mentioned qualities, though I profess it sounds oddly to say that sugar is not sweet.

Philonous. But, for your farther satisfaction, take this along with you: that which at other times seems sweet shall, to a distempered palate, appear bitter. And nothing can be plainer than that divers persons perceive different tastes in the same food, since that which one man delights in, another abhors. And how could this be if the taste was something really inherent in the food?

Hylas. I acknowledge I know not how.

Philonous. In the next place, odours are to be considered. And with regard to these I would fain know whether what hath been said of tastes does not exactly agree to them? Are they not so many pleasing or displeasing sensations?

Hylas. They are.

Philonous. Can you then conceive it possible that they should exist in an unperceiving thing?

Hylas. I cannot.

Philonous. Or can you imagine that filth and ordure affect those brute animals that feed on them out of choice with the same smells which we perceive in them?

Hylas. By no means.

Philonous. May we not therefore conclude of smells, as of the other forementioned qualities, that they cannot exist in any but a perceiving substance or mind?

Hylas. I think so.

Philonous. Then as to *sounds,* what must we think of them: are they accidents really inherent in external bodies or not?

Hylas. That they inhere not in the sonorous bodies is plain from hence; because a bell struck in the exhausted receiver of an air-pump sends forth no sound. The air, therefore, must be thought the subject of sound.

Philonous. What reason is there for that, Hylas?

Hylas. Because, when any motion is raised in the air, we perceive a sound greater or lesser, in proportion to the air's motion; but without some motion in the air we never hear any sound at all.

Philonous. And granting that we never hear a sound but when some motion is produced in the air, yet I do not see how you can infer from thence that the sound itself is in the air.

Hylas. It is this very motion in the external air that produces in the mind the sensation of *sound.* For, striking on the drum of the ear, it causeth a vibration which by the auditory nerves being communicated to the brain, the soul is thereupon affected with the sensation called *sound.*

Philonous. What! is sound then a sensation?

Hylas. I tell you, as perceived by us it is a particular sensation in the mind.

Philonous. And can any sensation exist without the mind?

Hylas. No, certainly.

Philonous. How then can sound, being a sensation, exist in the air if by the *air* you mean a senseless substance existing without the mind?

Hylas. You must distinguish, Philonous, between sound as it is perceived by us, and as it is in itself; or (which is the same thing) between the sound we immediately perceive and that which exists without us. The former, indeed, is a particular kind of sensation, but the latter is merely a vibrative or undulatory motion in the air.

Philonous. I thought I had already obviated that distinction by the answer I gave when you were applying it in a like case before. But, to say no more of that, are you sure then that sound is really nothing but motion?

Hylas. I am.

Philonous. Whatever, therefore, agrees to real sound may with truth be attributed to motion?

Hylas. It may.

Philonous. It is then good sense to speak of *motion* as of a thing that is *loud, sweet, acute,* or *grave.*

Hylas. I see you are resolved not to understand me. Is it not evident those accidents or modes belong only to sensible sound, or *sound* in the common acceptation of the word, but not to *sound* in the real and philosophic sense, which, as I just now told you, is nothing but a certain motion of the air?

Philonous. It seems then there are two sorts of sound—the one vulgar, or that which is heard, the other philosophical and real?

Hylas. Even so.

Philonous. And the latter consists in motion?

Hylas. I told you so before.

Philonous. Tell me, Hylas, to which of the senses, think you, the idea of motion belongs? To the hearing?

Hylas. No, certainly; but to the sight and touch.

Philonous. It should follow then that, according to you, real sounds may possibly be *seen* or *felt,* but never *heard.*

Hylas. Look you, Philonous, you may, if you please, make a jest of my opinion, but that will not alter the truth of things. I own, indeed, the inferences you draw me into sound something oddly, but common language, you know, is framed by, and for the use of, the vulgar. We must not therefore wonder if expressions adapted to exact philosophic notions seem uncouth and out of the way.

Philonous. Is it come to that? I assure you I imagine myself to have gained no small point since you make so light of departing from common phrases and opinions, it being a main part of our inquiry to examine whose notions are widest of the common road and most repugnant to the general sense of the world. But can you think it no more than a philosophical paradox to say that *real sounds are never heard,* and that the idea of them is obtained by some other sense? And is there nothing in this contrary to nature and the truth of things?

Hylas. To deal ingenuously, I do not like it. And, after the concessions already made, I had as well grant that sounds, too, have no real being without the mind.

Philonous. And I hope you will make no difficulty to acknowledge the same of *colours.*

Hylas. Pardon me; the case of colours is very different. Can anything be plainer than that we see them on the objects?

Philonous. The objects you speak of are, I suppose, corporeal substances existing without the mind?

Hylas. They are.

Philonous. And have true and real colours inhering in them?

Hylas. Each visible object has that colour which we see in it.

Philonous. How! is there anything visible but what we perceive by sight?

Hylas. There is not.

Philonous. And do we perceive anything by sense which we do not perceive immediately?

Hylas. How often must I be obliged to repeat the same thing? I tell you, we do not.

Philonous. Have patience, good Hylas, and tell me once more whether there is anything immediately perceived by the senses except sensible qualities. I know you asserted there was not; but I would now be informed whether you still persist in the same opinion.

Hylas. I do.

Philonous. Pray, is your corporeal substance either a sensible quality or made up of sensible qualities?

Hylas. What a question that is! Who ever thought it was?

Philonous. My reason for asking was, because in saying *each visible object has that colour which we see in it,* you make visible objects to be corporeal substances, which implies either that corporeal substances are sensible qualities or else that there is something besides sensible qualities perceived by sight; but as this point was formerly agreed between us, and is still maintained by you, it is a clear consequence that your *corporeal substance* is nothing distinct from *sensible qualities.*

Hylas. You may draw as many absurd consequences as you please and endeavour to perplex the plainest things, but you shall never persuade me out of my senses. I clearly understand my own meaning.

Philonous. I wish you would make me understand it, too. But, since you are unwilling to have your notion of corporeal substance examined, I shall urge that point no farther. Only be pleased to let me know whether the same colours which we see exist in external bodies or some other.

Hylas. The very same.

Philonous. What! are then the beautiful red and purple we see on yonder clouds really in them? Or do you imagine they have in themselves any other form than that of a dark mist or vapour?

Hylas. I must own, Philonous, those colours are not really in the clouds as they seem to be at this distance. They are only apparent colours.

Philonous. *Apparent* call you them? How shall we distinguish these apparent colours from real?

Hylas. Very easily. Those are to be thought apparent which, appearing only at a distance, vanish upon a nearer approach.

Philonous. And those, I suppose, are to be thought real which are discovered by the most near and exact survey.

Hylas. Right.

Philonous. Is the nearest and exactest survey made by the help of a microscope or by the naked eye?

Hylas. By a microscope, doubtless.

Philonous. But a microscope often discovers colours in an object different from those perceived by the unassisted sight. And, in case we had microscopes magnifying to any assigned degree, it is certain that no object whatsoever, viewed through them, would appear in the same colour which it exhibits to the naked eye.

Hylas. And what will you conclude from all this? You cannot argue that there are really and naturally no colours on objects because by artificial managements they may be altered or made to vanish.

Philonous. I think it may evidently be concluded from your own concessions that all the colours we see with our naked eyes are only apparent as those on the clouds, since they vanish upon a more close and accurate inspection which is afforded us by a microscope. Then, as to what you say by way of prevention: I ask you whether the real and natural state of an object is better discovered by a very sharp and piercing sight or by one which is less sharp?

Hylas. By the former without doubt.

Philonous. Is it not plain from *Dioptrics* that microscopes make the sight more penetrating and represent objects as they would appear to the eye in case it were naturally endowed with a most exquisite sharpness?

Hylas. It is.

Philonous. Consequently, the microscopical representation is to be thought that which best sets forth the real nature of the thing, or what it is in itself. The colours, therefore, by it perceived are more genuine and real than those perceived otherwise.

Hylas. I confess there is something in what you say.

Philonous. Besides, it is not only possible but manifest that there actually are animals whose eyes are by nature framed to perceive those things which by reason of their minuteness escape our sight. What think you of those inconceivably small animals perceived by glasses? Must we suppose they are all stark blind? Or, in case they see, can it be imagined their sight has not the same use in preserving their bodies from injuries which appears in that of all other animals? And if it hath, is it not evident they must see particles less than their own bodies, which will present them with a far different view in each object from that which strikes our senses? Even our own eyes do not always represent objects to us after the same manner. In the jaundice everyone knows that all things seem yellow. Is it not therefore highly probable those animals in whose eyes we discern a very different texture from that of ours, and whose bodies aboundwith different humours, do not see the same colours in every object that we do? From all which should it not seem to follow that all colours are equally apparent, and that none of those which we perceive are really inherent in any outward object?

Hylas. It should.

Philonous. The point will be past all doubt if you consider that, in case colours were real properties or affections inherent in external bodies, they could admit of no alteration without some change wrought in the very bodies themselves; but is it not evident from what has been said that, upon the use of microscopes, upon a change happening in the humours of the eye, or a variation of distance, without any manner of real alteration in the thing itself, the colours of any object are either changed or totally disappear? Nay, all other circumstances remaining the same, change but the situation of some objects and they shall present different colours to the eye. The same thing happens upon viewing an object in various degrees of light. And what is more known than that the same bodies appear differently coloured by candlelight from what they do in the open day? Add to these the experiment of a prism which, separating the heterogeneous rays of light, alters the colour of any object and will cause the whitest to appear of a deep blue or red to the naked eye. And now tell me whether you are still of opinion that every body has its true real colour inhering in it; and if you think it has, I would fain know farther from you what certain distance and position of the object, what peculiar texture and formation of the eye, what degree or kind of light is necessary for ascertaining that true colour and distinguishing it from apparent ones.

Hylas. I own myself entirely satisfied that they are all equally apparent and that there is no such thing as colour really inhering in external bodies, but that it is altogether in the light. And what confirms me in this opinion is that in proportion to the light colours are still more or less vivid; and if there be no light, then are there no colours perceived. Besides, allowing there are colours on external objects, yet, how is it possible for us to perceive them? For no external body affects the mind unless it acts first on our organs of sense. But the only action of bodies is motion, and motion cannot be communicated otherwise than by impulse. A distant object, therefore, cannot act on the eye, nor consequently make itself or its properties perceivable to the soul. Whence it plainly follows that it is immediately some contiguous substance which, operating on the eye, occasions a perception of colours; and such is light.

Philonous. How! is light then a substance?

Hylas. I tell you, Philonous, external light is nothing but a thin fluid substance whose minute particles, being agitated with a brisk motion and in various manners reflected from the different surfaces of outward objects to the eyes, communicate different motions to the optic nerves; which, being propagated to the brain, cause therein various impressions, and these are attended with the sensations of red, blue, yellow, etc.

Philonous. It seems, then, the light doth no more than shake the optic nerves.

Hylas. Nothing else.

Philonous. And, consequent to each particular motion of the nerves, the mind is affected with a sensation which is some particular colour.

Hylas. Right.

234

Philonous. And these sensations have no existence without the mind.

Hylas. They have not.

Philonous. How then do you affirm that colours are in the light, since by *light* you understand a corporeal substance external to the mind?

Hylas. Light and colours, as immediately perceived by us, I grant cannot exist without the mind. But in themselves they are only the motions and configurations of certain insensible particles of matter.

Philonous. Colours, then, in the vulgar sense, or taken for the immediate objects of sight, cannot agree to any but a perceiving substance.

Hylas. That is what I say.

Philonous. Well then, since you give up the point as to those sensible qualities which are alone thought colours by all mankind besides, you may hold what you please with regard to those invisible ones of the philosophers. It is not my business to dispute about *them;* only I would advise you to bethink yourself whether, considering the inquiry we are upon, it be prudent for you to affirm— *the red and blue which we see are not real colours, but certain unknown motions and figures which no man ever did or can see are truly so.* Are not these shocking notions, and are not they subject to as many ridiculous inferences as those you were obliged to renounce before in the case of sounds?

Hylas. I frankly own, Philonous, that it is in vain to stand out any longer. Colours, sounds, tastes, in a word, all those termed *secondary qualities,* have certainly no existence without the mind. But by this acknowledgment I must not be supposed to derogate anything from the reality of Matter, or external objects; seeing it is no more than several philosophers maintain, who nevertheless are the farthest imaginable from denying Matter. For the clearer understanding of this you must know sensible qualities are by philosophers divided into *primary* and *secondary.* The former are Extension, Figure, Solidity, Gravity, Motion, and Rest. And these they hold exist really in bodies. The latter are those above enumerated, or, briefly, *all sensible qualities besides the Primary,* which they assert are only so many sensations or ideas existing nowhere but in the mind. But all this, I doubt not, you are already apprised of. For my part I have been a long time sensible there was such an opinion current among philosophers, but was never thoroughly convinced of its truth till now.

Philonous. You are still then of opinion that *extension* and *figures* are inherent in external unthinking substances?

Hylas. I am.

Philonous. But what if the same arguments which are brought against secondary qualities will hold good against these also?

Hylas. Why then I shall be obliged to think they too exist only in the mind.

Philonous. Is it your opinion the very figure and extension which you perceive by sense exist in the outward object or material substance?

Hylas. It is.

Philonous. Have all other animals as good grounds to think the same of the figure and extension which they see and feel?

Hylas. Without doubt, if they have any thought at all.

Philonous. Answer me, Hylas. Think you the senses were bestowed upon all animals for their preservation and well-being in life? Or were they given to men alone for this end?

Hylas. I make no question but they have the same use in all other animals.

Philonous. If so, is it not necessary they should be enabled by them to perceive their own limbs and those bodies which are capable of harming them?

Hylas. Certainly.

Philonous. A mite therefore must be supposed to see his own foot, and things equal or even less than it, as bodies of some considerable dimension, though at the same time they appear to you scarce discernible, or at best as so many visible points?

Hylas. I cannot deny it.

Philonous. And to creatures less than the mite they will seem yet larger?

Hylas. They will.

Philonous. Insomuch that what you can hardly discern will to another extremely minute animal appear as some huge mountain?

Hylas. All this I grant.

Philonous. Can one and the same thing be at the same time in itself of different dimensions?

Hylas. That were absurd to imagine.

Philonous. But from what you have laid down it follows that both the extension by you perceived and that perceived by the mite itself, as likewise all those perceived by lesser animals, are each of them the true extension of the mite's foot; that is to say, by your own principles you are led into an absurdity.

Hylas. There seems to be some difficulty in the point.

Philonous. Again, have you not acknowledged that no real inherent property of any object can be changed without some change in the thing itself?

Hylas. I have.

Philonous. But, as we approach to or recede from an object, the visible extension varies, being at one distance ten or a hundred times greater than at another. Doth it not therefore follow from hence likewise that it is not really inherent in the object?

Hylas. I own I am at a loss what to think.

Philonous. Your judgment will soon be determined if you will venture to think as freely concerning this quality as you have done concerning the rest. Was it not admitted as a good argument that neither heat nor cold was in the water because it seemed warm to one hand and cold to the other?

Hylas. It was.

Philonous. Is it not the very same reasoning to conclude there is no extension or figure in an object because to one eye it shall seem little, smooth, and round, when at the same time it appears to the other great, uneven, and angular?

Hylas. The very same. But does this latter fact ever happen?

Philonous. You may at any time make the experiment by looking with one eye bare, and with the other through a microscope.

Hylas. I know not how to maintain it, and yet I am loath to give up *extension;* I see so many odd consequences following upon such a concession.

Philonous. Odd, say you? After the concessions already made, I hope you will stick at nothing for its oddness. But, on the other hand, should it not seem very odd if the general reasoning which includes all other sensible qualities did not also include extension? If it be allowed that no idea nor anything like an idea can exist in an unperceiving substance, then surely it follows that no figure or mode of extension, which we can either perceive or imagine, or have any idea of, can be really inherent in Matter, not to mention the peculiar difficulty there must be in conceiving a material substance, prior to and distinct from extension, to be the *substratum* of extension. Be the sensible quality what it will—figure or sound or colour—it seems alike impossible it should subsist in that which doth not perceive it.

Hylas. I give up the point for the present, reserving still a right to retract my opinion in case I shall hereafter discover any false step in my progress to it.

Philonous. That is a right you cannot be denied. Figures and extension being dispatched, we proceed next to *motion.* Can a real motion in any external body be at the same time both very swift and very slow?

Hylas. It cannot.

Philonous. Is not the motion of a body swift in a reciprocal proportion to the time it takes up in describing any given space? Thus a body that describes a mile in an hour moves three times faster than it would in case it described only a mile in three hours.

Hylas. I agree with you.

Philonous. And is not time measured by the succession of ideas in our minds?

Hylas. It is.

Philonous. And is it not possible ideas should succeed one another twice as fast in your mind as they do in mine, or in that of some spirit of another kind?

Hylas. I own it.

Philonous. Consequently, the same body may to another seem to perform its motion over any space in half the time that it does to you. And the same reasoning will hold as to any other proportion; that is to say, according to your principles (since the motions perceived are both really in the object) it is possible one and the same body shall be really moved the same way at once, both very swift and very slow. How is this consistent either with common sense or with what you just now granted?

Hylas. I have nothing to say to it.

Philonous. Then as for *solidity;* either you do not mean any sensible quality by that word, and so it is beside our inquiry; or if you do, it must be either hardness or resistance. But both the one and the other are plainly relative to our senses: it being evident that what seems hard to one animal may appear soft to another who hath greater force and firmness of limbs. Nor is it less plain that the resistance I feel is not in the body.

Hylas. I own the very *sensation* of resistance, which is all you immediately perceive, is not in the body, but the *cause* of that sensation is.

Philonous. But the causes of our sensations are not things immediately perceived, and therefore not sensible. This point I thought had been already determined.

Hylas. I own it was; but you will pardon me if I seem a little embarrassed; I know not how to quit my old notions.

Philonous. To help you out, do but consider that if *extension* be once acknowledged to have no existence without the mind, the same must necessarily be granted of motion, solidity, and gravity, since they all evidently suppose extension. It is therefore superfluous to inquire particularly concerning each of them. In denying extension, you have denied them all to have any real existence.

Hylas. I wonder, Philonous, if what you say be true, why those philosophers who deny the Secondary Qualities any real existence should yet attribute it to the Primary. If there is no difference between them, how can this be accounted for?

Philonous. It is not my business to account for every opinion of the philosophers. But, among other reasons which may be assigned for this, it seems probable that pleasure and pain being rather annexed to the former than the latter may be one. Heat and cold, tastes and smells have something more vividly pleasing or disagreeable than the ideas of extension, figure, and motion affect us with. And, it being too visibly absurd to hold that pain or pleasure can be in an unperceiving Substance, men are more easily weaned from believing the external existence of the Secondary than the Primary Qualities. You will be satisfied there is something in this if you recollect the difference you made between an intense and more moderate degree of heat, allowing the one a real existence while you denied it to the other. But, after all, there is no rational ground for that distinction, for surely an indifferent sensation is as truly a *sensation* as one more pleasing or painful, and consequently should not any more than they be supposed to exist in an unthinking subject.

Hylas. It is just come into my head, Philonous, that I have somewhere heard of a distinction between *absolute* and *sensible* extension. Now though it be acknowledged that *great* and *small,* consisting merely in the relation which other extended beings have to the parts of our own bodies, do not really inhere in the substances themselves, yet nothing obliges us to hold the same with regard to *absolute extension,* which is something abstracted from *great* and *small,* from this or that particular magnitude or figure. So likewise as to motion: *swift* and *slow* are altogether relative to the succession of ideas in our own minds. But it does not follow, because those modifications of motion exist not without the mind, that therefore absolute motion abstracted from them doth not.

Philonous. Pray what is it that distinguishes one motion, or one part of extension, from another? Is it not something sensible, as some degree of swiftness or slowness, some certain magnitude or figure peculiar to each?

Hylas. I think so.

Philonous. These qualities, therefore, stripped of all sensible properties, are without all specific and numerical differences, as the schools call them.

Hylas. They are.

Philonous. That is to say, they are extension in general, and motion in general.

Hylas. Let it be so.

Philonous. But it is a universally received maxim that *Everything which exists is particular.* How then can motion in general, or extension in general, exist in any corporeal substance?

Hylas. I will take time to solve your difficulty.

Philonous. But I think the point may be speedily decided. Without doubt you can tell whether you are able to frame this or that idea. Now I am content to put our dispute on this issue. If you can frame in your thoughts a distinct *abstract idea* of motion or extension divested of all those sensible modes as swift and slow, great and small, round and square, and the like, which are acknowledged to exist only in the mind, I will then yield the point you contend for. But if you cannot, it will be unreasonable on your side to insist any longer upon what you have no notion of.

Hylas. To confess ingenuously, I cannot.

Philonous. Can you even separate the ideas of extension and motion from the ideas of all those qualities which they who make the distinction term *secondary?*

Hylas. What! Is it not an easy matter to consider extension and motion by themselves, abstracted from all other sensible qualities? Pray how do the mathematicians treat of them?

Philonous. I acknowledge, Hylas, it is not difficult to form general propositions
and reasonings about those qualities without mentioning any other, and, in this
sense, to consider or treat of them abstractedly. But how doth it follow that,
because I can pronounce the word *motion* by itself, I can form the idea of it in
my mind exclusive of body? Or because theorems may be made of extension
and figures, without any mention of *great* or *small,* or any other sensible mode
or quality, that therefore it is possible such an abstract idea of extension,
without any particular size or figure or sensible quality, should be distinctly
formed and apprehended by the mind? Mathematicians treat of quantity without regarding what other sensible qualities it is attended with, as being altogether indifferent to their demonstrations. But when, laying aside the words,
they contemplate the bare ideas, I believe you will find they are not the pure
abstracted ideas of extension.

Hylas. But what say you to *pure intellect?* May not abstracted ideas be framed by
that faculty?

Philonous. Since I cannot frame abstract ideas at all, it is plain I cannot frame
them by the help of *pure intellect,* whatsoever faculty you understand by those
words. Besides, not to inquire into the nature of pure intellect and its spiritual
objects, as *virtue, reason, God,* or the like, thus much seems manifest that
sensible things are only to be perceived by sense or represented by the imagination. Figures, therefore, and extension, being originally perceived by sense, do
not belong to pure intellect; but, for your further satisfaction, try if you can
frame the idea of any figure abstracted from all particularities of size or even
from other sensible qualities.

Hylas. Let me think a little—I do not find that I can.

Philonous. And can you think it possible that should really exist in nature which
implies a repugnancy in its conception?

Hylas. By no means.

Philonous. Since therefore it is impossible even for the mind to disunite the ideas
of extension and motion from all other sensible qualities, doth it not follow
that where the one exist there necessarily the other exist likewise?

Hylas. It should seem so.

Philonous. Consequently, the very same arguments which you admitted as conclusive against the Secondary Qualities are, without any further application of
force, against the Primary, too. Besides, if you will trust your senses, is it not
plain all sensible qualities coexist, or to them appear as being in the same place?
Do they ever represent a motion or figure as being divested of all other visible
and tangible qualities?

Hylas. You need say no more on this head. I am free to own, if there be no secret error or oversight in our proceedings hitherto, that *all* sensible qualities are alike to be denied existence without the mind. But my fear is that I have been too liberal in my former concessions, or overlooked some fallacy or other. In short, I did not take time to think.

Philonous. For that matter, Hylas, you may take what time you please in reviewing the progress of our inquiry. You are at liberty to recover any slips you might have made, or offer whatever you have omitted which makes for your first opinion.

Hylas. One great oversight I take to be this—that I did not sufficiently distinguish the *object* from the *sensation.* Now, though this latter may not exist without the mind, yet it will not thence follow that the former cannot.

Philonous. What object do you mean? The object of the senses?

Hylas. The same.

Philonous. It is then immediately perceived?

Hylas. Right.

Philonous. Make me to understand the difference between what is immediately perceived and a sensation.

Hylas. The sensation I take to be an act of the mind perceiving; besides which there is something perceived, and this I call the *object.* For example, there is red and yellow on that tulip. But then the act of perceiving those colours is in me only, and not in the tulip.

Philonous. What tulip do you speak of? Is it that which you see?

Hylas. The same.

Philonous. And what do you see besides colour, figure, and extension?

Hylas. Nothing.

Philonous. What you would say then is that the red and yellow are coexistent with the extension; is it not?

Hylas. That is not all; I would say they have a real existence without the mind, in some unthinking substance.

Philonous. That the colours are really in the tulip which I see is manifest. Neither can it be denied that this tulip may exist independent of your mind or mine; but that any immediate object of the senses—that is, any idea, or combination of ideas—should exist in an unthinking substance, or exterior to *all* minds, is in itself an evident contradiction. Nor can I imagine how this follows from what you said just now, to wit, that the red and yellow were on the tulip *you saw,* since you do not pretend to *see* that unthinking substance.

Hylas. You have an artful way, Philonous, of diverting our inquiry from the subject.

Philonous. I see you have no mind to be pressed that way. To return then to your distinction between *sensation* and *object;* if I take you right, you distinguish in every perception two things, the one an action of the mind, the other not.

Hylas. True.

Philonous. And this action cannot exist in, or belong to, any unthinking thing, but whatever besides is implied in a perception may?

Hylas. That is my meaning.

Philonous. So that if there was a perception without any act of the mind, it were possible such a perception should exist in an unthinking substance?

Hylas. I grant it. But it is impossible there should be such a perception.

Philonous. When is the mind said to be active?

Hylas. When it produces, puts an end to, or changes anything.

Philonous. Can the mind produce, discontinue, or change anything but by an act of the will?

Hylas. It cannot.

Philonous. The mind therefore is to be accounted *active* in its perceptions so far forth as *volition* is included in them?

Hylas. It is.

Philonous. In plucking this flower I am active, because I do it by the motion of my hand, which was consequent upon my volition; so likewise in applying it to my nose. But is either of these smelling?

Hylas. No.

Philonous. I act, too, in drawing the air through my nose, because my breathing so rather than otherwise is the effect of my volition. But neither can this be called *smelling,* for if it were I should smell every time I breathed in that manner?

Hylas. True.

Philonous. Smelling then is somewhat consequent to all this?

Hylas. It is.

Philonous. But I do not find my will concerned any farther. Whatever more there is—as that I perceive such a particular smell, or any smell at all—this is independent of my will, and therein I am altogether passive. Do you find it otherwise with you, Hylas?

Hylas. No, the very same.

Philonous.   Then, as to seeing, is it not in your power to open your eyes or keep them shut, to turn them this or that way?

Hylas.   Without doubt.

Philonous.   But doth it in like manner depend on *your* will that in looking on this flower you perceive *white* rather than any other colour? Or, directing your open eyes toward yonder part of the heaven, can you avoid seeing the sun? Or is light or darkness the effect of your volition?

Hylas.   No, certainly.

Philonous.   You are then in these respects altogether passive?

Hylas.   I am.

Philonous.   Tell me now whether *seeing* consists in perceiving light and colours or in opening and turning the eyes?

Hylas.   Without doubt, in the former.

Philonous.   Since, therefore, you are in the very perception of light and colours altogether passive, what is become of that action you were speaking of as an ingredient in every sensation? And does it not follow from your own concessions that the perception of light and colours, including no action in it, may exist in an unperceiving substance? And is not this a plain contradiction?

Hylas.   I know not what to think of it.

Philonous.   Besides, since you distinguish the *active* and *passive* in every perception, you must do it in that of pain. But how is it possible that pain, be it as little active as you please, should exist in an unperceiving substance? In short, do but consider the point and then confess ingenuously whether light and colours, tastes, sounds, etc. are not all equally passions or sensations in the soul. You may indeed call them *external objects* and give them in words what subsistence you please. But examine your own thoughts and then tell me whether it be not as I say?

Hylas.   I acknowledge, Philonous, that, upon a fair observation of what passes in my mind, I can discover nothing else but that I am a thinking being affected with variety of sensations, neither is it possible to conceive how a sensation should exist in an unperceiving substance. But then, on the other hand, when I look on sensible things in a different view, considering them as so many modes and qualities, I find it necessary to suppose a *material substratum,* without which they cannot be conceived to exist.

Philonous.   *Material substratum* call you it? Pray, by which of your senses came you acquainted with that being?

Hylas.   It is not itself sensible; its modes and qualities only being perceived by the senses.

Philonous. I presume then it was by reflection and reason you obtained the idea of it?

Hylas. I do not pretend to any proper positive *idea* of it. However, I conclude it exists because qualities cannot be conceived to exist without a support.

Philonous. It seems then you have only a relative *notion* of it, or that you conceive it not otherwise than by conceiving the relation it bears to sensible qualities?

Hylas. Right.

Philonous. Be pleased, therefore, to let me know wherein that relation consists.

Hylas. Is it not sufficiently expressed in the term *substratum* or *substance?*

Philonous. If so, the word *substratum* should import that it is spread under the sensible qualities or accidents?

Hylas. True.

Philonous. And consequently under extension?

Hylas. I own it.

Philonous. It is therefore somewhat in its own nature entirely distinct from extension?

Hylas. I tell you extension is only a mode, and Matter is something that supports modes. And is it not evident the thing supported is different from the thing supporting?

Philonous. So that something distinct from, and exclusive of, extension is supposed to be the *substratum* of extension?

Hylas. Just so.

Philonous. Answer me, Hylas, can a thing be spread without extension, or is not the idea of extension necessarily included in *spreading?*

Hylas. It is.

Philonous. Whatsoever therefore you suppose spread under anything must have in itself an extension distinct from the extension of that thing under which it is spread?

Hylas. It must.

Philonous. Consequently, every corporeal substance being the *substratum* of extension must have in itself another extension by which it is qualified to be a *substratum,* and so on to infinity? And I ask whether this be not absurd in itself and repugnant to what you granted just now, to wit, that the *substratum* was something distinct from and exclusive of extension?

Hylas. Aye, but, Philonous, you take me wrong. I do not mean that Matter is *spread* in a gross literal sense under extension. The word *substratum* is used only to express in general the same thing with *substance*.

Philonous. Well then, let us examine the relation implied in the term *substance.* Is it not that it stands under accidents?

Hylas. The very same.

Philonous. But that one thing may stand under or support another, must it not be extended?

Hylas. It must.

Philonous. Is not therefore this supposition liable to the same absurdity with the former?

Hylas. You still take things in a strict literal sense; that is not fair, Philonous.

Philonous. I am not for imposing any sense on your words; you are at liberty to explain them as you please. Only, I beseech you, make me understand something by them. You tell me Matter supports or stands under accidents. How! is it as your legs support your body?

Hylas. No; that is the literal sense.

Philonous. Pray let me know any sense, literal or not literal, that you understand it in.—How long must I wait for an answer, Hylas?

Hylas. I declare I know not what to say. I once thought I understood well enough what was meant by Matter's supporting accidents. But now, the more I think on it, the less can I comprehend it; in short, I find that I know nothing of it.

Philonous. It seems then you have no idea at all, neither relative nor positive, of Matter; you know neither what it is in itself nor what relation it bears to accidents?

Hylas. I acknowledge it.

Philonous. And yet you asserted that you could not conceive how qualities or accidents should really exist without conceiving at the same time a material support of them?

Hylas. I did.

Philonous. That is to say, when you conceive the *real* existence of qualities, you do withal conceive Something which you cannot conceive?

Hylas. It was wrong I own. But still I fear there is some fallacy or other. Pray, what think you of this? It is just come into my head that the ground of all our mistake lies in your treating of each quality by itself. Now I grant that each quality cannot singly subsist without the mind. Colour cannot without extension, neither can figure without some other sensible quality. But, as the several qualities united or blended together form entire sensible things, nothing hinders why such things may not be supposed to exist without the mind.

Philonous. Either, Hylas, you are jesting or have a very bad memory. Though, indeed, we went through all the qualities by name one after another, yet my arguments, or rather your concessions, nowhere tended to prove that the Secondary Qualities did not subsist each alone by itself, but that they were not *at all* without the mind. Indeed, in treating of figure and motion we concluded they could not exist without the mind, because it was impossible even in thought to separate them from all secondary qualities, so as to conceive them existing by themselves. But then this was not the only argument made use of upon that occasion. But (to pass by all that hath been hitherto said and reckon it for nothing, if you will have it so) I am content to put the whole upon this issue. If you can conceive it possible for any mixture or combination of qualities, or any sensible object whatever, to exist without the mind, then I will grant it actually to be so.

Hylas. If it comes to that the point will soon be decided. What more easy than to conceive a tree or house existing by itself, independent of, and unperceived by, any mind whatsoever? I do at this present time conceive them existing after that manner.

Philonous. How say you, Hylas, can you see a thing which is at the same time unseen?

Hylas. No, that were a contradiction.

Philonous. Is it not as great a contradiction to talk of *conceiving* a thing which is *unconceived?*

Hylas. It is.

Philonous. The tree or house, therefore, which you think of is conceived by you?

Hylas. How should it be otherwise?

Philonous. And what is conceived is surely in the mind?

Hylas. Without question, that which is conceived is in the mind.

Philonous. How then came you to say you conceived a house or tree existing independent and out of all minds whatsoever?

Hylas. That was I own an oversight, but stay, let me consider what led me into it.—It is a pleasant mistake enough. As I was thinking of a tree in a solitary place where no one was present to see it, methought that was to conceive a tree as existing unperceived or unthought of, not considering that I myself conceived it all the while. But now I plainly see that all I can do is to frame ideas in my own mind. I may indeed conceive in my own thoughts the idea of a tree, or a house, or a mountain, but that is all. And this is far from proving that I can conceive them *existing out of the minds of all Spirits.*

Philonous. You acknowledge then that you cannot possibly conceive how any one corporeal sensible thing should exist otherwise than in a mind?

Hylas. I do.

Philonous. And yet you will earnestly contend for the truth of that which you cannot so much as conceive?

Hylas. I profess I know not what to think; but still there are some scruples remain with me. Is it not certain I *see things at a distance?* Do we not perceive the stars and moon, for example, to be a great way off? Is not this, I say, manifest to the senses?

Philonous. Do you not in a dream, too, perceive those or the like objects?

Hylas. I do.

Philonous. And have they not then the same appearance of being distant?

Hylas. They have.

Philonous. But you do not thence conclude the apparitions in a dream to be without the mind?

Hylas. By no means.

Philonous. You ought not therefore to conclude that sensible objects are without the mind, from their appearance or manner wherein they are perceived.

Hylas. I acknowledge it. But does not my sense deceive me in those cases?

Philonous. By no means. The idea or thing which you immediately perceive, neither sense nor reason informs you that it actually exists without the mind. By sense you only know that you are affected with such certain sensations of light and colours, etc. And these you will not say are without the mind.

Hylas. True, but, besides all that, do you not think the sight suggests something of *outness* or *distance?*

Philonous. Upon approaching a distant object, do the visible size and figure change perpetually or do they appear the same at all distances?

Hylas. They are in a continual change.

Philonous. Sight, therefore, doth not suggest or any way inform you that the visible object you immediately perceive exists at a distance,[8] or will be perceived when you advance farther onward, there being a continued series of visible objects succeeding each other during the whole time of your approach.

Hylas. It doth not; but still I know, upon seeing an object, what object I shall perceive after having passed over a certain distance; no matter whether it be exactly the same or no, there is still something of distance suggested in the case.

Philonous. Good Hylas, do but reflect a little on the point, and then tell me whether there be any more in it than this. From the ideas you actually perceive by sight, you have by experience learned to collect what other ideas you will

---

8. See the *Essay toward a New Theory of Vision* [1709], and its *Vindication* [*The Theory of Vision Vindicated and Explained,* 1733] – Note by Berkeley in the third or 1734 edition.

(according to the standing order of nature) be affected with, after such a certain succession of time and motion.

Hylas. Upon the whole, I take it to be nothing else.

Philonous. Now is it not plain that if we suppose a man born blind was on a sudden made to see, he could at first have no experience of what may be *suggested* by sight?

Hylas. It is.

Philonous. He would not then, according to you, have any notion of distance annexed to the things he saw, but would take them for a new set of sensations existing only in his mind?

Hylas. It is undeniable.

Philonous. But to make it still more plain: is not *distance* a line turned endwise to the eye?

Hylas. It is.

Philonous. And can a line so situated be perceived by sight?

Hylas. It cannot.

Philonous. Doth it not therefore follow that distance is not properly and immediately perceived by sight?

Hylas. It should seem so.

Philonous. Again, it is your opinion that colours are at a distance?

Hylas. It must be acknowledged they are only in the mind..

Philonous. But do not colours appear to the eye as coexisting in the same place with extension and figures?

Hylas. They do.

Philonous. How can you then conclude from sight that figures exist without, when you acknowledge colours do not; the sensible appearance being the very same with regard to both?

Hylas. I know not what to answer.

Philonous. But allowing that distance was truly and immediately perceived by the mind, yet it would not thence follow it existed out of the mind. For whatever is immediately perceived is an idea; and can any *idea* exist out of the mind?

Hylas. To suppose that were absurd; but, inform me, Philonous, can we perceive or know nothing besides our ideas?

Philonous. As for the rational deducing of causes from effects, that is beside our inquiry. And by the senses you can best tell whether you perceive anything which is not immediately perceived. And I ask you whether the things immediately perceived are other than your own sensations or ideas? You have indeed more than once, in the course of this conversation, declared yourself on those points, but you seem, by this last question, to have departed from what you then thought.

Hylas. To speak the truth, Philonous, I think there are two kinds of objects: the one perceived immediately, which are likewise called *ideas;* the other are real things or external objects, perceived by the mediation of ideas which are their images and representations. Now I own ideas do not exist without the mind, but the latter sort of objects do. I am sorry I did not think of this distinction sooner; it would probably have cut short your discourse.

Philonous. Are those external objects perceived by sense or by some other faculty?

Hylas. They are perceived by sense.

Philonous. How! Is there anything perceived by sense which is not immediately perceived?

Hylas. Yes, Philonous, in some sort there is. For example, when I look on a picture or statue of Julius Caesar, I may be said, after a manner, to perceive him (though not immediately) by my senses.

Philonous. It seems then you will have our ideas, which alone are immediately perceived, to be pictures of external things: and that these also are perceived by sense inasmuch as they have a conformity or resemblance to our ideas?

Hylas. That is my meaning.

Philonous. And in the same way that Julius Caesar, in himself invisible, is nevertheless perceived by sight, real things, in themselves imperceptible, are perceived by sense.

Hylas. In the very same.

Philonous. Tell me, Hylas, when you behold the picture of Julius Caesar, do you see with your eyes any more than some colours and figures, with a certain symmetry and composition of the whole?

Hylas. Nothing else.

Philonous. And would not a man who had never known anything of Julius Caesar see as much?

Hylas. He would.

Philonous. Consequently, he hath his sight and the use of it in as perfect a degree as you?

Hylas. I agree with you.

Philonous. Whence comes it then that your thoughts are directed to the Roman emperor, and his are not? This cannot proceed from the sensations or ideas of sense by you then perceived, since you acknowledge you have no advantage over him in that respect. It should seem therefore to proceed from reason and memory, should it not?

Hylas. It should.

Philonous. Consequently, it will not follow from that instance that anything is perceived by sense which is not immediately perceived. Though I grant we may, in one acceptation, be said to perceive sensible things mediately by sense—that is, when, from a frequently perceived connexion, the immediate perception of ideas by one sense *suggests* to the mind others, perhaps belonging to another sense, which are wont to be connected with them. For instance, when I hear a coach drive along the streets, immediately I perceive only the sound; but from the experience I have had that such a sound is connected with a coach, I am said to hear the coach. It is nevertheless evident that, in truth and strictness, nothing can be *heard* but *sound;* and the coach is not then properly perceived by sense, but suggested from experience. So likewise when we are said to see a red-hot bar of iron; the solidity and heat of the iron are not the objects of sight, but suggested to the imagination by the colour and figure which are properly perceived by that sense. In short, those things alone are actually and strictly perceived by any sense which would have been perceived in case that same sense had then been first conferred on us. As for other things, it is plain they are only suggested to the mind by experience grounded on former perceptions. But, to return to your comparison of Caesar's picture, it is plain, if you keep to that, you must hold the real things or archetypes of our ideas are not perceived by sense, but by some internal faculty of the soul, as reason or memory. I would, therefore, fain know what arguments you can draw from reason for the existence of what you call *real things* or *material objects,* or whether you remember to have seen them formerly as they are in themselves, or if you have heard or read of anyone that did.

Hylas. I see, Philonous, you are disposed to raillery; but that will never convince me.

Philonous. My aim is only to learn from you the way to come at the knowledge of *material beings.* Whatever we perceive is perceived either immediately or mediately—by sense, or by reason and reflexion. But, as you have excluded sense, pray show me what reason you have to believe their existence, or what *medium* you can possibly make use of to prove it, either to mine or your own understanding.

Hylas. To deal ingenuously, Philonous, now I consider the point, I do not find I can give you any good reason for it. But this much seems pretty plain, that it is at least possible such things may really exist. And as long as there is no absurdity in supposing them, I am resolved to believe as I did, till you bring good reasons to the contrary.

Philonous. What! Is it come to this, that you only *believe* the existence of material objects, and that your belief is founded barely on the possibility of its being true? Then you will have me bring reasons against it, though another would think it reasonable the proof should lie on him who holds the affirmative. And, after all, this very point which you are now resolved to maintain, without any reason, is in effect what you have more than once during this discourse seen good reason to give up. But to pass over all this—if I understand you rightly, you say our ideas do not exist without the mind, but that they are copies, images, or representations of certain originals that do?

Hylas. You take me right.

Philonous. They are then like external things?

Hylas. They are.

Philonous. Have those things a stable and permanent nature, independent of our senses, or are they in a perpetual change, upon our producing any motions in our bodies, suspending, exerting, or altering our faculties or organs of sense?

Hylas. Real things, it is plain, have a fixed and real nature, which remains the same notwithstanding any change in our senses or in the posture and motion of our bodies; which indeed may affect the ideas in our minds, but it were absurd to think they had the same effect on things existing without the mind.

Philonous. How then is it possible that things perpetually fleeting and variable as our ideas should be copies or images of anything fixed and constant? Or, in other words, since all sensible qualities, as size, figure, colour, etc., that is, our ideas, are continually changing upon every alteration in the distance, medium, or instruments of sensation—how can any determinate material objects be properly represented or painted forth by several distinct things each of which is so different from and unlike the rest? Or, if you say it resembles some one only of our ideas, how shall we be able to distinguish the true copy from all the false ones?

Hylas. I profess, Philonous, I am at a loss. I know not what to say to this.

Philonous. But neither is this all. Which are material objects in themselves—perceptible or imperceptible?

Hylas. Properly and immediately nothing can be perceived but ideas. All material things, therefore, are in themselves insensible and to be perceived only by their ideas.

Philonous. Ideas then are sensible, and their archetypes or originals insensible?

Hylas. Right.

Philonous. But how can that which is sensible be *like* that which is insensible? Can a real thing, in itself *invisible,* be like a *colour,* or a real thing which is not *audible* be like a *sound?* In a word, can anything be like a sensation or idea, but another sensation or idea?

Hylas. I must own, I think not.

Philonous. Is it possible there should be any doubt on the point? Do you not perfectly know your own ideas?

Hylas. I know them perfectly, since what I do not perceive or know can be no part of my idea.

Philonous. Consider, therefore, and examine them, and then tell me if there be anything in them which can exist without the mind, or if you can conceive anything like them existing without the mind?

Hylas. Upon inquiry I find it is impossible for me to conceive or understand how anything but an idea can be like an idea. And it is most evident that *no idea can exist without the mind.*

Philonous. You are, therefore, by your principles forced to deny the *reality* of sensible things, since you made it to consist in an absolute existence exterior to the mind. That is to say, you are a downright sceptic. So I have gained my point, which was to show your principles led to scepticism.

Hylas. For the present I am, if not entirely convinced, at least silenced.

Philonous. I would fain know what more you would require in order to [attain] a perfect conviction. Have you not had the liberty of explaining yourself all manner of ways? Were any little slips in discourse laid hold and insisted on? Or were you not allowed to retract or reinforce anything you had offered, as best served your purpose? Hath not everything you could say been heard and examined with all the fairness imaginable? In a word, have you not in every point been convinced out of your own mouth? And, if you can at present discover any flaw in any of your former concessions, or think of any remaining subterfuge, any new distinction, colour, or comment whatsoever, why do you not produce it?

Hylas. A little patience, Philonous. I am at present so amazed to see myself ensnared, and as it were imprisoned in the labyrinths you have drawn me into, that on the sudden it cannot be expected I should find my way out. You must give me time to look about me and recollect myself.

Philonous. Hark; is not this the college bell?

Hylas. It rings for prayers.

Philonous. We will go in then, if you please, and meet here again tomorrow morning. In the meantime, you may employ your thoughts on this morning's discourse and try if you can find any fallacy in it, or invent any new means to extricate yourself.

Hylas. Agreed.

The Second Dialogue

Hylas. I beg your pardon, Philonous, for not meeting you sooner. All this morning my head was so filled with our late conversation that I had not leisure to think of the time of the day, or indeed of anything else.

Philonous. I am glad you were so intent upon it, in hopes if there were any mistakes in your concessions, or fallacies in my reasonings from them, you will now discover them to me.

Hylas. I assure you I have done nothing ever since I saw you but search after mistakes and fallacies, and, with that [in] view, have minutely examined the whole series of yesterday's discourse; but all in vain, for the notions it led me into, upon review, appear still more clear and evident; and the more I consider them, the more irresistibly do they force my assent.

Philonous. And is not this, think you, a sign that they are genuine, that they proceed from nature and are conformable to right reason? Truth and beauty are in this alike, that the strictest survey sets them both off to advantage, while the false luster of error and disguise cannot endure being reviewed or too nearly inspected.

Hylas. I own there is a great deal in what you say. Nor can anyone be more entirely satisfied of the truth of those odd consequences so long as I have in view the reasonings that lead to them. But when these are out of my thoughts, there seems, on the other hand, something so satisfactory, so natural and intelligible in the modern way of explaining things that I profess I know not how to reject it.

Philonous. I know not what you mean.

Hylas. I mean the way of accounting for our sensations or ideas.

Philonous. How is that?

Hylas. It is supposed the soul makes her residence in some part of the brain, from which the nerves take their rise, and are thence extended to all parts of the body; and that outward objects, by the different impressions they make on the organs of sense, communicate certain vibrative motions to the nerves, and these, being filled with spirits, propagate them to the brain or seat of the soul, which, according to the various impressions or traces thereby made in the brain, is variously affected with ideas.

Philonous. And call you this an explication of the manner whereby we are affected with ideas?

Hylas. Why not, Philonous; have you anything to object against it?

Philonous. I would first know whether I rightly understand your hypothesis. You make certain traces in the brain to be the causes or occasions of our ideas. Pray tell me whether by the *brain* you mean any sensible thing.

Hylas. What else think you I could mean?

Philonous. Sensible things are all immediately perceivable; and those things which are immediately perceivable are ideas, and these exist only in the mind. This much you have, if I mistake not, long since agreed to.

Hylas. I do not deny it.

Philonous. The brain therefore you speak of, being a sensible thing, exists only in the mind. Now I would fain know whether you think it reasonable to suppose that one idea or thing existing in the mind occasions all other ideas. And if you think so, pray how do you account for the origin of that primary idea or brain itself?

Hylas. I do not explain the origin of our ideas by that brain which is perceivable to sense, this being itself only a combination of sensible ideas, but by another which I imagine.

Philonous. But are not things imagined as truly *in the mind* as things perceived?

Hylas. I must confess they are.

Philonous. It comes, therefore, to the same thing; and you have been all this while accounting for ideas by certain motions or impressions of the brain, that is, by some alterations in an idea, whether sensible or imaginable it matters not.

Hylas. I begin to suspect my hypothesis.

Philonous. Besides spirits, all that we know or conceive are our own ideas. When, therefore, you say all ideas are occasioned by impressions in the brain, do you conceive this brain or no? If you do, then you talk of ideas imprinted in an idea causing that same idea, which is absurd. If you do not conceive it, you talk unintelligibly, instead of forming a reasonable hypothesis.

Hylas. I now clearly see it was a mere dream. There is nothing in it.

Philonous. You need not be much concerned at it, for, after all, this way of explaining things, as you called it, could never have satisfied any reasonable man. What connexion is there between a motion in the nerves and the sensations of sound or colour in the mind? Or how is it possible these should be the effect of that?

Hylas. But I could never think it had so little in it as now it seems to have.

Philonous. Well then, are you at length satisfied that no sensible things have a real existence, and that you are in truth an arrant sceptic?

Hylas. It is too plain to be denied.

Philonous. Look! Are not the fields covered with a delightful verdure? Is there not something in the woods and groves, in the rivers and clear springs, that soothes, that delights, that transports the soul? At the prospect of the wide and deep ocean, or some huge mountain whose top is lost in the clouds, or of an old gloomy forest, are not our minds filled with a pleasing horror? Even in rocks and deserts is there not an agreeable wildness? How sincere a pleasure is it to behold the natural beauties of the earth! To preserve and renew our relish for them, is not the veil of night alternately drawn over her face, and doth she not change her dress with the seasons? How aptly are the elements disposed! What variety and use in the meanest productions of nature! What delicacy, what beauty, what contrivance in animal and vegetable bodies! How exquisitely are all things suited, as well to their particular ends as to constitute apposite parts of the whole! And while they mutually aid and support, do they not also set off and illustrate each other? Raise now your thoughts from this ball of earth to all those glorious luminaries that adorn the high arch of heaven. The motion and situation of the planets, are they not admirable for use and order? Were those (miscalled *erratic*) globes ever known to stray in their repeated journeys through the pathless void? Do they not measure areas round the sun ever proportioned to the times? So fixed, so immutable are the laws by which the unseen Author of nature actuates the universe. How vivid and radiant is the luster of the fixed stars! How magnificent and rich that negligent profusion with which they appear to be scattered throughout the whole azure vault! Yet, if you take the telescope, it brings into your sight a new host of stars that escape the naked eye. Here they seem contiguous and minute, but to a nearer view, immense orbs of light at various distances, far sunk in the abyss of space. Now you must call imagination to your aid. The feeble narrow sense cannot descry innumerable worlds revolving round the central fires, and in those worlds the energy of an all-perfect Mind displayed in endless forms. But neither sense nor imagination are big enough to comprehend the boundless extent with all its glittering furniture. Though the labouring mind exert and strain each power to its utmost reach, there still stands out ungrasped a surplusage immeasurable. Yet all the vast bodies that compose this mighty frame, how distant and remote soever, are by some secret mechanism, some divine art and force linked in a mutual dependence and intercourse with each other, even with this earth, which was almost slipt from my thoughts and lost in the crowd of worlds. Is not the whole system immense, beautiful, glorious beyond expression and beyond thought! What treatment, then, do those philosophers deserve who would deprive these noble and delightful scenes of all *reality?* How should those Principles be entertained that lead us to think all the visible beauty of the creation a false imaginary glare? To be plain, can you expect this Scepticism of yours will not be thought extravagantly absurd by all men of sense?

Hylas. Other men may think as they please, but for your part you have nothing to reproach me with. My comfort is you are as much a sceptic as I am.

Philonous. There, Hylas, I must beg leave to differ from you.

Hylas. What! have you all along agreed to the premises, and do you now deny the conclusion and leave me to maintain those paradoxes by myself which you led me into? This surely is not fair.

Philonous. I deny that I agreed with you in those notions that led to Scepticism. You indeed said the *reality* of sensible things consisted in an *absolute existence* out of the minds of spirits, or distinct from their being perceived. And, pursuant to this notion of reality, *you* are obliged to deny sensible things any real existence; that is, according to your own definition, you profess yourself a sceptic. But I neither said nor thought the reality of sensible things was to be defined after that manner. To me it is evident, for the reasons you allow of, that sensible things cannot exist otherwise than in a mind or spirit. Whence I conclude, not that they have no real existence, but that, seeing they depend not on my thought and have an existence distinct from being perceived by me, *there must be some other Mind wherein they exist.* As sure, therefore, as the sensible world really exists, so sure is there an infinite omnipresent Spirit, who contains and supports it.

Hylas. What! This is no more than I and all Christians hold; nay, and all others, too, who believe there is a God and that He knows and comprehends all things.

Philonous. Aye, but here lies the difference. Men commonly believe that all things are known or perceived by God, because they believe the being of a God; whereas I, on the other side, immediately and necessarily conclude the being of a God, because all sensible things must be perceived by him.

Hylas. But so long as we all believe the same thing, what matter is it how we come by that belief?

Philonous. But neither do we agree in the same opinion. For philosophers, though they acknowledge all corporeal beings to be perceived by God, yet they attribute to them an absolute subsistence distinct from their being perceived by any mind whatever, which I do not. Besides, is there no difference between saying, *There is a God, therefore He perceives all things,* and saying, *Sensible things do really exist; and if they really exist, they are necessarily perceived by an infinite Mind: therefore there is an infinite Mind, or God?* This furnishes you with a direct and immediate demonstration, from a most evident principle, of the *being of a God.* Divines and philosophers had proved beyond all controversy, from the beauty and usefulness of the several parts of the creation, that it was the workmanship of God. But that—setting aside all help of astronomy and natural philosophy, all contemplation of the contrivance, order and adjustment of things—an infinite Mind should be necessarily inferred from the bare *existence of the sensible world* is an advantage peculiar to them only who have made this easy reflexion, that the sensible world is that which we perceive by our several senses; and that nothing is perceived by the senses besides ideas; and that no idea or archetype of an idea can exist otherwise than in a mind. You may now, without any laborious search into the sciences, without any subtlety of reason or tedious length of discourse, oppose and baffle the most strenuous advocate for Atheism, those miserable refuges, whether in an eternal succession of unthinking causes and effects or in a fortuitous concourse of atoms; those wild imaginations of Vanini, Hobbes, and Spinoza: in a word, the whole system of Atheism, is it not entirely overthrown by this single reflexion on the repugnancy included in supposing the whole or any part, even the most rude and shapeless, of the visible world to exist without a Mind? Let any one of those abettors of impiety but look into his own thoughts, and there try if he can conceive how so much as a rock, a desert, a chaos, or confused jumble of atoms, how anything at all, either sensible or imaginable, can exist independent of a Mind, and he need go no farther to be convinced of his folly. Can anything be fairer than to put a dispute on such an issue and leave it to a man himself to see if he can conceive, even in thought, what he holds to be true in fact, and from a notional to allow it a real existence?

Hylas. It cannot be denied there is something highly serviceable to religion in what you advance. But do you not think it looks very like a notion entertained by some eminent moderns, of *seeing all things in God?*

Philonous. I would gladly know that opinion; pray explain it to me.

Hylas. They conceive that the soul, being immaterial, is incapable of being united with material things so as to perceive them in themselves, but that she perceives them by her union with the substance of God, which, being spiritual, is therefore purely intelligible, or capable of being the immediate object of a spirit's thought. Besides, the Divine essence contains in it perfections correspondent to each created being, and which are, for that reason, proper to exhibit or represent them to the mind.

Philonous. I do not understand how our ideas, which are things altogether passive and inert, can be the essence or any part (or like any part) of the essence or substance of God, who is an impassive, indivisible, purely active being. Many more difficulties and objections there are which occur at first view against this hypothesis; but I shall only add that it is liable to all the absurdities of the common hypothesis, in making a created world exist otherwise than in the mind of a Spirit. Beside all which it hath this peculiar to itself that it makes that material world serve to no purpose. And if it pass for a good argument against other hypotheses in the sciences that they suppose Nature or the Divine wisdom to make something in vain, or do that by tedious roundabout methods which might have been performed in a much more easy and compendious way, what shall we think of that hypothesis which supposes the whole world made in vain?

Hylas. But what say you, are not you too of opinion that we see all things in God? If I mistake not, what you advance comes near it.

Philonous. Few men think, yet all have opinions. Hence men's opinions are superficial and confused. It is nothing strange that tenets which in themselves are ever so different should nevertheless be confounded with each other by those who do not consider them attentively. I shall not therefore be surprised if some men imagine that I run into the enthusiasm of Malebranche, though in truth I am very remote from it. He builds on the most abstract general ideas, which I entirely disclaim. He asserts an absolute external world, which I deny. He maintains that we are deceived by our senses and know not the real natures or the true forms and figures of extended beings; of all which I hold the direct contrary. So that upon the whole there are no Principles more fundamentally opposite than his and mine. It must be owned. I entirely agree with what the holy Scripture says, "That in God we live and move and have our being." But that we see things in His essence, after the manner above set forth, I am far from believing. Take here in brief my meaning: It is evident that the things I perceive are my own ideas, and that no idea can exist unless it be in a mind. Nor is it less plain that these ideas or things by me perceived, either themselves or their archetypes, exist independently of *my* mind; since I know myself not to be their author, it being out of my power to determine at pleasure what particular ideas I shall be affected with upon opening my eyes or ears. They must therefore exist in some other Mind, whose will it is they should be exhibited to me. The things, I say, immediately perceived are ideas or sensations, call them which you will. But how can any idea or sensation exist in, or be produced by, anything but a mind or spirit? This indeed is inconceivable; and to assert that which is inconceivable is to talk nonsense, is it not?

Hylas. Without doubt.

Philonous. But, on the other hand, it is very conceivable that they should exist in and be produced by a Spirit, since this is no more than I daily experience in myself, inasmuch as I perceive numberless ideas, and, by an act of my will, can form a great variety of them and raise them up in my imagination; though, it must be confessed, these creatures of the fancy are not altogether so distinct, so strong, vivid, and permanent as those perceived by my senses, which latter are called *real things*. From all which I conclude, *there is a Mind which affects me every moment with all the sensible impressions I perceive*. And from the variety, order, and manner of these I conclude the *Author of them to be wise, powerful, and good beyond comprehension*. Mark it well; I do not say I see things by perceiving that which represents them in the intelligible Substance of God. This I do not understand; but I say the things by me perceived are known by the understanding and produced by the will of an infinite Spirit. And is not all this most plain and evident? Is there any more in it than what a little observation of our own minds, and that which passeth in them, not only enableth us to conceive but also obligeth us to acknowledge?

Hylas. I think I understand you very clearly and own the proof you give of a Deity seems no less evident than it is surprising. But allowing that God is the supreme and universal Cause of all things, yet may there not be still a Third Nature besides Spirits and Ideas? May we not admit a subordinate and limited cause of our ideas? In a word, may there not for all that be *Matter?*

Philonous. How often must I inculcate the same thing? You allow the things immediately perceived by sense to exist nowhere without the mind; but there is nothing perceived by sense which is not perceived immediately: therefore there is nothing sensible that exists without the mind. The Matter, therefore, which you still insist on is something intelligible, I suppose; something that may be discovered by reason, and not by sense.

Hylas. You are in the right.

Philonous. Pray let me know what reasoning your belief of Matter is grounded on, and what this Matter is in your present sense of it.

Hylas. I find myself affected with various ideas whereof I know I am not the cause; neither are they the cause of themselves or of one another, or capable of subsisting by themselves, as being altogether inactive, fleeting, dependent beings. They have therefore *some* cause distinct from me and them, of which I pretend to know no more than that it is *the cause of my ideas*. And this thing, whatever it be, I call *Matter*.

Philonous. Tell me, Hylas, hath everyone a liberty to change the current proper signification annexed to a common name in any language? For example, suppose a traveller should tell you that in a certain country men pass unhurt through the fire; and, upon explaining himself, you found he meant by the word *fire* that which others call *water;* or, if he should assert that there are trees that walk upon two legs, meaning men by the term *trees.* Would you think this reasonable?

Hylas. No, I should think it very absurd. Common custom is the standard of propriety in language. And for any man to affect speaking improperly is to pervert the use of speech, and can never serve to a better purpose than to protract and multiply disputes where there is no difference in opinion.

Philonous. And doth not *Matter,* in the common current acceptation of the word, signify an extended, solid, movable, unthinking, inactive Substance?

Hylas. It doth.

Philonous. And hath it not been made evident that no *such* substance can possibly exist? And though it should be allowed to exist, yet how can that which is *inactive* be a *cause,* or that which is *unthinking* be a *cause of thought?* You may, indeed, if you please, annex to the word *Matter* a contrary meaning to what is vulgarly received, and tell me you understand by it an unextended, thinking, active being which is the cause of our ideas. But what else is this than to play with words and run into that very fault you just now condemned with so much reason? I do by no means find fault with your reasoning, in that you collect *a* cause from the phenomena; but I deny that *the* cause deducible by reason can properly be termed Matter.

Hylas. There is indeed something in what you say. . . .

The Third Dialogue

Philonous. Tell me, Hylas, what are the fruits of yesterday's meditation? Has it confirmed you in the same mind you were in at parting, or have you since seen cause to change your opinion?

Hylas. Truly my opinion is that all our opinions are alike vain and uncertain. What we approve today, we condemn tomorrow. We keep a stir about knowledge and spend our lives in the pursuit of it, when, alas! we know nothing all the while; nor do I think it possible for us ever to know anything in this life. Our faculties are too narrow and too few. Nature certainly never intended us for speculation.

Philonous. What! say you we can know nothing, Hylas?

Hylas. There is not that single thing in the world whereof we can know the real nature, or what it is in itself.

Philonous. Will you tell me I do not really know what fire or water is?

Hylas. You may indeed know that fire appears hot, and water fluid; but this is no more than knowing what sensations are produced in your own mind upon the application of fire and water to your organs of sense. Their internal constitution, their true and real nature, you are utterly in the dark as to *that*.

Philonous. Do I not know this to be a real stone that I stand on, and that which I see before my eyes to be a real tree?

Hylas. Know? No, it is impossible you or any man alive should know it. All you know is that you have such a certain idea or appearance in your own mind. But what is this to the real tree or stone? I tell you that colour, figure, and hardness, which you perceive, are not the real natures of those things, or in the least like them. The same may be said of all other real things or corporeal substances which compose the world. They have, none of them, anything [in] themselves, like those sensible qualities by us perceived. We should not, therefore, pretend to affirm or know anything of them, as they are in their own nature.

Philonous. But surely, Hylas, I can distinguish gold, for example, from iron; and how could this be if I knew not what either truly was?

Hylas. Believe me, Philonous, you can only distinguish between your own ideas. That yellowness, that weight, and other sensible qualities, think you they are really in the gold? They are only relative to the senses and have no absolute existence in nature. And in pretending to distinguish the species of real things by the appearances in your mind, you may perhaps act as wisely as he that should conclude two men were of a different species because their clothes were not of the same colour.

Philonous. It seems, then, we are altogether put off with the appearances of things, and those false ones, too. The very meat I eat, and the cloth I wear, have nothing in them like what I see and feel.

Hylas. Even so.

Philonous. But is it not strange the whole world should be thus imposed on and so foolish as to believe their senses? And yet I know not how it is, but men eat, and drink, and sleep, and perform all the offices of life as comfortably and conveniently as if they really knew the things they are conversant about.

Hylas. They do so; but you know ordinary practice does not require a nicety of speculative knowledge. Hence the vulgar retain their mistakes, and for all that make a shift to bustle through the affairs of life. But philosophers know better things.

Philonous. You mean they *know* that they *know nothing.*

Hylas. That is the very top and perfection of human knowledge.

Philonous. But are you all this while in earnest, Hylas; and are you seriously persuaded that you know nothing real in the world? Suppose you are going to write, would you not call for pen, ink, and paper, like another man; and do you not know what it is you call for?

Hylas. How often must I tell you that I know not the real nature of any one thing in the universe? I may indeed upon occasion make use of pen, ink, and paper. But what any one of them is in its own true nature, I declare positively I know not. And the same is true with regard to every other corporeal thing. And what is more, we are not only ignorant of the true and real nature of things, but even of their existence. It cannot be denied that we perceive such certain appearances or ideas, but it cannot be concluded from thence that bodies really exist. Nay, now I think on it, I must, agreeably to my former concessions, farther declare that it is impossible any *real* corporeal thing should exist in nature.

Philonous. You amaze me. Was ever anything more wild and extravagant than the notions you now maintain? And is it not evident you are led into all these extravagances by the belief of *material substance?* This makes you dream of those unknown natures in everything. It is this occasions your distinguishing between the reality and sensible appearances of things. It is to this you are indebted for being ignorant of what everybody else knows perfectly well. Nor is this all: you are not only ignorant of the true nature of everything, but you know not whether any thing really exists or whether there are any true natures at all, forasmuch as you attribute to your material beings an absolute or external existence wherein you suppose their reality consists. And as you are forced in the end to acknowledge such an existence means either a direct repugnancy or nothing at all, it follows that you are obliged to pull down your own hypothesis of material Substance and positively to deny the real existence of any part of the universe. And so you are plunged into the deepest and most deplorable scepticism that ever man was. Tell me, Hylas, is it not as I say?

Hylas. I agree with you. *Material substance* was no more than an hypothesis, and a false and groundless one, too. I will no longer spend my breath in defence of it. But whatever hypothesis you advance or whatsoever scheme of things you introduce in its stead, I doubt not it will appear every whit as false; let me but be allowed to question you upon it. That is, suffer me to serve you in your own kind, and I warrant it shall conduct you through as many perplexities and contradictions to the very same state of scepticism that I myself am in at present.

Philonous. I assure you, Hylas, I do not pretend to frame any hypothesis at all. I am of a vulgar cast, simple enough to believe my senses and leave things as I find them. To be plain, it is my opinion that the real things are those very things I see and feel, and perceive by my senses. These I know and, finding they answer all the necessities and purposes of life, have no reason to be solicitous about any other unknown beings. A piece of sensible bread, for instance, would stay my stomach better than ten thousand times as much of that insensible, unintelligible real bread you speak of. It is likewise my opinion that colours and other sensible qualities are on the objects. I cannot for my life help thinking that snow is white, and fire hot. You, indeed, who by *snow* and *fire* mean certain external, unperceived, unperceiving substances are in the right to deny whiteness or heat to be affections inherent in *them.* But I who understand by those words the things I see and feel am obliged to think like other folks. And as I am no sceptic with regard to the nature of things, so neither am I as to their existence. That a thing should be really perceived by my senses and at the same time not really exist is to me a plain contradiction, since I cannot prescind or abstract, even in thought, the existence of a sensible thing from its being perceived. Wood, stones, fire, water, flesh, iron, and the like things which I name and discourse of are things that I know. And I should not have known them but that I perceived them by my senses; and things perceived by the senses are immediately perceived; and things immediately perceived are ideas; and ideas cannot exist without the mind; their existence therefore consists in being perceived; when, therefore, they are actually perceived, there can be no doubt of their existence. Away then with all that scepticism, all those ridiculous philosophical doubts. What a jest is it for a philosopher to question the existence of sensible things till he hath it proved to him from the veracity of God, or to pretend our knowledge in this point falls short of intuition or demonstration! I might as well doubt of my own being as of the being of those things I actually see and feel.

Hylas. Not so fast, Philonous: You say you cannot conceive how sensible things should exist without the mind. Do you not?

Philonous. I do.

Hylas. Supposing you were annihilated, cannot you conceive it possible that things perceivable by sense may still exist?

Philonous. I can, but then it must be in another mind. When I deny sensible things an existence out of the mind, I do not mean my mind in particular, but all minds. Now it is plain they have an existence exterior to my mind, since I find them by experience to be independent of it. There is therefore some other Mind wherein they exist during the intervals between the times of my perceiving them, as likewise they did before my birth, and would do after my supposed annihilation. And as the same is true with regard to all other finite created spirits, it necessarily follows there is an *omnipresent eternal Mind* which knows and comprehends all things, and exhibits them to our view in such a manner and according to such rules as He Himself hath ordained and are by us termed the *laws of nature.*

Hylas. Answer me, Philonous. Are all our ideas perfectly inert beings? Or have they any agency included in them?

Philonous. They are altogether passive and inert.

Hylas. And is not God an agent, a being purely active?

Philonous. I acknowledge it.

Hylas. No idea, therefore, can be like unto or represent the nature of God.

Philonous. It cannot.

Hylas. Since, therefore, you have no idea of the mind of God, how can you conceive it possible that things should exist in His mind? Or, if you can conceive the mind of God without having an idea of it, why may not I be allowed to conceive the existence of Matter, notwithstanding I have no idea of it?

Philonous.   As to your first question: I own I have properly no *idea* either of God or any other spirit; for these, being active, cannot be represented by things perfectly inert as our ideas are. I do nevertheless know that I, who am a spirit or thinking substance, exist as certainly as I know my ideas exist. Farther, I know what I mean by the terms *I* and *myself;* and I know this immediately or intuitively, though I do not perceive it as I perceive a triangle, a colour, or a sound. The Mind, Spirit, or Soul is that indivisible unextended thing which thinks, acts, and perceives. I say *indivisible,* because unextended; and *unextended,* because extended, figured, movable things are ideas; and that which perceives ideas, which thinks and wills, is plainly itself no idea, nor like an idea. Ideas are things inactive and perceived. And Spirits a sort of beings altogether different from them. I do not therefore say my soul is an idea, or like an idea. However, taking the word *idea* in a large sense, my soul may be said to furnish me with an idea, that is, an image or likeness of God, though indeed extremely inadequate. For all the notion I have of God is obtained by reflecting on my own soul, heightening its powers, and removing its imperfections. I have, therefore, though not an inactive idea, yet in *myself* some sort of an active thinking image of the Deity. And though I perceive Him not by sense, yet I have a notion of Him, or know Him by reflexion and reasoning. My own mind and my own ideas I have an immediate knowledge of; and, by the help of these, do mediately apprehend the possibility of the existence of other spirits and ideas. Farther, from my own being, and from the dependency I find in myself and my ideas, I do, by an act of reason, necessarily infer the existence of a God and of all created things in the mind of God. So much for your first question. For the second: I suppose by this time you can answer it yourself. For you neither perceive Matter objectively, as you do an inactive being or idea, nor know it, as you do yourself by a reflex act; neither do you mediately apprehend it by similitude of the one or the other, nor yet collect it by reasoning from that which you know immediately. All which makes the case of *Matter* widely different from that of the *Deity.*

Hylas.   You say your own soul supplies you with some sort of an idea or image of God. But, at the same time, you acknowledge you have, properly speaking, no *idea* of your own soul. You even affirm that spirits are a sort of beings altogether different from ideas. Consequently, that no idea can be like a spirit. We have, therefore, no idea of any spirit. You admit nevertheless that there is spiritual Substance, although you have no idea of it, while you deny there can be such a thing as material Substance, because you have no notion or idea of it. Is this fair dealing? To act consistently, you must either admit Matter or reject Spirit. What say you to this?

Philonous.   I say, in the first place, that I do not deny the existence of material substance merely because I have no notion of it, but because the notion of it is inconsistent, or, in other words, because it is repugnant that there should be a notion of it. Many things, for aught I know, may exist whereof neither I nor any other man hath or can have any idea of notion whatsoever. But then those things must be possible, that is, nothing inconsistent must be included in their definition. I say, secondly, that, although we believe things to exist which we do not perceive, yet we may not believe that any particular thing exists without some reason for such belief; but I have no reason for believing the existence of Matter. I have no immediate intuition thereof, neither can I immediately from my sensations, ideas, notions, actions, or passions infer an unthinking, unperceiving, inactive Substance, either by probable deduction or necessary consequence. Whereas the being of my Self, that is, my own soul, mind, or thinking principle, I evidently know by reflexion. You will forgive me if I repeat the same things in answer to the same objections. In the very notion or definition of *material Substance* there is included a manifest repugnance and inconsistency. But this cannot be said of the notion of spirit. That ideas should exist in what doth not perceive, or be produced by what doth not act, is repugnant. But it is no repugnancy to say that a perceiving thing should be the subject of ideas, or an active thing the cause of them. It is granted we have neither an immediate evidence nor a demonstrative knowledge of the existence of other finite spirits, but it will not thence follow that such spirits are on a foot with material substances, if to suppose the one be inconsistent, and it be not inconsistent to suppose the other; if the one can be inferred by no argument, and there is a probability for the other; if we see signs and effects indicating distinct finite agents like ourselves, and see no sign or symptom whatever that leads to a rational belief of Matter. I say, lastly, that I have a notion of Spirit, though I have not, strictly speaking, an idea of it. I do not perceive it as an idea, or by means of an idea, but know it by reflexion.

Hylas.   Notwithstanding all you have said, to me it seems that, according to your own way of thinking, and in consequence of your own principles, it should follow that *you* are only a system of floating ideas without any substance to support them. Words are not to be used without a meaning. And, as there is no more meaning in *spiritual substance* than in *material substance,* the one is to be exploded as well as the other.

Philonous.   How often must I repeat that I know or am conscious of my own being, and that *I myself* am not my ideas, but somewhat else, a thinking, active principle that perceives, knows, wills, and operates about ideas. I know that I, one and the same self, perceive both colours and sounds, that a colour cannot perceive a sound, nor a sound a colour, that I am therefore one individual principle distinct from colour and sound, and, for the same reason, from all other sensible things and inert ideas. But I am not in like manner conscious either of the existence or essence of Matter. On the contrary, I know that nothing inconsistent can exist, and that the existence of Matter implies an inconsistency. Farther, I know what I mean when I affirm that there is a spiritual substance or support of ideas, that is, that a spirit knows and perceives ideas. But I do not know what is meant when it is said that an unperceiving substance has inherent in it and supports either ideas or the archetypes of ideas. There is, therefore, upon the whole no parity of case between Spirit and Matter.

Hylas. I own myself satisfied in this point. But do you in earnest think the real existence of sensible things consists in their being actually perceived? If so, how comes it that all mankind distinguish between them? Ask the first man you meet, and he shall tell you, *to be perceived* is one thing, and *to exist* is another.

Philonous. I am content, Hylas, to appeal to the common sense of the world for the truth of my notion. Ask the gardener why he thinks yonder cherry tree exists in the garden, and he shall tell you, because he sees and feels it; in a word, because he perceives it by his senses. Ask him why he thinks an orange tree not to be there, and he shall tell you, because he does not perceive it. What he perceives by sense, that he terms a real being and saith it *is* or *exists;* but that which is not perceivable, the same, he saith, hath no being.

Hylas. Yes, Philonous, I grant the existence of a sensible thing consists in being perceivable, but not in being actually perceived.

Philonous. And what is perceivable but an idea? And can an idea exist without being actually perceived? These are points long since agreed between us.

Hylas. But be your opinion never so true, yet surely you will not deny it is shocking and contrary to the common sense of men. Ask the fellow whether yonder tree hath an existence out of his mind; what answer think you he would make?

Philonous. The same that I should myself, to wit, that it doth exist out of his mind. But then to a Christian it cannot surely be shocking to say, the real tree, existing without his mind, is truly known and comprehended by (that is, *exists in*) the infinite mind of God. Probably he may not at first glance be aware of the direct and immediate proof there is of this, inasmuch as the very being of a tree, or any other sensible thing, implies a mind wherein it is. But the point itself he cannot deny. The question between the Materialists and me is not whether things have a *real* existence out of the mind of this or that person, but, whether they have an *absolute* existence, distinct from being perceived by God, and exterior to *all* minds. This, indeed, some heathens and philosophers have affirmed, but whoever entertains notions of the Deity suitable to the Holy Scriptures will be of another opinion.

Hylas. But, according to your notions, what difference is there between real things and chimeras formed by the imagination, or the visions of a dream, since they are all equally in the mind?

Philonous. The ideas formed by the imagination are faint and indistinct; they have, besides, an entire dependence on the will. But the ideas perceived by sense, that is, real things, are more vivid and clear, and, being imprinted on the mind by a spirit distinct from us, have not the like dependence on our will. There is, therefore, no danger of confounding these with the foregoing, and there is as little of confounding them with the visions of a dream, which are dim, irregular, and confused. And though they should happen to be never so lively and natural, yet, by their not being connected and of a piece with the preceding and subsequent transaction of our lives, they might easily be dis-

265

tinguished from realities. In short, by whatever method you distinguish *things* from *chimeras* on your own scheme, the same, it is evident, will hold also upon mine. For it must be, I presume, by some perceived difference, and I am not for depriving you of any one thing that you perceive.

Hylas. But still, Philonous, you hold there is nothing in the world but spirits and ideas. And this you must needs acknowledge sounds very oddly.

Philonous. I own the word *idea,* not being commonly used for *thing,* sounds something out of the way. My reason for using it was because a necessary relation to the mind is understood to be implied by the term; and it is now commonly used by philosophers to denote the immediate objects of the understanding. But however oddly the proposition may sound in words, yet it includes nothing so very strange or shocking in its sense, which in effect amounts to no more than this, to wit, that there are only things perceiving and things perceived, or that every unthinking being is necessarily, and from the very nature of its existence, perceived by some mind, if not by any finite created mind, yet certainly by the infinite mind of God, in whom "we live, and move, and have our being." Is this as strange as to say the sensible qualities are not on the object or that we cannot be sure of the existence of things, or know anything of their real natures, though we both see and feel them and perceive them by all our senses?

Hylas. And, in consequence of this, must we not think there are no such things as physical or corporeal causes, but that a Spirit is the immediate cause of all the phenomena in nature? Can there be anything more extravagant than this?

Philonous. Yes, it is infinitely more extravagant to say a thing which is inert operates on the mind, and which is unperceiving is the cause of our perceptions. Besides, that which to you I know not for what reason seems so extravagant is no more than the Holy Scriptures assert in a hundred places. In them God is represented as the sole and immediate Author of all those effects which some heathens and philosophers are wont to ascribe to Nature, Matter, Fate, or the like unthinking principle. This is so much the constant language of Scripture that it were needless to confirm it by citations.

Hylas. You are not aware, Philonous, that, in making God the immediate Author of all the motions in nature, you make Him the Author of murder, sacrilege, adultery, and the like heinous sins.

Philonous. In answer to that I observe, first, that the imputation of guilt is the same whether a person commits an action with or without an instrument. In case, therefore, you suppose God to act by the mediation of an instrument or occasion called *Matter,* you as truly make Him the author of sin as I, who think Him the immediate agent in all those operations vulgarly ascribed to Nature. I farther observe that sin or moral turpitude doth not consist in the outward physical action or motion, but in the internal deviation of the will from the laws of reason and religion. This is plain, in that the killing an enemy in a battle or putting a criminal legally to death is not thought sinful, though the outward act be the very same with that in the case of murder. Since, therefore, sin doth not consist in the physical action, the making God an immediate cause of all such actions is not making Him the Author of sin. Lastly, I have nowhere said that God is the only agent who produces all the motions in bodies. It is true I have denied there are any other agents besides spirits, but this is very consistent with allowing to thinking rational beings, in the production of motions, the use of limited powers, ultimately, indeed, derived from God but immediately under the direction of their own wills, which is sufficient to entitle them to all the guilt of their actions.

Hylas. But the denying Matter, Philonous, or corporeal Substance, there is the point. You can never persuade me that this is not repugnant to the universal sense of mankind. Were our dispute to be determined by most voices, I am confident you would give up the point without gathering the votes.

Philonous. I wish both our opinions were fairly stated and submitted to the judgment of men who had plain common sense, without the prejudices of a learned education. Let me be represented as one who trusts his senses, who thinks he knows the things he sees and feels, and entertains no doubts of their existence; and you fairly set forth with all your doubts, your paradoxes, and your scepticism about you, and I shall willingly acquiesce in the determination of any indifferent person. That there is no substance wherein ideas can exist besides spirit is to me evident. And that the objects immediately perceived are ideas is on all hands agreed. And that sensible qualities are objects immediately perceived no one can deny. It is therefore evident there can be no *substratum* of those qualities but spirit, *in* which they exist, not by way of mode or property, but as a thing perceived in that which perceives it. I deny, therefore, that there is any unthinking *substratum* of the objects of sense, and *in that acceptation* that there is any material substance. But if by *material substance* is meant only *sensible body,* that which is seen and felt (and the unphilosophical part of the world, I dare say, mean no more), then I am more certain of matter's existence than you or any other philosopher pretend to be. If there be anything which makes the generality of mankind averse from the notions I espouse, it is a misapprehension that I deny the reality of sensible things; but as it is you who are guilty of that and not I, it follows that in truth their aversion is against your notions and not mine. I do therefore assert that I am as certain as of my own being that there are bodies or corporeal substances (meaning the things I perceive by my senses), and that, granting this, the bulk of mankind will take no thought about, nor think themselves at all concerned in the fate of, those unknown natures and philosophical quiddities which some men are so fond of.

Hylas. What say you to this? Since, according to you, men judge of the reality of things by their senses, how can a man be mistaken in thinking the moon a plain lucid surface, about a foot in diameter, or a square tower, seen at a distance, round, or an oar, with one end in the water, crooked?

Philonous. He is not mistaken with regard to the ideas he actually perceives, but in the inferences he makes from his present perceptions. Thus, in the case of the oar, what he immediately perceives by sight is certainly crooked, and so far he is in the right. But if he thence concludes that upon taking the oar out of the water he shall perceive the same crookedness, or that it would affect his touch as crooked things are wont to do, in that he is mistaken. In like manner, if he shall conclude, from what he perceives in one station, that, in case he advances toward the moon or tower, he should still be affected with the like ideas, he is mistaken. But his mistake lies not in what he perceives immediately and at present (it being a manifest contradiction to suppose he should err in respect of that), but in the wrong judgment he makes concerning the ideas he apprehends to be connected with those immediately perceived, or, concerning the ideas, that from what he perceives at present he imagines would be perceived in other circumstances. The case is the same with regard to the Copernican system. We do not here perceive any motion of the earth, but it were erroneous thence to conclude that, in case we were placed at as great a distance from that as we are now from the other planets, we should not then perceive its motion.

Hylas. I understand you and must needs own you say things plausible enough, but give me leave to put you in mind of one thing. Pray, Philonous, were you not formerly as positive that Matter existed as you are now that it does not?

Philonous. I was. But here lies the difference. Before, my positiveness was founded, without examination, upon prejudice, but now, after inquiry, upon evidence.

Hylas. After all, it seems our dispute is rather about words than things. We agree in the thing, but differ in the name. That we are affected with ideas *from without* is evident; and it is no less evident that there must be (I will not say archetypes, but) Powers without the mind corresponding to those ideas. And as these Powers cannot subsist by themselves, there is some subject of them necessarily to be admitted, which I call *Matter,* and you call *Spirit.* This is all the difference.

Philonous. Pray, Hylas, is that powerful Being, or subject of powers, extended?

Hylas. It has not extension, but it hath the power to raise in you the idea of extension.

Philonous. It is therefore itself unextended?

Hylas. I grant it.

Philonous. Is it not also active?

Hylas. Without doubt; otherwise, how could we attribute powers to it?

Philonous. Now let me ask you two questions: *First,* whether it be agreeable to the usage either of philosophers or others to give the name *Matter* to an unextended active being? And, *secondly,* whether it be not ridiculously absurd to misapply names contrary to the common use of language?

Hylas. Well then, let it not be called Matter, since you will have it so, but some *Third Nature,* distinct from Matter and Spirit. For what reason is there why you should call it Spirit? Does not the notion of spirit imply that it is thinking as well as active and unextended?

Philonous. My reason is this: because I have a mind to have some notion or meaning in what I say, but I have no notion of any action distinct from volition, neither can I conceive volition to be anywhere but in a spirit; therefore, when I speak of an active being I am obliged to mean a Spirit. Beside, what can be plainer than that a thing which hath no ideas in itself cannot impart them to me; and, if it hath ideas, surely it must be a Spirit. To make you comprehend the point still more clearly, if it be possible: I assert as well as you that, since we are affected from without, we must allow Powers to be without, in a Being distinct from ourselves. So far we are agreed. But then we differ as to the kind of this powerful Being. I will have it to be Spirit, you Matter or I know not what (I may add, too, you know not what) Third Nature. Thus I prove it to be Spirit. From the effects I see produced I conclude there are actions; and because actions, volitions; and because there are volitions, there must be a *will.* Again, the things I perceive must have an existence, they or their archetypes, out of *my* mind; but, being ideas, neither they nor their archetypes can exist otherwise than in an understanding; there is therefore an *understanding.* But will and understanding constitute in the strictest sense a mind or spirit. The powerful cause, therefore, of my ideas is in strict propriety of speech a *Spirit. . . .*

Hylas. . . . Do you think . . . you shall persuade me the natural philosophers have been dreaming all this while? Pray what becomes of all their hypotheses and explications of the phenomena which suppose the existence of Matter?

Philonous. What mean you, Hylas, by the *phenomena?*

Hylas. I mean the appearances which I perceive by my senses.

Philonous. And the appearances perceived by sense, are they not ideas?

Hylas. I have told you so a hundred times.

Philonous. Therefore, to explain the phenomena is to show how we come to be affected with ideas in that manner and order wherein they are imprinted on our senses. Is it not?

Hylas. It is.

Philonous. Now, if you can prove that any philosopher has explained the production of any one idea in our minds by the help of *Matter,* I shall forever acquiesce and look on all that has been said against it as nothing; but if you cannot, it is vain to urge the explication of phenomena. That a Being endowed with knowledge and will should produce or exhibit ideas is easily understood. But that a being which is utterly destitute of these faculties should be able to produce ideas, or in any sort to affect an intelligence, this I can never understand. This I say, though we had some positive conception of Matter, though we knew its qualities and could comprehend its existence, would yet be so far from explaining things that it is itself the most inexplicable thing in the world. And yet, for all this, it will not follow that philosophers have been doing nothing; for by observing and reasoning upon the connexion of ideas, they discover the laws and methods of nature, which is a part of knowledge both useful and entertaining.

Hylas. After all, can it be supposed God would deceive all mankind? Do you imagine He would have induced the whole world to believe the being of Matter if there was no such thing?

Philonous. That every epidemical opinion arising from prejudice, or passion, or thoughtlessness may be imputed to God, as the Author of it, I believe you will not affirm. Whatsoever opinion we father on Him, it must be either because He has discovered it to us by supernatural revelation or because it is so evident to our natural faculties, which were framed and given us by God, that it is impossible we should withhold our assent from it. But where is the revelation? Or where is the evidence that extorts the belief of Matter? Nay, how does it appear that Matter, *taken for something distinct from what we perceive by our senses,* is thought to exist by all mankind, or, indeed, by any except a few philosophers who do not know what they would be at? Your question supposes these points are clear; and, when you have cleared them, I shall think myself obliged to give you another answer. In the meantime let it suffice that I tell you I do not suppose God has deceived mankind at all.

Hylas. But the novelty, Philonous, the novelty! There lies the danger. New notions should always be discountenanced; they unsettle men's minds, and nobody knows where they will end.

Philonous. Why the rejecting a notion that has no foundation, either in sense or in reason or in Divine authority, should be thought to unsettle the belief of such opinions as are grounded on all or any of these, I cannot imagine. That innovations in government and religion are dangerous and ought to be discountenanced, I freely own. But is there the like reason why they should be discouraged in philosophy? The making anything known which was unknown before is an innovation in knowledge; and if all such innovations had been forbidden, men would [not] have made a notable progress in the arts and sciences. But it is none of my business to plead for novelties and paradoxes. That the qualities we perceive are not on the objects, that we must not believe our senses, that we know nothing of the real nature of things and can never be assured even of their existence, that real colours and sounds are nothing but certain unknown figures and motions, that motions are in themselves neither swift nor slow, that there are in bodies absolute extensions without any particular magnitude or figure, that a thing stupid, thoughtless, and inactive operates on a spirit, that the least particle of a body contains innumerable extended parts—these are the novelties, these are the strange notions which shock the genuine uncorrupted judgment of all mankind, and, being once admitted, embarrass the mind with endless doubts and difficulties. And it is against these and the like innovations I endeavor to vindicate Common Sense. It is true, in doing this I may, perhaps, be obliged to use some *ambages,* and ways of speech not common. But if my notions are once thoroughly understood, that which is most singular in them will, in effect, be found to amount to no more than this—that it is absolutely impossible and a plain contradiction to suppose any unthinking Being should exist without being perceived by a Mind. And if this notion be singular, it is a shame it should be so at this time of day and in a Christian country.

Hylas. As for the difficulties other opinions may be liable to, those are out of the question. It is your business to defend your own opinion. Can anything be plainer than that you are for changing all things into ideas? You, I say, who are not ashamed to charge me with *scepticism.* This is so plain, there is no denying it.

Philonous. You mistake me. I am not for changing things into ideas but rather ideas into things, since those immediate objects of perception, which, according to you, are only appearances of things, I take to be the real things themselves.

Hylas. Things! you may pretend what you please; but it is certain you leave us nothing but the empty forms of things, the outside only which strikes the senses.

Philonous. What you call the empty forms and outside of things seem to me the very things themselves. Nor are they empty or incomplete otherwise than upon your supposition that Matter is an essential part of all corporeal things. We both, therefore, agree in this, that we perceive only sensible forms; but herein we differ: you will have them to be empty appearances, I real beings. In short, you do not trust your senses, I do.

Hylas. You say you believe your senses, and seem to applaud yourself that in this you agree with the vulgar. According to you, therefore, the true nature of a thing is discovered by the senses. If so, whence comes that disagreement? Why, is not the same figure, and other sensible qualities, perceived all manner of ways? And why should we use a microscope the better to discover the true nature of a body, if it were discoverable to the naked eye?

Philonous. Strictly speaking, Hylas, we do not see the same object that we feel; neither is the same object perceived by the microscope which was by the naked eye. But in case every variation was thought sufficient to constitute a new kind or individual, the endless number or confusion of names would render language impracticable. Therefore, to avoid this as well as other inconveniences which are obvious upon a little thought, men combine together several ideas, apprehended by divers senses, or by the same sense at different times or in different circumstances, but observed, however, to have some connexion in nature, either with respect to coexistence or succession; all which they refer to one name and consider as one thing. Hence it follows that when I examine by my other senses a thing I have seen, it is not in order to understand better the same object which I had perceived by sight, the object of one sense not being perceived by the other senses. And when I look through a microscope, it is not that I may perceive more clearly what I perceived already with my bare eyes, the object perceived by the glass being quite different from the former. But in both cases my aim is only to know what ideas are connected together; and the more a man knows of the connexion of ideas, the more he is said to know of the nature of things. What, therefore, if our ideas are variable, what if our senses are not in all circumstances affected with the same appearances? It will not thence follow they are not to be trusted or that they are inconsistent either with themselves or anything else, except it be with your preconceived notion of (I know not what) one single, unchanged, unperceivable, real Nature, marked by each name; which prejudice seems to have taken its rise from not rightly understanding the common language of men speaking of several distinct ideas as united into one thing by the mind. And, indeed, there is cause to suspect several erroneous conceits of the philosophers are owing to the same original: while they began to build their schemes not so much on notions as words which were framed by the vulgar merely for convenience and dispatch in the common actions of life, without any regard to speculation.

Hylas.   Methinks I apprehend your meaning.

Philonous.   It is your opinion the ideas we perceive by our senses are not real things, but images or copies of them. Our knowledge, therefore, is no farther real than as our ideas are the true *representations* of those *originals*. But as these supposed originals are in themselves unknown, it is impossible to know how far our ideas resemble them, or whether they resemble them at all. We cannot, therefore, be sure we have any real knowledge. Farther, as our ideas are perpetually varied, without any change in the supposed real things, it necessarily follows they cannot all be true copies of them, or, if some are and others are not, it is impossible to distinguish the former from the latter. And this plunges us yet deeper in uncertainty. Again, when we consider the point, we cannot conceive how any idea, or anything like an idea, should have an absolute existence out of a mind, nor consequently, according to you, how there should be any real thing in nature. The result of all which is that we are thrown into the most hopeless and abandoned scepticism. Now give me leave to ask you, *first,* whether your referring ideas to certain absolutely existing unperceived substances, as their originals, be not the source of all this scepticism? *Secondly,* whether you are informed, either by sense or reason, of the existence of those unknown originals? And in case you are not, whether it be not absurd to suppose them? *Thirdly,* whether, upon inquiry, you find there is anything distinctly conceived or meant by the *absolute or external existence of unperceiving substances? Lastly,* whether, the premises considered, it be not the wisest way to follow nature, trust your senses, and, laying aside all anxious thought about unknown natures or substances, admit with the vulgar those for real things which are perceived by the senses?

Hylas.   For the present I have no inclination to the answering part. I would much rather see how you can get over what follows. Pray, are not the objects perceived by the *senses* of one likewise perceivable to others present? If there were a hundred more here, they would all see the garden, the trees and flowers, as I see them. But they are not in the same manner affected with the ideas I frame in my *imagination*. Does not this make a difference between the former sort of objects and the latter?

Philonous. I grant it does. Nor have I ever denied a difference between the objects of sense and those of imagination. But what would you infer from thence? You cannot say that sensible objects exist unperceived because they are perceived by many.

Hylas. I own I can make nothing of that objection, but it has led me into another. Is it not your opinion that by our senses we perceive only the ideas existing in our minds?

Philonous. It is.

Hylas. But the same idea which is in my mind cannot be in yours or in any other mind. Doth it not, therefore, follow from your principles that no two can see the same thing? And is not this highly absurd?

Philonous. If the term *same* be taken in the vulgar acceptation, it is certain (and not at all repugnant to the principles I maintain) that different persons may perceive the same thing, or the same thing or idea exist in different minds. Words are of arbitrary imposition; and since men are used to apply the word *same* where no distinction or variety is perceived, and I do not pretend to alter their perceptions, it follows that, as men have said before, *several saw the same thing,* so they may, upon like occasions, still continue to use the same phrase without any deviation either from propriety of language or the truth of things. But if the term *same* be used in the acceptation of philosophers who pretend to an abstracted notion of identity, then, according to their sundry definitions of this notion (for it is not yet agreed wherein that philosophic identity consists), it may or may not be possible for divers persons to perceive the same thing. But whether philosophers shall think fit to call a thing the *same* or no is, I conceive, of small importance. Let us suppose several men together, all endued with the same faculties, and consequently affected in like sort by their senses, and who had yet never known the use of language; they would without question agree in their perceptions. Though perhaps, when they came to the use of speech, some regarding the uniformness of what was perceived might call it the *same* thing; others, especially regarding the diversity of persons who perceived, might choose the denomination of *different* things. But who sees not that all the dispute is about a word, to wit, whether what is perceived by different persons may yet have the term *same* applied to it? Or suppose a house whose walls or outward shell remaining unaltered, the chambers are all pulled down, and new ones built in their place, and that you should call this the *same,* and I should say it was not the *same* house—would we not, for all this, perfectly agree in our thoughts of the house considered in itself? And would not all the difference consist in a sound? If you should say we differed in our notions, for that you superadded to your idea of the house the simple abstracted idea of identity, whereas I did not, I would tell you I know not what you mean by that *ab-*

stracted idea of identity, and should desire you to look into your own thoughts and be sure you understood yourself.—Why so silent, Hylas? Are you not yet satisfied men may dispute about identity and diversity without any real difference in their thoughts and opinions abstracted from names? Take this further reflexion with you—that, whether Matter be allowed to exist or no, the case is exactly the same as to the point in hand. For the Materialists themselves acknowledge what we immediately perceive by our senses to be our own ideas. Your difficulty, therefore, that no two see the same thing makes equally against the Materialists and me.

Hylas. But they suppose an external archetype to which referring their several ideas they may truly be said to perceive the same thing.

Philonous. And (not to mention your having discarded those archetypes) so may you suppose an external archetype on my principles; *external, I mean, to your own mind,* though, indeed, it must be supposed to exist in that Mind which comprehends all things; but then, this serves all the ends of *identity,* as well as if it existed out of a mind. And I am sure you yourself will not say it is less intelligible.

Hylas. You have indeed clearly satisfied me either that there is no difficulty at bottom in this point or, if there be, that is makes equally against both opinions.

Philonous. But that which makes equally against two contradictory opinions can be a proof against neither.

Hylas. I acknowledge it. But, after all, Philonous, when I consider the substance of what you advance against *Scepticism,* it amounts to no more than this: we are sure that we really see, hear, feel, in a word, that we are affected with sensible impressions.

Philonous. And how are *we* concerned any farther? I see this cherry, I feel it, I taste it, and I am sure *nothing* cannot be seen or felt or tasted; it is therefore *real.* Take away the sensations of softness, moisture, redness, tartness, and you take away the cherry. Since it is not a being distinct from sensations, a cherry, I say, is nothing but a congeries of sensible impressions, or ideas perceived by various senses, which ideas are united into one thing (or have one name given them) by the mind because they are observed to attend each other. Thus, when the palate is affected with such a particular taste, the sight is affected with a red colour, the touch with roundness, softness, etc. Hence, when I see and feel and taste in sundry certain manners, I am sure the cherry exists or is real, its reality being in my opinion nothing abstracted from those sensations. But if by the word *cherry* you mean an unknown nature distinct from all those sensible qualities, and by its *existence* something distinct from its being perceived, then, indeed, I own neither you nor I, nor anyone else, can be sure it exists.

Hylas. But what would you say, Philonous, if I should bring the very same reasons against the existence of sensible things *in a mind* which you have offered against their existing *in a material substratum?*

Philonous. When I see your reasons, you shall hear what I have to say to them.

Hylas. Is the mind extended or unextended?

Philonous. Unextended, without doubt.

Hylas. Do you say the things you perceive are in your mind?

Philonous. They are.

Hylas. Again, have I not heard you speak of sensible impressions?

Philonous. I believe you may.

Hylas. Explain to me now, O Philonous! how is it possible there should be room for all those trees and houses to exist in your mind. Can extended things be contained in that which is unextended? Or are we to imagine impressions made on a thing void of all solidity? You cannot say objects are in your mind, as books in your study, or that things are imprinted on it, as the figure of a seal upon wax. In what sense, therefore, are we to understand those expressions? Explain me this if you can, and I shall then be able to answer all those queries you formerly put to me about my *substratum.*

Philonous. Look you, Hylas, when I speak of objects as existing in the mind or imprinted on the senses, I would not be understood in the gross literal sense—as when bodies are said to exist in a place or a seal to make an impression upon wax. My meaning is only that the mind comprehends or perceives them, and that it is affected from without or by some being distinct from itself. This is my explication of your difficulty; and how it can serve to make your tenet of an unperceiving material *substratum* intelligible, I would fain know.

Hylas. Nay, if that be all, I confess I do not see what use can be made of it. But are you not guilty of some abuse of language in this?

Philonous. None at all. It is no more than common custom, which you know is the rule of language, hath authorised, nothing being more usual than for philosophers to speak of the immediate objects of the understanding as things existing in the mind. Nor is there anything in this but what is conformable to the general analogy of language; most part of the mental operations being signified by words borrowed from sensible things, as is plain in the terms *comprehend, reflect, discourse,* etc., which, being applied to the mind, must not be taken in their gross original sense.

Hylas. You have, I own, satisfied me in this point. . . .

Hylas. . . . It is plain, I do not now think with the philosophers, nor yet altogether with the vulgar. I would know how the case stands in that respect, precisely what you have added to or altered in my former notions.

Philonous. I do not pretend to be a setter-up of new notions. My endeavours tend only to unite and place in a clearer light that truth which was before shared between the vulgar and the philosophers, the former being of opinion that *those things they immediately perceive are the real things,* and the latter, that *the things immediately perceived are ideas which exist only in the mind.* Which two notions put together do, in effect, constitute the substance of what I advance.

Hylas. I have been a long time distrusting my senses; methought I saw things by a dim light and through false glasses. Now the glasses are removed and a new light breaks in upon my understanding. I am clearly convinced that I see things in their native forms and am no longer in pain about their *unknown natures* or *absolute existence.* This is the state I find myself in at present, though, indeed, the course that brought me to it I do not yet thoroughly comprehend. You set out upon the same principles that Academics, Cartesians, and the like sects usually do, and for a long time it looked as if you were advancing their philosophical Scepticism; but, in the end, your conclusions are directly opposite to theirs.

Philonous. You see, Hylas, the water of yonder fountain, how it is forced upwards, in a round column, to a certain height, at which it breaks and falls back into the basin from whence it rose, its ascent as well as descent proceeding from the same uniform law or principle of gravitation. Just so, the same Principles which, at first view, lead to Scepticism, pursued to a certain point, bring men back to Common Sense.

COMPARATIVE STUDY QUESTIONS

Review Questions

1. By denying that matter exists, is Berkeley (Philonous) denying that "things" exist?
2. Restate Philonous' argument to the effect that heat cannot, any more than pain, be supposed to exist in an "unperceiving corporeal substance."
3. What point is Berkeley trying to establish by his experiment involving the submersion of both hands in a bucket of water?
4. Are perceived sounds reducible to motions or vibrations, according to Berkeley?
5. Do colors exist on the objects we see? According to Berkeley, are roses red even apart from anyone's perception of them?
6. By what argument does Berkeley prove that primary qualities too are relative to the observer?
7. What does Berkeley (Philonous) mean by an "abstract idea"?
8. What does Berkeley mean by "idea"? "thing"? "mind" or "spirit"?
9. Toward the end of the first dialogue, Philonous accuses Hylas of being the sceptic. Why so?
10. Explain the significance of Berkeley's statement, "I am not for changing things into ideas but rather ideas into things."

Discussion Questions

1. Would Descartes agree with Berkeley's view that "secondary qualities" are mind-dependent (i.e., that they do not exist independently of someone's mind or experience)?
2. Explain how Berkeley would analyze Descartes' example of the wax in order to establish that all the differently perceived qualities relate to the same thing.
3. Hylas proposes a distinction between "sensation" and "object." Assess Philonous' criticism of such a distinction.
4. Restate the argument for God's existence in the second dialogue. What **kind** of a God does it purportedly prove to exist? Is the proof convincing? Is it better than previous arguments by Descartes, Spinoza, and Leibniz?
5. Are Berkeley's indictments of Hobbes and Spinoza as atheists justified?
6. Is it Berkeley's overall strategy to prove that the concept of matter is inherently self-contradictory, that the concept is meaningless, or that we simply have no evidence for supposing that such a thing exists?
7. Does Berkeley have an **idea** of God? Compare this discussion with Hobbes' criticism of Descartes' claim to have an idea of God.

8. Similarly, does Berkeley have an **idea** of himself (his mind)? What kind of knowledge does he have of himself? Of other finite selves or minds?
9. Hylas complains that he does not see how "there should be room for all those trees and houses to exist in your mind." What is the criticism, and do you find Philonous' reply satisfactory?
10. Complete the reply to the following limerick (by Ronald Knox)[9] regarding Berkeley's theory of material objects:

> There was a young man who said, "God
> Must think it exceedingly odd
> If he finds that this tree
> Continues to be
> When there's no one about in the Quad."

Reply

Dear Sir:
 Your astonishment's odd:
I am always about in the Quad.
 And that's why the tree
 Will continue to be,
Since observed by
  Yours faithfully,
  _?_

9. From Bertrand Russell, *A History of Western Philosophy* (New York: Simon and Schuster, 1945), p. 648. Used by permission of Simon and Schuster, Inc., and George Allen and Unwin Ltd.

David Hume
(1711 – 1776)

THE GROUNDS FOR SCEPTICISM

Mr. David Hume

> Apart from any reference to existing religions as they are,
> or as they ought to be, we must investigate dispassionately
> what the metaphysical principles, here developed, require
> on these points, as to the nature of God. . . . What follows
> is merely an attempt to add another speaker to that master-
> piece, Hume's *Dialogues Concerning Natural Religion.*
>
> Alfred North Whitehead, *Process and Reality*
> (1929)

One of the most curious documents in the world is James Boswell's last interview with David Hume. It is an extraordinary document not only because it concerns a deathbed interrogation of Hume by Boswell, but also because the reporter seems not to have realized just how much fun Hume was having at his expense.

According to the account,[1] it was a Sunday morning on the seventh of July, 1776. Boswell had risen too late for church and decided instead to visit David Hume who had recently returned from London to Edinburgh. He found him at his home on St. David's Street, alone in his drawing room, and in Boswell's own phrase, "just a-dying." Hume had lost weight and looked ghastly, but to Boswell's surprise, he was placid and even cheerful.

Somehow Boswell managed to introduce the topic of immortality into the conversation.[2] Hume admitted that he had entertained a belief in religion in his

---

1. "An Account of My Last Interview with David Hume, Esq.," reprinted in *Boswell in Extremes 1776–1778,* edited by Charles McC. Weis and Frederick A. Pottle (copyright 1970 by Yale University) and published by McGraw-Hill Book Company. Used by permission.

2. What follows is both close paraphrase and direct quotation, together with dialogue excerpted from Boswell's journal or reconstructed from the text. I am wholly responsible for the statements in the "author typeface" which are not found in the original account, but are supplied in order to clarify the discussion. Double quotation marks and indentation are used to indicate direct quotation. Where changes are required to convert Boswell's report of his conversation to dialogue, I have used single quotation marks to indicate my literal, but I hope not significant, divergence from the text. In order to capture some of the eighteenth-century flavor of the conversation, and also some of Boswell's intended meaning, I have occasionally reverted to Boswell's capitalization and spelling, as found in *The Private Papers of James Boswell from Malahide Castle in the Collection of Lt-Col. Ralph Heyward Isham,* Volume XII.

JAMES BOSWELL

youth, but not since he began to read Locke and Clarke.[3] At one time he had even made an abstract of a catalogue of vices which he found at the end of a book of religious instruction. Leaving out Murder and Theft, which he thought he had no chance of committing, he then conducted a self-examination. Apparently Hume failed the examination, or the examination failed him, for he concluded that it was "strange work" to try to have no pride or vanity while at the same time excelling his school-fellows. It was, he said, "absurd and contrary to fixed principles and necessary consequences."

To Boswell's utter dismay, Hume pronounced the morality of every religion bad, and Boswell thought he was really "not jocular" when Hume reversed the common remark about infidels and said, 'When I hear that a man is religious, I conclude that he is a rascal, though I have known some instances of very good men being religious.'

Boswell then reports that he had a "strong curiosity" to be satisfied whether Hume persisted in disbelieving in a future state even when he had death before his eyes. Boswell gathered from what Hume said and his manner of saying it that he did persist. The rest of the conversation between them, on this occasion, may be reconstructed from Boswell's account as follows:

> *Boswell.* 'Is it not possible that there might be a future state?'
>
> *Hume.* 'It is possible that a piece of coal put upon the fire would not burn, but that we should exist forever is a most unreasonable fancy.'
>
> *Boswell.* Why do you think so?

---

3. John Locke (1632–1704) and Samuel Clarke (1675–1729), both of whom, incidentally, were strong supporters of religion!

Hume. 'Because if there is any immortality at all, it must be general. It must include even those who lack any intellectual qualities: those who die in infancy before being possessed of reason; the porter who gets drunk by ten o'clock with gin; the trash of every age. New universes would have to be created to contain such infinite numbers.'

Boswell. "An unphilosophical objection, Mr. Hume. You know Spirit does not take up space."

Hume. [No response reported. Perhaps only a smile like the one Boswell says Wilkes[4] later expressed when told of Hume's opinion that, if any were, Wilkes and his mob must be immortal.]

Boswell. 'Does the thought of Annihilation ever give you any uneasiness?'

Hume. 'Not the least; no more, as Lucretius observes, than the thought that I might never have been.'

Boswell. "Well, Mr. Hume, I hope to triumph over you when I meet you in a future state; and remember you are not to pretend that you was joking with all this infidelity."

Hume. "No, no. But I shall have been so long there before you come that it will be nothing new."

Boswell had a few qualms of conscience about bedeviling Hume at such a time regarding "so aweful" a subject, but he said, "As nobody was present, I thought it could have no bad effect." He himself, however, experienced a few giddy feelings:

I . . . felt a degree of horror, mixed with a sort of wild, strange, hurrying recollection of my excellent mother's pious instructions, of Dr. Johnson's noble lessons, and of my religious sentiments and affections during the course of my life. I was like a man in sudden danger eagerly seeking his defensive arms; and I could not but be assailed by momentary doubts while I had actually before me a man of such strong abilities and extensive inquiry dying in the persuasion of being annihilated. But I maintained my faith.

Boswell. 'I believe the Christian Religion as I believe History.'

Hume. "You do not believe it as you believe the Revolution."

Boswell. "Yes, but the difference is that I am not so much interested in the truth of the Revolution; otherwise I should have

4. John Wilkes (1727–1797) described by Boswell as one "who either is, or affects to be, an infidel," was a radical member of Parliament during the reign of George III.

> anxious doubts concerning it. A man who is in love has doubts of the affections of his mistress, without cause."

After some discussion of the question of whether a future state was a pleasing idea (Hume thought it was not) and whether it would be agreeable to see deceased friends again (Hume owned it would be), Boswell somehow or other brought Dr. Johnson's name into the conversation.

> *Hume.* "Johnson should be pleased with my *History.*"

> *Boswell* (nettled by Hume's frequent attacks upon his revered friend in former conversations). 'Dr. Johnson does not allow you much credit, for he said, "Sir, the fellow is a Tory by chance."' But no matter, "If I were you, I should regret Annihilation. Had I written such an admirable history, I should be sorry to leave it."

> *Hume.* "I shall leave that history, of which you are pleased to speak so favourably, as perfect as I can."

Hume died on August 25, 1776, leaving the manuscript of his **Dialogues Concerning Natural Religion** unpublished, but like his **History**, in as "perfect" a condition as he could. He had hoped to publish the **Dialogues** himself before his death, but ill health prevented that, so he annotated it with precise instructions and tried to arrange its publication through his will. The trouble was that his friends, who had read the more or less completed manuscript years before, all counseled him against publication, fearing the public criticism it might bring him and themselves should they be associated with it. Even Hume's close friend, Adam Smith, had "scruples" about becoming Hume's literary executor. Hume regarded all such scruples as groundless, but in a codicil to his will finally left the manuscript to the publisher of his **History** and **Essays,** Mr. William Strahan, with the proviso that if it were not published within two and a half years after his death, it should become the property of his namesake nephew, David, whose duty it would be to publish the manuscript as the last request of his uncle. Surely no one, Hume thought, could object to the performance of such a family obligation. Strahan himself later decided that it would be more fitting for Hume's nephew to edit the book for publication. Thereupon the younger David Hume faithfully executed his famous uncle's wishes. The book appeared in 1779, three years after Hume's death in 1776.

The **Dialogues** have as their nominal topic of discussion the nature and existence of God. The positions of Demea, the orthodox believer, Philo, the sceptic, and Cleanthes, the religious rationalist, represent diverse and interesting positions regarding these substantive questions. But of equal or greater philosophical importance are the more general methodological considerations which are introduced. What is the role of evidence in matters of religious belief? What makes analogical reasoning valid? Can we validly reason from what we have experienced to something we have never experienced? Are all inferences regarding matters of fact founded on the supposition that similar causes prove similar effects, and similar effects similar causes? Do metaphysical conceptions, that is, views about the nature of the world as a whole, have specifically religious implications? What grounds, if any, do we have for thinking such metaphysical speculations true?

One final and unavoidable question: Who speaks for Hume in the **Dialogues**? Scholars have long differed regarding the answer to this question. Norman Kemp Smith contends that "Philo, from start to finish, represents Hume."[5] Others favor Cleanthes; still others Pamphilus, who reports the conversations. Some commentators believe that Hume is completely noncommittal, but at least one, J. Y. T. Greig, thinks the answer is: "Each now and then, but none always."[6]

---

5. For a discussion of this controversy and the variety of viewpoints which have been held, see Kemp Smith's comments in his edition of the *Dialogues*, Library of Liberal Arts (Indianapolis: Bobbs-Merrill), pp. 57–59; also, Charles W. Hendel's *Studies in the Philosophy of David Hume*, Library of Liberal Arts (Indianapolis: Bobbs-Merrill, 1963), p. 272.

6. *David Hume* (New York: Oxford University Press, 1931), p. 235.

HUME

*Dialogues Concerning Natural Religion**

Pamphilus to Hermippus

It has been remarked, my Hermippus, that, though the ancient philosophers conveyed most of their instruction in the form of dialogue, this method of composition has been little practised in later ages, and has seldom succeeded in the hands of those who have attempted it. Accurate and regular argument, indeed, such as is now expected of philosophical inquirers, naturally throws a man into the methodical and didactic manner, where he can immediately, without preparation, explain the point at which he aims; and thence proceed, without interruption, to deduce the proofs on which it is established. To deliver a *system* in conversation scarcely appears natural; and, while the dialogue writer desires, by departing from the direct style of composition, to give a freer air to his performance, and avoid the appearance of *author* and *reader,* he is apt to run into a worse inconvenience and convey the image of *pedagogue* and *pupil.* Or, if he carries on the dispute in the natural spirit of good company, by throwing in a variety of topics and preserving a proper balance among the speakers, he often loses so much time in preparations and transitions that the reader will scarcely think himself compensated, by all the graces of dialogue, for the order, brevity, and precision, which are sacrificed to them.

There are some subjects, however, to which dialogue-writing is peculiarly adapted, and where it is still preferable to the direct and simple method of composition.

Any point of doctrine which is so *obvious* that it scarcely admits of dispute, but at the same time so *important* that it cannot be too often inculcated, seems to require some such method of handling it; where the novelty of the manner may compensate the triteness of the subject; where the vivacity of conversation may enforce the precept; and where the variety of lights, presented by various personages and characters, may appear neither tedious nor redundant.

Any question of philosophy, on the other hand, which is so *obscure* and *uncertain* that human reason can reach no fixed determination with regard to it—if it should be treated at all—seems to lead us naturally into the style of dialogue and conversation. Reasonable men may be allowed to differ where no one can reasonably be positive. Opposite sentiments, even without any decision, afford an agreeable amusement; and if the subject be curious and interesting, the book carries us, in a manner, into company and unites the two greatest and purest pleasures of human life, study and society.

---

*From the first edition published in 1779, with some modernization of the punctuation and capitalization. Since Pamphilus' report of the conversations is not given in strict dialogue form, the names of the three principal speakers are printed in boldface type whenever required to identify their respective statements more easily. Pamphilus' own interspersed comments have not been so identified.

Happily, these circumstances are all to be found in the subject of *natural religion*. What truth so obvious, so certain, as the *being* of a God, which the most ignorant ages have acknowledged, for which the most refined geniuses have ambitiously striven to produce new proofs and arguments? What truth so important as this, which is the ground of all our hopes, the surest foundation of morality, the firmest support of society, and the only principle which ought never to be a moment absent from our thoughts and meditations? But, in treating of this obvious and important truth, what obscure questions occur concerning the *nature* of that Divine Being, his attributes, his decrees, his plan of providence? These have been always subjected to the disputations of men; concerning these human reason has not reached any certain determination. But these are topics so interesting that we cannot restrain our restless inquiry with regard to them, though nothing but doubt, uncertainty, and contradiction have as yet been the result of our most accurate researches.

This I had lately occasion to observe, while I passed, as usual, part of the summer season with Cleanthes, and was present at those conversations of his with Philo and Demea, of which I gave you lately some imperfect account. Your curiosity, you then told me, was so excited that I must, of necessity, enter into a more exact detail of their reasonings, and display those various systems which they advanced with regard to so delicate a subject as that of natural religion. The remarkable contrast in their characters still further raised your expectations, while you opposed the accurate philosophical turn of Cleanthes to the careless scepticism of Philo, or compared either of their dispositions with the rigid inflexible orthodoxy of Demea. My youth rendered me a mere auditor of their disputes; and that curiosity, natural to the early season of life, has so deeply imprinted in my memory the whole chain and connexion of their arguments that, I hope, I shall not omit or confound any considerable part of them in the recital.

Part I

After I joined the company whom I found sitting in Cleanthes' library, **Demea** paid Cleanthes some compliments on the great care which he took of my education, and on his unwearied perseverance and constancy in all his friendships. The father of Pamphilus, said he, was your intimate friend; the son is your pupil, and may indeed be regarded as your adopted son were we to judge by the pains which you bestow in conveying to him every useful branch of literature and science. You are no more wanting, I am persuaded, in prudence than in industry. I shall, therefore, communicate to you a maxim which I have observed with regard to my own children, that I may learn how far it agrees with your practice. The method I follow in their education is founded on the saying of an ancient, "That students of philosophy ought first to learn logics, then ethics, next physics, last of all the nature of the gods."[7] This science of natural theology, according to him, being the most pro-

---

7. Chrysippus *apud* Plut., *De repug. Stoicorum.*

found and abstruse of any, required the maturest judgment in its students; and none but a mind enriched with all the other sciences can safely be entrusted with it.

Are you so late, says **Philo,** in teaching your children the principles of religion? Is there no danger of their neglecting or rejecting altogether those opinions of which they have heard so little during the whole course of their education? It is only as a science, replied **Demea,** subjected to human reasoning and disputation, that I postpone the study of natural theology. To season their minds with early piety is my chief care; and by continual precept and instruction and, I hope, too, by example, I imprint deeply on their tender minds an habitual reverence for all the principles of religion. While they pass through every other science, I still remark the uncertainty of each part; the eternal disputations of men; the obscurity of all philosophy; and the strange, ridiculous conclusions which some of the greatest geniuses have derived from the principles of mere human reason. Having thus tamed their mind to a proper submission and self-diffidence, I have no longer any scruple of opening to them the greatest mysteries of religion, nor apprehend any danger from that assuming arrogance of philosophy, which may lead them to reject the most established doctrines and opinions.

Your precaution, says **Philo,** of seasoning your children's minds early with piety is certainly very reasonable, and no more than is requisite in this profane and irreligious age. But what I chiefly admire in your plan of education is your method of drawing advantage from the very principles of philosophy and learning which, by inspiring pride and self-sufficiency, have commonly, in all ages, been found so destructive to the principles of religion. The vulgar, indeed, we may remark, who are unacquainted with science and profound inquiry, observing the endless disputes of the learned, have commonly a thorough contempt for philosophy, and rivet themselves the faster, by that means, in the great points of theology which have been taught them. Those who enter a little into study and inquiry, finding many appearances of evidence in doctrines the newest and most extraordinary, think nothing too difficult for human reason and, presumptuously breaking through all fences, profane the inmost sanctuaries of the temple. But Cleanthes will, I hope, agree with me that, after we have abandoned ignorance, the surest remedy, there is still one expedient left to prevent this profane liberty. Let Demea's principles be improved and cultivated; let us become thoroughly sensible of the weakness, blindness, and narrow limits of human reason; let us duly consider its uncertainty and endless contrarieties, even in subjects of common life and practice; let the errors and deceits of our very senses be set before us; the insuperable difficulties which attend first principles in all systems; the contradictions which adhere to the very ideas of matter, cause and effect, extension, space, time, motion, and, in a word, quantity of all kinds, the object of the only science that can fairly pretend to any certainty or evidence. When these topics are displayed in their full light, as they are by some philosophers and almost all divines, who can retain such confidence in this frail faculty of reason as to pay any regard to its determinations in points so sublime, so abstruse, so remote from common life and experience? When the coherence of the parts of a stone, or even that composition of parts which renders it extended; when these familiar objects, I say, are so inexplicable, and contain circumstances so repugnant and contradictory, with what assurance can we decide concerning the origin of worlds or trace their history from eternity to eternity?

While Philo pronounced these words, I could observe a smile in the countenance both of Demea and Cleanthes. That of Demea seemed to imply an unreserved satisfaction in the doctrines delivered; but in Cleanthes' features I could distinguish an air of finesse, as if he perceived some raillery of artificial malice in the reasonings of Philo.

You propose then, Philo, said **Cleanthes,** to erect religious faith on philosophical scepticism; and you think that, if certainty or evidence be expelled from every other subject of inquiry, it will all retire to these theological doctrines, and there acquire a superior force and authority. Whether your scepticism be as absolute and sincere as you pretend, we shall learn by and by, when the company breaks up; we shall then see whether you go out at the door or the window, and whether you really doubt if your body has gravity or can be injured by its fall, according to popular opinion derived from our fallacious senses and more fallacious experience. And this consideration, Demea, may, I think, fairly serve to abate our ill-will to this humorous sect of the sceptics. If they be thoroughly in earnest, they will not long trouble the world with their doubts, cavils, and disputes; if they be only in jest, they are, perhaps, bad railers, but can never be very dangerous, either to the state, to philosophy, or to religion.

In reality, Philo, continued he, it seems certain that, though a man, in a flush of humour, after intense reflection on the many contradictions and imperfections of human reason, may entirely renounce all belief and opinion, it is impossible for him to persevere in this total scepticism or make it appear in his conduct for a few hours. External objects press in upon him; passions solicit him; his philosophical melancholy dissipates; and even the utmost violence upon his own temper will not be able, during any time, to preserve the poor appearance of scepticism. And for what reason impose on himself such a violence? This is a point in which it will be impossible for him ever to satisfy himself, consistently with his sceptical principles. So that, upon the whole, nothing could be more ridiculous than the principles of the ancient Pyrrhonians if, in reality, they endeavoured, as is pretended, to extend throughout the same scepticism which they had learned from the declamations of their schools, and which they ought to have confined to them.

In this view, there appears a great resemblance between the sects of the Stoics and Pyrrhonians, though perpetual antagonists; and both of them seem founded on this erroneous maxim that what a man can perform sometimes, and in some dispositions, he can perform always and in every disposition. When the mind, by Stoical reflections, is elevated into a sublime enthusiasm of virtue and strongly smit with any *species* of honour or public good, the utmost bodily pain and sufferings will not prevail over such a high sense of duty; and it is possible, perhaps, by its means, even to smile and exult in the midst of tortures. If this sometimes may be the case in fact and reality, much more may a philosopher, in his school or even in his closet, work himself up to such an enthusiasm and support, in imagination, the acutest pain or most calamitous event which he can possibly conceive. But how shall he support this enthusiasm itself? The bent of his mind relaxes and cannot be recalled at pleasure; avocations lead him astray; misfortunes attack him unawares; and the *philosopher* sinks, by degrees, into the *plebeian.*

I allow of your comparison between the Stoics and Sceptics, replied **Philo.** But you may observe, at the same time, that though the mind cannot, in Stoicism, support the highest flights of philosophy, yet, even when it sinks lower, it still retains somewhat of its former disposition; and the effects of the Stoic's reasoning will appear in his conduct in common life, and through the whole tenor of his actions. The ancient schools, particularly that of Zeno, produced examples of virtue and constancy which seem astonishing to present times.

> *Vain Wisdom all and false Philosophy.*
> *Yet with a pleasing sorcery could charm*
> *Pain, for a while, or anguish; and excite*
> *Fallacious Hope, or arm the obdurate breast*
> *With stubborn Patience, as with triple steel.*[8]

In like manner, if a man has accustomed himself to sceptical considerations on the uncertainty and narrow limits of reason, he will not entirely forget them when he turns his reflection on other subjects; but in all his philosophical principles and reasoning, I dare not say in his common conduct, he will be found different from those who either never formed any opinions in the case or have entertained sentiments more favourable to human reason.

To whatever length any one may push his speculative principles of scepticism, he must act, I own, and live, and converse, like other men; and for this conduct he is not obliged to give any other reason than the absolute necessity he lies under of so doing. If he ever carries his speculations farther than this necessity constrains him, and philosophises either on natural or moral subjects, he is allured by a certain pleasure and satisfaction which he finds in employing himself after that manner. He considers, besides, that everyone, even in common life, is constrained to have more or less of this philosophy; that from our earliest infancy we make continual advances in forming more general principles of conduct and reasoning; that the larger experience we acquire, and the stronger reason we are endued with, we always render our principles the more general and comprehensive; and that what we call *philosophy* is nothing but a more regular and methodical operation of the same kind. To philosophise on such subjects is nothing essentially different from reasoning on common life, and we may only expect greater stability, if not greater truth, from our philosophy on account of its exacter and more scrupulous method of proceeding.

But when we look beyond human affairs and the properties of the surrounding bodies; when we carry our speculations into the two eternities, before and after the present state of things; into the creation and formation of the universe, the existence and properties of spirits, the powers and operations of one universal Spirit existing without beginning and without end, omnipotent, omniscient, im-

---

8. [Milton, *Paradise Lost*, Bk. II.]

mutable, infinite, and incomprehensible—we must be far removed from the smallest tendency to scepticism not to be apprehensive that we have here got quite beyond the reach of our faculties. So long as we confine our speculations to trade, or morals, or politics, or criticism, we make appeals, every moment, to common sense and experience, which strengthen our philosophical conclusions and remove (at least in part) the suspicion which we so justly entertain with regard to every reasoning that is very subtile and refined. But, in theological reasonings, we have not this advantage; while at the same time we are employed upon objects which, we must be sensible, are too large for our grasp and, of all others, require most to be familiarized to our apprehension. We are like foreigners in a strange country to whom everything must seem suspicious, and who are in danger every moment of transgressing against the laws and customs of the people with whom they live and converse. We know not how far we ought to trust our vulgar methods of reasoning in such a subject, since, even in common life, and in that province which is peculiarly appropriated to them, we cannot account for them and are entirely guided by a kind of instinct or necessity in employing them.

All sceptics pretend that, if reason be considered in an abstract view, it furnishes invincible arguments against itself, and that we could never retain any conviction or assurance, on any subject, were not the sceptical reasonings so refined and subtile that they are not able to counterpoise the more solid and more natural arguments derived from the senses and experience. But it is evident, whenever our arguments lose this advantage and run wide of common life, that the most refined scepticism comes to be upon a footing with them, and is able to oppose and counterbalance them. The one has no more weight than the other. The mind must remain in suspense between them; and it is that very suspense or balance which is the triumph of scepticism.

But I observe, says **Cleanthes,** with regard to you, Philo, and all speculative sceptics that your doctrine and practice are as much at variance in the most abstruse points of theory as in the conduct of common life. Wherever evidence discovers itself, you adhere to it, notwithstanding your pretended scepticism; and I can observe, too, some of your sect to be as decisive as those who make greater professions of certainty and assurance. In reality, would not a man be ridiculous who pretended to reject Newton's explication of the wonderful phenomenon of the rainbow because that explication gives a minute anatomy of the rays of light, a subject, forsooth, too refined for human comprehension? And what would you say to one who, having nothing particular to object to the arguments of Copernicus and Galileo for the motion of the earth, should withhold his assent on that general principle that these subjects were too magnificent and remote to be explained by the narrow and fallacious reason of mankind?

There is indeed a kind of brutish and ignorant scepticism, as you well observed, which gives the vulgar a general prejudice against what they do not easily understand, and makes them reject every principle which requires elaborate reasoning to prove and establish it. This species of scepticism is fatal to knowledge, not to religion; since we find that those who make greatest profession of it give often their assent, not only to the great truths of theism and natural theology, but even to the most absurd tenets which a traditional superstition has recommended to them.

They firmly believe in witches, though they will not believe nor attend to the most simple proposition of Euclid. But the refined and philosophical sceptics fall into an inconsistency of an opposite nature. They push their researches into the most abstruse corners of science, and their assent attends them in every step, proportioned to the evidence which they meet with. They are even obliged to acknowledge that the most abstruse and remote objects are those which are best explained by philosophy. Light is in reality anatomized; the true system of the heavenly bodies is discovered and ascertained. But the nourishment of bodies by food is still an inexplicable mystery; the cohesion of the parts of matter is still incomprehensible. These sceptics, therefore, are obliged, in every question, to consider each particular evidence apart, and proportion their assent to the precise degree of evidence which occurs. This is their practice in all natural, mathematical, moral, and political science. And why not the same, I ask, in the theological and religious? Why must conclusions of this nature be alone rejected on the general presumption of the insufficiency of human reason, without any particular discussion of the evidence? Is not such an unequal conduct a plain proof of prejudice and passion?

Our senses, you say, are fallacious; our understanding erroneous; our ideas, even of the most familiar objects, extension, duration, motion, full of absurdities and contradictions. You defy me to solve the difficulties or reconcile the repugnancies which you discover in them. I have not capacity for so great an undertaking; I have not leisure for it. I perceive it to be superfluous. Your own conduct, in every circumstance, refutes your principles, and shows the firmest reliance on all the received maxims of science, morals, prudence, and behaviour.

I shall never assent to so harsh an opinion as that of a celebrated writer,[9] who says that the Sceptics are not a sect of philosophers: they are only a sect of liars. I may, however, affirm (I hope without offence) that they are a sect of jesters or railers. But for my part, whenever I find myself disposed to mirth and amusement, I shall certainly choose my entertainment of a less perplexing and abstruse nature. A comedy, a novel, or, at most, a history seems a more natural recreation than such metaphysical subtilties and abstractions.

In vain would the sceptic make a distinction between science and common life, or between one science and another. The arguments employed in all, if just, are of a similar nature and contain the same force and evidence. Or if there be any difference among them, the advantage lies entirely on the side of theology and natural religion. Many principles of mechanics are founded on very abstruse reasoning, yet no man who has any pretensions to science, even no speculative sceptic, pretends to entertain the least doubt with regard to them. The Copernican system contains the most surprising paradox, and the most contrary to our natural conceptions, to appearances, and to our very senses, yet even monks and inquisitors are now constrained to withdraw their opposition to it. And shall Philo, a man of so liberal a genius and extensive knowledge, entertain any general undistinguished scruples with regard to the religious hypothesis, which is founded on the simplest and most obvious arguments and, unless it meets with artificial obstacles, has such easy access and admission into the mind of man?

---

9. *L'art de penser* [Antoine Arnauld: *La Logique ou l'art de penser*, 1662.]

And here we may observe, continued he, turning himself towards Demea, a pretty curious circumstance in the history of the sciences. After the union of philosophy with the popular religion, upon the first establishment of Christianity, nothing was more usual, among all religious teachers, than declamations against reason, against the senses, against every principle derived merely from human research and inquiry. All the topics of the ancient Academics were adopted by the Fathers, and thence propagated for several ages in every school and pulpit throughout Christendom. The Reformers embraced the same principles of reasoning or rather declamation; and all panegyrics on the excellence of faith were sure to be interlarded with some severe strokes of satire against natural reason. A celebrated prelate, too,[10] of the Romish communion, a man of the most extensive learning, who wrote a demonstration of Christianity, has also composed a treatise which contains all the cavils of the boldest and most determined Pyrrhonism. Locke seems to have been the first Christian who ventured openly to assert that *faith* was nothing but a species of *reason;* that religion was only a branch of philosophy; and that a chain of arguments, similar to that which established any truth in morals, politics, or physics, was always employed in discovering all the principles of theology, natural and revealed. The ill use which Bayle and other libertines made of the philosophical scepticism of the Fathers and first Reformers still further propagated the judicious sentiment of Mr. Locke. And it is now in a manner avowed, by all pretenders to reasoning and philosophy, that *atheist* and *sceptic* are almost synonymous. And as it is certain that no man is in earnest when he professes the latter principle, I would fain hope that there are as few who seriously maintain the former.

Don't you remember, said **Philo,** the excellent saying of Lord Bacon on this head? That a little philosophy, replied **Cleanthes,** makes a man an atheist; a great deal converts him to religion. That is a very judicious remark, too, said **Philo**. But what I have in my eye is another passage, where, having mentioned David's fool, who said in his heart there is no God, this great philosopher observes that the atheists nowadays have a double share of folly, for they are not contented to say in their hearts there is no God, but they also utter that impiety with their lips, and are thereby guilty of multiplied indiscretion and imprudence. Such people, though they were ever so much in earnest, cannot, methinks, be very formidable.

But though you should rank me in this class of fools, I cannot forbear communicating a remark that occurs to me, from the history of the religious and irreligious scepticism with which you have entertained us. It appears to me that there are strong symptoms of priestcraft in the whole progress of this affair. During ignorant ages, such as those which followed the dissolution of the ancient schools, the priests perceived that atheism, deism, or heresy of any kind, could only proceed from the presumptuous questioning of received opinions, and from a belief that human reason was equal to everything. Education had then a mighty influence over the minds of men, and was almost equal in force to those suggestions of the senses and common understanding by which the most determined sceptic must allow himself to be governed. But at present, when the influence of education is much diminished

---

10. Mons. Huet.

292

and men, from a more open commerce of the world, have learned to compare the popular principles of different nations and ages, our sagacious divines have changed their whole system of philosophy and talk the language of Stoics, Platonists, and Peripatetics, not that of Pyrrhonians and Academics. If we distrust human reason we have now no other principle to lead us into religion. Thus sceptics in one age, dogmatists in another—whichever system best suits the purpose of these reverend gentlemen in giving them an ascendant over mankind—they are sure to make it their favourite principle and established tenet.

It is very natural, said **Cleanthes,** for men to embrace those principles by which they find they can best defend their doctrines, nor need we have any recourse to priestcraft to account for so reasonable an expedient. And surely nothing can afford a stronger presumption that any set of principles are true and ought to be embraced than to observe that they tend to the confirmation of true religion, and serve to confound the cavils of atheists, libertines, and free-thinkers of all denominations.

Part II

I must own, Cleanthes, said **Demea,** that nothing can more surprise me than the light in which you have all along put this argument. By the whole tenor of your discourse, one would imagine that you were maintaining the Being of a God against the cavils of atheists and infidels, and were necessitated to become a champion for that fundamental principle of all religion. But this, I hope, is not by any means a question among us. No man, no man at least of common sense, I am persuaded, ever entertained a serious doubt with regard to a truth so certain and self-evident. The question is not concerning the *being* but the *nature* of God. This I affirm, from the infirmities of human understanding, to be altogether incomprehensible and unknown to us. The essence of that supreme Mind, his attributes, the manner of his existence, the very nature of his duration—these and every particular which regards so divine a Being—are mysterious to men. Finite, weak, and blind creatures, we ought to humble ourselves in his august presence, and, conscious of our frailties, adore in silence his infinite perfections which eye hath not seen, ear hath not heard, neither hath it entered into the heart of man to conceive. They are covered in a deep cloud from human curiosity; it is profaneness to attempt penetrating through these sacred obscurities, and, next to the impiety of denying his existence, is the temerity of prying into his nature and essence, decrees and attributes.

But lest you should think that my *piety* has here got the better of my *philosophy,* I shall support my opinion, if it needs any support, by a very great authority. I might cite all the divines, almost from the foundation of Christianity, who have ever treated of this or any other theological subject; but I shall confine myself, at present, to one equally celebrated for piety and philosophy. It is Father Malebranche who, I remember, thus expresses himself.[11] "One ought not so much," says he, "to call God a spirit in order to express positively what he is, as in order to signify that he is not matter. He is a Being infinitely perfect: of this we cannot

---

11. *Recherche de la Vérité,* liv. 3, chap. 9.

doubt. But in the same manner as we ought not to imagine, even supposing him corporeal, that he is clothed with a human body, as the anthropomorphites asserted, under colour that that figure was the most perfect of any, so neither ought we to imagine that the spirit of God has human ideas or bears *any* resemblance to our spirit, under colour that we know nothing more perfect than a human mind. We ought rather to believe that as he comprehends the perfections of matter without being material . . . he comprehends also the perfections of created spirits without being spirit, in the manner we conceive spirit: that his true name is *He that is,* or, in other words, Being without restriction, All Being, the Being infinite and universal."

After so great an authority, Demea, replied **Philo,** as that which you have produced, and a thousand more which you might produce, it would appear ridiculous in me to add my sentiment or express my approbation of your doctrine. But surely, where reasonable men treat these subjects, the question can never be concerning the *being* but only the *nature* of the Deity. The former truth, as you well observe, is unquestionable and self-evident. Nothing exists without a cause; and the original cause of this universe (whatever it be) we call God, and piously ascribe to him every species of perfection. Whoever scruples this fundamental truth deserves every punishment which can be inflicted among philosophers, to wit, the greatest ridicule, contempt, and disapprobation. But as all perfection is entirely relative, we ought never to imagine that we comprehend the attributes of this divine Being, or to suppose that his perfections have any analogy or likeness to the perfections of a human creature. Wisdom, thought, design, knowledge, these we justly ascribe to him because these words are honourable among men, and we have no other language or other conceptions by which we can express our adoration of him. But let us beware lest we think that our ideas anywise correspond to his perfections, or that his attributes have any resemblance to these qualities among men. He is infinitely superior to our limited view and comprehension, and is more the object of worship in the temple than of disputation in the schools.

In reality, Cleanthes, continued he, there is no need of having recourse to that affected scepticism so displeasing to you in order to come at this determination. Our ideas reach no farther than our experience. We have no experience of divine attributes and operations. I need not conclude my syllogism, you can draw the inference yourself. And it is a pleasure to me (and I hope to you, too) that just reasoning and sound piety here concur in the same conclusion, and both of them establish the adorably mysterious and incomprehensible nature of the Supreme Being.

Not to lose any time in circumlocutions, said **Cleanthes,** addressing himself to Demea, much less in replying to the pious declamations of Philo, I shall briefly explain how I conceive this matter. Look round the world, contemplate the whole and every part of it: you will find it to be nothing but one great machine, subdivided into an infinite number of lesser machines, which again admit of subdivisions to a degree beyond what human senses and faculties can trace and explain. All these various machines, and even their most minute parts, are adjusted to each other with an accuracy which ravishes into admiration all men who have ever contemplated them. The curious adapting of means to ends, throughout all nature, resembles exactly, though it much exceeds, the productions of human contrivance, of human design, thought, wisdom, and intelligence. Since therefore the effects resemble each other, we are led to infer, by all the rules of analogy, that the causes also resemble, and that the Author of nature is somewhat similar to the mind of man, though possessed of much larger faculties, proportioned to the grandeur of the work which he has executed. By this argument *a posteriori,* and by this argument alone, do we prove at once the existence of a Deity and his similarity to human mind and intelligence.

I shall be so free, Cleanthes, said **Demea**, as to tell you that from the beginning I could not approve of your conclusion concerning the similarity of the Deity to men, still less can I approve of the mediums by which you endeavour to establish it. What! No demonstration of the being of God! No abstract arguments! No proofs *a priori!* Are these which have hitherto been so much insisted on by philosophers all fallacy, all sophism? Can we reach no farther in this subject than experience and probability? I will not say that this is betraying the cause of a Deity; but surely, by this affected candour, you give advantages to atheists which they never could obtain by the mere dint of argument and reasoning.

What I chiefly scruple in this subject, said **Philo**, is not so much that all religious arguments are by Cleanthes reduced to experience, as that they appear not to be even the most certain and irrefragable of that inferior kind. That a stone will fall, that fire will burn, that the earth has solidity, we have observed a thousand and a thousand times; and when any new instance of this nature is presented, we draw without hesitation the accustomed inference. The exact similarity of the cases gives us a perfect assurance of a similar event, and a stronger evidence is never desired nor sought after. But wherever you depart, in the least, from the similarity of the cases, you diminish proportionably the evidence, and may at last bring it to a very weak *analogy,* which is confessedly liable to error and uncertainty. After having experienced the circulation of the blood in human creatures, we make no doubt that it takes place in Titius and Maevius; but from its circulation in frogs and fishes it is only a presumption, though a strong one, from analogy that it takes place in men and other animals. The analogical reasoning is much weaker when we infer the circulation of the sap in vegetables from our experience that the blood circulates in animals; and those who hastily followed that imperfect analogy are found, by more accurate experiments, to have been mistaken.

If we see a house, Cleanthes, we conclude, with the greatest certainty, that it had an architect or builder, because this is precisely that species of effect which we have experienced to proceed from that species of cause. But surely you will not affirm that the universe bears such a resemblance to a house that we can with the same certainty infer a similar cause, or that the analogy is here entire and perfect. The dissimilitude is so striking that the utmost you can here pretend to is a guess, a conjecture, a presumption concerning a similar cause; and how that pretension will be received in the world, I leave you to consider.

It would surely be very ill received, replied **Cleanthes**; and I should be deservedly blamed and detested did I allow that the proofs of a Deity amounted to no more than a guess or conjecture. But is the whole adjustment of means to ends in a house and in the universe so slight a resemblance? The economy of final causes? The order, proportion, and arrangement of every part? Steps of a stair are plainly contrived, that human legs may use them in mounting; and this inference is certain and infallible. Human legs are also contrived for walking and mounting; and this inference, I allow, is not altogether so certain, because of the dissimilarity which you remark; but does it, therefore, deserve the name only of presumption or conjecture?

Good God! cried **Demea**, interrupting him, where are we? Zealous defenders of religion allow that the proofs of a Deity fall short of perfect evidence! And you, Philo, on whose assistance I depended in proving the adorable mysteriousness of the Divine Nature, do you assent to all these extravagant opinions of Cleanthes? For what other name can I give them? Or, why spare my censure when such principles are advanced, supported by such an authority, before so young a man as Pamphilus?

You seem not to apprehend, replied **Philo**, that I argue with Cleanthes in his own way, and, by showing him the dangerous consequences of his tenets, hope at last to reduce him to our opinion. But what sticks most with you, I observe, is the representation which Cleanthes has made of the argument *a posteriori;* and, finding that that argument is likely to escape your hold and vanish into air, you think it so disguised that you can scarcely believe it to be set in its true light. Now, however much I may dissent, in other respects, from the dangerous principle of Cleanthes, I must allow that he has fairly represented that argument, and I shall endeavour so to state the matter to you that you will entertain no further scruples with regard to it.

Were a man to abstract from everything which he knows or has seen, he would be altogether incapable, merely from his own ideas, to determine what kind of scene the universe must be, or to give the preference to one state or situation of things above another. For as nothing which he clearly conceives could be esteemed impossible or implying a contradiction, every chimera of his fancy would be upon an equal footing; nor could he assign any just reason why he adheres to one idea or system, and rejects the others which are equally possible.

Again, after he opens his eyes and contemplates the world as it really is, it would be impossible for him at first to assign the cause of any one event, much less of the whole of things, or of the universe. He might set his fancy a rambling, and she might bring him in an infinite variety of reports and representations. These would all be possible, but, being all equally possible, he would never of himself give a satisfactory account for his preferring one of them to the rest. Experience alone can point out to him the true cause of any phenomenon.

Now, according to this method of reasoning, Demea, it follows (and is, indeed, tacitly allowed by Cleanthes himself) that order, arrangement, or the adjustment of final causes, is not of itself any proof of design, but only so far as it has been experienced to proceed from that principle. For aught we can know *a priori,* matter may contain the source or spring of order originally within itself, as well as mind does; and there is no more difficulty in conceiving that the several elements, from an internal unknown cause, may fall into the most exquisite arrangement, than to conceive that their ideas, in the great universal mind, from a like internal unknown cause, fall into that arrangement. The equal possibility of both these suppositions is allowed. But, by experience, we find (according to Cleanthes) that there is a difference between them. Throw several pieces of steel together, without shape or form; they will never arrange themselves so as to compose a watch. Stone and mortar and wood, without an architect, never erect a house. But the ideas in a human mind, we see, by an unknown, inexplicable economy, arrange themselves so as to form the plan of a watch or house. Experience, therefore, proves that there is an original principle of order in mind, not in matter. From similar effects we infer similar causes. The adjustment of means to ends is alike in the universe, as in a machine of human contrivance. The causes, therefore, must be resembling.

I was from the beginning scandalized, I must own, with this resemblance which is asserted between the Deity and human creatures, and must conceive it to imply such a degradation of the Supreme Being as no sound theist could endure. With your assistance, therefore, Demea, I shall endeavour to defend what you justly call the adorable mysteriousness of the Divine Nature, and shall refute this reasoning of Cleanthes, provided he allows that I have made a fair representation of it.

When Cleanthes had assented, **Philo,** after a short pause, proceeded in the following manner.

That all inferences, Cleanthes, concerning fact are founded on experience, and that all experimental reasonings are founded on the supposition that similar causes prove similar effects, and similar effects similar causes, I shall not at present much dispute with you. But observe, I entreat you, with what extreme caution all just reasoners proceed in the transferring of experiments to similar cases. Unless the cases be exactly similar, they repose no perfect confidence in applying their past observation to any particular phenomenon. Every alteration of circumstances occasions a doubt concerning the event; and it requires new experiments to prove certainly that the new circumstances are of no moment or importance. A change in bulk, situation, arrangement, age, disposition of the air, or surrounding bodies, any of these particulars may be attended with the most unexpected consequences. And unless the objects be quite familiar to us, it is the highest temerity to expect with assurance, after any of these changes, an event similar to that which before fell under our observation. The slow and deliberate steps of philosophers here, if anywhere, are distinguished from the precipitate march of the vulgar, who, hurried on by the smallest similitude, are incapable of all discernment or consideration.

But can you think, Cleanthes, that your usual phlegm and philosophy have been preserved in so wide a step as you have taken when you compared to the universe houses, ships, furniture, machines, and, from their similarity in some circumstances, inferred a similarity in their causes? Thought, design, intelligence, such as we discover in men and other animals, is no more than one of the springs and principles of the universe, as well as heat or cold, attraction or repulsion, and a hundred others which fall under daily observation. It is an active cause by which some particular parts of nature, we find, produce alterations on other parts. But can a conclusion, with any propriety, be transferred from parts to the whole? Does not the great disproportion bar all comparison and inference? From observing the growth of a hair, can we learn anything concerning the generation of a man? Would the manner of a leaf's blowing, even though perfectly known, afford us any instruction concerning the vegetation of a tree?

But allowing that we were to take the *operations* of one part of nature upon another for the foundation of our judgment concerning the *origin* of the whole (which never can be admitted), yet why select so minute, so weak, so bounded a principle as the reason and design of animals is found to be upon this planet? What peculiar privilege has this little agitation of the brain which we call *thought,* that we must thus make it the model of the whole universe? Our partiality in our own favour does indeed present it on all occasions, but sound philosophy ought carefully to guard against so natural an illusion.

So far from admitting, continued **Philo,** that the operations of a part can afford us any just conclusion concerning the origin of the whole, I will not allow any one part to form a rule for another part if the latter be very remote from the former. Is there any reasonable ground to conclude that the inhabitants of other planets possess thought, intelligence, reason, or anything similar to these faculties in men? When nature has so extremely diversified her manner of operation in this small globe, can we imagine that she incessantly copies herself throughout so immense a universe? And if thought, as we may well suppose, be confined merely to this narrow corner and has even there so limited a sphere of action, with what propriety can we assign it for the original cause of all things? The narrow views of a peasant who makes his domestic economy the rule for the government of kingdoms is in comparison a pardonable sophism.

But were we ever so much assured that a thought and reason resembling the human were to be found throughout the whole universe, and were its activity elsewhere vastly greater and more commanding than it appears in this globe, yet I cannot see why the operations of a world constituted, arranged, adjusted, can with any propriety be extended to a world which is in its embryo state, and is advancing towards that constitution and arrangement. By observation we know somewhat of the economy, action, and nourishment of a finished animal, but we must transfer with great caution that observation to the growth of a foetus in the womb, and still more to the formation of an animalcule in the loins of its male parent. Nature, we find, even from our limited experience, possesses an infinite number of springs and principles which incessantly discover themselves on every change of her position and situation. And what new and unknown principles would actuate her in so new and unknown a situation as that of the formation of a universe, we cannot, without the utmost temerity, pretend to determine.

A very small part of this great system, during a very short time, is very imperfectly discovered to us; and do we thence pronounce decisively concerning the origin of the whole?

Admirable conclusion! Stone, wood, brick, iron, brass, have not, at this time, in this minute globe of earth, an order or arrangement without human art and contrivance; therefore, the universe could not originally attain its order and arrangement without something similar to human art. But is a part of nature a rule for another part very wide of the former? Is it a rule for the whole? Is a very small part a rule for the universe? Is nature in one situation a certain rule for nature in another situation vastly different from the former?

And can you blame me, Cleanthes, if I here imitate the prudent reserve of Simonides, who, according to the noted story, being asked by Hiero, *What God was?* desired a day to think of it, and then two days more; and after that manner continually prolonged the term, without ever bringing in his definition or description? Could you even blame me if I had answered, at first, *that I did not know,* and was sensible that this subject lay vastly beyond the reach of my faculties? You might cry out sceptic and rallier, as much as you pleased; but, having found in so many other subjects much more familiar the imperfections and even contradictions of human reason, I never should expect any success from its feeble conjectures in a subject so sublime and so remote from the sphere of our observation. When two *species* of objects have always been observed to be conjoined together, I can *infer,* by custom, the existence of one wherever I *see* the existence of the other; and this I call an argument from experience. But how this argument can have place where the objects, as in the present case, are single, individual, without parallel or specific resemblance, may be difficult to explain. And will any man tell me with a serious countenance that an orderly universe must arise from some thought and art like the human because we have experience of it? To ascertain this reasoning it were requisite that we had experience of the origin of worlds; and it is not sufficient, surely, that we have seen ships and cities arise from human art and contrivance.

Philo was proceeding in this vehement manner, somewhat between jest and earnest, as it appeared to me, when he observed some signs of impatience in Cleanthes, and then immediately stopped short. What I had to suggest, said **Cleanthes,** is only that you would not abuse terms, or make use of popular expressions to subvert philosophical reasonings. You know that the vulgar often distinguish reason from experience, even where the question relates only to matter of fact and existence, though it is found, where that *reason* is properly analyzed, that it is nothing but a species of experience. To prove by experience the origin of the universe from mind is not more contrary to common speech than to prove the motion of the earth from the same principle. And a caviller might raise all the same objections to the Copernican system which you have urged against my reasonings. Have you other earths, might he say, which you have seen to move? Have. . . .

Yes! cried **Philo,** interrupting him, we have other earths. Is not the moon another earth, which we see to turn round its centre? Is not Venus another earth, where we observe the same phenomenon? Are not the revolutions of the sun also a confirmation, from analogy, of the same theory? All the planets, are they not earths which revolve about the sun? Are not the satellites moons which move round Jupiter and Saturn, and along with these primary planets round the sun? These analogies and resemblances, with others which I have not mentioned, are the sole proofs of the Copernican system; and to you it belongs to consider whether you have any analogies of the same kind to support your theory.

In reality, Cleanthes, continued he, the modern system of astronomy is now so much received by all inquirers, and has become so essential a part even of our earliest education, that we are not commonly very scrupulous in examining the reasons upon which it is founded. It is now become a matter of mere curiosity to study the first writers on that subject who had the full force of prejudice to encounter, and were obliged to turn their arguments on every side in order to render them popular and convincing. But if we peruse Galileo's famous *Dialogues* concerning the system of the world, we shall find that that great genius, one of the sublimest that ever existed, first bent all his endeavours to prove that there was no foundation for the distinction commonly made between elementary and celestial substances. The schools, proceeding from the illusions of sense, had carried this distinction very far; and had established the latter substances to be ingenerable, incorruptible, unalterable, impassible; and had assigned all the opposite qualities to the former. But Galileo, beginning with the moon, proved its similarity in every particular to the earth: its convex figure, its natural darkness when not illuminated, its density, its distinction into solid and liquid, the variations of its phases, the mutual illuminations of the earth and moon, their mutual eclipses, the inequalities of the lunar surface, etc. After many instances of this kind, with regard to all the planets, men plainly saw that these bodies became proper objects of experience, and that the similarity of their nature enabled us to extend the same arguments and phenomena from one to the other.

In this cautious proceeding of the astronomers you may read your own condemnation, Cleanthes, or rather may see that the subject in which you are engaged exceeds all human reason and inquiry. Can you pretend to show any such similarity between the fabric of a house and the generation of a universe? Have you ever seen nature in any such situation as resembles the first arrangement of the elements? Have worlds ever been formed under your eye, and have you had leisure to observe the whole progress of the phenomenon, from the first appearance of order to its final consummation? If you have, then cite your experience and deliver your theory.

Part III

How the most absurd argument, replied **Cleanthes,** in the hands of a man of ingenuity and invention, may acquire an air of probability! Are you not aware, Philo, that it became necessary for Copernicus and his first disciples to prove the similarity of the terrestrial and celestial matter because several philosophers, blinded by old systems and supported by some sensible appearances, had denied this similarity? But that it is by no means necessary that theists should prove the similarity of the works of nature to those of art because this similarity is self-evident and undeniable? The same matter, a like form; what more is requisite to show an analogy between their causes, and to ascertain the origin of all things from a divine purpose and intention? Your objections, I must freely tell you, are no better than the abstruse cavils of those philosophers who denied motion, and ought to be refuted in the same manner, by illustrations, examples, and instances rather than by serious argument and philosophy.

Suppose, therefore, that an articulate voice were heard in the clouds, much louder and more melodious than any which human art could ever reach; suppose that this voice were extended in the same instant over all nations and spoke to each nation in its own language and dialect; suppose that the words delivered not only contain a just sense and meaning, but convey some instruction altogether worthy of a benevolent Being superior to mankind. Could you possibly hesitate a moment concerning the cause of this voice, and must you not instantly ascribe it to some design or purpose? Yet I cannot see but all the same objections (if they merit that appellation) which lie against the system of theism may also be produced against this inference.

Might you not say that all conclusions concerning fact were founded on experience; that, when we hear an articulate voice in the dark and thence infer a man, it is only the resemblance of the effects which leads us to conclude that there is a like resemblance in the cause; but that this extraordinary voice, by its loudness, extent, and flexibility to all languages, bears so little analogy to any human voice that we have no reason to suppose any analogy in their causes; and, consequently, that a rational, wise, coherent speech proceeded, you know not whence, from some accidental whistling of the winds, not from any divine reason or intelligence? You see clearly your own objections in these cavils, and I hope too you see clearly that they cannot possibly have more force in the one case than in the other.

But to bring the case still nearer the present one of the universe, I shall make two suppositions which imply not any absurdity or impossibility. Suppose that there is a natural, universal, invariable language, common to every individual of human race, and that books are natural productions which perpetuate themselves in the same manner with animals and vegetables, by descent and propagation. Several expressions of our passions contain a universal language: all brute animals have a natural speech, which, however limited, is very intelligible to their own species. And as there are infinitely fewer parts and less contrivance in the finest composition of eloquence than in the coarsest organized body, the propagation of an *Iliad* or *Aeneid* is an easier supposition than that of any plant or animal.

Suppose, therefore, that you enter into your library thus peopled by natural volumes containing the most refined reason and most exquisite beauty; could you possibly open one of them and doubt that its original cause bore the strongest analogy to mind and intelligence? When it reasons and discourses; when it expostulates, argues, and enforces its views and topics; when it applies sometimes to the pure intellect, sometimes to the affections; when it collects, disposes, and adorns every consideration suited to the subject; could you persist in asserting that all this, at the bottom, had really no meaning, and that the first formation of this volume in the loins of its original parent proceeded not from thought and design? Your obstinacy, I know, reaches not that degree of firmness; even your sceptical play and wantonness would be abashed at so glaring an absurdity.

But if there be any difference, Philo, between this supposed case and the real one of the universe, it is all to the advantage of the latter. The anatomy of an animal affords many stronger instances of design than the perusal of Livy or Tacitus; and any objection which you start in the former case, by carrying me back to so unusual and extraordinary a scene as the first formation of worlds, the same objection has place on the supposition of our vegetating library. Choose, then, your party, Philo, without ambiguity or evasion; assert either that a rational volume is no prof of a rational cause or admit of a similar cause to all the works of nature.

Let me here observe, too, continued **Cleanthes**, that this religious argument, instead of being weakened by that scepticism so much affected by you, rather acquires force from it and becomes more firm and undisputed. To exclude all argument or reasoning of every kind is either affectation or madness. The declared profession of every reasonable sceptic is only to reject abstruse, remote, and refined arguments; to adhere to common sense and the plain instincts of nature; and to assent, wherever any reasons strike him with so full a force that he cannot, without the greatest violence, prevent it. Now the arguments for natural religion are plainly of this kind; and nothing but the most perverse, obstinate metaphysics can reject them. Consider, anatomize the eye, survey its structure and contrivance, and tell me, from your own feeling, if the idea of a contriver does not immediately flow in upon you with a force like that of sensation. The most obvious conclusion, surely, is in favour of design; and it requires time, reflection, and study, to summon up those frivolous though abstruse objections which can support infidelity. Who can behold the male and female of each species, the correspondence of their parts and instincts, their passions and whole course of life before and after generation, but must be sensible that the propagation of the species is intended by nature? Millions and millions of such instances present themselves through every part of the universe, and no language can convey a more intelligible irresistible meaning than the curious adjustment of final causes. To what degree, therefore, of blind dogmatism must one have attained to reject such natural and such convincing arguments?

Some beauties in writing we may meet with which seem contrary to rules, and which gain the affections and animate the imagination in opposition to all the precepts of criticism and to the authority of the established masters of art. And if the argument for theism be, as you pretend, contradictory to the principles of logic, its universal, its irresistible influence proves clearly that there may be arguments of a like irregular nature. Whatever cavils may be urged, an orderly world, as well as a coherent, articulate speech, will still be received as an incontestable proof of design and intention.

It sometimes happens, I own, that the religious arguments have not their due influence on an ignorant savage and barbarian, not because they are obscure and difficult, but because he never asks himself any question with regard to them. Whence arises the curious structure of an animal? From the copulation of its parents. And these whence? From *their* parents? A few removes set the objects at such a distance that to him they are lost in darkness and confusion; nor is he actuated by any curiosity to trace them farther. But this is neither dogmatism nor scepticism, but stupidity: a state of mind very different from your sifting, inquisitive disposition, my ingenious friend. You can trace causes from effects; you can compare the most distant and remote objects; and your greatest errors proceed not from barrenness of thought and invention, but from too luxuriant a fertility which suppresses your natural good sense by a profusion of unnecessary scruples and objections.

Here I could observe, Hermippus, that Philo was a little embarrassed and confounded; but, while he hesitated in delivering an answer, luckily for him, **Demea** broke in upon the discourse and saved his countenance.

Your instance, Cleanthes, said he, drawn from books and language, being familiar, has, I confess, so much more force on that account; but is there not some danger, too, in this very circumstance, and may it not render us presumptuous, by making us imagine we comprehend the Deity and have some adequate idea of his nature and attributes? When I read a volume, I enter into the mind and intention of the author; I become him, in a manner, for the instant, and have an immediate feeling and conception of those ideas which revolved in his imagination while employed in that composition. But so near an approach we never surely can make to the Deity. His ways are not our ways. His attributes are perfect but incomprehensible. And this volume of nature contains a great and inexplicable riddle, more than any intelligible discourse or reasoning.

The ancient Platonists, you know, were the most religious and devout of all the pagan philosophers, yet many of them, particularly Plotinus, expressly declare that intellect or understanding is not to be ascribed to the Deity, and that our most perfect worship of him consists, not in acts of veneration, reverence, gratitude, or love, but in a certain mysterious self-annihilation or total extinction of all our faculties. These ideas are, perhaps, too far stretched, but still it must be acknowledged that, by representing the Deity as so intelligible and comprehensible, and so similar to a human mind, we are guilty of the grossest and most narrow partiality, and make ourselves the model of the whole universe.

All the *sentiments* of the human mind, gratitude, resentment, love, friendship, approbation, blame, pity, emulation, envy, have a plain reference to the state and situation of man, and are calculated for preserving the existence and promoting the activity of such a being in such circumstances. It seems, therefore, unreasonable to transfer such sentiments to a supreme existence or to suppose him actuated by them; and the phenomena, besides, of the universe will not support us in such a theory. All our *ideas* derived from the senses are confessedly false and illusive, and cannot therefore be supposed to have place in a supreme intelligence. And as the ideas of internal sentiment, added to those of the external senses, compose the whole furniture of human understanding, we may conclude that none of the *materials* of thought are in any respect similar in the human and in the divine intelligence. Now, as to the *manner* of thinking, how can we make any comparison between them or suppose them anywise resembling? Our thought is fluctuating, uncertain, fleeting, successive, and compounded; and were we to remove these circumstances, we absolutely annihilate its essence, and it would in such a case be an abuse of terms to apply to it the name of thought or reason. At least, if it appear more pious and respectful (as it really is) still to retain these terms when we mention the Supreme Being, we ought to acknowledge that their meaning, in that case, is totally incomprehensible, and that the infirmities of our nature do not permit us to reach any ideas which in the least correspond to the ineffable sublimity of the Divine attributes.

Part IV

It seems strange to me, said **Cleanthes**, that you, Demea, who are so sincere in the cause of religion, should still maintain the mysterious, incomprehensible nature of the Deity, and should insist so strenuously that he has no manner of likeness or resemblance to human creatures. The Deity, I can readily allow, possesses many powers and attributes of which we can have no comprehension; but, if our ideas, so far as they go, be not just and adequate and correspondent to his real nature, I know not what there is in this subject worth insisting on. Is the name, without any meaning, of such mighty importance? Or how do you mystics, who maintain the absolute incomprehensibility of the Deity, differ from sceptics or atheists, who assert that the first cause of all is unknown and unintelligible? Their temerity must be very great if, after rejecting the production by a mind; I mean a mind resembling the human (for I know of no other), they pretend to assign, with certainty, any other specific intelligible cause; and their conscience must be very scrupulous, indeed, if they refuse to call the universal unknown cause a God or Deity, and to bestow on him as many sublime eulogies and unmeaning epithets as you shall please to require of them.

Who could imagine, replied **Demea**, that Cleanthes, the calm philosophical Cleanthes, would attempt to refute his antagonists by affixing a nickname to them, and, like the common bigots and inquisitors of the age, have recourse to invective and declamation instead of reasoning? Or does he not perceive that these topics are easily retorted, and that *anthropomorphite* is an appellation as invidious, and implies as dangerous consequences, as the epithet of *mystic* with which he has honoured us? In reality, Cleanthes, consider what it is you assert when you represent the Deity as similar to a human mind and understanding. What is the soul of man? A composition of various faculties, passions, sentiments, ideas; united, indeed, into one self or person, but still distinct from each other. When it reasons, the ideas which are the parts of its discourse arrange themselves in a certain form or order which is not preserved entire for a moment, but immediately gives place to another arrangement. New opinions, new passions, new affections, new feelings arise which continually diversify the mental scene and produce in it the greatest variety and most rapid succession imaginable. How is this compatible with that perfect immutability and simplicity which all true theists ascribe to the Deity? By the same act, say they, he sees past, present, and future; his love and hatred, his mercy and justice, are one individual operation; he is entire in every point of space, and complete in every instant of duration. No succession, no change, no acquisition, no diminution. What he is implies not in it any shadow of distinction or diversity. And what he is this moment he ever has been and ever will be, without any new judgment, sentiment, or operation. He stands fixed in one simple, perfect state; nor can you ever say, with any propriety, that this act of his is different from that other, or that this judgment or idea has been lately formed and will give place, by succession, to any different judgment or idea.

I can readily allow, said **Cleanthes**, that those who maintain the perfect simplicity of the Supreme Being, to the extent in which you have explained it, are complete mystics, and chargeable with all the consequences which I have drawn from their opinion. They are, in a word, atheists, without knowing it. For though it be allowed that the Deity possesses attributes of which we have no comprehension, yet ought we never to ascribe to him any attributes which are absolutely incompatible with that intelligent nature essential to him. A mind whose acts and sentiments and ideas are not distinct and successive, one that is wholly simple and totally immutable, is a mind which has no thought, no reason, no will, no sentiment, no love, no hatred; or, in a word, is no mind at all. It is an abuse of terms to give it that appellation, and we may as well speak of limited extension without figure, or of number without composition.

Pray consider, said **Philo**, whom you are at present inveighing against. You are honouring with the appellation of *atheist* all the sound, orthodox divines, almost, who have treated of this subject; and you will at last be, yourself, found, according to your reckoning, the only sound theist in the world. But if idolaters be atheists, as, I think, may justly be asserted, and Christian theologians the same, what becomes of the argument, so much celebrated, derived from the universal consent of mankind?

But because I know you are not much swayed by names and authorities, I shall endeavour to show you, a little more distinctly, the inconveniences of that anthropomorphism which you have embraced, and shall prove that there is no ground to suppose a plan of the world to be formed in the divine mind, consisting of distinct ideas, differently arranged, in the same manner as an architect forms in his head the plan of a house which he intends to execute.

It is not easy, I own, to see what is gained by this supposition, whether we judge of the matter by *reason* or by *experience*. We are still obliged to mount higher in order to find the cause of this cause which you had assigned as satisfactory and conclusive.

If *reason* (I mean abstract reason derived from inquiries *a priori*) be not alike mute with regard to all questions concerning cause and effect, this sentence at least it will venture to pronounce: that a mental world or universe of ideas requires a cause as much as does a material world or universe of objects, and, if similar in its arrangement, must require a similar cause. For what is there in this subject which should occasion a different conclusion or inference? In an abstract view, they are entirely alike; and no difficulty attends the one supposition which is not common to both of them.

Again, when we will needs force *experience* to pronounce some sentence, even on these subjects which lie beyond her sphere, neither can she perceive any material difference in this particular between these two kinds of worlds, but finds them to be governed by similar principles, and to depend upon an equal variety of causes in their operations. We have specimens in miniature of both of them. Our own mind resembles the one; a vegetable or animal body the other. Let experience, therefore, judge from these samples. Nothing seems more delicate, with regard to its causes, than thought; and as these causes never operate in two persons after the same manner, so we never find two persons who think exactly alike. Nor indeed does the same person think exactly alike at any two different periods of time. A difference of age, of the disposition of his body, of weather, of food, of company, of books, of passions, any of these particulars, or others more minute, are sufficient to alter the curious machinery of thought and communicate to it very different movements and operations. As far as we can judge, vegetables and animal bodies are not more delicate in their motions, nor depend upon a greater variety or more curious adjustment of springs and principles.

How, therefore, shall we satisfy ourselves concerning the cause of that Being whom you suppose the Author of nature, or, according to your system of anthropomorphism, the ideal world into which you trace the material? Have we not the same reason to trace that ideal world into another ideal world or new intelligent principle? But if we stop and go no farther, why go so far? Why not stop at the material world? How can we satisfy ourselves without going on *in infinitum?* And, after all, what satisfaction is there in that infinite progression? Let us remember the story of the Indian philosopher and his elephant. It was never more applicable than to the present subject. If the material world rests upon a similar ideal world, this ideal world must rest upon some other, and so on without end. It were better, therefore, never to look beyond the present material world. By supposing it to contain the principle of its order within itself, we really assert it to be God; and the sooner we arrive at that Divine Being, so much the better. When you go one step beyond the mundane system, you only excite an inquisitive humour which it is impossible ever to satisfy.

To say that the different ideas which compose the reason of the Supreme Being fall into order of themselves and by their own nature is really to talk without any precise meaning. If it has a meaning, I would fain know why it is not as good sense to say that the parts of the material world fall into order of themselves and by their own nature. Can the one opinion be intelligible, while the other is not so?

We have, indeed, experience of ideas which fall into order of themselves and without any *known* cause. But, I am sure, we have a much larger experience of matter which does the same, as in all instances of generation and vegetation where the accurate analysis of the cause exceeds all human comprehension. We have also experience of particular systems of thought and of matter which have no order; of the first in madness, of the second in corruption. Why, then, should we think that order is more essential to one than the other? And if it requires a cause in both, what do we gain by your system, in tracing the universe of objects into a similar universe of ideas? The first step which we make leads us on for ever. It were, therefore, wise in us to limit all our inquiries to the present world, without looking farther. No satisfaction can ever be attained by these speculations which so far exceed the narrow bounds of human understanding.

It was usual with the Peripatetics, you know, Cleanthes, when the cause of any phenomenon was demanded, to have recourse to their *faculties* or *occult qualities,* and to say, for instance, that bread nourished by its nutritive faculty, and senna purged by its purgative. But it has been discovered that this subterfuge was nothing but the disguise of ignorance, and that these philosophers, though less ingenuous, really said the same thing with the sceptics or the vulgar who fairly confessed that they knew not the cause of these phenomena. In like manner, when it is asked, what cause produces order in the ideas of the Supreme Being, can any other reason be assigned by you, anthropomorphites, than that it is a *rational* faculty, and that such is the nature of the Deity? But why a similar answer will not be equally satisfactory in accounting for the order of the world, without having recourse to any such intelligent creator as you insist on, may be difficult to determine. It is only to say that *such* is the nature of material objects, and that they are all originally possessed of a *faculty* of order and proportion. These are only more learned and elaborate ways of confessing our ignorance; nor has the one hypothesis any real advantage above the other, except in its greater conformity to vulgar prejudices.

You have displayed this argument with great emphasis, replied **Cleanthes:** You seem not sensible how easy it is to answer it. Even in common life, if I assign a cause for any event, is it any objection, Philo, that I cannot assign the cause of that cause, and answer every new question which may incessantly be started? And what philosophers could possibly submit to so rigid a rule, philosophers who confess ultimate causes to be totally unknown, and are sensible that the most refined principles into which they trace the phenomena are still to them as inexplicable as these phenomena themselves are to the vulgar? The order and arrangement of nature, the curious adjustment of final causes, the plain use and intention of every part and organ; all these bespeak in the clearest language an intelligent cause or author. The heavens and the earth join in the same testimony: The whole chorus of nature raises one hymn to the praises of its Creator. You alone, or almost alone, disturb this general harmony. You start abstruse doubts, cavils, and objections; you ask me what is the cause of this cause? I know not; I care not; that concerns not me. I have found a Deity; and here I stop my inquiry. Let those go farther who are wiser or more enterprising.

I pretend to be neither, replied **Philo**; and for that very reason I should never, perhaps, have attempted to go so far, especially when I am sensible that I must at last be contented to sit down with the same answer which, without further trouble, might have satisfied me from the beginning. If I am still to remain in utter ignorance of causes and can absolutely give an explication of nothing, I shall never esteem it any advantage to shove off for a moment a difficulty which you acknowledge must immediately, in its full force, recur upon me. Naturalists indeed very justly explain particular effects by more general causes, though these general causes themselves should remain in the end totally inexplicable, but they never surely thought it satisfactory to explain a particular effect by a particular cause which was no more to be accounted for than the effect itself. An ideal system, arranged of itself, without a precedent design, is not a whit more explicable than a material one which attains its order in a like manner; nor is there any more difficulty in the latter supposition than in the former.

Part V

But to show you still more inconveniences, continued **Philo,** in your anthropomorphism, please to take a new survey of your principles. *Like effects prove like causes.* This is the experimental argument; and this, you say too, is the sole theological argument. Now it is certain that the liker the effects are which are seen and the liker the causes which are inferred, the stronger is the argument. Every departure on either side diminishes the probability and renders the experiment less conclusive. You cannot doubt of the principle; neither ought you to reject its consequences.

All the new discoveries in astronomy which prove the immense grandeur and magnificence of the works of nature are so many additional arguments for a Deity; according to the true system of theism; but, according to your hypothesis of experimental theism, they become so many objections, by removing the effect still farther from all resemblance to the effects of human art and contrivance. For if Lucretius,[12] even following the old system of the world, could exclaim:

---

12. [*De Rerum Natura*], Lib. [II], 109[5]. ["Who can rule the sum total of the immeasurable? Who can hold with a sure hand the mighty reins of the unfathomable? Who can make all the heavens turn at once, and arouse all the fertile lands with ethereal fires? Who can be present at all times in all places?"—P. E. D.]

Quis regere immensi summam, quis habere profundi
Indu manu validas potis est moderanter habenas?
Quis pariter coelos omnes convertere? et omnes
Ignibus aetheriis terras suffire feraces?
Omnibus inque locis esse omni tempore praesto?

If Tully[13] esteemed this reasoning so natural as to put it into the mouth of his Epicurean:

Quibus enim oculis animi intueri potuit vester Plato fabricam illam tanti operis, qua construi a Deo atque aedificari mundum facit? quae molitio? quae ferramenta? qui vectes? quae machinae? qui ministri tanti muneris fuerunt? quemadmodum autem oboedire et parere voluntati architecti aer, ignis, aqua, terra potuerunt?

If this argument, I say, had any force in former ages, how much greater must it have at present when the bounds of nature are so infinitely enlarged and such a magnificent scene is opened to us? It is still more unreasonable to form our idea of so unlimited a cause from our experience of the narrow productions of human design and invention.

The discoveries by microscopes, as they open a new universe in miniature, are still objections, according to you, arguments, according to me. The farther we push our researches of this kind, we are still led to infer the universal cause of all to be vastly different from mankind, or from any object of human experience and observation.

And what say you to the discoveries in anatomy, chemistry, botany? ... These surely are no objections, replied **Cleanthes;** they only discover new instances of art and contrivance. It is still the image of mind reflected on us from innumerable objects. Add a mind *like the human,* said **Philo.** I know of no other, replied **Cleanthes.** And the liker, the better, insisted **Philo.** To be sure, said **Cleanthes.**

Now, Cleanthes, said **Philo,** with an air of alacrity and triumph, mark the consequences. *First,* by this method of reasoning you renounce all claim to infinity in any of the attributes of the Deity. For, as the cause ought only to be proportioned to the effect, and the effect, so far as it falls under our cognizance, is not infinite, what pretensions have we, upon your suppositions, to ascribe that attribute to the Divine Being? You will still insist that, by removing him so much from all similarity to human creatures, we give in to the most arbitrary hypothesis, and at the same time weaken all proofs of his existence.

Secondly, you have no reason, on your theory, for ascribing perfection to the Deity, even in his finite capacity, or for supposing him free from every error, mistake, or incoherence, in his undertakings. There are many inexplicable diffi-

---

13. [Cicero] *De Nat[ura] Deor[um]*, Lib. I. ["For with what eyes of the mind could your Plato imagine a workshop of such productive capacity that in it a whole world could be put together and built by God? What building materials, what tools, what levers, what machines, what helpers were employed in so great a work? How could it happen that air, fire, water, and earth yield to the will of the architect and obey?"–P. E. D.]

Mr. David Hume

culties in the works of nature which, if we allow a perfect author to be proved *a priori,* are easily solved, and become only seeming difficulties from the narrow capacity of man, who cannot trace infinite relations. But according to your method of reasoning, these difficulties become all real, and, perhaps, will be insisted on as new instances of likeness to human art and contrivance. At least, you must acknowledge that it is impossible for us to tell, from our limited views, whether this system contains any great faults or deserves any considerable praise if compared to other possible and even real systems. Could a peasant, if the *Aeneid* were read to him, pronounce that poem to be absolutely faultless, or even assign to it its proper rank among the productions of human wit, he who had never seen any other production?

But were this world ever so perfect a production, it must still remain uncertain whether all the excellences of the work can justly be ascribed to the workman. If we survey a ship, what an exalted idea must we form of the ingenuity of the carpenter who framed so complicated, useful, and beautiful a machine? And what surprise must we feel when we find him a stupid mechanic who imitated others, and copied an art which, through a long succession of ages, after multiplied trials, mistakes, corrections, deliberations, and controversies, had been gradually improving? Many worlds might have been botched and bungled, throughout an eternity, ere this system was struck out; much labour lost, many fruitless trials made, and a slow but continued improvement carried on during infinite ages in the art of world-making. In such subjects, who can determine where the truth, nay, who can conjecture where the probability lies, amidst a great number of hypotheses which may be proposed, and a still greater which may be imagined?

And what shadow of an argument, continued **Philo,** can you produce from your hypothesis to prove the unity of the Deity? A great number of men join in building a house or ship, in rearing a city, in framing a commonwealth; why may not several deities combine in contriving and framing a world? This is only so much greater similarity to human affairs. By sharing the work among several, we may so much further limit the attributes of each, and get rid of that extensive power and knowledge which must be supposed in one deity, and which, according to you, can only serve to weaken the proof of his existence. And if such foolish, such vicious creatures as man can yet often unite in framing and executing one plan, how much more those deities or demons, whom we may suppose several degrees more perfect!

To multiply causes without necessity is indeed contrary to true philosophy, but this principle applies not to the present case. Were one deity antecedently proved by your theory who were possessed of every attribute requisite to the production of the universe, it would be needless, I own, (though not absurd) to suppose any other deity existent. But while it is still a question whether all these attributes are united in one subject or dispersed among several independent beings, by what phenomena in nature can we pretend to decide the controversy? Where we see a body raised in a scale, we are sure that there is in the opposite scale, however concealed from sight, some counterpoising weight equal to it; but it is still allowed to doubt whether that weight be an aggregate of several distinct bodies or one uniform united mass. And if the weight requisite very much exceeds anything which we have ever seen conjoined in any single body, the former supposition becomes still more probable and natural. An intelligent being of such vast power and capacity as is necessary to produce the universe, or, to speak in the language of ancient philosophy, so prodigious an animal exceeds all analogy and even comprehension.

But farther, Cleanthes, men are mortal, and renew their species by generation; and this is common to all living creatures. The two great sexes of male and female, says Milton, animate the world. Why must this circumstance, so universal, so essential, be excluded from those numerous and limited deities? Behold, then, the theogony of ancient times brought back upon us.

And why not become a perfect anthropomorphite? Why not assert the deity or deities to be corporeal, and to have eyes, a nose, mouth, ears, etc.? Epicurus maintained that no man had ever seen reason but in a human figure; therefore, the gods must have a human figure. And this argument, which is deservedly so much ridiculed by Cicero, becomes, according to you, solid and philosophical.

In a word, Cleanthes, a man who follows your hypothesis is able, perhaps, to assert or conjecture that the universe sometime arose from something like design; but beyond that position he cannot ascertain one single circumstance, and is left afterwards to fix every point of his theology by the utmost license of fancy and hypothesis. This world, for aught he knows, is very faulty and imperfect, compared to a superior standard, and was only the first rude essay of some infant deity who afterwards abandoned it, ashamed of his lame performance; it is the work only of some dependent, inferior deity, and is the object of derision to his superiors; it is the production of old age and dotage in some superannuated deity, and ever since his death has run on at adventures, from the first impulse and active force which it received from him. You justly give signs of horror, Demea, at these strange suppositions; but these, and a thousand more of the same kind, are Cleanthes' suppositions, not mine. From the moment the attributes of the Deity are supposed finite, all these have place. And I cannot, for my part, think that so wild and unsettled a system of theology is, in any respect, preferable to none at all.

These suppositions I absolutely disown, cried **Cleanthes;** they strike me, however, with no horror, especially when proposed in that rambling way in which they drop from you. On the contrary, they give me pleasure when I see that, by the utmost indulgence of your imagination, you never get rid of the hypothesis of design in the universe, but are obliged at every turn to have recourse to it. To this concession I adhere steadily; and this I regard as a sufficient foundation for religion.

Part VI

It must be a slight fabric, indeed, said **Demea,** which can be erected on so tottering a foundation. While we are uncertain whether there is one deity or many, whether the deity or deities, to whom we owe our existence, be perfect or imperfect, subordinate or supreme, dead or alive, what trust or confidence can we repose in them? What devotion or worship address to them? What veneration or obedience pay them? To all the purposes of life the theory of religion becomes altogether useless; and even with regard to speculative consequences its uncertainty, according to you, must render it totally precarious and unsatisfactory.

To render it still more unsatisfactory, said **Philo,** there occurs to me another hypothesis which must acquire an air of probability from the method of reasoning so much insisted on by Cleanthes. That like effects arise from like causes: this principle he supposes the foundation of all religion. But there is another principle of the same kind, no less certain and derived from the same source of experience, that where several known circumstances are *observed* to be similar, the unknown will also be *found* similar. Thus, if we see the limbs of a human body, we conclude that it is also attended with a human head, though hid from us. Thus, if we see, through a chink in a wall, a small part of the sun, we conclude that were the wall removed we should see the whole body. In short, this method of reasoning is so obvious and familiar that no scruple can ever be made with regard to its solidity.

Now if we survey the universe, so far as it falls under our knowledge, it bears a great resemblance to an animal or organized body, and seems actuated with a like principle of life and motion. A continual circulation of matter in it produces no disorder; a continual waste in every part is incessantly repaired; the closest sympathy is perceived throughout the entire system; and each part or member, in performing its proper offices, operates both to its own preservation and to that of the whole. The world, therefore, I infer, is an animal; and the Deity is the *soul* of the world, actuating it, and actuated by it.

You have too much learning, Cleanthes, to be at all surprised at this opinion which, you know, was maintained by almost all the theists of antiquity, and chiefly prevails in their discourses and reasonings. For though, sometimes, the ancient philosophers reason from final causes, as if they thought the world the workmanship of God, yet it appears rather their favourite notion to consider it as his body whose organization renders it subservient to him. And it must be confessed that, as the universe resembles more a human body than it does the works of human art and contrivance, if our limited analogy could ever, with any propriety, be extended to the whole of nature, the inference seems juster in favour of the ancient than the modern theory.

There are many other advantages, too, in the former theory which recommended it to the ancient theologians. Nothing more repugnant to all their notions because nothing more repugnant to common experience than mind without body, a mere spiritual substance which fell not under their senses nor comprehension, and of which they had not observed one single instance throughout all nature. Mind and body they knew because they felt both; an order, arrangement, organization, or internal machinery, in both they likewise knew, after the same manner; and it could not but seem reasonable to transfer this experience to the universe, and to suppose the divine mind and body to be also coeval and to have, both of them, order and arrangement naturally inherent in them and inseparable from them.

Here, therefore, is a new species of *anthropomorphism,* Cleanthes, on which you may deliberate, and a theory which seems not liable to any considerable difficulties. You are too much superior, surely, to *systematical prejudices* to find any more difficulty in supposing an animal body to be, originally, of itself or from unknown causes, possessed of order and organization, than in supposing a similar order to belong to mind. But the *vulgar prejudice* that body and mind ought always to accompany each other ought not, one should think, to be entirely neglected;

since it is founded on *vulgar experience,* the only guide which you profess to follow in all these theological inquiries. And if you assert that our limited experience is an unequal standard by which to judge of the unlimited extent of nature, you entirely abandon your own hypothesis, and must thenceforward adopt our mysticism, as you call it, and admit of the absolute incomprehensibility of the Divine Nature.

This theory, I own, replied **Cleanthes,** has never before occurred to me, though a pretty natural one; and I cannot readily, upon so short an examination and reflection, deliver any opinion with regard to it. You are very scrupulous, indeed, said **Philo,** were I to examine any system of yours, I should not have acted with half that caution and reserve, in starting objections and difficulties to it. However, if anything occur to you, you will oblige us by proposing it.

Why then, replied **Cleanthes,** it seems to me that, though the world does, in many circumstances, resemble an animal body, yet is the analogy also defective in many circumstances the most material: no organs of sense; no seat of thought or reason; no one precise origin of motion and action. In short, it seems to bear a stronger resemblance to a vegetable than to an animal, and your inference would be so far inconclusive in favour of the soul of the world.

But, in the next place, your theory seems to imply the eternity of the world; and that is a principle which, I think, can be refuted by the strongest reasons and probabilities. I shall suggest an argument to this purpose which, I believe, has not been insisted on by any writer. Those who reason from the late origin of arts and sciences, though their inference wants not force, may perhaps be refuted by considerations derived from the nature of human society, which is in continual revolution between ignorance and knowledge, liberty and slavery, riches and poverty; so that it is impossible for us, from our limited experience, to foretell with assurance what events may or may not be expected. Ancient learning and history seem to have been in great danger of entirely perishing after the inundation of the barbarous nations; and had these convulsions continued a little longer or been a little more violent, we should not probably have now known what passed in the world a few centuries before us. Nay, were it not for the superstition of the popes, who preserved a little jargon of Latin in order to support the appearance of an ancient and universal church, that tongue must have been utterly lost; in which case the Western world, being totally barbarous, would not have been in a fit disposition for receiving the Greek language and learning, which was conveyed to them after the sacking of Constantinople. When learning and books had been extinguished, even the mechanical arts would have fallen considerably to decay; and it is easily imagined that fable or tradition might ascribe to them a much later origin than the true one. This vulgar argument, therefore, against the eternity of the world seems a little precarious.

But here appears to be the foundation of a better argument. Lucullus was the first that brought cherry-trees from Asia to Europe, though that tree thrives so well in many European climates that it grows in the woods without any culture. Is it possible that, throughout a whole eternity, no European had ever passed into Asia and thought of transplanting so delicious a fruit into his own country? Or if the tree was once transplanted and propagated, how could it ever afterwards perish? Empires may rise and fall, liberty and slavery succeed alternately, ignorance and knowledge give place to each other; but the cherry-tree will still remain in the woods of Greece, Spain, and Italy, and will never be affected by the revolutions of human society.

It is not two thousand years since vines were transplanted into France, though there is no climate in the world more favourable to them. It is not three centuries since horses, cows, sheep, swine, dogs, corn, were known in America. Is it possible that during the revolutions of a whole eternity there never arose a Columbus who might open the communication between Europe and that continent? We may as well imagine that all men would wear stockings for ten thousand years, and never have the sense to think of garters to tie them. All these seem convincing proofs of the youth or rather infancy of the world, as being founded on the operation of principles more constant and steady than those by which human society is governed and directed. Nothing less than a total convulsion of the elements will ever destroy all the European animals and vegetables which are now to be found in the Western world.

And what argument have you against such convulsions? replied **Philo.** Strong and almost incontestable proofs may be traced over the whole earth that every part of this globe has continued for many ages entirely covered with water. And though order were supposed inseparable from matter, and inherent in it, yet may matter be susceptible of many and great revolutions, through the endless periods of eternal duration. The incessant changes to which every part of it is subject seem to intimate some such general transformations; though, at the same time, it is observable that all the changes and corruptions of which we have ever had experience are but passages from one state of order to another; nor can matter ever rest in total deformity and confusion. What we see in the parts, we may infer in the whole; at least, that is the method of reasoning on which you rest your whole theory. And were I obliged to defend any particular system of this nature, which I never willingly should do, I esteem none more plausible than that which ascribes an eternal inherent principle of order to the world, though attended with great and continual revolutions and alterations. This at once solves all difficulties; and if the solution, by being so general, is not entirely complete and satisfactory, it is at least a theory that we must sooner or later have recourse to, whatever system we embrace. How could things have been as they are, were there not an original inherent principle of order somewhere, in thought or in matter? And it is very indifferent to which of these we give the preference. Chance has no place, on any hypothesis, sceptical or religious. Everything is surely governed by steady, inviolable laws. And were the inmost essence of things laid open to us, we should then discover a scene of which, at present, we can have no idea. Instead of admiring the order of natural beings, we should clearly see that it was absolutely impossible for them, in the smallest article, ever to admit of any other disposition.

Were anyone inclined to revive the ancient pagan theology which maintained, as we learn from Hesiod, that this globe was governed by 30,000 deities, who arose from the unknown powers of nature, you would naturally object, Cleanthes, that nothing is gained by this hypothesis; and that it is as easy to suppose all men animals, beings more numerous but less perfect, to have sprung immediately from a like origin. Push the same inference a step further, and you will find a numerous society of deities as explicable as one universal deity who possesses within himself the powers and perfections of the whole society. All these systems, then, of scepticism, polytheism, and theism, you must allow, on your principles, to be on a like footing, and that no one of them has any advantage over the others. You may thence learn the fallacy of your principles.

Part VII

But here, continued **Philo**, in examining the ancient system of the soul of the world there strikes me, all on a sudden, a new idea which, if just, must go near to subvert all your reasoning, and destroy even your first inferences on which you repose such confidence. If the universe bears a greater likeness to animal bodies and to vegetables than to the works of human art, it is more probable that its cause resembles the cause of the former than that of the latter, and its origin ought rather to be ascribed to generation or vegetation than to reason or design. Your conclusion, even according to your own principles, is therefore lame and defective.

Pray open up this argument a little further, said **Demea**, for I do not rightly apprehend it in that concise manner in which you have expressed it.

Our friend Cleanthes, replied **Philo**, as you have heard, asserts that, since no question of fact can be proved otherwise than by experience, the existence of a Deity admits not of proof from any other medium. The world, says he, resembles the works of human contrivance; therefore its cause must also resemble that of the other. Here we may remark that the operation of one very small part of nature, to wit, man, upon another very small part, to wit, that inanimate matter lying within his reach, is the rule by which Cleanthes judges of the origin of the whole; and he measures objects, so widely disproportioned, by the same individual standard. But to waive all objections drawn from this topic, I affirm that there are other parts of the universe (besides the machines of human invention) which bear still a greater resemblance to the fabric of the world, and which, therefore, afford a better conjecture concerning the universal origin of this system. These parts are animals and vegetables. The world plainly resembles more an animal or a vegetable than it does a watch or a knitting-loom. Its cause, therefore, it is more probable, resembles the cause of the former. The cause of the former is generation or vegetation. The cause, therefore, of the world we may infer to be something similar or analogous to generation or vegetation.

But how is it conceivable, said **Demea**, that the world can arise from anything similar to vegetation or generation?

Very easily, replied **Philo**. In like manner as a tree sheds its seed into the neighbouring fields and produces other trees, so the great vegetable, the world, or this planetary system, produces within itself certain seeds which, being scattered into the surrounding chaos, vegetate into new worlds. A comet, for instance, is the seed of a world; and after it has been fully ripened, by passing from sun to sun, and star to star, it is, at last, tossed into the unformed elements which everywhere surround this universe, and immediately sprouts up into a new system.

Or if, for the sake of variety (for I see no other advantage), we should suppose this world to be an animal: a comet is the egg of this animal; and in like manner as an ostrich lays its egg in the sand, which, without any further care, hatches the egg and produces a new animal, so. . . . I understand you, says **Demea**. But what wild, arbitrary suppositions are these! What *data* have you for such extraordinary conclusions? And is the slight, imaginary resemblance of the world to a vegetable or an animal sufficient to establish the same inference with regard to both? Objects which are in general so widely different ought they to be a standard for each other?

Right, cries **Philo**: This is the topic on which I have all along insisted. I have still asserted that we have no *data* to establish any system of cosmogony. Our experience, so imperfect in itself and so limited both in extent and duration, can afford us no probable conjecture concerning the whole of things. But if we must needs fix on some hypothesis, by what rule, pray, ought we to determine our choice? Is there any other rule than the greater similarity of the objects compared? And does not a plant or an animal, which springs from vegetation or generation, bear a stronger resemblance to the world than does any artificial machine, which arises from reason and design?

But what is this vegetation and generation of which you talk? said **Demea**. Can you explain their operations, and anatomize that fine internal structure on which they depend?

As much, at least, replied **Philo**, as Cleanthes can explain the operations of reason, or anatomize that internal structure on which it depends. But without any such elaborate disquisitions, when I see an animal, I infer that it sprang from generation; and that with as great certainty as you conclude a house to have been reared by design. These words *generation, reason* mark only certain powers and energies in nature whose effects are known, but whose essence is incomprehensible; and one of these principles, more than the other, has no privilege for being made a standard to the whole of nature.

In reality, Demea, it may reasonably be expected that the larger the views are which we take of things, the better will they conduct us in our conclusions concerning such extraordinary and such magnificent subjects. In this little corner of the world alone, there are four principles, *reason, instinct, generation, vegetation,* which are similar to each other, and are the causes of similar effects. What a number of other principles may we naturally suppose in the immense extent and variety of the universe could we travel from planet to planet, and from system to system, in order to examine each part of this mighty fabric? Any one of these four principles above mentioned (and a hundred others which lie open to our conjecture) may afford us a theory by which to judge of the origin of the world; and it is a palpable and egregious partiality to confine our view entirely to that principle by which our own minds operate. Were this principle more intelligible on that account, such a partiality might be somewhat excusable; but reason, in its internal fabric and structure, is really as little known to us as instinct or vegetation; and, perhaps, even that vague, undeterminate word *nature* to which the vulgar refer everything is not at the bottom more inexplicable. The effects of these principles are all known to us from experience; but the principles themselves and their manner of operation are totally unknown; nor is it less intelligible or less conformable to experience to say that the world arose by vegetation, from a seed shed by another world, than to say that it arose from a divine reason or contrivance, according to the sense in which Cleanthes understands it.

But methinks, said **Demea,** if the world had a vegetative quality and could sow the seeds of new worlds into the infinite chaos, this power would be still an additional argument for design in its author. For whence could arise so wonderful a faculty but from design? Or how can order spring from anything which perceives not that order which it bestows?

You need only look around you, replied **Philo,** to satisfy yourself with regard to this question. A tree bestows order and organization on that tree which springs from it, without knowing the order; an animal in the same manner on its offspring; a bird on its nest; and instances of this kind are even more frequent in the world than those of order which arise from reason and contrivance. To say that all this order in animals and vegetables proceeds ultimately from design is begging the question; nor can that great point be ascertained otherwise than by proving, *a priori,* both that order is, from its nature, inseparably attached to thought and that it can never of itself or from original unknown principles belong to matter.

But farther, Demea, this objection which you urge can never be made use of by Cleanthes, without renouncing a defence which he has already made against one of my objections. When I inquired concerning the cause of that supreme reason and intelligence into which he resolves everything, he told me that the impossibility of satisfying such inquiries could never be admitted as an objection in any species of philosophy. *We must stop somewhere,* says he; *nor is it ever within the reach of human capacity to explain ultimate causes or show the last connections of any objects. It is sufficient if any steps, so far as we go, are supported by experience and observation.* Now that vegetation and generation, as well as reason, are experienced to be principles of order in nature is undeniable. If I rest my system of cosmogony on the former, preferably to the latter, it is at my choice. The matter seems entirely arbitrary. And when Cleanthes asks me what is the cause of my great vegetative or generative faculty, I am equally entitled to ask him the cause of his great reasoning principle. These questions we have agreed to forbear on both sides; and it is chiefly his interest on the present occasion to stick to this agreement. Judging by our limited and imperfect experience, generation has some privileges above reason; for we see every day the latter arise from the former, never the former from the latter.

Compare, I beseech you, the consequences on both sides. The world, say I, resembles an animal; therefore it is an animal, therefore it arose from generation. The steps, I confess, are wide, yet there is some small appearance of analogy in each step. The world, says Cleanthes, resembles a machine; therefore it is a machine, therefore it arose from design. The steps are here equally wide, and the analogy less striking. And if he pretends to carry on *my* hypothesis a step further, and to infer design or reason from the great principle of generation on which I insist, I may, with better authority, use the same freedom to push further *his* hypothesis, and infer a divine generation or theogony from his principle of reason. I have at least some faint shadow of experience, which is the utmost that can ever be attained in the present subject. Reason, in innumerable instances, is observed to arise from the principle of generation, and never to arise from any other principle.

Hesiod and all the ancient mythologists were so struck with this analogy that they universally explained the origin of nature from an animal birth, and copulation. Plato, too, so far as he is intelligible, seems to have adopted some such notion in his *Timaeus*.

The Brahmins assert that the world arose from an infinite spider, who spun this whole complicated mass from his bowels, and annihilates afterwards the whole or any part of it, by absorbing it again and resolving it into his own essence. Here is a species of cosmogony which appears to us ridiculous because a spider is a little contemptible animal whose operations we are never likely to take for a model of the whole universe. But still here is a new species of analogy, even in our globe. And were there a planet wholly inhabited by spiders (which is very possible), this inference would there appear as natural and irrefragable as that which in our planet ascribes the origin of all things to design and intelligence, as explained by Cleanthes. Why an orderly system may not be spun from the belly as well as from the brain, it will be difficult for him to give a satisfactory reason.

I must confess, Philo, replied **Cleanthes**, that, of all men living, the task which you have undertaken, of raising doubts and objections, suits you best and seems, in a manner, natural and unavoidable to you. So great is your fertility of invention that I am not ashamed to acknowledge myself unable, on a sudden, to solve regularly such out-of-the-way difficulties as you incessantly start upon me, though I clearly see, in general, their fallacy and error. And I question not, but you are yourself, at present, in the same case, and have not the solution so ready as the objection, while you must be sensible that common sense and reason are entirely against you, and that such whimsies as you have delivered may puzzle but never can convince us. . . .

COMPARATIVE STUDY QUESTIONS

Review Questions

1. According to Cleanthes, Philo proposes to erect religious faith on philosophical scepticism. Explain what he means.
2. Why is it impossible for anyone to persevere in total scepticism, according to Philo?
3. Are the methods of reasoning in matters of religion and theology necessarily different from those we employ in ordinary life situations and the sciences? What is Philo's opinion? Does Cleanthes agree?
4. Although Demea, the orthodox believer, and Philo, the sceptic, agree that there can be no question regarding the **being** but only regarding the **nature** of God, their reasons are somewhat different. Explain how "just reasoning and sound piety concur in the same conclusion."
5. State Cleanthes' **a posteriori** argument for the existence (and nature) of God. What are Demea's reservations regarding it? What is Philo's objection to it?
6. Are either Cleanthes or Philo prepared to admit that the existence of order among things is, by itself, a proof of intelligence or design?
7. Restate Philo's criticism of the design argument based on Cleanthes' analogical inference from part to whole.
8. Are there other causes or principles of order in the universe besides thought and intelligent purpose, according to Philo?
9. Why does Demea reject the idea that we can read the mind and intentions of Deity from the world in the same manner that we can enter into the mind and intentions of an author of a book?
10. On what basis does Cleanthes charge that mystics like Demea are no different from sceptics or atheists?

Discussion Questions

1. Compare Berkeley's Philonous with Hume's Demea and Cleanthes. Which character does Philonous most resemble?
2. In response to Philo, Cleanthes argues in effect that it is no more contrary to common speech to infer the origin of the whole universe by examining its parts than to infer the motion of the earth as a whole from our experiences of particular motions. What presupposition does he make regarding "reason" in this context? How does Philo respond?
3. Cleanthes proposes to refute Philo "by illustrations, examples, and instances rather than by serious argument and philosophy," and proceeds to talk about

a "natural library," the structure of the eye, and the "correspondence of male and female in each species." How persuasive are these "natural arguments"?

4. If we try to explain the material world by reference to an ideal world, do we not become committed to an infinite regress? What is Cleanthes' reply to the objection? Is it convincing?

5. In Part V Philo argues that Cleanthes' view makes God a finite being, and perhaps not the only deity. May not the deity (or deities) on Cleanthes' hypothesis also be corporeal and limited in power and intelligence? Trace Philo's reasoning.

6. In Part VI Philo, using Cleanthes' method of reasoning, draws the conclusion that the world is an animal and deity is its soul. Cleanthes argues that the world has a stronger resemblance to a vegetable. Both notions are developed and discussed by Philo in Part VII. What is the point which Hume is here attempting to make regarding all such metaphysical speculations?

7. Demea wonders whether the order bestowed on the world by vegetation and animal generation might themselves be a product of intelligent design. Philo accuses him of begging the question. How so?

8. Is Philo's aim simply to oppose Cleanthes' assumption that reason or intelligence is the only ultimate principle of order in the world; or does he mean to go further and suggest that reason itself is subordinate to and a product of the generative principle; or is Cleanthes correct in his supposition that Philo has "not the solution so ready as the objection"?

9. In line with the suggestion of A. N. Whitehead, can you imagine another speaker (or position) besides the three which Hume has invented?

10. Examine the claim Hume made during his final interview with Boswell to the effect that a belief in history (e.g., regarding the Revolution) is far different from a belief in religion (e.g., regarding immortality).

Immanuel Kant
(1724-1804)

A DEFENSE OF SCIENCE

A Critic of Hume's Philosophy
and Herr Professor Immanuel Kant

> Domestic animals expect food when they see the person
> who usually feeds them. We know that all these rather crude
> expectations of uniformity are liable to be misleading. The
> man who has fed the chicken every day throughout its life
> at last wrings its neck instead, showing that more refined
> views as to the uniformity of nature would have been useful
> to the chicken.
>
> Bertrand Russell, *The Problems of
> Philosophy* (1912)

It was David Hume, says Kant, who "first interrupted my dogmatic slumber." Or to quote him more accurately, it was his "recollection" of David Hume which interrupted his dogmatic slumber and gave his philosophy a new direction. The German expression Kant uses is **Erinnerung** and has been translated variously as "recollection," "remembrance," "recalling," "reminder," and even more freely as "suggestion" and "challenge." The problem is more than merely one of proper translation, however. It is both historical and philosophical.

The historical side of the problem concerns how Kant could have been influenced by Hume. The two philosophers never met, never corresponded, and it is reported that Kant was "imperfectly acquainted with the English language."[1] How can you "remember" or "recall" someone whom you have never met, never corresponded with, and whose written works you have never read?

There have been several attempted explanations. One is that Kant had in fact read Hume's **Enquiry** in German translation sometime between 1756 and 1762. (A German translation of Hume's **Essays,** including the **Enquiries,** appeared in 1754–1756.) But even if we suppose that he did read Hume's **Enquiry Concerning Human Understanding** in that form at about that time, there are two difficulties with this theory. One is that in a letter to Marcus Herz, dated February 21, 1772, Kant indicated that his thought was just then beginning to take a new and different turn.

---

1. Norman Kemp Smith, *A Commentary to Kant's Critique of Pure Reason* (New York: Humanities Press, 1962), p. xxviii.

The other is that although the **Enquiry,** which Kant may have read in German, does raise doubts about our reasoning from effects to causes in particular cases, it does not question, as the **Treatise** explicitly does in Book I, Part III, Section III, the universal causal principle that "whatever begins to exist must have a cause." Yet it is precisely this issue which later governs much of Kant's thinking. No German translation of the **Treatise** was available until 1790–1791, long after Kant published his **Critique of Pure Reason** in 1781.

Of course one can suppose that given the tendency of Kant's own thought, the "hint" provided by Hume's **Enquiry** was sufficient to suggest to Kant his central problem. Perhaps he reread the **Enquiry,** or simply recalled reading it, just prior to February, 1772, and perhaps this was enough to confirm a process already begun. This suggestion is supported by the fact that in another letter to Christian Garve, dated September 21, 1798, Kant claims to have been aroused from his dogmatic slumber by his thinking about the "antinomies of pure reason," that is to say, the kind of metaphysical disputes which philosophers have perennially engaged in regarding whether the world has a beginning in time or a limit in space; whether everything in the world consists of simple parts; whether everything takes place necessarily and according to the laws of nature, or not. Was Kant twice "awakened" from his dogmatic slumber, or did the recollection of (reading?) Hume merely complete or confirm a process already begun?

It is difficult, perhaps impossible to say, but even if we suppose that the extent of Hume's influence has been exaggerated, it is still an influence which needs to be accounted for. After all, there remains the question of what caused the recollection. What specifically reminded Kant of Hume's problem? Professor Norman Kemp Smith, in his **Commentary to Kant's Critique of Pure Reason,** has argued quite convincingly that it was Kant's acquaintance with James Beattie's **Essay on the Nature and Immutability of Truth** which first acquainted him with Hume's doubts about the validity of the universal principle of causality. Beattie's **Essay** contains not only a critique of Hume, but more importantly, a selection of crucial passages from both the **Enquiry** and the **Treatise,** precisely the ones which might very well have had a profound impact on Kant.

But did Kant actually read Beattie? The circumstantial evidence is quite substantial. Beattie's book, first published in 1770, went through at least six editions in English, and was translated into German in 1772, the same year Kant had indicated in his letter to Marcus Herz that his mind was moving in quite new directions. Kant makes several explicit references to Beattie in the **Prolegomena.** Furthermore, Beattie, a Professor at Marischal College, University of Aberdeen, was immensely popular in his day as a defender of Christianity, and was widely known, not only for his **Essay,** but also for his poems, particularly "The Minstrel." He sat for Sir Joshua Reynolds' painting, "The Triumph of Truth," became a member of Dr. Samuel Johnson's London circle, and was even granted a lifetime pension by King George III. It would be more surprising if Kant had not taken an interest in the writings of such a man.

There is an additional consideration which tends to support the thesis that Kant's primary acquaintance with Hume's thought was via an intermediary. Kant was an avid reader of magazine and newspaper reviews, not only of his own publications but of those of others as well. He added an Appendix to the **Prolegomena** in answer to an unfavorable and anonymous review of his **Critique** in the **Göttingische gelehrte Anzeigen.** He wrote an essay, "On A Supposed Right to Tell Lies From Benevolent Motives," in response to an article by Benjamin Constant in the journal **France.** In his correspondence Kant often refers to critical reviews of others' books. The notoriety which Beattie had achieved by his critique of Hume's philosophy must have been quite enough to make Kant want to read it.

But now for the more philosophical side of Kant's relationship to Hume. There are basically two questions. First, what "dogmatic slumber" did Hume interrupt? Second, what was Hume's problem which Kant set himself to solve?

The "slumber" of which Kant speaks refers to his rationalistic (largely Leibnizian) assumption that the categories or concepts of the mind, although underived from experience, were capable of being applied directly to things in themselves. Take, for example, the concepts of cause and effect. Leibniz had taught that we do not acquire these or any other such epistemological notions from the confused images of sense. They are all supplied entirely by the mind. Kant agreed and for a time at least was convinced that it made sense to apply them, for instance, to the question of God's creation of the world, as well as to ordinary questions about what specific objects or events in the world are causes of other natural objects or events.

Hume's analysis of the limits of the human understanding impressed Kant (awoke him) in two ways. He realized that the proposition, "Everything must have a cause," is not and cannot be shown to be either intuitively or demonstratively certain. Second, Hume made Kant realize that unless some reason other than mere habit or custom accounts for our imputation of causal relations or other categories of the understanding to the world, none of our reasonings regarding matters of empirical fact, nor any of our metaphysical claims regarding God, the world as a whole, or freedom could ever be justified. Science, and especially any metaphysics which claimed scientific status, would be wholly suspect. That, in short, is the problem with which Hume "challenges" Kant.

Although Kant agrees with Hume's scepticism regarding the derivation of "necessary connections" from experience, and his claim that they are beyond logical demonstration in the usual sense, he disagrees with Hume's contention that our only basis for attributing the terms "cause" and "effect" is a mental habit acquired after certain repetitive experiences. He also disagrees with Hume's narrow conception of the problem. The problem, Kant maintains, is not simply whether there are necessary connections discoverable in experience, or how we come by the notions of cause and effect. It is broader than that. **How are any synthetic propositions** (i.e., propositions which do more than merely repeat or analyze what we already know) **a priori possible?** Or put another way, how are synthetic judgments applicable to a world of objects from which their basic conceptual constituents are not derived? The concept of causal connection, which preoccupies Hume, is only one such problematic concept. There are, says Kant, eleven others.

Kant's "answer" to Hume involves showing that without synthetic a priori judgments neither mathematics nor empirical science are possible. But if we understand the role of such synthetic a priori judgments in mathematics and physics, then we should be able to discern the grounds for similar a priori judgments and categories in metaphysics. That is the philosophical task which Kant sets himself to do, and which constitutes his response to Hume's scepticism regarding not only the possibility of metaphysics, but also, and perhaps more importantly, the validity of all inductive inferences based on the relation of cause and effect.

HUME

*An Enquiry Concerning Human Understanding**

Section II

Of the Origin of Ideas

Everyone will readily allow that there is a considerable difference between the perceptions of the mind, when a man feels the pain of excessive heat, or the pleasure of moderate warmth, and when he afterwards recalls to his memory this sensation, or anticipates it by his imagination. These faculties may mimic or copy the perceptions of the senses; but they never can entirely reach the force and vivacity of the original sentiment. The utmost we say of them, even when they operate with greatest vigor, is, that they represent their object in so lively a manner, that we could *almost* say we feel or see it: But, except the mind be disordered by disease or madness, they never can arrive at such a pitch of vivacity, as to render these perceptions altogether undistinguishable. All the colors of poetry, however splendid, can never paint natural objects in such a manner as to make the description be taken for a real landscape. The most lively thought is still inferior to the dullest sensation.

We may observe a like distinction to run through all the other perceptions of the mind. A man in a fit of anger, is actuated in a very different manner from one who only thinks of that emotion. If you tell me, that any person is in love, I easily understand your meaning, and form a just conception of his situation; but never can mistake that conception for the real disorders and agitations of the passion. When we reflect on our past sentiments and affections, our thought is a faithful

---

*From the edition first published in 1748.

mirror, and copies its objects truly; but the colors which it employs are faint and dull, in comparison of those in which our original perceptions were clothed. It requires no nice discernment or metaphysical head to mark the distinction between them.

Here therefore we may divide all the perceptions of the mind into two classes or species, which are distinguished by their different degrees of force and vivacity. The less forcible and lively are commonly denominated *thoughts* or *ideas*. The other species want a name in our language, and in most others; I suppose, because it was not requisite for any, but philosophical purposes, to rank them under a general term or appellation. Let us, therefore, use a little freedom, and call them *impressions;* employing that word in a sense somewhat different from the usual. By the term *impression,* then, I mean all our more lively perceptions, when we hear, or see, or feel, or love, or hate, or desire, or will. And impressions are distinguished from ideas, which are the less lively perceptions, of which we are conscious, when we reflect on any of those sensations or movements above mentioned.

Nothing, at first view, may seem more unbounded than the thought of man, which not only escapes all human power and authority, but is not even restrained within the limits of nature and reality. To form monsters, and join incongruous shapes and appearances, costs the imagination no more trouble than to conceive the most natural and familiar objects. And while the body is confined to one planet, along which it creeps with pain and difficulty; the thought can in an instant transport us into the most distant regions of the universe; or even beyond the universe, into the unbounded chaos, where nature is supposed to lie in total confusion. What never was seen, or heard of, may yet be conceived; nor is anything beyond the power of thought, except what implies an absolute contradiction.

But though our thought seems to possess this unbounded liberty, we shall find, upon a nearer examination, that it is really confined within very narrow limits, and that all this creative power of the mind amounts to no more than the faculty of compounding, transposing, augmenting, or diminishing the materials afforded us by the senses and experience. When we think of a golden mountain, we only join two consistent ideas, *gold,* and *mountain,* with which we were formerly acquainted. A virtuous horse we can conceive; because, from our own feeling, we can conceive virtue; and this we may unite to the figure and shape of a horse, which is an animal familiar to us. In short, all the materials of thinking are derived either from our outward or inward sentiment: the mixture and composition of these belongs alone to the mind and will. Or, to express myself in philosophical language, all our ideas or more feeble perceptions are copies of our impressions or more lively ones.

To prove this, the two following arguments will, I hope, be sufficient. First, when we analyze our thoughts or ideas, however compounded or sublime, we always find that they resolve themselves into such simple ideas as were copied from a precedent feeling or sentiment. Even those ideas, which, at first view, seem the most wide of this origin, are found, upon a nearer scrutiny, to be derived from it. The idea of God, as meaning an infinitely intelligent, wise, and good Being, arises from reflecting on the operations of our own mind, and augmenting, without limit, those qualities of goodness and wisdom. We may prosecute this inquiry to what length we please; where we shall always find, that every idea which we examine is copied from a similar impression. Those who would assert that this position is not universally true nor without exception, have only one, and that an easy method of refuting it; by producing that idea, which, in their opinion, is not derived from this source. It will then be incumbent on us, if we would maintain our doctrine, to produce the impression, or lively perception, which corresponds to it.

Secondly. If it happen, from a defect of the organ, that a man is not susceptible of any species of sensation, we always find that he is as little susceptible of the correspondent ideas. A blind man can form no notion of colors; a deaf man of sounds. Restore either of them that sense in which he is deficient; by opening this new inlet for his sensations, you also open an inlet for the ideas; and he finds no difficulty in conceiving these objects. The case is the same, if the object, proper for exciting any sensation, has never been applied to the organ. A Laplander or Negro has no notion of the relish of wine. And though there are few or no instances of a like deficiency in the mind, where a person has never felt or is wholly incapable of a sentiment or passion that belongs to his species; yet we find the same observation to take place in a less degree. A man of mild manners can form no idea of inveterate revenge or cruelty; nor can a selfish heart easily conceive the heights of friendship and generosity. It is readily allowed, that other beings may possess many senses of which we can have no conception; because the ideas of them have never been introduced to us in the only manner by which an idea can have access to the mind, to wit, by the actual feeling and sensation.

There is, however, one contradictory phenomenon, which may prove that it is not absolutely impossible for ideas to arise, independent of their correspondent impressions. I believe it will readily be allowed, that the several distinct ideas of color, which enter by the eye, or those of sound, which are conveyed by the ear, are really different from each other; though, at the same time, resembling. Now if this be true of different colors, it must be no less so of the different shades of the same color; and each shade produces a distinct idea, independent of the rest. For if this should be denied, it is possible, by the continual gradation of shades, to run a color insensibly into what is most remote from it; and if you will not allow any of the means to be different, you cannot, without absurdity, deny the extremes to be the same. Suppose, therefore, a person to have enjoyed his sight for thirty years, and to have become perfectly acquainted with colors of all kinds except one particular shade of blue, for instance, which it never has been his fortune to meet with. Let all the different shades of that color, except that single one, be placed before him, descending gradually from the deepest to the lightest; it is plain that he will perceive a blank, where that shade is wanting, and will be sensible that there is a greater distance in that place between the contiguous colors than in any other. Now I ask, whether it be possible for him, from his own imagination, to supply this deficiency, and raise up to himself the idea of that particular shade, though it had never been conveyed to him by his senses? I believe there are few but will be of opinion that he can: and this may serve as a proof that the simple ideas are not always, in every instance, derived from the correspondent impressions; though this instance is so singular, that it is scarcely worth our observing, and does not merit that for it alone we should alter our general maxim.

Here, therefore, is a proposition, which not only seems, in itself, simple and intelligible; but, if a proper use were made of it, might render every dispute equally intelligible, and banish all that jargon, which has so long taken possession of metaphysical reasonings, and drawn disgrace upon them. All ideas, especially abstract ones, are naturally faint and obscure: the mind has but a slender hold of them: they are apt to be confounded with other resembling ideas; and when we have often employed any term, though without a distinct meaning, we are apt to imagine it has a determinate idea annexed to it. On the contrary, all impressions, that is, all sensations, either outward or inward, are strong and vivid: the limits between them are more exactly determined: nor is it easy to fall into any error or mistake with regard to them. When we entertain, therefore, any suspicion that a philosophical term is employed without any meaning or idea (as is but too frequent), we need but inquire, *from what impression is that supposed idea derived?* And if it be impossible to assign any, this will serve to confirm our suspicion. By bringing ideas into so clear a light we may reasonably hope to remove all dispute, which may arise, concerning their nature and reality.

Section IV

Sceptical Doubts Concerning the Operations of the Understanding

Part I

All the objects of human reason or inquiry may naturally be divided into two kinds, to wit, *relations of ideas,* and *matters of fact.* Of the first kind are the sciences of geometry, algebra, and arithmetic; and in short, every affirmation which is either intuitively or demonstratively certain. *That the square of the hypoteneuse is equal to the squares of the two sides,* is a proposition which expresses a relation between these figures. *That three times five is equal to the half of thirty,* expresses a relation between these numbers. Propositions of this kind are discoverable by the mere operation of thought, without dependence on what is anywhere existent in the universe. Though there never were a circle or triangle in nature, the truths demonstrated by Euclid would for ever retain their certainty and evidence.

Matters of fact, which are the second objects of human reason, are not ascertained in the same manner; nor is our evidence of their truth, however great, of a like nature with the foregoing. The contrary of every matter of fact is still possible; because it can never imply a contradiction, and is conceived by the mind with the same facility and distinctness, as if ever so conformable to reality. *That the sun will not rise tomorrow* is no less intelligible a proposition, and implies no more contradiction than the affirmation, *that it will rise.* We should in vain, therefore, attempt to demonstrate its falsehood. Were it demonstratively false, it would imply a contradiction, and could never be distinctly conceived by the mind.

It may, therefore, be a subject worthy of curiosity, to inquire what is the nature of that evidence which assures us of any real existence and matter of fact, beyond the present testimony of our senses, or the records of our memory. This part of philosophy, it is observable, has been little cultivated, either by the ancients or moderns; and therefore our doubts and errors, in the prosecution of so important an inquiry, may be the more excusable; while we march through such difficult paths without any guide or direction. They may even prove useful, by exciting curiosity, and destroying that implicit faith and security, which is the bane of all reasoning and free inquiry. The discovery of defects in the common philosophy, if any such there be, will not, I presume, be a discouragement, but rather an incitement, as is usual, to attempt something more full and satisfactory than has yet been proposed to the public.

All reasonings concerning matter of fact seem to be founded on the relation of *cause and effect.* By means of that relation alone we can go beyond the evidence of our memory and senses. If you were to ask a man, why he believes any matter of fact, which is absent; for instance, that his friend is in the country, or in France; he would give you a reason; and this reason would be some other fact; as a letter received from him, or the knowledge of his former resolutions and promises. A man finding a watch or any other machine in a desert island, would conclude that there had once been men in that island. All our reasonings concerning fact are of the same nature. And here it is constantly supposed that there is a connection between the present fact and that which is inferred from it. Were there nothing to bind them together, the inference would be entirely precarious. The hearing of an articulate voice and rational discourse in the dark assures us of the presence of some person: Why? because these are the effects of the human make and fabric, and closely connected with it. If we anatomize all the other reasonings of this nature, we shall find that they are founded on the relation of cause and effect, and that this relation is either near or remote, direct or collateral. Heat and light are collateral effects of fire, and the one effect may justly be inferred from the other.

If we would satisfy ourselves, therefore, concerning the nature of that evidence, which assures us of matters of fact, we must inquire how we arrive at the knowledge of cause and effect.

I shall venture to affirm, as a general proposition, which admits of no exception, that the knowledge of this relation is not, in any instance, attained by reasonings *a priori;* but arises entirely from experience, when we find that any particular objects are constantly conjoined with each other. Let an object be presented to a man of ever so strong natural reason and abilities; if that object be entirely new to him, he will not be able, by the most accurate examination of its sensible qualities, to discover any of its causes or effects. Adam, though his rational faculties be supposed, at the very first, entirely perfect, could not have inferred from the fluidity and transparency of water that it would suffocate him, or from the light and warmth of fire that it would consume him. No object ever discovers, by the qualities which appear to the senses, either the causes which produced it, or the effects which will arise from it; nor can our reason, unassisted by experience, ever draw any inference concerning real existence and matter of fact.

This proposition, *that causes and effects are discoverable, not by reason but by experience,* will readily be admitted with regard to such objects, as we remember to have once been altogether unknown to us; since we must be conscious of the utter inability, which we then lay under, of foretelling what would arise from them. Present two smooth pieces of marble to a man who has no tincture of natural philosophy; he will never discover that they will adhere together in such a manner as to require great force to separate them in a direct line, while they make so small a resistance to a lateral pressure. Such events, as bear little analogy to the common course of nature, are also readily confessed to be known only by experience; nor does any man imagine that the explosion of gunpowder, or the attraction of a loadstone, could ever be discovered by arguments *a priori*. In like manner, when an effect is supposed to depend upon an intricate machinery or secret structure of parts, we make no difficulty in attributing all our knowledge of it to experience. Who will assert that he can give the ultimate reason, why milk or bread is proper nourishment for a man, not for a lion or a tiger?

But the same truth may not appear, at first sight, to have the same evidence with regard to events, which have become familiar to us from our first appearance in the world, which bear a close analogy to the whole course of nature, and which are supposed to depend on the simple qualities of objects, without any secret structure of parts. We are apt to imagine that we could discover these effects by the mere operation of our reason, without experience. We fancy, that were we brought on a sudden into this world, we could at first have inferred that one billiard ball would communicate motion to another upon impulse; and that we needed not to have waited for the event, in order to pronounce with certainty concerning it. Such is the influence of custom, that, where it is strongest, it not only covers our natural ignorance, but even conceals itself, and seems not to take place, merely because it is found in the highest degree.

But to convince us that all the laws of nature, and all the operations of bodies without exception, are known only by experience, the following reflections may, perhaps, suffice. Were any object presented to us, and were we required to pronounce concerning the effect, which will result from it, without consulting past observation; after what manner, I beseech you, must the mind proceed in this operation? It must invent or imagine some event, which it ascribes to the object as its effect; and it is plain that this invention must be entirely arbitrary. The mind can never possibly find the effect in the supposed cause, by the most accurate scrutiny and examination. For the effect is totally different from the cause, and consequently can never by discovered in it. Motion in the second billiard ball is a quite distinct event from motion in the first: nor is there anything in the one to suggest the smallest hint of the other. A stone or piece of metal raised into the air, and left without any support, immediately falls: but to consider the matter *a priori,* is there anything we discover in this situation which can beget the idea of a downward, rather than an upward, or any other motion, in the stone or metal?

And as the first imagination or invention of a particular effect, in all natural operations, is arbitrary, where we consult not experience; so must we also esteem the supposed tie or connection between the cause and effect, which binds them together, and renders it impossible that any other effect could result from the operation of that cause. When I see, for instance, a billiard ball moving in a straight line towards another; even suppose motion in the second ball should by accident be suggested to me, as the result of their contact or impulse; may I not conceive, that a hundred different events might as well follow from that cause? May not both these balls remain at absolute rest? May not the first ball return in a straight line, or leap off from the second in any line or direction? All these suppositions are consistent and conceivable. Why then should we give the preference to one, which is no more consistent or conceivable than the rest? All our reasonings *a priori* will never be able to show us any foundation for this preference.

In a word, then, every effect is a distinct event from its cause. It could not, therefore, be discovered in the cause, and the first invention or conception of it, *a priori,* must be entirely arbitrary. And even after it is suggested, the conjunction of it with the cause must appear equally arbitrary; since there are always many other effects, which, to reason, must seem fully as consistent and natural. In vain, therefore, should we pretend to determine any single event, or infer any cause or effect, without the assistance of observation and experience.

Hence we may discover the reason why no philosopher, who is rational and modest, has ever pretended to assign the ultimate cause of any natural operation, or to show distinctly the action of that power, which produces any single effect in the universe. It is confessed, that the utmost effort of human reason is to reduce the principles, productive of natural phenomena, to a greater simplicity, and to resolve the many particular effects into a few general causes, by means of reasonings from analogy, experience, and observation. But as to the causes of these general causes, we should in vain attempt their discovery; nor shall we ever be able to satisfy ourselves, by any particular explication of them. These ultimate springs and principles are totally shut up from human curiosity and inquiry. Elasticity, gravity, cohesion of parts, communication of motion by impulse; these are probably the ultimate causes and principles which we ever discover in nature; and we may esteem ourselves sufficiently happy, if, by accurate inquiry and reasoning, we can trace up the particular phenomena to, or near to, these general principles. The most perfect philosophy of the natural kind only staves off our ignorance a little longer: as perhaps the most perfect philosophy of the moral or metaphysical kind serves only to discover larger portions of it. Thus the observation of human blindness and weakness is the result of all philosophy, and meets us at every turn, in spite of our endeavors to elude or avoid it.

Nor is geometry, when taken into the assistance of natural philosophy, ever able to remedy this defect, or lead us into the knowledge of ultimate causes, by all that accuracy of reasoning for which it is so justly celebrated. Every part of mixed mathematics proceeds upon the supposition that certain laws are established by nature in her operations; and abstract reasonings are employed, either to assist experience in the discovery of these laws, or to determine their influence in particular instances, where it depends upon any precise degree of distance and quantity. Thus, it is a law of motion, discovered by experience, that the moment or force of any body in motion is in the compound ratio or proportion of its solid contents and its velocity; and consequently, that a small force may remove the greatest obstacle or raise the greatest weight, if, by any contrivance or machinery, we can increase the velocity of that force, so as to make it an overmatch for its antagonist. Geometry assists us in the application of this law, by giving us the just dimensions of all the parts and figures which can enter into any species of machine; but still the discovery of the law itself is owing merely to experience, and all the abstract reasonings in the world could never lead us one step towards the knowledge of it. When we reason *a priori,* and consider merely any object or cause, as it appears to the mind, independent of all observation, it never could suggest to us the notion of any distinct object, such as its effect; much less, show us the inseparable and inviolable connection between them. A man must be very sagacious who could discover by reasoning that crystal is the effect of heat, and ice of cold, without being previously acquainted with the operation of these qualities.

Part II

But we have not yet attained any tolerable satisfaction with regard to the question first proposed. Each solution still gives rise to a new question as difficult as the foregoing, and leads us on to farther inquiries. When it is asked, *What is the nature of all our reasonings concerning matter of fact?* the proper answer seems to be, that they are founded on the relation of cause and effect. When again it is asked, *What is the foundation of all our reasonings and conclusions concerning that relation?* it may be replied in one word, *experience.* But if we still carry on our sifting humor, and ask, *What is the foundation of all conclusions from experience?* this implies a new question, which may be of more difficult solution and explication. Philosophers, that give themselves airs of superior wisdom and sufficiency, have a hard task when they encounter persons of inquisitive dispositions, who push them from every corner to which they retreat, and who are sure at last to bring them to some dangerous dilemma. The best expedient to prevent this confusion, is to be modest in our pretensions; and even to discover the difficulty ourselves before it is objected to us. By this means, we may make a kind of merit of our very ignorance.

I shall content myself, in this section, with an easy task, and shall pretend only to give a negative answer to the question here proposed. I say then, that, even after we have experience of the operations of cause and effect, our conclusions from that experience are *not* founded on reasoning, or any process of the understanding. This answer we must endeavor both to explain and to defend.

It must certainly be allowed, that nature has kept us at a great distance from all her secrets, and has afforded us only the knowledge of a few superficial qualities of objects; while she conceals from us those powers and principles on which the influence of those objects entirely depends. Our senses inform us of the color, weight, and consistence of bread; but neither sense nor reason can ever inform us of those qualities which fit it for the nourishment and support of a human body. Sight or feeling conveys an idea of the actual motion of bodies; but as to that wonderful force or power, which would carry on a moving body for ever in a continued change of place, and which bodies never lose but by communicating it to others; of this we cannot form the most distant conception. But notwithstanding this ignorance of natural powers[2] and principles, we always presume, when we see like sensible qualities, that they have like secret powers, and expect that effects, similar to those which we have experienced, will follow from them. If a body of like color and consistence with that bread, which we have formerly eaten, be presented to us, we make no scruple of repeating the experiment, and foresee, with certainty, like

---

2. The word, *power,* is here used in a loose and popular sense. The more accurate explication of it would give additional evidence to this argument. See Sect. VII.

nourishment and support. Now this is a process of the mind or thought, of which I would willingly know the foundation. It is allowed on all hands that there is no known connection between the sensible qualities and the secret powers; and consequently, that the mind is not led to form such a conclusion concerning their constant and regular conjunction, by anything which it knows of their nature. As to past *experience,* it can be allowed to give *direct* and *certain* information of those precise objects only, and that precise period of time, which fell under its cognizance: but why this experience should be extended to future times, and to other objects, which, for aught we know, may be only in appearance similar; this is the main question on which I would insist. The bread, which I formerly eat, nourished me; that is, a body of such sensible qualities was, at that time, endued with such secret powers: but does it follow, that other bread must also nourish me at another time, and that like sensible qualities must always be attended with like secret powers? The consequence seems nowise necessary. At least, it must be acknowledged that there is here a consequence drawn by the mind; that there is a certain step taken; a process of thought, and an inference, which wants to be explained. These two propositions are far from being the same, *I have found that such an object has always been attended with such an effect,* and *I foresee, that other objects, which are, in appearance, similar, will be attended with similar effects.* I shall allow, if you please, that the one proposition may justly be inferred from the other; I know, in fact, that it always is inferred. But if you insist that the inference is made by a chain of reasoning, I desire you to produce that reasoning. The connection between these propositions is not intuitive. There is required a medium, which may enable the mind to draw such an inference, if indeed it be drawn by reasoning and argument. What that medium is, I confess, passes my comprehension; and it is incumbent on those to produce it, who assert that it really exists, and is the origin of all our conclusions concerning matter of fact.

This negative argument must certainly, in process of time, become altogether convincing, if many penetrating and able philosophers shall turn their inquiries this way and no one be ever able to discover any connecting proposition or intermediate step, which supports the understanding in this conclusion. But as the question is yet new, every reader may not trust so far to his own penetration, as to conclude, because an argument escapes his inquiry, that therefore it does not really exist. For this reason it may be requisite to venture upon a more difficult task; and enumerating all the branches of human knowledge, endeavor to show that none of them can afford such an argument.

All reasonings may be divided into two kinds, namely demonstrative reasoning, or that concerning relations of ideas, and moral reasoning, or that concerning matter of fact and existence. That there are no demonstrative arguments in the case seems evident; since it implies no contradiction that the course of nature may change, and that an object, seemingly like those which we have experienced, may be attended with different or contrary effects. May I not clearly and distinctly conceive that a body, falling from the clouds, and which, in all other respects, resembles snow, has yet the taste of salt or feeling of fire? Is there any more intelligible proposition than to affirm, that all the trees will flourish in December and January, and decay in May and June? Now whatever is intelligible, and can be distinctly conceived, implies no contradiction, and can never be proved false by any demonstrative argument or abstract reasoning *a priori*.

If we be, therefore, engaged by arguments to put trust in past experience, and make it the standard of our future judgment, these arguments must be probable only, or such as regard matter of fact and real existence, according to the division above mentioned. But that there is no argument of this kind, must appear, if our explication of that species of reasoning be admitted as solid and satisfactory. We have said that all arguments concerning existence are founded on the relation of cause and effect; that our knowledge of that relation is derived entirely from experience; and that all our experimental conclusions proceed upon the supposition that the future will be conformable to the past. To endeavor, therefore, the proof of this last supposition by probable arguments, or arguments regarding existence, must be evidently going in a circle, and taking that for granted, which is the very point in question.

In reality, all arguments from experience are founded on the similarity which we discover among natural objects, and by which we are induced to expect effects similar to those which we have found to follow from such objects. And though none but a fool or madman will ever pretend to dispute the authority of experience, or to reject that great guide of human life, it may surely be allowed a philosopher to have so much curiosity at least as to examine the principle of human nature, which gives this mighty authority to experience, and makes us draw advantage from that similarity which nature has placed among different objects. From causes which appear *similar* we expect similar effects. This is the sum of all our experimental conclusions. Now it seems evident that, if this conclusion were formed by reason, it would be as perfect at first, and upon one instance, as after ever so long a course of experience. But the case is far otherwise. Nothing so like as eggs; yet no one, on account of this appearing similarity, expects the same taste and relish in all of them. It is only after a long course of uniform experiments in any kind, that we attain a firm reliance and security with regard to a particular event. Now where is that process of reasoning which, from one instance, draws a conclusion, so different from that which it infers from a hundred instances that are nowise different from that single one? This question I propose as much for the sake of information, as with an intention of raising difficulties. I cannot find, I cannot imagine any such reasoning. But I keep my mind still open to instruction, if anyone will vouchsafe to bestow it on me.

Should it be said that, from a number of uniform experiments, we *infer* a connection between the sensible qualities and the secret powers; this, I must confess, seems the same difficulty, couched in different terms. The question still recurs, on what process of argument this *inference* is founded? Where is the medium, the interposing ideas, which join propositions so very wide of each other? It is confessed that the color, consistence, and other sensible qualities of bread appear not, of themselves, to have any connection with the secret powers of nourishment and support. For otherwise we could infer these secret powers from the first appearance of these sensible qualities, without the aid of experience; contrary to the sentiment of all philosophers, and contrary to plain matter of fact. Here, then, is our natural state of ignorance with regard to the powers and influence of all objects. How is this remedied by experience? It only shows us a number of uniform effects, resulting from certain objects, and teaches us that those particular objects, at that particular time, were endowed with such powers and forces. When a new object, endowed with similar sensible qualities, is produced, we expect similar powers and forces, and look for a like effect. From a body of like color and consistence with bread we expect like nourishment and support. But this surely is a step or progress of the mind, which wants to be explained. When a man says, *I have found, in all past instances, such sensible qualities conjoined with such secret powers:* And when he says, *Similar sensible qualities will always be conjoined with similar secret powers,* he is not guilty of a tautology, nor are these propositions in any respect the same. You say that the one proposition is an inference from the other. But you must confess that the inference is not intuitive; neither is it demonstrative: Of what nature is it, then? To say it is experimental, is begging the question. For all inferences from experience suppose, as their foundation, that the future will resemble the past, and that similar powers will be conjoined with similar sensible qualities. If there be any suspicion that the course of nature may change, and that the past may be no rule for the future, all experience becomes useless, and can give rise to no inference or conclusion. It is impossible, therefore, that any arguments from experience can prove this resemblance of the past to the future; since all these arguments are founded on the supposition of that resemblance. Let the course of things be allowed hitherto ever so regular; that alone, without some new argument or inference, proves not that, for the future, it will continue so. In vain do you pretend to have learned the nature of bodies from your past experience. Their secret nature, and consequently all their effects and influence, may change, without any change in their sensible qualities. This happens sometimes, and with regard to some objects: Why may it not happen always, and with regard to all objects? What logic, what process of argument secures you against this supposition? My practice, you say, refutes my doubts. But you mistake the purport of my question. As an agent, I am quite satisfied in the point; but as a philosopher, who has some share of curiosity, I will not say scepticism, I want to learn the foundation of this inference. No reading, no inquiry has yet been able to remove my difficulty, or give me satisfaction in a matter of such importance. Can I do better than propose the difficulty to the public, even though, perhaps, I have small hopes of obtaining a solution? We shall, at least, by this means, be sensible of our ignorance, if we do not augment our knowledge.

I must confess that a man is guilty of unpardonable arrogance who concludes, because an argument has escaped his own investigation, that therefore it does not really exist. I must also confess that, though all the learned, for several ages, should have employed themselves in fruitless search upon any subject, it may still, perhaps, be rash to conclude positively that the subject must, therefore, pass all human comprehension. Even though we examine all the sources of our knowledge, and conclude them unfit for such a subject, there may still remain a suspicion, that the enumeration is not complete, or the examination not accurate. But with regard to the present subject, there are some considerations which seem to remove all this accusation of arrogance or suspicion of mistake.

It is certain that the most ignorant and stupid peasants—nay infants, nay even brute beasts—improve by experience, and learn the qualities of natural objects, by observing the effects which result from them. When a child has felt the sensation of

335

pain from touching the flame of a candle, he will be careful not to put his hand near any candle; but will expect a similar effect from a cause which is similar in its sensible qualities and appearance. If you assert, therefore, that the understanding of the child is led into this conclusion by any process of argument or ratiocination, I may justly require you to produce that argument; nor have you any pretense to refuse so equitable a demand. You cannot say that the argument is abstruse, and may possibly escape your inquiry; since you confess that it is obvious to the capacity of a mere infant. If you hesitate, therefore, a moment, or if, after reflection, you produce any intricate or profound argument, you, in a manner, give up the question, and confess that it is not reasoning which engages us to suppose the past resembling the future, and to expect similar effects from causes which are, to appearance, similar. This is the proposition which I intended to enforce in the present section. If I be right, I pretend not to have made any mighty discovery. And if I be wrong, I must acknowledge myself to be indeed a very backward scholar; since I cannot now discover an argument which, it seems, was perfectly familiar to me long before I was out of my cradle.

Section VII

Of the Idea of Necessary Connection

Part I

The great advantage of the mathematical sciences above the moral consists in this, that the ideas of the former, being sensible, are always clear and determinate, the smallest distinction between them is immediately perceptible, and the same terms are still expressive of the same ideas, without ambiguity or variation. An oval is never mistaken for a circle, nor an hyperbola for an ellipsis. The isosceles and scalenum are distinguished by boundaries more exact than vice and virtue, right and wrong. If any term be defined in geometry, the mind readily, of itself, substitutes, on all occasions, the definition for the term defined: or even when no definition is employed, the object itself may be presented to the senses, and by that means be steadily and clearly apprehended. But the finer sentiments of the mind, the operations of the understanding, the various agitations of the passions, though really in themselves distinct, easily escape us, when surveyed by reflection; nor is it in our power to recall the original object, as often as we have occasion to contemplate it. Ambiguity, by this means, is gradually introduced into our reasonings: similar objects are readily taken to be the same: and the conclusion becomes at last very wide of the premises.

One may safely, however, affirm, that, if we consider these sciences in a proper light, their advantages and disadvantages nearly compensate each other, and reduce both of them to a state of equality. If the mind, with greater facility, retains the ideas of geometry clear and determinate, it must carry on a much longer and more intricate chain of reasoning, and compare ideas much wider of each other, in order to reach the abstruser truths of that science. And if moral ideas are apt, without extreme care, to fall into obscurity and confusion, the inferences are always much shorter in these disquisitions, and the intermediate steps, which lead to the conclusion, much fewer than in the sciences which treat of quantity and number. In reality, there is scarcely a proposition in Euclid so simple, as not to consist of more parts, than are to be found in any moral reasoning which runs not into chimera and conceit. Where we trace the principles of the human mind through a few steps, we may be very well satisfied with our progress; considering how soon nature throws a bar to all our inquiries concerning causes, and reduces us to an acknowledgment of our ignorance. The chief obstacle, therefore, to our improvement in the moral or metaphysical sciences is the obscurity of the ideas, and ambiguity of the terms. The principal difficulty in the mathematics is the length of inferences and compass of thought, requisite to the forming of any conclusion. And, perhaps, our progress in natural philosophy is chiefly retarded by the want of proper experiments and phenomena, which are often discovered by chance, and cannot always be found, when requisite, even by the most diligent and prudent inquiry. As moral philosophy seems hitherto to have received less improvement than either geometry or physics, we may conclude, that, if there be any difference in this respect among these sciences, the difficulties, which obstruct the progress of the former, require superior care and capacity to be surmounted.

There are no ideas, which occur in metaphysics more obscure and uncertain, than those of *power, force, energy* or *necessary connection,* of which it is every moment necessary for us to treat in all our disquisitions. We shall, therefore, endeavor, in this section, to fix, if possible, the precise meaning of these terms, and thereby remove some part of that obscurity, which is so much complained of in this species of philosophy.

It seems a proposition, which will not admit of much dispute, that all our ideas are nothing but copies of our impressions, or, in other words, that it is impossible for us to *think* of anything, which we have not antecedently *felt,* either by our external or internal senses. I have endeavored[3] to explain and prove this proposition, and have expressed my hopes, that, by a proper application of it, men may reach a greater clearness and precision in philosophical reasonings, than what they have hitherto been able to attain. Complex ideas may, perhaps, be well known by definition, which is nothing but an enumeration of those parts or simple ideas, that compose them. But when we have pushed up definitions to the most simple ideas, and find still some ambiguity and obscurity; what resource are we then possessed of? By what invention can we throw light upon these ideas, and render them altogether precise and determinate to our intellectual view! Produce the impressions or original sentiments, from which the ideas are copied. These impressions are all strong and sensible. They admit not of ambiguity. They are not only placed in a full light themselves, but may throw light on their correspondent ideas, which lie in obscurity. And by this means, we may, perhaps, attain a new microscope or species of optics, by which, in the moral sciences, the most minute, and most simple ideas may be so enlarged as to fall readily under our apprehension, and be

---

3. Section II.

equally known with the grossest and most sensible ideas, that can be the object of our inquiry.

To be fully acquainted, therefore, with the idea of power or necessary connection, let us examine its impression; and in order to find the impression with greater certainty, let us search for it in all the sources, from which it may possibly be derived.

When we look about us towards external objects, and consider the operation of causes, we are never able, in a single instance, to discover any power or necessary connection; any quality, which binds the effect to the cause, and renders the one an infallible consequence of the other. We only find, that the one does actually, in fact, follow the other. The impulse of one billiard ball is attended with motion in the second. This is the whole that appears to the *outward* senses. The mind feels no sentiment or *inward* impression from this succession of objects: consequently there is not, in any single, particular instance of cause and effect, anything which can suggest the idea of power or necessary connection.

From the first appearance of an object, we never can conjecture what effect will result from it. But were the power or energy of any cause discoverable by the mind, we could foresee the effect, even without experience; and might, at first, pronounce with certainty concerning it, by mere dint of thought and reasoning.

In reality, there is no part of matter, that does ever, by its sensible qualities, discover any power or energy, or give us ground to imagine, that it could produce anything, or be followed by any other object, which we could denominate its effect. Solidity, extension, motion; these qualities are all complete in themselves, and never point out any other event which may result from them. The scenes of the universe are continually shifting, and one object follows another in an uninterrupted succession; but the power of force, which actuates the whole machine, is entirely concealed from us, and never discovers itself in any of the sensible qualities of body. We know, that, in fact, heat is a constant attendant of flame; but what is the connection between them, we have no room so much as to conjecture or imagine. It is impossible, therefore, that the idea of power can be derived from the contemplation of bodies, in single instances of their operation; because no bodies ever discover any power, which can be the original of this idea.[4]

Since, therefore, external objects as they appear to the senses, give us no idea of power or necessary connection, by their operation in particular instances, let us see, whether this idea be derived from reflection on the operations of our own minds, and be copied from any internal impression. It may be said, that we are every moment conscious of internal power; while we feel, that, by the simple command of our will, we can move the organs of our body, or direct the faculties of our mind. An act of volition produces motion in our limbs, or raises a new idea in our imagination. This influence of the will we know by consciousness. Hence we acquire the idea of power or energy; and are certain, that we ourselves and all other

---

4. Mr. Locke, in his chapter on power, says, that, finding from experience, that there are several new productions in matter, and concluding that there must somewhere be a power capable of producing them, we arrive at last by this reasoning at the idea of power. But no reasoning can ever give us a new original, simple idea; as this philosopher himself confesses. This, therefore, can never be the origin of that idea.

intelligent beings are possessed of power. This idea, then, is an idea of reflection, since it arises from reflecting on the operations of our own mind, and on the command which is exercised by will, both over the organs of the body and faculties of the soul.

We shall proceed to examine this pretension; and first with regard to the influence of volition over the organs of the body. This influence, we may observe, is a fact, which, like all other natural events, can be known only by experience, and can never be foreseen from any apparent energy or power in the cause, which connects it with the effect, and renders the one an infallible consequence of the other. The motion of our body follows upon the command of our will. Of this we are every moment conscious. But the means, by which this is effected; the energy, by which the will performs so extraordinary an operation; of this we are so far from being immediately conscious, that it must for ever escape our most diligent inquiry.

For *first,* Is there any principle in all nature more mysterious than the union of soul with body; by which a supposed spiritual substance acquires such an influence over a material one, that the most refined thought is able to actuate the grossest matter? Were we empowered, by a secret wish, to remove mountains, or control the planets in their orbit; this extensive authority would not be more extraordinary, nor more beyond our comprehension. But if by consciousness we perceived any power or energy in the will, we must know this power; we must know its connection with the effect; we must know the secret union of soul and body, and the nature of both these substances; by which the one is able to operate, in so many instances, upon the other.

Secondly, We are not able to move all the organs of the body with a like authority; though we cannot assign any reason besides experience, for so remarkable a difference between one and the other. Why has the will an influence over the tongue and fingers, not over the heart and liver? This question would never embarrass us, were we conscious of a power in the former case, not in the latter. We should then perceive, independent of experience, why the authority of will over the organs of the body is circumscribed within such particular limits. Being in that case fully acquainted with the power or force, by which it operates, we should also know, why its influence reaches precisely to such boundaries, and no farther.

A man, suddenly struck with palsy in the leg or arm, or who had newly lost those members, frequently endeavors, at first to move them, and employ them in their usual offices. Here he is as much conscious of power to command such limbs, as a man in perfect health is conscious of power to actuate any member which remains in its natural state and condition. But consciousness never deceives. Consequently, neither in the one case nor in the other, are we ever conscious of any power. We learn the influence of our will from experience alone. And experience only teaches us, how one event constantly follows another; without instructing us in the secret connection, which binds them together, and renders them inseparable.

Thirdly, We learn from anatomy, that the immediate object of power in voluntary motion, is not the member itself which is moved, but certain muscles, and nerves, and animal spirits, and, perhaps, something still more minute and more unknown, through which the motion is successfully propagated, ere it reach the member itself whose motion is the immediate object of volition. Can there be a more certain proof that the power, by which this whole operation is performed, so far from being directly and fully known by an inward sentiment or consciousness, is, to the last degree, mysterious and unintelligible? Here the mind wills a certain event: immediately another event, unknown to ourselves, and totally different from the one intended, is produced: this event produces another, equally unknown: till at last, through a long succession, the desired event is produced. But if the original power were felt, it must be known: were it known, its effect also must be known; since all power is relative to its effect. And *vice versa*, if the effect be not known, the power cannot be known nor felt. How indeed can we be conscious of a power to move our limbs, when we have no such power; but only that to move certain animal spirits, which, though they produce at last the motion of our limbs, yet operate in such a manner as is wholly beyond our comprehension?

We may, therefore, conclude from the whole, I hope, without any temerity, though with assurance; that our idea of power is not copied from any sentiment or consciousness of power within ourselves, when we give rise to animal motion, or apply our limbs, to their proper use and office. That their motion follows the command of the will is a matter of common experience, like other natural events: but the power or energy by which this is effected, like that in other natural events, is unknown and inconceivable.[5]

Shall we then assert, that we are conscious of a power or energy in our own minds, when, by an act or command of our will, we raise up a new idea, fix the mind to the contemplation of it, turn it on all sides, and at last dismiss it for some other idea, when we think that we have surveyed it with sufficient accuracy? I believe the same arguments will prove, that even this command of the will gives us no real idea of force or energy.

First, It must be allowed, that, when we know a power, we know that very circumstance in the cause, by which it is enabled to produce the effect: for these are supposed to be synonymous. We must, therefore, know both the cause and effect, and the relation between them. But do we pretend to be acquainted with the nature of the human soul and the nature of an idea, or the aptitude of the one to produce the other? This is a real creation; a production of something out of nothing: which implies a power so great, that it may seem, at first sight, beyond the reach of any being, less than infinite. At least it must be owned, that such a power is not felt, nor known, nor even conceivable by the mind. We only feel the event, namely, the existence of an idea, consequent to a command of the will: but the

---

5. It may be pretended, that the resistance which we meet with in bodies, obliging us frequently to exert our force, and call up all our power, this gives us the idea of force and power. It is this *nisus,* or strong endeavor, of which we are conscious, that is the original impression from which this idea is copied. But, *first,* We attribute power to a vast number of objects, where we never can suppose this resistance or exertion of force to take place; to the Supreme Being, who never meets with any resistance; to the mind in its command over its ideas and limbs, in common thinking and motion, where the effect follows immediately upon the will, without any exertion or summoning up of force; to inanimate matter, which is not capable of this sentiment. *Secondly,* This sentiment of an endeavor to overcome resistance has no known connection with any event: what follows it, we know by experience; but could not know it *a priori.* It must, however, be confessed, that the animal *nisus,* which we experience, though it can afford no accurate precise idea of power, enters very much into that vulgar, inaccurate idea, which is formed of it.

manner, in which this operation is performed, the power by which it is produced, is entirely beyond our comprehension.

Secondly, The command of the mind over itself is limited, as well as its command over the body; and these limits are not known by reason, or any acquaintance with the nature of cause and effect, but only by experience and observation, as in all other natural events and in the operation of external objects. Our authority over our sentiments and passions is much weaker than that over our ideas; and even the latter authority is circumscribed within very narrow boundaries. Will anyone pretend to assign the ultimate reason of these boundaries, or show why the power is deficient in one case, not in another?

Thirdly, This self-command is very different at different times. A man in health possesses more of it than one languishing with sickness. We are more master of our thoughts in the morning than in the evening; fasting, than after a full meal. Can we give any reason for these variations, except experience? Where then is the power, of which we pretend to be conscious? . . .

Part II

But to hasten to a conclusion of this argument, which is already drawn out to too great a length: we have sought in vain for an idea of power or necessary connection in all the sources from which we could suppose it to be derived. It appears that, in single instances of the operation of bodies, we never can, by our utmost scrutiny, discover anything but one event following another, without being able to comprehend any force or power by which the cause operates, or any connection between it and its supposed effect. The same difficulty occurs in contemplating the operations of mind on body—where we observe the motion of the latter to follow upon the volition of the former, but are not able to observe or conceive the tie which binds together the motion and volition, or the energy by which the mind produces this effect. The authority of the will over its own faculties and ideas is not a whit more comprehensible: so that, upon the whole, there appears not, throughout all nature, any one instance of connection which is conceivable by us. All events seem entirely loose and separate. One event follows another; but we never can observe any tie between them. They seem *conjoined,* but never *connected.* And as we can have no idea of anything which never appeared to our outward sense or inward sentiment, the necessary conclusion *seems* to be that we have no idea of connection or power at all, and that these words are absolutely without any meaning, when employed either in philosophical reasonings or common life.

But there still remains one method of avoiding this conclusion, and one source which we have not yet examined. When any natural object or event is presented, it is impossible for us, by any sagacity or penetration, to discover, or even conjecture, without experience, what event will result from it, or to carry our foresight beyond that object which is immediately present to the memory and senses. Even after one instance or experiment where we have observed a particular event to follow upon another, we are not entitled to form a general rule, or foretell what will happen in like cases; it being justly esteemed an unpardonable temerity to judge of the whole course of nature from one single experiment, however accurate or certain. But when one particular species of event has always, in all instances, been conjoined with another, we make no longer any scruple of foretelling one upon the appearance of the other, and of employing that reasoning which can alone assure us of any matter of fact or existence. We then call the one object, *cause;* the other, *effect*. We suppose that there is some connection between them; some power in the one, by which it infallibly produces the other, and operates with the greatest certainty and strongest necessity.

It appears, then, that this idea of a necessary connection among events arises from a number of similar instances which occur of the constant conjunction of these events; nor can that idea ever be suggested by any one of these instances, surveyed in all possible lights and positions. But there is nothing in a number of instances, different from every single instance, which is supposed to be exactly similar; except only, that after a repetition of similar instances, the mind is carried by habit, upon the appearance of one event, to expect its usual attendant, and to believe that it will exist. This connection, therefore, which we *feel* in the mind, this customary transition of the imagination from one object to its usual attendant, is the sentiment or impression from which we form the idea of power or necessary connection. Nothing farther is in the case. Contemplate the subject on all sides; you will never find any other origin of that idea. This is the sole difference between one instance, from which we can never receive the idea of connection, and a number of similar instances, by which it is suggested. The first time a man saw the communication of motion by impulse, as by the shock of two billiard balls, he could not pronounce that the event was *connected;* but only that it was *conjoined* with the other. After he has observed several instances of this nature, he than pronounces them to be *connected*. What alteration has happened to give rise to this new idea of *connection?* Nothing but that he now *feels* these events to be *connected* in his imagination, and can readily foretell the existence of one from the appearance of the other. When we say, therefore, that one object is connected with another, we mean only that they have acquired a connection in our thought, and give rise to this inference, by which they become proofs of each other's existence: a conclusion which is somewhat extraordinary, but which seems founded on sufficient evidence. Nor will its evidence be weakened by any general diffidence of the understanding, or sceptical suspicion concerning every conclusion which is new and extraordinary. No conclusions can be more agreeable to scepticism than such as make discoveries concerning the weakness and narrow limits of human reason and capacity.

And what stronger instance can be produced of the surprising ignorance and weakness of the understanding than the present? For surely, if there be any relation among objects which it imports to us to know perfectly, it is that of cause and effect. On this are founded all our reasonings concerning matter of fact or existence. By means of it alone we attain any assurance concerning objects which are removed from the present testimony of our memory and senses. The only immediate utility of all sciences, is to teach us, how to control and regulate future events by their causes. Our thoughts and inquiries are, therefore, every moment, employed about this relation: yet so imperfect are the ideas which we form concerning it, that it is impossible to give any just definition of cause, except what is drawn from something extraneous and foreign to it. Similar objects are always conjoined with similar. Of this we have experience. Suitably to this experience, therefore, we may define a cause to be *an object, followed by another, and where all the objects similar to the first are followed by objects similar to the second.* Or in other words *where, if the first object had not been, the second never had existed.* The appearance of a cause always conveys the mind, by a customary transition, to the idea of the effect. Of this also we have experience. We may, therefore, suitably to this experience, form another definition of cause, and call it, *an object followed by another and whose appearance always conveys the thought to that other.* . . .

To recapitulate, therefore, the reasonings of this section: every idea is copied from some preceding impression or sentiment; and where we cannot find any impression, we may be certain that there is no idea. In all single instances of the operation of bodies or minds, there is nothing that produces any impression, nor consequently can suggest any idea of power or necessary connection. But when many uniform instances appear, and the same object is always followed by the same event; we then begin to entertain the notion of cause and connection. We then feel a new sentiment or impression, to wit, a customary connection in the thought or imagination between one object and its usual attendant; and this sentiment is the original of that idea which we seek for. For as this idea arises from a number of similar instances, and not from any single instance, it must arise from that circumstance, in which the number of instances differ from every individual instance. But this customary connection or transition of the imagination is the only circumstance in which they differ. In every other particular they are alike. The first instance which we saw of motion communicated by the shock of two billiard balls (to return to this obvious illustration) is exactly similar to any instance that may, at present, occur to us, except only, that we could not, at first, *infer* one event from the other; which we are enabled to do at present, after so long a course of uniform experience. I know not whether the reader will readily apprehend this reasoning. I am afraid that, should I multiply words about it, or throw it into a greater variety of lights, it would only become more obscure and intricate. In all abstract reasonings there is one point of view which, if we can happily hit, we shall go farther towards illustrating the subject than by all the eloquence in the world. This point of view we should endeavor to reach, and reserve the flowers of rhetoric for subjects which are more adapted to them.

BEATTIE

An Essay on the Nature and Immutability of Truth *

Preface

. . . I had finished all these papers for the press, when a friend at London sent me an *Advertisement,* which had just then appeared prefixed to a new Edition of Mr. Hume's *Essays;* and which, in justice to that Author, I shall here insert, subjoining a few remarks in justice to myself.

> Most of the principles and reasonings contained in this volume were published in a work in three volumes, intitled, *A Treatise of Human Nature:* a work, which the author had projected before he left college, and which he wrote and published not long after. But not finding it successful, he was sensible of his error in going to the press too early, and he cast the whole anew in the following pieces; where some negligences in his former reasoning, and more in the expression, are, he hopes, corrected. Yet several writers, who have honoured the author's philosophy with answers, have taken care to direct all their batteries against that juvenile work, which the author never acknowledged; and have affected to triumph in any advantages which, they imagined, they had obtained over it: a practice very contrary to all rules of candour and fair-dealing, and a strong instance of those polemical artifices, which a bigotted zeal thinks itself authorised to employ. Henceforth the author desires, that the following pieces may alone be regarded as containing his philosophical sentiments and principles.

Thus far Mr. Hume.

I do not think it was with an evil purpose, that any of those who attacked this author's philosophy directed their batteries against the *Treatise of Human Nature.* In regard to myself, the case was briefly this.

Ever since I began to attend to matters of this kind, I had heard Mr. Hume's philosophy mentioned as a system very unfriendly to religion both revealed and natural, as well as to science; and its author spoken of as a teacher of sceptical and atheistical doctrines, and withal as a most acute and ingenious writer. I had reason to believe, that his arguments, and his influence as a great literary character, had done harm, by subverting or weakening the good principles of some, and countenancing the licentious opinions of others. Being honoured with the care of a part of the British youth; and considering it as my indispensable duty (from which I trust I

---

*From James Beattie, *An Essay on the Nature and Immutability of Truth, In Opposition to Sophistry and Scepticism,* revised ed. 1776, in James Beattie, *Essays,* a facsimile published by Garland Publishing, Inc., N.Y. 1971, pp. xi–xiv, 64–68, 193–201. Some citations and footnotes have been deleted. Used by permission.

JAMES BEATTIE

shall never deviate) to guard their minds against impiety and error, I endeavoured, among other studies that belonged to my office, to form a right estimate of Mr. Hume's philosophy, so as not only to understand his peculiar tenets, but also to preceive their *connection* and *consequences.*

In forming this estimate, I thought it at once the surest and the fairest method to begin with the *Treatise of Human Nature,* which was allowed, and is well known to be, the ground-work of the whole; and in which some of the principles and reasonings are more fully prosecuted, and their connection and consequences more clearly seen by an attentive reader (notwithstanding some inferiority in point of style), than in those more elegant republications of the system, that have appeared in the form of *Essays.* Every sound argument that may have been urged against the paradoxes of the *Treatise,* particularly against its first principles, does, in my opinion, tend to discredit the system; as every successful attempt to weaken the foundation of a building does in effect promote the downfall of the superstructure. Paradoxes there are in the *Treatise,* which are not in the *Essays;* and, in like manner, there are licentious doctrines in these, which are not in the other: and therefore I have not directed *all* my batteries against the first. . . .

For these eighteen years past (and before that period I knew nothing of this author's writings), I have always heard the *Treatise of Human Nature* spoken of as the work of Mr. Hume. Till after publishing the *Essay on Truth,* I knew not that it had ever been said, or insinuated, or even suspected, that he either did not acknowledge that Treatise, or wished it to be considered as a work which he did not acknowledge. On the contrary, from his reprinting so often, in *Essays* that bore his name, most of the principles and reasonings contained in it; and never, so far as I had heard, disavowing any part of it; I could not but think, that he set a very high value upon it. By the literary people with whom I was then acquainted it had been much read; and by many people it was much admired. And, in general, it was considered as the author's chief work in philosophy, and as one of the most curious systems of human nature that had ever appeared. Those who favoured his principles spoke of it as an unanswerable performance. And whatever its success might have been as an article of sale (a circumstance which I did not think it material to inquire into), I had reason to believe, that as a system of licentious doctrine it had been but *too successful;* and that to the author's reputation as a philosopher, and to his influence as a promoter of infidelity, it had contributed not a little.

Our author certainly merits praise, for thus publicly disowning, though late, his *Treatise of Human Nature;* though I am sorry to observe, from the tenor of his declaration, that he still seems inclined to adhere to "most of the reasonings and principles contained in that Treatise." But if he now at last renounced any one of his errors, I congratulate him upon it with all my heart. He has many good as well as great qualities; and I rejoice in the hope, that he may yet be prevailed on to relinquish totally a system, which I should think would be as uncomfortable to him, as it is unsatisfactory to others. In consequence of his Advertisement, I thought it right to mitigate in this Edition some of the censures that more especially refer to the *Treatise of Human Nature:* but as that Treatise is still extant, and will probably be read as long at least as any thing I write, I did not think it expedient to make any material change in the reasoning or in the plan of this performance.

April 30, 1776.

Part I

Chapter II. All Reasoning Terminates in First Principles. All Evidence Ultimately Intuitive. Common Sense the Standard of Truth to Man.

Section V. Of Reasoning from the Effect to the Cause

... I pronounce it ... to be an axiom, clear, certain, and undeniable, that "whatever beginneth to exist, proceedeth from some cause." I cannot bring myself to think, that the reverse of any geometrical axiom is more incredible than the reverse of this; and therefore I am as certain of the truth of this, as I can be of the truth of the other; and cannot, without contradicting myself, and doing violence to my nature, even attempt to believe otherwise.

Whether this maxim be intuitive or demonstrable, may perhaps admit of some dispute; but the determination of that point will not in the least affect the truth of the maxim. If it be demonstrable, we can then assign a reason for our belief of it: if it be intuitive, it is on the same footing with other intuitive axioms; that is, we believe it, because the law of our nature renders it impossible for us to disbelieve it.

In proof of this maxim it has been said, that nothing can produce itself. But this truth is not more evident than the truth to be proved, and therefore is no proof at all. Nay, this last proposition seems to be only a different, and less proper, way of expressing the same thing:—Nothing can produce itself;—that is, every thing produced, must be produced by some other thing;—that is, every effect must proceed from a cause;—and that is (for all effects being posterior to their causes, must necessarily have a beginning), "every thing beginning to exist proceeds from some cause." Other arguments have been offered in proof of this maxim, which I think are sufficiently confuted by Mr. Hume, in his *Treatise of Human Nature.*[6] This maxim therefore he affirms, and I allow, to be not demonstrably certain. But he further affirms, that it is not intuitively certain; in which I cannot agree with him. "All certainty," says he, "arises from the comparison of ideas, and from the discovery of such relations as are unalterable so long as the ideas continue the same; but the only relations of this kind are resemblance, proportion in quantity and number, degrees of any quality, and contrariety; none of which is implied in the maxim, *Whatever begins to exist, proceeds from some cause:*—that maxim therefore is not intuitively certain."—This argument, if it prove any thing at all, would prove, that the maxim is not even certain; for we are here told, that it has not that character or quality from which all certainty arises.

But, if I mistake not, both the premises of this syllogism are false. In the first place, I cannot admit, that all certainty arises from a comparison of ideas. I am certain of the existence of myself, and of the other things that affect my senses; I am certain, that "whatever is, is;" and yet I cannot conceive, that any comparison of ideas is necessary to produce these convictions in my mind. . . .

Secondly, I apprehend, that our author has not enumerated all the relations which, when discovered, give rise to certainty. I am certain, that I am the same person to-day I was yesterday. This indeed our author denies. I cannot help it; I am certain notwithstanding; and I flatter myself, there are not many persons in the world who would think this sentiment of mine a paradox. I say, then, I am certain, that I am the same person to-day I was yesterday. Now, the relation expressed in this proposition is not resemblance, nor proportion in quantity and number, nor degrees of any common quality, nor contrariety: it is a relation different from all these; it is identity or sameness. . . .

Again, that the foregoing maxim is neither intuitively nor demonstrably certain, our author attempts to prove from this consideration, that we cannot demonstrate the impossibility of the contrary. Nay, the contrary, he says, is not inconceivable: "For we can conceive an object non-existent this moment, and

6. Book I, part 3, sect. 3.

existent the next, without joining it to the idea of a cause, which is an idea altogether distinct and different." But this, I presume, is not a fair state of the case. Can we conceive a thing beginning to exist, and yet bring ourselves to think that a cause is not necessary to the production of such a thing? If we cannot, (I am sure I cannot), then is the contrary of this maxim, when fairly stated, found to be truly and properly inconceivable.

But whether the contrary of this maxim be inconceivable or not, the maxim itself may be intuitively certain. Of intuitive, as well as of demonstrable truths, there are different kinds. It is a character of some, that their contraries are inconceivable: such are the axioms of geometry. But of many other intuitive truths, the contraries are conceivable. "I do feel a hard body;"—"I do not feel a hard body;"—these propositions are equally conceivable: the first is true, for I have a pen between my fingers; but I cannot prove its truth by argument; therefore its truth is preceived intuitively. . . .

Section III.[7] Of Liberty and Necessity

. . . All ideas, according to Mr. Hume's fundamental hypothesis, are derived from and represent impressions: But we have never any impression that contains any power or efficacy: We never, therefore, have any idea of power. In proof of the minor proposition of this syllogism, he remarks, That

> When we think we perceive our mind acting on matter, or one piece of matter acting upon another, we do in fact perceive only two objects or events contiguous and successive, the second of which is always found in experience to follow the first; but that we never perceive, either by external sense, or by consciousness, that power, energy, or efficacy, which connects the one event with the other. By observing that the two events do always accompany each other, the imagination acquires a habit of going readily from the first to the second, and from the second to the first; and hence we are led to conceive a kind of necessary connection between them. But in fact there is neither necessity nor power in the objects we consider, but only in the mind that considers them; and even in the mind, this power of necessity is nothing but a determination of the fancy, acquired by habit, to pass from the idea of an object to that of its usual attendant.

So that what we call the efficacy of a cause to produce an effect, is neither in the cause nor in the effect, but only in the imagination, which has contracted a habit of passing from the object called the cause, to the object called the effect, and thus associating them together. Has the fire a power to melt lead? No; but the fancy is determined by habit to pass from the idea of fire to that of melted lead, on account of our having always perceived them contiguous and successive;—and this is the whole matter. Have I a power to move my arm? No; the volition that precedes the

---

7. Part II, Chapter II.

motion of my arm has no connection with that motion; but the motion having been always observed to follow the volition, comes to be associated with it in the fancy; and what we call the power, or necessary connection, has nothing to do, either with the volition, or with the motion, but is merely a determination of my fancy, or your fancy, or any body's fancy, to associate the idea or impression of my volition with the impression or idea of the motion of my arm.—I am sorry I cannot express myself more clearly; but I should not do justice to my author, if I did not imitate his language on the present occasion: plain words will never do, when one has an unintelligible doctrine to support.

What shall we say to this collection of strange phrases? or what name shall we give it? Shall we call it a most ingenious discovery, illustrated by a most ingenious argument? This would be complimenting the author at a very great expence; for this would imply, not only that he is the wisest of mortal men, but also that he is the only individual of that species of animals who is not a fool. Certain it is, that all men have in all ages talked, and argued, and acted, from a persuasion that they had a very distinct notion of power. If our author can prove, that they had no such notion, he can also prove, that all human discourse is nonsense, all human actions absurdity, and all human compositions (his own not excepted) words without meaning. The boldness of this theory will, however, pass with many, for a proof of its being ingenious. Be it so, Gentlemen, I dispute not about epithets; if you will have it, that genius consisteth in the art of putting words together so as to form absurd propositions, I have nothing more to say. Others will admire this doctrine, because the words by which the author means to illustrate and prove it, if printed on a good paper and with an elegant type, would of themselves make a pretty sizeable volume. It were pity to deprive these people of the pleasure of admiring; otherwise I might tell them, that nothing is more easy than this method of composition; for. that I would undertake, at a very short warning (if it could be done innocently, and without prejudice to my health), to write as many pages with equal appearance of reason and argument, and with equal advantage to philosophy and mankind, in vindication of any given absurdity; provided only, that (like the absurdity in question) it were expressed in words of which one at least is ambiguous.

In truth, I am so little disposed to admire this extraordinary paradox, that nothing could make me believe its author to have been in earnest, if I had not found him drawing inferences from it too serious to be jested with by any person who is not absolutely distracted. It is one of Mr. Hume's maxims, "That we can never have reason to believe, that any object, or quality of an object, exists, of which we cannot form an idea." But, according to this astonishing theory of power, and causation, "we have *no idea* of power, nor of a being endowed with any power, *much less* of one endowed with infinite power." The inference is but too glaring; and though our author does not plainly and avowedly express it, he once and again puts his reader in mind, that this inference, or something very like it, is deducible from his theory:—for which, no doubt, every friend to truth, virtue, and human nature, is infinitely obliged to him!

But what do you say in opposition to my theory? You affect to treat it with a contempt which hardly becomes you, and which my philosophy has not met with from your betters! pray let us hear your arguments.—And do you, Sir, really think it incumbent on me to prove by argument, that I, and all other men, have a notion of power; and that the efficacy of a cause (of fire, for instance, to melt lead) is in the cause, and not in my mind? Would you think it incumbent on me to confute you with arguments, if you were pleased to affirm, that all men have tails and cloven feet; and that it was I who produced the earthquake that destroyed Lisbon, the plague that depopulates Constantinople, the heat that scorches the wilds of Africa, and the cold that freezes the Hyperborean ocean? Truly, Sir, I have not the face to undertake a direct confutation of what I do not understand; and I am so far from comprehending this part of your system, that I will venture to pronounce it perfectly unintelligible. I know there are some who say they understand it; but I also know, that there are some who speak, and read, and write too, with very little expence of thought.

These are all but evasions, you exclaim; and insist on my coming to the point. Never fear, Sir; I am too deeply interested in some of the consequences of this theory of yours, to put you off with evasions. To come therefore to the point, I shall first state your doctrine in your own words, that there may be no risk of misrepresentation; and then, if I should not be able *directly* to prove it false (for the reason already given), I shall demonstrate, *indirectly* at least, or by the apagogical method, that it is not, and cannot be true.

> As the necessity which makes two times two equal to four, or three angles of a triangle equal to two right ones, lies only in the act of the understanding, by which we consider and compare these ideas[8]; in a like manner, the necessity or power which unites causes and effects, lies in the determination of the mind to pass from the one to the other. The efficacy, or energy, of causes, is neither placed in the causes themselves, nor in the Deity, nor in the concurrence of these two principles; but belongs entirely to the soul, which considers the union of two or more objects in all past instances. It is here that the real power of causes is placed, along with their connection and necessity.

To find that his principles lead to Atheism, would stagger an ordinary philosopher, and make him suspect his fundamental hypothesis, and all his subsequent reasonings. But the author now quoted is not apt to be staggered by considerations of this kind. On the contrary, he is so intoxicated with his discovery, that, however sceptical in other points, he seems willing to admit this as one certain conclusion.

If a man reconcile himself to Atheism, which is the greatest of all absurdities, I fear I shall hardly put him out of conceit with his doctrine, when I show him, that other less enormous absurdities are implied in it. We may make the trial however. Gentlemen are sometimes pleased to entertain unaccountable prejudices against their Maker; who yet, in other matters, where neither fashion nor hypothesis inter-

---

8. What! Is it an act of my understanding that makes two and two equal to four! Was it not so before I was born, and would it not be so though all intelligence were to cease throughout the universe!—But it is idle to spend time in confuting what every child who has learned the very first elements of science, knows to be absurd.

fere, condescend to acknowledge, that the good old distinction between truth and falsehood is not altogether without foundation.

On the supposition that we have no idea of power or energy, and that the preceding theory of causation is just, our author gives the following definition of a cause; which seems to be fairly deduced from his theory, and which he says is the best that he can give. "A cause is an object precedent and contiguous to another, and so united with it, that the idea of the one determines the mind to form the idea of the other, and the impression of the one to form a more lively idea of the other."[9] There are now in my view two contiguous houses, one of which was built last summer, and the other two years ago. By seeing them constantly together for several months, I find, that the idea of the one determines my mind to form the idea of the other, and the impression of the one to form a more lively idea of the other. So that, according to our author's definition, the one house is the cause, and the other the effect!—Again, day and night have always been contiguous and successive; the imagination naturally runs from the idea or impression of the one to the idea of the other: consequently, according to the same profound theory and definition, either day is the cause of night, or night the cause of day, just as we consider the one or the other to have been originally prior in time; that is, in other words, light is either the cause or the effect of darkness; and its being the one or the other depends entirely on my imagination! Let those admire this discovery who understand it.

Causation implies more than priority and contiguity of the cause to the effect. This relation cannot be conceived at all, without a supposition of power or energy in the cause. Let the reader recollect two things that stand related as cause and effect; let him contemplate them with a view to this relation; then let him conceive the cause divested of all power; and he must at the same instant conceive, that it is a cause no longer: for a cause divested of power, is divested of that by which it is a cause. If a man, after examining his notion of causation in this manner, is conscious that he has an idea of power, then I say he has that idea. If all men, in all ages, have used the word *power,* or something synonymous to it, and if all men know what they mean when they speak of power, I maintain, that all men have a notion, conception, or idea of power, in whatever way they came by it; and I also maintain, that no true philosopher ever denied the existence or reality of any thing, merely because he could not give an account of its origin, or because the opinion commonly received concerning its origin did not happen to quadrate with his system.

---

9. ... This is not the only definition of a cause which Mr. Hume has given. But his other definitions are all, in my opinion, inadequate; being all founded on the same absurd theory. My business, however, at present is, not to criticise Mr. Hume's definitions, but to confute (if I can) his licentious doctrines. These will be allowed to be absurd, if they be found to lead to absurd consequences. So Mr. Hume himself, in another place, very justly determines: "When any opinion leads into absurdities, it is certainly false." *Essay on Liberty and Necessity,* part 2.—The definition of a cause, here quoted, is a consequence drawn by Mr. Hume himself (and in my opinion fairly drawn) from his theory of power and causation By proving that consequence to be absurd, I prove (according to Mr. Hume's own rules of logic) the absurdity of the opinion that leads to it. This is all that I mean by quoting it; and this I presume is enough. A doctrine is sufficiently confuted, if it be shown to lead into *one absurdity.*

KANT

Prolegomena to Any Future Metaphysics*

Introduction

Since the *Essays* of Locke and Leibniz, or rather since the origin of metaphysics so far as we know its history, nothing has ever happened which was more decisive to its fate than the attack made upon it by David Hume. He threw no light on this species of knowledge, but he certainly struck a spark from which light might have been obtained, had it caught some inflammable substance and had its smouldering fire been carefully nursed and developed.

Hume started from a single but important concept in Metaphysics, viz., that of Cause and Effect (including its derivatives force and action, etc.). He challenges reason, which pretends to have given birth to this idea from herself, to answer him by what right she thinks anything to be so constituted, that if that thing be posited, something else also must necessarily be posited; for this is the meaning of the concept of cause. He demonstrated irrefutably that it was perfectly impossible for reason to think *a priori* and by means of concepts a combination involving necessity. We cannot at all see why, in consequence of the existence of one thing, another must necessarily exist, or how the concept of such a combination can arise *a priori*. Hence he inferred, that reason was altogether deluded with reference to this concept, which she erroneously considered as one of her children, whereas in reality it was nothing but a bastard of imagination, impregnated by experience, which subsumed certain representations under the Law of Association, and mistook the subjective necessity of habit for an objective necessity arising from insight. Hence he inferred that reason had no power to think such combinations, even generally, because her concepts would then be purely fictitious, and all her pretended *a priori* cognitions nothing but common experiences marked with a false stamp. In plain language there is not, and cannot be, any such thing as metaphysics at all. [10]

However hasty and mistaken Hume's conclusion may appear, it was at least founded upon investigation, and this investigation deserved the concentrated attention of the brighter spirits of his day as well as determined efforts on their part to

---

*From Immanuel Kant, *Prolegomena To Any Future Metaphysics*, edited in English by Paul Carus, 1902.

10. Nevertheless Hume called this very destructive science metaphysics and attached to it great value. Metaphysics and morals [he declares in the fourth part of his Essays] are the most important branches of science; mathematics and physics are not nearly so important. But the acute man merely regarded the negative use arising from the moderation of extravagant claims of speculative reason, and the complete settlement of the many endless and troublesome controversies that mislead mankind. He overlooked the positive injury which results, if reason be deprived of its most important prospects, which can alone supply to the will the highest aim for all its endeavor.

discover, if possible, a happier solution of the problem in the sense proposed by him, all of which would have speedily resulted in a complete reform of the science.

But Hume suffered the usual misfortune of metaphysicians, of not being understood. It is positively painful to see how utterly his opponents, Reid, Oswald, Beattie, and lastly Priestley, missed the point of the problem; for while they were ever taking for granted that which he doubted, and demonstrating with zeal and often with impudence that which he never thought of doubting, they so misconstrued his valuable suggestion that everything remained in its old condition, as if nothing had happened.

The question was not whether the concept of cause was right, useful, and even indispensable for our knowledge of nature, for this Hume had never doubted; but whether that concept could be thought by reason *a priori,* and consequently whether it possessed an inner truth, independent of all experience, implying a wider application than merely to the objects of experience. This was Hume's problem. It was a question concerning the *origin,* not concerning the *indispensable need* of the concept. Were the former decided, the conditions of the use and the sphere of its valid application would have been determined as a matter of course.

But to satisfy the conditions of the problem, the opponents of the great thinker should have penetrated very deeply into the nature of reason, so far as it is concerned with pure thinking,—a task which did not suit them. They found a more convenient method of being defiant without any insight, viz., the appeal to *common sense.* It is indeed a great gift of God, to possess right, or (as they now call it) plain common sense. But this common sense must be shown practically, by well-considered and reasonable thoughts and words, not by appealing to it as an oracle, when no rational justification can be advanced. To appeal to common sense, when insight and science fail, and no sooner—this is one of the subtle discoveries of modern times, by means of which the most superficial ranter can safely enter the lists with the most thorough thinker, and hold his own. But as long as a particle of insight remains, no one would think of having recourse to this subterfuge. For what is it but an appeal to the opinion of the multitude, of whose applause the philosopher is ashamed, while the popular charlatan glories and confides in it? I should think that Hume might fairly have laid as much claim to common sense as Beattie, and in addition to a critical reason (such as the latter did not possess), which keeps common sense in check and prevents it from speculating, or, if speculations are under discussion, restrains the desire to decide because it cannot satisfy itself concerning its own arguments. By this means alone can common sense remain sound. Chisels and hammers may suffice to work a piece of wood, but for steel-engraving we require an engraver's needle. Thus common sense and speculative understanding are each serviceable in their own way, the former in judgments which apply immediately to experience, the latter when we judge universally from mere concepts, as in metaphysics, where sound common sense, so called in spite of the inapplicability of the word, has no right to judge at all.

I openly confess, the suggestion of David Hume was the very thing, which many years ago first interrupted my dogmatic slumber, and gave my investigations in the field of speculative philosophy quite a new direction. I was far from following him in the conclusions at which he arrived by regarding, not the whole of his problem, but a part, which by itself can give us no information. If we start from a well-founded, but undeveloped, thought, which another has bequeathed to us, we may well hope by continued reflection to advance farther than the acute man, to whom we owe the first spark of light.

I therefore first tried whether Hume's objection could not be put into a general form, and soon found that the concept of the connexion of cause and effect was by no means the only idea by which the understanding thinks the connexion of things *a priori,* but rather that metaphysics consists altogether of such connexions. I sought to ascertain their number, and when I had satisfactorily succeeded in this by starting from a single principle, I proceeded to the deduction of these concepts, which I was now certain were not deduced from experience, as Hume had apprehended, but sprang from the pure understanding. This deduction (which seemed impossible to my acute predecessor, which had never even occurred to any one else, though no one had hesitated to use the concepts without investigating the basis of their objective validity) was the most difficult task ever undertaken in the service of metaphysics; and the worst was that metaphysics, such as it then existed, could not assist me in the least, because this deduction alone can render metaphysics possible. But as soon as I had succeeded in solving Hume's problem not merely in a particular case, but with respect to the whole faculty of pure reason, I could proceed safely, though slowly, to determine the whole sphere of pure reason completely and from general principles, in its circumference as well as in its contents. This was required for metaphysics in order to construct its system according to a reliable method.

But I fear that the execution of Hume's problem in its widest extent (viz., my *Critique of the Pure Reason*) will fare as the problem itself fared, when first proposed. It will be misjudged because it is misunderstood, and misunderstood because men choose to skim through the book, and not to think through it—a disagreeable task, because the work is dry, obscure, opposed to all ordinary notions, and moreover long-winded. I confess, however, I did not expect to hear from philosophers complaints of want of popularity, entertainment, and facility, when the existence of a highly prized and indispensable cognition is at stake, which cannot be established otherwise than by .the strictest rules of methodic precision. Popularity may follow, but is inadmissible at the beginning. Yet as regards a certain obscurity, arising partly from the diffuseness of the plan, owing to which the principal points of the investigation are easily lost sight of, the complaint is just, and I intend to remove it by the present *Prolegomena.*

The first-mentioned work, which discusses the pure faculty of reason in its whole compass and bounds, will remain the foundation, to which the *Prolegomena,* as a preliminary exercise, refer; for our critique must first be established as a complete and perfected science, before we can think of letting Metaphysics appear on the scene, or even have the most distant hope of attaining it.

We have been long accustomed to seeing antiquated knowledge produced as new by taking it out of its former context, and reducing it to a system in a new suit of any fancy pattern under new titles. Most readers will set out by expecting nothing else from the *Critique;* but these *Prolegomena* may persuade him that it is a perfectly new science, of which no one has ever even thought, the very idea of which was unknown, and for which nothing hitherto accomplished can be of the smallest use, except it be the suggestion of Hume's doubts. Yet even he did not suspect such a formal science, but ran his ship ashore, for safety's sake, landing on scepticism, there to let it lie and rot; whereas my object is rather to give it a pilot, who, by means of safe astronomical principles drawn from a knowledge of the globe, and provided with a complete chart and compass, may steer the ship safely, whither he listeth.

If in a new science, which is wholly isolated and unique in its kind, we started with the prejudice that we can judge of things by means of our previously acquired knowledge, which is precisely what has first to be called in question, we should only fancy we saw everywhere what we had already known, the expressions, having a similar sound, only that all would appear utterly metamorphosed, senseless and unintelligible, because we should have as a foundation our own notions, made by long habit a second nature, instead of the author's. But the longwindedness of the work, so far as it depends on the subject, and not the exposition, its consequent unavoidable dryness and its scholastic precision are qualities which can only benefit the science, though they may discredit the book.

Few writers are gifted with the subtilty, and at the same time with the grace, of David Hume, or with the depth, as well as the elegance, of Moses Mendelssohn. Yet I flatter myself I might have made my own exposition popular, had my object been merely to sketch out a plan and leave its completion to others, instead of having my heart in the welfare of the science, to which I had devoted myself so long; in truth, it required no little constancy, and even self-denial, to postpone the sweets of an immediate success to the prospect of a slower, but more lasting, reputation.

Making plans is often the occupation of an opulent and boastful mind, which thus obtains the reputation of a creative genius, by demanding what it cannot itself supply; by censuring, what it cannot improve; and by proposing, what it knows not where to find. And yet something more should belong to a sound plan of a general critique of pure reason than mere conjectures, if this plan is to be other than the usual declamations of pious aspirations. But pure reason is a sphere so separate and self-contained, that we cannot touch a part without affecting all the rest. We can therefore do nothing without first determining the position of each part, and its relation to the rest; for, as our judgment cannot be corrected by anything without, the validity and use of every part depends upon the relation in which it stands to all the rest within the domain of reason.

So in the structure of an organized body, the end of each member can only be deduced from the full conception of the whole. It may, then, be said of such a critique that it is never trustworthy except it be perfectly complete, down to the smallest elements of pure reason. In the sphere of this faculty you can determine either everything or nothing.

But although a mere sketch, preceding the *Critique of Pure Reason,* would be unintelligible, unreliable, and useless, it is all the more useful as a sequel. For so we are able to grasp the whole, to examine in detail the chief points of importance in the science, and to improve in many respects our exposition, as compared with the first execution of the work.

After the completion of the work I offer here such a plan which is sketched out after an analytical method, while the work itself had to be executed in the synthetical style, in order that the science may present all its articulations, as the structure of a peculiar cognitive faculty, in their natural combination. But should any reader find this plan, which I publish as the *Prolegomena to any future Metaphysics,* still obscure, let him consider that not every one is bound to study Metaphysics, that many minds will succeed very well, in the exact and even in deep sciences, more closely allied to practical experience,[11] while they cannot succeed in investigations dealing exclusively with abstract concepts. In such cases men should apply their talents to other subjects. But he who undertakes to judge, or still more, to construct, a system of Metaphysics, must satisfy the demands here made, either by adopting my solution, or by thoroughly refuting it, and substituting another. To evade it is impossible. . . .

Prolegomena

Preamble on the Peculiarities
of All Metaphysical Cognition

§1. *Of the Sources of Metaphysics*

If it becomes desirable to formulate any cognition as science, it will be necessary first to determine accurately those peculiar features which no other science has in common with it, constituting its characteristics; otherwise the boundaries of all sciences become confused, and none of them can be treated thoroughly according to its nature.

The characteristics of a science may consist of a simple difference of object, or of the sources of cognition, or of the kind of cognition, or perhaps of all three conjointly. On this, therefore, depends the idea of a possible science and its territory.

First, as concerns the sources of metaphysical cognition, its very concept implies that they cannot be empirical. Its principles (including not only its maxims but its basic notions) must never be derived from experience. It must not be physical but metaphysical knowledge, viz., knowledge lying beyond experience. It can therefore have for its basis neither external experience, which is the source of physics proper, nor internal, which is the basis of empirical psychology. It is therefore *a priori* knowledge, coming from pure Understanding and pure Reason.

But so far Metaphysics would not be distinguishable from pure Mathematics; it must therefore be called pure philosophical cognition; and for the meaning of this term I refer to the *Critique of the Pure Reason* (II. "Method of Transcendentalism," Chap. I., Sec. i), where the distinction between these two employments of the reason is sufficiently explained. So far concerning the sources of metaphysical cognition.

---

11. The term *Anschauung* here used means sense-perception. It is that which is given to the senses and apprehended immediately, as an object is seen by merely looking at it. The translation *intuition,* though etymologically correct, is misleading. In the present passage the term is not used in its technical ·ignificance but means "practical experience."–Carus.

§2. Concerning the Kind of Cognition
which can alone be called Metaphysical

a. Of the Distinction between Analytical and Synthetical Judgments in general. —
The peculiarity of its sources demands that metaphysical cognition must consist of
nothing but *a priori* judgments. But whatever be their origin, or their logical form,
there is a distinction in judgments, as to their content, according to which they are
either merely explicative, adding nothing to the content of the cognition, or expan-
sive, increasing the given cognition: the former may be called analytical, the latter
synthetical, judgments.

Analytical judgments express nothing in the predicate but what has been
already actually thought in the concept of the subject, though not so distinctly or
with the same (full) consciousness. When I say: *All bodies are extended,* I have not
amplified in the least my concept of body, but have only analysed it, as extension
was really thought to belong to that concept before the judgment was made,
though it was not expressed; this judgment is therefore analytical. On the contrary,
this judgment, *All bodies have weight,* contains in its predicate something not
actually thought in the general concept of the body; it amplifies my knowledge by
adding something to my concept, and must therefore be called synthetical.

*b. The Common Principle of all Analytical Judgments is the Law of Contra-
diction.* — All analytical judgments depend wholly on the law of Contradiction, and
are in their nature *a priori* cognitions, whether the concepts that supply them with
matter be empirical or not. For the predicate of an affirmative analytical judgment
is already contained in the concept of the subject, of which it cannot be denied
without contradiction. In the same way its opposite is necessarily denied of the
subject in an analytical, but negative, judgment, by the same law of contradiction.
Such is the nature of the judgments: *all bodies are extended,* and *no bodies are
unextended* (i.e., *simple*).

For this very reason all analytical judgments are *a priori* even when the
concepts are empirical, as, for example, *Gold is a yellow metal*; for to know this I
require no experience beyond my concept of gold as a yellow metal: it is, in fact,
the very concept, and I need only analyse it, without looking beyond it elsewhere.

*c. Synthetical Judgments require a different Principle from the Law of Con-
tradiction.* — There are synthetical *a posteriori* judgments of empirical origin; but
there are also others which are proved to be certain *a priori,* and which spring from
pure Understanding and Reason. Yet they both agree in this, that they cannot
possibly spring from the principle of analysis, viz., the law of contradiction, alone;
they require a quite different principle, though, from whatever they may be deduced, they must be subject to the law of contradiction, which must never be
violated, even though everything cannot be deduced from it. I shall first classify
synthetical judgments.

1. Empirical Judgments are always synthetical. For it would be absurd to base
an analytical judgment on experience, as our concept suffices for the purpose

without requiring any testimony from experience. That body is extended, is a judgment established *a priori,* and not an empirical judgment. For before appealing to experience, we already have all the conditions of the judgment in the concept, from which we have but to elicit the predicate according to the law of contradiction, and thereby to become conscious of the necessity of the judgment, which experience could not even teach us.

2. Mathematical Judgments are all synthetical. This fact seems hitherto to have altogether escaped the observation of those who have analysed human reason; it even seems directly opposed to all their conjectures, though incontestably certain, and most important in its consequences. For as it was found that the conclusions of mathematicians all proceed according to the law of contradiction (as is demanded by all apodeictic certainty), men persuaded themselves that the fundamental principles were known from the same law. This was a great mistake, for a synthetical proposition can indeed be comprehended according to the law of contradiction, but only by presupposing another synthetical proposition from which it follows, but never in itself.

First of all, we must observe that all proper mathematical judgments are *a priori,* and not empirical, because they carry with them necessity, which cannot be obtained from experience. But if this be not conceded to me, very good; I shall confine my assertion to *pure Mathematics,* the very notion of which implies that it contains pure *a priori* and not empirical cognitions.

It must at first be thought that the proposition 7 + 5 = 12 is a mere analytical judgment, following from the concept of the sum of seven and five, according to the law of contradiction. But on closer examination it appears that the concept of the sum of 7 + 5 contains merely their union in a single number, without its being at all thought what the particular number is that unites them. The concept of twelve is by no means thought by merely thinking of the combination of seven and five; and analyse this possible sum as we may, we shall not discover twelve in the concept. We must go beyond these concepts, by calling to our aid some concrete image (*Anschauung*), i.e., either our five fingers, or five points (as Segner has it in his Arithmetic), and we must add successively the units of the five, given in some concrete image (*Anschauung*), to the concept of seven. Hence our concept is really amplified by the proposition 7 + 5 = 12, and we add to the first a second, not thought in it. Arithmetical judgments are therefore synthetical, and the more plainly according as we take larger numbers; for in such cases it is clear that, however closely we analyse our concepts without calling visual images (*Anschauung*) to our aid, we can never find the sum by such mere dissection.

All principles of geometry are no less analytical. That a straight line is the shortest path between two points, is a synthetical proposition. For my concept of straight contains nothing of quantity, but only a quality. The attribute of shortness is therefore altogether additional, and cannot be obtained by any analysis of the concept. Here, too, visualisation (*Anschauung*) must come to aid us. It alone makes the synthesis possible.

Some other principles, assumed by geometers, are indeed actually analytical, and depend on the law of contradiction; but they only serve, as identical propositions, as a method of concatenation, and not as principles, e.g., $a = a$, the whole is equal to itself, or $a + b > a$, the whole is greater than its part. And yet even these, though they are recognised as valid from mere concepts, are only admitted in mathematics, because they can be represented in some visual form (*Anschauung*). What usually makes us believe that the predicate of such apodeictic[12] judgments is already contained in our concept, and that the judgment is therefore analytical, is the duplicity of the expression, requesting us to think a certain predicate as of necessity implied in the thought of a given concept, which necessity attaches to the concept. But the question is not what we are requested to join in thought *to* the given concept, but what we actually think together with and in it, though obscurely; and so it appears that the predicate belongs to these concepts necessarily indeed, yet not directly but indirectly by an added visualisation (*Anschauung*).[13]

The essential and distinguishing feature of pure mathematical cognition among all other *a priori* cognitions is, that it cannot at all proceed from concepts, but only by means of the construction of concepts (see *Critique* II., Method of Transcendentalism, chap. I., sect. I). As therefore in its judgments it must proceed beyond the concept to that which its corresponding visualisation (*Anschauung*) contains, these judgments neither can, nor ought to, arise analytically, by dissecting the concept, but are all synthetical.

I cannot refrain from pointing out the disadvantage resulting to philosophy from the neglect of this easy and apparently insignificant observation. Hume being prompted (a task worthy of a philosopher) to cast his eye over the whole field of *a priori* cognitions in which human understanding claims such mighty possessions, heedlessly severed from it a whole, and indeed its most valuable, province, viz., pure mathematics; for he thought its nature, or, so to speak, the state-constitution of this empire, depended on totally different principles, namely, on the law of contradiction alone; and although he did not divide judgments in this manner formally and universally as I have done here, what he said was equivalent to this: that mathematics contains only analytical, but metaphysics synthetical, *a priori* judgments. In this, however, he was greatly mistaken, and the mistake had a decidedly injurious effect upon his whole conception. But for this, he would have extended his question concerning the origin of our synthetical judgments far beyond the metaphysical concept of Causality, and included in it the possibility of mathematics *a priori* also, for this latter he must have assumed to be equally synthetical. And then he could not have based his metaphysical judgments on mere experience without subjecting the axioms of mathematics equally to experience, a thing which he was far too acute to do. The good company into which metaphysics would thus have been brought, would have saved it from the danger of a contemptuous ill-treatment, for the thrust intended for it must have reached mathematics, which was

---

12. The term *apodeictic* is borrowed by Kant from Aristotle who uses it in the sense of "certain beyond dispute." The word is . . . contrasted to dialectic propositions, i.e., such statements as admit of controversy.—Carus.

13. The following five paragraphs from section four have been inserted here in accordance with a revision first proposed by Hans Vaihinger and concurred in by later translators Carl J. Friedrich and Lewis W. Beck. Paul Carus did not reorder the passages in this way, but it appears reasonable to do so.—P.E.D.

not and could not have been Hume's intention. Thus that acute man would have been led into considerations which must needs be similar to those that now occupy us, but which would have gained inestimably by his inimitably elegant style.

[3.] Metaphysical Judgments, properly so called, are all synthetical. We must distinguish judgments pertaining to metaphysics from metaphysical judgments properly so called. Many of the former are analytical, but they only afford the means for metaphysical judgments, which are the whole end of the science, and which are always synthetical. For if there be concepts pertaining to metaphysics (as, for example, that of substance), the judgments springing from simple analysis of them also pertain to metaphysics, as, for example, substance is that which only exists as subject; and by means of several such analytical judgments, we seek to approach the definition of the concept. But as the analysis of a pure concept of the understanding pertaining to metaphysics, does not proceed in any different manner from the dissection of any other, even empirical, concepts, not pertaining to metaphysics (such as: air is an elastic fluid, the elasticity of which is not destroyed by any known degree of cold), it follows that the concept indeed, but not the analytical judgment, is properly metaphysical. This science has something peculiar in the production of its *a priori* cognitions, which must therefore be distinguished from the features it has in common with other rational knowledge. Thus the judgment, that all the substance in things is permanent, is a synthetical and properly metaphysical judgment.

If the *a priori* principles, which constitute the materials of metaphysics, have first been collected according to fixed principles, then their analysis will be of great value; it might be taught as a particular part (as a *philosophia definitiva*), containing nothing but analytical judgments pertaining to metaphysics, and could be treated separately from the synthetical which constitute metaphysics proper. For indeed these analyses are not elsewhere of much value, except in metaphysics, i.e., as regards the synthetical judgments, which are to be generated by these previously analysed concepts.

The conclusion drawn in this section then is, that metaphysics is properly concerned with synthetical propositions *a priori,* and these alone constitute its end, for which it indeed requires various dissections of its concepts, viz., of its analytical judgments, but wherein the procedure is not different from that in every other kind of knowledge, in which we merely seek to render our concepts distinct by analysis. But the generation of *a priori* cognition by concrete images as well as by concepts, in fine of synthetical propositions *a priori* in philosophical cognition, constitutes the essential subject of Metaphysics.

§3. *A Remark on the General Division
of Judgments into Analytical and Synthetical*

This division is indispensable, as concerns the critique of human understanding, and therefore deserves to be called classical, though otherwise it is of little use, but this is the reason why dogmatic philosophers, who always seek the sources of metaphysical judgments in Metaphysics itself, and not apart from it, in the pure laws of reason generally, altogether neglected this apparently obvious distinction. Thus the celebrated Wolff, and his acute follower Baumgarten, came to seek the proof of the principle of Sufficient Reason, which is clearly synthetical, in the principle of Contradiction. In Locke's *Essay,* however, I find an indication of my division. For in the fourth book (chap. iii. §9, seq.), having discussed the various connexions of representations in judgments, and their sources, one of which he makes "identity and contradiction" (analytical judgments), and another the coexistence of representations in a subject, he confesses (§ 10) that our *a priori* knowledge of the latter is very narrow, and almost nothing. But in his remarks on this species of cognition, there is so little of what is definite, and reduced to rules, that we cannot wonder if no one, not even Hume, was led to make investigations concerning this sort of judgments. For such general and yet definite principles are not easily learned from other men, who have had them obscurely in their minds. We must hit on them first by our own reflexion, then we find them elsewhere, where we could not possibly have found them at first, because the authors themselves did not know that such an idea lay at the basis of their observations. Men who never think independently have nevertheless the acuteness to discover everything, after it has been once shown them, in what was said long since, though no one ever saw it there before.

§ 4. The General Question of the Prolegomena— Is Metaphysics at all Possible?

Were a metaphysics, which could maintain its place as a science, really in existence; could we say, "Here is metaphysics, learn it, and it will convince you irresistibly and irrevocably of its truth"; this question would be useless, and there would only remain that other question (which would rather be a test of our acuteness, than a proof of the existence of the thing itself), "How is the science possible, and how does reason come to attain it?" But human reason has not been so fortunate in this case. There is no single book to which you can point as you do to Euclid, and say: "This is Metaphysics; here you may find the noblest objects of this science, the knowledge of a highest Being, and of a future existence, proved from principles of pure reason." We can be shown indeed many judgments, demonstrably certain, and never questioned; but these are all analytical, and rather concern the materials and the scaffolding for Metaphysics, than the extension of knowledge, which is our proper object in studying it (§ 2). Even supposing you produce synthetical judgments (such as the law of Sufficient Reason, which you have never proved, as you ought to, from pure reason *a priori,* though we gladly concede its truth), you lapse when they come to be employed for your principal object, into such doubtful assertions, that in all ages one Metaphysics has contradicted another, either in its assertions, or their proofs, and thus has itself destroyed its own claim to lasting assent. Nay, the very attempts to set up such a science are the main cause of the early appearance of scepticism, a mental attitude in which reason treats itself with such violence that it could never have arisen save from complete despair of ever satisfying our most important aspirations. For long before men began to inquire into nature methodically, they consulted abstract reason, which had to some extent been exercised by means of ordinary experience; for reason is ever present, while laws of nature must usually be discovered with labor. So Metaphysics floated to the surface, like foam, which dissolved the moment it was scooped off. But immediately there appeared a new supply on the surface, to be ever eagerly gathered up by some, while others, instead of seeking in the depths the cause of the phenomenon, thought they showed their wisdom by ridiculing the idle labor of their neighbors. . . .

But it happens fortunately, that though we cannot assume metaphysics to be an actual science, we can say with confidence that certain pure *a priori* synthetical cognitions, pure Mathematics and pure Physics are actual and given; for both contain propositions, which are thoroughly recognised as apodeictically certain, partly by mere reason, partly by general consent arising from experience, and yet as independent of experience. We have therefore some at least uncontested synthetical knowledge *a priori,* and need not ask *whether* it be possible, for it is actual, but *how* it is possible, in order that we may deduce from the principle which makes the given cognitions possible the possibility of all the rest.

§5. The General Problem: How is Cognition from Pure Reason Possible?

We have above learned the significant distinction between analytical and synthetical judgments. The possibility of analytical propositions was easily comprehended, being entirely founded on the law of contradiction. The possibility of synthetical *a posteriori* judgments, of those which are gathered from experience, also requires no particular explanation; for experience is nothing but a continual synthesis of perceptions. There remain therefore only synthetical propositions *a priori,* of which the possibility must be sought or investigated, because they must depend upon other principles than the law of contradiction.

But here we need not first establish the possibility of such propositions so as to ask whether they are possible. For there are enough of them which indeed are of undoubted certainty, and as our present method is analytical, we shall start from the fact, that such synthetical but purely rational cognition actually exists; but we must now inquire into the reason of this possibility, and ask, *how* such cognition is possible, in order that we may from the principles of its possibility be enabled to determine the conditions of its use, its sphere and its limits. The proper problem upon which all depends, when expressed with scholastic precision, is therefore: *How are Synthetic Propositions* a priori *possible?* . . .

Metaphysics stands or falls with the solution of this problem: its very existence depends upon it. Let any one make metaphysical assertions with ever so much plausibility, let him overwhelm us with conclusions, if he has not previously proved able to answer this question satisfactorily, I have a right to say: This is all vain baseless philosophy and false wisdom. You speak through pure reason, and claim, as it were to create cognitions *a priori* by not only dissecting given concepts, but also by asserting connexions which do not rest upon the law of contradiction, and which you believe you conceive quite independently of all experience; how do you arrive at this, and how will you justify your pretensions? An appeal to the consent of the common sense of mankind cannot be allowed; for that is a witness whose authority depends merely upon rumor. Says Horace:

Quodcunque ostendis mihi sic, incredulus odi. (To all that which thou provest me thus, I refuse to give credence.)

The answer to this question, though indispensable, is difficult; and though the principal reason that it was not made long ago is, that the possibility of the question never occurred to anybody, there is yet another reason, which is this that a satisfactory answer to this one question requires a much more persistent, profound, and painstaking reflexion, than the most diffuse work on Metaphysics, which on its first appearance promised immortality to its author. And every intelligent reader, when he carefully reflects what this problem requires, must at first be struck with its difficulty, and would regard it as insoluble and even impossible, did there not actually exist pure synthetical cognitions *a priori.* This actually happened to David Hume, though he did not conceive the question in its entire universality as is done here, and as must be done, should the answer be decisive for all Metaphysics. For how is it possible, says that acute man, that when a concept is given me, I can go beyond it and connect with it another, which is not contained in it, in such a manner as if the latter necessarily belonged to the former? Nothing but experience can furnish us with such connexions (thus he concluded from the difficulty which he took to be an impossibility), and all that vaunted necessity, or, what is the same thing, all cognition assumed to be *a priori,* is nothing but a long habit of accepting something as true, and hence of mistaking subjective necessity for objective.

Should my reader complain of the difficulty and the trouble which I occasion him in the solution of this problem, he is at liberty to solve it himself in an easier way. Perhaps he will then feel under obligation to the person who has undertaken for him a labor of so profound research, and will rather be surprised at the facility with which, considering the nature of the subject, the solution has been attained. Yet it has cost years of work to solve the problem in its whole universality (using the term in the mathematical sense, viz., for that which is sufficient for all cases), and finally to exhibit it in the analytical form, as the reader finds it here.

All metaphysicians are therefore solemnly and legally suspended from their occupations till they shall have answered in a satisfactory manner the question, "How are synthetic cognitions *a priori* possible?" For the answer contains the only credentials which they must show when they have anything to offer in the name of pure reason. But if they do not possess these credentials, they can expect nothing else of reasonable people, who have been deceived so often, than to be dismissed without further ado. . . .

As we now proceed to this solution according to the analytical method, in which we assume that such cognitions from pure reasons actually exist, we can only appeal to two sciences of theoretical cognition (which alone is under consideration here), pure mathematics and pure natural science (physics). For these alone can exhibit to us objects in a definite and actualisable form (*in der Anschauung*), and consequently (if there should occur in them a cognition *a priori*) can show the truth or conformity of the cognition to the object *in concreto,* that is, its actuality, from which we could proceed to the reason of its possibility by the analytic method. This facilitates our work greatly, for here universal considerations are not only applied to facts, but even start from them, while in a synthetic procedure they must strictly be derived *in abstracto* from concepts. . . .

First Part of the
Transcendental Problem

How Is Pure Mathematics Possible?

§6. Here is a great and established branch of knowledge, encompassing even now a wonderfully large domain and promising an unlimited extension in the future. Yet it carries with it thoroughly apodeictical certainty, i.e., absolute necessity, which therefore rests upon no empirical grounds. Consequently it is a pure product of reason, and moreover is thoroughly synthetical. [Here the question arises:]

"How then is it possible for human reason to produce a cognition of this nature entirely *a priori?*"

Does not this faculty [which produces mathematics], as it neither is nor can be based upon experience, presuppose some ground of cognition *a priori,* which lies deeply hidden, but which might reveal itself by these its effects, if their first beginnings were but diligently ferreted out?

§7. But we find that all mathematical cognition has this peculiarity: it must first exhibit its concept in a visual form (*Anschauung*) and indeed *a priori,* therefore in a visual form which is not empirical, but pure. Without this mathematics cannot take a single step; hence its judgments are always visual, viz., "intuitive"; whereas philosophy must be satisfied with discursive judgments from mere concepts, and though it may illustrate its doctrines through a visual figure, can never derive them from it. This observation on the nature of mathematics gives us a clue to the first and highest condition of its possibility, which is, that some non-sensuous visualisation (called pure intuition, or *reine Anschauung*) must form its basis, in which all its concepts can be exhibited or constructed, *in concreto* and yet *a priori.* If we can find out this pure intuition and its possibility, we may thence easily explain how synthetical propositions *a priori* are possible in pure mathematics, and consequently how this science itself is possible. Empirical intuition [viz., sense-perception] enables us without difficulty to enlarge the concept which we frame of an object of intuition [or sense-perception], by new predicates, which intuition [i.e., sense-perception] itself presents synthetically in experience. Pure intuition [viz., the visualisation of forms in our imagination, from which every thing sensual, i.e., every thought of material qualities, is excluded] does so likewise, only with this difference, that in the latter case the synthetical judgment is *a priori* certain and apodeictical, in the former, only *a posteriori* and empirically certain; because this latter contains only that which occurs in contingent empirical intuition, but the former, that which must necessarily be discovered in pure intuition. Here intuition, being an intuition *a priori,* is *before all experience,* viz., before any perception of particular objects, inseparably conjoined with its concept.

§8. But with this step our perplexity seems rather to increase than to lessen. For the question now is, "How is it possible to intuite [in a visual form] anything *a priori?"* An intuition [viz., a visual sense-perception] is such a representation as immediately depends upon the presence of the object. Hence it seems impossible to intuite from the outset *a priori,* because intuition would in that event take place without either a former or a present object to refer to, and by consequence could not be intuition. Concepts indeed are such, that we can easily form some of them *a priori,* viz., such as contain nothing but the thought of an object in general; and we need not find ourselves in an immediate relation to the object. Take, for instance, the concepts of Quantity, of Cause, etc. But even these require, in order to make them understood, a certain concrete use—that is, an application to some sense-experience (*Anschauung*), by which an object of them is given us. But how can the intuition of the object [its visualisation] precede the object itself?

§9. If our intuition [i.e., our sense-experience] were perforce of such a nature as to represent things as they are in themselves, there would not be any intuition *a priori,* but intuition would be always empirical. For I can only know what is contained in the object in itself when it is present and given to me. It is indeed even then incomprehensible how the visualisation (*Anschauung*) of a present thing should make me know this thing as it is in itself, as its properties cannot migrate into my faculty of representation. But even granting this possibility, a visualising of that sort would not take place *a priori,* that is, before the object were presented to me; for without this latter fact no reason of a relation between my representation and the object can be imagined, unless it depend upon a direct inspiration.

*Therefore in one way only can my intuition (*Anschauung*) anticipate the actuality of the object, and be a cognition* a priori, *viz.: if my intuition contains nothing but the form of sensibility, antedating in my subjectivity all the actual impressions through which I am affected by objects.*

For that objects of sense can only be intuited according to this form of sensibility I can know *a priori.* Hence it follows: that propositions, which concern this form of sensuous intuition only, are possible and valid for objects of the senses; as also, conversely, that intuitions which are possible *a priori* can never concern any other things than objects of our senses.

§10. Accordingly, it is only the form of sensuous intuition by which we can intuite things *a priori,* but by which we can know objects only as they *appear* to us (to our senses), not as they are in themselves; and this assumption is absolutely necessary if synthetical propositions *a priori* be granted as possible, or if, in case they actually occur, their possibility is to be comprehended and determined beforehand.

Now, the intuitions which pure mathematics lays at the foundation of all its cognitions and judgments which appear at once apodeictic and necessary are Space and Time. For mathematics must first have all its concepts in intuition, and pure mathematics in pure intuition, that is, it must construct them. If it proceeded in any other way, it would be impossible to make any headway, for mathematics proceeds, not analytically by dissection of concepts, but synthetically, and if pure intuition be wanting, there is nothing in which the matter for synthetical judgments *a priori* can be given. Geometry is based upon the pure intuition of space. Arithmetic accomplishes its concept of number by the successive addition of units in time; and pure mechanics especially cannot attain its concepts of motion without employing the representation of time. Both representations, however, are only intuitions; for if we omit from the empirical intuitions of bodies and their alterations (motion) everything empirical, or belonging to sensation, space and time still remain, which are therefore pure intuitions that lie *a priori* at the basis of the empirical. Hence they can never be omitted, but at the same time, by their being pure intuitions *a priori,* they prove that they are mere forms of our sensibility, which must precede all empirical intuition, or perception of actual objects, and conformably to which objects can be known *a priori*, but only as they appear to us.

§11. The problem of the present section is therefore solved. Pure mathematics, as synthetical cognition *a priori,* is only possibly by referring to no other objects than those of the senses. At the basis of their empirical intuition lies a pure intuition (of space and of time) which is *a priori.* This is possible, because the latter intuition is nothing but the mere form of sensibility, which precedes the actual appearance of the objects, in that it, in fact, makes them possible. Yet this faculty of intuiting *a priori* affects not the matter of the phenomenon (that is, the sense-element in it, for this constitutes that which is empirical), but its form, viz., space and time. Should any man venture to doubt that these are determinations adhering not to things in themselves, but to their relation to our sensibility, I should be glad to know how it can be possible to know the constitution of things *a priori*, viz., before we have any acquaintance with them and before they are presented to us. Such, however, is the case with space and time. But this is quite comprehensible as soon as both count for nothing more than formal conditions of our sensibility, while the objects count merely as phenomena; for then the form of the phenomenon, i.e., pure intuition, can by all means be represented as proceeding from ourselves, that is, *a priori.*

§12. In order to add something by way of illustration and confirmation, we need only watch the ordinary and necessary procedure of geometers. All proofs of the complete congruence of two given figures (where the one can in every respect be substituted for the other) come ultimately to this that they may be made to coincide; which is evidently nothing else than a synthetical proposition resting upon immediate intuition, and this intuition must be pure, or given *a priori,* otherwise the proposition could not rank as apodeictically certain, but would have empirical certainty only. In that case, it could only be said that it is always found to be so, and holds good only as far as our perception reaches. That everywhere space (which [in its entirety] is itself no longer the boundary of another space) has three dimensions, and that space cannot in any way have more, is based on the proposition that not more than three lines can intersect at right angles in one point; but this proposition cannot by any means be shown from concepts, but rests immediately on intuition, and indeed on pure and *a priori* intuition, because it is apodeictically certain. That we can require a line to be drawn to infinity (*in indefinitum*), or that a series of changes (for example, spaces traversed by motion) shall be infinitely continued, presupposes a representation of space and time, which can only attach to intuition, namely, so far as it in itself is bounded by nothing, for from concepts it could never be inferred. Consequently, the basis of mathematics actually [is] pure intuitions, which make its synthetical and apodeictically valid propositions possible. Hence our transcendental deduction of the notions of space and of time explains at the same time the possibility of pure mathematics. Without some such deduction its truth may be granted, but its existence could by no means be understood, and we must assume "that everything which can be given to our senses (to the external senses in space, to the internal one in time) is intuited by us as it appears to us, not as it is in itself."

§13. Those who cannot yet rid themselves of the notion that space and time are actual qualities inhering in things in themselves, may exercise their acumen on the following paradox. When they have in vain attempted its solution, and are free from prejudices at least for a few moments, they will suspect that the degradation of space and of time to mere forms of our sensuous intuition may perhaps be well founded.

If two things are quite equal in all respects as much as can be ascertained by all means possible, quantitatively and qualitatively, it must follow, that the one can in all cases and under all circumstances replace the other, and this substitution would not occasion the least perceptible difference. This in fact is true of plane figures in geometry; but some spherical figures exhibit, notwithstanding a complete internal agreement, such a contrast in their external relation, that the one figure cannot possibly be put in the place of the other. For instance, two spherical triangles on opposite hemispheres, which have an arc of the equator as their common base, may be quite equal, both as regards sides and angles, so that nothing is to be found in either, if it be described for itself alone and completed, that would not equally be applicable to both; and yet the one cannot be put in the place of the other (being situated upon the opposite hemisphere). Here then is an internal difference between the two triangles, which difference our understanding cannot describe as internal, and which only manifests itself by external relations in space.

But I shall adduce examples, taken from common life, that are more obvious still.

What can be more similar in every respect and in every part more alike to my hand and to my ear, than their images in a mirror? And yet I cannot put such a hand as is seen in the glass in the place of its archetype; for if this is a right hand, that in the glass is a left one, and the image or reflexion of the right ear is a left one which never can serve as a substitute for the other. There are in this case no internal differences which our understanding could determine by thinking alone. Yet the differences are internal as the senses teach, for, notwithstanding their complete equality and similarity, the left hand cannot be enclosed in the same bounds as the right one (they are not congruent); the glove of one hand cannot be used for the other. What is the solution? These objects are not representations of things as they are in themselves, and as the pure understanding would cognise them, but sensuous intuitions, that is, appearances, the possibility of which rests upon the relation of certain things unknown in themselves to something else, viz., to our sensibility. Space is the form of the external intuition of this sensibility, and the internal determination of every space is only possible by the determination of its external relation to the whole space, of which it is a part (in other words, by its relation to the external sense). That is to say, the part is only possible through the whole, which is never the case with things in themselves, as objects of the mere understanding, but with appearances only. Hence the difference between similar and equal things, which are yet not congruent (for instance, two symmetric helices), cannot be made intelligible by any concept, but only by the relation to the right and the left hands which immediately refers to intuition. . . .

Second Part of the
Transcendental Problem

How Is the Science of Nature Possible?

§14. Nature is the existence of things, so far as it is determined according to universal laws. Should nature signify the existence of things in themselves, we could never cognise it either *a priori* or *a posteriori*. Not *a priori*, for how can we know what belongs to things in themselves, since this never can be done by the dissection of our concepts (in analytical judgments)? We do not want to know what is contained in our concept of a thing (for the [concept describes what] belongs to its logical being), but what is in the actuality of the thing superadded to our concept, and by what the thing itself is determined in its existence outside the concept. Our understanding, and the conditions on which alone it can connect the determinations of things in their existence, do not prescribe any rule to things themselves; these do not conform to our understanding, but it must conform itself to them; they must therefore be first given us in order to gather these determinations from them, wherefore they would not be cognised *a priori*.

A cognition of the nature of things in themselves *a posteriori* would be equally impossible. For, if experience is to teach us laws, to which the existence of things is subject, these laws, if they regard things in themselves, must belong to them of necessity even outside our experience. But experience teaches us what exists and how it exists, but never that it must necessarily exist so and not otherwise. Experience therefore can never teach us the nature of things in themselves.

§15. We nevertheless actually possess a pure science of nature in which are propounded, *a priori* and with all the necessity requisite to apodeictical propositions, laws to which nature is subject. I need only call to witness that propaedeutic of natural science which, under the title of the universal Science of

Nature, precedes all Physics (which is founded upon empirical principles). In it we have Mathematics applied to appearance, and also merely discursive principles (or those derived from concepts), which constitute the philosophical part of the pure cognition of nature. But there are several things in it, which are not quite pure and independent of empirical sources: such as the concept of *motion,* that of *impenetrability* (upon which the empirical concept of matter rests), that of *inertia,* and many others, which prevent its being called a perfectly pure science of nature. Besides, it only refers to objects of the external sense, and therefore does not give an example of a universal science of nature, in the strict sense, for such a science must reduce nature in general, whether it regards the object of the external or that of the internal sense (the object of Physics as well as Psychology), to universal laws. But among the principles of this universal physics there are a few which actually have the required universality; for instance, the propositions that "substance is permanent," and that "every event is determined by a cause according to constant laws," etc. These are actually universal laws of nature, which subsist completely *a priori.* There is then in fact a pure science of nature, and the question arises, *How is it possible?*

§16. The word "nature" assumes yet another meaning, which determines the object, whereas in the former sense it only denotes the conformity to law [*Gesetzmässigkeit*] of the determinations of the existence of things generally. If we consider it *materialiter* (i.e., in the matter that forms its objects) "nature is the complex of all the objects of experience." And with this only are we now concerned, for besides, things which can never be objects of experience, if they must be cognised as to their nature, would oblige us to have recourse to concepts whose meaning could never be given *in concreto* (by any example of possible experience). Consequently we must form for ourselves a list of concepts of their nature, the reality whereof (i.e., whether they actually refer to objects, or are mere creations of thought) could never be determined. The cognition of what cannot be an object of experience would be hyperphysical, and with things hyperphysical we are here not concerned, but only with the cognition of nature, the actuality of which can be confirmed by experience, though it [the cognition of nature] is possible *a priori* and precedes all experience.

§17. The formal [aspect] of nature in this narrower sense is therefore the conformity to law of all the objects of experience, and so far as it is cognised *a priori,* their necessary conformity. But it has just been shown that the laws of nature can never be cognised *a priori* in objects so far as they are considered not in reference to possible experience, but as things in themselves. And our inquiry here extends not to things in themselves (the properties of which we pass by), but to things as objects of possible experience, and the complex of these is what we properly designate as nature. And now I ask, when the possibility of a cognition of nature *a priori* is in question, whether it is better to arrange the problem thus: How can we cognise *a priori* that things as objects of experience necessarily conform to law? or thus: How is it possible to cognise *a priori* the necessary conformity to law of experience itself as regards all its objects generally?

Closely considered, the solution of the problem, represented in either way, amounts, with regard to the pure cognition of nature (which is the point of the question at issue), entirely to the same thing. For the subjective laws, under which alone an empirical cognition of things is possible, hold good of these things, as objects of possible experience (not as things in themselves, which are not considered here). Either of the following statements means quite the same:

A judgment of observation can never rank as experience, without the law, that "whenever an event is observed, it is always referred to some antecedent, which it follows according to a universal rule."

"Everything, of which experience teaches that it happens, must have a cause."

It is, however, more commendable to choose the first formula. For we can *a priori* and previous to all given objects have a cognition of those conditions, on which alone experience is possible, but never of the laws to which things may in themselves be subject, without reference to possible experience. We cannot therefore study the nature of things *a priori* otherwise than by investigating the conditions and the universal (though subjective) laws, under which alone such a cognition as experience (as to mere form) is possible, and we determine accordingly the possibility of things, as objects of experience. For if I should choose the second formula, and seek the conditions *a priori,* on which nature as an object of experience is possible, I might easily fall into error, and fancy that I was speaking of nature as a thing in itself, and then move round in endless circles, in a vain search for laws concerning things of which nothing is given me.

Accordingly we shall here be concerned with experience only, and the universal conditions of its possibility which are given *a priori.* Thence we shall determine nature as the whole object of all possible experience. I think it will be understood that I here do not mean the rules of the observation of a nature that is already given, for these already presuppose experience. I do not mean how (through experience) we can study the laws of nature; for these would not then be laws *a priori,* and would yield us no pure science of nature; but [I mean to ask] how the conditions *a priori* of the possibility of experience are at the same time the sources from which all the universal laws of nature must be derived.

§ 18. In the first place we must state that, while all judgments of experience (*Erfahrungsurtheile*) are empirical (i.e., have their ground in immediate sense-perception), *vice versa,* all empirical judgments (*empirische Urtheile*) are not judgments of experience, but, besides the empirical, and in general besides what is given to the sensuous intuition, particular concepts must yet be superadded—concepts which have their origin quite *a priori* in the pure understanding, and under which every perception must be first of all subsumed and then by their means changed into experience.

Empirical judgments, so far as they have objective validity, are **judgments of experience**; but those which are only subjectively valid, I name mere **judgments of perception**. The latter require no pure concept of the understanding, but only the logical connexion of perception in a thinking subject. But the former always require, besides the representation of the sensuous intuition, particular *concepts* *originally begotten in the understanding,* which produce the objective validity of the judgment of experience.

All our judgments are at first merely judgments of perception; they hold good only for us (i.e., for our subject), and we do not till afterwards give them a new reference (to an object), and desire that they shall always hold good for us and in the same way for everybody else; for when a judgment agrees with an object, all judgments concerning the same object must likewise agree among themselves, and thus the objective validity of the judgment of experience signifies nothing else than its necessary universality of application. And conversely when we have reason to consider a judgment necessarily universal (which never depends upon perception, but upon the pure concept of the understanding, under which the perception is subsumed), we must consider it objective also, that is, that it expresses not merely a reference of our perception to a subject, but a quality of the object. For there would be no reason for the judgments of other men necessarily agreeing with mine, if it were not the unity of the object to which they all refer, and with which they accord; hence they must all agree with one another.

§19. Therefore objective validity and necessary universality (for everybody) are equivalent terms, and though we do not know the object in itself, yet when we consider a judgment as universal, and also necessary, we understand it to have objective validity. By this judgment we cognise the object (though it remains unknown as it is in itself) by the universal and necessary connexion of the given perceptions. As this is the case with all objects of sense, judgments of experience take their objective validity not from the immediate cognition of the object (which is impossible), but from the condition of universal validity in empirical judgments, which, as already said, never rests upon empirical, or, in short, sensuous conditions, but upon a pure concept of the understanding. The object always remains unknown in itself; but when by the concept of the understanding the connexion of the representations of the object, which are given to our sensibility, is determined as universally valid, the object is determined by this relation, and it is the judgment that is objective.

To illustrate the matter: When we say, "The room is warm, sugar sweet, and wormwood bitter,"[14] —we have only subjectively valid judgments. I do not at all expect that I or any other person shall always find it as I now do; each of these sentences only expresses a relation of two sensations to the same subject, to myself, and that only in my present state of perception; consequently they are not valid of the object. Such are judgments of perception. Judgments of experience are of quite

---

14. I freely grant that these examples do not represent such judgments of perception as ever could become judgments of experience, even though a concept of the understanding were superadded, because they refer merely to feeling, which everybody knows to be merely subjective, and which of course can never be attributed to the object, and consequently never become objective. I only wished to give here an example of a judgment that is merely subjectively valid, containing no ground for universal validity, and thereby for a relation to the object. An example of the judgments of perception, which become judgments of experience by superadded concepts of the understanding, will be given in the next note.

a different nature. What experience teaches me under certain circumstances, it must always teach me and everybody; and its validity is not limited to the subject nor to its state at a particular time. Hence I pronounce all such judgments as being objectively valid. For instance, when I say, "The air is elastic," this judgment is as yet a judgment of perception only—I do nothing but refer two of my sensations to one another. But, if I would have it called a judgment of experience, I require this connexion to stand under a condition, which makes it universally valid. I desire therefore that I and everybody else should always connect necessarily the same perceptions under the same circumstances.

§20. We must consequently analyse experience in order to see what is contained in this product of the senses and of the understanding, and how the judgment of experience itself is possible. The foundation is the intuition of which I become conscious, i.e., perception (*perceptio*), which pertains merely to the senses. But in the next place, there are acts of judging (which belong only to the understanding). But this judging may be twofold—first, I may merely compare perceptions and connect them in a particular state of my consciousness; or, secondly, I may connect them in consciousness generally. The former judgment is merely a judgment of perception,and of subjective validity only: it is merely a connexion of perceptions in my mental state, without reference to the object. Hence it is not, as is commonly imagined, enough for experience to compare perceptions and to connect them in consciousness through judgment; there arises no universality and necessity, for which alone judgments can become objectively valid and be called experience.

Quite another judgment therefore is required before perception can become experience. The given intuition must be subsumed under a concept, which determines the form of judging in general relatively to the intuition, connects its empirical consciousness in consciousness generally, and thereby procures universal validity for empirical judgments. A concept of this nature is a pure *a priori* concept of the Understanding, which does nothing but determine for an intuition the general way in which it can be used for judgments. Let the concept be that of cause, then it determines the intuition which is subsumed under it, e.g., that of air, relative to judgments in general, viz., the concept of air serves with regard to its expansion in the relation of antecedent to consequent in a hypothetical judgment. The concept of cause accordingly is a pure concept of the understanding, which is totally disparate from all possible perception, and only serves to determine the representation subsumed under it, relatively to judgments in general, and so to make a universally valid judgment possible.

Before, therefore, a judgment of perception can become a judgment of experience, it is requisite that the perception should be subsumed under some such a concept of the understanding; for instance, air ranks under the concept of causes, which determines our judgment about it in regard to its expansion as hypothetical.[15] Thereby the expansion of the air is represented not as merely belonging

---

15. As an easier example, we may take the following: "When the sun shines on the stone, it grows warm." This judgment, however often I and others may have perceived it, is a mere

to the perception of the air in my present state or in several states of mine, or in the state of perception of others, but as belonging to it necessarily. The judgment, "The air is elastic," becomes universally valid, and a judgment of experience, only by certain judgments preceding it, which subsume the intuition of air under the concept of cause and effect: and they thereby determine the perceptions not merely as regards one another in me, but relatively to the form of judging in general, which is here hypothetical, and in this way they render the empirical judgment universally valid.

If all our synthetical judgments are analysed so far as they are objectively valid, it will be found that they never consist of mere intuitions connected only (as is commonly believed) by comparison into a judgment; but that they would be impossible were not a pure concept of the understanding superadded to the concepts abstracted from intuition, under which concept these latter are subsumed, and in this manner only combined into an objectively valid judgment. Even the judgments of pure mathematics in their simplest axioms are not exempt from this condition. The principle, "A straight line is the shortest between two points," presupposes that the line is subsumed under the concept of quantity, which certainly is no mere intuition, but has its seat in the understanding alone, and serves to determine the intuition (of the line) with regard to the judgments which may be made about it, relatively to their quantity, that is, to plurality (as *judicia plurativa*).[16] For under them it is understood that in a given intuition there is contained a plurality of homogenous parts.

§21. To prove, then, the possibility of experience so far as it rests upon pure concepts of the understanding *a priori,* we must first represent what belongs to judgments in general and the various functions of the understanding, in a complete table. For the pure concepts of the understanding must run parallel to these functions, as such concepts are nothing more than concepts of intuitions in general, so far as these are determined by one or other of these functions of judging, in themselves, that is, necessarily and universally. Hereby also the *a priori* principles of the possibility of all experience, as of an objectively valid empirical cognition, will be precisely determined. For they are nothing but propositions by which all perception is (under certain universal conditions of intuition) subsumed under those pure concepts of the understanding.

§21a. In order to comprise the whole matter in one idea, it is first necessary

---

judgment of perception, and contains no necessity; perceptions are only usually conjoined in this manner. But if I say, "The sun warms the stone," I add to the perception a concept of the understanding, viz., that of cause, which connects with the concept of sunshine that of heat as a necessary consequence, and the synthetical judgment becomes of necessity universally valid, viz., objective, and is converted from a perception into experience.

16. This name seems preferable to the term *particularia*, which is used for these judgments in logic. For the latter implies the idea that they are not universal. But when I start from unity (in single judgments) and so proceed to universality, I must not [even indirectly and negatively] imply any reference to universality. I think plurality merely without universality, and not the exception from universality. This is necessary, if logical considerations shall form the basis of the pure concepts of the understanding. However, there is no need of making changes in logic.

LOGICAL TABLE OF JUDGMENTS.

1.	**2.**
As to Quantity.	*As to Quality.*
Universal.	Affirmative.
Particular.	Negative.
Singular.	Infinite.
3.	**4.**
As to Relation.	*As to Modality.*
Categorical.	Problematical.
Hypothetical.	Assertorical.
Disjunctive.	Apodeictical.

TRANSCENDENTAL TABLE OF THE PURE CONCEPTS OF THE UNDERSTANDING.

1.	**2.**
As to Quantity.	*As to Quality.*
Unity (the Measure).	Reality.
Plurality (the Quantity).	Negation.
Totality (the Whole).	Limitation.
3.	**4.**
As to Relation.	*As to Modality.*
Substance.	Possibility.
Cause.	Existence.
Community.	Necessity.

PURE PHYSIOLOGICAL TABLE OF THE UNIVERSAL PRINCIPLES OF THE SCIENCE OF NATURE.

1.	**2.**
Axioms of Intuition.	Anticipations of Perception.
3.	**4.**
Analogies of Experience.	Postulates of Empirical Thinking generally.

to remind the reader that we are discussing not the origin of experience, but of that which lies in experience. The former pertains to empirical psychology, and would even then never be adequately explained without the latter, which belongs to the critique of cognition, and particularly of the understanding.

Experience consists of intuitions, which belong to the sensibility, and of judgments, which are entirely a work of the understanding. But the judgments, which the understanding forms alone from sensuous intuitions, are far from being judgments of experience. For in the one case the judgment connects only the perceptions as they are given in the sensuous intuition, while in the other the judgments must express what experience in general, and not what the mere perception (which possesses only subjective validity) contains. The judgment of experience must therefore add to the sensuous intuition and its logical connexion in a judgment (after it has been rendered universal by comparison) something that determines the synthetical judgment as necessary and therefore as universally valid. This can be nothing else than that concept which represents the intuition as determined in itself with regard to one form of judgment rather than another, viz., a concept of that synthetical unity of intuitions which can only be represented by a given logical function of judgments.

§22. The sum of the matter is this: the business of the senses is to intuite—that of the understanding is to think. But thinking is uniting representations in one consciousness. This union originates either merely relative to the subject, and is accidental and subjective, or is absolute, and is necessary or objective. The union of representations in one consciousness is judgment. Thinking therefore is the same as judging, or referring representations to judgments in general. Hence judgments are either merely subjective, when representations are referred to a consciousness in one subject only, and united in it, or objective, when they are united in a consciousness generally, that is, necessarily. The logical functions of all judgments are but various modes of uniting representations in consciousness. But if they serve for concepts, they are concepts of their necessary union in a consciousness, and so principles of objectively valid judgments. This union in a consciousness is either analytical, by identity, or synthetical, by the combination and addition of various representations one to another. Experience consists in the synthetical connexion of phenomena (perceptions) in consciousness, so far as this connexion is necessary. Hence the pure concepts of the understanding are those under which all perceptions must be subsumed ere they can serve for judgments of experience, in which the synthetical unity of the perceptions is represented as necessary and universally valid.[17]

§23. Judgments, when considered merely as the condition of the union of given representations in a consciousness, are rules. These rules, so far as they repre-

---

17. But how does this proposition, that "judgments of experience contain necessity in the synthesis of perceptions," agree with my statement so often before inculcated, that "experience as cognition *a posteriori* can afford contingent judgments only"? When I say that experience teaches me something, I mean only the perception that lies in experience,—for example, that heat always follows the shining of the sun on a stone; consequently the proposition of experience is always so far accidental. That this heat necessarily follows the shining of the sun is contained indeed in the judgment of experience (by means of the concept of cause), yet is a fact not learned by experience; for conversely, experience is first of all generated by this addition of the concept of the understanding (of cause) to perception. How perception attains this addition may be seen by referring in the *Critique* itself to the section on the Transcendental Faculty of Judgment [viz., in the first edition, *Von dem Schematismus der reinen Verstandsbegriffe*].

sent the union as necessary, are rules *a priori,* and so far as they cannot be deduced from higher rules, are fundamental principles. But in regard to the possibility of all experience, merely in relation to the form of thinking in it, no conditions of judgments of experience are higher than those which bring the phenomena, according to the various form of their intuition, under pure concepts of the understanding, and render the empirical judgment objectively valid. These concepts are therefore the *a priori* principles of possible experience.

The principles of possible experience are then at the same time universal laws of nature, which can be cognised *a priori.* And thus the problem in our second question, "How is the pure Science of Nature possible?" is solved. For the system which is required for the form of a science is to be met with in perfection here, because, beyond the above-mentioned formal conditions of all judgments in general offered in logic, no others are possible, and these constitute a logical system. The concepts grounded thereupon, which contain the *a priori* conditions of all synthetical and necessary judgments, accordingly constitute a transcendental system. Finally the principles, by means of which all phenomena are subsumed under these concepts, constitute a physical[18] system, that is, a system of nature, which precedes all empirical cognition of nature, makes it even possible, and hence may in strictness be denominated the universal and pure science of nature. . . .

§27. Now we are prepared to remove Hume's doubt. He justly maintains, that we cannot comprehend by reason the possibility of Causality, that is, of the reference of the existence of one thing to the existence of another, which is necessitated by the former. I add, that we comprehend just as little the concept of Subsistence, that is, the necessity that at the foundation of the existence of things there lies a subject which cannot itself be a predicate of any other thing; nay, we cannot even form a notion of the possibility of such a thing (though we can point out examples of its use in experience). The very same incomprehensibility affects the Community of things, as we cannot comprehend how from the state of one thing an inference to the state of quite another thing beyond it, and *vice versa,* can be drawn, and how substances which have each their own separate existence should depend upon one another necessarily. But I am very far from holding these concepts to be derived merely from experience, and the necessity represented in them, to be imaginary and a mere illusion produced in us by long habit. On the contrary, I have amply shown, that they and the theorems derived from them are firmly established *a priori,* or before all experience, and have their undoubted objective value, though only with regard to experience.

§28. Though I have no notion of such a connexion of things in themselves, that they can either exist as substances, or act as causes, or stand in community with others (as parts of a real whole), and I can just as little conceive such properties in appearances as such (because those concepts contain nothing that lies in the

---

18. [Kant uses the term physiological in its etymological meaning as "pertaining to the science of physics," i.e., nature in general, not as we use the term now as "pertaining to the functions of the living body." Accordingly it has been translated "physical."—Carus]

appearances, but only what the understanding alone must think): we have yet a notion of such a connexion of representations in our understanding, and in judgments generally; consisting in this that representations appear in one sort of judgments as subject in relation to predicates, in another as reason in relation to consequences, and in a third as parts, which constitute together a total possible cognition. Besides we cognise *a priori* that without considering the representation of an object as determined in some of these respects, we can have no valid cognition of the object, and, if we should occupy ourselves about the object in itself, there is no possible attribute, by which I could know that it is determined under any of these aspects, that is, under the concept either of substance, or of cause, or (in relation to other substances) of community, for I have no notion of the possibility of such a connexion of existence. But the question is not how things in themselves, but how the empirical cognition of things is determined, as regards the above aspects of judgments in general, that is, how things, as objects of experience, can and shall be subsumed under these concepts of the understanding. And then it is clear, that I completely comprehend not only the possibility, but also the necessity of subsuming all phenomena under these concepts, that is, of using them for principles of the possibility of experience.

§29. When making an experiment with Hume's problematical concept (his *crux metaphysicorum*), the concept of cause, we have, in the first place, given *a priori*, by means of logic, the form of a conditional judgment in general, i.e., we have one given cognition as antecedent and another as consequence. But it is possible, that in perception we may meet with a rule of relation, which runs thus: that a certain phenomenon is constantly followed by another (though not conversely), and this is a case for me to use the hypothetical judgment, and, for instance, to say, if the sun shines long enough upon a body, it grows warm. Here there is indeed as yet no necessity of connexion, or concept of cause. But I proceed and say, that if this proposition, which is merely a subjective connexion of perceptions, is to be a judgment of experience, it must be considered as necessary and universally valid. Such a proposition would be, "The sun is by its light the cause of heat." The empirical rule is now considered as a law, and as valid not merely of appearances but valid of them for the purposes of a possible experience which requires universal and therefore necessarily valid rules. I therefore easily comprehend the concept of cause, as a concept necessarily belonging to the mere form of experience, and its possibility as a synthetical union of perceptions in consciousness generally; but I do not at all comprehend the possibility of a thing generally as a cause, because the concept of cause denotes a condition not at all belonging to things, but to experience. It is nothing in fact but an objectively valid cognition of appearances and of their succession, so far as the antecedent can be conjoined with the consequent according to the rule of hypothetical judgments.

§30. Hence if the pure concepts of the understanding do not refer to objects of experience but to things in themselves (*noumena*), they have no signification whatever. They serve, as it were, only to decipher appearances, that we may be able to read them as experience. The principles which arise from their reference to the sensible world, only serve our understanding for empirical use. Beyond this they are arbitrary combinations, without objective reality, and we can neither cognise their possibility *a priori*, nor verify their reference to objects, let alone make it intelligible by any example; because examples can only be borrowed from some possible experience, consequently the objects of these concepts can be found nowhere but in a possible experience.

This complete (though to its originator unexpected) solution of Hume's problem rescues for the pure concepts of the understanding their *a priori* origin, and for the universal laws of nature their validity, as laws of the understanding, yet in such a way as to limit their use to experience, because their possibility depends solely on the reference of the understanding to experience, but with a completely reversed mode of connexion which never occurred to Hume, not by deriving them from experience, but by deriving experience from them.

This is therefore the result of all our foregoing inquiries: "All synthetical principles *a priori* are nothing more than principles of possible experience, and can never be referred to things in themselves, but to appearances as objects of experience. And hence pure mathematics as well as a pure science of nature can never be referred to anything more than mere appearances, and can only represent either that which makes experience generally possible, or else that which, as it is derived from these principles, must always be capable of being represented in some possible experience."

§31. And thus we have at last something definite, upon which to depend in all metaphysical enterprises, which have hitherto, boldly enough but always at random, attempted everything without discrimination.

COMPARATIVE STUDY QUESTIONS

Review Questions

1. Explain Hume's distinction between "impressions" and "ideas."
2. In connection with his thesis that all our ideas are copies of impressions, Hume admits "one contradictory phenomenon." What significance does it have for his theory?
3. All reasoning regarding matters of fact, according to Hume, are founded on what kind of relation?
4. Evaluate Beattie's criticisms of Hume's view that all ideas are derived from and represent impressions.
5. Why does Hume say that "there are no ideas, which occur in metaphysics, more obscure and uncertain, than those of **power, force, energy,** or **necessary connection**"?
6. State one of Hume's own definitions of "cause."
7. What do Hume and Kant mean by the term "a priori"?
8. Explain Kant's distinction between analytical and synthetical judgments.
9. How does Kant understand the nature of space and time?
10. Explain Kant's distinction between "judgments of experience" and "judgments of perception."

Discussion Questions

1. According to Hume, the maxim, "Whatever begins to exist must have a cause," is neither intuitively nor demonstrably certain. Beattie "allows" that it is not demonstrable, but disagrees with Hume regarding its intuitive certainty. Assess Beattie's criticisms.
2. Kant finds it "positively painful" to see how utterly Hume's opponents, including Beattie, misunderstood Hume's position and the point of his problem. What did they misunderstand, and what was the point of his problem?
3. Beattie upholds common sense as the standard of truth, and regards all evidence as ultimately intuitive in character. Compare this position with what Kant has to say about it in his Introduction to the **Prolegomena.**
4. Does Hume deny that the concept of cause is totally without meaning, or that it is useless for scientific investigations? In what respects, if any, does his own conception of causality differ from Kant's?
5. To what extent does Kant think that Hume was correct in his analysis of the causal problem, and in what respects was he wrong?
6. Why is an adequate account of reasoning concerning matters of fact based on the relation of cause and effect so essential to an understanding of inductive inferences such as the following: "The sun will rise tomorrow"?

7. How do Hume and Kant differ in their conceptions of the status and character of mathematical knowledge?

8. Some critics have described Kant's Table of the Pure Concepts (or Categories) of the Understanding as a kind of "intellectual hatrack." What do you suppose Kant was trying to do by formulating such a classification?

9. How would you express the general problem of knowledge as Kant sees it? More specifically, what is the question on whose answer depends the very existence of metaphysics, according to Kant? Would Hume have understood this way of putting the problem?

10. Briefly sketch or summarize Kant's solution of Hume's problem. Do you think he has succeeded in "answering" Hume's scepticism regarding the possibility of empirical science?

Immanuel Kant
(1724 – 1804)

THE MORAL LAW WITHIN

A Student of Ethics and Professor Immanuel Kant

> Everyone knows that unless a child is properly brought up
> he will probably not behave properly when grown up; and
> if he is properly brought up he is quite likely to behave
> properly when grown up. Everyone knows, too, that
> though certain actions of lunatics, epileptics, kleptomaniacs
> and drowning men are regrettable, they are not reprehensible
> or, of course, commendable either, where similar actions of
> a normal adult in normal situations are both regrettable and
> reprehensible. Yet if a person's bad conduct reflects his bad
> upbringing, it seems to follow that not he but his parents
> should be blamed—and then, of course, in their turn, his
> grandparents, his great-grandparents, and in the end nobody
> at all. We feel quite sure both that a person can be made
> *moral* and that he cannot be *made* moral; and yet that both
> cannot be true.
>
> Gilbert Ryle, *Dilemmas* (1954)

Despite the fact that Immanuel Kant is the only major philosopher of the modern period who was by profession a teacher, relatively little attention has been paid to his views regarding education. No one is likely to deny that he was interested in methods of knowing. It could even be argued that methodology, in the broadest sense, was the only thing he ever wrote about. What is often overlooked, however, is that Kant distinguished two kinds of methodology: one is the study of the procedures we use to systematize our theoretical knowledge; the other is the study of the procedures we use, as he says, "to make objective principles **subjectively** practical."[1] The latter kind of methodology involves pedagogy, and specifically **moral** education.

Kant's own moral upbringing was rather strict. His parents were members of a religious sect called Pietists, who were known for their emphasis on the practical moral virtues of truthfulness, kindliness, and tolerance, and for their devout prayers and diligent Bible study. The family, being poor, also taught their son the virtues of frugality, industry, and punctuality.

---

1. Cf. *Critique of Practical Reason*, translated by Lewis White Beck, Library of Liberal Arts (Indianapolis: Bobbs-Merrill, 1956), Part II, "Methodology of Pure Practical Reason," pp. 155–157.

At the age of eight, and for the next eight years (1732–1740), Kant attended a Pietist academy known as the Collegium Fridericianum. The school day, which began early in the morning and lasted until late in the evening, was punctuated with religious instruction and prayers. The Bible served as a major textbook for the teaching of history and Greek; Latin, geography, and mathematics were also taught. Discipline at the school was harsh, so much so in fact, that in later years Kant spoke of the "slavery" of his youth.[2]

When he enrolled at the University of Königsberg at the age of sixteen, Kant entered as a theological student. Instead of theology, however, he became absorbed in philosophy, mathematics, and the classics, particularly Latin. By the time he had completed his course in the Faculty of Theology, apparently having taken the minimum number of theological classes, he decided against a career in the ministry. His father's death about this time forced him in any case to support himself by instructing some of his fellow students in a variety of subjects including science or "natural philosophy" as it was then called. Later he became a resident tutor for children in various eminent households in and around Königsberg. He was so employed for nine years. He finally obtained an appointment at the University as a **privat-docent,** an underpaid but overworked instructor. His first lectures were on mathematics and physics and later on philosophy (logic, metaphysics, ethics), natural theology, physical geography, anthropology, and of all things, "fortifications." He held this position of privat-docent for fifteen years before he became a Professor of Logic and Metaphysics at the age of forty-six.

The point of reciting these facts about Kant's own education and early career is to indicate that, in addition to the tutoring he did while a student, and even before he became a professor, he had some twenty-four years of experience teaching young people a variety of very different subjects. Was he a good instructor? If his lectures resembled even slightly the works for which he is best known—his three **Critiques**—we can safely assume that his audiences were small and the student response at best lukewarm. In fact, however, just the opposite was the case. Although he himself was dissatisfied with his performance as a family tutor ("There was hardly ever a tutor with a better theory or a worse practice," he said), he was reportedly loved by his pupils and respected by their parents. His lectures as privat-docent were extremely popular, attracting not only students, but townspeople and even out-of-town visitors as well. One of Kant's former students, Johann Gottfried von Herder, gave the following account:

> I have had the good fortune to know a philosopher who was my teacher; he had the happy sprightliness of a youth. . . . His open, thoughtful brow was the seat of unruffled calmness and joy; discourse full of thought flowed from his lips; jest and wit and humour were at his command; and his lecture was the most entertaining conversation. With the same genius with which he criticized Leibnitz, Wolf, Crusius, Hume, and expounded the laws of

---

2. Quoted by Karl Vorländer, *Immanuel Kant's Leben;* cited and translated by Theodore M. Greene in *Religion Within the Limits of Reason Alone* (La Salle, Ill.: Open Court, 1934), p. xxviii.

Newton and Kepler, he would also take up the writings of Rousseau, or any recent discovery in nature, give his estimate of them, and come back again to the knowledge of nature and to the moral worth of man. Natural history, natural philosophy, the history of nations and human nature, mathematics, and experience—these were the sources from which he enlivened his lectures and his conversation.[3]

Kant's lectures on anthropology are said to have been especially interesting. Unlike some of his later publications, they were full of entertaining allusions, examples, and anecdotes. Even his lectures on metaphysics were clear and intelligible. It is reported that he sought, as he himself expressed it, to teach "not philosophy, but to philosophize."[4]

If Kant's lectures were so lucid, witty, and entertaining, why are his major philosophical writings, including some of his writings on ethics, so dense, dry, and fatiguing? Although Kant never laid claim to as lucid a style as Hume's or Berkeley's, he did aim at intelligibility and completeness. He knew that he could indeed make his works more attractive by the addition of examples and anecdotes, but he feared that as they became more voluminous, they would lose their intelligibility. Furthermore, he realized that he had to choose between popularity and completeness. The latter, he felt, could not be achieved otherwise than by a dry treatment.

One might wonder whether this typically German penchant for thoroughness and completeness is something we might very well do without in philosophy. Kant obviously did not think so, and in fact, aside from logical and aesthetic considerations, he offered still another, specifically methodological, reason for it. In an essay entitled, "Concerning the Common Saying: This May Be True in Theory, But Does Not Apply to Practice," Kant suggests that a theory might fail practically either because of bad judgment on the part of the one attempting to apply it, or because the theory itself lacks completeness. Regarding the first fault nothing much can be done. One is either born with a capacity for good judgment or is not; it is not something that can be taught by means of a fixed set of rules. On the other hand, if the fault lies in the theory, its incompleteness, then it may only be necessary to supplement it in order to make it applicable. For example, in order for a theory of general mechanics to be of use to a machinist, it needs to be supplemented by a theory of friction; and in order for the theory of ballistics to be of use to an artilleryman, it needs to be supplemented by a theory of air resistance. The practical utility of any theory, even a philosophical one, depends, therefore, not simply on an intelligent understanding of the theory to be applied, or a natural gift of judgment, but also on the completeness of the theory itself.

According to Kant, the common saying (that a theory may be true but unrelated to practice) is less likely to be true in the case of ethical theories than in the case of scientific or even metaphysical theories. For the concepts and principles

---

3. Quoted in T. K. Abbott, *Kant's Critique of Practical Reason and Other Works on the Theory of Ethics*, 1873 (6th ed. 1909, Longmans, Green and Co.), "Memoir of Kant," pp. xxx–xxxi.
4. *Ibid.*, p. xxxiii.

of morality, particularly the central notions of "duty" and "goodwill," are inherently practical, i.e., capable of directly affecting our actions and creating a **practice.**[5] What is required in the case of ethical theories, however, is not the **teaching** of these notions as one would the empirical concepts of physics, but the systematic **clarification** of the moral ideas which exist already, Kant thinks, in the sound, natural understanding.[6] Once completely presented and understood, they can influence our conduct if only we freely allow them to do so. The task of the moral educator, therefore, whose function is to make the objective principles of moral theory subjectively practical, is to elicit these basic moral ideas by calling them to the student's attention. When properly confronted with the notion of pure duty, the student will become conscious of his inner freedom and his independence of circumstances and wants. He will thus acquire a new respect for himself, and, Kant believes, a new reverence for the moral law.

KANT

Acquiring Good Dispositions *

Student of Ethics. Tell me, Professor, can moral virtue be taught, or can persons only be induced to be good through punishment or enticement?

Professor Kant. It cannot indeed be denied that in order to bring an uncultivated or degraded mind into the track of moral goodness some preparatory guidance is necessary, to attract it by a view of its own advantage, or to alarm it by fear of loss; but as soon as this mechanical work, these leading-strings, have produced some effect, then we must bring before the mind the pure moral motive, which, not only because it is the only one that can be the foundation of a

---

5. Which he defines in the essay as follows: "An activity which is the realization of an end conceived as a result of following certain general principles of procedure."

6. Cf. Kant, *Fundamental Principles of the Metaphysics of Morals*, translated by T. K. Abbott, *op. cit.*, p. 13.

*The following conversation is based on Kant's discussion of methodology in his *Critique of Practical Reason* (1788) Abbott translation, 1873, sixth ed. 1909. The dialogue format and the names of the participants are superimposed on Kant's discussion. As in the other constructed dialogues in this book, the "editorial typeface" words are either paraphrases of Kant's language or entirely my own.—P.E.D.

character (a practically consistent habit of mind with unchangeable maxims), but also because it teaches a man to feel his own dignity, gives the mind a power unexpected even by himself, to tear himself from all sensible attachments so far as they would fain have the rule, and to find a rich compensation for the sacrifice he offers, in the independence of his rational nature and the greatness of soul to which he sees that he is destined. We will therefore show, by such observations as every one can make, that this property of our minds, this receptivity for a pure moral interest, and consequently the moving force of the pure conception of virtue, when it is properly applied to the human heart, is the most powerful spring, and, when a continued and punctual observance of moral maxims is in question, the only spring of good conduct. It must, however, be remembered that if these observations only prove the reality of such a feeling, but do not show any moral improvement brought about by it, this is no argument against the only method that exists of making the objectively practical laws of pure reason subjectively practical, through the mere force of the conception of duty; nor does it prove that this method is a vain delusion. For as it has never yet come into vogue, experience can say nothing of its results; one can only ask for proofs of the receptivity for such springs.

Student. I am most anxious to hear these proofs. Would you please briefly present them and then sketch your method of founding and cultivating genuine moral dispositions?

Professor. I would be glad to. When we attend to the course of conversation in mixed companies, consisting not merely of learned persons and subtle reasoners, but also of men of business or of women, we observe that, besides story-telling and jesting, another kind of entertainment finds a place in them, namely, argument; for stories, if they are to have novelty and interest, are soon exhausted, and jesting is likely to become insipid. Now of all argument there is none in which persons are more ready to join who find any other subtle discussion tedious, none that brings more liveliness into the company, than that which concerns the *moral worth* of this or that action by which the character of some person is to be made out. Persons, to whom in other cases anything subtle and speculative in theoretical questions is dry and irksome, presently join in when the question is to make out the moral import of a good or bad action that has been related, and they display an exactness, a refinement, a subtlety, in excogitating everything that can lessen the purity of purpose, and consequently the degree of virtue in it, which we do not expect from them in any other kind of speculation. In these criticisms persons who are passing judgment on others often reveal their own character: some, in exercising their judicial office, especially upon the dead, seem inclined chiefly to defend the goodness that is related of this or that deed against all injurious charges of insincerity, and ultimately to defend the whole moral worth of the person against the reproach of dissimulation and secret wickedness; others, on the contrary, turn their thoughts more upon attacking this worth by accusation and fault-finding. We cannot always, however, attribute to these latter the intention of arguing away virtue altogether out of all human examples in order to make it an empty name:

often, on the contrary, it is only well-meant strictness in determining the true moral import of actions according to an uncompromising law. Comparison with such a law, instead of with examples, lowers self-conceit in moral matters very much, and not merely teaches humility, but makes everyone feel it when he examines himself closely. Nevertheless, we can for the most part observe in those who defend the purity of purpose in given examples, that where there is the presumption of uprightness they are anxious to remove even the least spot, lest, if all examples had their truthfulness disputed, and if the purity of all human virtue were denied, it might in the end be regarded as a mere phantom, and so all effort to attain it be made light of as vain affectation and delusive conceit.

Student. Why haven't parents and other teachers made more use of this method?

Professor. I do not know why the educators of youth have not long since made use of this propensity of reason to enter with pleasure upon the most subtle examination of the practical questions that are thrown up; and why they have not, after first laying the foundation of a purely moral catechism, searched through the biographies of ancient and modern times with the view of having at hand instances of the duties laid down, in which, especially by comparison of similar actions under different circumstances, they might exercise the critical judgment of their scholars in remarking their greater or less moral significance. This is a thing in which they would find that even early youth, which is still unripe for speculation of other kinds, would soon become very acute and not a little interested, because it feels the progress of its faculty of judgment; and what is most important, they could hope with confidence that the frequent practice of knowing and approving good conduct in all its purity, and on the other hand of remarking with regret or contempt the least deviation from it, although it may be pursued only as a sport in which children may compete with one another, yet will leave a lasting impression of esteem on the one hand and disgust on the other; and so, by the mere habit of looking on such actions as deserving approval or blame, a good foundation would be laid for uprightness in the future course of life. Only I wish they would spare them the example of so-called *noble* (super-meritorious) actions in which our sentimental books so much abound, and would refer all to duty merely, and to the worth that a man can and must give himself in his own eyes by the consciousness of not having transgressed it, since whatever runs up into empty wishes and longings after inaccessible perfection produces mere heroes of romance, who, while they pique themselves on their feeling for transcendent greatness, release themselves in return from the observance of common and every-day obligations, which then seem to them petty and insignificant.

Student. What then is really **pure** morality, by which as a touchstone we must test the moral significance of every action?

Professor. I must admit that it is only philosophers that can make the decision of this question doubtful, for to common sense it has been decided long ago, not indeed by abstract general formulae, but by habitual use, like the distinction between the right and left hand. We will then point out the criterion of pure virtue in an example first, and imagining that it is set before a boy of, say, ten years old, for his judgment, we will see whether he would necessarily judge so of himself without being guided by his teacher. Tell him the history of an honest man whom men want to persuade to join the calumniators of an innocent and powerless person (say, Anne Boleyn, accused by Henry VIII of England). He is offered advantages, great gifts, or high rank; he rejects them. This will excite mere approbation and applause in the mind of the hearer. Now begins the threatening of loss. Amongst these traducers are his best friends, who now renounce his friendship; near kinsfolk, who threaten to disinherit him (he being without fortune): powerful persons, who can persecute and harass him in all places and circumstances; a prince who threatens him with loss of freedom, yea, loss of life. Then to fill the measure of suffering, and that he may feel the pain that only the morally good heart can feel very deeply, let us conceive his family threatened with extreme distress and want, *entreating him to yield;* conceive himself, though upright, yet with feelings not hard or insensible either to compassion or to his own distress; conceive him, I say, at the moment when he wishes that he had never lived to see the day that exposed him to such unutterable anguish, yet remaining true to his uprightness of purpose, without wavering or even doubting; then will my youthful hearer be raised gradually from mere approval to admiration, from that to amazement, and finally to the greatest veneration, and a lively wish that he himself could be such a man (though certainly not in such circumstances). Yet virtue is here worth so much only because it costs so much, not because it brings any profit. All the admiration, and even the endeavour to resemble this character, rest wholly on the purity of the moral principle, which can only be strikingly shown by removing from the springs of action everything that men may regard as part of happiness. Morality then must have the more power over the human heart the more purely it is exhibited. Whence it follows that if the law of morality and the image of holiness and virtue are to exercise any influence at all on our souls, they can do so only so far as they are laid to heart in their purity as motives, unmixed with any view to prosperity, for it is in suffering that they display themselves most nobly. Now that whose removal strengthens the effect of a moving force must have been a hindrance, consequently every admixture of motives taken from our own happiness is a hindrance to the influence of the moral law on the heart. I affirm further, that even in that admired action, if the motive from which it was done was a high regard for duty, then it is just this respect for the law that has the greatest influence on the mind of the spectator, not any pretension to a supposed inward greatness of mind or noble meritorious sentiments; consequently duty, not merit, must have not only the most definite, but, when it is represented in the true light of its inviolability, the most penetrating influence on the mind.

It is more necessary than ever to direct attention to this method in our times, when men hope to produce more effect on the mind with soft, tender feelings, or high-flown, puffing-up pretensions, which rather wither the heart than strengthen it, than by a plain and earnest representation of duty, which is more suited to human imperfection and to progress in goodness. To set before children, as a pattern, actions that are called noble, magnanimous, meritorious, with the notion of captivating them by infusing an enthusiasm for such actions, is to defeat our end. For as they are still so backward in the observance of the commonest duty, and even in the correct estimation of it, this means simply to make them fantastical romancers betimes. But, even with the instructed and experienced part of mankind, this supposed spring has, if not an injurious, at least no genuine moral effect on the heart, which, however, is what it was desired to produce.

All *feelings,* especially those that are to produce unwonted exertions, must accomplish their effect at the moment they are at their height, and before they calm down; otherwise they effect nothing; for as there was nothing to strengthen the heart, but only to excite it, it naturally returns to its normal moderate tone, and thus falls back into its previous languor. *Principles* must be built on conceptions; on any other basis there can only be paroxysms, which can give the person no moral worth, nay, not even confidence in himself, without which the highest good in man, consciousness of the morality of his mind and character, cannot exist. Now if these conceptions are to become subjectively practical, we must not rest satisfied with admiring the objective law of morality, and esteeming it highly in reference to humanity, but we must consider the conception of it in relation to man as an individual, and then this law appears in a form indeed that is highly deserving of respect, but not so pleasant as if it belonged to the element to which he is naturally accustomed, but, on the contrary, as often compelling him to quit this element, not without self-denial, and to betake himself to a higher, in which he can only maintain himself with trouble and with unceasing apprehension of a relapse. In a word, the moral law demands obedience, from duty, not from predilection, which cannot and ought not to be pre-supposed at all.

Student. I find it difficult to imagine a case in which the duty motive alone is stronger than a predilection. Could you perhaps supply an illustration?

Professor. Yes, I think so. Let us see. We want an example in which the conception of an action as a noble and magnanimous one has less subjective moving power than if the action is conceived merely as duty in relation to the solemn law of morality.

The action by which a man endeavours at the greatest peril of life to rescue people from shipwreck, at last losing his life in the attempt, is reckoned on one side as duty, but on the other and for the most part as a meritorious action, but our esteem for it is much weakened by the notion of *duty to himself,* which seems in this case to be somewhat infringed. More decisive is the magnanimous sacrifice of life for the safety of one's country; and yet there still remains some scruple whether it is a perfect duty to devote one's self to this purpose spontaneously and unbidden, and the action has not in itself the full force of a pattern and impulse to imitation. But if an indispensable duty be in question, the transgression of which violates the moral law itself, and without regard to the welfare of mankind, and as it were tramples on its holiness (such as are usually called duties to God, because in Him we conceive the ideal of holiness in substance), then we give our most perfect esteem to the pursuit of it at the sacrifice of all that can have any value for the dearest inclinations, and we find our soul strengthened and elevated by such an example, when we convince ourselves by contemplation of it that human nature is capable of so great an elevation above every motive that nature can oppose to it. Juvenal describes such an example in a climax which makes the reader feel vividly the force of the spring that is contained in the pure law of duty, as duty:

> *Esto bonus miles, tutor bonus, arbiter idem*
> *Integer; ambiguae si quando citabere testis*
> *Incertaeque rei, Phalaris licet imperet ut sis*
> *Falsus, et admoto dictet periuria tauro,*
> *Summum crede nefas animam praeferre pudori,*
> *Et propter vitam vivendi perdere causas.* [7]

When we can bring any flattering thought of merit into our action, then the motive is already somewhat alloyed with self-love, and has therefore some assistance from the side of the sensibility. But to postpone everything to the holiness of duty alone, and to be conscious that we *can* because our own reason recognizes this as its command and says that we *ought* to do it, this is, as it were, to raise ourselves altogether above the world of sense, and there is inseparably involved in the same a consciousness of the law, as a spring of a faculty *that controls the sensibility;* and although this is not always attended with effect, yet frequent engagement with this spring, and the at first minor attempts at using it, give hope that this effect may be wrought, and that by degrees the greatest, and that a purely moral interest in it may be produced in us.

Student. What course does the method then take?

Professor. The method then takes the following course. At first we are only concerned to make the judging of actions by moral laws a natural employment accompanying all our own free actions as well as the observation of those of others, and to make it, as it were, a habit, and to sharpen this judgment, asking first whether the action *conforms* objectively *to the moral law,* and to what law; and we distinguish the law that merely furnishes a *principle* of obligation from that which is really *obligatory* (*leges obligandi a legibus obligantibus*); as, for instance, the law of what men's *wants* require from me, as contrasted with that which their *rights* demand, the latter of which prescribes essential, the former only non-essential duties; and thus we teach how to distinguish different

---

7. *Satires,* viii. "Be a good soldier, guardian and incorruptible judge. If summoned to testify in a questionable and uncertain case, then even though threatened with torture and death (literally: even though Phalaris commands you and brings up his bull) unless you speak falsely and commit perjury, consider it the highest and most shameful crime to prefer breath to honor, and so destroy, for the sake of life, the very reason for living." Phalaris, a tyrant in Sicily during the sixth century B.C., reportedly roasted his opponents alive in a brazen bull, constructed expressly for the purpose.—P.E.D.

kinds of duties which meet in the same action. The other point to which attention must be directed is the question whether the action was also (subjectively) done *for the sake of the moral law,* so that it not only is morally correct as a deed, but also, by the maxim from which it is done, has moral worth as a disposition. Now there is no doubt that this practice, and the resulting culture of our reason in judging merely of the practical, must gradually produce a certain interest even in the law of reason, and consequently in morally good actions. For we ultimately take a liking for a thing, the contemplation of which makes us feel that the use of our cognitive faculties is extended, and this extension is especially furthered by that in which we find moral correctness, since it is only in such an order of things that reason, with its faculty of determining *a priori* on principle what ought to be done, can find satisfaction. An observer of nature takes liking at last to objects that at first offended his senses, when he discovers in them the great adaptation of their organization to design, so that his reason finds food in its contemplation. So Leibniz spared an insect that he had carefully examined with the microscope, and replaced it on its leaf, because he had found himself instructed by the view of it, and had as it were received a benefit from it.

Student.   I take it that this employment of the faculty of judgment, which makes us feel our own cognitive powers, is the same as the interest in actions from the standpoint of morality itself.

Professor.   No. I am afraid that you are mistaken. It is not yet that interest. The employment of the faculty of judgment merely causes us to take pleasure in engaging in such criticism, and it gives to virtue or the disposition that conforms to moral laws a form of beauty, which is admired, but not on that account sought after (*laudatur et alget*); as everything the contemplation of which produces a consciousness of the harmony of our powers of conception, and in which we feel the whole of our faculty of knowledge (understanding and imagination) strengthened, produces a satisfaction, which may also be communicated to others, while nevertheless the existence of the object remains indifferent to us, being only regarded as the occasion of our becoming aware of the capacities in us which are elevated above mere animal nature. Now, however, the *second* exercise comes in, the living exhibition of morality of character by examples, in which attention is directed to purity of will, first only as a negative perfection, in so far as in an action done from duty no motives of inclination have any influence in determining it. By this the pupil's attention is fixed upon the consciousness of his *freedom,* and although this renunciation at first excites a feeling of pain, nevertheless, by its withdrawing the pupil from the constraint of even real wants, there is proclaimed to him at the same time a deliverance from the manifold dissatisfaction in which all these wants entangle him, and the mind is made capable of receiving the sensation of satisfaction from other sources. The heart is freed and lightened of a burden that always secretly presses on it, when instances of pure moral resolutions reveal to the man an inner faculty of which otherwise he has no right knowledge, *the inward freedom* to release himself from the boisterous importunity of inclinations, to such a degree that none of them, not even the dearest, shall have any influence on a resolution, for which we are now to employ our reason.

Student. Could you be a little more specific, Professor?

Professor. Well, suppose a case where *I alone* know that the wrong is on my side, and although a free confession of it and the offer of satisfaction are so strongly opposed by vanity, selfishness, and even an otherwise not illegitimate antipathy to the man whose rights are impaired by me, I am nevertheless able to discard all these considerations; in this there is implied a consciousness of independence [of] inclinations and circumstances, and of the possibility of being sufficient for myself, which is salutary to me in general for other purposes also. And now the law of duty, in consequence of the positive worth which obedience to it makes us feel, finds easier access through the *respect for ourselves* in the consciousness of our freedom. When this is well established, when a man dreads nothing more than to find himself, on self-examination, worthless and contemptible in his own eyes, then every good moral disposition can be grafted on it, because this is the best, nay, the only guard that can keep off from the mind the pressure of ignoble and corrupting motives.

Student. The achievement of self-respect by becoming conscious of our inherent freedom is surely a most attractive goal. But I imagine that it is a somewhat more complicated process than you have so far suggested.

Professor. Yes, indeed it is. I have only pointed out the most general maxims of the methodology of moral cultivation and exercise. As the manifold variety of duties requires special rules for each kind, and this would be a prolix affair, please excuse me if in these preliminary remarks, I content myself with these outlines.

Eliciting Moral Concepts*

The fact that virtue must be acquired (and is not innate) is contained already in the concept of virtue, and needs no appeal to anthropological information gleaned from experience. The moral capacity of man would not be virtue if it were not actualized by the strength of one's resolution in conflict with powerful opposing inclinations. Virtue is the product of pure practical reason insofar as the latter, in the consciousness of its superiority (through freedom), gains mastery over the inclinations.

That virtue can and must be taught follows from the fact that it is not innate; the philosophy of virtue [*Tugendlehre*] is thus a doctrine [*Doktrin*]. But because the power of exercising virtue's rules is not gained merely by instruction in how one should conduct himself to conform to the concept of virtue, the Stoics thought that virtue could not be taught by simple representations of duty or by exhorta-

---

*From *The Metaphysical Principles of Virtue* by Immanuel Kant, translated by James Ellington, copyright © 1964 by The Bobbs-Merrill Company, Inc., reprinted by permission of the publisher.

tions, but that it must be cultivated and exercised by seeking to combat the internal foe within man (ascetically). For one cannot straightway do whatever he wills if he has not tried and exercised his powers beforehand. However, the determination to do what one wills must be embraced completely and all at once; otherwise that disposition (*animus*) which so capitulates to vice as to give it up gradually would be in itself impure and even vicious, and, consequently, could produce no virtue (since virtue is founded upon a single principle).

Now, as for the method of this doctrine (and every scientific study must be methodical, else the treatment would be chaotic), it cannot be fragmentary but must be systematic, if the philosophy of virtue is to be represented as a science. The treatment can be either acroamatic, where all but the teacher are mere auditors, or erotematic, in which the teacher asks of his pupils what he wants to teach them. This erotematic procedure in turn is either that of *dialogue,* in which the instructor seeks what he wants to teach in his pupils' reason, or that of *catechism,* which asks merely of the memory what is to be taught. For if anyone wants to ask something of another's reason, he can only do it through dialogue, i.e., teacher and student mutually questioning and answering one another. The teacher's questions direct his pupil's train of thought merely by developing the pupil's predisposition to grasp certain concepts through proposed cases (he is the midwife for his pupil's thoughts). The pupil, who thus becomes aware that he too is able to think, by his counterquestions (about obscurities or about his doubts that stand in the way of the propositions advanced) teaches his teacher how to question well; we learn by teaching (*docendo discimus*), as the saying goes. (For there is a demand made of logic—not yet sufficiently taken to heart—that it provide rules of inquiry appropriate to the aim of the inquirer, not always for determinant judgments only, but also for preparatory judgments (*judicia praevia*), by which a person is led to new thoughts. This is a subject which can indicate discoveries even to the mathematician and which is also often applied by him.)

For the pupil who is still a novice, the first and most necessary doctrinal instrument of the philosophy of virtue is a moral catechism. This must precede the religious catechism, and cannot be expounded merely as an insertion interwoven with religious instruction, but must be separated as a self-sufficient whole; for the transition from the philosophy of virtue to religion can be made only through pure moral principles, since otherwise the avowals of religion would be impure. For that reason, even the greatest and most estimable theologians have hesitated to draw up and at the same time vouch for a catechism for statutory religious dogma, though one would think that the least he would be entitled to expect from the vast stores of their learning.

A moral catechism, on the other hand, as a fundamental doctrine [*Lehre*] of the duties of virtue, involves no such scruples or difficulty, because it can be developed (as far as its content is concerned) from common human reason and only needs to be adapted (formally) to the didactic rules of instruction. However, the formal principle of such instruction does not permit the use of the Socratic dialogue for this purpose because .the student does not even know how he should put his questions; and so the teacher alone is the interrogator. But the answer which he methodically elicits from his pupil's reason must be drawn up and kept in definite terms that are not easily altered, so that it can be entrusted to the pupil's memory. In this way the catechistic method of teaching differs from the acroamatic method (where only the teacher speaks) and from the dialogistic (where both teacher and pupil question and answer one another).

The experimental (technical) means for the cultivation of virtue is the good example of the teacher himself (his own conduct being exemplary) and the admonitory example of other people; for imitation is, for the still uncultivated man, the first determination of the will to accept maxims which he later makes for himself. Habituation is the establishment of a firm inclination by its more frequent gratification and without the use of any maxims; such habituation is a mechanism of sense rather than a principle of thought (whereby unlearning becomes subsequently more difficult than learning). But as for the power of an example (be it an example for good or bad) and what it offers for the propensity to imitate or be warned, we must say that whatever others give us can be the foundation of no maxims of virtue. For these maxims consist just in the subjective autonomy of every man's practical reason; consequently the law, not the conduct of other men, must serve us as an incentive. The instructor therefore will not say to his bad pupil, "Take an example from that good (orderly, diligent) boy!" For that will only cause the pupil to hate the boy for putting himself in a prejudicial light.[8] The good example (exemplary behavior) should not serve as a model but only as proof of the feasibility of what is in accordance with duty. Thus, it is not comparison with any other man (as he is) but with the idea of humanity (as he ought to be), and so with the law, which must supply the teacher with an infallible standard for education.

Remark

Fragments of a Moral Catechism

The teacher seeks in his pupil's reason what he wants to teach him; and if perhaps the student does not know the answer to the question, then (directing his student's reason) he suggests it to him.

1. Teacher: What is your greatest, yes, your whole desire in life?
    Student: (remains silent).
    Teacher: That everything should always go according to your wish and will.
2. What does one call such a condition?
    Student: (remains silent).
    Teacher: It is called happiness (constant well-being, a pleasant life, complete satisfaction with one's condition).

---

8. Mark Twain said it too: "Few things are harder to put up with than the annoyance of a good example." *Pudd'nhead Wilson's Calendar*—P.E.D.

3. If you had all happiness (all that is possible in the world) in your possession, would you keep it all for yourself or share it with your fellow men?

   Student: I would share it and make other people happy and contented also.

4. Teacher: That shows quite well that you have a good heart. But let us see if you have good understanding. Would you give the sluggard soft pillows to while away his life in sweet idleness? Or the drunkard wine and other intoxicating spirits? Or the deceiver a charming appearance and captivating manners so as to dupe others? Or the violent person audacity and a hard fist so as to be able to overpower others? These are all so many means which each of these people wishes in order to be happy in his fashion.

   Student: No, not that.

5. Teacher: So, you see, if you had all happiness at your disposal and the best will besides, you still would not, without reflection, bestow that happiness upon everyone who sought it, but would first inquire to what extent each person was worthy of happiness. But as for yourself, you would probably have no hesitation about first providing yourself with everything you reckon in your happiness?

   Student: Yes.

   Teacher: But does it not also occur to you to ask whether you yourself might be worthy of happiness?

   Student: By all means.

   Teacher: That something in you which strains after happiness is inclination. But that which restricts your inclination, on condition that you first be worthy of happiness, is your reason, and your being able by means of your reason to restrain and subdue your inclination is the freedom of your will.

6. The rule and direction for knowing how you go about sharing in happiness, without also becoming unworthy of it, lies entirely in your reason. This amounts to saying that you don't have to learn this rule of conduct by experience or from other people's instruction; your own reason teaches and even tells you what you have to do. For instance, if a situation presents itself in which you can get yourself or a friend a great advantage by an artfully thought out lie (and without hurting anybody else either), what does your reason say to that?

   Student: I should not lie, though the advantage to me and my friend be as great as ever you please. Lying is mean and makes a man unworthy to be happy. Here is an unconditional constraint by a command (or prohibition) of reason, which I must obey. In the face of this, all my inclinations must be silent.

   Teacher: What does one call this necessity, laid upon man directly by his reason, to act in accordance with its law?

   Student: It is called duty.

Teacher: Accordingly, the observance of man's duty is the universal and sole condition of his worthiness to be happy; and these two are one and the same.

7. But if, besides, we are conscious of such a good and efficacious will, by which we think ourselves worthy (at least not unworthy) to be happy, can we make this the foundation of any secure hope of sharing in happiness?

Student: No, not upon that alone. For it is not always within our power to provide ourselves with it. Moreover, the course of nature does not adjust itself to our merit; the fortunes of life (our welfare generally) depend upon circumstances which are far from being all within the power of man. Our happiness, therefore, remains always only a wish, which can never even become a hope unless some other power is added.

8. Teacher: Has reason its own grounds for assuming that there really is such a power that distributes happiness according to the merit and guilt of men, governs the whole of nature, and rules the world with supreme wisdom, i.e., for believing in God?

Student: Yes. For we see in those works of nature which we can judge of such extensive and profound wisdom that we cannot explain it to ourselves otherwise than as the inexpressibly great art of a Creator. From this Creator we also have cause to promise ourselves a no less wise regulation of the moral order, the supreme ornament of the world: a regulation, namely, that if we do not make ourselves unworthy of happiness by violating our duty, then we can hope to become partakers of it.

In this catechism, which ought to go through all the articles of virtue and vice, the greatest attention must be paid to the consideration that a command of duty is not founded upon the advantages or disadvantages of observing it, either for the man it ought to obligate or even for other people, but, rather, is founded quite purely upon moral principle. Any mention of advantages or disadvantages is only incidental, as a supplement that is dispensable in itself, but serves as a vehicle for the taste of those who are frail by nature. The ignominy of vice, not the harmfulness of it (for the agent himself), must above all be strikingly represented. For if the dignity of virtue in action is not exalted above everything else, the very concept of duty disappears and dissolves into mere pragmatic prescriptions. Then the nobility of man in his own consciousness disappears, and he is for sale, to be bought at any price which tempting inclinations may offer him.

When these things have been wisely and accurately evolved from man's own reason according to the variety of the circumstances of age, sex, and rank which are encountered, then there is still something which must make the decision, which inwardly moves the soul and sets man in a position in which he cannot but regard himself with the greatest admiration for the original predisposition residing within him, the impression of which never fades away. When, at the conclusion of the student's instruction, his duties in their order are once more summarily enumerated (recapitulated) for him, when in each one of these duties he is made mindful of the fact that no evil, hardship, nor any of life's suffering, nor even threat of death—any or all of which might be inflicted upon him for remaining true to his duties—can rob him of his consciousness of being superior to such evils and being master of them, then the following question lies very close to him: What is that in you which may dare to do battle against all the forces of nature within you and round about you, and to conquer them when they come into conflict with your moral principles? When this question, whose solution completely transcends the power of speculative reason, but which nonetheless presents itself of its own accord, is taken to heart, then even the incomprehensibility of this self-knowledge must give the soul an exaltation which only animates it into more strongly holding its duty sacred the more it is assailed.

In this catechistic moral instruction it would be of the greatest advantage to moral education to present some casuistical questions with every analysis of a duty, and to let the assembled students test their understanding by having each one of them declare how he thinks the captious problem proposed to him might be solved. This is so not only because such a procedure is a cultivation of the reason especially suited to the ability of a beginner (inasmuch as these questions, which concern what duty is, can be resolved far more easily than questions of speculation), and is, accordingly, the most appropriate kind of procedure for generally sharpening the understanding of the young; but this is especially so because it lies in the nature of man to love what he by his own work has brought to the condition of a science (whose outcome he now knows), and so the student by such exercises is drawn imperceptibly to serve the interest of morality.

But it is of the greatest importance in education not to intermix (amalgamate) the moral catechism with the religious catechism, still less to let it follow upon the latter, but always to bring the moral catechism to a state of the clearest insight and indeed with the greatest diligence and minuteness of detail. For otherwise nothing will come of religion later on but the hypocrisy of acknowledging one's duties from fear, and of feigning an interest in them which is not of the heart.

Conclusion*

Two things fill the mind with ever new and increasing admiration and awe, the oftener and the more steadily we reflect on them: *the starry heavens above and the moral law within.* I have not to search for them and conjecture them as though they were veiled in darkness or were in the transcendent region beyond my horizon; I see them before me and connect them directly with the consciousness of my existence. The former begins from the place I occupy in the external world of sense, and enlarges my connexion therein to an unbounded extent with worlds upon worlds and systems of systems, and moreover into limitless times of their periodic motion,

---

*From *The Critique of Practical Reason,* Abbott trans. 1873.

its beginning and continuance. The second begins from my invisible self, my personality, and exhibits me in a world which has true infinity, but which is traceable only by the understanding, and with which I discern that I am not in a merely contingent but in a universal and necessary connexion, as I am also thereby with all those visible worlds. The former view of a countless multitude of worlds annihilates, as it were, my importance as an *animal creature,* which after it has been for a short time provided with vital power, one knows not how, must again give back the matter of which it was formed to the planet it inhabits (a mere speck in the universe). The second, on the contrary, infinitely elevates my worth as an *intelligence* by my personality, in which the moral law reveals to me a life independent [of] animality and even [of] the whole sensible world—at least so far as may be inferred from the destination assigned to my existence by this law, a destination not restricted to conditions and limits of this life, but reaching into the infinite.

COMPARATIVE STUDY QUESTIONS

Review Questions

1. In the process of moral education, do rewards and punishments have any function at all, according to Kant?
2. What does Kant mean by the "pure moral motive"?
3. Of what use are biographies in moral education, according to Kant?
4. How does Kant perceive the relation between what we **can** do and what we **ought** to do?
5. What point does Kant mean to make by his story about Leibniz and the insect?
6. How may we become conscious of our inward freedom, according to Kant?
7. Does Kant believe that virtue is innate or is it acquired? What follows from this fact?
8. On what point do both Immanuel Kant and Mark Twain agree?
9. What is Kant's objection to the telling of lies, even of those that are harmless to others?
10. Does Kant believe that if we are moral we are, by that fact alone, assured of happy lives?

Discussion Questions

1. If you are acquainted with Plato's dialogues (especially the **Meno**), compare Kant's approach to the question of moral education with Plato's.
2. Is there any reason to hope that those who are made **worthy** of happiness by leading a good life will ever be rewarded, according to Kant? What sort of reason does he suggest?
3. How does Kant distinguish a moral catechism from (1) a Socratic dialogue, (2) the "acroamatic" method of moral education, and (3) a religious catechism?
4. How would Kant go about reeducating a confirmed egoist, one who never does anything "unless there's something in it for me"? Do you think he would be successful?
5. Someone once expressed astonishment that Kant should have been so impressed with the "starry heavens above." They are big, he said, but so what? Do you find his astonishment odd?

A Recommended Bibliography

Francis Bacon

Anderson, F.,H. **The Philosophy of Francis Bacon.** Chicago: University of Chicago Press, 1948.

———. **Francis Bacon: His Career and Thought.** Los Angeles: University of Southern California Press, 1962.

Bowen, Catherine Drinker. **Francis Bacon: The Temper of a Man.** Boston: Little, Brown, 1963.

Broad, C. D. **The Philosophy of Francis Bacon.** Cambridge: University Press, 1926.

Crowther, J. G. **Francis Bacon: The First Statesman of Science.** London: The Cresset Press, 1960.

Eisely, Loren. **Francis Bacon and the Modern Dilemma.** Lincoln: University of Nebraska Press, 1962.

Farrington, Benjamin. **Francis Bacon: Philosopher of Industrial Science.** New York: Henry Schuman, 1949.

Green, A. Wigfall. **Sir Francis Bacon: His Life and Works.** Denver: Alan Swallow, 1952. Contains bibliography.

———. **Sir Francis Bacon.** New York: Twayne Publishers, Inc., 1966.

Rossi, Paolo. **Francis Bacon: From Magic to Science.** Translated by Sacha Rabinovitch. Chicago: University of Chicago Press, 1968. Italian edition, 1957.

Thomas Hobbes

Brown, K. C., ed. **Hobbes Studies.** Cambridge: Harvard University Press, 1965.

Hobbes, Thomas. **The Metaphysical System of Hobbes: Selections.** Edited by Mary Whiton Calkins. Second edition. La Salle, Ill.: Open Court, 1948. First edition 1905. Contains Hobbes' Latin autobiography.

———. **Body, Man, and Citizen: Selections from Thomas Hobbes.** Edited with an introduction by Richard S. Peters. Collier Books. New York: Macmillan, 1962.

———. **A Dialogue Between A Philosopher and A Student of the Common Laws of England.** Edited with an introduction by Joseph Cropsey. Chicago and London: University of Chicago Press, 1971.

Mintz, Samuel I. **The Hunting of Leviathan: Seventeenth-Century Reactions to the Materialism and Moral Philosophy of Thomas Hobbes.** Cambridge: University Press, 1962. Contains bibliography of books relating to the times.

Peters, Richard. **Hobbes.** Harmondsworth, Middlesex, and Baltimore: Penguin Books, 1956.

Spragens, Thomas A., Jr. **The Politics of Motion: The World of Thomas Hobbes.** Lexington: University of Kentucky Press, 1973.

Stephen, Sir Leslie. **Hobbes.** New York and London: Macmillan, 1904.

Taylor, A. E. **Thomas Hobbes.** Port Washington, New York, and London: Kennikat Press, 1970. First published 1908.

Woodbridge, Frederick J. E., ed. **Hobbes Selections.** New York: Charles Scribner's Sons, 1930.

René Descartes

Balz, Albert G. A. **Cartesian Studies.** New York: Columbia University Press, 1951.

———. **Descartes and the Modern Mind.** New Haven: Yale University Press, 1952.

Beck, L. J. **The Method of Descartes: A Study of the** Regulae. Oxford: Clarendon Press, 1952.

———. **The Metaphysics of Descartes: A Study of the** Meditations. Oxford: Clarendon Press, 1965.

Butler, R. J., ed. **Cartesian Studies.** Oxford: Basil Blackwell, 1972.

Descartes, René. **The Philosophical Works of Descartes.** Translated by Elizabeth S. Haldane and G. R. T. Ross. 2 vols. Cambridge: University Press, 1911; corrected edition 1934. Reprinted by Dover Publications, Inc., 1955.

Gibson, A. Boyce. **The Philosophy of Descartes.** London: Methuen, 1932. Reissued by Russell and Russell, 1967.

Maritain, Jacques. **The Dream of Descartes.** Translated by M. L. Andison. New York: Philosophical Library, 1944.

Smith, Norman Kemp. **New Studies in the Philosophy of Descartes: Descartes as Pioneer.** London: Macmillan, 1953.

Valéry, Paul. **Les Pages Immortelles de Descartes.** Paris: Buchet/Chastel, 1961. Contains pictures of Descartes at different ages, his birthplace in La Haye, and some of his associates.

John Locke

Aaron, Richard I. **John Locke.** 3rd ed. Oxford: Clarendon Press, 1971.

Bourne, H. R. Fox. **The Life of John Locke.** 2 vols. London: 1876. Reprinted by Scientia Verlag Aalen, 1969.

Cox, Richard H. **Locke on War and Peace.** Oxford: Clarendon Press, 1960.

Cranston, Maurice. **John Locke: A Biography.** London: Longmans, Green, 1957.

Dunn, John. **The Political Thought of John Locke.** Cambridge: University Press, 1969. Contains useful bibliography.

Gough, J. W. **John Locke's Political Philosophy.** 2nd. ed. Oxford: Clarendon Press, 1973.

Lamprecht, Sterling Power. **The Moral and Political Philosophy of John Locke.** New York: Russell and Russell, 1962. First published 1918.

Locke, John. **An Essay Concerning Human Understanding.** Abridged and edited by A. S. Pringle-Pattison. Oxford: Clarendon Press, 1924.

———. **Two Treatises of Government.** Edited with an introduction by Thomas I. Cook. New York: Hafner Publishing Co., 1947. Also includes Filmer's **Patriarcha** as a supplement.

———. **The Second Treatise of Government** and **A Letter Concerning Toleration.** Edited with a revised introduction by J. W. Gough. Oxford: Basil Blackwell, 1966.

———. **Two Treatises of Government.** A critical edition with an introduction and Apparatus Criticus by Peter Laslett. 2nd ed. Cambridge: University Press, 1970. Also published as a Mentor paperback by The New American Library.

Mabbot, J. D. **John Locke.** London and Basingstoke: Macmillan, 1973.

Martin, C. B., and Armstrong, D. M., eds. **Locke and Berkeley: A Collection of Critical Essays.** Notre Dame and London: University of Notre Dame Press, 1968.

Pollock, Sir Frederick. "Locke's Theory of the State," in **Essays in the Law.** Hamden, Ct.: Archon Books, 1969.

Yolton, John W. **Locke and the Compass of Human Understanding: A Selective Commentary on the "Essay."** Cambridge: University Press, 1970.

Baruch de Spinoza

Curley, E. M. **Spinoza's Metaphysics: An Essay in Interpretation.** Cambridge: Harvard University Press, 1969.

de Deugd, C. **The Significance of Spinoza's First Kind of Knowledge.** Assen: Van Gorcum, 1966.

Grene, Marjorie, ed. **Spinoza: A Collection of Critical Essays.** Anchor Books. Garden City, N.Y.: Doubleday, 1973.

Hallett, H. F. **Aeternitas: A Spinozistic Study.** Oxford: Clarendon Press, 1930.

———. **Benedict de Spinoza: The Elements of His Philosophy.** London: Athlone Press, 1957.

Hampshire, Stuart. **Spinoza.** Harmondsworth, Middlesex, and Baltimore: Penguin Books, 1951.

Joachim, H. H. **A Study of the Ethics of Spinoza.** Oxford: Clarendon Press, 1901.

Kashap, S. Paul, ed. **Studies in Spinoza: Critical and Interpretive Essays.** Berkeley: University of California Press, 1972.

Pollock, Sir Frederick. **Spinoza: His Life and Philosophy.** London: C. Kegan Paul, 1880. 2nd ed. 1899. A longer work than the one below.

———. **Spinoza.** London: Duckworth, 1935. An excellent little book about Spinoza's life.

Roth, Leon. **Spinoza.** Boston: Little, Brown, 1929.

Wolfson, Harry A. **The Philosophy of Spinoza,** 2 vols. Cambridge: Harvard University Press, 1934. 1 vol. ed. 1948.

Gottfried Wilhelm Leibniz

Broad, C. D. **Leibniz: An Introduction.** Edited by C. Lewy. London and New York: Cambridge University Press, 1975.

Carr, Herbert W. **Leibniz.** Boston: Little Brown, 1929.

Dewey, John. **Leibniz's New Essays Concerning the Human Understanding: A Critical Exposition.** New York: Hillary House, Reprinted 1961. First edition 1888.

Frankfurt, Harry G. **Leibniz: A Collection of Critical Essays.** Garden City, N.Y.: Doubleday, 1972.

Joseph, H. W. B. **Lectures on the Philosophy of Leibniz.** Oxford: Clarendon Press, 1949.

Leibniz, G. W. **The Monadology and Other Philosophical Writings.** Translated by Robert Latta. London: Oxford University Press, 1898.

———. **Philosophical Writings.** Translated by Mary Morris. Everyman's Library. London: J. M. Dent; New York: E. P. Dutton, 1934.

———. **Die philosophischen Schriften.** Edited by C. J. Gerhardt, 7 vols. Hildesheim: George Olm, 1960–62.

———. **Philosophical Papers and Letters.** Translated and edited by Leroy E. Loemker. 2nd ed. Dordrecht, Holland: D. Reidel Publishing Co., 1969.

Mason, H. T., editor and translator. **The Leibniz-Arnauld Correspondence.** Manchester: Manchester University Press, 1967.

Martin, Gottfried. **Leibniz: Logic and Metaphysics.** Translated by K. J. Northcott and P. G. Lucas. Manchester: Manchester University Press, 1964.

Rescher, Nicholas. **The Philosophy of Leibniz.** Englewood Cliffs, N.J.: Prentice-Hall, 1967.

Russell, Bertrand. **A Critical Exposition of the Philosophy of Leibniz.** London: George Allen & Unwin, Ltd., 1900. 2nd ed. 1937.

Saw, Ruth Lydia. **Leibniz.** Harmondsworth, Middlesex, and Baltimore: Penguin Books, 1954.

George Berkeley

Berkeley, George. **Principles, Dialogues, and Philosophical Correspondence.** Edited with an introduction by Colin Murray Turbayne. Library of Liberal Arts. Indianapolis and New York: Bobbs-Merrill, 1965.

Fraser, A. C. **Life and Letters of George Berkeley.** Oxford: Clarendon Press, 1871.

Hicks, G. Dawes. **Berkeley.** London: Oxford University Press, 1932.

Jessop, T. E. **George Berkeley.** London: Longmans, Green, 1959.

Johnston, G. A. **The Development of Berkeley's Philosophy.** London: Macmillan, 1923. Reissued Russell and Russell, 1965.

Luce, A. A. **The Life of George Berkeley, Bishop of Cloyne.** Edinburgh: Thomas Nelson & Sons, 1949.

———. The Dialectic of Immaterialism: An Account of the Making of Berkeley's **Principles.** London: Hodder & Stoughton, 1963.

Martin, C. B., and Armstrong, D. M., eds. **Locke and Berkeley: A Collection of Critical Essays.** Notre Dame and London: University of Notre Dame Press, 1968.

Rand, Benjamin. **Berkeley and Percival.** Cambridge: University Press, 1914.

———. **Berkeley's American Sojourn.** Cambridge: Harvard University Press, 1932.

Ritchie, A. D. **George Berkeley: A Reappraisal.** Edited by G. E. Davie. Manchester: Manchester University Press, 1967.

Tipton, J. C. **Berkeley: The Philosophy of Immaterialism.** London: Methuen, 1974.

Warnock, G. J. **Berkeley.** Harmondsworth, Middlesex, and Baltimore: Penguin Books, 1953.

Wild, John. **George Berkeley: A Study of His Life and Philosophy.** Cambridge: Harvard University Press, 1936.

Wisdom, J. O. **The Unconscious Origins of Berkeley's Philosophy.** London: Hogarth, 1953; New York: Hillary House, 1957.

David Hume

Basson, A. **David Hume.** Harmondsworth, Middlesex, and Baltimore: Penguin Books, 1958.

Chappell, V. C., ed. **Hume: A Collection of Critical Essays.** Garden City, N.Y.: Doubleday, 1966.

Church, Ralph W. **Hume's Theory of the Understanding.** London: George Allen & Unwin, Ltd., 1935. Reissued by Archon Books, 1968.

Flew, Antony. **Hume's Philosophy of Belief: A Study of His First** Inquiry. New York: Humanities Press, 1961.

Greig, J. Y. T. **David Hume.** New York: Oxford University Press, 1931.

Hendel, Charles W. **Studies in the Philosophy of David Hume.** Princeton: Princeton University Press, 1925. New edition: Library of Liberal Arts. Indianapolis and New York: Bobbs-Merrill, 1963.

Hume, David. **Dialogues Concerning Natural Religion.** Edited with an introduction by Norman Kemp Smith. Edinburgh: Thomas Nelson and Sons, Ltd. 2nd ed. 1947. Reprinted by Library of Liberal Arts. Contains text of Boswell's interview with Hume and a critical analysis of the argument of the **Dialogues.**

———. **An Inquiry Concerning Human Understanding.** Edited with an introduction by Charles W. Hendel. Library of Liberal Arts. Indianapolis and New york: Bobbs-Merrill, 1955. Contains as a supplement **An Abstract of a Treatise of Human Nature.**

Macnabb, D. G. C. **David Hume: His Theory of Knowledge and Morality.** Hamden, Ct.: Archon Books, 1951. 2nd ed. 1966.

Mossner, Ernest Campbell. **The Life of David Hume.** Austin: University of Texas Press, 1954.

Noxon, James. **Hume's Philosophical Development: A Study of His Methods.** Oxford: Clarendon Press, 1973.

Price, H. H. **Hume's Theory of the External World.** Oxford: Clarendon Press, 1940.

Smith, Norman Kemp. **The Philosophy of David Hume: A Critical Study of Its Origins and Central Doctrines.** London: Macmillan, 1941.

Immanuel Kant

Beck, Lewis White, ed. **Kant Studies Today.** La Salle, Ill.: Open Court, 1969.

Buchner, Edward F. **The Educational Theory of Immanuel Kant.** Philadelphia and London: J. B. Lippincott, 1908. Contains an introduction and a translation of Kant's writings on education.

Copleston, Frederick. **A History of Philosophy,** Vol. 6: **Modern Philosophy,** Part II: **Kant.** Image Book. Garden City, N.Y.: Doubleday, 1964.

Friedrich, Carl J., ed. **The Philosophy of Kant: Immanuel Kant's Moral and Political Writings.** New York: Random House, 1949. Modern Library edition. Contains selections from most of Kant's major works.

Kant, Immanuel. **Critique of Practical Reason.** Translated by Lewis White Beck. Library of Liberal Arts. Indianapolis and New York: Bobbs-Merrill, 1956.

———. **Education.** Translated by Annette Churton. Ann Arbor: University of Michigan Press, 1960.

———. **Religion Within the Limits of Reason Alone.** Translated with an introduction and notes by Theodore M. Greene and Hoyt H. Hudson, with a new essay, "The Ethical Significance of Kant's **Religion**," by John R. Silber. New York: Harper & Row, 1960. Translation first published in 1934 by Open Court.

———. **The Metaphysical Principles of Virtue.** Translated by James Ellington. Library of Liberal Arts. Indianapolis and New York: Bobbs-Merrill, 1964. Contains an excellent introduction on "Kant's Moral Philosophy" by Warner Wick.

———. **On the Old Saw: That May Be Right in Theory But It Won't Work in Practice.** Translated by E. B. Ashton; introduction by George Miller. Philadelphia: University of Pennsylvania Press, 1974.

Klinke, Willibald. **Kant For Everyman: An Introduction for the General Reader.** Translated by Michael Bullock. London: Macmillan, 1951. Reprinted by Collier Books, 1962.

Körner, S. **Kant.** Harmondsworth, Middlesex, and Baltimore: Penguin Books, 1955.

Schilpp, Paul Arthur. **Kant's Pre-Critical Ethics.** 2nd ed. Evanston: Northwestern University Press, 1960.

Strawson, P. F. **The Bounds of Sense: An Essay on Kant's Critique of Pure Reason.** London: Methuen, 1966.

Wolff, Robert Paul, ed. **Kant: A Collection of Critical Essays.** Garden City, N.Y.: Doubleday, 1967.

Zweig, Arnulf, ed. and trans. **Kant: Philosophical Correspondence 1759–99.** Chicago: University of Chicago Press, 1967.

Background and Comparative Studies

Aubrey, John. **Brief Lives and Other Selected Writings.** Edited with an introduction and notes by Anthony Powell. London: The Cresset Press, 1949.

———. **Brief Lives.** Edited by Oliver Lawson Dick. London: Secker and Warburg, 1950. The "life" of Hobbes in this edition is considerably different from the one in the Powell edition.

Barber, W. H. **Leibniz in France: From Arnauld to Voltaire: A Study in French Reaction to Leibnizianism, 1670–1760.** Oxford: Clarendon Press, 1955.

Bennett, Jonathan. **Locke, Berkeley, Hume: Central Themes.** Oxford: Clarendon Press, 1971.

Blondel, Maurice. **Dialogue avec les philosophes: Descartes-Spinoza-Malebranche-Pascal-Saint Augustin.** Paris: Editions Aubier-Montaigne, 1966.

Bowen, Catherine Drinker. **The Lion and the Throne: The Life and Times of Sir Edward Coke.** Boston: Little, Brown, 1956. Extensive bibliography, notes, and source references.

Burtt, E. A. **The Metaphysical Foundations of Modern Physical Science: A Historical and Critical Essay.** Rev. ed. London: Routledge & Kegan Paul, 1932.

Calkins, M. W. **The Persistent Problems of Philosophy: An Introduction to Metaphysics Through the Study of Modern Systems.** 5th ed. New York: Macmillan, 1925.

Collingwood, R. G. **The Idea of Nature.** Oxford: Clarendon Press, 1945.

———. **The Idea of History.** Oxford: Clarendon Press, 1946. A Galaxy paperback since 1956.

Filmer, Robert. **Patriarcha and Other Political Works of Sir Robert Filmer.** Edited by Peter Laslett. Oxford: Clarendon Press, 1949.

Kuypers, M. S. **Studies in the Eighteenth Century Background of Hume's Empiricism.** Minneapolis: University of Minnesota Press, 1930.

Loemker, Leroy E. **Struggle For Synthesis: The Seventeenth Century Background of Leibniz's Synthesis of Order and Freedom.** Cambridge: Harvard University Press, 1972.

Rescher, Nicholas. **The Primacy of Practice: Essay Toward a Pragmatically Kantian Theory of Empirical Knowledge.** Oxford: Basil Blackwell, 1973.

Russell, Bertrand. **A History of Western Philosophy.** New York: Simon and Schuster, 1945.

Strauss, Leo. **Natural Right and History.** Chicago: University of Chicago Press, 1953. Contains interesting discussions of both Locke and Hobbes.

Weis, Charles McC., and Pottle, Frederick A., eds. **Boswell in Extremes 1776–1778.** New York: McGraw-Hill, 1970.

Whitehead, A. N. **Science and the Modern World.** New York: Macmillan, 1925. Available in Mentor paperback since 1948.

Willey, Basil. **The Eighteenth Century Background.** Anchor Books. Garden City, N.Y.: Doubleday, 1953.

INDEX OF NAMES

INDEX OF SUBJECTS